1 MONTH OF
FREE
READING

at

www.ForgottenBooks.com

By purchasing this book you are eligible for one month membership to ForgottenBooks.com, giving you unlimited access to our entire collection of over 1,000,000 titles via our web site and mobile apps.

To claim your free month visit:

www.forgottenbooks.com/free931952

ISBN 978-0-260-16465-0
PIBN 10931952

For support please visit www.forgottenbooks.com

IN THE

COURT OF COMMON PLEAS

AND

EXCHEQUER CHAMBER.

BY

JOHN SCOTT,

OF THE INNER TEMPLE, ESQ., BARRISTER AT LAW.

VOL. III.

EASTER AND TRINITY TERMS, 6 WILL. IV, AND MICHAELMAS TERM,
7 WILL. IV.

LONDON:

S. SWEET, 1, CHANCERY LANE, FLEET STREET,
LAW BOOKSELLER AND PUBLISHER;
AND MILLIKEN & SON, GRAFTON STREET, DUBLIN.

1837.

LONDON:
W. M'DOWALL, PEMBERTON ROW,
GOUGH SQUARE.

JUDGES

OF

THE COURT OF COMMON PLEAS.

———◆———

The Right Hon. Sir NICOLAS CONYNGHAM TINDAL, Knt., L. C. J.
The Hon. Sir JAMES ALLAN PARK, Knt.
The Hon. Sir STEPHEN GASELEE, Knt.
The Right Hon. Sir JOHN VAUGHAN, Knt.
The Right Hon. Sir JOHN BERNARD BOSANQUET, Knt.

TABLE OF CASES.

ERRATA.

Page 11, marginal note, line 9, for "c. xlii" read "c. xi."

90, ——————— line 6, add " Will. 4."

REGULÆ GENERALES

HILARY AND EASTER TERMS, 6 WILL. IV.

𝕳ilary 𝕿erm, 6 WILL. IV.

---

1. **W**HEREAS, by the stat. 4 Hen. 4, c. 18, it was enacted, " That all the attorneys shall be examined by the justices, and by their discretion their names put on the roll, and they that be good and vertuous and of good fame shall be received and sworn well and truly to serve in their offices." And whereas by the stat. 3 Jac. 1, c. 7, s. 2, it was enacted, " That none shall from henceforth be admitted attorneys in any of the king's courts of record but such as have been brought up in the same courts, or otherwise well practised in soliciting of causes, and have been found by their dealings to be skilful and of honest disposition, and that none be suffered to solicit any cause or causes in any of the courts aforesaid but only such as are known to be men of sufficient and honest disposition." And whereas by a rule made in Michaelmas Terms, 1654, in the courts of King's Bench and Common Pleas, it was ordered that the courts " should once in every year, in Michaelmas Term, nominate twelve or more able and credible practisers, to continue for the ensuing year, to examine such persons as should desire to be admitted attorneys, and appoint convenient times and

[margin notes: 1836. Recitals. 4 H. 4, c. 18, 3 Jac. 1, c. 7, s. 2. Reg. gen. M. T. 1654.]

2 Geo. 2, c.
23, s. 2.

Appointment of
examiners.

No person to be
admitted an at-
torney without
a certificate
from the exa-
miners.

places for the examination: and the persons desiring to
be admitted were first to attend with their proofs of service, then to repair to the persons appointed to examine,
and, being approved, to be presented to the court and
sworn." And whereas by the stat. 2 Geo. 2, c. 23, s. 2, it
was enacted, "That the judges, or any one or more of
them, should, and they were thereby authorized and required, before they should admit such person to take the
oath, to examine and inquire, by such ways and means
as they should think proper, touching his fitness and
capacity to act as an attorney: and if such judge or judges
respectively should be thereby satisfied that such person
is duly qualified to be admitted to act as an attorney, then,
and not otherwise, the said judge or judges of the said
courts respectively should, and they were thereby authorized to administer to such persons the oath thereinafter
directed to be taken by attorneys, and, after such oath
taken, to cause him to be admitted an attorney of such
court respectively." And whereas, in order to carry the
last-mentioned statute more fully into effect, it is expedient annually to appoint examiners, subject to the control of the judges in manner hereinafter mentioned, It is
ordered that the several masters and prothonotaries for
the time being of the courts of King's Bench, Common
Pleas, or Exchequer respectively, together with twelve
attorneys or solicitors, be appointed, by a rule of court in
Easter Term in every year, to be examiners for one year:
any five of whom (one whereof to be one of the said masters or prothonotaries) shall be competent to conduct the
examination; and that, from and after the last day of next
Easter Term, subject to such appeal as hereinafter mentioned, no person shall be admitted to be sworn an attorney of any of the courts, except on production of a certificate signed by the major part of such examiners actually
present at and conducting his examination, testifying his
fitness and capacity to act as an attorney; such certificate

to be in force only to the end of the term next following
the date thereof, unless such time shall be specially extended by the order of a judge.

2. It is further ordered, that the examiners so to be ap- Regulations to
pointed shall conduct the said examinations under regula- be approved by the judges.
tions to be first submitted to and approved by the judges.

3. And it is further ordered, that, in case any person Appeal from
shall be dissatisfied with the refusal of the examiners to examiners' decision.
grant such certificate, he shall be at liberty to apply for
admission by petition in writing to the judges, to be delivered to the clerk of the Lord Chief Justice of the court
of King's Bench, upon which no fee or gratuity shall be
received, which application shall be heard in Serjeant's
Inn Hall, by not less than three of the judges.

4. And whereas the Hall or building of the Incorpo- Place of examination.
rated Law Society of the United Kingdom, in Chancery
Lane, will be a fit and convenient place for holding the
said examination, and the said society have consented to
allow the same to be used for that purpose : it is further
ordered, that, until further order, such examinations be Time.
there held on such days, being within the last ten days of
every term, as the said examiners or any five of them
shall appoint; and that any person not previously ad- Notice to the examiners.
mitted an attorney of any of the three courts, and de-
sirous of being admitted, shall, in addition to the notices
already required, give a term's notice to the said examiners of his intention to apply for examination, by
leaving the same with the secretary of the said society
at their said Hall; which notice shall also state his place Form of notice.
or places of residence or service for the last preceding
twelve months; and, in case of application to be admitted
on a refusal of the certificate, shall give ten days' notice,
to be served in like manner, of the day appointed for
hearing the same.

5. And it is further ordered, that, three days at the Notices of application to be
least before the commencement of the term next preced- admitted, re-

1836.

REG. GEN.
quisites of, and
to whom de-
livered.

ing that in which any person not before admitted shall propose to be admitted an attorney of either of the courts, he shall cause to be delivered at the masters' or prothonotaries' office, as the case may be, instead of affixing the same on the walls of the courts as now required, the usual written notices, which shall state, in addition to the particulars now required, his place or places of abode or service for the last preceding twelve months; and the master or prothonotary, as the case may be, shall reduce all such notices as in this rule first mentioned into an alphabetical table or tables under convenient heads, and affix the same, on the first day of term, in some conspicuous place within or near to and on the outside of each court.

Affidavit and
notices on ap-
plication for re-
admission.

6. And whereas it is expedient, that, upon the re-admission of attornies, the judges should have further means of inquiring as to the circumstances under which persons applying to be re-admitted discontinued to practise, and as to their conduct and employment during the time of such discontinuance; it is further ordered, that, at the time of giving the usual notice of the intention to apply for such re-admission, the party shall cause to be filed the affidavit on which he seeks to be re-admitted, with the master or prothonotary, as the case may be; which affidavit shall contain, in addition to the particulars now required, a statement of his place or places of abode during the last preceding year; and such person shall also at the same time cause to be left a copy of such affidavit with the clerk of the Lord Chief Justice of the court of King's Bench; and the rule for the re-admission of such person shall be drawn up on reading such affidavit, and also an affidavit of such copy having been left in compliance with this rule.

(Signed by all the Judges.)

1836.

REG. GEN.
Holidays to be
kept in the law
offices.

WHEREAS by the act of the 3 & 4 Will. 4, c. 42, s. 43, it is enacted, that none of the several days mentioned in the statute passed in the sessions of parliament holden in the 5th and 6th year of the reign of King Edward the 6th, intituled, "An Act for keeping Holidays and Fasting Days," shall be kept or observed in the courts of common law, or in the several offices belonging thereto, except Sundays, the day of the Nativity of our Lord, and the three following days, and Monday and Tuesday in Easter week: it is hereby ordered, that, henceforth, in addition to the said days, the following and none other shall be observed or kept as holidays in the several offices belonging to the said courts, viz. Good Friday and Easter Eve, and such of the five days following as may not fall in the time of term, but not otherwise; the Birthday of our Lord the King, the Birthday of our Lady the Queen, the day of the Accession of our Lord the King, Whit Monday, and Whit Tuesday.

(Signed by all the Judges.)

Hilary Term, 6 WILL. IV.

EXAMINATION OF ATTORNEYS.

Regulations approved by the Judges in Easter Term, 1836, for the Examination of Persons applying to be admitted as Attorneys of the courts of King's Bench, Common Pleas, or Exchequer, pursuant to the rule of court made in Hilary Term, 1836.

WHEREAS, by a rule of the courts of King's Bench, Common Pleas, and Exchequer, made in Hilary Term, 1836, it was ordered, that the several masters and prothonotaries for the time being of the said courts respectively, together with twelve attorneys or solicitors, should be appointed by a rule of court in Easter Term in every year, to be examiners, for one year, of persons applying

Recital of rules
of Hilary Term.

to be admitted attorneys of the said courts, any five of
whom (one whereof to be one of the said masters or prothonotaries) should be competent to conduct the examination ; and that, from and after the last day of the present
Easter Term, subject to such appeal as thereinafter mentioned, no person should be admitted to be sworn an attorney of any of the said courts, except on production of a
certificate, signed by the major part of such examiners
actually present at and conducting his examination, testifying his fitness and capacity to act as an attorney ; such
certificate to be in force only to the end of the term next
following the date thereof, unless such time should be
specially extended by the order of a judge : And it was
further ordered, that the examiners so to be appointed
should conduct the said examinations under regulations
to be first submitted to and approved by the judges; and
that, until further order, such examinations should be
held in the hall or building of the Incorporated Law
Society of the United Kingdom, in Chancery Lane, on
such days (being within the last ten days of every term) as
the said examiners, or any five of them, should appoint;
and that any person not previously admitted of any of the
three courts, and desirous of being admitted, should give
a term's notice of his intention to apply for examination,
by leaving the same with the secretary of the said society,
at their said hall :

Appointment of examiners.

And whereas, by a rule of all the said courts, made in
this present Easter Term, it was ordered, that the several
masters and prothonotaries for the time being of the said
courts respectively, together with Thomas Adlington,
Jonathan Brundrett, George Frere, James William Freshfield, James Hall, Bryan Holme, William Lowe, Edward
Rowland Pickering, Samuel White Sweet, William Tooke,
Richard White, and Edward Archer Wilde, gentlemen,
attorneys, should be, and the same were thereby appointed
examiners for one year then next ensuing, to examine all

such persons as should desire to be admitted attorneys of all or either of the said courts from and after the last day of that term; and that any five of the said examiners, one of them being one of the said masters or prothonotaries, should be competent to conduct the said examination, in pursuance of and subject to the provisions of the said rule of Hilary Term last:

In pursuance of the said rules, the following regulations for conducting the said examinations have been submitted to and approved by the judges of the said courts.

1. That every person applying to be admitted an attorney of any of the said courts pursuant to the said rules, shall, within the first seven days of the term in which he is desirous of being admitted, leave or cause to be left with the secretary of the said Incorporated Law Society, his articles of clerkship, duly stamped, and also any assignment which may have been made thereof, together with answers to the several questions hereunto annexed, signed by the applicant, and also by the attorney or attorneys with whom he shall have served his clerkship.

2. That, in case the applicant shall shew sufficient cause, to the satisfaction of the examiners, why the first regulation cannot be fully complied with, it shall be in the power of the said examiners, upon sufficient proof being given of the same, to dispense with any part of the first regulation that they may think fit and reasonable.

3. That every person applying for admission shall also, if required, sign and leave, or cause to be left, with the secretary of the said society, answers in writing to such other written or printed questions as shall be proposed by the said examiners touching his said service and conduct; and shall also, if required, attend the said examiners personally, for the purpose of giving further explanation touching the same; and shall also, if required, procure the attorney or attorneys with whom he shall have served his clerkship as aforesaid, to answer, either personally or

Side notes:

1836.
REG. GEN.

Regulations for examination.

Articles &c. to be previously left with the secretary of the Law Society.

Power to examiners to dispense with any part of the first regulation.

Answers to questions, and personal attendance.

in writing, any question touching such service or conduct, or shall make proof to the satisfaction of the said examiners of his inability to procure the same.

Examination.

4. That every person so applying shall also attend the said examiners at the hall of the said society, at such time or times as shall be appointed for that purpose, pursuant to the said rule, as the said examiners shall appoint, and shall answer such questions as the said examiners shall then and there put to him by written or printed papers, touching his fitness and capacity to act as an attorney.

Certificate to be given by the examiners.

5. That, upon compliance with the aforesaid regulations, and if the major part of the said examiners actually present at and conducting the said examination (one of them being one of the said masters or prothonotaries) shall be satisfied as to the fitness and capacity of the person so applying to act as an attorney, the said examiners present, or the major part of them, shall certify the same under their hands in the following form, viz. :—

" In pursuance of the rules made in Hilary and Easter Terms, 1836, of the courts of King's Bench, Common Pleas, and Exchequer, We, being the major part of the examiners actually present at and conducting the examination of A. B., of &c., do hereby certify that we have examined the said A. B., as required by the said rules: and we do testify that the said A. B. is fit and capable to act as an attorney of the said courts."

(Signed by all the Judges).

QUESTIONS AS TO DUE SERVICE, TO BE ANSWERED BY THE CLERK.

1. What was your age on the day of the date of your articles?

2. Have you served the whole term of your articles at the office where the attorney or attorneys to whom you were articled or assigned carried on his or their business? and, if not, state the reason.

3. Have you, at any time during the term of your articles, been absent without the permission of the attorney or attorneys to whom you were

articled or assigned? and, if so, state the length and occasions of such absence.

4. Have you, during the period of your articles, been engaged or concerned in any profession, business, or employment, other than your professional employment as clerk to the attorney or attorneys to whom you were articled or assigned?

5. Have you, since the expiration of your articles, been engaged or concerned, and for how long time, in any and what profession, trade, business, or employment, other than the profession of an attorney or solicitor?

————

QUESTIONS AS TO DUE SERVICE, TO BE ANSWERED BY THE ATTORNEY.

1. Has A. B. served the whole term of his articles at the office where you carry on your business? and, if not, state the reason.

2. Has the said A. B., at any time during the term of his articles, been absent without your permission? and, if so, state the length and occasions of such absence.

3. Has the said A. B., during the period of his articles, been engaged or concerned in any profession, business, or employment, other than his professional employment as your articled clerk?

4. Has the said A. B., during the whole term of his clerkship, with the exceptions above mentioned, been faithfully and diligently employed in your professional business of an attorney or solicitor?

5. Has the said A. B., since the expiration of his articles, been engaged or concerned, and for how long time, in any and what profession, trade, business, or employment, other than the profession of an attorney and solicitor?

And I do hereby certify that the said A. B. hath duly and faithfully served under his articles of clerkship, (or assignment, *as the case may be*), bearing date &c., for the term therein expressed; and that he is a fit and proper person to be admitted an attorney.

———◆———

The following notice has been posted up in the Common Law Courts, and at the Judges' Chambers, and all the law offices:—

EXAMINATION OF ATTORNEYS UNDER THE RULES OF HILARY AND EASTER TERMS, 1836.

THE articles of clerkship, and answers to questions touching the due service and good conduct of persons applying

to be admitted attorneys, are to be left with the secretary
of the Incorporated Law Society, at the Hall in Chancery
Lane, within the first seven days of term (viz. between
the 23rd and 30th May inclusive).

The first examination will take place at the Hall of the
Incorporated Law Society, on Saturday, the 4th of June,
and commence at ten o'clock in the forenoon. The ap-
plicants are required to attend in the Hall at half-past
nine on the day of examination.

Application for further information may be made to the
secretary.

17th May, 1836.   R. Maugham.

MEMORANDUM.

The Judges who sat in the Court of Common Pleas
during Easter Term, were—

Lord Chief Justice Tindal,
Mr. Justice Park,
Mr. Justice Vaughan,
and
Mr. Justice Bosanquet.

IN THE COMMON PLEAS.

EASTER TERM, 6 WILL. IV.

BATTERSBY, Treasurer of The BRISTOL DOCK COMPANY, *v.* KIRK.

1836.

Friday,
Jan. 29th.

THIS was an action of indebitatus assumpsit for rates and duties due and payable from and by the defendant to the Bristol Dock Company for goods, wares, and merchandize imported into the port of Bristol, consigned to the defendant, and by him there received as consignee. The defendant pleaded non assumpsit, under the direction of an order made on the 3rd April, 1835, by Bosanquet, J., by consent, impowering the defendant under that plea to give in evidence any matter of defence which tended to shew that the money specified in the plaintiff's particulars of demand was not due. The particulars of demand claimed the sum of 5*s.* for rates and duties on two boxes of Irish linen therein alleged to have been imported into the port of Bristol on the 15th November, 1834, by the Express steam packet from Dublin, consigned to the defendant, and by him received as such consignee. By consent of the parties, and by order of Vaughan, J., bearing date the 25th August, 1835, the facts were stated for the opinion of the court in the following case :—

" By an act of parliament passed in the 43 Geo. 3 (c. 140),

In relation to the rates and duties payable on goods imported into the port of Bristol, by the Bristol Dock act, 48 Geo. 3, c. xii, Ireland is in parts beyond the seas.

43 G. 3, c. 140.

1836.

BATTERSBY
v.
KIRK.

46 Geo. 3, c. 35.

48 Geo. 3, c. 11.

Section 38.

intituled 'An act for improving and rendering more commodious the port and harbour of Bristol,' the mayor,
burgesses, and commonalty of Bristol and their successors,
the master, wardens, and commonalty of merchant ven-
turers of the said city and their successors, and the persons
therein named, subscribers towards a joint stock for the
purposes of the act, and others, possessors for the time
being of any part of such stock, were united into a company of proprietors of the works thereby authorized and
of the premises thereto belonging, to be known by the
stile of 'The Bristol Dock Company,' and were invested
with various powers and authorities to enable them to ful-
fil the objects indicated in the title of the act; and certain
rates and duties were thereby made payable to the company after the completion of the works, for all goods imported from *parts beyond the seas*, but *not brought coastwise*, or *by inland navigation*, into the said port of Bristol,
except articles of provision.   By an act passed in the
46 Geo. 3 (c. 35), intituled 'An act to alter and amend an
act passed in the 43 Geo. 3, intituled—An act for improving and rendering more commodious the port and harbour
of Bristol—and for extending the powers and provisions
of the said act,' various provisions were made as to calls
on shares and other matters relative to the purposes of
the former act, and certain further works were directed.
By an act passed in the 48 Geo. 3 (c. 11), intituled 'An act
for completing the improvement of the port of Bristol,'
and in which the former acts hereinbefore stated were recited, further provisions were made, and further works
directed.   The 38th section enacts—'That, from and after
such completion of the said intended works as aforesaid,
and the completion thereof shall have been so allowed and
certified by the magistrates in quarter sessions, and advertized as aforesaid, in case the same shall be so completed, certified, and advertized on or by the said 1st May,
1809, and, in case the same shall not be then so completed,

certified, and advertized, then from and after the expiration of three calendar months after the said works shall have been so completed and finished, and certified and advertized as hereinbefore directed, there shall be paid and payable to the said company or their collectors or deputies for their use (in lieu of the rates on merchandize imposed by the said first-recited act), for all goods, wares, or merchandizes imported from *parts beyond the seas*, and *not brought by inland navigation*, into the port of Bristol (except corn, flour, rice, and other articles of provision), and also for all goods, wares, and merchandizes that shall be brought coastwise into the said port, *of foreign growth or importation*, but *not of British growth or manufacture*, except from.Cardiff, Newport, and other ports to the eastward of the Holmes, and except corn, flour, rice; and other articles of provision, and except foreign goods brought coastwise which shall not be discharged for sale at the quays, but passing or going to or from the Bath River Navigation, or Kennet and Avon canal, or any part thereof, by the owner or owners, consignee or consignees of such goods, wares, or merchandizes, or other commodities, the several rates and duties particularly rated, specified, and set forth in the schedule hereunto annexed, as far as such goods, wares, and merchandizes are therein particularized.' The 41st section gives power to the directors of the company, with the consent of the justices of the peace in and for the city of Bristol and county of the same city, in sessions assembled, to be certified by an order of the said sessions, to lessen any or either of the said rates and duties payable for or chargeable on any article or articles imported into the said port of Bristol, and again to alter and increase them, not exceeding the respective rates by this or the recited acts made payable. Annexed to this act is a schedule intituled 'Schedule of rates and duties on goods and merchandizes imported into

Section 41.

Schedule of rates
and duties.

1836.

BATTERSBY
v.
KIRK.

49 Geo. 3. c. 17.

Public acts.

the port of Bristol, imposed by the foregoing act.' In this schedule are, among others, the following items:—

"'Linen in transitu, per pack or box . . . . 1*s*. 6*d*.
'Linen not in transitu, per pack or box . . . 3*s*. 6*d*.'

" By another act passed in the 49 Geo. 3 (c. 17), intitu-led 'An act to enable the Bristol Dock Company to bor-row a further sum of money for completing the improve-ments of the port and harbour of Bristol,' certain further provisions were made. Each of the acts before mentioned contains a clause in the usual form declaring it to be a public act.

" In the year 1809, the works directed by the several Bristol Dock acts hereinbefore referred to were com-pleted, and the completion thereof proved, allowed, certi-fied, and advertized, according to the enactments of those acts. From that time until the month of August, 1834, no alteration was made in the rate or duty of 3*s*. 6*d*. per pack or box of linen not in transitu, particularized in the schedule subjoined to the statute 48 Geo. 3, c. 11, above referred to. By an order made on the 27th August, 1834, the justices in and for the city and county of Bristol, in quarter sessions assembled, declared their consent and approbation that it should be lawful for the Directors of the Bristol Dock Company to lessen the rates and duties which by the said act of the 48 Geo. 3 were payable on the several articles imported into the said port of Bristol specified and set forth in the schedule under the said order written, to the several sums therein set opposite to the said respective articles; and in this schedule there is the following item:—

"'Linen not in transitu, per box . . . . . . 2*s*. 6*d*.'

"These duties were then lessened by the directors ac-cordingly. The monies borrowed under the before-men-tioued acts, together with the capital stock advanced, still remains unpaid and undischarged; and the duties imposed and made payable by the said acts are still vested in and payable to the said Bristol Dock Company.

"The plaintiff is the treasurer for the time being of the Bristol Dock Company, who by the before-mentioned acts, are impowered to sue in the name of their treasurer. The defendant is a natural born subject of the United Kingdom of Great Britain and Ireland, born in Ireland, and from his birth during all the times hereinafter mentioned, except while he was at Bristol as hereinafter mentioned, was resident at Armale, in the county of Armagh, in Ireland, where he carried on the trade of a bleacher of linens. On the 1st November, 1834, he was the owner of 108 pieces of Irish linen which had been woven in Ireland by Irish subjects, from yarn or thread spun in Ireland by Irish subjects, out of flax which had been raised and dressed in Ireland by Irish subjects; and, having packed the same in two wooden boxes manufactured in Ireland by Irish subjects, the defendant on that day shipped the same from the port of Dublin, in Ireland, in a certain vessel built in England and belonging to and navigated by certain natural born subjects of the United Kingdom resident in England, and called the Express steam packet, to be carried therein to the port of Bristol, being one of the ports of the realm within England, consigned, and there to be delivered to himself the said defendant. The same linens and boxes never were carried from Ireland to any other realm or country than England, nor to any other port of England than Bristol, nor ever were brought into England or Bristol from any other realm or country than Ireland aforesaid, nor from any other port or place than Dublin aforesaid, nor in any other vessel than the same Express steam packet. And the said linens and boxes so being put on board the same vessel, were afterwards on the same day carried therein by the direct and usual course from the said port of Dublin towards and unto the said port of Bristol, whereat they arrived on the

15th November aforesaid, and were there on that day delivered to and received and accepted by the defendant, he the said defendant during all the times aforesaid knowing that the duty of 2s. 6d. per box on such goods was claimed by the company, and being such owner and such consignee thereof, and such subject and so domiciled in Ireland as aforesaid. The goods so imported were not in transitu. Two days after the defendant had so received the same linens and boxes, the Bristol Dock Company demanded of the defendant the sum of 5s. as and for the rate and duty of 2s. 6d. by them alleged to be payable by him by virtue of the said Bristol Dock acts and the said order of justices and act of the said directors, in respect of each of the said two boxes of Irish linens; which sum the defendant refused to pay, or to pay any other duty or sum whatever for the same. The plaintiff claimed the duty of 2s. 6d. per box under the acts above referred to.

"The defendant referred to and relied on the same acts, and particularly the 43 Geo. 3, c. 140, s. 74, and the schedule of rates and duties thereto annexed—the 48 Geo. 3, c. 11, s. 48, and the schedule of rates and duties thereto annexed—and also on the several statutes of Ireland, of Great Britain, and of the United Kingdom of Great Britain and Ireland generally, and in particular upon the statute of Ireland, 40 Geo. 3, c. 38; touching which the parties mutually agreed to admit that an act intituled ' An act for the union of Great Britain and Ireland' was made and passed by the parliament of the kingdom of Ireland and his late majesty king George the Third, of Great Britain and Ireland, king, in the 40th year of his said late majesty's reign; and that the same received his said majesty's royal assent before the 1st January, 1801, viz. on the 1st August, 1800; and further that it should be lawful for either of the parties hereto to refer in their arguments to any parts or part of the same act, or of any other acts of the Irish parliament as being proved to be passed and the contents thereof to be evidenced by any print or copy of the same purporting to be printed by any printer authorized, or in the same print or otherwise expressed to be authorized, to print and publish statutes, by any king of Great Britain and Ireland or of the united kingdom of Great Britain and Ireland, in like manner as if the whole of the same statutes had been set out in this case. And the defendant particularly referred to the articles 1, 2, 3, 4, 5, 6, 7, and 8, and the 10th section, of the Irish act 40 Geo. 3, c. 38, and the schedule of reciprocal duties thereto annexed, the statute of Great Britain 39 & 40 Geo. 3, c. 67, intituled ' An act for the union of Great Britain and Ireland,' and the articles 1, 2, 3, 4, 5, 6, 7, and 8, and the 10th section, and the schedule of reciprocal duties thereto annexed.

" It was admitted and agreed, that, on the argument, any part of any of the above mentioned or any other public acts of Ireland, Great Britain, or the united kingdom of Great Britain and Ireland, might be referred to on the part of either party."

The question for the opinion of the court was—" Whether the rate and duty so demanded and refused was payable to the Bristol Dock Company. If the court should be of opinion that it was so payable, then judgment was to be entered for the plaintiff by confession for the sum of five shillings, and costs: but, if the court should be of a contrary opinion, then judgment of nolle prosequi (with costs) was to be entered for the defendant."

The case was argued in Michaelmas Term last.

The points marked for argument on the part of the plaintiff were—That the goods imported from Ireland, as stated in the case, were liable to the duty claimed under the local acts mentioned in the case, and more particularly under the words of the 48 Geo. 3, c. xi, s. 38, describing

the goods liable to the duty thereby given—"All goods,
wares, or merchandizes imported from parts beyond the
seas, and not brought by inland navigation, into the port
of Bristol (except corn, flour, rice, and other articles of
provision); and also all goods, wares, and merchandizes
that shall be brought coastwise into the said port, of foreign growth or importation, but not of British growth or
manufacture:" and that the right to the duty claimed under the before-mentioned statutes was not affected, abrogated, or controlled by any previous or subsequent statute,
either local or general.

For the defendant—1. That Irish linens are exempted
by the English and Irish Union acts, 39 & 40 Geo. 3, c. 67,
English, Art. 8, and 40 Geo. 3, c. 38, Irish, which are not
repealed by the Bristol local act, from duty, on importation
into Bristol, to which Scotch linens are not subjected.
2. That Irish linens are exempted by the English and
Irish Union acts from duty on importation into Bristol;
because, if duty was payable, they could not be exported
through England to foreign countries at the like charges
subject whereto they may be exported from Ireland. 3.
That the particular and positive enactments of the Union
acts, excepting Irish goods from duty, are not repealed by
any implication arising on general words in a local statute,
48 Geo. 3, c. xi. 4. That Ireland and Irish interests are
not to be affected or bound by any statute in which Ireland is not named. 5. That, if the international contract
between Great Britain and Ireland be ambiguous, it is to
be expounded in favour of Ireland, as the weaker nation.
6. That, in this Bristol local act, made since the Union,
the phrase "parts beyond the seas" does not designate or
comprehend Ireland. 7. That Irish linens are not since
the Union goods of foreign growth or importation. 8. That
Irish linens are since the Union goods of British growth
and manufacture.

Stephen, Serjeant (*Wilde*, Serjeant, was with him), for the plaintiff.—The Bristol Dock Company being impowered by act of parliament (more particularly by the 48 Geo. 3, c. xi,) to levy certain duties on goods " imported from parts beyond the seas, *and not brought by inland navigation*, into the port of Bristol, except corn, flour, rice, and other articles of provision;" and also on goods " brought coastwise into the said port, *of foreign growth* or importation, but not of British growth or manufacture," &c. &c.; the question is whether or not they are impowered to levy such duties on goods imported from Ireland.

That Ireland is, within the popular meaning of the term, " beyond the seas," cannot be questioned so long as St. George's Channel shall flow between them. And, even if the legal and technical sense of those words be different from their popular sense; yet, upon the construction of this act, Ireland must be intended to be beyond the seas: for, the words " and not brought by inland navigation," shew the meaning of the words that precede, and amount to a legislative declaration, that, for the purposes of this act, that which is not brought by inland navigation is from parts beyond the seas. The words are inserted as mere matter of description; and there can be no reason for excepting Ireland from the operation of an act, the object of which was to enable the company to improve the port and harbour of Bristol, the duties collected under the authority of the act to be applied to pay the principal and dividends or interest on the money advanced for that purpose by the parties constituting the company. These duties, therefore, are in the nature of private tolls. That Ireland also falls within the strict legal meaning of the words " parts beyond the seas," is clear from a variety of authorities. In Co. Litt. 244. a., it is said: " By the common law, if the husband be within the four seas, that is, within the jurisdiction of the king of England, if the wife hath issue, no proof is to be

admitted to prove the child a bastard (a), for, in that case,
filiatio non protest probari, unless," &c.: and Jenkins
says, 1 Cent. pl. 18; "Husband and wife, if the husband
be in Ireland or Scotland for a year, and the wife in England during this time has issue, this issue is a bastard. It
seems to me that at this day 'tis otherwise for Scotland,
for both are become under one king, and they make one
continent of land. Absence over sea takes away all presumption that the husband might be privately and secretly
with his wife; as he might if he were in England, although she had eloped and lived with an adulterer." In
Nightingale v. *Adams*, Holt, 426, S. C. *Anonymous*, 1
Show. 91, it was held by Holt, C. J., upon the statute of
limitations, "that Dublin or any other place in Ireland
is beyond sea, within the meaning of that clause in that
statute." The reporter adds—"Ruled so by him upon
consideration." This ruling is confirmed by *Baker* v.
Dormer, 1 Show. 197; and its correctness recognized by
the 3 & 4 Will. 4, c. 27, s. 19, and the 3 & 4 Will. 4, c. 42,
s. 7, which respectively enact that Ireland, amongst other
places, shall not be deemed to be beyond seas within the
meaning of those acts, or (3 & 4 Will. 4, c. 42, s. 7) of
the 21 Jac. 1, c. 16, s. 7. By the 10 Anne, c. 26, s. 34—
"for the better securing the duties upon coffee imported
from any foreign parts, and all such tea as shall be imported from any place within the limits of the charter
granted to the East India Company, by that and other
acts of parliament imposed; and to the intent the same
might not be too burdensome on the importers of such
coffee and tea as should again be exported to *parts beyond
the seas*"—it is provided and enacted that all such coffee
as should be imported into *Great Britain* from any

(a) The law upon this subject
is otherwise at the present day:
see Shelley v.———, 13 Ves. 58;
Head v. Head, 1 Turn. & R. 138,
1 Sim. & Stu. 150; Morris v.
Davies, 3 C. & P. 427; Cope v.
Cope, 5 C. & P. 604, 1 M. & Rob.
269.

foreign parts, and all such tea as should be imported &c., should be bonded, &c., and such of the said coffee and tea as should be for exportation to parts beyond the seas should be delivered out of such warehouse unto the importers or buyers &c. upon sufficient security to be first given to her majesty, her heirs and successors, that the same and every part thereof should be exported, and not relanded in Great Britain; which securities should be discharged without fee or reward, upon certificate returned or produced to the commissioners of the customs &c., under the common seal of the chief magistrate in any place or places in parts beyond the seas, or under the hands and seals of two known British merchants then being at such place or places, that such coffee or tea was there landed, or upon proof by credible persons that such coffee or tea was taken by enemies or perished in the seas. The 5 Geo. 1, c. 11, s. 5, reciting the 10 Anne, c. 26, enacts "that, from and after the 1st May, 1719, no such bond given for the exportation of coffee, tea, or other certificate goods exported to Ireland, shall be delivered up, or any drawback allowed for any goods entitled thereto, until a certificate shall be produced under the hands and seals of the collector, controller, and surveyor of the customs of some port in Ireland, or any two of them, where such goods shall be landed, testifying the landing thereof." This provision clearly demonstrates that in the preceding statute Ireland was deemed to be in "parts beyond the seas." Again, by the 13 & 14 Car. 2, c. 11, s. 3, it is enacted "that no captain, master, purser, or any other person or persons taking charge of any ship or vessel bound for the parts beyond the seas, *or into the kingdom of Scotland,* whether the same ship or vessel shall have commission from or belong unto the king's majesty that now is, his heirs or successors, or shall belong to or have commission from any foreign prince or state, or otherwise, shall take in, or suffer to be taken into or

laden aboard any such ship or vessel, any English goods,
wares, or merchandize to be exported into the parts beyond the seas, or into the kingdom of Scotland, until such
captain, &c., shall have entered such ship or ships in the
book of the commissioners, customer or collector and
comptroller outwards of such port where he shall load or
take in goods, together with the name of such captain or
master, &c.; and, before he or they shall depart with his
or their ship or vessel out of such port or place, shall
bring and deliver unto the said person or persons which
are or shall be appointed by his majesty for managing the
customs, the customer or collector and comptroller of
such port or place, a content in writing, under his or their
hands, of the names of every merchant and other person
or persons that shall have laden and put on board any
such ship or vessel any such goods or merchandize, together
with the marks and numbers of such goods and merchandize," &c. &c. "Great Britain" there is put in opposition to "parts beyond the seas." By the 43 Geo. 3, c.
128, s. 1 (upon the same subject), it is enacted, that, from
and after a day therein mentioned, "it shall not be lawful
for any person or persons whatever to lade or put or
cause to be laden or put off or from any quay, wharf, or
other place on land, into any ship, &c., any goods, wares,
or merchandize whatever, with intent to export the same
to *parts beyond the seas,* until such person or persons
shall deliver or cause to be delivered to the comptrolling
searchers of his majesty's customs, or some one of them, a
true and correct copy in writing of the cocquet or entry
(together with the indorsement thereon) for all such
goods, wares, and merchandize so intended to be exported." In that statute "Ireland" is put in opposition to
"Great Britain;" and it has always been the practice to
deliver a copy of the cocquet or entry upon exports of
goods to Ireland. The 43 Geo. 3, c. 68, contains an express legislative declaration that Ireland is in parts beyond

the seas: the 2nd section imposes upon "goods, wares, or merchandizes imported and brought into Great Britain from parts beyond the seas" the several duties set forth in the schedule and tables annexed to the act; and by Sched. A., Table 1, certain duties are declared to be payable on the importation of corn *except from Ireland*, and Table 2. gives the duties payable on the importation of corn from that country. [*Tindal*, C. J.—The two statutes last cited are more apposite, inasmuch as they were passed subsequently to the Union.] The exception of Ireland from Sched. A., Table 1, of the 43 Geo. 3, c. 68, was perfectly idle, unless Ireland were for all commercial purposes, notwithstanding the act of Union, still considered to be "in parts beyond the seas."

But, supposing the court to be of opinion that Ireland is not beyond seas for the purpose and within the meaning of the act now under consideration; still these goods were liable to the duty claimed as goods brought coastwise into the port of Bristol, of foreign growth, and not of British manufacture. Since the Union, Ireland is bound by all acts of the imperial parliament, unless actually and expressly excluded. The act of Union has relation only to public rights and international questions: it does not in any degree affect the private claims of corporations for tolls for improvements in their own ports. Lord Chief Justice Hale, in his treatise De Jure Maris et Brachiorum ejusdem, Part 1, c. 4 (1 Hargr. Tracts, 132), recognizes the validity of such customs: he says—"Customs by prescription belonging to ports were various, according as the usage and custom was. Some were in respect of ships or vessels themselves that came into the port, as anchorage and culage or keelage, which were certains sums taken for the ships, in some places more, in some places less. Vid. P. 40. E. 3. Rot. 73. The Earl of Surrey, as lord of the town and port of Poole, claimed by prescription quasdam custumas, viz. pro anchoragio et

culagio de quâlibet nave in portu prædictâ applicante
duos denarios, et diversas alias custumas, &c., and brought
his action for disturbance. Again, some were in respect
of goods imported into the port. Thus, in the former record, the same earl claimed by prescription diversas alias
custumas, viz. de quolibet dolio vini in nave infrà portum
prædictum applicante duos denarios, de quâlibet centenâ
averii ponderis duos denarios, de quolibet mille alecis ru-
beæ unum denarium; and brings his action against them
that disturbed his minister in collecting them." The duties
claimed in the present case are of this last description.
The case of *Jones* v. *Smart*, 1 T.R. 44, strongly illus-
trates the position now contended for. It was there held
that a diploma conferring the degree of doctor of physic,
granted by either of the universities in Scotland, does not
give a qualification to kill game, under the 22 & 23 Car.
2, c. 25. In the course of the argument the defendant's
claim to the qualification was rested mainly on the fourth
article of the act of Union (Scotch); as to which Lord Mansfield says: "There is not a colour for saying that the defendant is qualified by the act of Union. It is true, that, by the
fourth article of that act, the Scotch have the same general privileges as the English; but then they must have the
same qualifications, otherwise they come not within the
same description; for, the general article, which declares
there shall be a communication of all privileges, can only
mean such as are of a general nature. A burgess of London is endued with certain privileges to which a burgess of
Edinburgh has no claim: so, in every case where a privilege is of a qualified nature, it must be understood with
that qualification. A doctor of the English universities
may become a member of the college of physicians, may
plead in Doctors Commons, and has various other privileges, from all of which a Scotch doctor, as such, is excluded. The qualification therefore must be from Oxford

or Cambridge (*b*). In like manner, the statute allowing men of certain degrees to have dispensations for holding two livings, necessarily refers to such degrees only as are obtained in an English university; for, the Church of Scotland is distinct from ours, and admits not of the same rules." By the 4 Geo. 4, c. 72, s. 6, it is enacted, "that, at any time after the passing of that act, it should and might be lawful for the lord high treasurer, or for the commissioners of his majesty's treasury of the united kingdom of Great Britain and Ireland, or any three of them, by any warrant or order in writing signed by him or them, and published in the London and Dublin Gazettes, to direct and declare, that, from a day to be named in such warrant or order, the trade between Great Britain and Ireland should be taken and deemed to be a coasting trade, and from and after the day mentioned in such warrant or order, such trade should be and become a coasting trade accordingly;" and by the 6 Geo. 4, c. 107, s. 100 (repealed by 3 & 4 Will. 4, c. 50, s. 2, and re-enacted in the same terms by 3 & 4 Will. 4, c. 52, s. 105), it is enacted " that all trade by sea from any one part of the united kingdom to any other part thereof, or from one part of the Isle of Man to another thereof, shall be deemed to be a coasting trade, and all ships while employed therein shall be deemed to be coasting ships; and that no part of the united kingdom, however situated with regard to any other part thereof, shall be deemed in law, with reference to each other, to be parts beyond the seas, in any matter relating to the trade, or navigation, or revenue of this realm." But these statutes never could have been intended to affect private rights of toll like the present; and they shew conclusively, that, at the time of the passing of the Bristol Dock acts, the trade between this country and Ireland was not con-

(*b*) This case, it must be observed, was decided several years before the union of Great Britain with Ireland.

sidered a coasting trade. If the construction contended
for on the other side were to prevail, this absurd consequence would follow—foreign goods brought into the
port of Bristol from Scotland would be subjected to duties
from which the same goods brought there from Ireland
would be exempted.

Sir *John Campbell*, A. G. (*W. P. Taunton* was with him),
for the defendant.—The parties who are represented by
the plaintiff in this action are a company who have entered
into a certain adventure for their own benefit, and claim
certain tolls or duties upon all goods imported into their
port. It is incumbent on them to shew that the duty they
seek to inforce is imposed by the plain, unambiguous, and
unequivocal language of the legislature: if there be the
smallest scintilla of doubt, the defendant is entitled to the
benefit of it. In *Keen* v. *Waterhouse*, 4 B. & C. 208, 6 D.
& R. 257, which was an action for tolls for passing along
a turnpike road, Bayley, J., says: "Where there is an
ambiguity in the language used, the construction must be
in favour of the public, because it is a general rule, that,
where the public are to be charged with a burden, the intention of the legislature to impose that burden must be
explicitly and distinctly shewn." And in *Denn d. Mani-
fold* v. *Diamond*, 6 D. & R. 328, 4 B. & C. 243, on a question arising upon the construction of the stamp act, the
same learned judge observes: "It is a well settled rule of
law, that every charge upon the subject must be imposed
by clear and unambiguous terms." A still more strict rule
of construction is applied to acts of parliament brought in
by adventurers who for their own individual benefit acquire a right to construct works, and to derive a pecuniary profit from charges on the public: in these cases
the language employed is to be taken most strongly against
the adventurers and in favour of the public. This is
clearly ascertained by the case of *The Stourbridge Canal*

Company v. *Wheeley*, 2 B. & Ad. 792. It was there held,
that, where a canal is made pursuant to act of parliament,
the right of the proprietors to toll is derived entirely from
the act; and is to be considered as if there was a bargain
between them and the public, the terms of which are expressed in the statute; and the rule of construction is, that
any ambiguity in the terms of the contract must operate
against the company of adventurers, and in favour of the
public: the proprietors therefore can claim nothing which
is not clearly given to them by the act. Lord Tenterden,
delivering the judgment of the court, there says: " The
canal having been made under the provisions of an act of
parliament, the rights of the plaintiffs are derived entirely
from that act. This, like many other cases, is a bargain
between a company of adventurers and the public, the
terms of which are expressed in the statute; and the rule
of construction in all such cases is now fully established
to be this—that any ambiguity in the terms of the contract must operate against the adventurers and in favour of
the public; and the plaintiffs can claim nothing which is
not *clearly* given to them by the act. The rule is laid
down in distinct terms by the court in the case of *The
Hull Dock Company* v. *La Marche*, 8 B. & C. 51, 2 M. &
R. 107, where some previous authorities are cited; and·it
was also acted upon in the case of *The Leeds and Liverpool Canal Company*, v. *Hustler*, 1 B. & C. 424, 2 D & R.
556. Adopting this rule, we are to decide whether a
right to demand some compensation for the use of this
part of the canal is *clearly and unambiguously* given to
the plaintiffs by this act of parliament." So, here, it is
incumbent on the plaintiff to shew that the acts of parliament upon which the company rest their claim contain
words unequivocally and undeniably imposing the duty
demanded for these goods. Allowing that the duty in question is clearly imposed by the words of the 48 Geo. 3, c. xi,
does that act operate so as to supersede the act of Union,

39 & 40 Geo. 3, c. 67? At the time of the passing of the Bristol Dock acts, the trade of Ireland was of but little account. Can it be supposed that the legislature contemplated imposing upon goods imported in British ships from Dublin into Bristol larger duties than upon similar importations from Scotland? The 6th article of the act of Union enacts "that his majesty's subjects of Great Britain and Ireland shall, from and after the 1st January, 1801, be entitled to the same privileges, and be on the same footing, as to encouragements and bounties on the like articles being the growth, produce, or manufacture of either country respectively, and generally in respect of trade and navigation in all ports and places in the united kingdom and its dependencies"—clearly shewing the anxiety of the legislature to place the trade and commerce of the three kingdoms upon an equal footing. The argument on the other side goes the length of saying that the Isle of Wight is, and the Isle of Anglesea was, before the ingenuity of Mr. Telford united it with the main land by the celebrated Menai Bridge, in parts beyond the seas. From the whole tenor and scope of the act of Union, it is perfectly clear that from the moment of the passing of that act Ireland ceased to be beyond the seas. What is the just and rational meaning of that term? Simply this—that "beyond the seas" means without the seas that divide the country legislated for from foreign countries. Were this not so, the king, who cannot depart the realm, would be prevented from visiting his Irish dominions. The parliament that passed the acts by which the Bristol Dock Company was incoporated, might have sat in Dublin: would Ireland in that case have been beyond the seas? Throughout the Bristol Dock acts, it will be found, that, wherever a duty is imposed upon importations from Ireland or Scotland, those countries are spcifically mentioned. The 75th section of the 43 Geo. 3, c. cxl., amounts to a declaration that ships coming from Ireland would have

been considered coasters unless before specifically mentioned. The authority cited from Co. Litt. 244. a. affords no key to the construction of a modern act of parliament: and Ireland was to all intents and purposes a separate and independent kingdom at the time of the decision of *Nightingale* v. *Adams*. So, for the same reason, the statutes 13 & 14 Car. 2, c. 11, 10 Ann. c. 26, and 5 Geo. 1, c. 11, have no influence on the question; for the purposes of those acts, it may be admitted that Ireland was at the time they were passed beyond the seas: and there is no evidence that the provisions of the 43 Geo. 3, c. 128, have ever been applied to Irish voyages. It is equally impossible to say that Ireland is embraced by the enacting clause (s. 2) of the 43 Geo. 3, c. 68; though Ireland is ex abundanti cautelâ mentioned in the schedule thereto: and the 3rd section contains an express provision that that act shall not repeal or alter the provisions of the acts of Union between Great Britain and Ireland respecting duties on goods imported or exported. Many statutes, both English and Irish, might be cited to shew that, " out of the realm," " beyond the seas," and " out of this kingdom" are convertible terms: for example, the 32 Hen. 8, c. 1—English; and the 33 Hen. 8, c. 12, 10 Car. 1, sess. 1, c. 6, ss. 1, 8, 9, 13, 10 Car. 1, sess. 3, c. 21, and 6 Ann. c. 10, s. 17 — Irish. So, in *King* v. *Walker*, 1 W. Bl. 286 " in foreign parts," " out of the realm," and " beyond the seas," are supposed to be synonymous. Many statutes passed since the Union use the words " beyond the seas" in contradistinction to the united kingdom. Thus, the 43 Geo. 3, c. 56, s. 1, regulates the mode of conveyance of emigrants "from any port or place in the united kingdom of Great Britain and Ireland to any parts beyond the seas." So, the 5 Geo. 4, c. 84, an act for the transportation of offenders from Great Britain, contains in ss. 3, 5, 6, 8, provisions regulating the conveyance of convicts to parts beyond the seas ; and upon the construction

1836.

BATTERSBY
v.
KIRK.

of that act it would be absurd to say that Ireland was included within the term "beyond the seas." Again, the provisions in the 6 Geo. 4, c. 107, s. 100, and the 3 & 4 Will.
4, c. 52, s. 105—which declare "that all trade by sea
from any one part of the united kingdom to any other
part thereof, or from one part of the Isle of Man to
another thereof, shall be deemed to be a coasting trade,
and all ships while employed therein shall be deemed to
be coasting ships; and that no part of the united kingdom, however situate with regard to any other part thereof, shall be deemed in law, with reference to each other,
to be parts beyond the seas in any matter relating to the
trade, or navigation, or revenue of this realm"—lead irre-
sistibly to the same conclusion. The customs' act, 3 & 4
Will. 4, c. 52, contains repeated instances of the exclusion
of Ireland from "parts beyond the seas:" such are to be
found in sections 2, 3, 5, 10, 15, 35, 62, 63, 64, 65, 72, 78,
and 80. Throughout that act, Irish are included in the
term "British ships"—sections 2, 3, 6, 8, 16, 44, 56, 83,
84, and 112. The statutes 3 & 4 Will. 4, c. 53, ss. 28,
49, 74, 77, 80, 3 & 4 Will. 4, c. 54, ss. 7, 8, 9, 12, and
3 & 4 Will. 4, c. 55, s. 3, severally contain provisions to
the like effect. And the Liverpool Dock act, 51 Geo. 3,
c. cxliii, s. 16, applies the term "coastwise" to voyages
from one part of the *united kingdom* to another.

Then it is said that the goods in question are at all
events liable to the duty claimed, inasmuch as they are
goods of "foreign growth," and not of "British growth or
manufacture." The 3 & 4 Will. 4, c. 52, ss. 33, 40, 53,
56, and 113, however, distinguish "foreign goods" from
goods the produce or manufacture of Ireland. And in
The Attorney-General v. *M'Kenzie*, 11 Price, 284, it was
expressly held, that, where spirituous liquors distilled and
made in Ireland are imported from that country into England, they become British spirits, and are entitled as such
to all the advantages of British spirits. [*Tindal*, C. J.—

Do not the words in the 48 Geo. 3, c. xi, s. 88, " and not brought by inland navigation, " give some sense and meaning to the expression " beyond the seas ?"]   Those words afford no stronger argument as to goods from Ireland than with respect to goods coming from Glasgow.

Stephen, Serjeant, in reply.—It seems to be conceded that Ireland before the Union was in parts beyond the seas.   How, then, for the purposes of an act like the present, can it be said to have ceased to be so?   There can be no reason why those words should not upon the present occasion receive a construction agreeable with the sense in which they are understood in common parlance. Several Irish acts have been cited to shew that " out of the realm," " beyond the seas," and " out of this kingdom," are used synonymously: as to Ireland, this need not be disputed.   The parliament of the united kingdom, in contemplation of law, sits at Westminster; though there are instances of its having sat elsewhere—as, for instance, the statutes of Marlebridge, of Gloucester, of Acton Burnel, &c.   The 43 Geo. 3, c. 68, s. 2, is decisive of the question : it affords a clear and indubitable contemporaneous exposition of the intention of the legislature.   The provisions in the 6 Geo. 4, c. 107, s. 100, and the 3 & 4 Will. 4, c. 52, s. 105, declaring the trade with Ireland to be a coasting trade, must be construed with reference only to the immediate purposes of those acts: they never could be intended to interfere with or supersede any of the provisions in the Bristol Dock acts; and they tend materially to strengthen the argument, that, before the first of those acts passed, the trade of Ireland with this country was not a coasting trade.   It may be admitted, that, for the purpose of revenue regulations, Irish ships and Irish goods may be respectively British ships and goods.   But, upon the construction of the 46 Geo. 3, c. xi, it is perfectly clear that that which is not of

British is of foreign manufacture. *The Attorney-General
v. M'Kenzie* has no reference whatever to the question
now before the court: the decision there turned upon the
language of the 26 Geo. 3, c. 73, s. 34.

Cur. adv. vult.

TINDAL, C. J.—Upon this special case the question is
whether linens the produce and manufacture of Ireland,
imported from Dublin, in Ireland, into the port of Bristol,
are or are not liable to the duty imposed by the 38th section of the Bristol Dock act, 48 Geo. 3, c. xi. The duty is
imposed by that section " on goods, wares, or merchandizes imported from parts beyond the seas, and not brought
by inland navigation, into the port of Bristol," and also
" on goods, wares, and merchandizes brought coastwise into
the said port, of foreign growth or importation, but not of
British growth or manufacture." The plaintiff contends
that the goods in question fall within the first branch of
the description. The defendant, on the other hand, contends that they fall under neither of the heads above
referred to: not under the first, because Ireland at the
time of passing this act was not, within the meaning of
the statute, " beyond the seas:" nor under the second,
because, although the goods in question were carried *coastwise* (as he the defendant contends they were), *they were
not " of foreign growth or importation, but not of British
growth or manufacture,"* so as to fill up this second description of goods liable to the duty.

With respect to the duty imposed on goods falling within
the second description, we cannot bring ourselves to the
opinion that goods imported from any port in Ireland into
Bristol can be considered to be goods brought coastwise
within the meaning of the act. The words are incapable
of such a construction in their natural and popular sense:
and there is no technical meaning annexed to the expression. It is urged in argument, that, by the 6 Geo. 4, c. 107,

s. 100, the legislature has enacted that all trade from any one part of the United Kingdom to any other part shall be deemed to be a *coasting trade*. But that enactment is expressly declared to be made " for the purposes of trade and navigation, and the revenue of the realm.". And we are of opinion that a legislative enactment for that purpose cannot have the effect of indirectly repealing a duty or toll imposed by a former statute, such duty not being any part of the public revenue of the realm, but granted by the legislature to private individuals for good and valuable service rendered by them to the public: so far, therefore, as the claim to the duty imposed by the statute 48 Geo. 3 is concerned, we think the same meaning belongs to the term "coastwise" at the present time as it had at the time of passing that act. The only question, therefore, which we propose to consider is, whether the goods in question were imported " from parts beyond the seas."

Before we proceed, however, to state the grounds of the opinion at which we have arrived after the best consideration we have been able to bring to a case of considerable difficulty, it may be useful to observe that the terms employed by the legislature in imposing the duty, both in the 43 Geo. 3, c. cxl, s. 75, and also in the 48 Geo. 3, c. xi, above referred to, are substantially the same. The two acts differ, indeed, from each other in one very important particular: that whereas, by the former act, goods brought coastwise are exempted from duty; by the latter, goods brought coastwise are made liable to the duty if of foreign growth or importation. But each of the acts, in imposing the duty, uses precisely the same expressions—viz. goods imported from parts beyond the seas, goods brought coastwise, and goods brought by inland navigation. So that there can be no doubt but that the legislature, in using the words " goods imported from parts beyond the seas into the port of Bristol," intended one and the same subjectmatter of duty in both the acts. What such meaning and intention of the legislature was, we are called upon to declare.

If these words are to be taken in their plain, natural, and popular sense, without reference to any technical meaning acquired by legal use, there could be no difficulty in their interpretation. No one would hesitate to say that they were intended to express the importing of goods into the port of Bristol in vessels which arrived from any port or place not being in England or Scotland. For, as the clause which imposes the duty, both in the earlier and later act, specifies and distinguishes the three modes by which only goods and merchandise can be imported into the port of Bristol by water—that is to say, by inland navigation, by vessels sailing coastwise, and by vessels from "parts beyond the seas"—the latter expression must be taken to comprehend every mode of importation of goods not included in the former two. And, as the coastwise navigation comprehends the navigation from all parts of England and Scotland, and as the inland navigation comprehends all importation from any part of the interior, the importation "from parts beyond the seas" must comprehend the bringing in of goods by sea from all other places whatsoever, and consequently the ports of Ireland equally with those of America and France. Such being the natural and ordinary interpretation of the words of the statute, it is not to be lost sight of during the whole of the inquiry; for, unless there is some technical sense in which the words are used, or unless the construction of other parts of the act does of necessity give a different meaning to these words, there is no safer mode of construing a statute than by interpreting the words employed therein according to their ordinary and familiar signification. The argument, however, on the part of the defendant is, that the phrase " parts beyond the seas" is used by the legislature in these statutes in the technical sense in which it was well known by the English law; that the acknowledged meaning of that expression was the same as "out of the realm of England;" and that, although Ireland was at one time, and for certain purposes, clearly held to be " beyond the seas" in such legal sense, yet that, since the passing of the act of Union, Ireland has become a component part of the same realm with England, and consequently from that time has ceased to be beyond the seas as to England, within the proper legal meaning of the expression.

That Ireland before the Union was held to be "beyond the seas," with reference to England, is certain. It was beyond the seas within the meaning of the exception in the statute of limitations, 21 Jac. 1, c. 16. It was so ruled by Holt, C. J., and, as the reporter says, upon consideration—*Nightingale* v. *Adams*, 1 Show. 91. It is stated to be beyond seas for the purpose of presuming non-access to the wife, if the husband be in Ireland for a year, and the wife in England during that time has issue—Jenk. Cent. 1, ca. 18; Co. Litt. 244. a. So, it was held to be beyond the seas with respect to the exceptions of disabilities under the statutes relating to fines; and in some other instances. It is also clear that the expression in the books, " beyond the seas," may be taken to be the same in effect as " out of the realm of England," for, so Lord Coke explains the phrase in his commentary on Litt. s. 677— Littleton there saying, " if the husband goeth beyond sea;" and Lord Coke saying, " if he had been *within the realm*, it doth not alter the case." And the expressions " beyond the sea" and " within the land" or " within the realm," appear to be used indiscriminately for each other in the statutes relating to fines—see 18 Ed. 1, st. 4; 4 Hen. 7, c. 24, s. 5; in which latter statute parties are excepted who are described as " out of this land," and who are afterwards in the same statute directed to make their claim within ten years next after their " coming into this realm," and at no time after. To the same effect also, in 27 Eliz. c. 9, s. 3, the statute makes provision for persons " beyond

the seas," so as "such person beyond the seas" shall,
within seven years next after the return of such person
"within the realm of England," or the death of such person,
if he shall before his return die " in any foreign country."
It appears, from these and other authorities which might
be cited, that Ireland was at the several periods of time to
which they respectively refer considered to be " in parts
beyond the seas," that is " out of this realm of England."
It follows, therefore, as an undeniable consequence, that,
if the act imposing the duty in question had been passed
before the act of Union, the laying of the duty on
goods imported " from parts beyond the seas" would have
attached upon goods imported from Ireland ; that country
being unquestionably before the Union " beyond the seas,"
whether the words are taken in their natural and ordinary
sense, or in the legal meaning of the phrase, " out of this
land," or " out of this realm of England." But, as the
Bristol Dock acts were passed *after* the Union, the great
question in this case arises upon the effect and operation
of the act of Union upon the construction of those words.
The defendant argues, that, from the moment the act of
Union was passed, Ireland was no longer " beyond the
seas" with reference to England, but part of one and the
the same realm, viz. part of the united kingdom of Great
Britain and Ireland ; that, whereas before Ireland was
divided from England by St. George's Channel, now it is
no otherwise divided from it than the Isle of Wight from
the county of Southampton; and, consequently, that,
when the statute 48 Geo. 3, c. xi, which was passed subsequently to the act of Union, imposed a duty on all
goods imported from parts beyond the seas, it could not
comprehend the importation of goods from Ireland. There
appears to be no provision contained in either of the statutes, 43 Geo. 3, c. cxl, or 48 Geo. 3. c. xi, which throws
any certain light on the intention of the legislature with
respect to this disputed question: we must therefore have

1836.

BATTERSBY
v.
KIRK.

recourse to the act of Union itself, and must further consider different acts of the legislature relating to this subject matter which have passed since the period of the Union, in order to discover if possible such indications of the intention of the legislature upon the subject in dispute as may enable us to come to a safe conclusion thereon.

The part of the act of Union (39 & 40 Geo. 3, c. 67) which has been chiefly relied on by the defendant is article 6. It is not contended that there is any part of the act of Union which in terms brings Ireland into the realm of England, so as to make it literally " part of the same land" or "within the realm," according to the equivalent expression in the older authorities before adverted to: but it is argued, and with great appearance of reason, that, by incorporating the two countries into one new united kingdom, the same legal consequences ought to follow which undoubtedly would have followed if that country had by the act of the legislature been expressly declared to form part of the realm of England alone; and it is insisted more particularly that the 6th article of the Union, enacting that the subjects of the two countries are placed upon the same footing generally in respect of trade and navigation in all ports and places in the united kingdom and its dependencies, declares in effect that goods the produce or manufacture of Ireland shall not be made subject by any future act to a larger duty for entering any port in England than similar goods from any part of Great Britain. We feel the full force of this argument; and, if the determination of the question before us had turned upon the construction of the act of Union alone, we should have thought it extremely difficult to avoid the conclusion above contended for. But several statutes have been referred to by the plaintiff as having passed since the act of Union, and which are by him insisted upon to be inconsistent with the defendant's inference that the effect of the Union of the two kingdoms was to prevent Ireland from continuing "beyond the seas" with reference to England. The whole strength of the argument on the part of the defendant rests, it must be recollected, upon that assumption; and if it should, upon reference to those statutes, appear that since the act of Union, and notwithstanding its provisions, Ireland has been recognized by the legislature as still being "beyond the seas" with respect to England, the inference drawn from the passing of the act of Union must fall to the ground, and the legislature itself will have afforded an exposition of the sense and meaning which it attached to that phrase where in occurs in the two statutes now under consideration. And, upon reference to those statutes subsequently passed, we think such is the necessary conclusion, and, consequently, that we are bound to adopt such legislative exposition, and to submit our private judgment in expounding the two statutes to the same authority by which they were enacted.

3 & 4 Will. 4,
c. 42, s. 7.

First, let us advert to the statute passed in the 3 & 4 Will. 4, c. 42. The 7th section enacts that after the act shall commence no part of the united kingdom of Great Britain and Ireland shall be deemed to be beyond the seas within the meaning of the statute 21 Jac. 1. Now, if by the simple operation of the act of Union, Ireland had become, as contended by the defendant, no longer "beyond the seas" with reference to England, such an enactment would seem to have been unnecessary. The making of such enactment, therefore, affords reasonable ground for the inference, that, in the judgment of the legislature, such consequence had not followed. A similar observation arises on the statute 3 & 4 Will. 4, c. 27. By the 16th section of that act, an exception is made in favor of a person under disability by reason of his being "absent beyond seas" at the time of the right first accruing; and in the 19th section it is further enacted that no part of the united kingdom of Great Britain or Ireland shall be deemed to be "beyond seas" within the mean-

3 & 4 Will. 4,
c. 27, s. 16.

ing of that act. Where was the necessity for this enactment, if Ireland had already ceased to be beyond the
seas? But, if these provisions should be argued to be
made pro majori cautelâ only, let us next advert to the
statute 6 Geo. 4, c. 107, s. 100. By that statute it is enacted " that no part of the united kingdom, however situated with regard to any other part thereof, shall be
deemed in law, with reference to each other, to be ' parts
beyond the seas' in any matter relating to the trade or
navigation or revenue of the realm." Upon this statute
two observations arise—first, that, when compared with
the 6th article of the act of Union, it is found to apply
distinctly and closely to the main object of that article,
viz. the equalization of the king's subjects of Great Britain and Ireland in respect of trade and navigation in all
ports and places of the united kingdom and its dependencies: and therefore the inference arises, that the
legislature did not consider that Ireland had ceased to be
"in parts beyond the seas" from the time of the Union;
for, had such been the consequence, there would then
have existed no necessity to make a subsequent enactment expressly to that effect. The second observation is,
that, although this statute makes every part of Great Britain and Ireland cease to be beyond the seas with respect to
any other part, yet it is only so enacted with respect to the
object and purpose declared in the same section, that is,
"in any matter relating to the trade or navigation or revenue of the realm;" and such an enactment for general and
public purposes could not operate a repeal of a duty or toll
already granted to a private company by a former act.
Ireland might therefore cease to be " beyond the seas"
for the purposes of the one statute, but continue " beyond
the seas" for the purposes of the other.

But the statute 43 Geo. 3, c. 68, is the act by which we
feel ourselves most strongly pressed to the conclusion that
the legislature has in effect declared that at that time

Ireland was still considered as "beyond the seas" with reference to England; and has thereby itself expounded by a contemporaneous enactment the meaning of the clause in the two Bristol Dock acts, the 43 Geo. 3, c. cxl, and the subsequent act of the 48 Geo. 3, c. xi. By the 2nd section of the act now referred to, certain duties of customs are granted to the king upon goods imported and brought into Great Britain " from parts beyond the seas." By s. 4, it is enacted that nothing in the act contained shall extend to repeal or alter any of the provisions contained in the act of Union. The schedule A. which is annexed to the act, contains the duties of customs payable on the importation into Great Britain of certain goods &c.: and, when the article "corn" occurs, two tables are subjoined, of which table 1. is stated to contain the duties payable on different kinds of corn on importation, *except from Ireland*, and table 2. is stated to contain the duties payable on corn on *importation from Ireland*. Now, the duty of customs being granted expressly upon goods imported into Great Britain " from parts beyond the seas," the question arises with respect to table No. 1—why should the importation from Ireland be excepted, if Ireland was already by the operation of the act of Union no longer " beyond the seas" with reference to Great Britain? And, again, with reference to table No. 2—the duties of customs having been only granted on goods imported from " beyond, the seas," the table of particular duties upon corn imported into Great Britain from Ireland, is equivalent to an express declaration that Ireland comes within the general description of places the importation of goods from whence renders them liable to the duty imposed by the act. The observation appears the stronger from the reference that is made to the effect of the act of Union, which cannot therefore be supposed to have been out of the view of the legislature at the time. And, further, the act now under consideration is strictly contemporaneous with the first of the

Bristol Dock acts; the royal assent having been given to the one in June, and to the other in August, of the very same year.

We cannot but consider these legislative enactments as forming a glossary for the proper interpretation of the expression's in the Bristol Dock act which are considered to be left in doubt; and that the effect of the several statutes above referred to, is sufficient to destroy the inference upon which the whole of the defendant's argument rests, viz. that, by the act of Union, Ireland ceased for all purposes to be considered in parts beyond the seas.

Upon the whole of the question it appears to us, that, if the words " parts beyond the seas" are to be taken in their plain and natural sense, as denoting the relative locality of the ports from which goods are sent, and the port of Bristol, into which they are sent, Ireland in that sense of the words is manifestly " in parts beyond the seas;" that, if the words are to be taken in their legal technical sense, then, undoubtedly, before the Union, Ireland was in parts beyond the seas; and that, although the act of Union, if taken separately and alone, might lead to the inference that Ireland after the Union was no longer to be considered " beyond the seas," yet that the legislature has, by divers acts passed since the act of Union, at once rebutted such inference, and afforded its own exposition of the sense in which the phrase " parts beyond the seas" was still to be understood with respect to Ireland: and, feeling ourselves bound to attend to such exposition, we hold that the proper interpretation of the statutes relating to the Bristol Docks, is, that goods imported from Ireland into the port of Bristol are " goods imported from parts beyond the seas," and therefore liable to the duty claimed. For these reasons, we give—

Judgment for the plaintiff.

1836.

Saturday,
April 16th.

On a reference
to arbitration of
an action of
ejectment and
all matters in
difference be-
tween the par-
ties, the arbi-
trator directed
that a sum of
50*l.* should be
paid by the
lessor of the
plaintiff to the
defendants by
way of compen-
sation for certain
buildings erect-
ed by them, and
that a verdict
should be en-
tered for the
former. On mo-
tion, the court
directed the
sum awarded to
the defendants
to be set off
against the costs
of the lessor of
the plaintiff,
saving the lien
of their attor-
ney.

DOE d. SWINTON v. SINCLAIR and Others.

THIS was an action of ejectment, which, with all matters in difference between the parties, had been referred to an arbitrator, who had directed the verdict to be entered for the lessor of the plaintiff, but awarded two sums of 30*l.* and 20*l.* to be paid by him to the defendants by way of compensation for certain buildings erected upon the demised premises.

G. T. White, in the last term, obtained a rule, on the part of the lessor of the plaintiff, calling upon the defendants to shew cause why the sums so awarded to them should not be set off against the costs in the cause.

Humfrey and *Heaton* shewed cause.—They produced an affidavit wherein it was sworn that a greater sum than 50*l.* was due from the defendants to their attorney; and they submitted, that, inasmuch as the payment of the money was made a condition by the award, it should have been paid before any question as to costs could arise, and therefore that, even as between the parties to the suit, it could not properly form the subject of a set-off; but that, at all events, inasmuch as it was sworn that the attorney's lien exceeded the sum awarded to the defendants, he was entitled to retain it as against all parties. They cited and relied on the cases of *Newton* v. *Newton*, 1 M. & Scott, 366, 8 Bing. 202, 1 Dowl. 264, and *Watson* v. *Maskell*, ante, Vol. 1, p. 286, 658, 1 New Cases, 366, 727, 2 Dowl. 10, and also referred to 1 Reg. Gen. Hilary Term, 2 Will. 4, s. 93, which provides that " no set-off of damages or costs between parties shall be allowed to the prejudice of the lien of the attorney for costs in the particular suit against which the set-off is sought."

G. T. White, in support of his rule.—As between the parties themselves, the set-off is clearly allowable—*Doe* d. *Hope* v. *Carter*, 1 M. & Scott, 516, 8 Bing. 330: the only question is, as to how far it is affected by the attorney's lien. In *Howell* v. *Harding*, 8 East, 362, it was held that the plaintiff was entitled to set off interlocutory costs in the same cause payable by him to the defendant, against the debt and costs recovered by him on the final result of the cause, notwithstanding the objection of the defendant's attorney on the ground of his lien, which only attaches on the general result of the costs &c. of the cause. *George* v. *Elston*, ante, Vol. 1, 518, 1 New Cases, 513, 3 Dowl. 419, recognizes the principle laid down in *Howell* v. *Harding*: there, a verdict was found against one of three defendants and in favour of the other two, and this court deducted the costs of the two out of the plaintiff's costs and damages against the one, without regard to the plaintiff's attorney's lien. And in *Figes* v. *Adams*, 4 Taunt. 632, it was held, that, if upon the reference of an action in this court, the arbitrator award the costs of a nonsuit to be paid by the one party, and a larger sum to be paid as a debt by the other party, the party awarded to pay the smaller sum is entitled to a set-off, without motion.

Tindal, C. J.—It appears to me that this rule should be made absolute, saving the lien of the defendant's attorney for costs in the suit. The first question is whether these sums awarded to the defendants in the nature of damages can properly form the subject of a set-off. *Newton* v. *Newton* is an authority to shew that they may. There, by an order of Nisi Prius, it was agreed that a verdict should be entered for the plaintiff for nominal damages and the costs of the action, and that the plaintiff should pay the defendant a sum of 70*l.* due to her from him: and the court permitted the 70*l.* to be set off against the costs in the cause. If the 50*l.* awarded in this case can properly be considered as in the nature of damages, there is an end of the question.

Vaughan, J.—The case seems to me to fall within the spirit of the rule referred to.

The rest of the court concurring—

Rule absolute accordingly.

———◆———

HUMPHREY and Another v. MITCHELL.

A ca. sa. against one G. was delivered to the sheriff, who thereupon made his warrant commanding one W. a bailiff to arrest G. The bailiff W. and his assistant R. proceeded to execute the warrant. The latter, in the absence of the former, arrested G., and, in order to secure him till he could procure the attendance of W. who had the warrant in his possession, placed him in the custody of a policeman on a false charge of felony, and caused him to be conveyed to a police-station. R. then fetched W., who, with full knowledge of the illegal manner in which the caption had been effected, took G. on the warrant and carried him to prison:—Held, that these facts were sufficient to establish the affirmative of an issue as to whether or not W. illegally seized and imprisoned G.

THIS was an action brought by the plaintiffs, late sheriffs of London, against the defendant on a bond executed by him as surety for one William Jackson, a sheriff's officer, in the penal sum of 2000l. The bond was set out on oyer in the plea, and was conditioned for the performance of the covenants in an indenture bearing even date with the bond, between the plaintiffs of the one part, and the defendant and William Jackson and four others of the other part, whereby, after reciting that the plaintiffs, then sheriffs of London, at the request of the defendant and others, and upon their undertaking to indemnify the plaintiffs, had appointed William Jackson to be one of the plaintiffs' serjeants-at-mace, the defendant covenanted with the plaintiffs that Jackson should duly discharge his duties of serjeant-at-mace, &c. &c., detailing them: the plea then averred performance of all the covenants contained in that indenture.

The plaintiffs replied, that, on the 26th November, 1833, R. M. Casberd, G. Daniell, and H. Tripp, sued out a ca. sa. directed to the sheriffs of London, and commanding them to take one George to satisfy a debt of 200*l.*; that the writ was delivered to the plaintiffs as sheriffs to be executed, and that they made out their warrant to William Jackson to take George according to the tenor of the writ; that William Jackson afterwards, to wit, on the 31st December, in the year aforesaid, took upon himself the execution of the warrant, and, acting in his said office of serjeant-at-mace of the plaintiffs, and under color of the said warrant, illegally seized and imprisoned George, he, George, then and at the time of such seizure being illegally imprisoned by one Richard Jackson, who acted in aid of the said William Jackson on the occasion, and who had previously seized and imprisoned George without any sufficient authority in that behalf; and of which illegal imprisonment William Jackson knowingly availed himself; that William Jackson having so illegally imprisoned George, he afterwards, to wit, on &c., conveyed George to a certain prison, to wit, White Cross Street prison, being a prison of the plaintiffs as such sheriffs of London, and there delivered him to the plaintiffs as such sheriffs, who detained him in custody there under the supposed authority of the said writ of ca. sa., they the plaintiffs being wholly ignorant and without notice of the illegal manner in which he had been so seized and imprisoned by William Jackson; that afterwards, to wit, on the 29th January, 1833, George, in an action brought by him in the court of Common Pleas, impleaded the plaintiffs and William Jackson and Richard Jackson for and in respect of the said illegal seizure and imprisonment of him George, and such proceedings were thereupon had that they the plaintiffs, in order to relieve themselves from the said action, and to settle the same, necessarily and properly, and for the benefit and advantage, as well of the defendant and the other persons parties to the said writing obligatory and the said indenture, as of themselves, paid to George a certain large sum of money, to wit, the sum of

1836.

HUMPHREY
v.
MITCHELL.

80*l.*, for his damages by reason of the illegal seizure and imprisonment, and his costs in the action; and the plaintiffs were also compelled and necessarily became liable to pay a certain other large sum of money, to wit, the sum of other 80*l.* for their costs in and about defending and settling and putting an end to the said action: of all which premises the defendant and the said other persons parties to the said writing obligatory and indenture had notice, and were afterwards, to wit, on &c., requested by the plaintiffs to save and indemnify them from the said damages, costs, charges, and expenses which they so incurred and paid, and to which they were so put by reason of the illegal conduct of William Jackson as aforesaid; but neither the defendant nor the said other persons, nor any other person or persons whatsoever on his or their behalf did or would, when so requested, or at any other time whatsoever, so save and indemnify the plaintiffs as aforesaid, or pay them the said sums of 80*l.* and 80*l.*, or any part thereof, but to do so wholly refused and still do refuse, contrary to the form and effect of the said indenture and also contrary to the form and effect of the condition of the said writing obligatory.

The defendant rejoined that the said W. Jackson did not illegally seize or imprison George in manner and form as the plaintiffs had above in their replication in that behalf stated, &c.

The cause was tried before Tindal, C. J., at the Sittings in London after the last term, when the following facts appeared in evidence:—A ca. sa. against George at the suit of Casberd and others having been delivered to the plaintiffs as sheriffs of London, to be executed, they thereupon made their warrant to William Jackson, a serjeant-at-mace, who assisted by his son Richard proceeded to the neighbourhood of the residence of George, in the Temple, in order to arrest him. The warrant was in the possession of William Jackson. Richard Jackson

seeing George proceeding towards Fleet Street, followed
and seized him there, and, being asked by George to shew
him his warrant, called a policeman to aid him in arresting George on a pretended charge of felony. They then
proceeded together to the police-station in Black Horse
Court, where Richard Jackson, on being called upon
to specify the charge in order to its being entered in the
book kept for that purpose at the station, stated that
George had escaped from custody on civil process. Richard Jackson then proceeded to the Temple, accompanied
by the policeman, to seek his father. On the way back
to the station, Richard Jackson said to his father, " Give
me the warrant, and then they will not know but that I
had it all the time." The warrant was accordingly handed
to Richard Jackson; and when they arrived at the police-
station, the charge of felony was abandoned, and George
was taken by William Jackson in pursuance of the warrant, and carried to White Cross Street prison, where he
was detained about a month under the above mentioned
ca. sa. and under process at the suit of several other persons which were at the same time in the hands of the sheriffs. George having been discharged from custody on
the ground of the illegality of the original caption (a),
afterwards brought an action against the sheriffs and the
two Jacksons (b), which was ultimately settled on the terms
stated in the replication. The proceedings in the action
against the sheriffs were put in and proved. A verdict
having been found for the plaintiffs, damages 160l.—

Atcherley, Serjeant, now moved for a new trial.—The
arrest of George by Richard Jackson was not such an
arrest as satisfies the allegation on the record that William
Jackson, acting in his office as serjeant-at-mace of the
plaintiffs, and under color of the warrant, illegally seized

(a) See Barratt v. Price, 2 M. &   (b) See Price v. Peek, ante, Vol.
Scott, 634, 9 Bing. 566.   1, p. 205, 1 New Cases, 380.

and imprisoned George, he, George, then being illegally imprisoned by one Richard Jackson, who acted in aid of the said William Jackson on the occasion, and who had previously seized and imprisoned George without any sufficient authority in that behalf; the then state of George not being a state of illegal imprisonment according to the above allegation.   It is not necessary that the caption should be made by the person named in the warrant, or in his presence.   Holt, C. J., in *Wilson* v. *Gary*, 6 Mod. 211, doubted whether an arrest made under circumstances similar to those of the present case was good: but in *Blatch* v. *Archer*, Cowp. 65, and in *Fenton's* case, Lofft. 524, it is expressly laid down that an arrest must be made by the authority and direction of the bailiff; but it need not be his hand that actually arrests, nor need it take place in his presence and in his sight, nor is there any precise distance from the person arrested within which he must be at the time; so that he be come for that purpose, and be near enough to be in readiness to act if occasion requires.   Lord Mansfield says, in *Blatch* v. *Archer:* " Several objections have been made—first, that the arrest was not by the sheriff's officer himself, for that the father was the officer, and the son the hand that arrested.   That the officer must be the *authority* to arrest is certain; but he need not be the hand that arrests, nor in the presence of the person arrested, nor actually in sight; nor is any exact distance prescribed."   Aston, J., said: " It is not necessary that the bailiff should be actually in sight, but he must be so near as to be near at hand and acting in the arrest."   And Ashhurst, J., said: " The jury have found that the officer was so near as to be acting in the arrest, which is sufficient."   Here, the son had authority to effect the caption.   If so, at what precise moment did he become a trespasser—when he first captured George in Fleet Street, or when he resorted to the stratagem of charging him with felony in order the better to secure him?   If the arrest was originally lawful, the subsequent misconduct of Richard Jackson will not render it illegal: if it would, every falsehood told by an officer in the course of effecting a caption will render the sheriff liable to an action for false imprisonment. Then, did the father, William Jackson, knowingly avail himself of the illegal seizure and imprisonment of George by Richard Jackson? There was nothing in the evidence to shew that William Jackson was at all cognisant of any illegality in the conduct of the arrest by his son. For anything that appears, he may have supposed that an assault had been committed, or that George had attempted to escape, or that there was reason to apprehend a rescue.

TINDAL, C. J.—The only question before us is, whether or not the issue joined on this record has been made out by the evidence—whether or not William Jackson illegally seized and imprisoned George. It appears that a ca. sa. had issued commanding the sheriffs to take George; that the sheriffs thereupon made their warrant to William Jackson, who proceeded to execute it assisted by his son Richard; and that the father and the son were watching in the neighbourhood of the residence of George in the Temple, when the son, seeing George come out, followed him into Fleet Street, and there, in order to effect a caption, falsely charged him with felony, and caused him to be conveyed by a policeman on such false charge to the police-station in Black Horse Court, and to be there detained in custody until he could procure the attendance of his father, who with the warrant in his possession had remained all this time watching in the Temple. Now, the first part of the evidence that affects William Jackson is that which occurred at the police-station. Arrived there, the charge of felony was abandoned, and the party taken upon the civil process by William Jackson and carried to White Cross Street prison. The question is whether or

1836.

HUMPHREY
v.
MITCHELL.

not George was legally in custody at the police-station.
It has been urged on the part of the defendant that
Richard Jackson originally had George legally in custody,
inasmuch as he had a right, being at hand and acting in
aid of his father, to arrest George. It is unnecessary now
to decide whether or not he had such right; for, if he
had, he by his own act determined such legal custody, and
voluntarily placed George in a situation of illegal restraint.
Admitting, for the sake of argument, that Richard Jackson might legally have called the policeman to assist him
if his strength were unequal to the effecting the caption,
or if he had reason to apprehend a rescue; yet here the
aid of a policeman was not called for for any such purpose; he was called to assist in taking a felon: from that
moment the detention of George was clearly illegal. From
the evidence of the policeman it appeared, that, when
they got to the station, and Richard Jackson was required to specify the charge in order to its being entered
in the book kept for that purpose, he said that if George
had not been guilty of felony it was something as bad, for
he had escaped from civil custody. This was false within his knowledge. When William Jackson arrived at the
police-station, and found George there in custody, he
possibly might have imagined that there had been an attempt to rescue: but that would be a fact for the jury.
And, from the whole evidence, there is no room for doubting that William Jackson perfectly well knew how matters
stood; for, it appears that whilst on the way Richard the
son said to his father—" Give me the warrant, and then
they will not know but that I had it all the time." Knowing, therefore, that the arrest was made by his son without
the warrant, can one doubt for a moment that William
Jackson was aware that the custody of George was illegal:
he saw the false charge entered in the book. Upon the
whole it seems to me to have been sufficiently proved that
George was illegally seized and imprisoned by Richard

Jackson, and that the fact was known to and improperly taken advantage of by William Jackson. Where the sheriff is cognizant of such an illegality in the mode of effecting a caption, and avails himself of it, the arrest itself is illegal.

PARK, J., concurred.

VAUGHAN, J.—I certainly should feel some difficulty in saying that the original caption by Richard Jackson was illegal, had not the charge of felony been made (c): that, however, clearly made the subsequent detention of the party illegal. I also think it is well established by the evidence that the illegality of the arrest was known to the father when he availed himself of it.

BOSANQUET, J.—I am also of opinion that the arrest of George was illegally effected. The declarations made by Richard Jackson at the time the party was first taken shew that he was not professing to act under the authority of the civil process in the hands of his father, and in his aid. His subsequent conduct, both in the Temple and at the police-station, confirms this view of the case. And I am clearly of opinion that Richard Jackson knew at the time he availed himself of it that the original caption was illegal.

Rule refused.

(c) Mr. Justice Park afterwards desired that he might not be understood to concur in the opinion that the first caption was legal.

Thursday,
April 21st.

A bailable writ
having been
sued out of
this court
against an at-
torney of the
King's Bench,
he, after some
attempts to
compromise,
obtained a
judge's order
to stay the pro-
ceedings on
payment of the
debt and such
costs as the
prothonotary
should under
the circumstan-
ces think rea-
sonable. The
prothonotary
having allowed
the costs of
bailable pro-
cess :—Held,
that the parties
were concluded
by his determi-
nation.

The writ is-
sued on the 5th
September, and
was sent to the
under-sheriff
of Hants on the
16th October.
The order for a
stay of proceed-
ings was made
on the 20th, on
which day the
plaintiff's
attorney wrote
to the under-
sheriff at Win-
chester, desiring

MEGGS *v.* BINNS.

BOMPAS, Serjeant, on a former day, obtained a rule calling on the plaintiff's late attorney to shew cause why he should not pay to the plaintiff or to his present attorney the sum of 9*l.* 6*s.* 6*d.*, with the costs of the motion. From the affidavits in support of the application, it appeared that the defendant was an attorney of the court of King's Bench; that Mr. Healey, the plaintiff's late attorney, on the 5th of September, 1835, issued *bailable* process against the defendant; that, after a sum of 30*l.* had been paid to Healey on account of the debt and costs in the action, a summons was taken out to stay proceedings on payment of the balance of the debt, together with the costs of a *serviceable writ* only; that, on the 20th October, an order was thereupon made by Gaselee, J., for staying the proceedings upon payment of the debt, 75*l.* 16*s.* 7½*d.*, together with such costs as the prothonotary should think right under the circumstances; that the costs were accordingly taxed, and the debt and costs (7*l.* 1*s.*) paid to Healey on the 31st of October; that, after the debt and costs had been so paid, viz. on the 4th of November, the defendant was arrested by the sheriff of Hants upon a capias in- dorsed for 105*l.* 16*s.* 7½*d.* and 15*l.* costs; that a judge's order was thereupon obtained to cancel the bail-bond given upon that arrest, for irregularity, with costs to be paid by the plaintiff; that these costs were afterwards taxed at 9*l.* 6*s.* 6*d.*, which sum was accordingly paid to the defen- dant's agent by the plaintiff, who now sought to recover it by this motion from Healey.

to be informed what was the amount of his and the officer's charges, and informing the under- sheriff that a judge's order had been obtained for staying the proceedings. The debt and costs were paid on the 31st October. On the 4th November, the defendant was arrested on the same writ in Hampshire, and gave a bail-bond. A judge's order having been obtained for cancelling the bail-bond, with costs, and those costs having been paid by the plaintiff, he obtained a rule calling upon his attorney to shew cause why he should not repay to him the sum so paid for costs :—Held, that the attorney had not under the circumstances been guilty of such a degree of negligence as to render him liable—at least on motion.

F. Kelly shewed cause, upon affidavits which disclosed the following facts:—On the 20th October, immediately after Mr. Justice Gaselee's order was pronounced, the plaintiff's then attorney (Healey) wrote to the under-sheriff at Winchester a letter to the following effect:— "*Meggs* v. *Binns.* The defendant has this day obtained a judge's order for the stay of proceedings herein on payment of debt and costs to be taxed. Favor me with an account of your own and the officer's charges." On the 23rd of October, Healey received from the under-sheriff a letter in answer, as follows:—"*Meggs* v. *Binns.* My charges for warrant, &c., are 8*s.*, and the officer's 1*l.* 1*s.*, which I shall feel obliged by your paying to my deputies, Messrs. Hicks & Braikenridge." On the 31st Healey attended with the defendant's agent before the prothonotary to tax the costs; when the prothonotary allowed the costs of a *bailable capias,* which costs were paid by the defendant without objection. It further appeared that the defendant was not an attorney of this court; that a bailable writ was issued at the express desire of the plaintiff, and transmitted to the sheriff of Hants on the 16th of October; that Healey, in his instructions to the under-sheriff, directed him to issue a warrant, but did not state the name or residence of any officer or other person to whom it was to be sent, but desired the under-sheriff to give the defendant credit for the 30*l.* paid on account.

The learned counsel submitted that an action on the case will not lie against a party suing out a writ if he neglect to countermand it after payment of the debt and costs, at least malice must be averred—citing *Scheibel* v. *Fairbain,* 1 B. & P. 388, *Page* v. *Wiple,* 3 East, 314; that the court would not indirectly give on motion a relief that a party would not be entitled to in an action; and that Healey had done all that he was bound to do, to prevent the arrest, it being the defendant's duty to require a countermand under the circumstances.

1836.

MEGGS
v.
BINNS.

Bompas, Serjeant, in support of his rule.—It may be conceded that a defendant cannot complain of the absence of a countermand where he does not ask for it, when the debt and costs are paid by mere arrangement between the parties : but the case is different where, as here, the payment is made under the order of a judge; for, in that case, it is the plaintiff's duty to obey that order by staying the proceedings; he is guilty of a contempt if he does not do so. The plaintiff's attorney ought not to ·have issued bailable process at all.

TINDAL, C. J.—The parties having been before the prothonotary, and the costs of bailable process having been allowed, and not objected to, I think the time for mooting that objection is gone by. The only question therefore is, whether or not the plaintiff ought to recover from Healey, his late attorney, the 9*l.* 6*s.* 6*d.* which he (the plaintiff) has been compelled to pay to the defendant under the second judge's order. To entitle the plaintiff to succeed in this motion, it should be made appear to us that the attorney against whom the application is made has been guilty of gross negligence. If any doubt exists, the party has a right to have the matter submitted to a jury. Upon looking at the facts sworn to on both sides, I am of opinion that there is not such clear evidence of negligence on his part as will justify us in interfering in a summary manner. It appears that the writ issued on the 5th of September; that a considerable period was allowed to elapse before the defendant took any steps to effect a settlement; and that it was not until the 20th October that the order was obtained for staying the proceedings on payment of the debt and costs. Upon this state of facts, the first observation that arises is, that the proceedings are not stayed upon an order of this description until the debt and costs are actually paid. The payment took place on the 31st of October: and the question is

whether Healey, in omitting to countermand his instructions to the sheriff of Hants, has been guilty of such a
degree of negligence as would deprive him of any defence to an action for a malicious arrest.   The writ was
sent to the under-sheriff of Hampshire, on the 16th of
October.   On the 20th, after my Brother Gaselee's order
was made, Healey wrote to the under-sheriff to ascertain
the amount of his charges.   At this time he had no
right to interpose and prevent the writ being executed:
it would have been a breach of his duty to his client so
to do.   It is to be observed also that Healey had no
knowledge of the officer, and therefore could only communicate with the under-sheriff.   If he had written to
the under-sheriff on the 2nd of November (the first being
Sunday) to apprise him that the debt and costs had been
paid, who is to say that the officer was so near at hand
that the under-sheriff could have communicated that fact
to him in time to prevent the defendant's arrest on the
4th?   Under these circumstances, I cannot say that the
attorney has been guilty of gross negligence.   It is at least
extremely doubtful whether this mere nonfeazance would
make the attorney chargeable at all.   Is the defendant
himself to do nothing?   I think it was his duty to ask for
a countermand.   At the most, I am of opinion (though
even that is by no means clear) that there has been a very
venial degree of negligence: but in that the party himself has been to a certain extent a sharer.   The rule must
therefore be discharged, with costs.

The rest of the court concurring—

Rule discharged, with costs.

1836.

Thursday,
April 21st.

An allegation
that the plain-
tiff was pos-
sessed of a
messuage and
premises, is
supported by
proof of his
occupation of
a part of a
house; the word
"messuage"
importing no
more than
"dwelling-
house."

FENN *v.* GRAFTON and Another.

CASE for disturbing the plaintiff in the possession of certain rooms &c. in a dwelling-house. The declaration stated that the plaintiff before and at and after the time of committing the grievances thereinafter mentioned, was lawfully possessed of *a certain messuage* and premises with the appurtenances situate in Coleman Street in the city of London, and in which said messuage and premises the plaintiff and his family had during all the time aforesaid resided and dwelt; nevertheless, the defendants, contriving and wrongfully and unjustly intending to injure, prejudice, and aggrieve the plaintiff in the possession, use, occupation, and enjoyment of *his said messuage* and premises, and to render the same incommodious, unfit for habitation, and of little or no use or value to the plaintiff, whilst the plaintiff was so possessed thereof, and so resided or dwelt with his family aforesaid, to wit, on &c., wrongfully and unjustly threw, poured, or spilt, and caused and procured to be thrown, poured, or spilled, large quantities of water near *a certain room or rooms of the plaintiff in, upon, and belonging to the said messuage* or premises of the plaintiff, in so careless, negligent, and improper a manner, that, by reason thereof, afterwards, to wit, on &c., and on divers other times afterwards and before the commencement of this suit, divers large quantities of water ran and flowed from the landing place or stairs down to, upon, against, and into *the said room and rooms in the said messuage and premises of the plaintiff*, and the walls, floors, wainscoatings, furniture, carpets, carpeting, papering, stairs, doors, and other parts thereof and therein being, and thereby greatly weakened, injured, wetted, and damaged *the said messuage and premises of the said plaintiff*, and the said walls, floors, &c., thereof, and wrongfully and improperly made great noises and disturbances near to and adjoining

*the plaintiff's dwelling-house and rooms thereof respect-
ively belonging to the said plaintiff;* and by reason of the
premises *the said room and rooms in the said messuage
and premises of the said plaintiff* became and were incommodious and less fit for habitation; and also by reason of
the premises, &c. the plaintiff lost a lodger.

The defendant pleaded, amongst other pleas, secondly,
that the plaintiff was not possessed of the messuage and
premises, with the appurtenances, in the declaration mentioned, in manner and form as he had in that behalf above
alleged &c.

The cause was tried before Tindal, C. J., at the Sittings
in London after the last term, when the following facts
appeared in evidence:—In the course of the year 1830,
the defendant took under an agreement from one Wallen
certain rooms of a house in Coleman Street (the premises
in question); and, in 1832, the plaintiff also took under
an agreement from Wallen the shop and attic, and, at a
subsequent period, the remainder of the house with the
exception of the rooms occupied by the defendants, over
which he had no control.

On the part of the defendant it was contended that this
evidence did not support the issue raised by the second
plea. A verdict having been found for the plaintiff,
damages 20*l.*, with liberty to the defendant to move to
enter a nonsuit—

Bompas, Serjeant, on a former day moved accordingly,
on the ground above stated, and also on the ground of
want of certainty in the declaration by reason of the improper use of the word " messuage," which, he submitted,
meant an entire house, and not the partial possession or
interest of a mere lodger.

Cur. adv. vult.

Tindal, C. J.—The only question was, whether the
issue raised by the second plea has been supported by the

evidence; for, as to any objection to the declaration on
the ground of want of certainty by the improper use of
the word messuage, such an objection affords a ground of
special demurrer only. Now, the issue raised was "whether the plaintiff was possessed of the messuage and premises with the appurtenances in the declaration mentioned,
modo et formâ." It appeared upon the evidence that the
plaintiff was not possessed of the *whole messuage*, but
that he had the separate use and occupation of the first
floor and some other parts of the house, the defendants
having also the separate use and occupation of the remainder: and the objection is, that such evidence negatives the allegation that the plaintiff was possessed of *the
messuage*. But we think, that, although the word "messuage" *may*, there is no necessity that it *must*, import
more than the word "dwelling-house," with which word
it is frequently put in apposition and used synonimously.
The ordinary language of conveyances is a sufficient proof
of this, in which "all that messuage or dwelling-house"
occurs as a constant description; and, if the declaration
had stated that the plaintiff was lawfully possessed of a
certain dwelling-house, there can be no doubt, upon the
authority of Lord Coke, 3 Inst. 65, and many other authorities, the evidence would have supported the allegation.
"Likewise," he says, "a chamber or room, be it upper or
lower, wherein any person does inhabit or dwell, is domus
mansionalis in law." If the word "messuage" is referred
to in the old book called "Termes de la Ley," it will be
found that "a house and a messuage differ in that a house
cannot be intended other than the matter of building,
but a messuage shall be said all the mansion place, and
the curtilage shall be taken as parcel of the messuage;"
shewing only that it is more comprehensive where there
is anything besides the building: and Spelman, in his
Glossary, tit. *Messuagium*, after stating that it is properly
a dwelling-house with land, adds—"transfertur ad hones-

tum quodvis domicilium sine prædio: unde et ædes urbicas 'messuagia' nuncupamur." We therefore think the word messuage in this declaration is satisfied by the evidence, and that the verdict ought not to be disturbed.

1836.

FENN
v.
GRAFTON.

Rule refused.

————◆————

SHACKELL v. ROSIER.

Friday,
April 22nd.

THIS was an action of assumpsit brought by the plaintiff, the proprietor of the John Bull newspaper, against the defendant on a promise to indemnify the plaintiff against the consequences of publishing a libel, the defendant asserting that it was true.

The first count of the declaration stated, that, before and at the time of the making of the promise and undertaking of the defendant as thereinafter mentioned, the plaintiff and Thomas Arrowsmith (since deceased) were the proprietors and publishers of a certain newspaper called the John Bull, and, being such proprietors and publishers, they, at the solicitation and request of the defendant, had theretofore, to wit, on the 27th January, 1833, published in the said newspaper a certain statement and paragraph as follows, that is to say—" Verily, the whigs select choice subjects for the exercise of his majesty's grace. A few weeks since the town was astonished at the respite from death of two men who had been found guilty of a murder under circumstances of peculiar atrocity. It was then suggested that the respite was granted to court the favour of the mobocracy of Lambeth, as Lord Palmerston had then some intention of standing for that borough. In the Times of Friday is the following, from a correspondent—' Mr. Chalmers, who was convicted of forgery at the sessions of May last at the Old Bailey, has received his majesty's gracious pardon. The case was reserved by

The plaintiff
published a
libel at the
request of the
defendant, and
on his under-
taking to in-
demnify him
against the
consequences
of such publi-
cation, and
defended an
action brought
against him
for the libel at
the defendant's
request and on
his promise to
indemnify him
against the
costs of such
action:—Held,
that the con-
sideration was
illegal, and
the promise
void.

the court over several sessions for the opinion of the
judges on various points of law, which were ultimately decided against him, and he was at length sentenced to be
transported for life. Sentence having been passed, the
case became fit to be recognized by the Secretary of State,
on the merits; and the result of the investigation is, that
Mr. Chalmers has received a pardon under the Great Seal,
discharging him from all the consequences of the verdict,
and restoring him to the enjoyment of all his civil rights
and privileges, the same as if the conviction had not taken
place.' In the former case, the murderers were men of
such notorious bad characters, that the officers, when they
heard of the deed, immediately proceeded to take them
up on suspicion. In this case, we know that the crime of
forgery was not new to Mr. Free-pardon Patrick Chalmers:
and we think we can offer some reason for this act of whig-
liberal mercy. Mr. F. P. P. C. was, for some time previous to his incarceration on this charge, an eminent mob
leader in a small way. He called a public meeting in
Smithfield: he headed a deputation to the Lord Mayor to
call a meeting of the Livery to petition for the abolition of
the punishment of death for forgery; he . often took the
chair at the Rotunda; and he is or was the intimate friend
of that much persecuted and respectable publisher of
treason, Hetherington. These are surely convincing reasons that Mr. Patrick Chalmers is a fit subject for the
mercy of the sovereign: but, if these should fail to con-
vince, we have still one which must be unanswerable: the
Political Union met within these few weeks to petition for
this man's pardon, and he is pardoned accordingly." The
declaration then proceeded to state, that, at the time of
the defendant's making the said declaration and request,
the defendant represented to the plaintiff and the said
Thomas Arrowsmith, since deceased, that the contents of
the said statement and paragraph were correct and true;
that the plaintiff and Arrowsmith, confiding in the truth

of the defendant's representation, and not knowing that
the same was false, or that the said statement and paragraph were in its contents inaccurate or untrue, or that
the same was libellous, did accordingly, on the said 27th
January, 1833, publish the said statement and paragraph
in the said newspaper; that, afterwards, and before the
making of the promise and undertaking of the defendant
as theretofore mentioned, one Peter Charles Chalmers,
being the said person named Chalmers in the said statement and paragraph, to wit, on the 25th May, 1833, commenced an action on the case at his suit against Edward
Shackell, then the printer and publisher of the said newspaper, William Shackell the now plaintiff, and the said
Thomas Arrowsmith, since deceased, in the court of Common Pleas, for the said publication of the said statement
and paragraph, asserting and alleging that the same was a
false, scandalous, malicious, and defamatory libel of and
concerning the said Peter Charles Chalmers, and that he
had sustained damages to a large amount thereby; and
which said action, at the time of the making of the promise and undertaking of the defendant as thereinafter
mentioned, was depending in the said court, and the defendant had notice of the premises; and thereupon, theretofore, to wit, on the 6th June, 1833, in consideration of
the premises, and that the said E. Shackell, the said W.
Shackell the now plaintiff, and the said T. Arrowsmith,
would defend the said action, he, the defendant, undertook, and then faithfully promised the plaintiff and the
said T. Arrowsmith to save harmless and indemnify them
from and reimburse them all payments, damages, costs,
charges, and expenses which they should or might incur,
bear, pay, sustain, or be liable for, for or by reason of
their so as aforesaid publishing the said statement and
paragraph, and of their defending the said action; that the
plaintiff and the said T. Arrowsmith, confiding in the said
promise and undertaking of the defendant, did afterwards,

1836.

SHACKELL
v.
ROSIER.

to wit, on &c., accordingly defend the said action, and the same was so defended; that, afterwards, to wit, on the 4th July, 1834, certain issues before then joined in the said action between the parties thereto came on to be and were in due form of law tried at the Sittings at Nisi Prius of the said court after Trinity Term, 1834, held at Guildhall in and for the city of London, before Sir Nicolas Conyngham Tindal, knight, his majesty's Chief Justice of the Bench at Westminster, by and before a jury in that behalf chosen and sworn between the said parties; and the said jury then found a verdict in the said action upon the said issues for the said Peter Charles Chalmers, and upon their oath said that he had sustained damages for and by reason of the said publication of the said statement and paragraph, being a false, scandalous, malicious, and defamatory libel of and concerning him, to the amount of 30*l.*; and such proceedings were thereupon afterwards had in the said action, that the plaintiff W. Shackell, after the death of the said T. Arrowsmith, to wit, on the 5th November, 1834, applied to the said court to set aside the said verdict, and obtained a rule of the said court calling upon the said Peter Charles Chalmers to shew cause on a certain day therein named why the said verdict should not be set aside, and instead thereof a nonsuit be entered, or why the entry of final judgment on the said verdict should not be stayed; that the said T. Arrowsmith having died before the obtaining of the said rule nisi, and before the same was finally disposed of, to wit, on the 26th July, 1834, the plaintiff William Shackell, being advised by counsel learned in the law, and finding that he could not support the said rule and make it absolute, or set aside the said verdict, or arrest the said judgment, did, after the death of the said T. Arrowsmith, and with the leave and consent of the defendant Rosier, afterwards, to wit, on the 17th November, 1834, settle and compromise the said action with the said Peter Charles Chalmers, and thereupon became liable for and was forced and obliged to and did pay him a large sum, to wit, 60l., in satisfaction of the said damages so found by the said jury, and given by their verdict aforesaid, and of the costs and charges of the said Peter Charles Chalmers by him about his suit in that behalf expended; and by means of the premises the plaintiff, after the death of the said T. Arrowsmith, then became and was damnified and injured to the amount of the said sum of 60l.; and also by means of the premises the plaintiff and the said T. Arrowsmith, during the lifetime of the said T. Arrowsmith, and the plaintiff after his death, were put to, incurred, bore, and sustained, and became liable for and paid great costs, charges, and expenses, amounting to 300l., in and about the defending and compromising the said action, and in making the said application to the court; whereof the defendant afterwards, and after the death of the said T. Arrowsmith, to wit, on the 2nd December, 1834, had notice: yet the defendant, not regarding his said promise and undertaking, had not yet saved harmless and indemnified the plaintiff and the said T. Arrowsmith in his lifetime, or the plaintiff since his death, or reimbursed them or either of them the said payments, damages, costs, charges, and expenses so made, incurred, borne, paid, sustained, and become liable for as aforesaid, or any of them, or any part thereof, but so to do had hitherto wholly neglected and refused, and still did neglect and refuse.

The declaration also contained counts for money paid and for money found to be due upon an account stated.

The defendant pleaded—first, non assumpsit—secondly, that he did not represent to the plaintiff and the said T. Arrowsmith (since deceased) that the contents of the said statement and paragraph in the first count of the declaration mentioned were correct and true.

The cause was tried before Tindal, C. J., at the sittings in London after the last Trinity Term. It appeared that the paragraph in question had been left by the defendant at the John Bull office, together with his card, which was usually considered a voucher for the correctness of articles so left; and that, in January, 1835, Chalmers, the party libelled, having commenced an action against the printer and proprietors of the John Bull for the publication of the libel, the defendant was apprised of the fact, and afterwards called at the plaintiff's office and requested that the action might be defended, promising to indemnify the plaintiff and his late partner against the consequences. An indemnity was subsequently drawn up, but was never signed, neither was it stamped. A verdict was found for the plaintiff, damages 326*l.* 8*s.* 10*d.;* with liberty to the defendant to move to set it aside and enter a nonsuit, on the ground of the want of signature and stamp to the supposed indemnity.

Talfourd, Serjeant, accordingly, in Michaelmas Term last, moved for a rule nisi to enter a nonsuit on the point reserved, and also in arrest of judgment, on two grounds— first, that the consideration for the defendant's promise was illegal, part of it being the commission by the plaintiff of an indictable offence—secondly, that the defendant, if not privy to the publication of the libel by the plaintiff, was a stranger to the action brought against the latter and his partner, and therefore his promise to indemnify them against the damages and costs in that action was void on the ground of maintenance.

Alexander and *Butt* shewed cause.—The promise to indemnify need not have been in writing at all—*Thomas* v. *Cooke*, 3 M. & R. 444, 8 B. & C. 728 ; *Adams* v. *Dansey*, 4 M. & P. 245, 6 Bing. 506; such a promise not falling within either the words or the policy of the statute of frauds. And even supposing that it was necessary that the indemnity in this case should be in writing, still, inas-

much as it amounted at most only to a mere proposal or
prospective agreement, and was not produced as the
document upon which the action was founded, it did not
require a stamp, and, being unsigned, did not exclude
parol evidence of the defendant's promise. Thus, in
Hawkins v. *Warre*, 5 D & R. 512, 3 B & C. 690, where a
witness deposed that the settled draft of a lease was the
final agreement between the parties, for one of whom he
acted as agent; it was held that an unstamped memorandum written afterwards by himself, but not signed by anybody, was admissible in evidence as a mere proposal, to
shew that the settled draft was not the final agreement
between the parties. So, in *Doe* d. *Bingham* v. *Cartwright*,
3 B. & A. 326, where, upon the letting of premises to a
tenant, a memorandum of agreement was drawn up, the
terms of which were read over and assented to by him,
and it was then agreed that he should on a future day
bring a surety and sign the agreement, neither of which
he ever did; it was held that the memorandum was not
an agreement, but a mere unaccepted proposal, and that
the terms of the letting therefore might be proved by
parol evidence. In *Ramsbottom* v. *Tunbridge*, 2 M. & S. 434,
a written paper, not signed by the auctioneer, but delivered
by him to a bidder at a sale by auction, and which contained a description of the property sold, was held not to
be such a writing as would exclude parol evidence. And
in *The King* v. *Wrangle*, 4 N. & M. 375, 2 Ad. & E. 514,
it was held that an agreement for the hiring of a servant
may be proved by parol, although the terms of the agreement are, by the direction of the parties, written down by
a third person, such writing, though read over to the
parties, not being signed by them. Besides, in order to
render a stamp necessary, it must appear upon the face
of the instrument that "the matter thereof shall be of
the value of 20l. or upwards"—56 Geo. 3, c. 184, Sched.
Part 1; *Wrigley* v. *Smith*, 3 N. & M. 181, 5 B. & Ad. 1117,

and the cases there cited; *Marson* v. *Short*, ante, Vol. 1,
243.

Then, as to the arrest of judgment—The question now
presented for the decision of the court is essentially distinguishable from that which arose in *Colburn* v. *Patmore*,
1 C. M. & R. 73, 4 Tyr. 677; for, here the action had already been commenced against the plaintiff when the defendant gave his undertaking to indemnify him against the
damages and costs in that particular action: the case might
have been different had the party libelled proceeded by
indictment.   In *Merryweather.* v. *Nixan,* 8 T. R. 186, it
was held, that, if a plaintiff recover in an action of *tort*
against two defendants, and levy the whole damages on
one, that one cannot sue the other for contribution.   But
the doctrine has been considerably extended since that
case was decided: and the distinction now universally recognized is, that, where the act is clearly illegal, no contribution can be recovered amongst joint tort-feasors; but,
where the act is equivocal, and may be legal, it is otherwise.   Contribution and indemnity are convertible terms.
In *Fletcher* v. *Harcot,* Hutton, 55 (S. C. nom. *Battersey's*
case, Winch, 48), the defendant having arrested one Battersby under a lawful authority, as he affirmed, requested
the plaintiff to keep the prisoner in his inn during one
night, and promised to indemnify.   Battersby afterwards
brought an action for a false imprisonment against the
plaintiff, who spent 10*l.* in defending that action, and had
since applied to the defendant to indemnify him, which he
refused: upon motion in arrest of judgment, on the ground
that the arrest not appearing to have been lawful, there
was no consideration for the promise, the plaintiff had
judgment.   Lord Hobart took a distinction between a promise to indemnify in consideration of a promise to do an
act which is unlawful, as if one at the request of J. S. promised to *beat* J. D., and the case of a promise to save a
man harmless in consideration of his doing a thing which

may be lawful, and the illegality whereof *appears not to* the party doing it. The first case that broke through the rule laid down in *Merryweather* v. *Nixan* was that of *Woolley* v. *Batte*, 2 C. & P. 417, where it was held, that, if a party recover damages *in case* against one of two joint proprietors of a stage coach for an injury sustained by the negligence of their servants, such proprietor may maintain an action against his co-proprietor for contribution, if he prove at the trial that he was not personally present when the accident happened. That ruling has been fully supported since. Thus, in *Adamson* v. *Jervis*, 12 Moore, 241, 4 Bing. 66, a count in case stated that the defendant was possessed of certain cattle, and, being so possessed thereof, represented and affirmed to the plaintiff (an auctioneer) that he was legally entitled to sell the same, and requested him to put them up for sale by auction; that the plaintiff sold the cattle and paid over the net proceeds to the defendant; that the defendant deceived and defrauded the plaintiff in this, to wit, that he was not, *at the time of the said sale*, legally entitled to sell the cattle; and that the true owner afterwards sued the plaintiff, and recovered against him the value of the cattle so sold—breach, nonpayment by the defendant of the sum so recovered and costs: it was held that the count was sufficient after verdict. And Best, C. J., said: " From the inclination of the court in *Philips* v. *Biggs*, Hardres, 164, and from the concluding part of Lord Kenyon's judgment in *Merryweather* v. *Nixan*, and from reason, justice, and sound policy, the rule that wrong-doers cannot have redress or contribution against each other, is confined to cases where the person seeking redress must be presumed to have *known* that he was doing an unlawful act." And in a very late case, *Betts* v. *Gibbins*, 2 Ad. & E. 57, 4 N. & M. 64, it is laid down that the rule that a tort-feasor cannot recover upon a promise to indemnify made by the person at whose request the tortious act is committed, is confined to cases in which the act is of an *obviously* illegal character, and does not extend to a case in which there is any bonâ fide doubt whatever whether in point of law the act was authorized. Taunton, J., there says: "I accede to the case of *Merry-weather* v. *Nixan,* because I think the law laid down there is too plain to be mistaken, viz. that, where there are two *wrong-doers,* or tort-feasors, the law will not *imply* an indemnity; but I take it to be otherwise where the matter to be done is apparently a matter altogether *innocent,* and where it must depend on *subsequent* circumstances whether the law will affirm it or not." And Williams, J., said: "This is not like a case where a party seeks to be indemnified for the commission of an *obviously unlawful* act, as a breach of the peace, or any other of that description, nor of an act against public policy. The defendant requests the plaintiffs to do an act which at that time was undoubtedly equivocal, because it has been made a matter of some argument to-day whether they were or were not authorized in doing that act; but most certainly the act is so far doubtful as that there was not the least resemblance between this and any which are of a *notoriously illegal* character." Besides, the defendant who urges the objection was himself a party to the unlawful act, if unlawful it were. The statement of the premises in the declaration may be rejected, and a perfectly good consideration would still remain: it is no ground for avoiding a promise that a part of the consideration upon which it proceeded is illegal or void. In *Newman* v. *Newman,* 4 M. & S. 66, where a bond was conditioned for the payment of money, and also to present to a living, it was held, that, admitting that part of the condition for the presentation to be simoniacal, yet the bond was good for the payment of the money. So, in *Bradburne* v. *Bradburne,* Cro. Eliz. 149, the court said, that, where there are divers considerations alleged by the plaintiff, and some are frivolous and void, yet, if any of them be good, the plaintiff shall recover. *Crisp* v. *Gamel,*

Cro. Jac. 128, and Viner's Abridgment, Damages (Q), pl. 17, are authorities to the same effect. In the former it was held sufficient, in assumpsit, if one of two considerations be proved good, and that a void consideration need not be proved: and in the latter it is laid down, that, "where there are two considerations, whereof the one is good and the other is void, the damages given shall be intended to be all given for the good consideration." Here, the consideration on which the promise is founded has nothing to do with the original publication of the alleged libel: the undertaking stated in the declaration is an undertaking to indemnify the plaintiff against the costs of an action then already commenced against him. And there is no pretence for saying that the promise is void for maintenance. In *Williamson* v. *Henley*, 3 M & P. 731, 6 Bing. 299, the declaration stated, that, in consideration that the plaintiff, at the request of the defendant, would defend any action that might be brought by J. S. against the plaintiff, on account of certain money which the plaintiff had delivered to the defendant, he the defendant promised to save the plaintiff harmless from the consequences of such action; that J. S. afterwards brought an action, and obtained judgment against the plaintiff; and that a writ of ca. sa. was afterwards sued out on the judgment, under which the plaintiff was arrested and imprisoned, and was obliged to pay the sum recovered by J. S., in order to procure his, the plaintiff's, discharge: and it was holden that this count did not disclose a contract void on the ground of maintenance. At all events, such a defence ought to have been pleaded specially—*Potts* v. *Sparrow*, ante, Vol. 1, p. 578, 1 New Cases, 594.

Talfourd, Serjeant, and *Petersdorff*, in support of the rule.—It may be conceded that an indemnity as such requires no stamp. This, however, is not a mere indemnity; it is a promise by the defendant to pay costs already incurred or about to be incurred by the plaintiff in the defence of the action of libel. The plaintiff's case, it is said, was not founded upon the memorandum. But, it having been put in as part of his case, he was bound to prove it in the ordinary way. Nor can it be said to be a mere conditional or incomplete bargain. [The court intimating a strong opinion that the memorandum was a mere proposal not binding on the party, and therefore not requiring a stamp—this point was given up.] Then, the promise was either given partly in consideration of the publication of a libel (and not merely a libel against the individual by whom the action was brought, but also against the government, and against other individuals), a criminal act; or it was a promise, that, in consideration that the plaintiff would defend an action in which the party making the promise (the present defendant) was in no degree interested, he, the defendant, would indemnify him against the costs and damages &c.: and in either case equally illegal and void. The precise distinction applicable here is that taken in *Fletcher* v. *Harcot:* the publication of the libel was clearly an illegal act. Where the act done is palpably unlawful, the authorities already cited clearly shew that no contribution or indemnity can be enforced by the one against the others jointly concerned in its commission. The fact of an *action* having already been brought by Chalmers for the libel, makes no difference; for, he might still have indicted all or any of the parties: and there can no just distinction between an indemnity against the consequences of a libel already published, and one about to be published. Although the point was not directly decided in *Colburn* v. *Patmore,* the opinion of the court of Exchequer seems to have been clear that no contribution or indemnity can be enforced as between two libellers. Here, taking the consideration and the promise together, the whole forms one entire and indivisible consideration. In most cases of tort it is possible to assume an absence of illegality in the act: but not so the case of a libel. In *Betts* v. *Gibbins* the action was *trover*, and therefore there was not necessarily and obviously any illegality in the transaction out of which the action arose. Here, there could not be a doubt as to the import of the publication. In *Blackett* v. *Crissop*, 1 Ld. Raym. 278, a contract to indemnify the sheriff against the consequences of doing what he ought not to do, was held void. And in *Pitcher* v. *Bailey*, 8 East, 171, it was held, that, if an officer permit a prisoner to go at large on his promise to pay the debt to the creditor, in consequence of which he is obliged to pay the creditor himself, he cannot recover back the money from the debtor, having been guilty of a breach of duty out of which he cannot derive a cause of action. The only ground upon which the defendant in this case could be supposed to have any interest in the former action, would be, that he was a party to the criminal act: for, otherwise he was a mere stranger, and his undertaking clearly would fall within the definition given of maintenance by Hawkins, P. C., Book 1, c. 84, s. 5, and by all the later authorities. Mr. Justice Buller goes very fully into the law on the subject in the case of *Master* v. *Miller*, 4 T. R. 340. And in *Wallis* v. *The Duke of Portland*, 3 Ves. 494, the Lord Chancellor says: "Maintenance is not confined to supporting suits at common law. In the first book you open upon the subject (one naturally looks into Hawkins), it is stated to be either in pais, or by prosecuting suits. Maintenance in pais is punishable by indictment. Maintenance by prosecuting suits, without distinguishing what suits, is punishable by an action at common law. Statutes prohibiting particular species of maintenance add penalties; but it is laid down as a fundamental authority, that maintenance is not malum prohibitum, but malum in se: that parties shall not by their countenance aid the prosecution of suits of any kind ; which every person must bring upon his own bottom, and at his own expense. The manner in which it is considered at law, is strongly illustrated in *Pierson* v. *Hughes*, 1 Freem. 71, 81, which was an action of debt upon bond for money expended and to be expended in the prosecution of that suit. Upon the first argument it was held maintenance; that giving the bond was as great an evil as laying out money. Maynard, as amicus curiæ, stated, that to speak to a counsel or an attorney to encourage the suit wherein he had no interest, had been adjudged maintenance. Upon the second day, the argument took this turn; that, as only a bond was given, no maintenance was in fact committed, upon the common maxim 'Non officit conatus nisi sequatur effectus.' The answer of Vaughan was, that a bond given to maintain [maim?] or kill will be void, though the act never ensue. Atkyns, J., was of opinion that a bond given while the suit was depending, for what was already expended, was maintenance; because an encouragement to go on with the suit." And in Russell on Crimes, 2nd edit. Vol. 1, p. 176, it is said—"Maintenance seems to signify an unlawful taking in hand or upholding of quarrels or sides, to the disturbance or hindrance of common right. This may be, where a person assists another in his pretentions to lands, by taking or holding the possession of them for him by force or subtilty; or where a person stirs up quarrels and suits in *relation to matters wherein he is in no way concerned;* or it may be *where a person officiously intermeddles in a suit depending in a court of justice, and in no way belonging to him, by assisting either party with money, or otherwise, in the prosecution or defence of such suit.* Where there is no contract to have part of the thing in suit, the party so intermeddling is said to be guilty of maintenance generally; but, if the party stipulate to have part of the thing in suit, his offence is called champerty."

TINDAL, C. J.—After what has fallen from the court
in the course of the argument, our judgment may be confined to that part of the rule which seeks to arrest the
judgment: and I am of opinion that the judgment ought
to be arrested on two grounds—first, on the ground of
illegality in the consideration for the defendant's promise
—secondly, on the ground of the extent of the promise
itself. The declaration alleges that the plaintiff and his
partner were the proprietors and publishers of a newspaper called the John Bull, and, being such proprietors
and publishers, they, at the solicitation and request of
the defendant, published in such newspaper a certain
statement and paragraph which is set forth in the count,
and which is, undoubtedly, a gross libel on the individual
therein mentioned. The count then proceeds to allege
that that person commenced an action against E. Shackell,
then the printer and publisher of the newspaper, the
plaintiff, and his deceased partner, for the publication of
the libel, which action was depending at the time of the
making the promise and undertaking of the defendant
as thereinafter mentioned; and thereupon, in consideration
of the premises, and *that* the said E. Shackell, *the plaintiff*, and his late partner, *would defend the action*, the
defendant undertook and promised the plaintiff and his
partner to save harmless and indemnify them from and
reimburse them all payments, damages, costs, charges,
and expenses which they should or might incur, bear,
pay, sustain, or be liable for, for or by reason of their
so as aforesaid publishing the said statement and paragraph, and of their defending the said action. The consideration for the defendant's promise thus appears to
consist of two parts—first, *of the premises*, part of which
is that the plaintiff at the solicitation of the defendant
published the libellous paragraph. This the plaintiff contends may be rejected, and the promise to indemnify retained. But, if this part of the consideration be rejected,

no answer can be given to the argument urged on the part of the defendant, that the promise to indemnify the plaintiff and his partner against the damages and costs in the action for the libel was a promise by a mere stranger, and therefore void on the score of maintenance. If, however, this be not rejected, it appears upon the face of the declaration, that a part of the consideration for the defendant's promise was the publication of a libel by the plaintiff, a misdemeanor in all the principals. What is that, in effect, but saying that the plaintiff and defendant have been jointly concerned in the commission of a breach of the law, and making that breach of the law a part of the consideration for the defendant's promise to save the plaintiff harmless from the consequences thereof? It is said that the part of the consideration which involves the breach of the law may be rejected, and regard had only to that part which has reference to the damages and costs sustained by the plaintiff at the defendant's request. Undoubtedly there are cases in the books which shew, that, where a promise rests upon two considerations, and one of them is upon the face of it impossible or unintelligible and imperfect, that part of the consideration which is impossible may be rejected, and the promise may be referred to the other part. But in all the cases a distinction is taken between a merely void and an illegal consideration. This is distinctly laid down in *Featherston* v. *Hutchinson*, Cro. Eliz. 199. There, in assumpsit, the plaintiff declared that whereas he had taken the body of one H. in execution at the suit of J. S. by virtue of a warrant directed to him as special bailiff; the defendant, in consideration he would permit him to go at large, and of two shillings to the defendant paid &c., promised to pay the plaintiff all the money in which H. was condemned. Upon non-assumpsit it was found for the plaintiff. It was moved in arrest of judgment that the consideration is not good, being contrary to the statute 23 Hen. 6, c. 10, and that a

promise and obligation was all one. And though it be
joined with another consideration of two shillings, yet,
being void and against the statute for part, it is void in
all. Then it is said that the law recognises a distinction
between considerations that are void at common law and
those that are avoided by statute. But I can find no authority for such a distinction. Upon the whole, it appears
to me that a part of the consideration for the defendant's
promise in this case being founded upon a breach of the
law, the promise cannot be supported. Even if this were
not so, I hold the promise to be too large: it is not
merely a promise to indemnify the plaintiff against the
costs and damages in the action; but a general promise
to indemnify him against all the consequences that might
result from the publication of the libel—including fine,
imprisonment, &c. Upon public grounds, it seems to me
that a promise to indemnify a party against the legal consequences of the publication of a libel, is illegal and
void, inasmuch as it would be holding out a premium to
libellers; and therefore that such a promise cannot upon
any principle of law be supported. The rule for arresting
the judgment must be made absolute.

PARK, J.—I am of the same opinion. One cannot fail
to perceive, on reading the declaration in this case, that
the publication of the libel formed a material part of the
consideration for the defendant's promise. The declaration states in substance that the plaintiff, at the solicitation
and request of the defendant, published the libel in question; that the individual to whom the libel applied brought
an action against the plaintiff; and that the defendant, *in
consideration of the premises, and that the plaintiff would
defend the action*, undertook to save harmless and indemnify him from, and reimburse him all payments,
damages, costs, charges, and expenses which he should
or might incur, pay, sustain, or be liable for, for or
by reason of his so as aforesaid publishing the libel,

and of his defending the action. The whole appears to me to form one entire consideration. If the criminal matter be taken away, then the intervention of the defendant becomes the act of a mere stranger, and the promise void for maintenance. The main point in this case was much discussed in *Farebrother* v. *Ansley*, 1 Camp. 342, where the owner of goods recovered in trespass against a sheriff, the auctioneer, and others, who had taken and sold the goods under a fi. fa., and levied the whole damages on the auctioneer alone, who was only employed by the sheriff's officer: it was held that the auctioneer had no right of action for contribution against any of his co-defendants, and that there was no implied promise of indemnity on the part of the sheriff. *Fletcher* v. *Harcot* is not particularly applicable; but *Martin* v. *Blythman*, Yelv. 197, seems to me to apply pointedly to the present case. There " Holman fut en execution en Plymouth for 31*l*. al suit D., q' fut recover la devant le maior, &c. Blithman vient al Martin, et promise q' consideratio' il en voit mitter et suffer Holman d'aler a large, q' les 31*l*. sera port eins en court la p' Holman p' tiel jour a satisfier D., et q'il sauvera Martin harmeless de cest enlargement. D. recover vers Martin sur l'escape, et puis Martin port assumpsit vers Blithman sur le promise, et declare tout ut supra: et adjudg. vers le pl', car le consideration est encount' ley, viz. a suffer un en execution q'escaper." I agree with my Lord Chief Justice that it would be productive of infinite mischief and inconvenience if such an undertaking as that now under consideration could be enforced in a court of law. The case of *Merryweather* v. *Nixan* takes the very distinction we are now aiming at. That case was tried before Lord Chief Baron Thompson, a very eminent lawyer, who ruled that no contribution could be recovered from joint tort-feasors; and Lord Kenyon, on a new trial being afterwards moved for, observed that he had never heard of such an action—adding: " Our decision in this case will not affect cases of indemnity where one man employs another to do acts not unlawful in themselves." *Woolley* v. *Batte,* which is erroneously supposed to have overturned *Merryweather* v. *Nixan,* was a totally different case. Lord Lyndhurst asserts the same principle in the case of *Colburn* v. *Palmore.* " I know of no case," says his lordship, " in which a person who has committed an act declared by the law to be criminal has been permitted to recover compensation against a person who has acted jointly with him in the commission of the crime. It is not necessary to give any opinion upon this point; but I may say that I entertain little doubt that a person who is declared by the law to be guilty of a crime cannot be allowed to recover damages against another who has participated in its commission." I therefore agree with his lordship in thinking that the judgment in this case ought to be arrested.

VAUGHAN, J.—After the very clear and luminous exposition of the law by the Lord Chief Justice and my Brother Park, I should content myself with saying generally that I concur in the opinion they have pronounced, were not the subject one of such very general concern. I shall therefore add a few words. The matter was much discussed, though not decided, in the Court of Exchequer, in the case of *Colburn* v. *Palmore.* Lord Lyndhurst (with the concurrence of the Barons) expressed himself as entertaining little or no doubt that it was not competent to a man convicted of a criminal act to enforce by action a contract of indemnity against his associates in the crime. In the present case it has been suggested in argument that the illegal part of the consideration may be discarded. But, upon the face of the record, that part of the consideration is so interwoven with the rest, that I cannot conceive it possible to separate them. The declaration begins with stating that the plaintiff and his partner at the solicitation and request of the defendant published a certain libel: it then proceeds to state that an action against them for such publication being depending in this court, the defendant, in consideration of the premises (that is, of *all* the premises), and also in consideration that the plaintiff and his partner would defend the action, undertook and promised to save harmless and indemnify them from and reimburse them all payments, damages, costs, charges, and expenses which they should or might incur, bear, pay, sustain, or be liable for, for or by reason of their so as aforesaid publishing the libel and defending the action. It appears to me to be impossible to reject or to separate from the rest any part of the consideration there stated. With respect to the cases cited, none of them go the length of determining that part of an entire consideration, being illegal, may be discarded, and the residue retained. *Newman* v. *Newman* was a very different case: there, the bond was conditioned for the performance of two several and distinct acts, and, admitting one of them to be illegal, the bond was held capable of being enforced as to the other. *Crisp* v. *Gamel* is also clearly distinguishable: it was there held that one of two considerations being idle and vain need not be proved, because it was in vain to allege it. The court would be allowing itself to be made accessory to the publication of libels, if it were to hold that a contract of indemnity of this description may be enforced. I am clearly of opinion that the judgment ought to be arrested on the ground of illegality in the consideration for the defendant's promise: and if that objection were removed, still the promise would be void on the ground of maintenance.

BOSANQUET, J.—I am also of opinion that the consideration and promise in this case are both illegal and void for the reasons already stated. The consideration is the publication of a libel at the solicitation and request of the defendant; and the promise, in consideration of the premises, and that the plaintiff and his partner would defend an action that had been brought against them for the publication of the libel, to save harmless and indemnify them from and reimburse them all payments, damages, costs, charges, and expenses which they should or might incur, bear, pay, sustain, or be liable for, for or by reason of their so as aforesaid publishing the said libel and defending the said action. The publication in question was clearly a libel, and the act of publishing an offence against the public. It was not an act apparently innocent, so as to bring this within the case of *Betts* v. *Gibbins*, and others of the like description, which have somewhat tended to limit the doctrine of *Merryweather* v. *Nixan*. On the contrary, the publication of a libel is presumed illegal; and it is not until the justification is established in a civil action that the presumption of guilt is removed. Still, however, the public offence remains. He who concurs with another in the commission of an offence punishable criminally, must abide the consequences. The offence adverted to in *Betts* v. *Gibbins* might primâ facie be legal. In the present case, it appears to me that the expression " in consideration of the premises" involves all the preceding matter, and makes the publication of the libel a part of the consideration for the defendant's promise; tainting the whole consideration, and rendering it incapable of being supported. But, as has already been observed, even if the consideration might be confined to the defence of the action, the plaintiff is met by the objection that the defendant is a stranger voluntarily maintaining him in the defence of the action, and thereby obstructing the fair and legitimate course of justice; which clearly falls within Hawkins's definition of maintenance.

Rule absolute accordingly.

GREEN *v.* COBDEN.

Leaving a copy
of a monition
in a room of
the vicarage-
house is suffi-
cient service
whereon to
found a seques-
tration, al-
though the in-
cumbent do not
reside there,
but is absent
from the parish,
and his place
of abode un-
known—the
officiating mi-
nister being
the sequestra-
tor, and having
the original
monition in his
possession.

WILLIAM KILWICK, the vicar of Westbourne, in Sussex, charged his glebe with the payment of two annuities, which becoming in arrear, the defendant, assignee of the annuities, entered into possession under the annuity deed, and in 1829 demised the land to the plaintiff, who paid rent to the defendant as his landlord up to Michaelmas, 1831; but, for that which became due at Michaelmas, 1832, a distress was made by the defendant. Before the distress, George Agustus How had been licensed to perform the office of stipendiary curate of the parish by the Bishop of Chichester, who by the licence had assigned to him the yearly stipend of 75*l.*, payable quarterly, with the surplice fees; and the stipend being in arrear on the 20th January, 1832, a monition, and on the 10th March, 1832, a writ of sequestration, had been issued by the bishop; and, under the sequestration, How had demanded from the plaintiff, and the plaintiff had paid to How, as sequestrator, but without the assent or authority of the defendant, the rent due at Michaelmas, 1832. The service of the monition, upon which issue was taken in an action of replevin brought by the plaintiff upon the defendant's distress, was proved as follows:—

Thomas Baker was clerk of the parish of Bosham, and lived in the parish. The last time he saw Mr. Kilwick, the vicar, at the vicarage-house, was at Michaelmas, 1831; but he had been absent before that. That was the house wherein he resided when he came to the parish. His daughter lived with him in the vicarage-house before he went away; after he went, she lived in lodgings about one hundred yards from the vicarage-house, when the copy of the monition was served; and she lived in the vicarage-house at the time of the trial of the cause. Mr. Kilwick kept no servant: his daughter was his servant; a servant girl used to wait on her. About a week before the copy of the monition was served, Mr. How, who had been some years curate of the parish, directed Baker to make inquiries of Miss Kilwick where her father was. Baker did so, but could get no information from her, and he, Baker, did not know where Mr. Kilwick was. About a week after that, Baker was directed by Mr. How to serve a copy of the monition, and to lay it in the vicarage-house. He took it accordingly to the vicarage-house on the 31st January, 1832, and laid it on the mantle shelf in the front parlour, which was the room that Mr. Kilwick generally frequented when he was in the parish. He put it there that Mr. Kilwick or his daughter might see it if they came. The front door of the house was open, and nobody let Baker in: he could not say whether there were any chairs or table in the room. A fisherman's family were in the house, and they occupied the back parlour. Baker did not go again to see if the monition had been taken by anybody. The sequestration was read in the church, and stuck up at the church door, on the 10th of April, 1832.

The only question at the trial, which took place at the Summer Assizes, 1834, was, whether the monition had been duly served on W. Kilwick. A verdict was found for the avowant, subject to the opinion of the court on a special case upon that point.

By the statute 57 Geo. 3, c. 99, ss. 74, 75, it is enacted, that, "in every case in which jurisdiction is given to the bishop of the diocese, or to any archbishop, under the provisions of this act, and for the purposes thereof, and the enforcing the due execution of the provisions thereof, all other and concurrent jurisdiction in respect thereof shall wholly cease, and no other jurisdiction in relation to the provisions of this act shall be used, exercised, or enforced, save and except such jurisdiction of the bishop and archbishop under this act; anything in any act or acts of parliament, or law or laws, or usage or custom to

to the contrary notwithstanding, &c. &c. And that, in
all cases where proceedings under this act are directed by
monition and sequestration, such monition shall issue
under the hand and seal of the bishop, and, being duly
served, shall be returned, with a certificate of service,
into the registry of the Consistorial court of such bishop;
and thereupon it shall be competent for the party monished to shew cause by affidavit or otherwise, as the
case may require, against the sequestration issuing; and,
unless sufficient cause be shewn to the contrary, the
sequestration shall issue under the seal of the said Consistorial court, and in such form as is commonly used in
that behalf."

By section 26, it is enacted, "that, in every case in
which it shall appear to any such bishop as aforesaid, that
any spiritual person having or holding any benefice, and
not being licensed according to this act to be absent
therefrom, nor having any lawful cause of absence from
the same, does not sufficiently reside on the same respectively, it shall be lawful for such bishop to issue or cause
to be issued a monition to such spiritual person forthwith
to proceed to and reside thereon, and perform the duties
thereof; and to make a return to such monition within
a certain number of days after the issuing thereof, so as
that in every such case there shall be thirty days between
the time of delivering such monition to such spiritual person, or leaving the same at his then usual or last place of
abode, or, if not there to be found, with the officiating
minister or one of the churchwardens, and also a copy
thereof at the house of residence (if any such there be)
belonging to such benefice, to which any such spiritual
person shall be required by such monition to proceed and
reside thereon, and the time specified in such monition
for the return thereto; and a copy of every such monition
shall immediately on the issuing thereof be filed in the
registry of such bishop's court, and shall be open for in-

spection on the payment of 3s. and no more; and the
spiritual person to whom any such monition shall be sent
under this act, shall, within the time specified for that
purpose, make a return thereto into such registry, to be
there filed."

W. H. Watson, for the plaintiff.—There has been a due
service of the monition according to the provisions of the
statute—at the domicile of the party. This is all that is
required by the practice of the Ecclesiastical court. Personal service has never been considered indispensible.
By an ordinance or constitution of Otho (A. D. 1237),
Gibs. Cod. 1002, citations are required to be served on
the person *if he can be found,* or otherwise by publication
in the church. And by a constitution of Archbishop Mep-
ham (A. D. 1328), Gibs. 1003, it is provided that, in certain cases, they who cannot be cited personally, nor have
any dwelling, may be cited in the parish church or cathedral (a). [*Tindal,* C. J.—Are we bound judicially to
take notice of the practice of the Ecclesiastical courts?]
The court will give effect to the judgment of the Consistorial court, provided that court has not proceeded contrary to natural justice.—*Douglas* v. *Forrest,* 1 M. & P.
663, 6 Bing. 186; *Becquet* v. *MacCarthy,* 2 B. & Ad. 951,
and the cases there cited. In *Capel* v. *Child,* 2 Tyr. 689,
2 C. & J. 558, the requisition upon which the proceedings
were founded was clearly contrary to the first principles
of justice. Here, at all events, the requisitions of the
57 Geo. 3, c. 99, s. 26, have been complied with to the letter
in the service of the monition.

Platt, for the defendant.—The question is whether there
has been such a service of the monition upon the party as

(a) In Allen v. Brookbank, 2
Salk. 625, it was held that citation may be served by fixing on
the church door on Sunday.

the law requires; as to which the evidence was, that the
last time Mr. Kilwick was seen at the vicarage-house was
at Michaelmas, 1831; that, in January, 1832, the parish
clerk inquired of his daughter, who lived near the spot,
where her father was; but, not obtaining the desired information, he proceeded to the vicarage-house (which appears to have been a perfectly abandoned building), and
there left a copy of the monition. The practice of the
Ecclesiastical court should have appeared by evidence.
The service here, however, cannot be held good either
according to the rules of the Ecclesiastical law, or by
any analogy to the practice of our courts. In Burn's Eccl.
Law, 8th edit., by Trywhitt, Vol. 1, 417, the practice is
thus stated: "By the constitution of Otho, the person to
whom the citation is directed shall diligently seek the
party to be cited. And when he hath found him, he is to
shew to the party cited the citation under seal, and by
virtue thereof cite him to appear at the time and place
appointed: and it is usual also to leave a note with him,
expressing the contents thereof—1 Ought. 44, 45. But,
if it be returned upon the citation that the defendant
cannot be found, then the plaintiff's proctor petitioneth
that the defendant may be cited personally (if he can) to
appear and answer the contents of the former citation;
and if not personally, then by any other ways and means,
so as the party to be cited may come to the knowledge thereof.
And this is that which is called a citation viis et modis,
or a public citation, seeing it is executed either by public
edict, a copy thereof being affixed to the doors of the
house where the defendant dwells, or the doors of the
parish church where he inhabits, for the space of half an
hour in the time of divine service; or, by publication in the
church in time of divine service; or, as it hath been said,
by the tolling of a bell, or the sounding of a trumpet, or
the erecting of a banner. This being done, a certificate
must be made of the premises, and the citation brought

into court; and, if the party cited appear not, the plaintiff's proctor accuseth his contumacy (he being first three times called by the crier of the court), and, in penalty of such his contumacy, requesteth that he may be excommunicate." That this court will not interfere with the judgment of a court of competent jurisdiction, provided such judgment do not appear to be manifestly contrary to natural justice, cannot now be disputed. And if this question had been left to a jury, and they had found that the citation had come to the knowledge of the party, their finding would have been conclusive. But the simple question here is, whether or not the facts stated in the case do or do not constitute a due service. In all cases and in all courts the service of process or of rules is required to be either personal or at the usual place of abode of the party. In ejectment, the declaration and notice must be served upon the tenant, or (under certain circumstances) upon some member of his family, on the premises or at the place of his abode. If the outer door be found open, the mere leaving the declaration in a front parlour, as was done with the monition in this case, will not do: the court could not thence infer that the document had come to the knowledge of the party. The 26th section of the 57 Geo. 3, c. 99, has been cited to shew that the service in this case was correct. The very enactment shews, however, that the assistance of the legislature was required to render such a mode of service legal: and that clause has relation to quite a different state of things. In the absence of all evidence as to the practice of the Ecclesiastical courts upon the subject, this court clearly cannot hold good a service wanting every requisite to a valid service in any proceeding known to the common law courts.

W. H. Watson was heard in reply.

TINDAL, C. J.—This question comes before us upon a

precise issue raised upon the record, and the facts are
stated in the case for our guidance. The sole point to
be considered is whether or not the monition has been
duly served on William Kilwick, the vicar of Westbourne.
It appears to me that we may arrive at a proper judgment
upon this question without entering into many of the
arguments that have been urged before us on the part of
the defendant; and that upon the true construction of the
statute alone we may come to the conclusion that the
monition has been duly served. The 74th section of the
57 Geo. 3, c. 99, enacts, " that, in every case in which
jurisdiction is given to the bishop of the diocese, or to any
archbishop, under the provisions of the act, and for the
purposes thereof, and the enforcing the due execution of
the provisions thereof, all other and concurrent jurisdiction in respect thereof shall wholly cease, and no other
jurisdiction in relation to the provisions of the act shall be
used, exercised, or enforced, save and except such jurisdiction of the bishop and archbishop under this act; anything in any act or acts of parliament, or law or laws, or
usage or custom, to the contrary notwithstanding." And
the 75th section makes the due service of the monition a
condition precedent to the issuing of the sequestration:
it enacts, " that, in all cases where proceedings under the
act are directed by monition and sequestration, such monition shall issue under the hand and seal of the bishop,
and, being duly served, shall be returned with a certificate
of service into the registry of the Consistorial court of such
bishop; and thereupon it shall be competent for the party
monished to shew cause by affidavit or otherwise, as the
case may require, against the sequestration issuing; and,
unless sufficient cause be shewn to the contrary, the
sequestration shall issue under the seal of the said Consistorial court, and in such form as is commonly used in that
behalf." The 26th section, the object of which is the enforcing the residence of spiritual persons, condescends on

the particular modes of serving the monition: and the 75th section applying generally to *all* cases where proceedings under the act are directed by monition and sequestration, I can discover no reasonable principle upon which a mode of service pointed out in the one case should not equally apply in a subsequent case, when it clearly must have been in the view of the legislature at the time. By the 26th section, it is enacted, "that, in every case in which it shall appear to any such bishop as aforesaid that any spiritual person having or holding any benefice, and not being licensed according to this act to be absent therefrom, nor having any lawful cause of absence from the same, does not sufficiently reside on the same respectively, it shall be lawful for such bishop to issue or cause to be issued a monition to such spiritual person forthwith to proceed to and reside thereon, and perform the duties thereof; and to make a return to such monition within a certain number of days after the issuing thereof, so as that in every case there shall be thirty days between the time of *delivering such monition to such spiritual person,* or *leaving the same at his then usual or last place of abode,* or, *if not to be found, with the officiating minister or one of the churchwardens, and also a copy thereof at the house of residence (if any such there be) belonging to such benefice,* to which any such spiritual person shall be required by such monition to proceed and reside thereon, and the time specified in such monition for the return thereto; and a copy of every such monition shall immediately on the issuing thereof be filed in the registry of such bishop's court, and shall be open for inspection on the payment of 3*s.* and no more ; and the spiritual person to whom any such monition shall be sent under this act, shall, within the time specified for that purpose, make a return thereto into such registry, to be there filed." Thus, three distinct modes of service of monitions upon the parties are pointed out by the statute—first, by delivery to the spiritual person himself—secondly, by leaving the monition at his then usual or last place of abode—thirdly, if he is not to be found at his then usual or last place of abode, by leaving the monition with the officiating minister or one of the churchwardens, and also a copy at the house of residence belonging to the benefice. Now, how has the act been complied with in the present case? There is no pretence for saying that there has been a personal service; and, upon the facts, it appears rather doubtful whether or not the monition has been left at "the then usual or last place of abode" of the party. It appears that the last time Mr. Kilwick was seen at the vicarage-house was at Michaelmas, 1831; and, from that time down to the time of service of the monition, he was no more seen in the parish. I am not quite prepared to say, that, under the circumstances, the vicarage-house might not be considered the last place of abode of this gentleman. But, upon the third mode of service, it appears to me that the facts admit of no doubt. The evidence as to this is, that Baker, the person by whom the monition was served, about a week before the service, made application to Miss Kilwick as to where her father then was, but could get no information. Accordingly, one copy of the monition was left by Baker in that part of the vicarage-house to which Mr. Kilwick came when in the parish. Mr. How, the officiating curate, being the party moving, it could not be necessary to leave a copy with him. The evidence shews that there was a vicarage-house, in which the vicar resided when he came to the parish; that his daughter at the time of the service lived within a hundred yards of the place; and that she lived in the house at the time of the trial. Under these circumstances, how can it be said that the vicarage-house was not "the house of residence belonging to the benefice?" It appears to me that the monition has been duly served according to one at least of the modes pointed out by the legislature; and therefore that the plaintiff is entitled to judgment.

PARK, J.—I am of the same opinion. I see no ground for holding, that, because a parson chooses to absent himself from the place where by law he is bound to reside, it should not still be called his place of abode. The vicarage-house, however, according to the facts stated in the case, was Mr. Kilwick's place of abode: there was no evidence that he had any other. The 26th section of the statute directs the service of the monition to be made by delivering it to the party, or leaving it his then usual or last place of abode, or, if not there to be found (here, the Rev. Mr. Kilwick was not to be found at his usual or last place of abode, the vicarage-house, and his daughter would give no information as to where he could be seen), then the statute directs that the monition be left with the officiating minister or one of the churchwardens, and a copy thereof at the house of residence (if any such there be) belonging to the benefice. Now, what has been done in this case? Mr. How, the officiating minister, was the party who delivered the copy of the monition to Baker, the clerk, and such copy was left at the house of residence belonging to the benefice, which it appears was habitable and actually inhabited at the time of such service. I am · clearly of opinion that the monition has been duly served.

VAUGHAN, J.—I am also of opinion that there has in this case been as near a compliance with the directions of the statute as could under the circumstances be expected. Personal service was impossible, the party having absented himself. Perhaps it can hardly be said that the leaving a copy at the vicarage-house was a due service at the then usual or last place of abode of the party: at least I find some difficulty in saying so. In one sense, to be sure, the monition may be said to have been left with the officiating minister: but I should have been better satisfied had it been left with one of the churchwardens. Upon the whole, however, I think the service sufficiently proved.

BOSANQUET, J.—I am of opinion that the monition in this case has been duly served within the meaning of the 75th section of the act, in aid of the construction of which, as to the mode of service, I think the court are well warranted in having recourse to the 26th section. I am very much disposed to think that the vicarage-house may be considered the last place of abode of the vicar: it was the place at which he was bound to reside, and where he did reside before he went away; and he had no other known place of abode at the time. The original monition was in the possession of How, the officiating minister, and the copy left by the clerk at the vicarage-house was delivered to him by How for that purpose.

Judgment for the plaintiff.

———————◆———————

CLARKE v. STOCKEN.

A judge's order for the revocation of the authority of an arbitrator, under the 3 & 4, c. 42, s. 39, cannot issue upon an ex parte application.

BY the 3 & 4 Will. 4, c. 42, s. 39, after reciting that it is expedient to render references to arbitration more effectual, it is enacted, " that the power and authority of any arbitrator or umpire appointed by or in pursuance of any rule of court, or judge's order, or order of Nisi Prius, in any action now brought or which shall hereafter be brought, or by or in pursuance of any submission to reference containing an agreement that such submission shall be made a rule of any of his majesty's courts of record, shall not be revocable by any party to such reference, without the leave of the court by which such rule or order shall be made, or which shall be mentioned in such submission, *or by leave of a judge;* and the arbitrator or umpire shall and may and is hereby required to proceed with the reference notwith-standing any such revocation, and to make such award, al-though the person making such revocation shall not after-wards attend the reference; and that the court, or any judge thereof, may from time to time enlarge the term for any such arbitrator making his award."

This cause was referred to a barrister. The declara-tion was in assumpsit for goods sold and delivered.—Plea, the statute of limitations. The arbitrator having inti-mated an opinion adverse to the defendant, and having declined to state the matters specially on the face of his award, the defendant stated a case for the opinion of the Attorney-General. That learned person thinking the ar-bitrator was mistaken in the opinion he had expressed (no award having been made), the defendant upon an ex parte application, obtained from a judge, in pursuance of the statute, leave to revoke his submission.

Alexander, on a former day, obtained a rule calling upon the defendant to shew cause why the judge's order should not be rescinded.—He submitted that the very evils which the statute was intended to remedy would pre-vail even to a larger extent than before, if such orders could be obtained upon ex parte statements.

R. V. Richards shewed cause.—The court has no autho-rity to do that which this rule prays. The learned judge who made the order was aware that the application to him was ex parte. There is nothing in the act to give power to the court to interfere with the order of a judge, or to review his discretion in the matter. [*Bosanquet*, J. —The question is, not whether the court has power to review the decision of the judge, but whether the judge had power to make the order that has been obtained from him, upon an ex parte statement.] There are many cases wherein judges' orders are obtained upon ex parte applications: as, where it is sought to hold a defendant to bail a second time for the same cause of action (*Richards* v. *Stuart*, 3 M. & Scott, 778, 10 Bing. 319), or in trover, &c. If the leave of the court or a judge to revoke the submission must in all cases be made on a rule nisi or upon summons, and upon hearing both parties, the rule nisi or the summons will operate as a notice to the arbitrator to make his award. Besides, if the court rescind this order, will the authority of the arbitrator, which has been put an end to by the order, revive? If not, the rescinding of the order will be useless.

TINDAL, C. J.—The only question now before us is whether or not the order that has been made by the learned judge, giving the defendant leave to revoke his submission in this case, ought to be set aside. Upon the best construction I am able to put upon the statute, I think the rule for setting aside the order should be made absolute. The 39th section of the 3 & 4 Will. c. 42, enacts, " that the power and authority of any arbitrator or umpire appointed by or in pursuance of any rule of court or judge's order, or order of Nisi Prius, in any action now brought or which shall hereafter be brought, or by or in pursuance of any submission to reference containing an agreement that such submission shall be made a rule of any of his majesty's courts of record, shall not be revocable by any party to such reference, without the leave of the court by which such rule or order shall be made, or which shall be mentioned in such submission, or by leave of a judge." The statute, therefore, takes away from the parties the right to revoke the submission, except on leave obtained from the court or a judge. The section must be construed secundum subjectam materiem. It appears to me that no order can be pronounced by the court or by a judge unless both parties have been heard. Inasmuch, therefore, as in this case the order was obtained in the absence of the plaintiff, it is the same thing as if the order had never been pronounced at all. Where the application is made to the court, it is perfectly clear that the rule would be a rule nisi only in the first instance. What may be the effect of rescinding the order will be seen hereafter.

PARK, J.—In upholding an order obtained as this has been, we should be acting against the first principles of justice. I have always understood, that, before a party's rights are to be concluded by a rule or order, an opportunity must be given to him to be heard. (See *Capel* v. *Child*, 2 Tyr. 689, 2 C. & J. 558). The cases of a second arrest, or an arrest under a judge's order, are different: there, if the defendant had notice of the application, he would of course abscond. But, with respect to the application for leave to revoke a submission operating as notice to the arbitrator to expedite the publication of his award, that supposes gross corruption and partiality in him; and that I never will impute to any arbitrator, whether lawyer or layman.

VAUGHAN, J.—The provision in question is a very wholesome one, and highly conducive to justice and the saving of expense to suitors. Before the passing of the late act, cases frequently occurred where one party having contrived to learn the sense of the arbitrator, the submission was immediately revoked. Now, however, the revocation can only be effected by the order of the court or of a judge; and, according to every principle of law and justice, this leave should never be granted ex parte. Were it otherwise, the main object of the statute would not be attained. With respect to the authority of the court to review the decision of the judge, I think it clearly exists. Seeing the quantity and importance of the business that is now transacted at chambers, I think it of great importance that there should in all cases be a liberty of appeal.

BOSANQUET, J.—I am of opinion that the authority given by the act to the court or a judge is in no case to be exercised without notice to the opposite party. It is admitted on all hands, that, before this statute passed, the frequent and groundless revocation of the authority of the arbitrator when he was prepared to make his award, was an evil that called for a remedy. It seems to me, that, if parties may now go before a judge, and upon an ex parte statement obtain an order to revoke the submission, all the evils that existed under the old practice will remain in their full force. It is suggested that there might be danger in giving notice of the application, inasmuch as it would put the opposite party on the alert, and enable the arbitrator to defeat the application by making his award instanter. The court, however, cannot presume that the arbitrator will act corruptly. If such a case were to arise, the proper course would be to apply to the court to set aside the award.

Rule absolute.

Quære whether the refusal of an arbitrator to state the grounds of his decision upon the face of his award (where by the terms of the submission *authorized* to do so), is enough to induce the court to grant leave to revoke his authority, under the 3 & 4 W. 4, c. 42, s. 39.

R. V. Richards afterwards obtained a rule nisi to revoke the submission; against which cause was shewn by *Alexander;* and Sir *F. Pollock* and *Richards* were heard in support. The ground upon which it was suggested that leave to revoke should be given was, that the arbitrator had declined to state specially upon the face of his award the facts and grounds of his decision, which the submission *authorized* him to do.

THE COURT, expressly disclaiming to lay down any general rule upon the subject, but holding the application to be answered by the affidavits filed by the plaintiff—

Discharged the rule.

1836.

Tuesday,
April 26th.

CLARKE *v.* TAYLOR and Another.

THIS was an action on the case for a libel published by the defendants in a newspaper called the Manchester Guardian.

The declaration stated, that the plaintiff was a person of good name, fame, and credit, and had not ever been guilty, or, until the time of the committing of the several grievances by defendant as thereinafter mentioned, been suspected to have been guilty of the offences and misconduct thereinafter mentioned to have been charged upon and imputed to the plaintiff, or of any other such offences and misconduct: that, before and at the time of the committing the grievances thereinafter mentioned, the plaintiff used, exercised, and carried on the trade and business of a warehouseman, and had always conducted himself, in his said trade and business, in an upright, fair, and honourable manner, and was honestly acquiring great gains and profits in his said trade and business: yet the defendants, well knowing the premises, but wickedly and maliciously intending to injure the plaintiff, and to cause it to be suspected and believed that the plaintiff had been and was guilty of the offences and misconduct thereinafter mentioned to have been imputed to him, on the 27th of December, 1834, falsely, wickedly, and maliciously did com-

Where a libel contains several distinct charges, the defendant may justify a part only: but, if the part not justified contain libellous matter, he is liable in damages for that which is so left uncovered by the justification.

The defendants published in the Manchester Guardian a statement reflecting upon the plaintiff, and charging him with having been connected with a "grand swindling concern." The whole of the alleged libel related to transactions said to have taken place at Manchester, with the exception of the following passages: "As we have already stated, Clarke (the plaintiff) had been at Leeds for one or two days before his arrival in this town, and is supposed to have made considerable purchases there. It is hoped, however, that the detection of his plans in Manchester will be learnt in time to prevent any very serious losses from taking place."—"We have already stated that Clarke referred Mr. N. to a stockbroker in London, a Mr. P., we believe, to whom Mr. N. wrote for information respecting Clarke's circumstances. He received a reply from Mr. P., stating that Clarke had been introduced to him by a very respectable party; that he had sold stock for Clarke amounting to 1700*l.*, and had introduced him to Messrs. Jones, Lloyd, & Co., with whom he had opened an account by depositing 2000*l.* We believe there is not the slightest reason to doubt the truth of Mr. P.'s statement; and the probability is that Clarke had been furnished with the stock and an introduction to the stock-broker, for the purpose of giving colour to his proceedings here and in Yorkshire." The defendants, in their plea, justified the whole libel with the exception of the paragraph above set out. The declaration containing no allegation that the defendants intended to impute to the plaintiff the commission of any fraud at Leeds:—Held, that the passages not justified were not so clearly libellous as to entitle the plaintiff to a verdict thereon.

pose and publish, and caused and procured to be composed and published in a certain newspaper, to wit, the
Manchester Guardian, of and concerning the plaintiff,
and of and concerning him in relation to his said trade and
business, a certain false, scandalous, malicious, and defamatory libel, containing therein the false, scandalous, malicious, defamatory, and libellous matters following, of and concerning the plaintiff, and of and concerning him in relation
to his said trade and business, that is to say :—" Grand
swindling concern. During the present week a most artful
and deep laid scheme for obtaining goods without the intention of paying for them, has been detected in this town.
Generally speaking, plots of this nature are confined to
men equally destitute of property and of character; but
the one to which we now allude appears to have been devised by parties having the command of considerable funds,
and possessing thereby the means of giving to their ini-
quitous designs a sanction which they could not otherwise
have possessed. A few days ago there came to the Mosley
Arms inn, in this town, a person calling himself Mr. Edward Clarke (meaning the plaintiff), and professing to be
a principal in the firm of ' Edward Clarke & Co., warehousemen, Bucklersbury, London.' His (meaning the
plaintiff's) declared object here was to buy manufactured
goods; and he was accompanied by a Mr. Newman, as a
buyer of Manchester goods, and a Mr. Musgrove, as
buyer of woollens. It is, perhaps, necessary to state at
the outset, that there is not the slightest reason for believing that either of these individuals had any knowledge
of his (meaning the plaintiff's) real character, having been
engaged by him a very short time before his arrival here,
in consequence of an advertisement which he had inserted
in a newspaper. On their arrival in Manchester, Mr. Newman (who is known here, from the circumstance of his having previously been buyer for a respectable London firm) introduced Mr. Clarke (meaning the plaintiff) to a consider-

able number of houses in different branches of business. Clarke's (meaning the plaintiff's) story was, that he had a capital of about 3000*l.*, with which he was commencing business as a warehouseman; that his funds had been in the first instance transmitted to Leeds, where he had laid out the greater part of them, as from the state of business in that town he found he could obtain a greater discount than in Manchester. He (meaning the plaintiff) had, however, a credit on Messrs. Jones, Lloyd, & Co., to the extent of about 1000*l.* From two or three parties on whom he called small purchases were made, and were paid for by checks on Jones, Lloyd, & Co., which were duly honoured. From other parties he (meaning the plaintiff) proposed to buy largely on the terms of credit which are usual in the trade. Amongst others he (meaning the plaintiff) called on Messrs. Taylor, Son, & Gibson, of High Street, where he bought a parcel of woollens, &c., amounting to about 1000*l.*, referring them to their own establishment in London, where he said he was well known. He (meaning the plaintiff) went also to Messrs. Potters & Norris, Cannon Street, where he looked out goods worth about 1400*l.*, and gave them a reference to Taylor, Son, & Gibson. Mr. Norris, who had shewn him the goods, consequently sent to those gentlemen, who expressed their surprise at the reference, as they said Mr. Clarke (meaning the plaintiff) must know that they had not had time to receive an answer from London. In consequence of this reply, Mr. Norris sent for Newman, and he came accompanied by Clarke (meaning the plaintiff), who said that he supposed Mr. Norris might entertain some doubts, and he was therefore come to answer any inquiries that might be made. When told of the reply of Taylor, Son, & Gibson to the inquiry which had been made, Clarke (meaning the plaintiff) said that their house in London, to whom he was well known, had promised to write on his behalf to the house in Manchester, which he supposed

they had neglected to do. Mr. Norris then asked him
(meaning the plaintiff) for a reference to some party in
London to whom he could himself apply, and 'Clarke
gave the name of a stockbroker to whom he said he was
well known. He (meaning the plaintiff) also stated that
he had been some time in the service of a Mr. Jones,
a draper in Tottenham Court Road, London, whom he
left about eighteen months ago; and had since been living upon his property. It happened that there was also
at the time in Manchester, Mr. Truman, of the firm of
Llewelyn, Truman, & Co., warehousemen, who was about
returning to London, and Mr. Norris requested him to
make some inquiries from Mr. Jones, the draper in Tottenham Court Road, as to the character and circumstances of Mr. Edward Clarke (meaning the plaintiff). Mr.
Truman accordingly, on his arrival in London, sent a
clerk to make the necessary inquiries from Mr. Jones,
who stated that Clarke had lived with him three years,
and had left him about eighteen months ago; that his
conduct had always been unexceptionable; that he was
ignorant of the extent of his property, but knew that his
connections were highly respectable. The result of this
inquiry was communicated by Mr. Truman to Messrs.
Potters & Norris by the post which arrived here on
Tuesday last. By the same post there came to Manchester a letter directed to 'Mr. Clarke, Mosley Arms,
Manchester,' which was delivered according to its address. It very fortunately happened, however, that, in
addition to 'Mr. Edward Clarke' (meaning the plaintiff),
there was then stopping at the Mosley Arms another Mr.
Clarke, who was better known there, and to whom the
letter was by mistake delivered. It was without signature (though perhaps the writer may be guessed at),
and was in the following terms:—'Dear ——, I was very
anxious for your letter, which I received this morning,
and the rather as I received none yesterday, which augur-
ed badly. Your letter I considered as disasterous as

could be, inasmuch as it did not say that the 1000l. you
had selected at Gibson's would be sent—omitted all mention of Musgrove's brother—informed me you had expended 300l.'s worth in shooting at "birds in a bush;"
and finally I had received no letter by this post from the
house whom you had referred to me. Judge further of
my consternation, when, in the afternoon Llewelyn's clerk,
the Llewelyn, came up and said he was desired by their
house, requested by Potters & Somebody, to make inquiries into the respectability of Mr. Edward Clarke, who
had referred said Potters to me. Here was a Scylla and
Charybdis to steer betwixt! On the one hand to say
what was necessary, and the other to say nothing to commit myself. If I erred, it was by sailing too close to the
rocks of Scylla by saying too much; but I hope subsequent precaution will repair the damage, and preserve
our keel unbroken. They had no idea that it was the
Edward Clarke—the "real pig." It was not for me to
inform them it was the same, only in a new character. It
is, therefore, well you did not settle with them; and you
see in this another instance of the advantage of procras-
tination—my doctrine. If you had attempted to make the
donkey speak, you would have been swamped at once, and
have been blown directly. I have 200l. by me, and shall
have 50l. more on Monday night, and will pay 250l. into
Lloyd's on that day, but I shall give no orders respecting
it to them. Trust not to making 1000l. a year; 'tis falla-
cious. Llewelyns will know you when they see you; and
though they are paid by you, they will set themselves right
with the Potters. Deacon has been here bothering, but
I gave him his quietus. Buy all you can; don't trust to
second journies, and don't burn this letter. I must see it
destroyed when you return. I am in great haste, for the
postman is gone past some time. Mrs. C. was here just
now. I gave her your letter, and 5l. credit with me.'—
As may be readily supposed, the gentleman into whose

hands this precious epistle had fallen, was, at first, no
little puzzled with its contents; he therefore shewed it
to some other gentlemen who were in the commercial
room, and all they could make out of it was that some
scheme of roguery was in progress. They were engaged
in discussing it when Newman entered the room, and the
letter being handed to him, he at once perceived that he
had been made the unwilling instrument of a gang of
swindlers. He immediately took the course which any
honest man would take under the circumstances. He went
to all the parties from whom goods had been purchased,
and communicated to them the discovery which had taken
place. Fortunately this communication was in time to prevent any goods, except those which had been paid for,
from falling into the hands of Mr. Clarke's (meaning the
plaintiff's) London confederates. One or two parcels had
been delivered to the carriers, but the sellers were enabled
to stop them in transitu; and one person who had sold
some fustians to Clarke (meaning the plaintiff) obtained
the money from him on Wednesday morning, by threaten-
ing to hand him over to a police officer if the demand was
not complied with. Clarke (meaning the plaintiff) himself
departed for London by the Peveril coach on Wednesday,
having made a very bad speculation of his Manchester
trip, particularly as he had in one or two cases made a
part payment in cash for goods which he had bought, and
which are now held by the sellers for the balance. As we
have already stated, Clarke (meaning the plaintiff) had
been at Leeds for one or two days before his arrival in this
town, and is supposed to have made considerable purchases
there. It is hoped, however, that the detection of his
plans in Manchester will be learnt in time to prevent any
very serious losses from taking place. There is one circumstance connected with this business which shews how
deeply the scheme of fraud had been laid, and how cautious
parties should be in their inquiries respecting strangers.
We have already stated that Clarke (meaning the plaintiff)

· referred Mr. Norris to a stockbroker in London, a Mr. Peacock, we believe, to whom Mr. Norris wrote for information respecting Clarke's (meaning the plaintiff's) circumstances. He received a reply from Mr. Peacock, stating that Mr. Clarke (meaning the plaintiff) had been introduced to him by a very respectable party; that he had sold stock for Clarke, amounting to 1700*l*., and had introduced him to Messrs. Jones, Lloyd, & Co., with whom he had opened an account by depositing 2000*l*. We believe there is not the slightest reason to doubt the truth of Mr. Peacock's statement; and the probability is, that Clarke (meaning the plaintiff) had been furnished with the stock, and an introduction had been obtained to the stockbroker for the purpose of giving colour to his (meaning the plaintiff's) proceedings here and in Yorkshire."—By means of the committing of which said several grievances by the defendants as aforesaid the plaintiff was greatly injured in his said good name, fame, and credit, and in his said trade and business; and thereby also one Richard Musgrove, who otherwise would have entered into the plaintiff's employ in his said trade and business, then refused so to do, and the plaintiff was compelled to pay a large sum, to wit, 105*l*., in order to rescind a certain contract by him before then made in that behalf with the said Richard Musgrove.

The defendants pleaded, first, the general issue, and then a justification of the whole libel, with the exception of the following passages at the end: "As we have already stated, Clarke had been at Leeds for one or two days before his arrival in this town, and is supposed to have made considerable purchases there. It is hoped, however, that the detection of his plans in Manchester will be learnt in time to prevent any very serious losses from taking place." "We have already stated that Clarke referred Mr. Norris to a stockbroker in London, a Mr. Peacock, we believe, to whom Mr. Norris wrote for information respecting Clarke's circumstances. He received a reply from Mr. Peacock, stating that Mr. Clarke had been introduced to him by a very respectable party; that he had sold stock for Clarke amounting to 1700*l.*, and had introduced him to Messrs. Jones, Lloyd, & Co., with whom he had opened an account by depositing 2000*l.* We believe there is not the slightest reason to doubt the truth of Mr. Peacock's statement; and the probability is, that Clarke had been furnished with the stock, and an introduction had been obtained to the stock-broker, for the purpose of giving colour to his (meaning the plaintiff's) proceedings here and in Yorkshire."

The cause was tried before Tindal, C. J., at the sittings at Westminster after last Trinity Term. The publication of the libel by the defendants was admitted. The jury finding the justification proved, returned a verdict for the defendants.

Humfrey, in Michaelmas Term last, obtained a rule nisi to set aside this verdict, and enter a verdict for the plaintiff for that part of the libel which related to the alleged transactions in Yorkshire, with one farthing damages, on the ground that it was left uncovered by the justification; or for a new trial, on the ground that the justification quoad the transactions at Manchester was not made out by the evidence.—He cited *Higham* v. *Reynolds,* Cro. Eliz. 87; *Stiles* v. *Nokes,* 7 East, 493; *Lewis* v. *Clements,* 3 B. & A. 703; *Clements* v. *Lewis,* 7 Moore, 200, 3 B. & B. 297; *Lewis* v. *Walter,* 4 B. & A. 615; *Weaver* v. *Lloyd,* 2 B. & C. 678, 4 D. & R. 230, 1 C. & P. 295; *M'Gregor* v. *Thwaites,* 3 B. & C. 24, 4 D. & R. 695; *Duncan* v. *Thwaites,* 3 B. & C. 556, 5 D. & R. 447; *Clarkson* v. *Lawson,* 3 M. & P. 605, 6 Bing. 266; and *Mountney* v. *Watson,* 2 B. & Ad. 673.

Wightman and *W. H. Watson* shewed cause.—The defendants have in fact justified the entire libel, although they do not in terms condescend upon every particular:

and the justification as pleaded was clearly made out by the evidence they offered at the trial. It suffices that enough be shewn to satisfy the jury that the facts stated in the alleged libel are in substance proved. The plaintiff is charged with carrying on a grand swindling concern at Manchester. That which relates to the plaintiff's proceedings in Yorkshire, amounts to nothing, unless coupled with the rest of the libel : taken per se, there is nothing libellous in that part of the publication. Towards the close of the statement the writer observes :—" As we have already stated, Clarke had been at Leeds for one or two days before his arrival in this town, and is supposed to have made considerable purchases there. It is to be hoped, however, that the detection of his plans in Manchester will be learnt in time to prevent any very serious losses from taking place." This and the concluding part of the statement are not libellous unless the statement relative to the plaintiff's plans in Manchester be libellous : and that is justified. In *Clarkson* v. *Lawson*, the libel stated that the plaintiff had been thrice suspended from his office of proctor for extortion ; and the defendant by his plea only justified as to one suspension, and therefore the plea was properly held bad, inasmuch as the libel consisted of one entire charge, and not a general charge of extortion, setting forth instances, in which case it would have been competent to the defendant to select certain of those instances to form the subject of his justification. So, in *Weaver* v. *Lloyd*, the justification failed in a material point. There, to a declaration for a libel imputing to the plaintiff various acts of barbarous cruelty to his horse, and, amongst others, with knocking out an eye. The defendant pleaded in justification—first, that the charge was true in all its particulars—secondly, that it was true in substance and effect : and the jury found, that the first plea was true, with the exception of two statements containing particulars of aggravated cruelty to the horse, and that the eye was not knocked out; and that the second was true in substance and effect; and they gave a shilling damages, subject to the opinion of the court as to the propriety of their verdict : and the court held that the verdict was right, the justification not being proved. *Mountney* v. *Watton,* 2 B. & Ad. 673, is exactly the converse of the present case. The declaration there stated that the defendant, intending to cause it to be believed that the plaintiff was guilty of feloniously stealing a horse, published a libel concerning him : the libel as set out was headed " Horse-stealer," and then alleged that the plaintiff was taken up on suspicion of having stolen a horse, by a constable who was informed that " such a character " was at a certain public house : it then went on to state cicumstances of suspicion against the plaintiff, and ultimately, that, having obtained permission to go out of the constable's sight, he made his escape, but was re-taken, and confined in gaol for examination—innuendo, that the plaintiff was guilty of stealing a horse. The defendant pleaded the general issue, and then a justification as to all parts of the libel except the word "horse-stealer," setting out in this latter plea the several circumstances related in the libel: and the court held, that, as the declaration alleged that the libel was intended to convey a charge of felony, and that intent was not denied by the plea, the statement of circumstances of suspicion to excuse part of the libel, was no sufficient justification. Littledale, J., there says : " The gist of the whole matter imputed by the libel is contained in the word ' horse-stealer.' The rest is a statement of facts from which the imputation contained in that word is deduced. And the declaration avers, in the beginning, and in conclusion by way of innuendo, that the intention was to impute felony. The justification only states circumstances which induce suspicion, and it is therefore no sufficient answer. And these circumstances all tend to the one conclusion which is contained in the word 'horse-stealer.' In such a case, I think a defendant cannot excuse parts of a libel as grounded on matter of suspicion, unless he can justify that which is the result of the whole." So, here, the sting of the libel is contained in the heading, "Grand swindling concern;" and that is justified. In *Edwards* v. *Bell*, 8 Moore, 467, 1 Bing. 403, the plaintiff (a dissenting minister) in his declaration charged the defendant with publishing of him the following libel—" A serious misunderstanding has recently taken place amongst the independent dissenters of Great Marlow and their pastor, in consequence of some personal invectives . publicly thrown from the pulpit by the latter against a young lady of distinguished merit and spotless reputation." The defendant in justification pleaded that the plaintiff, whilst officiating as minister, published from a part of the chapel assigned to him as minister for the delivery of a sermon, to and in the presence of his congregation, of and concerning one M. F., a teacher of a certain Sunday school, the scandalous words following: "I have something to say, which I have thought of saying for some time, namely, the improper conduct of one of the female teachers: her name is Miss F.: her conduct is a bad example and disgrace to the school; and if any of the children dare ask her to go home, she (meaning such child) shall be turned out of the school, and never enter it again : Miss F. does more harm than good :" and thereby gave great offence to divers of the dissenters, to wit, one A. B. and one C. D., and occasioned a serious misunderstanding among the dissenters. The jury having found a verdict for the defendant, it was held, on motion in arrest of judgment, that the plea was a sufficient answer to the libel. And Burrough, J., said : " The defendants were entitled to justify in this action by shewing that what they had alleged against the plaintiff was borne out in fact. In such a case, it is sufficient if the substance of the libellous statement

1836.

CLARKE
v.
TAYLOR.

be justified ; it is unnecessary to repeat every word which might have been the subject of the original comment. As much must be justified as meets the sting of the charge ; and if anything be contained in a charge which does not add to the sting of it, that need not be justified." In *Janson* v. *Stuart*, 1 T. R. 748, a plea that the plaintiff had been illegally, fraudulently, and dishonestly concerned and connected with and was one of a gang of swindlers and common informers, and had also been guilty of deceiving and defrauding divers persons with whom he had had dealings and transactions, wherefore the defendant printed and published the libel in question was held too general. And in *Newman* v. *Bailey*, 2 Chit. 665 (cited in *Janson* v. *Stuart*), it was held that a plea of justification for slandering the plaintiff, a justice of the peace, by charging him with pocketing fines of prisoners whom he had convicted, should state the names of the parties convicted and of whom the plaintiff had received the fines.

Platt and *Humfrey*, in support of the rule.—In order to constitute a perfect justification, the defendant is bound to assert the truth of the whole of the guilty acts charged in the libel. *Lewis* v. *Clement* and the other cases cited shew that the justification must be co-extensive with the slanderous matter. In the present case, it is impossible to read the libel without being satisfied that it imputes to the plaintiff having been guilty of fraudulent practices in Yorkshire as well as at Manchester. Two distinct charges of fraud are alleged to have been perpetrated in two different counties: and both should have been justified.

TINDAL, C. J.—A defendant undoubtedly may, in justifying the publication of a libel, separate and distinctly justify different parts of it, where each part imports a distinct and separate charge. This is well established by the case of *Stiles* v. *Nokes*, 7 East, 493, where Lawrence, J., says: "A plea of justification may be good, with a general reference to certain parts of the libel set forth in the declaration, if the court can see with certainty what parts are referred to; as, if the reference be to so much of the libel as imputes to the plaintiff such a crime (e. g. perjury), that would be sufficient without repeating all those parts again, which would lead to prolixity of pleading, and ought to be avoided." But it is equally certain, that, if the defendant omits to justify a part of the libel, he will be liable in damages for the part so left uncovered by the justification. Here, the plea does not profess to justify the whole of the alleged libel: it omits a part; and the question is whether the part so omitted would of itself afford ground for an action. It appears to me that that portion of the publication to which the justification does not apply, does not per se furnish a ground of action. The libel begins with a general charge that the plaintiff was connected with a grand swindling concern : and, from the general tone of the libel, it is clear that Manchester is primarily and substantially the arena of the alleged swindling. The newspaper which contained the libel, is published there. The libel begins—"During the present week, a most artful and deep-laid scheme for obtaining goods without the intention of paying for them, has been detected *in this town*." Further on, it states, that, "On their arrival in Manchester, Mr. Newman (who is known here from the circumstance of his having previously been buyer for a respectable London firm), introduced Mr. Clarke to a considerable number of houses in different branches of business. Clarke's story was, that he had a capital of about 3000*l*., with which he was commencing business as a warehouseman; that his funds had been in the first instance transmitted to Leeds, where he had laid out the greater part of them, as from the state of business in that town he found he could obtain a greater discount

1836.

CLARKE
v.
TAYLOR.

than in Manchester." Towards the end of the statement there is a passage that certainly looks something like a charge of fraud committed at Leeds; and, as the justification does not cover that, it is contended on the part of the plaintiff that he is at all events entitled to a verdict upon that part of the libel, with nominal damages. The passage in question is as follows: " As we have already stated, Clarke (meaning the plaintiff) had been at Leeds for one or two days before his arrival in this town, and is supposed to have made considerable purchases there. It is hoped, however, that the detection of his plans in Manchester will be learnt in time to prevent any very serious losses from taking place." It certainly is impossible to read this passage without perceiving it to be highly probable that the writer of the article meant to insinuate that the plaintiff had been at Leeds for no very good purpose. But the declaration does not allege any intention to impute to the plaintiff the commission of any fraud at the last-mentioned place. It is left in ambiguo: and I do not see why we should be called upon at this late hour to affix to the libel in this respect a meaning which the plaintiff himself has not thought fit to do. The libel then concludes as follows:—" We have already stated that Clarke referred Mr. Norris to a stockbroker in London, a Mr. Peacock, we believe, to whom Mr. Norris wrote for information respecting Clarke's circumstances. He received a reply from Mr. Peacock, stating that Mr. Clarke had been introduced to him by a very respectable party; that he had sold stock for Clarke amounting to 1700*l.*, and had introduced him to Messrs. Jones, Lloyd, & Co., with whom he had opened an account by depositing 2000*l.* We believe there is not the slightest reason to doubt the truth of Mr. Peacock's statement; and the probability is that Clarke had been furnished with the stock, and an introduction had been obtained to the stockbroker, for the purpose of giving colour to his proceedings here and in Yorkshire."

This unquestionably has a strong tendency the same way; but that is all: and when the plaintiff might, by a single allegation in his declaration, have made the passage libellous, and has omitted so to do, I think we are not warranted in saying that it of itself amounts to a libel. I therefore think the rule must be discharged.

PARK, J.—I am of the same opinion. The statement in the libel relating to the plaintiff's transactions at Leeds is not libellous in itself and without the aid of that part which relates to Manchester, and which is justified. One is rather led to suppose that the goods purchased at Leeds were paid for.

VAUGHAN, J.—I am also of opinion that the rule should be discharged. The question is whether the libel is not substantially justified. All that part of it which directly imputes fraud to the plaintiff relates solely to what took place at Manchester, and that is covered by the justification. With respect to Leeds, there is no averment or innuendo in the declaration to point the libel. The case of *Clarkson* v. *Lawson* was widely different from the present: the plaintiff was charged with having been thrice suspended from the office of proctor; and the plea only shewed one suspension, which was clearly no justification of the libel. In this case, however, I cannot discover in the alleged libel any distinct and clear substantive act of criminality charged, which the defendants' plea does not cover.

BOSANQUET, J.—If those parts of the libel that are not justified by the plea would not be actionable standing alone, it is admitted that the justification is sufficient. Looking at the libel, I am of opinion that those parts that are not covered by the plea are not libellous. The concluding paragraph is that which has made the greatest impression on my mind: but even there the language is ambiguous; and it does not appear to me, unaccompanied as it is by any averment or innuendo to give a meaning to it, so necessarily to involve a charge of fraudulent conduct as to entitle the plaintiff to maintain an action. It is not to be forgotten, that, under the general issue, it was for the jury to say whether or not anything fraudulent was intended to be thereby charged. Inasmuch, therefore, as all that which is excepted out of the justification is matter that is immaterial, the rule must be discharged.

Rule discharged.

POWELL v. HORTON.

The defendant contracted to sell to the plaintiff " Scott & Co., 75 barrels mess pork, at 53s. per barrel." At the trial it was proved that mess pork cured by Scott & Co. obtained in the market a higher price by 2s. 6d. per barrel than pork cured by any other house; and witnesses (connected with the trade) were allowed to state their construction of the contract:—Held, that, by the terms of the contract, the pork was expressly warranted to be pork *cured* by Scott & Co., and not merely *consigned* by that firm:—Held, also, that the witnesses were properly admitted to explain the meaning of the contract.

ASSUMPSIT for breach of a warranty on a sale of pork. The first count of the declaration stated, that, on the 15th August, 1834, in consideration that the plaintiff, at the request of the defendant, would buy of the defendant a certain quantity, to wit, 75 barrels, of pork, at 53s. per barrel, payable by bill at three months, less three months' discount, and fourteen days for delivery, the defendant promised the plaintiff that the said quantity of pork was then pork of a certain description, kind, and quality, to wit, mess pork of Scott & Co.; that the plaintiff, relying on the said promise of the defendant, did then buy the said quantity of pork of the defendant upon the terms aforesaid, and then paid him for the same at the rate and in manner aforesaid, and that the said quantity of pork was afterwards, to wit, at the expiration of the said period of fourteen days, delivered by the defendant to the plaintiff; yet the defendant, contriving and fraudulently intending to injure the plaintiff, did not perform or regard the promise so by the defendant made as aforesaid, but thereby craftily and subtilly defrauded the plaintiff in this, to wit, that the quantity of pork so sold and delivered as aforesaid was not at the time of such promise or delivery of the description, kind, and quality aforesaid, but, on the contrary thereof, was then pork of a different and inferior description, kind, and quality, that is to say, unmessed, and not pork of Scott & Co., and worth less to the plaintiff by a large sum of money, to wit, the sum of 100l., than the like quantity of pork of the description, kind, and quality promised by the defendant as aforesaid would have been; whereby the plaintiff had not only lost and been deprived of the benefit and advantage which might and otherwise would have accrued to him from the said purchase and from the possession of such quantity of pork of the description, kind, and quality promised by the defendant as aforesaid; but also, relying on the defendant's said promise, had been put fruitlessly and without advantage to great expense, amounting in the whole to a large sum of money, to wit, the sum of 100l., in and about the receiving, warehousing, and keeping the said pork, and in and about the endeavouring to sell and dispose thereof.

The defendant pleaded—first, non assumpsit—secondly, that the said pork so delivered to the plaintiff as in the said first count mentioned *was* mess pork of Scott & Co.

The cause was tried before Tindal, C. J., at the sittings in London after last Trinity Term. The facts were as follow:—The plaintiff was a provision merchant in London; the defendant an importer of Irish provisions, and agent for several Irish houses. On the 15th August, 1834, one Hawley, a provision inspector employed by the plaintiff, inspected under an order from one O'Ryan, the defendant's broker, certain pork lying at the wharf of Messrs. Pomeroy & Co., Horslydown. The order described the pork as " 75 barrels of best pork, per Vine; branded Scott & Co." On such inspection, Hawley had two or three of the barrels opened, and found them to contain pork of the best quality; and on his representation the plaintiff purchased the lot at 53*s.* per barrel, the highest price at that time given for prime mess pork. The sale note was as follows, signed by O'Ryan:—

"London, 15th August, 1834.

" Sold Mr. Henry Powell for account of Mr. Benjamin Horton, Scott & Co. 75 barrels mess pork, at 53*s.* per barrel: ex Vine: payable by bill at three months, less three months' discount; and fourteen days for delivery."

On the 29th August, the plaintiff gave the defendant his acceptance for 196*l.* 5*s.* 4*d.*, the amount of the invoice (which was in due course paid), and the pork was shortly afterwards removed to the plaintiff's wharf. On the 5th September, some of the barrels were opened for the inspection of an intended purchaser, when it was found that only five of them were of the description exhibited to Hawley at Pomeroy's wharf, the remaining seventy, branded W. at the top, being very inferior. The plaintiff immediately wrote to the defendant, stating the fact, and proposing to return the pork. The latter declined to receive it. Several ineffectual attempts were afterwards made to compromise the affair; and ultimately, on the 25th November, the pork was sold by the plaintiff at a loss of 5*s.* per barrel. The net proceeds of the sale amounted to 149*l.* 16*s.*, being 46*l.* 9*s.* 4*d.* less than the amount of the plaintiff's acceptance, which sum, together with certain charges, amounting in the whole to 70*l.* 15*s.* 1*d.*, the plaintiff sought to recover in this action.

It was admitted that the pork in question had not been cured by Scott & Co., whose high character in the market obtained for their pork 2*s.* 6*d.* per barrel more than was given for prime mess pork of any other house; but that it had been purchased from another curer, and shipped by Scott & Co.   ᵗ

On the part of the defendant it was submitted that the plaintiff had failed to make out his case; for that the contract contained no warranty that the pork in question was actually prepared or cured by Scott & Co., but was satisfied by the delivery of pork of the description usually called mess pork (which this was) consigned from the house of Scott & Co. His lordship expressed himself of opinion that the contract did imply a warranty that the pork was of the manufacture of Scott & Co., and admitted (subject to a motion) evidence to shew that pork purchased as the pork in question was, would be generally understood in the trade to mean pork manufactured or cured by Scott & Co.; and upon that evidence it was left to the jury to say whether or not the pork was warranted to be mess pork of the manufacture of Scott & Co.; and also whether or not, with reference to the damages, the pork had been held by the plaintiff for an unreasonable period. The jury found for the plaintiff—damages 52*l.*

Cresswell, in Michaelmas Term, in pursuance of the leave reserved to him, obtained a rule nisi to set aside the verdict and enter a nonsuit, on the ground urged at the trial, or to reduce the damages to 9*l.* 7*s.* 6*d.*, being 2*s.* 6*d.* per barrel, the difference in value between prime mess pork cured by Scott & Co., and mess pork of the manufacture of any other house.

Bampas, Serjeant, now shewed cause.—By the contract the pork was expressly warranted to be mess pork manufactured or cured by Scott & Co. The jury found that the pork was warranted to be of Scott & Co.'s curing, and that it had not been kept an unreasonable time; and they gave by way of damages the difference between the invoice price and the price produced on the sale, which under the circumstances was the only proper measure of damages. A representation in the contract of sale is a warranty. In *Gardiner* v. *Gray*, 4 Camp. 144, it was held, that, where before or at the time of sale a specimen is exhibited to the buyer, if there be a written contract which

merely describes the goods as of a particular denomination,
this is not a sale by sample, but there is an implied warranty that the goods shall be of a merchantable quality,
and of the denomination mentioned in the contract. So, in
Shepherd v. *Kain*, 5 B. & A. 240, where an advertisement
for the sale of a ship described her as "a copper-fastened
vessel," adding that she was to be taken with all faults,
without any allowance for any defects whatsoever, and it
appeared that she was only partially copper-fastened: it
was held, that, notwithstanding the words "with all faults,
and without any allowance for any defects whatsoever,"
the vendor was liable for the breach of the warranty.
Jones v. *Bowden*, 4 Taunt. 847, is a much stronger case
than the present. There—it being usual in the sale by
auction of drugs, if they are sea-damaged, to express it in
the broker's catalogue, and drugs which are re-packed or
the packages of which are discoloured by sea-water bearing an inferior price, although not damaged—the defendants, who had purchased some sea-damaged pimento,
re-packed it and advertised it in catalogues which did not
notice that it was sea-damaged or re-packed, but referred
it to be viewed (with little facility, however, of viewing it),
exhibited impartial samples of the quality, and sold it by
auction: it was held that this was equivalent to a sale of
goods as and for goods that were not sea-damaged, and
that an action lay for the fraud. Here, the question is
what was the meaning of the contract—what was understood in the trade by the words "mess pork of Scott &
Co." It was in evidence that pork branded "Scott & Co."
fetched a higher price by 2s. 6d. per barrel than pork cured
by any other dealers. If any doubt existed upon the construction of the sale note, it was removed by the evidence.
Undoubtedly, where the terms of a written contract are
clear and intelligible, parol evidence is not admissible to
vary or control them: but where, as in this case, the contract contains terms intelligible only to persons in the par-

ticular trade, the evidence of individuals of competent skill is admissible for the purpose of explaining the latent ambiguity.

Cresswell and *Wightman*, in support of the rule.—The contract was for a sale of mess pork of Scott & Co.; the declaration, if it had been intended to say that this involved a warranty that the pork was manipulated or cured by Scott & Co., should have so averred. Nothing of the kind, however, does appear upon the record: and the defendant's plea, that the pork delivered to the plaintiff was mess pork of Scott & Co., was clearly proved; for, it was shewn that the pork was mess pork, and that Scott & Co. were the consignors, which was all that was required to satisfy the terms of the contract: and therefore the defendant was clearly entitled to a nonsuit. This was not a sale by sample, but on an inspection of the bulk; and it has been held that a warranty does not extend to defects that are discoverable upon inspection—*Margetson* v. *Wright*, 5 M. & P. 606, 7 Bing. 603. In *Gray* v. *Cox*, 6 D. & R. 200, 4 B. & C. 108, 1 C. & P. 184, where the plaintiff declared in assumpsit upon a contract for the sale of copper sheathing, that the defendant undertook that it should be good, sound, substantial, and serviceable copper; and there was no proof that the defendant had given a warranty such as that declared on: it was held that he was not liable for any latent defects in the sheathing, although it was sold as copper sheathing. And Abbott, C. J., said, that, "if a person sold a commodity for a particular purpose, he would be understood to warrant it reasonably fit and proper for such purpose." Here, there is no complaint that the article was of bad quality; but merely that it was not of the manufacture of a particular house. In *Jones* v. *Bowden*, which is the strongest case to be found in favour of the plaintiff, Lord Chief Justice Gibbs differed from the rest of the court, a circumstance that must very materially

I 2

detracts from the value of that decision.—The witnesses whose testimony was objected to at the trial were not called for the purpose of proving any known usage of trade, but merely to put their own individual construction upon the terms of this contract. It clearly was not competent to the plaintiff by parol evidence to introduce into the contract a term which was not to be found in the declaration.—Then, as to the damages—The pork was kept three weeks without objection, and the sale did not take place until the 25th November, which was about ten weeks after the purchase—with a falling market, and a commodity of a perishable description. The jury were clearly not warranted in finding this delay reasonable. Parke, B., in a cause that was tried before him at the last Assizes at Liverpool, relative to a contract for the sale of palm oil, held a week to be a reasonable time for a re-sale. The proper measure of damages, therefore, in this case, supposing there has been a breach of warranty in the particular contended for, will be the difference in value between mess pork of Scott & Co., and mess pork of any other manufacturer—viz. 2s. 6d. per barrel.

TINDAL, C. J.—I am of opinion that this rule cannot be supported upon either of the grounds urged. The action is brought for an alleged breach of a warranty on a sale of pork, and the precise issue joined between the parties is, whether or not the pork delivered under the contract was mess pork of Scott & Co. The question is, what is the meaning of the warranty. Both parties are using the same language, but construe it differently. The proper construction of the words must therefore be ascertained either by the court or by the evidence of persons acquainted with the particular branch of trade to which the contract has reference. The meaning that the plaintiff attaches to the contract is, that the pork was warranted to be of the manufacture or curing of Scott & Co.: on the other hand, the defendant contends that the contract of warranty, if any such existed, was satisfied by the evidence that the article had been consigned by or passed through the hands of Scott & Co. It appeared, however, from the evidence that there was a commodity known on the market as Scott & Co.'s pork. The broker who made the contract, stated that he was acquainted with the brand of that firm, that he had examined the pork in question, and found that certain of the casks, bearing their brand only, contained pork of their manufacture, and that those that were marked with a W. on the head were not of Scott & Co.'s manufacture, but were merely pork that had passed through their hands. How could the broker make this distinction, unless the manufacture of Scott & Co. was well known in the market? The fact that Scott & Co.'s pork always produced 2s. 6d. per barrel more than that of any other house, leads to the same conclusion. Without reference, therefore, to any particular evidence of opinion, I have no hesitation in saying that this contract upon the face of it imports a warranty that the pork in question was mess pork, manufactured or cured by Scott & Co. Where an article is warranted to be of the fabric or manufacture of a particular house of character and celebrity, the real benefit to the purchaser consists in the assurance that the character of the maker stands pledged to him for the quality of the article. So, when one buys a picture as the work of a particular artist, he is entitled to have a picture painted by that artist, and the contract would not be satisfied by the delivery of one that had merely hung up in his studio. But, supposing the extent of the warranty to be left in doubt upon the face of the contract, is not this like the case of any other mercantile contract? It is the constant course, where any doubt arises upon such instruments, to call persons conversant with the trade for the purpose of explaining them. The only witnesses that were called with this view were called by the plaintiff;

and they stated that they would understand from the contract that the pork was warranted to be of the manufacture of Scott & Co. It is true that the declaration does not expresaly allege that as the legal effect of the contract; but it states as the breach of the contract that the pork delivered to the plaintiff was not of the description, kind, and quality contracted for, but, on the contrary, was of a different and inferior description, and not pork of Scott & Co. It would be too much to say, that, because the plaintiff sets out the contract in its terms, and complains of the consequence of the breach of it, he thereby gives up its legal effect.—With regard to the damages—it does not appear to me that the re-sale was, under the circumstances, unreasonably delayed. The parties appear to have been negotiating, and I think the plaintiff down to within a few days of the sale had a right to expect that the defendant would have taken back the pork. Upon the whole, therefore, I am not prepared to say that the jury have given an unreasonable measure of damages.

PARK, J.—I am of the same opinion. Upon the mere words of the contract, it appears to me to be impossible to entertain a doubt: but, assuming it to be ambiguous and doubtful, it clearly was proper to receive the evidence of mercantile men to explain such ambiguity. If such evidence be excluded, who is to decide the question? Both judge and jury were decidedly opposed to the construction contended for on the part of the defendant. As to the inspection, *Gardiner* v. *Gray* is precisely in point: it was there held, that, where before or at the time of sale, a specimen is exhibited to the buyer, if there be a written contract which merely describes the goods as of a particular denomination, this is not a sale by sample, but there is an implied warranty that the goods shall be of a merchantable quality, and of the denomination mentioned in the contract.

VAUGHAN, J.—I also am of opinion that the verdict in this case ought not to be disturbed. The single question is as to the proper construction of the contract. I have always understood, that, although an usage of trade cannot be set up in contravention of an express contract—*Yeats* v. *Pym*, 2 Marsh. 141, 6 Taunt. 446—still evidence is admissible to shew the general understanding of the particular trade, in order to explain an ambiguity in a mercantile contract. In the present case, it was entirely for the jury, assisted by the evidence of men acquainted with the Irish trade, to decide as to the meaning of this contract. The evidence upon the subject was all one way; and I think the jury were well warranted in adopting the construction given by the witnesses. The warranty was clearly proved to have been broken. With respect to the damages, I concur with the rest of the court in thinking that the jury have given the proper measure.

BOSANQUET, J.—I am of the same opinion. A contract for the sale of pork of Scott & Co., clearly means pork manufactured or cured by that firm. If I speak of a literary work and name the author, it is to be inferred that I represent the work to have been written by the individual named. So, with respect to the work of an artist, or the goods of a particular manufacturer. On the part of the defendant it is suggested that the warranty in this case imports no more than that the pork was consigned to this country by the house of Scott & Co. But I cannot subscribe to such a limited construction. It is the constant course at Nisi Prius to admit the testimony of mercantile men for the purpose of explaining commercial contracts.— Then, as to the damages—The article having been sold as pork of a particular description, and not answering that description, the proper measure of damages was that which the jury have given, viz. the difference between the invoice price and the sum produced on the re-sale';

1836.

POWELL
v.
HORTON.

and, under the circumstances, I think the sale was not delayed for an unjustifiably long period.

Rule discharged.

ll. 23: Hil. 556 — 7 C. B. 578.

PAGET and Another v. EMILY M. A. FOLEY, Executrix
of ANN CHAMBERS, Deceased.

*Wednesday,
April 27th.*

Quære whether
the limitation
of six years
imposed by the
3 & 4 Will. 4,
c. 27, s. 42, in
actions for " ar-
rears of rent
or of interest
in respect of
any sum of
money charged
upon or payable
out of land,"
applied to an
action of cove-
nant for arrears
of rent accruing
under an inden-
ture—Tindal,
C. J., and Bo-
sanquet, J.,
accord.—Park,
J., and Vaughan,
J., dis.
      The limita-
tion in actions
of covenant
for arrears of
rent under in-
denture, is
governed by
the 3 & 4 Will.
4, c. 42, s. 3,
this provision
being virtually
a repeal pro
tanto of the
former.

COVENANT by the assignee of the lessor against the executrix of the lessee, for arrears of rent accruing more than six years before the commencement of the action.

The declaration stated that one A. H. Chambers, before and at the time of the making of the indenture of demise thereinafter next mentioned, was lawfully possessed of the tenements with the appurtenances thereinafter mentioned to have been demised to Ann Chambers, that is to say, for the residue and remainder of a certain term of years whereof divers, to wit, twenty years would after the expiration of the lease thereafter mentioned be to come and unexpired; and being so possessed thereof, he the said A. H. Chambers theretofore, to wit, on the 2nd April, 1808, by a certain indenture then made between the said A. H. Chambers of the one part and the said Ann Chambers of the other part, he the said A. H. Chambers, for the consideration therein mentioned, did demise, lease, set, and to farm let unto the said Ann Chambers, her executors, administrators, and assigns, certain premises with the appurtenances particularly mentioned and described in the said indenture, to have and to hold the same unto the said Ann Chambers, her executors, &c., for sixty years from the 25th March then last past, yielding and paying therefor yearly and every year during such part of the said term as the said Ann Chambers should happen to live the rent or sum of 10l. 10s., and, in the like manner, yearly and every year for and during such part of the said term as should be to come and unexpired at and after the decease of the

said Ann Chambers, the rent or sum of 15*l.* 15*s.;* the said
rents to be paid on &c., free of taxes &c.: and the said
Ann Chambers, for herself, her heirs &c., did by the said
indenture promise and agree to and with the said A. H.
Chambers, his heirs and assigns, amongst other things; in
manner following, that is to say, that she the said Ann
Chambers, her executors &c., should and would well and
truly pay or cause to be paid unto the said A. H. Chambers, his heirs and assigns, the aforesaid two several rents
or sums of 10*l.* 10*s.* and 15*l.* 15*s*, at the days or times and
in manner thereinbefore limited and appointed for payment thereof, according to the true intent and meaning of
the said indenture &c.: by virtue of which said demise the
said Ann Chambers afterwards, to wit, on the day and
year first aforesaid, entered into and upon all and singular
the demised premises, with the appurtenances, and became and was possessed thereof for the said term so to her
thereof granted as aforesaid, and which said term is still
unexpired: And the said A. H. Chambers being so possessed as aforesaid, and the said lease having been so made
as aforesaid, afterwards, that is to say, on the 21st October, 1824, by a certain indenture made between the said
A. H. Chambers of the first part, one Joseph Pouget of
the second part, and the plaintiffs of the third part—pro-
fert—for the considerations therein mentioned, he the said
A. H. Chambers bargained, sold, assigned, transferred, and
set over unto the plaintiffs, their executors &c., among
other property, the said premises so demised as aforesaid
to the said Ann Chambers, to have and to hold the same,
and his mansion therein, to the plaintiffs, their executors
&c., for the residue of the said term of which he was so
possessed as aforesaid ; whereupon and whereby the plaintiffs became and were, and from thence hitherto had been,
and still were entitled to the said demised premises, with
the appurtenances, and all the interest of the said A. H.
Chambers therein ; and afterwards, to wit, on the 26th

Mortgage to
plaintiffs, 21
Oct. 1824.

February, 1826, the said Ann Chambers died: And although the said A. H. Chambers had always from the time of the making of the said indenture of demise until the making of the said indenture of assignment, and the plaintiffs from that time hitherto, had always well and duly performed, fulfilled, and kept all things in the said indenture contained on the part of the said A. H. Chambers to be performed, fulfilled, and kept, according to the tenor and effect, true intent, and meaning thereof; yet, protesting that Ann Chambers in her lifetime, and the defendant, executrix as aforesaid, since her decease, had not, nor had either of them, performed, fulfilled, or kept any thing in the said indenture contained on her part to be performed, fulfilled, and kept, the plaintiffs said, that, after the making of the said assignment to them, and in the lifetime of Ann Chambers, and during the term granted to her as aforesaid, to wit, on the 29th September, 1825, a large sum of money, to wit, 10*l*. 10*s*., of the rent aforesaid, for one year of the said term then elapsed, became and was due and owing, and still is in arrear and unpaid to the plaintiffs, contrary to the tenor and effect, true intent, and meaning of the said indenture, and of the said covenant of Ann Chambers by her in that behalf made as aforesaid: And the plaintiffs further said, that, after the making of the said assignment to them the plaintiffs, and after the death of Ann Chambers, and during the term granted to her as aforesaid, to wit, on the 25th March, 1835, a large sum of money, to wit, the sum of 149*l*. 2*s*. 6*d*. of the rent aforesaid, for nine years and one half of a year of the said term elapsed since the death of Ann Chambers, became and was due and owing, and still is in arrear and unpaid to the plaintiffs, contrary to the tenor and effect, true intent, and meaning of the said indenture, and of the covenant of the said Ann Chambers by her in that behalf made as aforesaid.

The defendant craved oyer of the indenture in the declaration secondly mentioned; which being set out, he

First breach—
nonpayment of
one year's rent
accruing during
the lifetime of
Ann Chambers.

Second breach
—nonpayment
for 9½ years
since the de-
cease of Ann
Chambers.

Pleas of the
statute of limi-
tations, 3 & 4

pleaded, as to the breach of covenant first above assigned, that the said sum of 10*l.* 10*s.* of rent aforesaid therein mentioned, did not, nor did any part thereof, become due at any time within six years next before the commencement of this suit, nor had any acknowledgment of the same in writing, signed by the defendant or her agent, been given to the plaintiffs or their agent, at any time within six years before the commencement of the suit: And, as to the breach of covenant secondly above assigned, except so far as the same related to the sum of 94*l.* 10*s.* of rent aforesaid for six years of the said term, ending on the 25th March, 1835, that the said rent in the second breach mentioned, except as in the introductory part of this plea was excepted, did not, nor did any part thereof, become due at any time within six years next before the commencement of this suit, nor had any acknowledgment of the same in writing, signed by the defendant or her agent, been given to the plaintiffs or their agent at any time within six years next before the commencement of this suit.

Demurrer and joinder.

R. V. Richards, for the plaintiffs.—The question is, whether or not an action of covenant may be maintained for the nonpayment of rent accrued due more than six years before the commencement of the action. Until very lately there was no limitation whatever in covenant or any other form of action on a deed: the jury might, it is true, presume a release, from lapse of time and other circumstances; but still there was no positive limitation. Two points present themselves for discussion—the one, whether or not an action upon a deed is comprehended within the statute 3 & 4 Will. 4. c. 27, s. 40—the other (supposing that it is), whether or not the subsequent enactment in the 3 & 4 Will. 4. c. 42, s. 3, for this purpose repeals the former provision. The first mentioned act received the royal assent on the 24th July, and the other on the 14th August, 1833.

1836.

PAGET
v.
FOLEY.

Will. 4, c. 27, s. 42.

Argument for plaintiff—That the period of six years is not any limitation in bar to an action upon a covenant.

The 3 & 4 Will. 4, c. 27, s. 42, enacts, " that no arrears of rent or of interest in respect of any sum of money charged upon or payable out of any land or rent, or in respect of any legacy, or any damages in respect of such arrears of rent or interest, shall be recovered by any distress, action, or suit, but within six years next after the same respectively shall have become due, or next after an acknowledgment of the same in writing shall have been given to the person entitled thereto, or his agent, signed by the person by whom the same was payable, or his agent (*a*)." There can be no pretence for holding a covenant for payment of rent to fall within this provision, it being perfectly clear that the clause has no operation whatever upon any other deed or upon any covenant except a covenant for securing the payment of rent, leaving the covenant to repair to the limitation of twenty years. The section could not have been intended to embrace any debt by specialty: its words are satisfied by applying them only to the case of rent claimed for use and occupation; for, it is well known that before the statute the remedy by distress was barred only by the statute 32 Hen. 8, c. 37. By the 21 Jac. 1, c. 16, s. 3, it is enacted " that all actions of debt for arrearages of rent &c. shall be commenced within six years next after the cause of such action." The words of the clause now under consideration are almost the same: the construction, therefore, put upon the former must govern the latter; and in *Freeman* and *Stacy's* case, Hutton, 109, it

---

(*a*) " Provided, nevertheless, that, where any prior mortgagee or other incumbrancer shall have been in possession of any land, or in the receipt of the profits thereof, within one year next before an action or suit shall be brought by any person entitled to a subsequent mortgage or other incumbrance on the same land, the person entitled to such subsequent mortgage or incumbrance may recover in such action or suit the arrears of interest which shall have become due during the whole time that such prior mortgagee or incumbrancer was in such possession or receipt as aforesaid, although such time may have exceeded the said term of six years.",

was holden expressly that the 3rd section of the 21 Jac. 1, c. 16, did not extend to rent reserved on an indenture.

In determining whether or not the 3 & 4 Will. 4, c. 42, s. 3, operates so as to repeal the previous enactment of the 3 & 4 Will. 4, s. 27, s. 42, the court will be guided by the same principle which induced the decision of the court of King's Bench in *The King* v. *The Justices of Middlesex*, 2 B. & Ad, 818, where it was held, that, where two acts of parliament, which passed during the same session, and were to come into operation the same day, are repugnant to each other, that which last received the royal assent must prevail, and be considered pro tanto a repeal of the other. The object of the 3 & 4 Will. 4, c. 42, s. 3, was, to supply the want of some statutory limitation in actions on specialties: it enacts " that all actions of debt for rent upon an indenture of demise, all actions of covenant or debt upon any bond or other specialty, and all actions of debt or scire facias upon any recognizance, and also all actions of debt upon any award where the submission is not by specialty, or for any fine due in respect of any copyhold estates, or for an escape, or for money levied on any fieri facias; and all actions for penalties, damages, or sums of money given to the party grieved by any statute now or hereafter to be in force, that shall be sued or brought at any time after the end of the present session of parliament, shall be commenced and sued within the time and limitation hereinafter expressed, and not after; that is to say, the said actions of debt for rent upon an indenture of demise, or covenant, or debt upon any bond or other specialty, actions of debt or scire facias upon recognizance, within *ten* years after the end of this present session or within *twenty* years after the cause of such actions or suits, but not after; the said actions by the party grieved one year after the end of this present session or within two years after the cause of such actions or suits, but not after; and the said other actions within three years after the end of this present session, or within six years after the cause of such actions or suits, but not after; provided that nothing therein contained shall extend to any action given by any statute where the time for bringing such action is or shall be by any statute specially limited." If the 3 & 4 Will. 4, c. 27, s. 42, did apply to actions of covenant, the 3 & 4 Will. 4, c. 42, s. 3, operates pro tanto a repeal of it. In *Paddon* v. *Bartlett*, 5 N. & M. 383, Lord Abinger, in the course of the argument, intimated an opinion that the two provisions now under consideration were repugnant and inconsistent.

Argument for defendant—That, by the 3 & 4 Will. 4, c. 27, s. 42, the plaintiffs were precluded from recovering any arrears of rent but within six years next after the same became due.

That the assignment of the term granted to A. H. Chambers was made to the plaintiffs by way of mortgage, and not otherwise.

Stephen, Serjeant, for the defendant.—If the 3 & 4 Will. 4, c. 27, s. 42, does not apply to rent accruing under an indenture, to what case of rent can it apply? for, the 21 Jac. 1, c. 16, s. 3, had already imposed a limitation on the action of debt on simple contract for arrearages of rent. If the last-mentioned statute had provided that all actions of debt for rent should be barred after six years, and rent accruing under an indenture was the only exception, the first-mentioned enactment was wholly unnecessary except as it affected claims of rent by indenture. That this is the only case to which the statute could have had any effective view, is so manifest that it has been suggested on the other side to apply to the case of a distress for rent. In *Freeman* and *Stacy's* case, the court expounded the second part of the 21 Jac. 1, c. 16, s. 3, by the first, and held it to apply only to arrearages of rent without specialty: but there was something left for the statute to operate upon; whereas here the clause, according to the plaintiff's argument, is perfectly without effect, and leaves the old provision (except as to distress) where it was. Much stress has been laid upon the apparent inconsistency that would arise from holding this act (c. 27) to extend to a covenant for rent, inasmuch as it

does not extend to a covenant to repair. The latter,
however, sounding in damages, could not have been
within the intention of the legislature: their object was
to relieve the land from incumbrances, to protect it
from claims in respect of rent under particular circumstances only—in respect of money charged upon or payable out of land: the statute has no reference *generally*
to a claim of rent under an indenture; but to rent payable in respect of money charged upon the land. The
entire act has exclusive reference to real property. The
2nd section provides " that no person shall make an *entry*
or *distress*, or *bring an action to recover any land or rent*,
but within *twenty years* next after the time at which the
right to make such entry or distress or to bring such action shall have first accrued to some person through whom
he claims; or, if such right shall not have accrued to any
person through whom he claims, then within twenty years
next after the time at which the right to make such entry
or distress or to bring such action shall have first accrued
to the person making or bringing the same:" and the
17th, " that no *entry*, *distress*, or *action*, shall be made or
brought by any person who, at the time at which his
right to make an entry or distress or to bring an action to
recover any land or rent shall have first accrued, shall be
under any of the disabilities thereinbefore mentioned
[infancy, coverture, idiotcy, lunacy, unsoundness of mind,
or absence beyond seas—s. 16], or by any person claiming
through him, but within *forty years* next after the time
at which such right shall have first accrued, although the
person under disability at such time may have remained
under one or more of such disabilities during the whole of
such forty years, or although the term of ten years from
the time at which he shall have ceased to be under any
such disability, or have died, shall not have expired."
The object of these provisions was, to discharge the land

from incumbrances, *to shorten abstracts* (*b*), to enable parties to make title after twenty or forty years at the furthest. The act then proceeds to discharge the land from various other incumbrances. The 40th section takes up a case that no prior part of the act had provided for, namely, the case of a sum of money charged upon land— " No action or suit or other proceeding shall be brought to recover any sum of money secured by any mortgage, judgment, or lien, or otherwise charged upon or payable out of any land or rent, at law or in equity, or any legacy, but within *twenty years* next after a present right to receive the same shall have accrued to some person capable of giving a discharge for or release of the same, unless in the meantime some part of the principal money, or some interest thereon, shall have been paid, or some acknowledgment of the right thereto shall have been given in writing, signed, &c.; and, in such case, no such action, or suit, or proceeding shall be brought but within twenty years after such payment or acknowledgment, or the last of such payments or acknowledgments, if more than one, was given." This clause is in perfect harmony with all the previous provisions of the act : it determines the right where there has been no claim within twenty

(*b*) " It is a mistake," says Mr. Brodie, Hayes's Intro. Conv. 3rd edit., Appendix, 240, 241, " and at present a very prevalent one amongst professional gentlemen who have not duly considered the subject, to suppose that in consequence of the new statute of limitations, a purchaser will not be warranted in requiring the abstract of title to go so far back as under the old system. It is a common notion that the present length of abstracts is with reference to the limitation of sixty years. This is quite a mistake. It is with *reference to the duration of human life;* and so long as the law will not allow a remainderman expectant on an estate for life to be barred by a possession adverse to the tenant for life, a purchaser will be entitled to require a title to be shewn for the same period as heretofore under the old law."

And see the subject very learnedly and elaborately discussed in the Treatise above referred to, pp. 193—202.

years. The 42nd section, which is strictly correlative with the 40th, advances a step further, having reference to a withdrawal of rent for a less period than twenty years. It enacts "that no arrears of rent [*no comma*] or of interest in respect of any sum of money charged upon or payable out of any land or rent, or in respect of any legacy, or any damages in respect of such arrears of rent or interest, shall be recovered by *any* distress, *action*, or suit, but within six years next after the same respectively shall have become due, or next after an acknowledgment of the same in writing shall have been given to the person entitled thereto, or his agent, signed by the person to whom the same was payable, or his agent." Still the provision is limited to money charged upon the land. [*Tindal*, C. J.—"Arrears of rent in respect of any sum of money charged upon or payable out of any land or rent," does not seem to be a very usual phrase.] Suppose the case of a rent charged by will, could there be a doubt as to its falling within the act (*a*)? Whether charged by will or by indenture can make no difference. [*Tindal*, C. J.— The argument applies to a rent-charge: this is a rent-service.] The case before the court satisfies the words of section. It was essential that some such provision should be made. The main object of the legislature was to discharge the land from all arrears of interest of money charged thereon, after the expiration of the limited period. Under this clause, the mortgagor would be entitled to redeem the land on tendering the mortgage money and six years' arrears of interest. Unless the act applies to a case like the present, the *tenant* would not have the benefit of the bar,

One statute is not to be held to operate a repeal of another, if by any reasonable construction they can be reconciled. Both the statues now under consideration

That the 3 & 4 Will. 4, c. 42, s. 3, has not the effect of repealing the 3 & 4 Will. 4, c. 27, s. 42, or any part thereof.

(*a*) See James v. Salter, ante, Vol. 1, 750.

passed in the same session, and in contemplation of law
are one and the same statute. The 3 & 4 Will. 4, c. 27,
relates exclusively to questions affecting real property;
the 3 & 4 Will. 4, c. 42, has relation to the general administration of the law: and both were introduced at the
suggestion of the commissioners.   If the second operates
a repeal of the first, it must be either designedly or by accident: it is well known that it was not designed to have
that effect; and to hold the last provision to be an accidental repeal of the former, would be to stultify the legislature.   There is, however, no collision, no necessary opposition between the two provisions.   The first is a special provision applicable to " arrears of rent or of interest
in respect of any sum of money charged upon or payable
out of any land or rent, or in respect of any legacy, or
any damages in respect of such arrears of rent or interest:"
the second is a general provision applying to claims on all
kinds of indentures, extending to scire facias upon recognizances, debt upon awards, &c.; it enacts that actions of
debt [not *covenant*] for rent upon an indenture of demise,
or covenant, or debt upon any bond or other specialty,
and actions of debt or scire facias upon recognizance,
shall be brought within ten years after the cause of such
actions or suits, but not after.   *Hill* v. *Filking*, 10 Mod.
481, was a case of alleged repugnancy between two clauses
in the same act.   *The King* v. *The Justices of Middlesex*
turned upon a repugnancy (as to which there could be no
reasonable doubt) between two turnpike acts.   In *Paddon*
v. *Bartlett*, which did not seem to be very much relied on,
the mere question was whether or not the statute 3 & 4
Will. 4, c. 27, s. 42, had a prospective operation.   Some
doubt is suggested by Lord Abinger as to whether or not
the 3 & 4 Will. 4, c. 42, s. 3, was not inconsistent with the
3 & 4 Will. 4, c. 27, s. 42; but that was extrajudicial.   In
Comyns's Digest, *Parliament*, (K. 9), it is said—" A later
statute, general and affirmative, does not abrogate a former

which is particular: as, the statute 5 Eliz. c. 4, that none use a trade without being apprentice, does not take away 4 & 5 Philip & Mary, c. 5, that no *weaver* use, &c. So, a subsequent act which may be reconciled with a former, shall not be a repeal of it, though there are negative words: as, the statute 1 & 2 Philip & Mary, c. 10, that all trials shall be according to the course of the common law, and not otherwise, does not take away 35 Eliz. c. 8, for trial of treason beyond sea." In Dr. *Foster's* case, 11 Rep. 63. a., Lord Coke says: "It must be known, forasmuch as acts of parliament are established with such gravity, wisdom, and universal consent of the whole realm, for the advancement of the common wealth, they ought not by any constrained construction out of the general and ambiguous words of a subsequent act to be abrogated; sed hujusmodi statuta tantâ solennitate et prudentia edita, as Fortescue speaks, ought to be maintained and supported with a benign and favourable construction: for, Fortescue saith, prudentiâ enim et sapientiâ ipsa esse referta putandum est, dum non unici, aut centum solum consultorum virorum prudentiâ, sed plusquam trecentorûm electorum hominum, quali numero olim senatus Romanorum regebatur, edita sunt. And where the statute of 16 Rio. c. 5 enacts that all the lands and tenements of one attainted in a præmunire shall be forfeited to the king, the case in Pasch. 21 Eliz. was, that one Trudgin, being tenant in tail of certain lands and tenements, was attainted in a præmunire; and the question before all the judges of England was, if the estate tail was barred or not: and it was resolved by all the judges that those general words had not repealed the statute of Donis Conditionalibus, but that he should forfeit only for his life, and the issue in tail should inherit." *Gregory's* case, 6 Rep. 20. b., is to the same effect. There, Gregory brought a writ of error against Blashfield, and the case was that Blashfield brought a plaint in the court of London, which was a court of record, against Gregory, tam pro dominâ reginâ quam pro seipso, on the statute of 4 & 5 Philip & Mary, c. 5, which prohibits that none shall weave any woollen cloth or kersies, unless he hath been apprentice, or exercised the trade, &c., by seven years, upon pain of forfeiture of such cloth, or the value of it, the penalty to be recovered by action &c. in any court of record &c.; and three errors were assigned, first, that the said branch of the act was abrogated and taken away by the statute of 5 Eliz. c. 4: Sed non allocatur; for, inspecto statuto, they both stand together; and it was said that a later statute in the affirmative shall not take away a former act; and eo potius if the former be particular and the latter general. *Stradling* v. *Morgan*, Plowd. 201, further confirms this position. By a statute made in 7 Ed. 6, c. 1, s. 15, it is enacted, "that, if any treasurer, receiver, or minister accountant, or their deputy or deputies, do take or receive of any person any sum or sums of money of or for the payment of any fees &c. more or otherwise than he or they may lawfully do by former laws and statutes in such case provided, then the said treasurer &c. so offending shall forfeit and lose for every penny or pennyworth so to be taken or received 6s. 8d. to the party grieved." The defendant was receiver of certain manors, and took more than was due. The point (whether the statute extended to the treasurers, receivers, or ministers accountant of any other person than the king) was argued by the counsel for the defendant; and also it was argued, and held by all the Barons, that treasurers, receivers, or ministers accountant of common persons, and their deputies, who receive money or other profit for payment of fees &c., are out of the provision and penalty of the statute. And yet they all agreed that such are within the words of the statute; for, the words are, "if any treasurer" &c. "But, if a man considers where the mischief lay before the statute and what it was that the parliament intended to redress, he will thereby perceive that the intent of the makers of the act was only to punish the treasurers &c. of the king, and not of common persons; for, from the former only the mischief grew. For, when monasteries, houses of religion, colleges, and chantries were dissolved, and came to the hands of Henry 8 and Edward 6, pensions were assigned to the abbots &c.: and the treasurers, receivers, &c. appointed by the kings to pay them, perceiving that so many were payable through their hands, made a gain of it," &c. "And the judges of the law in all times past have so far pursued the intent of the makers of statutes, that they have expounded acts which were general in words to be but particular where the intent was particular." After citing several authorities, the report proceeds—"From which cases it appears that the sages of the law heretofore have construed statutes quite contrary to the letter in some appearance; and those statutes which comprehend all things in the letter, they have expounded to extend but to some things; and those which generally prohibit all people from doing such an act, they have interpreted to permit some people to do it; and those which include every person in the letter, they have adjudged to reach to some persons only: which expositions have always been founded upon the intent of the legislature, which they have collected sometimes by considering the cause and necessity of making the act, sometimes by comparing one part of the act with another, and sometimes by foreign circumstances: so that they have ever been guided by the intent of the legislature, which they have always taken according to the necessity of the matter, and according to that which is consonant to reason and good discretion." The 3 & 4 Will. 4, c. 27, s. 42, provides that no arrears of rent &c. shall be recovered by any distress &c. And in the 3 & 4 Will. 4, c. 42, s. 3, nothing is said about distresses. Now, it is, at the least, extremely improbable that the legislature, if they had intended by the latter provision to repeal the former in any respect, would have left the case of a distress for arrears of rent where it was,

without either confirmation or repeal. [*Tindal*, C. J.—
Might not this reason be suggested—that whereas, in the
case of a distress, the cattle of one man might be taken
for the debt of another; in an action, the plaintiff would
only recover for the actual occupation?] It is not enough
that a possible case may be suggested in order to justify
an argument for the constructive repeal of a statute : but
the question is whether by any reasonable construction
the former act can be reconciled with the latter; if it can,
then both must stand.

R. V. Richards, in reply.—If the one provision is clearly
repugnant to the other, the later one must prevail. In all
the cases cited on the other side, the first enactment was
particular, the second general; whereas here, the first
is general, and the last particular. The court can only
collect the intention of the legislature, and the reasons for
the passing of the act, from the act itself. The 2nd section of the 3 & 4 Will. 4, c. 27, means no more than this,
that after twenty years the rent is altogether lost; s. 42
extending to other remedies, by distress, &c., the provisions
of the 21 Jac. 1, c. 16, s. 3. The construction attempted to
be put upon the 42nd section (founded upon the absence
of a comma after the words "arrears of rent,") is clearly
erroneous: the words of that clause are amply satisfied by
confining it to the case of rent accruing under a parol demise. It would, indeed, be a strange anomaly so to construe the section as to hold that actions of covenant for
non-repair are to be left as they were, but that actions of
covenant for non-payment of rent are to be limited to six
years. Then it is said that the main object of the act was
to relieve the land from incumbrances. But rent, properly speaking, is not an incumbrance: incumbrances
created by deed or by will are very different from rent.
Covenant on an indenture is as much within the 3 & 4 Will.
4, c. 42, s. 3, as the action of debt. *Paddon* v. *Bartlett*

shews the strong impression of Lord Abinger that the 3 & 4 Will. 4, c. 27, s. 42, is in this respect repealed by the 3 & 4 Will. 4, c. 42, s. 3.

1836.

PAGET
v.
FOLEY.

TINDAL, C. J.—In giving judgment for the plaintiffs in this case, I am disposed to rest the opinion I am about to pronounce solely on the construction of the 3 & 4 Will. 4, c. 42, s. 3. But, at the same time, I must observe, that, if called upon to decide whether or not the present case fell within the prior enactment, 3 & 4 Will. 4, c. 27, s. 42, I should feel disposed to hold the case not to be within that section. That act was passed "for the limitation of actions and suits relating to real property, and for simplifying the remedies for trying the rights thereto :" and it contains enactments much more pertinent to charges on land than to mere conventional rents; for, by the 1st section, it is enacted that "the word 'rent' shall extend to all heriots, and to all services and suits for which a distress may be made, and to all annuities and periodical sums of money charged upon or payable out of any land, except moduses or compositions belonging to a spiritual or eleemosynary corporation sole." This seems to shew that the act intended to deal with a subject matter having no affinity to rent reserved upon an indenture. The 2nd section provides that "no person shall make an entry or distress, or bring an action, to recover any land or rent, but within twenty years next after the time at which the right to make such entry or distress, or to bring such action, shall have first accrued to some person through whom he claims." It is clear that in that section the word "rent" is used with reference to charges on land, fee-farm rents, &c., for which an assize would lie. The 36th section abolishes all real and mixed actions except writs of right of dower, or writs of dower unde nihil habet, or quare impedit, or ejectment: and the act then proceeds to make regulations to govern the amount of damages. Section

40 enacts that " no action or suit or other proceeding shall
be brought to recover any sum of money secured by any
mortgage, judgment, or lien, or otherwise charged upon
or payable out of any land or rent, at law or in equity, or
any legacy, but within twenty years next after a present
right to receive the same shall have accrued to some person capable of giving a discharge for or release of the
same, unless" &c. Section 41, which relates to dower,
enacts that "no arrears of dower, nor any damages on account of such arrears, shall be recovered or obtained by
any action or suit, for a longer period than six years next
before the commencement of such action or suit." When,
therefore, the clause that immediately follows provides
" that no arrears of rent or of interest in respect of any
sum of money charged upon or payable out of any land or
rent, or in respect of any legacy, or any damages in respect
of such arrears of rent or interest, shall be recovered by
any distress, action, or suit, but within six years next after
the same respectively shall have become due, or next after
an acknowledgment of the same in writing shall have been
given to the person entitled thereto, or his agent, signed
by the person by whom the same was payable, or his
agent," I should rather feel inclined to refer it to arrears
of rent of the description before mentioned in the act. It
is, however, unnecessary on the present occasion to give a
definitive opinion upon the point; for, it seems to me to
be perfectly clear, that, if rent accruing under an indenture was intended to be embraced by the 3 & 4 Will. 4, c.
27, s. 42, the subsequent enactment in the 3 & 4 Will. 4,
c. 42, s. 3, expressly takes it out of the operation of the
former. The 3 & 4 Will. 4, c. 27, received the royal assent on the 24th July, 1833, and was to come in force on
the 1st January, 1834: the 3 & 4 Will. 4, c. 42, received
the royal assent on the 14th August, 1833, and was to
come in force on the 1st June, 1833 (see s. 44), or at all
events from the end of the session—long before the for-

mer act came into operation. If, therefore, there is anything in the second statute irreconcileable with the first,
it would be singular to hold that the second provision
should remain in force only until the end of the year
1833, and should then be superseded by the first. By the
3rd section of the 3 & 4 Will. 4, c. 42, it is enacted "that
all actions of debt for rent upon an indenture of demise,
all actions of covenant or debt upon any bond or other
specialty, and all actions of debt or scire facias upon any
recognizance, and also all actions of debt upon any award
where the submission is not by specialty, or for any fine
due in respect of any copyhold estates, or for an escape,
or for money levied on any fieri facias, and all actions for
penalties, damages, or sums of money, given to the party
grieved by any statute now or hereafter to be in force,
that shall be sued or brought at any time after the end
of the present session of parliament, shall be commenced
and sued within the time and limitation thereinafter expressed, and not after; that is to say, the said actions of
debt for rent upon an indenture of demise, or *covenant*, or
debt upon any bond or other specialty, actions of debt or
scire facias upon recognizance, within ten years after the
end of this present session, or within twenty years after
the cause of such actions or suits, but not after," &c. These
are not merely negative words: they import an affirmative
also, viz. that a party may sue for rent in arrear at the
time of the passing of the act, at any time within ten years
after the end of the then present session.   There is therefore in August, 1833, a legislative declaration that actions
of covenant for arrears of rent may be brought during the
continuance of that time.   If the provision in the 3 & 4
Will. 4, c. 27, s. 42, be a general enactment limiting the
right of action for arrears of rent to six years, I think the
subsequent declaration in the 3 & 4 Will. 4, c. 42, s. 3,
that an action of covenant may be brought at any time
within ten years, is virtually an exception of this subject of

limitation out of the former act. Without, therefore, impeaching the 3 & 4 Will. 4, c. 27, further than is necessary, I hold, for the reasons above given, that the plea in this case is bad, and that consequently the plaintiffs are entitled to judgment.

PARK, J.—This case has been argued on two grounds—first, that the 3 & 4 Will. 4, c. 27, s. 42, did not extend to rents reserved by indenture—secondly, that, if it did, that provision, as far as it regarded that subject-matter, is repealed by the subsequent provision in the 3 & 4 Will. 4, c. 42, s. 3. Upon the words of the enactment, and upon the authority quoted, I am inclined to think that this case was not intended to be embraced by the former statute. But it is not necessary to decide the point, we being clearly of opinion that the second act, 3 & 4 Will. 4, c. 42, s. 3, operates a virtual repeal of the former clause if it were applicable to actions for rent under an indenture. The words of s. 3. are express, declaring that " all actions of debt for rent upon any indenture of demise, or *covenant*, or debt upon any bond or other specialty," &c., shall be sued or brought " within ten years after the end of this present session, or within twenty years after the cause of such actions or suits, but not after." We can only collect the intention of the framers of the act from the language they have used in it. And when we find in the last act language totally inconsistent with the language of the first, we must (as, indeed, it is admitted on the part of the defendant) give such an interpretation as is consistent with the words and spirit of the later enactment. I am clearly of opinion that this action is under the 3 & 4 Will. 4, c. 42, s. 3, entitled to the ten years' limitation, and consequently that the plea is bad.

VAUGHAN, J.—I am of the same opinion. It would be very desirable to give effect to both the clauses in question, if by any reasonable interpretation we could do so: but, if we cannot do so, the later one must prevail. It is certainly very difficult to imagine, the one act so closely following the other, that any collision or contradiction between them was anticipated, or repeal intended. I must confess that I am very strongly inclined to read the 3 & 4 Will. 4, c. 27, as not applying to specialties. There certainly is difficulty in arriving at the true construction: still I think they may both stand. At all events, the language of the 3 & 4 Will. 4, c. 42, s. 3, so clearly embraces this case, that no doubt can exist but that ten years is the period of limitation in an action of covenant upon an indenture of demise. In *Cockram* v. *Welby*, 2 Mod. 212, it had been held that to an action of debt brought by an executor against the sheriff to recover money levied on a fieri facias under an execution sued out by the testator, the defendant could not plead the statute of limitations: and in *Hodsden* v. *Harridge*, 2 Saund. 64 d., it had been held that debt on an award was not within the statute of limitations, 21 Jac. 1, c. 16. To meet these and other difficulties, and to remedy what was found to be a defect in the administration of the law as to the limitation of actions, the statute 3 & 4 Will. 4, c. 42, was passed.

BOSANQUET, J.—When two acts of parliament can by any reasonable intendment be construed consistently with each other, both undoubtedly ought to receive full effect. If this be impossible, the later act must prevail. If the 3 & 4 Will. 4, c. 42, s. 3, had never passed, I very much doubt whether this action would not be restrained to the shorter period of limitation, six years. The 3 & 4 Will. 4, c. 27, s. 42, appears to me to include rent service. The 1st section of the statute enacts that " the word ' rent ' shall extend to all heriots, and to all *services* and suits for which a distress may be made." The 2nd section relates to the recovery of the estate in the rent itself: and the act contains other provisions applying to the recovery of the arrears. The 40th section enacts "that no action or suit or other proceeding shall be brought to recover any sum of money secured by any mortgage, judgment, or lien, or otherwise charged upon or payable out of any land or rent, at law or in equity, or any legacy, but within twenty years next after a present right to receive the same shall have accrued to some person capable of giving a discharge for or release of the same," unless &c. Section 41 enacts that "no arrears of dower, nor any damages on account of such arrears, shall be recovered or obtained by any action or suit, for a longer period than six years next before the commencement of such action or suit." Then comes the 42nd section, which enacts that "no arrears of rent or of interest in respect of any sum of money charged upon or payable out of any land or rent, or in respect of any legacy, or any damages in respect of such arrears of rent or interest, shall be recovered by any distress, action, or suit, but within six years next after the same respectively shall have become due," &c. It is contended that this enactment does not apply to rent reserved by specialty; and *Freeman* and *Stacy's* case, Hutton, 109, a case decided upon the 21 Jac. 1, c. 16, s. 3, is relied on in confirmation of the argument. But, if we look at the words with which "rent" is associated in the 3 & 4 Will. 4, c. 27, s. 42, I think it will be found to be very difficult to say that it is confined to rent accruing under a parol demise. The clause refers to "interest of money charged upon land," which cannot be by parol. If the case had rested upon this section, I should have entertained a strong opinion in support of the application of the six years' limitation to this case.

It is, however, unnecessary to come to a decision upon the point. It is not easy to discover which of the two acts is the more general in its language. But I feel no hesitation in saying that an action of covenant on an indenture of demise is within the 3 & 4 Will. c. 42, s. 3; that that

clause is wholly inconsistent and irreconcileable with the
3 & 4 Will. 4, c. 27, s. 42; and consequently that the limitation must be governed by the former and not by the latter act.

1836.

PAGET
v.
FOLEY.

Judgment for the plaintiff.

WELLS and Another v. PORTER.

Friday,
April 29th.

ASSUMPSIT for 1500*l.* for work done by the plaintiffs for the defendant at his request, and for commission due and payable from the defendant to the plaintiffs in respect thereof; for 500*l.* paid by the plaintiffs for the use of the defendant at his like request; for 1000*l.* for interest for the forbearance by the plaintiffs at the defendant's request of divers monies due and owing from the defendant to the plaintiffs; and for 1500*l.* found to be due from the defendant to the plaintiff on an account stated between them.

The stock-jobbing act, 7 Geo. 2, c. 8, is confined to the stocks of this country.

Time bargains in foreign funds are not illegal or void at the common law.

If they were so, semble that that the broker employed in effecting them would still be entitled to sue for his commission in respect thereof.

The defendant pleaded (amongst other pleas), sixthly— as to the promise of the defendant as to the sum of 1183*l.*, parcel of the sum of 1500*l.* in which the defendant was in the declaration alleged to be indebted to the plaintiffs for work done—that the said work so alleged to have been done by the plaintiffs was work done by the plaintiffs as brokers and agents in and about the making of divers contracts between the defendant and divers other persons for liberty to the defendant to put upon and to deliver, receive, accept, or refuse, certain public stocks of certain foreign states, that is to say, of the kingdoms of Spain and Portugal respectively, and certain parts, shares, and interest therein, the defendant and the other persons, parties to the contracts respectively not being possessed of or entitled to the same, or any part thereof, in their own right, or in their own names, or in the name or names of a trustee or trustees to their own use; the plaintiffs at the time of paying the said monies

Sixth plea— That the work declared for was done by the plaintiffs as brokers in the making of illegal contracts in the nature of puts and refusals for foreign stocks, the parties to the contracts not having any interest in such stocks.

well knowing that the defendant and the said other persons
parties to the contracts respectively were not possessed of
or entitled to the same, or any part thereof, either in their
own name or in their own right, or in the name or names
of a trustee or trustees to their use or in their right, &c.

Seventh plea—
That the work
was done by the
plaintiffs as
brokers in un-
lawfully nego-
tiating contracts
for the sale and
transfer of
foreign stocks
in which none
of the contract-
ing parties had
any interest.

Seventhly, as to the said sum of 1183*l.*, parcel &c., that
the said work so alleged to have been done by the plaintiffs
was work done by them as brokers and agents in unlawfully negotiating, transacting, and intermeddling in the
making and procuring to be made certain contracts and
agreements for buying, selling, assigning, and transferring
certain public stocks of certain foreign states, to wit, the
kingdoms of Spain and Portugal respectively, and certain
parts, shares, and interest therein, which the defendant
and the other persons contracting, and on whose behalf
the said several contracts and agreements were made to
sell, assign, and transfer the same, were not, nor was any
of them, at the time of the making of such contracts and
agreements respectively, actually possessed of or entitled
to, either in their own right or in their own names, or in
the name or names of a trustee or trustees or any other
person or persons to their use or in their right; the
plaintiffs at the time of the doing of the said work and of
the making of the said contracts and agreements well
knowing that the persons on whose behalf such contracts
and agreements were respectively made were not nor was
any of them possessed of or entitled to the said stocks,
parts, shares, or interests in respect of which such contracts and agreements, were respectively made, in his, her,
or their own name or names, or in the name or names of
a trustee or trustees, or any other person or persons for
their use or in their right, &c.

Demurrer.—
That the sixth
and seventh
pleas did not
traverse or con-
fess and avoid

To these two pleas the plaintiffs demurred specially;
assigning for causes—that the said pleas did not deny or
confess and avoid the part of the declaration to which
they were pleaded; that there was nothing in the said pleas

or either of them to shew that the contracts therein alleged were illegal or void by reason of any statute or otherwise, or without consideration: and also that the said pleas were respectively double, and contained a twofold answer to so much of the declaration as they professed to answer; in this, to wit, that the defendant had in each of the said pleas pleaded and alleged that the said supposed contracts in the said pleas respectively mentioned were in the nature of puts and refusals, and also that the respective parties thereto were not at the time of making the same in any way possessed of or entitled to the said stock in respect whereof the said supposed contracts were made: and also that the said sixth and seventh pleas were in other respects uncertain, informal, and insufficient &c.

1836.

WELLS
v.
PORTAL.

that part of the declaration to which they were pleaded; and that they did not show any illegality in the contracts mentioned.

The defendant joined in demurrer.

Butt, in support of the demurrer.—The question is whether or not the transactions out of which this action arises (time bargains in foreign funds) fall within the stock-jobbing act, 7 Geo. 2, c. 8—"An act to prevent the infamous practice of stock-jobbing." That statute—after reciting that "great inconveniences have arisen and do daily arise by the wicked, pernicious, and destructive practice of stock-jobbing, whereby many of his majesty's good subjects have been and are diverted from pursuing and exercising their lawful trades and vocations, to the utter ruin of themselves and families, to the great discouragement of industry, and to the manifest detriment of trade and commerce"—enacts "that all contracts and agreements whatsoever which shall, from and after the 1st June, 1734, be made or entered into by or between any person or persons whatsoever, upon which any premium or consideration in the nature of a premium shall be given or paid for liberty to put upon, or to deliver, receive, accept, or refuse any public or joint stock or public securities whatsoever, or any part, share, or interest therein, and also all wagers and contracts in the nature of wagers, and all contracts in the nature of putts and refusals, relating to the then present or future price or value of any such stock or securities as aforesaid, shall be null and void to all intents and purposes whatsoever; and all premiums, sum or sums of money whatsoever which shall be given, received, paid, or delivered upon all such con- tracts or agreements, or upon any such wagers or con- tracts in the nature of wagers as aforesaid, shall be re- stored and repaid to the person or persons who shall give, pay, or deliver the same, who shall be at liberty, within six months from and after the making such contract or agree- ment, or laying any such wager, to sue for and recover the same from the person or persons to whom the same is or shall be paid or delivered, with double costs of suit." And by the 2nd section parties sued for penalties under the act are compellable to answer on oath touching the contracts made by them. Foreign stocks are not men- tioned in the act; and, being an act of a highly penal de- scription, it is not to be pressed beyond that which can fairly be supposed to have been within the intention of the legislature. At the time the act passed, foreign stocks were not known in this country: consequently the words " public or joint stocks or public securities," must clearly have been intended to comprehend only the public stocks of this kingdom. The precise point arose in *Henderson* v. *Bise*, 3 Stark. 158, where it was expressly ruled by Lord Chief Justice Abbott that a trafficking in Columbian bonds was not within the statute. His lordship said he "was of opinion that the words ' public or joint stock' relate merely to stock of this country, and [the act] was made to prevent jobbing in the British funds. It did not appear what the nature of Columbian bonds was: it was probable that the trafficking in such instruments might be attended with as much mischief as jobbing in the funds of this country; and it might be desirous that a statute should be passed to restrain such practices; but, as they did not fall within the statute referred to, the plaintiff was entitled to recover." In *Mortimer* v. *Salkeld*, 4 Camp. 42, Lord Ellenborough ruled that a wager respecting the profits to be made by the contractors for a lottery could. not be brought within the provisions of the statute: and the plaintiff there had a verdict, which was acquiesced in. It may be contended on the other side that the contracts in respect of which the plaintiffs claim the right to recover commission were void at common law, as being in the nature of wagers: but it is to be observed that the plaintiffs, who are third parties, do not seek to enforce those contracts, but merely to recover a compensation for work and labour bestowed by them at the defendant's request in the making of the contracts.

J. Manning, contrà.—The contracts out of which arises the plaintiffs' claim to recover in this action are clearly void and illegal both at common law and by the statute.

First, as to the statute—It it assumed on the other side, that, at the time of the passing of the statute 7 Geo. 2, c. 8, foreign stocks were unknown in this country. This, how-ever, is erroneous; for, it is clear matter of history that stocks existed in France and in Holland long before their formation here, and that the stocks of those countries were the subject of purchase and sale here long before the reign of William the Third (a). The words of the act are "any public or joint stock or public securities:" and supposing the term "public or joint stock" applies to British stocks only, surely "public securities" must be held to include as well Spanish and Portuguese stocks as those of our own country. The preamble affords a key

(a) The practice of funding ap-pears to have been introduced by the Venetians and Genoese in the sixteenth century. The establish-ment of funds was not introduced in this country until after the re-volution in 1668.

to the meaning of the framers of the act; it recites that
"great inconveniences have arisen and do daily arise by
the wicked, pernicious, and destructive practice of stock-
jobbing, whereby many of his majesty's good subjects
have been and are diverted from pursuing their lawful trades and vocations, to the utter ruin of themselves
and families, to the great discouragement of industry, and
to the manifest detriment of trade and commerce." The
act is intituled "An act to prevent the infamous practice
of stock-jobbing." What difference in degree of infamy
can there be between jobbing in our own or in foreign
funds? Two Nisi Prius cases have been relied on to shew
that transactions of the kind in question are not within
the act, viz. *Henderson* v. *Bise* and *Mortimer* v. *Salkeld*.
The argument in *Henderson* v. *Bise* turned on the 7th
section of the act which *impowers* (but does not *require*)
the bonâ fide purchasers of stock to purchase when the
seller refuses to deliver the stock which he has contracted
to sell. The objection taken was, not that the defendant
(the vendor) was possessed of no Columbian bonds at the
time he contracted to sell them to the plaintiff; but that
the contract was void under the statute, the plaintiff not
having purchased the stock before the commencement of
the action; which clearly was not necessary in order to
enable him to maintain the action, and the omission to do
which could not render the contract void. The opinion
of Abbott, C. J., therefore was wholly extrajudicial. *Mortimer* v. *Salkeld* was a case arising out of a wager as to the
profits of a lottery, and therefore totally beside any question as to gambling in the funds.—Then, the statute is declaratory only of the infamy of the already existing practice
of stock-jobbing. [*Tindal*, C. J.—The word "enact" only
is used in the statute.] Can an act which the statute de-
signates as "infamous, wicked, pernicious, and destructive," be held legal? or can it be held to be illegal only with
reference to the prospective enactments of the statute?
[*Tindal*, C. J.—The statute clearly is prospective only: it

enacts a new state of the law.] Though not within the direct purview of the act, gambling or jobbing in foreign funds is within the mischief intended by the act to be remedied. The point also arose in a case of *Rossum* v. *Taylor* (Chitt. Stat. 1022, n.), tried before Dallas, C. J., at Guildhall, in 1823. There, the plaintiff sued for differences in dealings in Spanish stock, and the learned judge said that the question ought to undergo the consideration of a full court. Several other objections were taken, but the plaintiff had a verdict, and leave was reserved to the defendant to move to enter a nonsuit, which was accordingly done in the following term. Dallas, C. J., on granting the rule, said: " This is a case of stock-jobbing in the foreign funds, and not in our own: in my present opinion, it is not the less gambling because it is in this or that stock; however, Sir John Bernard's act is nominally applicable to the British funds only. But what is the title of that act? It is an act to prevent the infamous practice of stock-jobbing. The legislature, therefore, has pronounced the act infamous. The question, therefore, upon that point is still open." The case underwent no further discussion, a compromise having been effected between the parties. That, in the opinion of Lord Tenterden, such a contract would be illegal and void at common law, is clear from the case of *Bryan* v. *Lewis*, R. & M. 386, a case that occurred about three years after that of *Henderson* v. *Bise*. His lordship there said: " I have always thought, and shall continue to think until I am told by the House of Lords that I am wrong, that, if a man sells goods to be delivered on a future day, and neither has the goods at the time nor has entered into any prior contract to buy them, nor has any reasonable expectation of receiving them by consignment, but means to go into the market and to buy the goods which he has contracted to deliver, he cannot maintain an action upon such a contract: such a contract amounts, on the part of the vendor, to a wager on the price of the com-

modity, and is attended with the most mischievous consequences." And in Chitty on Contracts, 2nd edit. p. 332, n.,
the same learned judge is said to have ruled on a still
later occasion, that, " if two persons enter into a contract
under the semblance of a sale of goods, not intending
really to buy or sell the commodity, but merely as a gambling speculation, and to pay the difference of the market
price on a particular day, *like a time bargain in the stocks,*
such a contract is illegal and void at common law, and no
action will lie to enforce it." This is a much stronger case
than that. And if the transactions themselves were illegal and void, the brokers are not entitled to maintain an
action against their principal for monies paid by them on
account, or for commission in respect thereof—*Clayton* v.
Dilly, 4 Taunt. 165; *Josephs* v. *Pebrer,* 3 B. & C. 639,
5 D. & R. 542, 1 C. & P. 507.

Butt, in reply.—Unless it be clearly apparent that foreign stocks were intended to be embraced by the statute,
or if the words of the act are satisfied by confining its
operation to the funds of this country, foreign stocks cannot be held to be within it. The words " other securities" can have reference only to securities of the like kind
with those before intended by " public or joint-stocks."
The same public securities are meant throughout the act;
and the 10th section, which relates to purchases of stock
by the accountant-general, puts the matter beyond doubt,
that officer having no power to deal with any other than
the British funds. *Henderson* v. *Bise,* as far as its authority goes, and also *Rossum* v. *Taylor,* shew that this case
is not within the statute. The question here is, whether
these contracts are within the words and meaning of the
statute, not merely whether they are within the mischief
it was intended to remedy: *Mortimer* v. *Salkeld* was cited
for the mere purpose of shewing that the case there put
was as much within the mischief of the act as this can be.

Unless avoided by the statute, dealings in the nature of time bargains are perfectly legal. There are no words in the act declaratory of the illegality of the practice at common law. *Bryan* v. *Lewis* decided nothing: and the opinion there expressed by Lord Tenterden is not warranted to the extent to which it goes by any case to be found in the books. Even if it were good to the fullest extent, it is no authority to shew that the brokers employed would not be entitled to maintain an action for their work and labour. *Clayton* v. *Dilly* merely decided that a plaintiff who by the defendant's authority lays illegal bets in the defendant's name, and, losing, pays them without a subsequent express direction so to do, cannot recover from the defendant the amount of the money so paid. Here, it is admitted on the record that the work was done *at the request of the defendant.* The contracts, however, being clearly not illegal either at common law or under the statute, the plaintiffs are entitled to judgment.

TINDAL, C. J.—It appears to me that the pleas now under consideration do not furnish any answer to the declaration. The action is brought for work and labour and commission. The pleas state that the work alleged to have been done by the plaintiffs was work done by them as brokers and agents in making illegal contracts for the sale and transfer of foreign stocks, in which none of the contracting parties were at the time interested—in effect, pleas of the stock-jobbing act; and affording a complete answer to the action if foreign stocks or funds are within that act. Looking at the words of the statute, it appears to me that foreign stocks are not within either its words or meaning. In the first place, the statute was passed with a view to prevent a common practice that had been found to be destructive of the interests of the country. The title and preamble of the act sufficiently shew that its object was to put down a practice that had become extremely general and in its consequences pernicious. Before the passing of the act in question many statutes had existed relating to the public stocks of this country, which shew that there was a subject-matter upon which this statute could operate. But there is no evidence before us of the then existence of any foreign stocks. If the defendant intended to rely on the fact of the existence of other funds besides English funds at the time of the passing of the 7 Geo. 2, c. 8, he should at least have averred that fact. Seeing what the statute might and did relate to, viz. English stocks, and having no judicial knowledge or information to shew us that it could have been intended to embrace stocks of any other country, I feel myself bound to hold that the former only are within the act. Besides, the statute carries with it consequences highly penal: it imposes a penalty on parties guilty of the acts prohibited, and also renders them liable, by a bill in equity filed against them, to answer on oath touching the contracts they may have entered into. A statute so penal in its nature is not to be enlarged beyond the fair and obvious meaning of the words employed to express the intention of the legislature. The act containing no expressions to induce us to suppose it was designed to embrace any other than the stocks of this country, I think we should not be warranted in holding any others to fall within it. The 10th section contains a provision applicable to sales of stock with the privity of the accountant-general of the court of Chancery. Hence it would seem clear that the stocks of this kingdom only were the subject of legislation; for, it is well known that no purchases or sales of stock are made under the authority of the accountant-general other than domestic stocks. This, undoubtedly, is not a conclusive argument on the subject; but it is not by any means an unusual or improper rule, in the construction of a statute, to call in aid an exception. For these reasons it appears to me that, as far as the statute is concerned, time bargains in foreign stocks are not illegal.—It has been contended, however, that such transactions constitute an offence at common law, and therefore not capable of being made the foundation of an action like the present. The words of the statute are words of enactment, not declaratory of the common law: and it would be too much to say that an action for work and labour could not be maintained in respect of work done by a broker or agent in the making of a contract which is not illegal, but at the most void. It is enough for the present purpose to say that I do not see my way with sufficient clearness to hold the transactions in question illegal at common law; and therefore I think the plaintiffs are entitled to judgment.

PARK, J.—I am of the same opinion. Two questions arise in this case—first, whether contracts called time bargains in foreign stocks (Spanish bonds) arc by the statute made illegal—secondly, whether they are illegal at common law. Upon a full consideration of the statute, and of the authorities to which our attention has been more particularly called, I am of opinion that such transactions are not within the statute. It is clear, that, where a statute says nothing to the contrary, it applies only to the subjects of, and to contracts made in, this country There is nothing in this act to shew that it was intended to apply to foreign funds. The 10th section is not without its weight in the construction of a statute that has not before received a distinct judicial interpretation. That section relating to the sale of stocks by an officer who is authorized only to deal with the stocks of this country, affords, in my judgment, a strong presumption that such only were the stocks to which the statute was intended to apply. There are cases in the books in which the subject has come under consideration. In *Henderson v. Bise*, 3 Stark. 158, Lord Chief Justice Abbott expressed himself of opinion that the act applied only to the stocks of this country. The only authority that at all impugns that opinion is the dictum of Lord Chief Justice Dallas in *Rossum* v. *Taylor:* his lordship seems to have been inclined to think that foreign stocks are within the act: he says—" This is a case of stock-jobbing in the foreign funds, and not in our own: in my present opinion it is not the less gambling because it is in this or that stock; however, Sir John Bernard's act is nominally applicable to British funds only. But, what is the title of that act? It is an act to prevent the infamous practice of stock-jobbing. The legislature, therefore, has pronounced the act infamous. The question, therefore, upon that point is still open." *Rossum* v. *Taylor* is not an authority to be opposed to *Henderson* v. *Bise;* it was afterwards settled without coming before the court.—With respect to the second point—I do not find any authority for holding transactions like those out of which this action arises to be illegal at common law. If the legislature had so understood at the time of the passing of the 7 Geo. 2, c. 8, some intimation to that effect would doubtless have been found in its preamble. The preamble, however, merely recites the fact of the existence and daily increase of a pernicious practice, to *prevent* which the legislature proceed to enact that the contracts therein described shall from and after a given day be null and void, and the parties offending subjected to certain penalties. Although I do not approve of the practice of gambling in foreign funds, still I cannot perceive that it is an offence at common law so as to disentitle the broker making the contracts to maintain an action for his commission.

VAUGHAN, J.—I am also of opinion that making what are called time bargains in the foreign funds is not an offence either at common law or by the statute. In *Billing* v. *Flight,* 2 Marsh. 124, 6 Taunt. 419, the 7 Geo. 2, c. 8, was held to be a remedial rather than a penal act: but it cannot be denied that some of its clauses are in the highest degree penal; and I think there is nothing in its language to shew that it was intended to apply to foreign stocks. Then, was this an offence at common law? No authority has been adduced to shew that it has ever been so held; though it cannot be supposed that foreign stocks did not exist at the time this statute passed. The act is prospective in all its provisions. It must be remembered, too, that the plaintiffs are one step removed from a participation in the offence, if it were an offence.

BOSANQUET, J.—I am of opinion that the contract upon which the plaintiffs have declared is not void or illegal either by the common law or by the statute. The statute imposes penalties for the commission of those practices it was framed to prevent, and therefore is not to be extended beyond the strict and fair meaning of its words. Notwithstanding the recital the act is still prospective, and not declaratory of what the law was before its passing. The statute speaking generally of public stocks or securities, must necessarily be understood to mean the public stocks or securities of this country only. I cannot say that I rely upon the 10th section of the act so much as the rest of the court seem to do: it would have been equally necessary to insert the exception whether the statute embraced foreign funds or not. But we have the authority of Lord Tenterden that Columbian bonds are not within the act; and that is the only express judicial opinion upon the point.—Then, are transactions of this nature illegal at common law? The contract here is for work and labour stated in the declaration to have been performed at the request of the defendant: and this is admitted by the pleas. The authority of Lord Tenterden in *Bryan* v. *Lewis* has been pressed upon us to shew that this contract is of such a nature as to be void at common law. The decision, however, in that case did not turn upon that point: that for which it is cited is a mere dictum of Lord Tenterden; and the circumstances of the case were such that one cannot feel surprised at a strong expression of opinion on the part of the judge. His lordship says—"I have always thought, and shall continue to think until I am told by the House of Lords that I am wrong, that, if a man sells goods to be delivered on a future day, and has neither the goods at the time, nor has entered into any prior contract to buy them, nor has *any reasonable expectation of receiving them* by consignment, but means to go into the market and to buy the goods which he has contracted to deliver, he cannot maintain an action upon such a contract: such a contract amounts, on the part of the vendor, to a wager on the price of the commodity, and is attended with the most mischievous consequences." Comparing that opinion with what appears upon this record, it will be seen that there is a material distinction between the two cases. There the vendor had no reasonable expectation of getting the goods he contracted to deliver: here the plaintiffs were merely employed as brokers or agents, and the pleas do not negative the power of the vendors to become possessed of the stock, or aver the plaintiffs' cognizance of the vendors' want of power to become possessed. This is material when the opinion of the same learned judge in the former case is remembered, viz. that foreign stocks are not within the 7 Geo. 2, c. 8. Independently of this, I am not prepared to say that the plaintiffs are not entitled to recover in this action a compensation for their work and labour. The contracts upon which the labour was bestowed might be void: but still it would by no means follow that the brokers by whom the contracts were made would be precluded from recovering their commission.

Judgment for the plaintiffs (b).

(b) See Oakley v. Rigby, post, 194.

WESTON v. FOSTER.

ASSUMPSIT for money lent and money paid, interest, and for money due on an account stated.

The defendant pleaded—first, that he did not promise in manner and form as the plaintiff had above thereof complained against him—secondly, as to the sum of 406*l.* 0*s.* 6½*d.*, parcel &c., that, after the making of the promises in the declaration mentioned, and before the commencement of the suit, to wit, on the 5th August, 1834, an account was stated between the plaintiff and defendant of and concerning the said several sums of money in the declaration mentioned, being such account stated as in the declaration mentioned, and upon that accounting he the defendant was then found to be in arrear and indebted to the plaintiff in the said sum of 406*l.* 0*s.* 6½*d.* : And the defendant further said, that the causes of action in the declaration mentioned so far as the same related to the said sum of 406*l.* 0*s.* 6½*d.*, parcel &c., arose and accrued to the plaintiff for and in respect of certain disbursements made for and on account of a certain brig or vessel called the Elizabeth, whereof one R. Fortune was master and commander, then lying and being off Sierra Leone, on the coast of Africa, and monies supplied for the purpose of enabling her to sail and proceed on a certain then intended voyage on which she was about to proceed, to wit, from Sierra Leone aforesaid to England, and for interest on such monies respectively: And the defendant further said that afterwards, and after such account had been and was so stated as aforesaid, and before the said brig or vessel set sail from Sierra Leone aforesaid on her said intended voyage, and before the

In assumpsit for money lent, &c., the defendant pleaded—first, non assumpsit—secondly, that the causes of action arose out of disbursements made for and on account of a vessel belonging to the defendant, and that the master made and sealed a bottomry bond, which was accepted and received by the plaintiff in satisfaction of the promises in the declaration mentioned, &c. The plaintiff replied that he did not accept or receive the bond in satisfaction of the promises modo et formâ. At the trial it appeared that the bond was given by the master the day after the transaction as to the advances on the ship's account was closed, and by way of collateral security only : the issue thereon having been found for the plaintiff:— Held, that the plaintiff's right to sue the

owner in respect of the implied contract was not destroyed by his taking such *additional* security.

Held, also, that it was not competent to the defendant under non assumpsit to give in evidence the making and delivery of the bond.

commencement of the suit, to wit, on the said 5th August, 1834, he the said R. Fortune, so being such master and commander of the said brig or vessel as aforesaid, did for and on account of the said several causes of action in the declaration mentioned, so far as the same related to the said sum of 406*l*. 0*s.* 6½*d.*, parcel &c., make and seal, and as his act and deed deliver to the plaintiff, his, the said R. Fortune's, certain writing obligatory commonly called a bottomry bond, in the penal sum of 812*l*. 1*s.* 1*d.*, under and subject to a certain condition thereunder written, whereby, after recting that the good brig or vessel called the Elizabeth, of the burthen of 276 tons or thereabouts, whereof the said R. Fortune was master, was then bound home, and forthwith to depart on her return voyage to England, and that, in consequence of the great sickness and mortality that had prevailed amongst the crew of the said brig, and the detention and expense arising therefrom, the disbursements of the said vessel had amounted to an unusually large sum, and that the owner of the said brig had not furnished the said master with the means of paying the same and proceeding on his intended voyage, and thereupon the said master was necessitated to take up money for supplying the said brig for her said intended voyage, which said voyage and employment the owner of the said brig had consented and agreed to, and that the plaintiff had paid and lent unto the said master the sum of 406*l*. 0*s.* 6½*d.* of lawful money of that colony, and was contented and had agreed to stand to and bear the hazard and adventure thereof on the hull or body of the said ship during the said voyage, so as the same did not exceed three calendar months from the first day of the then present month of August to be accounted: the condition of the said writing obligatory was declared to be such, that, if the said vessel should and did accordingly with all convenient speed proceed and sail on her said voyage to England (the dangers and casualties of the seas excepted), and also if the said R. Fortune, his heirs, executors, and administrators, did and should within ten days next after the return and arrival of the said brig or vessel at her port of delivery from her said intended voyage, or at the end and expiration of three calendar months to be accounted as aforesaid, which of the said terms should first and next happen, well and truly pay or cause to be paid to the plaintiff, his executors, administrators, or assigns, the sum of 406l. 0s. 6 d., together with 20l. for every calendar month the said brig should be out on the said voyage over and above three calendar months, to the expiration of six calendar months to be accounted as aforesaid, and so in proportion for less than a month, or that if in the said voyage and within the said three calendar months, to be accounted as aforesaid, an utter loss of the said ship or vessel by fire, enemies, or casualties should unavoidably happen, to be sufficiently proved by the said R. Fortune, his heirs, executors, or administrators, then the said writing obligatory was to be void, otherwise to remain in full force and effect: which said writing obligatory the plaintiff then, to wit, on &c. aforesaid, accepted and received of and from the said R. Fortune in full satisfaction and discharge of the said several promises in the declaration mentioned as to the said sum of 406l. 0s. 6½d., parcel &c., and of all damages and sums of money thereupon due and owing or accrued: And the defendant further said, that the said brig or vessel did afterwards and with all convenient speed, to wit, on the 7th August in the year aforesaid, proceed and sail on her said voyage to England aforesaid, and that afterwards and whilst the said brig or vessel was proceeding on her said voyage, to wit, on &c. last aforesaid, and on divers other days and times between that day and the 3rd October then next following, the said brig or vessel by stormy and tempestuous weather and the perils and dangers of the seas became and was leaky and greatly broken and

damaged, insomuch that notwithstanding the great and
determined exertions of the master and crew, and the constant and continued working of the pumps thereof, the
said brig or vessel became and was greatly filled with water
and in immediate danger of sinking; by means whereof,
and in consequence of the leaky state of the said brig or
vessel continuing to increase notwithstanding such exertions as aforesaid, and the sick and exhausted state of the
master and the crew thereof, it then became and was expedient and indispensably necessary for the preservation
of the lives of the master and crew of the said brig or vessel, for them to leave and abandon the said brig or vessel;
and the said master and crew did then for the preservation
of their lives accordingly leave and abandon the same; and
the said brig or vessel was then and within the space of
three calendar months from the 1st August in the year
aforesaid, being the said month of August in the said condition of the said writing obligatory in that behalf mentioned, and before the arrival of the said brig or vessel at
England aforesaid, to wit, on &c. last aforesaid, by the
force and violence of the winds and waves, and the perils
of the sea, wrecked, foundered, and sunk, and became
and was utterly lost by casualties within the true intent
and meaning of the said condition of the said writing obligatory; and the said brig or vessel never did arrive in
England aforesaid or other port of delivery from her said
intended voyage: And the defendant further said that
such utter loss of the said brig or vessel by such casualties
as aforesaid was afterwards, to wit, on the 29th October
in the year last aforesaid, sufficiently proved by the said
R. Fortune according to the tenor and effect of the said
condition; of all which the plaintiff then had notice: And
this &c.

The plaintiff added a similiter to the first plea, and replied to the second, that he did not accept or receive of
and from the said R. Fortune the said writing obligatory

in full satisfaction and discharge of the said several promises in the declaration mentioned as to the said sum of 406*l.* 0*s.* 6½*d.*, parcel, &c., modo et formâ.

At the trial before Mr. Justice Park at the adjourned sittings at Guildhall after last Trinity Term, the following facts appeared in evidence:—The plaintiff is a merchant residing in London, and having establishments at Sierra Leone and other places on the coast of Africa, where he is represented by an agent named Craig. The defendant was the owner of the ship Neptune, Fortune, master, which was chartered by the defendant to the plaintiff on the 13th November, 1833, for a voyage from London to Sierra Leone and back to England. The vessel having arrived at Sierra Leone, and taken on board a cargo of timber, a claim was made upon the master by Craig, the plaintiff's agent, for a sum of 338*l.* 7*s.* 1½*d.*, for cash and goods paid and supplied by him for the ship's use during her stay at Sierra Leone. The master, to satisfy this demand, drew bills upon his owner for the amount in the usual course: and afterwards, *on the same or the next day*, Craig procured from the master a bottomry bond for 406*l.* 0*s.* 6½*d.*, being the sum claimed for the cash and supplies with the addition of 20*l.* per cent., the usual maritime interest. The vessel left Sierra Leone on her voyage to England on the 7th August, and on the 3rd October was abandoned by the master and crew, she being in imminent danger of foundering, off the island of Madeira; and she was never afterwards heard of. After the loss of the Neptune the bills drawn by the master at Sierra Leone were presented to the defendant for acceptance, but he refused to accept them, alleging the bond to have been taken in satisfaction of the sum the bills were given to secure.

On the part of the defendant it was contended, that the plaintiff, having at the same time taken a bottomry bond, with maritime interest (20*l.* per cent.), and bills drawn by the captain on the owner, his claim on the bills was destroyed, for he could not retain both. To which it was answered that the bond was void—Abbott on Shipping,' 5th edit. 125; case of *The Augusta*, 1 Dods. 283—and was not accepted in satisfaction of the bills; but merely as a collateral security, after the close of the transaction.

A verdict having been found for the plaintiff, on both issues—damages 338*l.* 7*s.* 1½*d.*—

Taddy, Serjeant, in Michaelmas Term last, obtained a rule nisi for a new trial, on the ground above stated.

F. Kelly and *Butt* now shewed cause.—It appeared from the evidence that the transaction was closed and the bills given by the captain before the execution of the bond: and whether the bond was accepted in satisfaction of the advances or merely as a collateral security, was a question of fact, and is concluded by the finding of the jury. Then, the other defence attempted to be set up, viz. that the acceptance of the bond operated an extinguishment of the original contract, was not admissible under non-assumpsit, but should have been pleaded specially—Reg. Gen. Hilary, 4 Will. 4, Assumpsit, 1, 3. It was a defence arising after the cause of action accrued: in the nature of a release. Had the whole been one transaction, not completed until the giving of the bond, the defence might have been available in the present state of the record: but the evidence shewed, and the finding of the jury has established, that the giving of the bills and the giving of the bond were separate and distinct transactions. The case of *The Augusta*, 1 Dods. 283, is an express authority to shew that the bond was void: it was there held, that a bond of hypothecation is good only where the ship and freight are the sole security; but not so where the lender looks to the personal security of the borrower.

Taddy and *Andrews*, Serjeants, in support of the rule.—

The facts clearly shew that the plaintiff did not rely on the personal responsibility of the owner. Whether the bills and the bond were given on the same day or not, is immaterial; they both bore date the same day, and constituted together one entire transaction. The case is not at all embarrassed by the new rules. Here was no express contract except on the bills or upon the bond: and the matter of fact whence the promise is to be implied must be the whole transaction. It is a clear and settled principle, that there cannot be an implied promise unless in the absence of an *express* promise between the parties. Where one takes a security reserving maritime interest, the case of *The Augusta* shews that the Admiralty Court will exercise its discretion as to whether or not it will under the circumstances enforce the bond: there, the bond was held void because many months had intervened between the contraction of the debt and the giving of the bond. But, in the case of *The Tartar*, 1 Hagg. 13, such a bond was enforced. The replication to the second plea here admits the bond to be good: all the allegations in that plea are admitted except that the bond was taken and accepted in satisfaction.

TINDAL, C. J.—It appears to me that this case may be disposed of upon one short ground. The action is for money lent, paid, &c.; to which the defendant has pleaded non assumpsit, and also a special plea stating in substance, that a bottomry bond with the usual maritime interest was given and received in satisfaction of the debt. To this latter plea the plaintiff replied that the bond was not accepted and received in satisfaction. On both issues the jury have found for the plaintiff. When the effect of the finding is to be considered, each plea must be taken separately. As to the second, the jury, who were the proper judges, found that the plaintiff did not accept the bond in satisfaction of the advances made on account of

the ship, but by way of collateral security only; and as far
as the evidence goes I think it warrants that finding.
Then, with respect to the first issue—The defendant insists that he is at liberty to shew that the money was advanced on a security other and different from his personal
responsibility, viz. on the security of the bond. But it
seems to me that that defence is excluded by the new
rules from being set up under non assumpsit. The rule
already referred to provides, that, "in all actions of assumpsit, except on bills of exchange and promissory notes,
the plea of non assumpsit shall operate only as a denial in
fact of the express contract or promise alleged, or of the
matters of fact from which the contract or promise alleged
may be implied by law;" and that, "in every species of
assumpsit, all matters in confession and avoidance, including not only those by way of discharge, but those
which shew the transaction to be either void or voidable
in point of law, on the ground of fraud or otherwise, shall
be specially pleaded; e. g. infancy, coverture, release, &c.,
and various other defences, must be pleaded." Now, here,
the only matter of fact asserted in the declaration is, that
the money was lent and paid. If the defendant meant to
shew that a bond was negotiated between the parties so
as to vary his responsibility upon the implied contract
arising out of the loan or payment, such defence should
have appeared specially upon the record. One instance
put by the new rules comes very near this: " In an action
of indebitatus assumpsit for goods sold and delivered, the
plea of non assumpsit will operate as a denial of the sale
and delivery in point of fact." That rule certainly would
not authorize a defendant to shew, that, *after* the goods
were sold, a bond had been given and received in satisfaction. Upon both issues, therefore, I think the verdict
right; and consequently that this rule ought to be discharged.

VAUGHAN, J.—I am of the same opinion. I think the

jury have not drawn an improper conclusion from the evidence before them: I do not see how they could find any other verdict. The advance of the money was all that was put in issue by the first plea. And, upon the second, all that was put in issue was, whether or not the bond was accepted and received in full satisfaction and discharge of the several promises in the declaration mentioned. As to this the evidence was all one way.

BOSANQUET, J.—I am of the same opinion. Non assumpsit is no longer a plea of the general issue; it is confined to a denial in fact of the express contract or promise alleged in the declaration, or of the matters of fact from which the contract or promise alleged may be implied by law. Here, it only operates as a denial of the lending. It is true, that, if the advance of the money and the giving of the bond were one and the same transaction, then no implied contract or promise to repay would arise, the money not having been advanced on the personal security of the borrower; and under the plea of non assumpsit, the defendant might have shewn those facts to rebut the implication of a promise. But here the bond was not given until after the transaction had been closed. The bond being incapable of being enforced, is the plaintiff to be deprived of the personal security of the defendant upon which the advances were made? It is true that the subsequent taking of such a security as was taken here, would destroy the implied promise, provided it were taken in satisfaction: but then it must be the subject matter of a special plea. The question upon the second issue was a mere matter of fact, whether or not the bond had been accepted and received by the plaintiff in satisfaction for the money advanced to the captain for the use of the ship. The jury have found that it was not, and I am not disposed to think they have judged erroneously. The plaintiff appears to have sought an *additional* security.

M 2

1836.

Weston
v.
Foster.

Park, J.—I am also of opinion that there is no pretence for disturbing the verdict. I was perfectly satisfied with it at the time, and am so still.

Rule discharged.

*Thursday,
May 5th.*

Where a cause is tried in vacation, a motion in arrest of judgment, in this court, must, pursuant to the old practice, be made within the first four days of the ensuing term.

Semble, that the Reg. Gen. Hilary, 2 Will. 4, s.65, as to motions in arrest of judgment, does not apply to the case of a trial out of term.

Taddy, Serjeant, on a subsequent day, moved for a rule nisi to arrest the judgment, or for a repleader. He submitted that the bond having been given after the making of the promise (whether express or implied was immaterial for the purposes of the motion), the promise thereby became merged or extinguished : citing Com. Dig. Pleader, (2 W. 46); and *Blyth* v. *Hill*, 1 Mod. 221, 225, where it was held, that, to debt on bond, the defendant cannot plead another bond given in satisfaction; but that, if the plaintiff take issue, and it is found against him, the defendant shall have judgment: and North, C. J., said—" If the second bond had been given by the obligor himself, it would not have discharged the former; but here, being given by the administrator, so that the plaintiff's security is bettered, and the administrator chargeable de bonis propriis, I conceive it may be a sufficient discharge of the first bond." [*Bosanquet*, J.—There the issue in fact was found for the defendant: here, for the plaintiff.—*Tindal*, C. J.—*White* v. *Culyer*, 6 T. R. 176, seems to approach very nearly to the present case: it was there held, that the deed of a surety does not extinguish the simple contract debt of the principal.] There, the contract was void as to the husband. [*Tindal*, C. J.—But not so as to the co-obligor.] In the present case there is an implied promise by the defendant. A bond is afterwards given by the captain (both acting in the *same* interest), which in its necessary effect extinguishes the promise. It is true, that generally speaking, where issue is taken on the defendant's plea, and is found against him, the plea is considered as if it were altogether expunged from the record.

But here the issue tendered admits that the bond was given for the same causes of action as those in respect of which the implied promise was made, and that the ship was lost. Whether the bond were accepted in satisfaction or not, is perfectly immaterial: in law, it operates a merger. The defendant is clearly entitled to have the judgment arrested, or at all events a repleader, for his was not the first default—2 Wms. Saund. 47, n.; Tidd's Practice, 9th edit. pp. 928, 929.

Butt, contrà, relied upon I Reg. Gen. H. T. 2 Will. 4, *s.* 65, by which it is provided that " no motion in arrest of judgment, or for judgment non obstante veredicto, shall be allowed after the expiration of four days from the time of trial, if there are so many days in term, nor in any case after the expiration of the term, provided the jury process be returnable in the same term;" and which rule is in affirmance of the previous practice in this court and in the Exchequer, disaffirming that of the King's Bench, where, it is said, the motion in arrest of judgment might be made any time before judgment was actually given.

Taddy, Serjeant, in support of his rule.—The rule referred to can only apply to causes tried in term: if the object of the rule were otherwise, the words used do not attain that object. This case, therefore, must stand upon the old practice. When the jury process was returnable in the same term in which the trial took place (*a*), the party was bound to move in that term, even though four

---

(*a*) Formerly, the jury process was tested and returnable in term time only: but now, by the 3 & 4 Will. 4, c. 67, s. 2, it is enacted " that the writ of venire facias juratores may be tested on the day on which the same shall be issued, and be made returnable forthwith, and that the writ of distringas juratores or habeas corpora juratorum may be tested in term or vacation on a day subsequent to the teste of the writ of venire facias juratores."

days did not remain: but, when the trial took place out of term, the party was allowed to move at any time before judgment was actually signed. In *Lyte* v. *Rivers*, Barnes, 445, " Hayward, for the defendant, offered to move in arrest of judgment July 5. But per Cur. the motion comes too late. Writ of hab. corp. jur. was returnable 15 Trin., and the motion in arrest of judgment ought to be made before or upon the appearance day of that return, which was July 4." [*Tindal*, C. J.—That case clearly applies to a case in term.] Otherwise the motion in arrest of judgment could never be made at all unless on the first day of the term succeeding the trial. [*Tindal*, C. J.— The universal practice is, to make the motion within the first four days.] The point has never been considered in this court; but it has in the King's Bench in *Taylor* v. *Whitehead*, Doug. 745. There, Lee objected that a motion to enter judgment non obstante veredicto had been ap- plied for too late, for that it was in the nature of a motion in arrest of judgment: and he said he had always under- stood the practice to be that such a motion could not be made after a new trial had been applied for, unless the court upon granting the rule for a new trial should have given leave, if that should be discharged, to follow it by a motion in arrest of judgment. It seemed, he said, very unreasonable that a party should be permitted to avail himself in so late a stage of the cause of an objection that might have been taken in the first instance by a demurrer to the plea, by which mode of proceeding, if the objection was founded in law, all the expense and vexation of the trial and the motion to set aside the verdict would have been avoided. In answer to this it was observed by Dun- ning that it would be extremely absurd if an objection should be stated to the court, and they should be con- vinced that the party had not by law a right to judgment in his favour, that they should yet be necessitated by any rule of practice to pronounce an erroneous judgment in

1836.

WESTON
v.
FOSTER.

his favour, and so force a party to bring a writ of error. After some consideration, and conference with the Master, the court declared their opinion that a motion in arrest of judgment may be made at any time before judgment is entered up; and that the present motion, being of the same nature, was not too late. In Tidd's Practice, 9th edit., pp. 928, 929, the practice is thus stated—"The motion in arrest of judgment, or for judgment non obstante veredicto, &c., may be made in the King's Bench at any time before judgment is given; though a new trial is previously moved for. In the Common Pleas, the motion in arrest of judgment must be made before or on the appearance day of the return of the habeas corpora juratorum (citing for this *Lyte* v. *Rivers*, Barnes, 445, which was the case of a trial in term). In the Exchequer, the motion in arrest of judgment must, it seems, be made within the first four days of the next term after the trial; and it cannot be made after an unsuccessful motion for a new trial"—citing *Lane* v. *Crockett*, 7 Price, 556: Man. Exch. Prac. 353, contra. [*Bosanquet*, J.—The above cited passage of Tidd was under consideration when the new rule was framed. The intention was to render the practice of the three courts uniform—to adopt that of this court and the Exchequer in this respect.] Inasmuch, therefore, as the practice in this court appears by no means established in accordance with the supposition in Tidd, and the reasoning in the case of *Taylor* v. *Whitehead* seems conclusive, and the permitting the motion would be mercy to the parties, as the expense of a writ of error may thereby be avoided, the motion ought to be allowed.

TINDAL, C. J.—The present case either falls within the new rule or must be governed by the old practice of the court. If it falls within the new rule (and I am not by any means clear that it does), the motion in arrest of judgment, where the cause has been tried at the sittings *out* of term, must be made within the first four days of the term ensuing the trial. But, supposing the rule to apply only to causes tried at the sittings *in* term, then it will become necessary for us to ascertain what was the former practice upon the point in this court. It appears to me from the authorities to which our attention has been called, and from a general understanding of the practice, that the defendant had only the first four days of the term in which to move in arrest of judgment. With respect to the case of *Taylor* v. *Whitehead*, I do not think it entitled to so much attention as it would have merited had it been a direct application to the court upon the point. That was an action of trespass, in which the defendant had pleaded the general issue and a justification under a claim of a right of way. The issue taken upon the first plea was found for the plaintiff, that upon the second for the defendant: the plaintiff, therefore, was entitled to the general judgment. A motion for a new trial was negatived; and the plaintiff then applied for leave to enter judgment non obstante veredicto upon the second issue. A plaintiff may apply at any time: he is not limited to make his application within the first four days. And the court there incidentally liken the case to that of a motion in arrest of judgment. The motion before the court did not call for a decision upon the point for which it is now cited: therefore I do not think that case a decisive authority for the position. And, when I learn from my Brother Park, whose long experience must have rendered him very familiar with the practice, that he has always understood the invariable practice to be to move in arrest of judgment within the first four days of the term following the sittings at which the cause is tried, I am still less disposed to be influenced by *Taylor* v. *Whitehead*. I think this rule must be discharged.

PARK, J.—I am of the same opinion. Speaking from

1836.

WESTON
v.
FOSTER.

an experience of nearly fifty years, I say, without hesitation or doubt, that the practice, in this court, at least, has always been as has been stated by his lordship. In the King's Bench, too, in my recollection, it was the practice, on obtaining a rule for a new trial, also to state the ground for a motion in arrest of judgment, and obtain a reservation of leave to make the motion in that form, in case the rule for a new trial should ultimately be discharged. When I came into this court, I found the course here was, to take the rule in the alternative—for a new trial, or in arrest of judgment. I abstain from offering any opinion upon the 65th rule of Hilary Term, 2 Will. 4; it being somewhat doubtful whether the language of that rule does go any further than is suggested. It is, however, enough to say, that, upon the old practice, this motion is out of time.

VAUGHAN, J.—On the construction of the rule referred to, it is very doubtful whether it applies to any other than trials in term.

BOSANQUET, J.—The old practice is clearly ascertained: but, whatever the intention of the framers of the new rule might have been, the language does not seem to convey it very clearly. Much countenance is given to the argument of my Brother Taddy by the modern books of practice.

Rule discharged.

HOULDITCH and Another v. SWINFEN.

Thursday,
April 28th.

BOMPAS, Serjeant, on a former day, obtained a rule calling upon the plaintiffs to shew cause why the outlawry in this case should not be set aside, on the grounds that

A motion to reverse an outlawry cannot be entertained, unless it expressly appear by the affidavits

that the attorney making the application is duly authorized by the outlaw.

1836.

HOULDITCH
v.
SWINFEN.

the affidavit to hold to bail was defective, and that the defendant had, to the knowledge of the plaintiff, been abroad during the whole time that the proceedings in the action were pending.

Petersdorff, contrà, submitted that the party was not in a situation to be heard, inasmuch as it did not appear upon the face of the affidavits upon which the motion was founded that the attorney who assumed to act for the defendant was properly constituted by the defendant. He cited *Plunkett* v. *Buchanan*, 3 B. & C. 376, 5 D. & R. 625, where it was held that an attorney making an affidavit in support of an application to reverse an outlawry against a defendant who does not appear personally, must shew in express terms that he is duly authorised by the outlaw to to make the application. [The Court thinking the authority of *Plunkett* v. *Buchanan* to be decisive]—

Bompas submitted that the rule should be discharged without costs, inasmuch as it would appear somewhat anomalous to visit with costs a party whom the court held not to be before them.

PER CURIAM.—The party should have come properly armed: the rule must be discharged with costs.

Rule discharged, with costs.

Monday,
May 9th.

The summons and distringas given by the statute 2 Will. 4, c. 39, are not the only mode of proceeding to outlawry.
   A bailable capias, upon which the defendant was outlawed, having issued upon a defective affidavit—The court, on motion, reversed the outlawry on payment of costs, the defendant entering a common appearance.

THE motion was on a subsequent day renewed, upon amended affidavits.

Petersdorff shewed cause.—To entitle the defendant to make his rule absolute, it is incumbent on him to shew that the affidavit of debt (which in this case, it may be con-

ceded, is irregular,) is an essential ingredient in the proceedings to outlawry. That, however, is not so. It
may be filed after the proceedings to outlawry are complete. In Tidd's Practice, 9th edit. p. 136—citing *Fow-
ney* v. *Allen*, M. 10 G. 2, it is said: "It is not necessary
that the affidavit should be made *before* the outlawry,
nor the sum sworn to be indorsed on the capias utlaga-
tum; but it is sufficient if there be an affidavit before the
defendant is discharged: the court having determined
that process of outlawry is not within the statutes for
preventing frivolous and vexatious arrests." The defendant is, besides, in no condition to make this application;
he has no locus standi in judicio, until he has appeared—
Summervil v. *Watkins*, 14 East, 586; *Solly* v *Forbes*, 2
Moore, 567.

Bompas, Serjeant, in support of his rule.—Notwithstanding the cases cited, it is clearly not necessary for the
defendant to appear before moving to reverse the outlawry. In *Garland* v. *Noble*, 1 Moore, 187, *Plunkett* v.
Buchanan, *Bryan* v. *Wagstaff*, 8 D. & R. 208, 5 B. & C.
314, R. & M. 329, 2 C. & P. 125, *Pigou* v. *Drummond*, 1
New Cases, 154, 1 Scott, 264, no appearance was entered:
and in *Graham* v. *Henry*, 1 B. & Ald. 131, it was expressly
held that the defendant need not appear before he moves to
reverse an outlawry. [*Tindal*, C. J.—There are many cases
where the courts have imposed upon the party the entering of
an appearance or the putting in of special bail as a condition of the reversal. But, where the affidavit is defective, it
would seem very hard to compel the defendant to put in
bail before he could be permitted to come to the court
and say that the plaintiff is not entitled to have bail at all.
I think the defendant ought to be allowed to have the
outlawry reversed on entering an appearance, and upon
payment of costs.] The defendant ought not to be compelled to pay the plaintiff the costs of the proceedings
that have been irregularly taken against him. The plain-

1836.

HOULDITCH
v.
SWINYEN.

tiff ought not to have issued a capias: he should have proceeded by distringas in the mode pointed out by the statute 2 Will. 4, c. 39—*Fraser* v. *Case*, 2 M. & Scott, 720.

TINDAL, C. J.—Notwithstanding the defective affidavit, the capias is still a valid writ. I do not find any words in the statute 2 Will. 4, c. 39, to compel a party to pursue the mode pointed out by that act instead of proceeding by capias, the object of which is that he may have the security of bail. This seems to me to be the ordinary case of a party coming by motion to reverse an outlawry. And this is uniformly done only on payment of costs. The court generally superadds that the party shall put in bail to the amount sworn to; but, inasmuch as the affidavit here is defective, that condition may be dispensed with. The justice of the case will I think be attained by setting aside the outlawry on payment of costs, and on the defendant's entering a common appearance.

The rest of the court concurring —

Rule absolute accordingly.

———◆———

SPARKES *v.* MARSHALL.

One B. contracted to sell to the plaintiff 500 to 700 barrels of oats, to be shipped by J. & Son at Youghall, and to be delivered at Portsmouth. Shortly afterwards, B. wrote to the plaintiff to inform him that room had been engaged in the G. Packet for about 600 barrels on his (the defendant's) account; and on the following day the plaintiff sent instructions to his agent in London to insure 400*l.* on oats per the G. Packet from Youghall to Southampton and Portsmouth. J. & Son shipped 486 barrels of oats on account of the above contract on board the G. Packet bound for Southampton, and transmitted a bill of lading (indorsed generally) to their agent there. The plaintiff insisting upon the vessel going round to Portsmouth, B. sold the oats to a third party. The G. Packet was afterwards lost:—Held, that the plaintiff having at the time of effecting the insurance an insurable interest in the oats shipped on board the G. Packet, no subsequent change in the property in the oats would relieve the underwriters from their liability on the policy.

THIS was an action of assumpsit upon a policy of insurance subscribed by the defendant as an underwriter for

200*l.* In the first count of the declaration it was averred that 500 barrels of oats were shipped at Youghall, on board the Gibraltar Packet, to be carried and conveyed to Southampton; that the plaintiff was interested therein to the amount of the monies insured; and that the vessel departed and set sail from Youghall aforesaid, on her voyage towards Southampton, and was totally lost, with the oats on board, by perils of the sea. The second count was to the same effect, except that the interest was averred to be in one F. B. Bamford. The declaration was delivered before the late rules came into operation. The defendant pleaded the general issue, upon which issue was joined. The parties to the action, by consent, and under a judge's order, stated the facts in the following special case, for the opinion of the court:—

The plaintiff was a corn merchant at Cosham, in Hampshire. In the month of October, 1831, F. B. Bamford, who was a corn dealer at Southampton, now deceased, contracted with Thomas John & Son, merchants of Youghall, in Ireland, through M'Cheane, who was the agent at Portsmouth of John & Son, for the purchase of a parcel of black oats—from 500 to 700 barrels—as appeared by the following correspondence between M'Cheane and John & Son.

M'Cheane to John & Son.—" Portsmouth, 22nd October, 1831. I wrote to you last on the 14th, and was yesterday favoured with yours of the 18th. I have sold for you to Mr. Bamford 500 to 700 barrels prepared black oats, as you can get a vessel to answer, at 11*s.* 6*d.* per barrel on board," &c.

John & Son to M'Cheane.—" 26th October, 1831. We observe your sale to Mr. Bamford of 500 to 700 barrels black oats at 11*s.* 6*d.* per barrel, which shall be shipped the first opportunity. The price low, as we now pay 12*s.* per barrel free on board here: you may sell 500 to 700 barrels more at 14*s.* 6*d.* per barrel," &c.

1836.

SPARKES
v.
MARSHALL.

Contract of sale.

On the 10th November, 1831, Bamford and the plaintiff entered into a negotiation (having met at Portsea) for the purchase by the plaintiff of some black oats, and the following note was written and signed by the plaintiff in a book belonging to Bamford, which was usually carried about by him whilst attending corn markets or fairs, and such book was then handed back to Bamford with such note entered therein:—" Bought of Mr. Bamford 500 to 700 barrels of prepared black oats at 11s. 9d. per barrel, to be shipped by Andrew Carbery of Dungarvon, and 500 to 700 barrels of prepared black oats at 11s. 9d. per barrel, to be shipped by Thomas John & Son of Youghall; both parcels free on board, and freight not to exceed 2s.; if it does, Mr. B. to pay the addition.   Portsea, 10th November, 1831.   This is to cancel a former sale."   At the same time Bamford wrote and signed in pencil, and handed to the plaintiff, the following note:—" Sold Mr. I. H. Sparkes 500 to 700 barrels prepared black oats, at 11s. 9d. per barrel, on board, to be shipped by Andrew Carbery, and 500 to 700 barrels prepared black oats, to be shipped by Thomas John & Son, at 11s. 9d. per barrel, at Youghall: freight not to exceed 2s. per quarter.   F. B. Bamford. Portsea, 10th November, 1831.   To cancel former sale to Mr. Sparkes, who is to have his bill returned."

At the time of signing and exchanging these notes, Bamford did not know in what vessel the oats ordered by him of John & Son, as before mentioned, would be shipped. The former sale referred to at the foot of the notes was a sale of oats by Bamford to Sparkes, to be delivered at Portsmouth; which delivery was not made, in consequence of the master of the vessel on board which those oats arrived refusing to proceed to Portsmouth, and insisting on landing them at Southampton.   To compensate Sparkes for this, M'Cheane negotiated the sale from Bamford to Sparkes mentioned in the above notes.   On the 14th November, 1831, Bamford received a letter from John & Son, dated and written at Youghall on the 10th of the same month, and which was as follows:—"We have commenced shipping the black oats sold to you through Mr. M'Cheane, per schooner Gibraltar Packet of Dartmouth, Thomas Wetherell master, for Southampton. She will take from 500 to 600 barrels; and our next will inclose invoice and bill of lading." On the same day, Bamford addressed the following letter to the plaintiff, which was received by him on the same day:—"Southampton, 14th November, 1831. I am this day advised by Thomas John & Son that they have engaged room in the schooner Gibraltar Packet of Dartmouth, to take about 600 barrels black oats on your account." On the following day, the 15th November, the plaintiff forwarded to his agent in London, Mr. W. B. Overton, the following letter:—"Have the goodness to insure 400*l.* on oats per the Gibraltar Packet of Dartmouth, from Youghall to Southampton and Portsmouth, supposed to be not yet loaded." In pursuance of the order contained in the above letter, a policy was effected on the 16th November, which was subscribed by the defendant as underwriter for the sum of 200*l.*, and was the policy declared on in this cause. The premium mentioned in the policy was paid by the plaintiff's agent to the defendant. No other insurance was ever effected upon the parcel of 486 barrels of oats hereinafter mentioned, or any part of it, either by Sparkes or Bamford, or any other person.

Messrs. John & Son shipped on board the Gibraltar Packet 486 barrels of black oats, being part of the oats referred to in their letter of the 14th November; and also another parcel of 250 barrels of black oats, and 200 barrels of barley; and the shipment was completed on the 14th November, 1831. The following bill of lading, relating to the first mentioned parcel only, was signed by the master; a separate bill of lading being made out for the two other parcels:—"Shipped in good order and con-

dition by Thomas John & Son, in and upon the good ship
called Gibraltar Packet, of Dartmouth, whereof is master
for the present voyage John Wetherell, and now riding at
anchor in the port of Youghall, and bound for Southampton, to say, 486 barrels of black oats, at fourteen stone
each, being marked and numbered as in the margin; and
are to be delivered in like good order and condition at the
aforesaid port of Southampton (the danger of the seas, fire,
rivers, and navigation, of whatsoever nature and kind, excepted) unto shippers' orders, or to assigns, he or they
paying freight for the said goods 2s. per quarter, with
primage and average accustomed. In witness whereof the
said master or purser of the said ship hath affirmed to
three bills of lading, all of this tenor and date, the one of
which being accomplished, the other two to stand void.
Dated in Youghall, November 14, 1831.   John Wetherell."

The above-mentioned bill of lading was indorsed generally by Messrs. John & Son, and forwarded to their agent
M'Cheane, together with the invoice of those 486 barrels
of oats; and another invoice of the other parcel of 250
barrels of oats (which last-mentioned parcel formed no part
of the 600 barrels referred to in the letter of Messrs. John
& Son of the 14th November, above set forth), and 200
barrels of barley by the same vessel; and, on receipt of
the letter inclosing those invoices and bill of lading,
M'Cheane addressed to Bamford the following letter:—
" I have an invoice from John & Son to-day of 486 barrels
of oats for you per Gibraltar Packet, which is all your
berth would hold, although they thought it would have
held 500 to 600 barrels. They also send me invoice of 250
barrels oats and 200 barrels barley per same vessel, freight
2s. oats, and barley 2s. 6d., which they desire me to give
you at 11s. 6d. and 14s. 6d. if you will relinquish all claim
on them for more barley; if not, I am to give you the 200
barrels barley, and the other barrels they will ship the

first opportunity. As this vessel will not come to Portsmouth, perhaps it will be as well for you to agree to their proposal, and supply Sparkes hereafter with others. Waiting your reply, &c."

Bamford to M'Cheane.—" Southampton, November 21st, 1831. Your favour of the 19th is now before me. I note what Johns have done, and what they propose; but I have a right to the whole of the oats, or nearly so, according to my contract; and also have a right to full 300 barrels of barley. Under these circumstances, however, I think it will be best to send Sparkes's invoice, and draw on him for 736 barrels oats per said vessel, and I will take the barley and exonerate Johns if Sparkes accepts. You are aware I have nothing to do with any vessel going to Portsmouth with either lot oats for Sparkes. Write me on this."

On Monday, the same 21st November, M'Cheane saw the plaintiff, and offered him the option of taking the 736 barrels mentioned in the above letter; but the plaintiff required that the Gibraltar Packet should make the discharge in Portsmouth; when M'Cheane wrote to Bamford as follows:—" Monday Evening. Mr. Sparkes will take the 736 barrels oats at 11s. 9d., but he insists on the vessel coming into Portsmouth. Every one that he has spoken to on the subject says you are bound to ship them for Portsmouth."

On the same 21st November, Bamford, unknown to Sparkes, entered into a treaty with E. L. Oke, a corn merchant of Southampton, to sell him 700 barrels of black oats; and upon that occasion a bought note was signed as follows:—" Southampton, November 21st, 1831. Bought of F. B. Bamford about 700 barrels prepared black oats, free on board at Youghall, shipped per the Gibraltar Packet, at 2s. freight, price 12s. 3d. per barrel. E. L. Oke." A sold note, in the same form, was signed by Bamford, and handed to Oke.

VOL. III.

The following letters then passed at the respective times at which they are dated:—

Bamford to the plaintiff.—" November 22nd, 1831.   I am exceedingly vexed that the Gibraltar Packet will not go to Portsmouth; though I am not bound to send her or any other vessel to any particular port, I should be glad that one would go to you of course. I shall ship your oats according to my contract, and do all I can to get a vessel engaged to meet your wishes in the interim. If you want black oats, I will supply you out of my store with as many quarters as would be 600 barrels, at 11s. 9d. on board at Youghall.   Can I do more?"

The plaintiff to Bamford.—" Cosham, near Portsmouth, 23rd November, 1831. By your letter of the 14th instant you informed me that Messrs. Thomas John & Son had engaged room in the Gibraltar Packet for about 600 barrels black oats on my account, and I immediately wrote to London for insurance to be effected on her for 400l., which was done at 20s. per cent. On Monday last Mr. M'Cheane told me there were two bulks on the Gibraltar Packet, amounting to 736 barrels, which he offered me the option of taking, and I accepted them both.   I must therefore insist on your sending on the Gibraltar Packet to Portsmouth."

M'Cheane to Bamford.—" Portsmouth, November 23rd, 1831. Your favor of the 22nd came to hand. My orders from Messrs. John & Son are, to give you the 250 barrels of oats at 11s. 6d., if you will exonerate them from shipping the 100 barrels barley which remain due to you (on your contract for 300 barrels) after the 200 barrels now on board Gibraltar Packet. Please say by post to-night if you agree to this.   I do not send documents, or draw, till I receive your answer, to save expense of stamps.   You said in your's of 21st instant, you will agree to John & Son's proposition if Sparkes accepted; but he has not, inasmuch as he insists on vessel coming to Portsmouth. The 250 barrels oats and 200 barley are insured for 340*l.* in London. You say in your's of 22nd, Sparkes should wait till the 736 barrels are offered him. I offered them to him per your orders given 21st instant. Sparkes is at Petersfield market to-day, but I fear he will not be satisfied unless vessel comes on."

M'Cheane to Bamford.—" Portsmouth, November 24th, 1831. I have your favour of the 23rd instant. I annex invoice of the 736 barrels of oats, 200 barrels barley, per Gibraltar Packet, and inclose bills of lading, and bill for amount, which please to return to me as soon as in your power." Invoice 24th November, on the back of the same letter.—" Invoice of 736 barrels oats and 200 barrels barley shipped by Messrs. John & Son, at Youghall, on board the Gibraltar Packet, of Dartmouth, John Wetherell master, for Southampton, for account and risk of Mr. F. B. Bamford, Southampton. [The particulars followed.] 340*l.* insured through Pim on 250 barrels oats and 200 barrels barley. 486 barrels not insured by me."

On the 24th November, Bamford indorsed the bill of lading for the 486 barrels of oats with the following indorsement:—" Deliver the within-named oats to Mr. E. L. Oke. F. B. Bamford." The bill of lading, with this indorsement, was, without Sparkes's knowledge, handed to Oke; and on the same day an invoice was made out by Bamford to Oke, of which the following is a copy:—
" Invoice of 736 barrels prepared black oats, shipped by Thomas John & Son, of Youghall, free on board the Gibraltar Packet of Dartmouth, John Wetherell master, for account and risk of Mr. Edward Langdon Oke, Southampton." Here followed particulars, and amongst others a charge of 5*l.* for insurance on 500*l.* The price at which the said oats were sold by Bamford to Oke, viz. 12*s.* 3*d.* per barrel, was the market value of the said oats on the 21st November, 1831. The value of the 486 barrels in question, with all the additional charges in the above last-

mentioned invoice (except the sum of 5*l.* 9*s.* 9*d.* for insurance) was 321*l.* 16*s.* 4*d.* Bamford had not in fact effected any policy for 500*l.*, as stated in the said invoice, but was an insurer to Oke of the 736 barrels of oats for that sum. On the same 24th of November, 1831, a bill was drawn by Bamford on Oke for 478*l.* 14*s.* 4*d.*, being the amount of the above invoice. That bill was accepted by Oke, and fell due on the 17th January, and was then paid in regular course.

The following letters were written, sent, and received according to their respective dates:—

The plaintiff to Oke, 26th November, 1831.—" I shall be obliged if you will inform me when the Gibraltar Packet arrives at Southampton from Youghall, and if you observe any one presuming to touch the black oats on board, which I shall endeavour to obtain coute qu'il coute."

Oke to Sparkes, 27th November, 1831.—" The black oats per Gibraltar Packet Mr. Bamford has sold to me, and insurance effected thereon."

The plaintiff to Oke, 28th November, 1831.—" It is very unpleasant to differ with one's friends; but I am determined to try the case with Mr. Bamford: therefore, if the Gibraltar Packet does not deliver the oats to me, I shall immediately take such steps as my attorney may advise."

About the 16th December, it was generally believed that the Gibraltar Packet was lost. She sailed from Youghall to Southampton, having the several parcels of oats and barley specified in the before-mentioned bills of lading on board, on the 16th November: but neither the master nor any of the crew had since been heard of; and it was admitted that she was totally lost. On the 16th November, 1831, the policy of insurance was sent to the plaintiff by his London agent; and about the 16th April, 1832, the same was, after a long dispute, handed over to Bamford, and the following indorsement put upon it, and

signed by the plaintiff and Bamford:—" By this indorsement the interest on the policy is vested in Mr. F. B. Bamford." At the time that indorsement was made, the plaintiff received in consideration for it the sum of 60*l*.

The defendant and the other underwriters had not in
any way assented to, or been apprised, until the action
was brought, of the above-mentioned indorsement being
put on the policy. The premium was paid into court.

The court was to decide as to the admissibility of all or
any of the foregoing letters; and also to form the same
conclusions as to all or any of the facts herein stated as a
jury would be at liberty to do at Nisi Prius. If the court
should decide that the plaintiff, under the circumstances,
was entitled to the whole sum of 400*l*. insured upon the
policy, the judgment was to be for 200*l*. If the court
should decide that the plaintiff was entitled only to such
a portion of the sum insured as 486, which was the quantity of oats actually on board, bore to 600, which was the
quantity of oats intended to be insured for 400*l*., the
judgment was to be entered for 162*l*. And, if the court
should decide that the plaintiff was not entitled to recover,
the judgment to be entered for the defendant.

Talfourd, Serjeant, for the plaintiff.—The question is
whether the plaintiff is entitled to recover the amount of
the loss in this case either upon the count averring interest in himself, or upon that which alleges the interest to
be in Bamford: either will suffice to support the action.
It will not be disputed that *any* interest in the plaintiff in
respect of which he might sustain a loss, is insurable—
Smith v. *Lascelles*, 2 T. R. 187; *Craufurd* v. *Hunter*, 8 T.
R. 13; *Lucena* v. *Craufurd*, 3 B. & P. 75, 2 N. R. 269.
Neither will it be disputed that the policy enures to the
benefit of the party really interested, and that the party
effecting the insurance may sue on the policy in respect
of the interest of such third person provided he after-

wards assents to and adopts the insurance—*Routh* v.
Thompson, 13 East, 274; *Hagedorn* v. *Oliverson*, 2 M. &
S. 485.   Here the plaintiff had an insurable interest.
Under the contract entered into on the 10th November,
1831, between the plaintiff and Bamford, and the letter of
the 14th, the oats which were the subject of the insurance were specifically appropriated to the plaintiff: and,
although the plaintiff was entitled to demand a larger
quantity than was actually shipped, yet no assent on his
part to receive the lesser quantity was necessary to complete the bargain; and, if it were, such assent is amply
evidenced by the fact of his writing immediately on receipt of advice of the shipment to desire his agent to
effect an insurance thereon.   The plaintiff all along insisted upon his right to the specific oats shipped on board
the Gibraltar Packet; and his right is not lessened by his
also insisting upon their being delivered at Portsmouth.

Maule, for the defendant.—The plaintiff had no insurable interest at the time of the loss in the oats on board
the Gibraltar Packet: he had no right to insist upon these
specific oats being sent to Portsmouth.   The fact of their
having been lost, leaves him precisely where he was; he
is not bound to pay for them: and if they had arrived in
safety, he would under the circumstances have been entitled to a return of premium.   The policy was effected
on a mistaken supposition on his part that he was interested in the goods: and it was not intended, nor could
it enure to protect the interest of Bamford, an adverse
party.   According to the contract, the plaintiff was entitled to require 700 barrels of oats to be delivered to
him at Portsmouth.   None were in fact ever shipped for
Portsmouth.   The contract of the 10th November was to
cancel a former sale by Bamford to Sparkes of oats that
were to have been delivered at Portsmouth.   Where a
bargain is made for a sale of goods at any given place,

unless the goods are expressed to be deliverable elsewhere, primâ facie they must be taken to be deliverable at the place where the contract is made. In *Idle* v. *Thornton*, 3 Camp. 274, it was held that a contract made in London for the sale of tallow then at sea, in which it was agreed that if the goods did not arrive by a certain time the bargain was to be void, means arrival in London and not elsewhere. In *Irving* v. *Richardson*, 2 B. & Ad. 193, a mortgagee effected policies at two offices on a ship valued in each policy at 3,000*l.*, and, the ship being lost, he received on the two insurances 3,700*l.* An action being brought against him by one set of underwriters to recover back their proportion of the sum paid above 3,000*l.*, and the question being whether the defendant had received more than the actual value of the ship insurable and insured by him, it was held that it was properly submitted to the jury, whether, in effecting the policies, the defendant meant to ensure his own interest only, or that of the mortgagor also; a mortgagee (at least since the register act, 6 Geo. 4, c. 110,) not being an owner to any greater extent than that of the value mortgaged, and the mortgagor continuing an owner.

Talfourd, Serjeant, in reply, cited *Alexander* v. *Gardner*, ante, Vol. 1, 630, 1 New Cases, 671. There, the plaintiffs sold to the defendants a quantity of Sligo butter, which it was provided by the contract should be shipped for London in October, and be paid for by bill at two months from the date of the landing. The butters were on the 6th November shipped by M. & S. of Sligo, addressed and invoiced to the plaintiffs, and by the bill of lading made deliverable to their order. On the 10th, the defendants were informed that the butters were not shipped within the time provided by the contract, and, though they at first demurred, they subsequently verbally consented to waive the objection, and accepted the invoice

and the bill of lading, which the plaintiffs indorsed to them.
The invoice specified the weights and prices of the several firkins. The vessel on board of which the butters
were shipped was wrecked, and part of the butters were
lost, and the remainder damaged. In indebitatus assumpsit for goods bargained and sold, the jury found that the
defendants had waived the performance of the condition
as to the shipment of the butters in October. It was held
that there was a sufficient appropriation and ascertain-
ment of the goods, and assent thereto by the defendants,
to vest the property in them, and consequently that the
action was maintainable.

Cur. adv. vult.

TINDAL, C. J., delivered the judgment of the court :—
Upon the facts stated in the special case, two objections
have been made by the defendant against the plaintiff's
right to recover—first, that, at the time of effecting the
insurance, the plaintiff had no insurable interest in the
oats shipped on board the Gibraltar Packet, and had sustained no loss in respect of them, so as to enable him to
maintain the action as to the first count—secondly, that
Bamford was a stranger to the insurance, and had no interest in the oats at the time of the supposed loss, and
had sustained no such damage as to entitle the plaintiff to
maintain the action on the second count of the declaration. If the first question is determined in favour of the
plaintiff, it becomes unnecessary to consider the second ;
for, if the plaintiff had an insurable interest at the time
the policy was effected, whatever change may have taken
place in the property in the oats since, can have no effect
in relieving the underwriters from their liability, as the
plaintiff may sue on the policy for the benefit of the party
to whom such property has passed. And we think, looking at the situation of the parties, and the effect of the
correspondence which has passed between them, that the

plaintiff had an insurable interest in the oats upon which
the policy was effected.   The question turns upon the
right of the plaintiff, at the time of effecting the policy, to
the specific cargo of oats on board the Gibraltar Packet.
The plaintiff contends these particular oats were appropriated to him: the defendant, on the other hand, contends that no specific cargo of oats was appropriated, that
he had only a right of action against Bamford on the
bought and sold notes for the nondelivery of oats at
Portsmouth, and that he could recover the same damages *now* in such action, notwithstanding the loss of the
Gibraltar Packet.   Under the bought and sold notes
which were entered into on the 10th November, there was
no interest acquired in any particular oats.   Nothing more
was specified than that they were oats to be shipped by
Thomas John & Son of Youghall; and (as we think must
be inferred from necessary intendment upon the face of
the contract) that the oats were to be delivered at Portsmouth.   This latter condition appears abundantly afterwards from the correspondence between the contracting
parties.   Four days afterwards, Bamford, the vendor, has
notice that the oats which he intended as the subject matter of the contract at the time such contract was entered
into, were shipping for him by Messrs. Thomas John &
Son, at Youghall, on board the Gibraltar Packet, bound
to Southampton; and, by the same post, Bamford writes
to the plaintiff that Messrs. Thomas John & Son have engaged room in the Gibraltar Packet to take about 600
barrels of oats on his account.   This letter appears to us
to be an unequivocal appropriation of the oats on board
the Gibraltar Packet by Bamford, the only person who had
the control over them: and this appropriation is assented
to and adopted by the plaintiff, who, on the following
day, gives instructions to his agent in London to effect
the policy on oats per Gibraltar Packet from Youghall
to Southampton and Portsmouth. It is true that Bam-

ford concealed from the plaintiff the fact that the vessel was bound only to Southampton: but, as he entered into a contract to deliver oats, which were afterwards fixed between the parties to be *these* oats, at Portsmouth, the plaintiff had the right to hold him to his bargain, and to call upon him either to procure the Gibraltar Packet to bring them on to Portsmouth, or to forward them by some other vessel to the place of delivery: as the concealment that the Gibraltar Packet was not bound to Portsmouth, could not upon any legal principle divest from the plaintiff the interest he had in these specific oats. Accordingly, the plaintiff continually from this time until after the loss of the oats, insists upon these particular oats being forwarded to Portsmouth. The letters from M'Cheane to Bamford of the 21st and 23rd of November, and the plaintiff's letter of the 23rd, are precise and peremptory on the point, insisting on these particular oats being forwarded by the Gibraltar Packet.

On looking at the whole of the transaction, we see no assent on the part of the plaintiff to vary his right or claim to these particular oats, until after the policy is effected and the loss known. And we are not aware of any principle on which a change in the interest, after the policy is effected, much less after the loss has happened, can be set up as an answer by the underwriters against a claim for such loss. We therefore think, upon the facts stated in this case, the plaintiff is entitled to judgment for 162*l.*

Judgment for the plaintiff accordingly.

1836.

*Thursday,
April 28th.*

Where a cause is referred and a verdict entered, a motion to impeach the award must be made within the first four days of the following term.

LYNG *v.* SUTTON.

THIS cause and all matters in difference between the parties were referred to an arbitrator. The arbitrator, in the course of the last vacation, directed a verdict to be entered for the plaintiff on the second count of the declaration, with 30*l.* damages.

Mansel, on a former day, obtained a rule nisi to refer the matter back to the arbitrator, on the ground that he had omitted to make any award touching a point in equity which was one of the matters in difference referred to him.

J. Manning, contrà, objected that the application, not having been made within the first four days of the term, could not be entertained. He relied on *Borrowdaile* v. *Hitchener*, 3 Bos. & Pull. 344, where it was held, that, if a verdict for a plaintiff be taken at Nisi Prius, subject to the award of an arbitrator, and the award be made before the term, the defendant can only impeach it within the first four days of the term.

Mansel, in support of his rule, submitted that the rule upon which *Borrowdaile* v. *Hitchener* turned applied only to cases where it was sought to impugn the verdict: whereas, here, if the equitable jurisdiction of the court failed the plaintiff, he would altogether lose his remedy in equity for that upon which the arbitrator had omitted to adjudicate.

PER CURIAM.—If the point suggested was intended to be referred, and by mistake was not referred, the plaintiff is not concluded as to that. The application should have been made within the first four days. We ought to be very tenacious of relaxing the rule.

Rule discharged, without costs.

1836.

Friday,
April 29th.

Upon writs of inquiry before the sheriff, where the damages are under 20*l.*, the costs are taxed on the same scale as upon trials before the sheriff.

HOOPPELL *v.* LEIGH.

THIS was an action of covenant for non-repair of the demised premises. The defendant suffered judgment by default, and the damages were assessed upon a writ of inquiry before the sheriff of Exeter, at 13*l.* 12*s.* The prothonotary having taxed the costs according the reduced scale directed by the rule of Hilary Term, 1834, 2 Dowl. P. C. 487, applicable to trials before the sheriff—

Hoggins, for the plaintiff, moved that the officer might review his taxation. He contended that the directions in question did not apply to writs of inquiry.

The Prothonotaries stated that it was the practice in the office to tax the costs upon writs of inquiry before the sheriff, where the damages were less than 20*l.*, upon the same principles as in cases tried before the sheriff under the statute 3 & 4 Will. 4, c. 42, ss. 17—20.

THE COURT said that the directions referred to did not in terms apply to writs of inquiry; but, inasmuch as it appeared to have been the practice in the office to tax such costs upon the like principle, the rule was

Refused.

———◆———

Friday,
April 29th.

In assumpsit for money paid to the use of the defendants, they pleaded specially circumstances shewing that the policy of insurance in respect of which the payments were made had been so framed as to be utterly unavailing. Upon special demurrer, on the ground, amongst others, that the plea was argumentative and amounted to the general issue—The court inclined to think the plea good, but allowed the plaintiff to withdraw his demurrer and reply de novo, without costs.

COLE and Another *v.* LE SOUEF and Another.

ASSUMPSIT for money paid, for interest, and for money due upon an account stated.

Pleas—first, non assumpsit—secondly, as to 173*l.* 5*s.* parcel of the sums of money in the first and third counts

1836.

COLE
v.
LE SOUEF.

mentioned, and the promises in the declaration mentioned
so far as related to the said sum of 173l. 5s.—that, theretofore, and before the plaintiffs were retained or employed
as thereinafter mentioned, certain goods of a large value,
to wit, of the value of 5,000l., had been and were at London shipped and loaded in and on board of a certain ship
or vessel called the Pomona, to be carried and conveyed
therein from London aforesaid to Falmouth, and from
thence on a voyage to a certain place beyond the seas, to
wit, to Oporto, and that the defendant, before and at and
after the time of retaining and employing the plaintiffs as
thereinafter mentioned, were interested in the said goods
to a large value and amount, to wit, to the value and
amount of all the monies which they retained and employed the plaintiffs as thereinafter mentioned to cause to
be insured thereon; of all which several premises the
plaintiffs before and at the time of their being retained
and employed as thereinafter mentioned, to wit, on &c.,
had notice: that, before and at the time when the plaintiffs were retained and employed as thereinafter mentioned, the plaintiffs were insurance brokers, and used,
exercised, and carried on the business and employment of
insurance brokers; and thereupon, theretofore, to wit, on
&c. last aforesaid, the defendants, at the plaintiffs' request, retained and employed the plaintiffs as insurance
brokers and agents in that behalf, for compensation and
reward to them in that behalf, to effect and cause to be
made for the benefit of the defendants an insurance to the
amount of a certain sum of money, to wit, 2,000l., upon
the said goods in the said ship or vessel, upon and for the
said voyage from Falmouth to Oporto; which said retainer and employment the plaintiffs then accepted, and in
consideration of the premises then promised the defendants
to do and perform their duty as such brokers and agents
as aforesaid in that behalf; and thereupon it then became
and was the duty of the plaintiffs as such brokers and

agents of the defendants as aforesaid, to use due and proper
care and skill in and about the effecting and causing to be
made such insurance as aforesaid: that the plaintiffs, well
knowing the premises, and that the said goods had been
shipped and loaded at London as aforesaid, and not at
Falmouth as aforesaid, but neglecting their duty in that
behalf, did not nor would use due or proper skill in and
about the effecting and causing to be made the same insurance, but wholly neglected so to do, and, on the contrary thereof, as and for the purpose of effecting such insurance as aforesaid, carelessly, negligently, unskilfully,
and improperly effected and caused to be made two policies of assurance, to wit, &c., which policies, by reason of
the carelessness, negligence, and want of skill of the plaintiffs in that behalf, were worded and expressed in such
words and manner as not to be, and the same were not,
nor was either of them, applicable or adapted to an insurance upon the said goods or any goods shipped and
loaded in and on board of the said ship or vessel at London
aforesaid; by means whereof the said policies of assurance
did not nor did either of them operate, and were not, nor
was either of them, an insurance upon the said goods or
upon any part thereof; and thereby the defendants were
prevented from having, and never had, any insurance on
the said goods or any part thereof, or any indemnity, benefit, or advantage whatever of or from the said policies of
assurance, and the said goods, by means of the premises,
and of the carelessness, negligence, and want of skill and
improper conduct of the plaintiffs as such insurance brokers
and agents of the defendants in that behalf as aforesaid,
were wholly uninsured of or for the said voyage from Falmouth to Oporto: and that the said sum of 173*l.* 5*s.* was
and is the amount of certain premiums of insurance and
expenses upon, of, and relating to the said policies of assurance, and paid and incurred by the plaintiffs in and

about and relative to the same and the effecting and causing
the same to be made—verification.

To the first plea the plaintiffs added the similiter, and
to the second demurred specially, assigning for causes—
that the defendants in and by their said second plea specially pleaded and relied upon matter amounting in effect
to a general traverse of the promise laid in the declaration
as far as such promise related to the causes of action in
the commencement of that plea referred to—that the plea
was a multifarious, argumentative, and insufficient mode of
pleading the plea of non assumpsit to the last-mentioned
causes of action—that the said second plea concluded with
a verification, and purported to be a special plea in avoidance of the last-mentioned causes of action, without in any
manner confessing even a primâ facie or colorable title or
right of action in the plaintiffs—that the said second plea
did not state any fact which arose after the causes of action
which it professed to answer had accrued to the plaintiffs,
nor did it contain any matter of law in answer to the last-
mentioned causes of action, nor did it state any matter of
law or of fact in avoidance of any or of any part of the
causes of action in the declaration alleged—that the said
second plea contained material allegations at variance and
inconsistent with each other, inasmuch as it contained aver-
ments shewing that the sum of 173l. 5s. therein and in the
declaration mentioned was paid by the plaintiffs as and for
certain premiums of insurance and expenses paid and incurred in consequence of the retainer of the defendants,
and yet attempted to state and to tender for issue certain
facts from which it was sought to be inferred that the same
payments and expenses were made and incurred in the
plaintiffs' own wrong, and without any request, retainer,
or instructions of or from the defendants—that, in and by
the said second plea, it was admitted that there was an
account stated between the plaintiffs and defendants as in
the declaration alleged, and it was also implied and ad-

1836.

COLE
v.
LE SOUEF.

mitted that the said sum of 173*l.* 5*s.* was an item in such account, and that upon such account a balance to that amount remained to the credit of the plaintiffs; and yet in and by the said second plea there was not shewn any matter or matters in avoidance of or as a set-off against the said item or sum of 173*l.* 5*s.*, but, in a subsequent part of the plea, it was attempted to be shewn that the said sum of 173*l.* 5*s.* never was a valid debt in account or otherwise from the defendants to the plaintiffs, and it was stated in effect, notwithstanding the implied admission of the said account and of the said sum of 173*l.* 5*s.* being such balance as aforesaid, that the said sum of 173*l.* 5*s.* consisted of certain payments made by the plaintiffs in their own wrong, and not at the request of the defendants, and for which said sum of 173*l.* 5*s.*, or any part thereof, it was attempted in and by the said second plea (but in an argumentative, indirect, and insufficient manner) to be shewn that the defendants never were or ought to be liable to the plaintiffs— and that the said second plea contained various allegations upon no one of which could the plaintiffs take issue without thereby admitting the truth of the other allegations in the plea, which, though wholly false or unfounded, would materially embarrass the plaintiffs on the trial of the cause, and in the recovery of their demand.—Joinder.

J. Manning, in support of the demurrer.—The plea is bad inasmuch as it does not confess and avoid the matters alleged in the declaration, and merely amounts to the general issue. It does not fall within either of the cases that form an exception to the general rule that that which may be given in evidence under non assumpsit cannot be pleaded specially. These exceptions are, first, where the matters alleged in the declaration are confessed by the plea and avoided by matter ex post facto; secondly, where the matters alleged are avoided by matter of law, that is, by matters of fact involving matters of law—*Carr* v. *Hinch-*

cliffe, 7 D. & R. 42, 4 B. & C. 547; *Maggs* v. *Ames*, 1 M. & P. 294, 4 Bing. 470, nom. *Maggs* v. *Anson*. The new rule of Hilary Term, 4 Will. 4, s. 1, which provides, that, "in all actions of assumpsit, except on bills of exchange and promissory notes, the plea of non assumpsit shall operate only as a denial in fact of the express contract or promise alleged, or of the matters of fact from which the contract or promise alleged may be implied by law," leaves the matter just where it was. Here, the plaintiffs declare for money paid to the use of the defendants. Under non assumpsit the defendants might have given in evidence any thing to shew that the money was not in fact paid to their use. [*Tindal*, C. J.—You might have put in a replication denying the whole of the matters alleged in the plea.] It may admit of great doubt whether we could safely have replied de injuria. We might have been embarrassed by the admission of some of the facts alleged in the plea. [*Tindal*, C. J.—The defence is, that the policy in respect of which the alleged payments were made was so framed by the plaintiffs as to be utterly useless to the defendants: if so, why may not that form the subject of a special plea? I think you had better amend.]

Manning expressed his willingness to amend without costs: but this was not acceded to by the other side.

Barstow, contrà.—It is by no means clear that this would not have been a good plea before the new rules. *Maggs* v. *Ames*, is an authority in its favour. But, at all events, since those rules, there can be no doubt. The general policy of the new rules was to encourage the putting of defences specially upon the record. Under non assumpsit, the proposed defence would have been excluded. The third rule, in assumpsit, provides that, "in every species of assumpsit, all matters in confession and avoidance, including not only those by way of discharge, but those which

1836.

COLE
*.
LE SOUEF.

shew the transaction to be either void or *voidable in point
of law, on the ground of fraud or otherwise,* shall be
specially pleaded." Here the transaction is *voidable* in
consequence of the neglect of the defendants.

TINDAL, C. J.—The plea admits an account stated in
point of fact after the transaction was closed. For anything that appears, the defendants are not damnified. I
think the plaintiffs should have leave to withdraw their
demurrer, and reply de novo, without payment of costs.

Rule accordingly.

———◆———

*Wednesday,
May 4th.*

The stock-job-
bing act, 7 Geo.
2, c. 8, operates
only upon time
bargains in the
funds of this
country.

Second plea.

Third plea.

OAKLEY *v.* RIGBY.

ASSUMPSIT for work done by the plaintiff for the defendant at his request, and for commission due and payable from the defendant to the plaintiff in respect thereof,
for money paid, for interest, and for money alleged to be
due from the defendant to the plaintiff on an account
stated.

Pleas—first, that the defendant did not promise modo
et forma—secondly, as to the counts in the declaration for
work done and for commission due in respect thereof, and
for money paid by the plaintiff for the use of the defendant, and for money found to be due on an account stated
—that the said work was done, and the said commission
became due, and the said money was paid, and the said
money was found to be due, for and in respect of certain contracts and agreements knowingly made by the plaintiff
upon which consideration in the nature of premium was
with the knowledge of the plaintiff given for liberty to accept or refuse certain public and joint stock, and certain
public securities, and shares and interests in certain public
securities, contrary to the form of the statute in such case
made and provided—verification. Thirdly (to the same

counts), that such work was done, and the said commission became due, and the said money was paid, and the
said money was found to be due, for and in respect of contracts in the nature of putts and refusals knowingly made
by the plaintiff relating to the then future price and value
of certain public and joint stock, and of certain public securities, contrary to the form of the statute &c. Fourthly,
as to the counts in the declaration for work done and for
commission due in respect thereof, and for money paid by
the plaintiff for the use of the defendant, that the promise
to pay made by the defendant was made by him upon the
faith of a statement before then made by the plaintiff to
the defendant that he the plaintiff had before then purchased for the defendant divers securities, to wit, regency
bonds, old Portuguese bonds, and Spanish bonds, and
had before then sold for him the defendant divers securities, to wit, regency bonds, old Portuguese bonds, and
Spanish bonds, and that the making of such stated purchases and sales was and is the work mentioned in the
declaration for which the commission mentioned in the
declaration became due, and that the money mentioned
in the declaration as paid by the plaintiff for the use of
the defendant is the money stated by the plaintiff as
aforesaid to have been paid by him for the use of the
defendant in making such stated purchases; and that
such statement so made by the plaintiff was wholly false
and untrue, and that, at the time of the making of the
said promise he the plaintiff had not purchased or sold for
the defendant any such securities, &c. Fifthly, to the
account stated, that the said account was so stated by the
defendant upon the faith of a statement before then made
by the plaintiff to the defendant that he the plaintiff had
before then purchased for the defendant divers securities,
to wit, regency bonds, old Portuguese bonds, and Spanish
bonds, and had before then sold for him the defendant
divers securities, to wit, regency bonds, old Portuguese

Marginalia:
1836.

OAKLEY
v.
RIGBY.

Fourth plea.

Fifth plea.

1836.

OAKLEY
v.
RIGBY.

bonds, and Spanish bonds; and that the money found to be due from the defendant to the plaintiff upon the stating of the said account was so found upon the faith that such purchases and sales had been made; and that such statement so made by the plaintiff was wholly false and untrue; and that, at the time of the stating of the said account, he the plaintiff had not purchased or sold for the defendant any such securities.

Replication to the second plea;

Similiter to the first plea. Replication to the second plea—that the said work was not done, nor was any part thereof done, the said commission did not nor did any part thereof become due, the said money was not nor was any part thereof paid, nor was the said money or any part thereof found to be due for or in respect of any contract or agreement knowingly made by the plaintiff upon which consideration in the nature of premium was with the knowledge of the plaintiff given for liberty to accept or refuse any public or joint stock or any public security or share or interest in any public security, contrary to the form of the statute, modo ac forma.

to the third plea;

To the third plea—that the said work was not nor was any part thereof done, the said commission did not nor did any part thereof become due, the said money was not nor was any part thereof paid, nor was the said money or any part thereof found to be due, for or in respect of any contract in the nature of wager, or contract in the nature of putt and refusal knowingly made by the plaintiff relating to the then future price and value of any public or joint stock or any public security, contrary to the form of the statute &c., modo ac forma.

to the fourth plea.

To the fourth plea—that the plaintiff, before the time of making the statement in the second plea mentioned, and also before the time of the making of the said promise, had purchased for the defendant divers securities, to wit, 30,000 regency bonds, 10,000 old Portuguese bonds, and 20,000 Spanish bonds, and had then also sold for the defendant divers other securities, to wit, 30,000 regency bonds, 10,000 old Portugese bonds, and

20,000 Spanish bonds.   There was a similar replication to the fifth plea.

The cause was tried before Tindal, C. J., at the sittings in London after last Trinity Term.   On the part of the plaintiff it was admitted that the amount sought to be recovered consisted of differences on time bargains in foreign funds, paid by the plaintiff as the broker of the defendant.   Three questions were raised on the part of the defendant, and the points reserved by his lordship: first, whether time bargains in the foreign funds are affected by the stock-jobbing act, 7 Geo. 2, c. 8, made perpetual by the 10 Geo. 2, c. 8—*Rossum* v. *Taylor*, Chit.Stat. 1032, *Henderson* v. *Bise*, 3 Stark. 158: secondly, whether or not such bargains were void at common law— *Bryan* v. *Lewis*, R. & M. 386: thirdly, whether or not a broker could recover differences voluntarily paid by him on account of his principal, in an action for money paid to to his use—*Child* v. *Morley*, 8 T. R. 610, confirmed by *Lightfoot* v. *Creed*, 2 Moore, 255, 8 Taunt. 268.

The jury finding that the plaintiff had been duly authorized by the defendant to enter into the transactions in question on his account, returned a verdict for the former, damages 529*l*. 17*s*.

Platt, in Michaelmas Term, obtained a rule nisi for a nonsuit or a new trial.

Sir *W. Follett*, *R. V. Richards*, and *Martin*, contra, relied upon *Wells* v. *Porter*, ante, p. 141.

Platt and *Barstow*, in support of the rule.—The 7 Geo. 2, c. 8, is a remedial rather than a penal act—*Billing* v. *Flight*, 6 Taunt. 419: but, whether the one or the other, still it must be construed to extend to all the mischief intended to be remedied.   The statute must be intended to apply to all those things that are popularly called stocks. The mischief is not the less because the transaction has relation to foreign funds; and there can be no valid reason for holding "public securities" to be confined to the public securities of England or of Great Britain. Jobbing in omnium has been held to be within the statute, the scrip receipts not being in the market at the time—*Brown* v. *Turner*, 1 Esp. 631, 7 T. R. 630. In *Olivierson* v. *Coles*, 1 Stark. 496, an agreement for selling out omnium to be replaced in stock was held not to be illegal: but, as Lord Ellenborough observed, "A person who has omnium is potentially in possession of stock." "The case," he says, "certainly differs from that of a sale of actually existing stock, but it does not come within the mischief intended to be guarded against by Sir John Bernard's act." *Brown* v. *Turner* was not adverted to in that case. As well might it be said that any newly invented game did not fall within the mischief of the 9 Ann. c. 14, as that foreign stocks are not within the stock-jobbing act, because not at the time of the passing of the act an article of traffic in this country. The transaction is in fact a mere wager on the future price of the stock. In The *Attorney-General* v. *Saggers*, 1 Price, 182, it was held the statute 8 Anne, c. 13, imposing a penalty on the importation of foreign goods, the importation of which into this country is prohibited, is prospective in its operation, and applies to goods the importation of which is prohibited by subsequent statutes. If the subject matter of a wager have an indecent or immoral tendency, it is clearly illegal. The legislature having declared the practice of stock-jobbing to be infamous, can it be said that the practice has not an immoral tendency? In Starkie on Evidence, 1st edit. Vol. 3, p. 1655, it is said: "In general, it seems that a wager is legal, and may be enforced in a court of law, if it be not an incitement to a breach of the peace or immorality, or affect the feelings or interest of a third person, or expose him to ridicule, or libel him; or if it be not against sound policy or the provisions of a statute." Here, the wager is clearly against sound policy, as well as against the provisions of the statute. If the practice of gambling in the funds of this country be infamous, gambling in foreign funds must of necessity be equally so. In *Gilbert* v. *Sykes*, 16 East, 150, a wager on the life of the first consul of the French republic was held to be illegal, on the ground of immorality and impolicy. A betting on the solvency of a state must be equally immoral and impolitic with a wager on the life of its governor. That which affects the value of any foreign fund, may to a certain extent affect the prosperity of this country. [*Tindal*, C. J.—A wager upon the *past* value of goods is not illegal—*Good* v. *Elliott*, 3 T. R. 693; why, then, should a wager upon the future value be illegal?] Lord Chief Justice Abbott in *Bryan* v. *Lewis*, R. & M. 386, ruled that a wager upon the future price of a commodity was contrary to sound policy, and could not be made the subject of an action. A wager upon the probable amount of any branch of the public revenue is illegal, because it tends to an improper discussion, and is contrary to sound policy—*Atherfold* v. *Beard*, 2 T. R. 610; *Shirley* v. *Sankey*, 2 B. & P. 130. So, a wager that the princess Victoria would ascend the throne within a given time, would clearly be illegal. At the time of the passing of the 7 Geo. 2, c. 8, Ireland had a distinct legislature. By the act of Union, 39 & 40 Geo. 3, c. 67, the Irish debt became merged in the British. Was Irish stock foreign at the time of the passing of the 7 Geo. 2, c. 8? and and, if so, when did it cease to be so? By the 2 & 3 Will. 4, c. 81, this country guarantees to Russia the payment of a portion of her old Dutch debt: would that fund be a public stock or security within the meaning of the 7 Geo. 2, c. 8? By the 2 & 3 Will. 4. c. 121, the loan contracted by Prince Otho of Bavaria, as King of Greece, is guaranteed, one third by this country, one third by France, and the remaining third by Russia: is the one third guaranteed by this country to be considered a British fund, and

1836.

Oakley
v.
Rigby.

within the stock-jobbing act, and the remaining two thirds foreign, and not within it? What was East India stock at the time the act passed? These instances shew the extreme difficulty there is in ascertaining with precision what particular stock is, and what is not, within the mischief intended by the legislature to be remedied. The consequence of holding time bargains in these and other foreign funds legal will be to convert the stock exchange into a licensed gambling house.—Notwithstanding the pleas all conclude " contrary to the form of the statute," these words may be rejected, if the transactions be illegal and void at common law—*Rex* v. *Urlyn*, 2 Saund. 308. [*Tindal*, C. J.—The special pleas are all framed on the statute: and though it is true, that, when the matter charged appears to be an offence at common law, the addition of the words " against the form of the statute" will not be an incurable defect; yet here the issues are joined on the statute.]

TINDAL, C. J.—It appears to me that this case involves precisely the same considerations as *Wells* v. *Porter* (ante, 141), which was decided in this court the other day. I am unwilling to go over the same ground again, not having heard anything in the argument to-day to induce me to alter the opinion I gave on that occasion. I shall therefore content myself with noticing two of the points made, viz. as to the statute 9 Anne, c. 14, and the argument founded upon the case of *The Attorney-General* v. *Saggers*. It is said, that, if the construction we have already put upon the 7 Geo. 2, c. 8, be applied to the statute 9 Anne, c. 14, we shall be involved in this dilemma—that games not known at the time of the passing of the last-mentioned statute, must be held not to fall within the mischief intended to be thereby remedied. But that argument is disposed of by a reference to the words of the act, which comprehend not merely games then in use, but embrace " any other games whatsoever." Then, as to *The At-*

torney-General v. *Saggers*, it is true the statute 8 Anne, c. 13, was there held to extend to goods upon which customs were at a subsequent period imposed: but there is nothing unreasonable in that, the statute imposing penalties for running uncustomed goods being merely a part of the machinery devised to aid the collection of the revenue, and applying from time to time as any new article of importation is subjected to customs. The statute 7 Geo. 2, c. 8, however, applies only to the public stocks or securities of this country. I am therefore of opinion that this rule should be discharged.

The rest of the court concurring—

Rule discharged (*a*).

(*a*) See 8 & 9 Will. 3, c. 32.

1836.

OAKLEY
v.
RIGBY.

DOBREE and Another *v.* NAPIER and Others.

*Monday,
May 9th.*

THIS was an action of trespass. The declaration alleged that the defendants, on the 12th September, 1833,

The only ground upon which the authority of a servant is traverseable in an action of trespass, is, the protection of the person or property of a party from the officious and wanton interference of a stranger, where the principal might have been willing to waive his right.

Where the act of the principal is lawful in the country where it is done, and the authority under which such act is done is complete, binding, and unquestionable there, the servant who does the act cannot be made responsible in the courts of this country (of which he is a subject) for the consequences of such act, merely by reason of a personal disability imposed by the law of this country upon him for contracting such engagement.

In trespass for seizing and converting the plaintiff's ship, the defendant pleaded—first, that he was retained in the service of the Queen of Portugal, being at peace with our sovereign; that enemies were waging war against her by sea and land; that the defendant by her command established and proclaimed an effective blockade along the coast of Portugal; that the plaintiff's ship broke the blockade; and that thereupon the defendant, as the servant and by the command of the Queen of Portugal, seized the ship—secondly, that the plaintiff's ship, laden with warlike stores, was on the high seas aiding and assisting the queen's enemies, wherefore the defendant, as the servant and by the command of the queen, seized her—thirdly, that the vessel was in a port in Portugal, and had just discharged a cargo there destined for the use of the queen's enemies, whereupon the defendant, as the servant and by the command of the queen, seized her as lawful prize, and that she was in due course and form of law condemned as lawful prize by a court of competent jurisdiction in that behalf. To these pleas the plaintiffs replied that they and the defendant were natural born subjects of the kingdom of England; that the vessel in question was a British registered vessel; and that the defendant, in breach of the foreign enlistment act, 59 Geo. 3, c. 69, s. 2, entered the service of the Queen of Portugal, and whilst in such service committed the trespass complained of:—Held, that, notwithstanding the statute, the authority of the Queen of Portugal was a justification of the seizure—whether " as prize," for breaking the blockade, or for supplying warlike stores to her enemies; and therefore that the pleas were a sufficient bar to the plaintiff's right of action.

with force and arms &c., seized and took a certain steam
vessel of the plaintiffs, called The Lord of the Isles, of
great value, to wit, of the value of 20,000l., and converted
and disposed of the same to their own use, to the damage
of the said plaintiffs of 20,000l. &c.

First plea.
Second plea.

The defendant Napier pleaded—first, not guilty—
secondly, that, before and at the time when &c. in the
declaration mentioned, he was employed and retained
in the service of Donna Maria, Queen of Portugal,
as an admiral in the Portuguese navy, and chief commander of a certain squadron thereof, the said Queen of
Portugal, during the time aforesaid, being at peace with
our sovereign lord William the Fourth, and that, before
and at the said time when &c., divers enemies of the said
queen were waging war against her, both by sea and
land, and thereupon, and before the said time when &c.,
the said queen had commanded the defendant Napier, as
such admiral and chief commander as aforesaid, to establish and proclaim a blockade along the coast of Portugal,
and that the defendant Napier, in obedience to the said
command of the said queen, had before the time when &c.
duly established and proclaimed a good and sufficient
blockade along the said coast of Portugal, and had put
and placed divers, to wit, fifty ships of war in and upon
the high seas along the said coast, for the purpose of supporting and maintaining the said blockade, and which said
blockade the last mentioned ships were sufficient duly to
maintain and support, and did in fact maintain and support; of all which premises the plaintiffs then had notice;
and the defendant Napier says, that, after the said blockade had been so established and proclaimed as aforesaid,
and while the same was so supported and maintained as
aforesaid, the said steam vessel in the declaration mentioned, just before the said time when &c., being on the
high seas, by and with the consent and under the authority and direction of the plaintiffs, did break the said

blockade, contrary to the law of nations in that behalf;
whereupon the defendant Napier, as such admiral and
such chief commander as aforesaid, and as the servant and
by the command of the said queen, at the said time when
&c., did seize and take the said steam vessel in the declaration mentioned, as he lawfully might for the cause aforesaid—verification.

The third plea stated, that, before and at the time *Third plea.*
when &c. in the declaration mentioned, the defendant
Napier was employed and retained in the service of Donna Maria, Queen of Portugal, as chief commander of a
certain squadron of the Portuguese navy, the said queen
then being at peace with our said sovereign lord the
king, and that, before and at the said time when &c.,
divers enemies of the said queen were waging war against
her both by sea and land, whereof the plaintiffs then had
notice; and that, just before the said time when &c., the
said ship or vessel in the declaration mentioned, laden
with warlike stores and ammunition, by and with the consent and under the direction and authority of the plaintiffs,
was on the high seas aiding and assisting the said enemies
of the said queen, whereupon the defendant Napier, as such
chief commander as last aforesaid, and as the servant and
by the command of the said queen, at the said time when
&c., attacked and captured, seized and took, the said
steam vessel in the declaration mentioned, as he lawfully
might for the cause aforesaid—verification.

Fourthly, that, before and at the said time when &c., *Fourth plea.*
the said steam vessel in the declaration mentioned was in a
certain port upon the coast of Portugal, to wit, the port
of Saint Martinho, and that the said steam vessel had,
just before the said time when &c., discharged a cargo at
the said port, destined for the use of certain persons
then being enemies of Donna Maria, Queen of Portugal,
the said queen then being at peace with our said sovereign
lord the king; and that thereupon the defendant Napier,

1896.

DOBREE
v.
NAPIER.

claiming to be and acting as admiral and chief commander of a certain squadron of the Portuguese navy, and servant of the said queen, and by her command, at the said time when &c., attacked, captured, seized, and took the said steam vessel in the declaration mentioned, as lawful prize; and such procedings were thereupon had according to the laws of Portugal in a certain court of law in the kingdom of Portugal of competent jurisdiction in that behalf, to wit, the Supreme Tribunal of Marine, at Lisbon, that afterwards, to wit, on the 27th September, 1833, at Lisbon, in the kingdom of Portugal, in and by the said court the said steam vessel in the declaration mentioned was adjudged to have been justly and lawfully taken, and was then in due course and form of law condemned as lawful prize, and as forfeited to the said Queen of Portugal—verification.

Fifth plea—
That the plaintiffs, contrary to
59 Geo. 3, c. 69,
s. 7, were, without the license or consent of his majesty, knowingly concerned in equipping the vessel, with intent that the same should be employed in the service of a foreign prince as a transport and store-ship; and that, by force of the statute, the vessel became forforfeited to his majesty. On special demurrer, for that the plea did not allege that the vessel was ever seized or con-

Fifthly, that the plaintiffs, after the 1st day of November which was in the year 1819, and during the reign of his present majesty, and before the said time when &c., not regarding the statute in such case made and provided, were within a certain port of the united kingdom of Great Britain and Ireland, to wit, within the port of London, without the leave and licence of his said majesty for that purpose first had and obtained, knowingly concerned in the equipping and furnishing of the said steam vessel in the said declaration mentioned, with intent that the same should be employed in the service of a certain foreign prince, to wit, Don Miguel, of Portugal, as a transport and store-ship, contrary to the said statute; and by virtue and force of the said statute, the said steam vessel in the said declaration mentioned, afterwards, and before the said time when &c., became and was forfeited to his said majesty—verification.

demned as forfeited, or that the defendant had any authority from his majesty to seize her:—Held, that the plea was insufficient, for want of the allegation of authority.

Sixthly, that the said steam vessel in the declaration mentioned, at the said time when &c., was not the property of the plaintiffs—concluding to the country.

Similar pleas were pleaded by the other defendants.

Replication to the second plea—that, before and at the said time when &c., they, the said plaintiffs, and also the said defendant Napier, were natural born subjects of his present majesty, King William the Fourth, and the said steam vessel in the said declaration and second plea mentioned was a British registered vessel, and entitled to all and every the privileges and advantages belonging to such British registered vessel; and that, after the 1st day of November which was in the year of our Lord 1819, and during the reign of his said present majesty, and before the said time when &c., the said Charles Napier, being such natural born subject of his majesty as aforesaid, and not regarding the statute in such case made and provided, without the leave or licence of his majesty in any form whatever, accepted a commission or appointment as an officer in the service of a certain foreign power, that is to say, accepted the office of admiral in the Portuguese navy, and chief commander of a squadron thereof in the service of the said Donna Maria, Queen of Portugal, as in the said second plea mentioned, and continually from thence until and at the said time when &c. was employed and engaged in the service of the said Donna Maria, and served in and on board divers ships and vessels of war of the said Donna Maria, and in and on board divers other ships and vessels used by her for warlike purposes and in her service, contrary to the said statute; and that the said Charles Napier, at the said time when &c., whilst he was such officer and so employed and engaged as aforesaid, and by virtue and in the course of such illegal employment and service, seized and took the said steam vessel of the plaintiffs as in the said declaration mentioned.

Replication to the third plea—that, before and at the

1836.

DOBREE
v.
NAPIER.

Replication to
the second plea.

Replication to
the third plea.

said time when &c., they, the plaintiffs, and also the said
defendant Napier, were natural born subjects of his present majesty king William the Fourth, and the said steam
vessel in the said declaration and third plea mentioned was
a British registered vessel, and entitled to all and every
the privileges and advantages belonging to such British
registered vessel; and that, after the 1st day of November, which was in the year of our Lord 1819, and during
the reign of his said present majesty, and before the said
time when &c., the said Charles Napier, being such natural born subject of his majesty as aforesaid, and not regarding the statute in such case made and provided, without the leave or license of his majesty in any form whatsoever, accepted a commission or appointment as an officer
in the service of a certain foreign power, that is to say,
accepted the office of chief commander of a squadron of
the Portuguese navy in the service of the said Donna
Maria, Queen of Portugal, as in the said third plea mentioned, and continually from thence until and at the said
time when &c. was employed and engaged in the service
of the said Donna Maria, and served in and on board
divers ships and vessels of war of the said Donna Maria,
and in and on board divers other ships and vessels used
by her for warlike purposes and in her service, contrary
to the said statute; and that the said Charles Napier, at
the said time when &c., whilst he was such officer and so
employed and engaged as aforesaid, and by virtue and in
the course of such illegal employment and service, seized
and took the said steam vessel as in the said declaration
mentioned.

Replication to
the fourth plea.

Replication to the fourth plea—That, before and at the
said time when &c., they, the said plaintiffs, and also the
said defendant Napier, were natural born subjects of his
present majesty King William the Fourth, and the said
steam vessel in the said declaration and fourth plea mentioned was a British registered vessel, and entitled to all

and every the privileges and advantages belonging to such
British registered vessel, and that, after the 1st day of
November, which was in the year of our Lord 1819, and
during the reign of his said present majesty, and before
the said time when &c., the said Charles Napier, being
such natural born subject of his majesty as aforesaid, and
not regarding the statute in such case made and provided,
without the leave or license of his majesty in any form
whatever, accepted a commission or appointment in the
service of a certain foreign power, that is to say, accepted
the office of admiral and chief commander of a squadron
of the Portuguese navy in the service of the said Donna
Maria, Queen of Portugal, as in the said fourth plea mentioned, and continually from thence until and at the said
time when &c. was employed and engaged in the service
of the said Donna Maria, and served in and on board
divers ships and vessels of war of the said Donna Maria,
and in and on board divers other ships and vessels used
by her for warlike purposes, and in her service, contrary
to the said statute; and that the said Charles Napier, at
the said time when &c., whilst he was such officer and so
employed and engaged as aforesaid, and by virtue and in
the course of such illegal employment and service, seized
and took the said steam vessel as in the said declaration
mentioned.

The plaintiffs demurred to the fifth and sixth pleas, assigning for causes—as to the fifth plea—that it is not
therein alleged that the said steam vessel was ever seized
or condemned as forfeited, or that the said defendant had
any authority from his majesty to seize the said steam
vessel; and, as to the last plea, that the said defendant
had not thereby traversed or denied or attempted to put
in issue any allegation contained in the declaration, but
had introduced and attempted to put in issue a matter of
fact not alleged or necessary to be alleged; and also that
the said last plea contained new matter not anywhere be-

Demurrer to
the fifth and
sixth pleas.

fore alleged, and concluded to the country, and not with a verification; and also that by the said last plea the defendant attempted to raise a question whether the vessel in the declaration mentioned was the property of the plaintiffs, whereas the action and the declaration of the plaintiffs would be supported by shewing a mere possession of the said vessel in the plaintiffs at the time the said trespass was committed; and also that the said last plea was no answer to the declaration, and was evasive, argumentative, and uncertain.

Demurrer to the replications to the 1st, 2nd, and 3rd pleas. Joinder.

The defendants demurred to the replications to the second, third, and fourth pleas; and joined in demurrer to the fifth and last pleas.

As to the 2nd, 3rd, and 4th pleas—That those pleas afford no answer to the action.

Stephen, Serjeant (*Wilde*, Serjeant, and *Martin*, were with him), for the plaintiffs.—To this action of trespass for seizing the plaintiff's ship, the defendant, in substance, pleads (2nd, 3rd, and 4th pleas) that he did so under the authority and by the command of the Queen of Portugal, in whose service he was retained and employed as an admiral. The plaintiffs reply that they as well as the defendant were natural born subjects of his present majesty, that the vessel in question was a British registered vessel, and that the defendant Napier, being such natural born subject of his majesty, not regarding the statute in such case made and provided, without the leave or license of his majesty, accepted a commission in the Portuguese navy, and while acting under such commission made the capture complained of. To this replication the defendant has demurred; and, upon this state of the record, the first question that presents itself is, whether the pleas above mentioned are sufficient in law, or, if so, whether they are not answered by the replication. It is perfectly clear that a defendant cannot justify a civil trespass by shewing that he was at the time of committing it engaged in the violation of a public act of parliament. Admiral Napier being punish-

able under the statute 59 Geo. 3, c. 69, can he be permitted to turn the statute into a ground of defence? Had
the death of a British subject ensued, whilst the admiral
was so engaged in the prosecution of an illegal design, he
would, according to circumstances, have been guilty either
of murder or of manslaughter: and if such a defence as
that now attempted to be set up would not avail him on
an indictment for murder or manslaughter, how can it
afford him a justification for a civil trespass? The statute
above referred to was in full force at the time the cause of
action accrued: it enacts, in s. 2, "That, if any natural
born subject of his majesty, his heirs and successors, without the leave or license of his majesty &c. for that purpose
first had and obtained under the sign manual of his majesty
&c., or signified by order in council, or by proclamation
of his majesty &c., shall take or accept, or shall agree to
take or accept any military commission, or shall otherwise
enter into the military service as a commissioned or non-
commissioned officer, or shall enlist or enter himself to enlist, or shall agree to enlist or to enter himself to serve as
a soldier, or to be employed, or shall serve in any warlike
or military operation in the service of or for or under or in
aid of any foreign prince, state, potentate, colony, province
or part of any province or people, or of any person or persons exercising or assuming to exercise the powers of
government in or over any foreign country, colony, province or part of any province or people, either as an officer
or soldier, or in any other military capacity; or if any
natural born subject of his majesty shall, without such
leave or license as aforesaid, accept or agree to take or
accept any commission, warrant, or appointment as an
officer, or shall enlist or enter himself,· or shall agree to
enlist or enter himself to serve as a sailor or marine, or to
be employed or engaged, or shall serve in and on board
any ship or vessel of war, or in and on board any ship or
vessel used or fitted out or equipped or intended to be used

for any warlike purpose, in the service of or for or under
or in aid of any foreign power &c.; or if any natural born
subject of his majesty shall, without such leave and license
as aforesaid, engage, contract, or agree to go, or shall go
to any foreign state &c. with an intent or in order to enlist
or enter himself to serve, or with intent to serve in any
warlike or military operation whatever, whether by land or
sea, in the service of or for or under or in aid of any foreign
prince &c., either as an officer or a soldier, or in any other
military capacity, or as an officer or sailor or marine in any
such ship or vessel as aforesaid, although no enlisting
money or pay or reward shall have been or shall be in any
or either of the cases aforesaid actually paid to or received
by him, or by any person to or for his use or benefit; or
if any person whatever, within the united kingdom of
Great Britain and Ireland, or in any part of his majesty's
dominions elsewhere, or in any country &c. belonging to
or subject to his majesty, shall hire, retain, engage, or
procure, or shall attempt or endeavour to hire &c. any
person or persons whatever to enlist or to enter or engage
to enlist or to serve or to be employed in any such service
or employment as aforesaid, as an officer &c., for or under
or in aid of any foreign prince &c., or to go or to agree to
go or embark from any part of his majesty's dominions for
the purpose or with intent to be so enlisted, &c.: in any
or either of such cases, every person so offending shall be
deemed guilty of a misdemeanor, and, upon being convicted
thereof upon any information or indictment, shall be punishable by fine or imprisonment, or either of them, at the discretion of the court before which such offender shall be
convicted." The replications to the 2nd, 3rd, and 4th
pleas shew that the service in which the defendant was
engaged at the time of committing the trespass complained
of was in contravention of the act of parliament: and no
authority to excuse the trespass is disclosed upon the face
of the pleas. One justifying under the command of an-

other, must shew a specific authority, otherwise his plea
fails. Here, Admiral Napier has not shewn that he acted
under the authority of the Queen of Portugal; for, it appears from the replications that his service under that
sovereign was one that the law, not only does not recognize,
but absolutely prohibits. It is therefore the same as if
there was an absence of authority de facto: the authority
shewn must be of a lawful kind; whereas, it is scarcely
possible to conceive a case of an authority more unlawful
than that set up by these pleas. Then, how stands the
case independently of the foreign enlistment act? Can a
subject of Great Britain justify jure belli against a fellow
subject? All that the pleas amount to is, that the vessel
of the plaintiffs at the time of the capture was breaking
the blockade, in violation of the rights of the belligerents.
How can a subject of the same country with those engaged
in breaking the blockade set up as a justification such
breach of blockade, or interfere to redress it? The allegation that the plaintiffs broke the blockade, *contrary to
the law of nations*, amounts to nothing: this court knows
nothing of the law of nations. It is well established that
no subject of any country whose prince is at peace can
lawfully enter into hostilities with the subjects of any other
power; and, even where war is proclaimed between two
countries, to justify seizure, the party must be commissioned. In Lord Chief Justice Hale's treatise "Concerning the Customs," part 3, c. 28, Hargr. Law Tracts, 245, it
is said: "When war is proclaimed by the king against a
foreign prince or state, the subjects of either side may not
take the goods of others without commission, which is
usually granted by the lord admiral. If he doth assail the
foreigners' ships otherwise than in his own defence without commission, it is a depredation; for, it is not a time
of absolute hostility, in respect especially of the king's
subjects, but qualified, viz. that commissions shall issue
of reprisal to them that desire it; and this qualification

P 2

is commonly in the proclamation that issues upon such occasion, although in truth there is another end of such commission, viz. that the parties employed in such acts of hostility as privateers, may be known, and may secure the shares belonging to the king or admiral of goods taken, and may be responsible for any miscarriage at sea under pretence of hostility." How much greater the crime in a party to assail the ships of his own nation, and that in the teeth of an act of parliament! It is contrary to every principle of law and to every legal analogy to suppose that a party may under any circumstances justify a mere gratuitous trespass. In Viner's Abridgment, (F. a. 4) pl. 9—" Trespass quare clausum fregit et averia cepit et asportavit, the defendant came and justified, and pleaded a by-law &c., and that he, *as bailiff*, took the beasts as a distress for breach of the by-law by the plaintiff. The plaintiff demurred, and in the resolution of the court Holt, C. J., said "that the pleadings are ill, because that the defendant had not shewn *a precept* to make the distress; for, he could not do it ex officio no more than a sheriff might execute a judgment of B. R. without a writ; and the command in this case is traverseable; for, this is the difference between a justification in trespass and an avowry in replevin, that the justification there is in the right, and therefore not traverseable; but in trespass it is only by way of excuse: also in trespass it is sufficient to say presentatum existit, but in avowry he ought to *shew the thing was done*, as well as presentatum existit "—*Lamb* v. *Mills*, Skin. 587. So, (G. a.), pl. 32—" If the sheriff has not any writ, and makes a warrant to J. D. to arrest J. S., an action lies for J. S. against J. D. for this arrest, and against the sheriff likewise "—*Girling's* case, Jo. 379, pl. 9. No action can arise out of any act or contract which is a violation of an act of parliament; neither can any man set up such violation as a justification or defence in a court of justice. This principle is established by

numerous authorities.   Thus, in *Langton* v. *Hughes*, 1 M.
& S. 593, where the plaintiff, a druggist, after the 42
Geo. 3, c. 38, but before the 51 Geo. 3, c. 87, sold and delivered drugs to the defendant, a brewer, *knowing that*
they were to be used in the brewery; it was held that he
could not recover the price of them.   Lord Ellenborough
there says: " By the 42 Geo. 3, the prohibition is express;
and this agreement, being in contravention of it, cannot be
enforced."   And Le Blanc, J.—"It is an established
principle, that the court will not lend its aid in order to
enforce a contract entered into with a view of carrying
into effect anything which is prohibited by law."   In
Lightfoot v. *Tenant*, 1 B. & P. 551, to debt on bond the
defendant pleaded that the bond was given to secure payment of the price of goods agreed to be sold and delivered
in London by the plaintiff to the defendant, to be by the
latter shipped to Ostend, and from thence re-shipped for
the East Indies, and there trafficked with clandestinely: and
it was held a sufficient bar to the action, the case being
within the 7 Geo. 1, c. 21, which avoids all contracts for
supplying cargoes to foreign ships in such a trade.   Eyre,
C. J., in delivering the judgment of the court, says: " The
ground of the defence to be collected from this plea is
thus opened by Lord Mansfield in *Holman* v. *Johnson*,
Cowp. 343—'The objection that a contract is immoral or
illegal sounds at all times very ill in the mouth of a defendant.   It is not for his sake, however, that the objection
is ever allowed; but it is founded in general principles of
policy, which the defendant has the advantage of contrary
to the real justice as between him and the plaintiff, by accident, if I may so say.   The principle of public policy is
this, ex dolo malo non oritur actio.   No court will lend
its aid to a man who founds his cause of action upon an
immoral or an illegal act.   If from the plaintiff's own
stating, or otherwise, the cause of action appears to arise
ex turpi causa, or the *transgression of a positive law of this* '

country, there the court says he has no right to be assisted.' After this introduction his lordship stated the
question in that cause to be 'whether the plaintiff's demand is founded upon the ground of any immoral act or
contract; *or upon the ground of his being guilty of any-*
thing which is prohibited by a positive law of this coun-
try.' And this is the question which arises between the
parties to this record." In *Bensley* v. *Bignold*, 5 B. & Ald.
335, it was held that a printer cannot recover for labour
or materials used in printing any work, unless he affixes
his name to it, pursuant to the 39 Geo. 3, c. 79, s. 27.
And Bayley, J., says: "The 39 Geo. 3, c. 79, establishes
several regulations for public purposes. It requires that
certain acts shall be done, and makes it penal for any person to neglect to do those acts. The omission to do them
is a direct violation of the law: and a party cannot be permitted, in a court of law, to recover for work and labour
done in direct violation of the law. Where a provision is
enacted for public purposes, I think it makes no difference whether the thing be prohibited absolutely or only
under a penalty." In *Wetherell* v. *Jones*, Lord Tenterden says (3 B. & Ad. 225)—"Where a contract which a
plaintiff seeks to enforce is expressly, or by implication,
forbidden by the statute or common law, no court will
lend its assistance to give it effect; and there are numerous cases in the books where an action on the contract
has failed, because either the consideration for the promise or the act to be done was illegal, as being against
the express provisions of the law, or contrary to justice,
morality, and sound policy." In *Montefiori* v. *Montefiori*,
1 W. Bl. 363, Lord Mansfield says: "No man shall set up
his own iniquity as a defence, any more than as a cause of
action." In *Robinson* v. *Mahon*, 1 Camp. 245, Lord Ellenborough held the defendant to be estopped to set up
bigamy as a bar to an action for necessaries supplied to a
woman whom he had married and held out to the world

as his wife, his real wife being still living. The general principle was admitted in *Allen* v. *Wood*, 1 New Cases, 8, 4 M. & Scott, 510. In *Doe* d. *Roberts* v. *Roberts*, 2 B. & Ald. 367, it was held that no man can be allowed to allege his own fraud to avoid his own deed; and therefore, where a deed of conveyance of an estate from one brother to another was executed to give the latter a colourable qualification to kill game, it was held, that, as against the parties to the deed, it was valid, and was sufficient to support an ejectment for the premises. From these several authorities may be deduced as a paramount principle that a transaction that is bottomed in fraud or is in contravention either of a statute or the common law, cannot afford either a ground of action or a ground of defence. In the present case, the seizure of the plaintiffs' ship by Admiral Napier was primâ facie unlawful: it is for him to justify the act, and to shew some *legal* excuse or authority. The admiral may have had a duty to discharge towards the Queen of Portugal: but it was also his duty, and in a much higher degree, to obey the laws of the country that gave him birth, and to which he owed a natural allegiance and subjection. Courtesy is due to the laws of a foreign state only where they clash not with our own—Huberus, De Conflictu Legum. In Hale's P. C., 68, it is said "That though there may be due from the same person *subordinate* allegiances, which, though they are not without an exception of the fidelity due to the superior prince, yet are in their kind sacramenta ligea fidelitatis, or subordinate allegiances, yet there cannot, or at least should not, be two or more co-ordinate absolute ligeances by one person to several independent or absolute princes; for, that lawful prince that hath the prior obligation of allegiance from his subject, cannot lose that interest without his own consent by his subject's resigning himself to the subjection of another; and hence it is that the natural born subject of one prince cannot by swearing allegiance to another prince put off or discharge him from that natural allegiance; for, this natural allegiance was intrinsic and primitive, and antecedent to the other, and cannot be devested without the concurrent act of that prince to whom it was first due: indeed, the subject of a prince, to whom he owes allegiance, may entangle himself by his absolute subjecting himself to another prince, which may bring him into great straits; but he cannot by such a subjection devest the right of subjection and allegiance that he first owed to his lawful prince."

As to the 5th plea.—Forfeiture of vessel.

The fifth plea is founded upon the 7th section of the 59 Geo. 3, c. 69, which enacts, " that, if any person within any part of the united kingdom, or in any part of his majesty's dominions beyond the seas, shall, without the leave and license of his majesty for that purpose first had and obtained as aforesaid, equip, furnish, fit out, or arm, or attempt or endeavour to equip &c., or procure to be equipped &c., or shall knowingly aid, assist, or be concerned in the equipping &c. of any ship or vessel with intent or in order that such ship or vessel shall be employed in the service of any foreign prince &c., as a transport or store-ship, or with intent to cruize or commit hostilities against any prince &c. with whom his majesty shall not then be at war; or shall, within the united kingdom &c., issue or deliver any commission for any ship or vessel to the intent that such ship or vessel shall be employed as aforesaid; every such person so offending shall be deemed guilty of a misdemeanor, and shall, upon conviction thereof upon any information or indictment, be punished by fine and imprisonment, or either of them, at the discretion of the court in which such offender shall be convicted; and every such ship or vessel, with the tackle &c., shall be forfeited; and it shall be lawful for any officer of his majesty's customs or excise, or any officer of his majesty's navy, who is by law impowered to make seizures for any forfeiture incurred under any of the laws of cus-

1836.

DOBREE
v.
NAPIER.

toms or excise, or the laws of trade or navigation, to seize such ships and vessels aforesaid, and in such places and in such manner in which the officers of his majesty's customs or excise and the officers of his majesty's navy are impowered respectively to make seizures under the laws of customs and excise, or under the laws of trade and navigation; and that every such ship and vessel, with the tackle &c., may be prosecuted and condemned in the like manner and in such courts as ships or vessels may be prosecuted and condemned for any breach of the laws made for the protection of the revenues of customs and excise, or of the laws of trade and navigation." This plea merely alleges that the vessel of the plaintiffs was *forfeited*, not that she was *seized*, or that the defendant had any warrant or authority to seize her. It states no circumstances to shew that the property in the vessel was ever devested out of the plaintiffs. She could not legally be seized for the alleged forfeiture without a solemn adjudication; for, the king has no title to property forfeited before office found—2 Bl. Com. 259. It is perfectly clear, therefore, that a mere forfeiture, without seizure, could not so divest the plaintiffs' property in the vessel as to entitle a mere wrong-doer to seize and convert her to his own use.

The sixth plea alleges that the vessel was not the *property* of the plaintiffs. To entitle them to maintain this action, it was not necessary that they should have the property, it is enough that they had the possession—*Heath* v. *Milward*, ante, Vol. 2, 160. In Com. Dig. *Pleader* (3 M. 9.) it is laid down that the declaration in trespass quare clausum fregit " must say that the property, or at least *the possession*, of the lands or goods &c. is in the plaintiff, and therefore, if in trespass, *ipsius quer'*, or *sua* is not inserted, it is bad." Again, in *Trespass* (B. 4.), it is said: " So not only he who has the property, but also he who has the possession of goods, shall maintain trespass for the goods; as, if a man has cattle to agist,

As to the 6th plea—Possession sufficient to maintain the action.

he shall have trespass against him who takes them." In *Brooke* v. *Brooke*, 1 Sid. 184, " in trespass p' prisel dun hooke &c. defendant plea que il ad un chimin a tiel bois sur le terre del plaintiff, et que il fuit passant la, et le plaintiff endeavor pur cutt ses harnesse et pur luy wound ove le dit hooke, et pur ceo il prist le dit hooke hors del maines del plaintiff et deliver ceo al constable &c. Et issue sur le chimin, et verdict pur plaintiff, et fuit move in arrest de judgment que plaintiff nad monstre in son declar' que le hooke fuit in son possession : et fuit agrée per curiam que si defendant .ad plead non culp' le judgment serroit arrest, quia plaintiff in son declar' ne dit hamum suum ne monstre que fuit in son possession. Mes in cest case le court fueront d'opinion que le defendant per son special plea fait le declar' bone, car defendant plead que il prist le hooke *extra possessionem* le plaintiff, pur que le plaintiff poit bien maintaine cest action sur son possession *sans ascun property*." So, in Vin. Abr. *Trespass* (L. a.), pl. 4: " If A. takes the cattle of W. S. without cause, it is not lawful for J. N. to take them from him; for, he has title against all unless against the very owner." And in *Sutton* v. *Buck*, 2 Taunt. 302, it was held that possession under a general bailment, is a sufficient title for a plaintiff in trover. *Pitt* v. *Graince*, 1 Salk. 10, is a distinct authority to the same effect. Great practical inconvenience may result from holding the traverse in this case to be sufficient. [*Tindal*, C. J.—Should not the plaintiffs have taken issue upon this plea : the damages so much depending upon it. I think you had better withdraw the demurrer, and reply, on payment of costs.] The learned Serjeant adopted the suggestion.

Crowder, for the defendant Napier.—This case is one of the first impression. It is an action arising out of an act done by a foreign power in the prosecution of a right recognized by the law of nations. This court, it is said, knows nothing of the law of nations. [*Tindal*, C. J.—The plaintiffs have come to the wrong court—*Le Caux* v. *Eden*, 2 Doug. 594.] Where an effective blockade is broken, the belligerent power has an undoubted right to seize anything on board the vessel engaged in the attempt. In Vattel, Book 3, c. 7, s. 117, it is said: " If I lay siege to a place, or even simply blockade it, I have a right to hinder any one from entering, and to treat as an enemy whoever attempts to enter the place or carry anything to the besieged without my leave; for, he opposes my undertaking, and may contribute to the miscarriage of it, and thus involve me in all the misfortunes of an unsuccessful war." It is said that the defendant shews no authority in himself to make the seizure. But that is not so; for the 2nd, 3rd, and 4th pleas each distinctly aver that the seizure was made under the authority and by the command of the Queen of Portugal, who had a clear and undoubted right to do the act. It was not the defendant Napier that asserted and attempted to prevent a breach of the blockade: it was the Queen of Portugal assisted by her admiral. The entering the service of a foreign state not at war with this country would, before the 59 Geo. 3, c. 69, be no violation of the party's allegiance to the king of England. It may be admitted that Admiral Napier, in entering the Portuguese service without a license, was guilty of a misdemeanor, for which he might have been fined or imprisoned. But the circumstance of his having committed an act which renders him amenable to· the.laws of his country, cannot have the effect of preventing him from justifying under the Queen of Portugal an act which that royal personage had a clear right to do. By the 5 Eliz. c. 4, s. 47, an apprentice absconding to a foreign shire is declared guilty of a misdemeanor: suppose such fugitive apprentice hired by another farmer, and employed by him to seize cattle trespassing upon his new master's land— would the apprentice be liable in trespass (the master be-

ing justified) merely because he was guilty of a misdemeanor in entering the second service? Or, suppose the
case of a deserter: would he be liable in trespass for anything done by him in obedience to the lawful commands
of a master into whose service he had no right to enter?
Here, the act itself and the command were clearly both
justifiable. Where an act is done by one at the command and under the authority of another, both must stand
or fall together : they cannot have separate justifications.
[*Tindal*, C. J.—The fact of Admiral Napier having no
right to place himself under the command of the Queen
of Portugal, is urged here as a ground of estoppel.] The defendant here sets up the right of a third party—the Queen
of Portugal; not his own wrong: and this distinguishes the
present case from all those that have been cited upon this
part of the argument. By the law of nations, the Queen
of Portugal was not bound to know anything of our acts
of parliament, or of any disability created thereby. The
4th plea alleges a seizure of the vessel in question as
lawful prize, and as forfeited to the Queen of Portugal,
and a condemnation in due course and form of law by the
Supreme Tribunal of Marine at Lisbon, a properly constituted court, whose decision binds every court in this
kingdom. By this seizure and condemnation the property
was changed.

According to the statement upon the record, Admiral
Napier has been guilty of piracy under the 11 & 12 Will. 3,
c. 7, s. 8 (*a*): the facts charged against him amount to fe-

(*a*) Which enacts, " that, if any
of his majesty's natural-born subjects, or denizens of this kingdom, shall commit any piracy or
robbery, or any act of hostility
against others his majesty's subjects upon the sea, under colour
of any commission from any foreign prince or state, or pretence

of authority from any person whatsoever, such offender and offenders, and every of them, shall be
deemed, adjudged, and taken to
be pirates, felons, and robbers;
and they and every of them being
duly convicted thereof according
to this act, or the aforesaid statute of King Henry the 8th, [28

lony, and therefore the plaintiffs are out of court, for the
civil remedy is merged. [*Tindal*, C. J.—The 11 & 12 Will.
3, c. 7, is diverso intuitu: it applies only to offences committed lucri causâ, with a felonious intent, and under
colour of a pretended commission. The whole record
must be taken together: the defendant justifies jure belli,
under a real commission.] Unless the defendant can
justify a civil trespass under the command of the Queen of
Portugal, he will be liable to be put upon his trial for
assault, false imprisonment, manslaughter, murder! The
command being in itself lawful, this would be an absurd
result.

The 5th plea, at all events, affords a perfect answer to
the plaintiff's case. It in effect shews that the plaintiffs
had no property in the vessel at the time of the seizure.
Being equipped for an illegal purpose (59 Geo. 3, c. 69, s.
7), she was forfeited; and the plaintiffs cannot complain
of her seizure. A printer who has neglected to comply
with the provision of the 39 Geo. 3, c. 7, s. 27, in affixing
his name to a work printed by him, cannot sue in respect
of labour or materials employed in the printing—*Bensley*
v. *Bignold*, 5 B. & Ald. 335: neither can the author or
publisher of a work of a libellous or immoral tendency,
have any legal property in it, or maintain an action for an
infringement of his supposed copyright in it—*Stockdale*
v. *Onwhyn*, 7 D. & R. 625, 5 B. & C. 173. Holroyd, J., there
said: "It would be equally preposterous and disgraceful to common sense and to the laws under which we live,
to hold that a work such as this was entitled to protection,
and that an act criminal and punishable in itself and its
author could furnish him with a cause of action against
any other individual." So, here, the plaintiffs having
been guilty of an act which has deprived them of all right

As to the 5th
plea.

Hen. 8, c. 15], shall have and suffer such pains of death, loss of
lands, goods, and chattels, as pi-

rates, felons, and robbers upon
the seas ought to have and suffer."

1836.

DOBREE
v.
NAPIER.

of property in the vessel, they cannot be permitted to come into a court of law and claim a compensation for the seizure. [*Tindal*, C. J.—You contend, that, by reason of the prohibition in the 7th section of the statute, the plaintiffs were strangers to the property. The plea is not large enough for the first part of your proposition. The act in which the plaintiffs are alleged to have been engaged in was not unlawful quoad the present defendant.] The plaintiffs, as we contend, seek compensation for the seizure of that in which, by reason of their own unlawful act, they were at the time of the seizure incapable of asserting any right of property. In *Du Bost* v. *Beresford*, 2 Camp. 511, to trespass for destroying a picture, the defendant pleaded, that it was a scandalous libel upon individuals, and, being publicly exhibited, he cut it to pieces by way of abating a nuisance; and Lord Ellenborough ruled that the owner of the picture was at the most only entitled to recover the value of the paint and canvass which formed its component parts. [*Park*, J.—I always thought that a very odd ruling.] *Wilkins* v. *Despard*, 5 T. R. 112, is precisely in point: it was there held, that, if a ship be seized as forfeited under the navigation act, 12 Car. 2, c. 18, by a governor of a foreign country belonging to Great Britain, the owner cannot maintain trespass against the party seizing, although the latter do not proceed to condemnation; for, by the forfeiture, the property is divested out of the owner. So, here, the property in the vessel was by the forfeiture divested out of the plaintiffs. Until office found, undoubtedly the property would not be vested in any one: but, for the purpose of the argument, it is enough to say that it is divested out of the plaintiffs.

Reply.

Stephen, Serjeant, in reply.—To say that the civil injury in this case is merged in the felony—that Admiral Napier is a pirate, a robber, a felon, and therefore not amenable to the law for a civil trespass—is a very extraordinary line of argument, and one that no man can be permitted to urge in his own defence. The statute 11 & 12 Will. 3, c. 7, however, could only apply to the case of a seizure made under colour of a false commission; and that act is virtually repealed by the foreign enlistment act. No British subject can justify jure belli against another British subject when this country is in a state of peace. The 59 Geo. 3, c. 69, is no more than a declaration of the common law: upon the face of it, it appears not to have been the first act of parliament on the subject; four acts are recited in it, by one of which, the 9 Geo. 2, c. 30, a party entering into foreign military or naval service was declared guilty of felony without benefit of clergy. The Irish and Scotch brigades in the service of France before and at the time of the revolution, were guilty of an infraction of the law. In the 3rd Inst. 144, Lord Coke says: " It is not lawful for any subject of the king of England to take a pension &c. of any foreign king, prince, or state (without the king's licence) albeit they be in league with the king of England; both for that they may become enemies, and for that also it is mischievous and dangerous to the king himself and his state, as it appeareth by this distichon,

> " Principe ab externo veniunt lethalia dona,
> " Quæ studii specie, fata, necemque ferunt."

The passage cited from Vattel has reference only to the violated rights of the belligerent power. Here, the belligerent power has not seized; for, Admiral Napier, as a subject of this kingdom, and more particularly as an officer in the service of his majesty, was estopped by the law from becoming an instrument in the hands of the Portuguese Queen. It is a perfectly clear and indubitable position, that one who justifies under another. must shew a lawful authority derived under that individual. The sheriff can only justify a seizure under an execution by bringing himself properly in connection with the execution creditor. Here, Admiral Napier was not *legally* the agent or servant of the Queen of Portugal: he was a mere stranger. Before a party can avail himself of a given position, he must arrive at it *lawfully*.

It is true that a court of law cannot enter into a question of prize or no prize: this is well established by *Le Caux* v. *Eden*, 2 Doug. 594, *Faith* v. *Pearson*, 6 Taunt. 439, *Mitchell* v. *Rodney*, 2 Bro. P. C. 423, and many other authorities. But the law has never been carried further than this, that a court of law has no jurisdiction because the question of prize or no prize depends upon the law of nations, of which the courts of common law can have no knowledge. Neither could the Supreme Tribunal of Marine at Lisbon take cognisance of our foreign enlistment act. In like manner, a court of common law will not entertain a question as to whether or not a given act is a breach of privilege of parliament; but they will decide as to whether or not a party is in a situation to avail himself of a defence arising out of such privilege—*Jay* v. *Topham*, cited in *Burdett* v. *Abbott*, 14 East, 1. So, here, whether the capture were lawful or not, still the question remains whether or not the defendant is at liberty to set it up as a defence. Then, as to the 5th plea—A violation of the law on the part of the plaintiffs cannot afford a justification for a violation of the law on the part of the defendant. No doubt, a man may be divested of his property without its being vested in another. But a mere forfeiture does not divest property. In *Du Bost* v. *Beresford*, and in *Stockdale* v. *Onwhyn*, the plaintiffs were asserting a right of property in things that were in themselves incapable of being lawful objects of property.

Cur. adv. vult.

TINDAL, C. J.—The plaintiffs declare in this action against the two defendants for seizing and taking a steam vessel of the plaintiffs, and converting the same to their use. The defendants sever in their pleading, but each puts upon the record substantially the same justifications, to which the answers given by the replications are the same, and the same questions of law are raised thereon. It will be sufficient, therefore, to consider the case as it is raised upon the pleadings with respect to the first named defendant, Charles Napier. The third special plea of the defendant Charles Napier alleges, that, as a servant of the Queen of Portugal, and by her command, he seized and took the steam vessel of the plaintiffs as lawful prize, and that such proceedings were thereupon had according to the laws of Portugal, in a court of law in the kingdom of Portugal, of competent jurisdiction in that behalf, that afterwards, in and by the said court, the said vessel was adjudged to have been justly and lawfully taken, and was then in due course and form of law condemned as lawful prize, and as forfeited to the Queen of Portugal. In answer to this plea, the plaintiffs in their replication allege certain facts, which bring the service of the defendant Charles Napier under the queen of Portugal upon the occasion in question within the restrictions of the statute 59 Geo. 3, c. 69, s. 2, generally known by the name of the foreign enlistment act; and to this replication the defendant demurs. We think it is perfectly clear, that, except for the facts introduced by the replication, the plea, standing alone and unanswered, would be a conclusive bar to the plaintiffs' right of action. The sentence of a foreign court of competent jurisdiction, condemning a neutral vessel taken in war as prize, is binding and conclusive on all the world; and no English court of law can call in question the propriety or the grounds of such condemnation. It is sufficient to refer to the case of *Hughes* v. *Cornelius and Others*, Sir T. Raymond, 473, as a decisive authority on that point. It follows, that, after the sentence of the court at Lisbon, it cannot be controverted in this or any other English court, that the steam vessel was rightly taken by the Queen of Portugal as prize, and that all the property of the plaintiffs therein became by such capture and condemnation forfeited to the queen, and vested in her. But the plaintiffs contend that the replication, by the facts therein disclosed, shews that the service of the defendant Charles Napier under the Queen of Portugal, by virtue of which service alone he justifies the seizing of the vessel, is made illegal by an English statute, viz. the statute 59 Geo. 3, c. 69; and that such illegality of the service prevents him from making any justification under the Queen of Portugal, and renders him liable to all the damages which the plaintiffs have sustained by reason of the seizure. And whether the conclusion which the plaintiffs draw from these premises is the just conclusion or not, is the question between these parties. The seizure by the Queen of Portugal must be admitted to be justifiable : no objection can be taken against the forfeiture of the property in this vessel to the queen, under the sentence of condemnation. The plaintiffs, therefore, in contemplation of law, have sustained no legal injury by reason of the seizure. Again, no one can dispute the right or power of the Queen of Portugal to appoint in her own dominions the defendant or any other person she may think proper to select as her officer or servant to seize a vessel which is afterwards condemned as prize ; or can deny that the relation of lord and servant de facto subsisted between the queen and the defendant Napier; for, the Queen of Portugal cannot be bound to take any notice of, much less owe any obedience to, the municipal laws of this country. Still, however, notwithstanding the loss by seizure is such that no court of law can consider it an injury, or give any redress for it, and that the service and employment of the defendant is a service and employment de facto, the plaintiffs contend that they can make the servant responsible for the whole loss, by reason of his being obnoxious to punishment in this country for having engaged in such service.

No case whatever has been cited which goes the length of this proposition; the authorities referred to establishing only, that, where an act prohibited by the law of this country has been done, the doer of such illegal act cannot claim the assistance of a court of law in this country to enforce such act, or any benefit to be derived from, or any contract founded upon it. To the full extent of these authorities we entirely accede; but we cannot consider the law to be, that, where the act of the principal is lawful in the country where it is done, and the authority under which such act is done is complete, binding, and unquestionable there; the servant who does the act can be made responsible in the courts of this country for the consequence of such act to the same extent as if it were originally unlawful, merely by reason of a personal liability imposed by the law of this country upon him for contracting such engagement. Such a construction would effect an unreasonable alteration in the situation and rights of the plaintiffs and the defendant. The plaintiffs would, without any merit on their part, recover against the servant the value of the property to which they had lost all claim and title by law against the principal: and the defendant, instead of the measure of punishment intended to be inflicted by the statute for the transgression of the law, might be made liable to damages of an incalculable amount. Again, the only ground upon which the authority of the servant is traversable at all in an action of trespass, is no more than this—to protect the person or property of a party from the officious and wanton interference of a stranger, where the principal might have been willing to waive his rights. It is obvious that the full benefit of this principle is secured to the plaintiffs, by allowing a traverse of the authority de facto, without permitting them to impeach it by a legal objection to its validity in another and a foreign country. And we think there is no material difference between the third and the first and second special

pleas on this record: for, as we hold the authority of
the queen to be a justification of the seizure "as prize,"
there is as little doubt but that she might direct a neutral
vessel to be seized when in the act of breaking a blockade
by her established, which is the substance of the first special
plea, or of supplying warlike stores to her enemies, which
is the substance of the second. We therefore give judgment on the first three special pleas for the defendants.

As the determination on these pleas in effect decides
the main question in the cause in favour of the defendants,
it becomes unnecessary to consider the special pleas which
are fifthly pleaded by each defendant, and to which the
plaintiffs have demurred, except so far as the costs of
those pleas may be concerned in the inquiry.

By the fifth plea, the defendants set up on their part,
as a bar to the plaintiffs' right of action, certain facts and
circumstances from which it appears that the plaintiffs
had themselves been guilty of a violation of the statute
59 Geo. 3, c. 69, whereby the steam vessel "became and
was forfeited to his majesty." Now, one of the objections
taken to the plea was, that the defendants shew no authority to seize the vessel. And we are of opinion that the
plea is insufficient upon this ground. No case can be cited
in which a justification in trespass is made under the right
of another person without alleging an authority from the
principal under whose right the act complained of was
committed. If the defendant justifies breaking a close, on
the ground that it is the freehold of another, he is bound
to state that he did so enter by the command and as the
servant of the owner of the close—*Chambers* v. *Donaldson*,
11 East, 65. So, where a man justifies seizing a heriot,
where the property is in the lord of the manor, he shews
his authority from the lord: for, in these and similar cases,
non constat that the party entitled would have ever insisted
on his right; and there can be no reason, if he thinks
proper to waive it, why a stranger should justify himself

in standing in his place. The case of *Wilkins and Others v. Despard*, 5 Term Rep. 112, has been cited as an authority to shew, that, where a ship has been forfeited by breach of the provisions of an act of parliament, the owner cannot maintain trespass against the party seizing it, although the latter do not proceed to condemnation; for, as it is said by the court, by the forfeiture the property is divested out of the owner. But the plea in that case will be found to stand clear of the objection urged against that which is now under consideration. In the case cited, the plea alleges that the defendant " seized the ship as forfeited to the use of his majesty and of himself the defendant." The defendant, therefore, was not a stranger, but had authority to seize in right of himself as to part of the ship. Here, the forfeiture is given to his majesty only; and the plea is so far from stating that the defendant was authorized by his majesty to seize, that it does not even state that it was seized for the use of the king, or even as forfeited. On this ground, we think the judgment of the court on the fifth pleas must be against the defendants. Upon the whole, the general judgment of the court is for the defendants.

1836.

DOBREE
v.
NAPIER.

Judgment for the defendants accordingly.

GIBSON and Others, Assignees of GREEN, a Bankrupt,
v. BOUTTS.

THIS was an action brought by the assignees of one Green, a bankrupt, to recover from the defendant a sum

Tuesday,
May 3rd.

Whether or not a voluntary payment made by a trader in insolvent circumstances and on the verge of bankruptcy to a particular creditor, is void as being a fraud upon the bankrupt laws, is a question of fact for the jury, depending upon the mind and intention of the party at the time of making the payment, to be collected from the surrounding circumstances. If his condition and conduct be such as to evince clearly a contemplation on the part of the trader that his embarrassments *must* of necessity end in *bankruptcy*, the jury will not be warranted in coming to any other conclusion than that the transaction is fraudulent. But, inasmuch as every man has down to the time of committing an act of bankruptcy the sole right of dominion over his property, such a payment cannot be held to be a fraudulent preference where the bankrupt at the time of making it appears to entertain a bonâ fide hope or expectation that he may be extricated from his difficulties without being made a bankrupt.

of 1533*l.* alleged to have been paid to him by Green
voluntarily and by way of fraudulent preference. The
cause was tried before Tindal, C. J., at the sittings at
Guildhall after last Trinity Term. The facts were as follow:—Green was a manchester warehouseman. He had
long supported his credit by negotiating accommodation
bills. Towards the close of August, 1834, his bills being
rejected, his means of raising money, and consequently his
ability to meet his coming engagements, failed. On the
4th, 5th, and 6th of September, his liabilities (on acceptances) amounted to between 3,000*l.* and 4,000*l.*, and in
the whole month to about 8,000*l.*: to meet which he possessed on the 2nd September 2100*l.* only, with no prospect of getting more. The whole of this sum of 2100*l.*
was appropriated by Green to the payment of monies borrowed by him of friends; and, amongst the rest, the sum
sought to be recovered in this action was handed over
(without any solicitation) to the present defendant. The
payment to the defendant was made on the 3rd September.
On the 5th or 6th September a fiat was taken out against
Green, which not being proceeded with, a second issued
on the 11th October, under which he was duly declared a
bankrupt. It appeared that both before and after the issuing of the first fiat, Green had studiously avoided committing an act of bankruptcy—desiring his clerk not to
deny him to any creditor; and had been endeavouring to
induce his creditors to accept a composition. In this he
had so far succeeded that all with the exception of one or
two had consented on condition of Boutts's restoring the
1533*l.* This Boutts refused to do, and consequently the
negotiation failed. It was stated, that, unless the offer
of the composition was acceded to, Green's bankruptcy
was inevitable.

　His lordship left it to the jury to say whether or not the
payment in question was made by Green voluntarily and
with a view of giving him an undue preference over the

rest of his creditors; telling them, that, if the bankrupt, at the time of making the payment, really expected that his creditors would come together and accept a composition, and did not actually contemplate bankruptcy, the payment did not in law amount to a fraudulent preference.

The jury returned a verdict for the defendant.

Bompas, Serjeant, in Michaelmas Term last, obtained a rule nisi for a new trial, on payment of costs, on the ground that the verdict was against evidence.

Atcherley, Serjeant, and *Addison*, shewed cause—If a preference or payment is to be held void as being a fraud upon the bankrupt laws, because it is made voluntarily and without pressure by a man in embarrassed circumstances, then undoubtedly the present verdict cannot be supported. That, however, is not the true definition of a fraudulent preference. It is necessary that the payment be not only *voluntary*, but also made by a party having bankruptcy in his contemplation at the time, intending to favour a particular creditor at the expense of the rest, and to defeat the fair and equal distribution of his property which it is the sole object of the bankrupt laws to enforce: upon these two points of law depends the question of fact. [*Bosanquet*, J.—Assuming the law to be as stated, the question here seems to be whether or not a payment made for the avowed purpose of securing the payee against the consequences of a *probable* bankruptcy, which the trader is exerting himself to avoid (with a very faint hope of success), amounts to a fraudulent preference.] If the party has fair ground to expect that bankruptcy may be avoided, a payment made by him cannot be said to have been made in contemplation of bankruptcy. [*Bosanquet*, J.—Suppose the payment made because the party fears he may not succeed in avoiding bankruptcy?] The question is what is the real motive and intent of the party.

There are chances in every situation in life. The motives of men are infinitely various. Until he has committed an act of bankruptcy, a trader has the sole right of dominion over his property. [*Tindal*, C. J.—Unless Green *expected* to be made a bankrupt, why should he, when most in want of money, have made the payment in question? When determining as to the probable motives of the individual, we must take into the account the fact that he is at the very moment committing an act that effectually prevents the execution of his presumed intention to effect a composition with his creditors.] In the absence of all evidence to shew an intention of bankruptcy, and the party appearing to be acting under a belief that bankruptcy may be avoided, although he is confessedly in such a situation that bankruptcy is extremely probable—does a voluntary payment made under such circumstances amount to a fraudulent preference *in contemplation of bankruptcy?* The court cannot speculate upon probabilities, except in so far as they may lead to a knowledge of the contemplation and intention of the bankrupt. In order to avoid the payment, the party must appear to have *contemplated*, to have *intended* to become bankrupt; that is, he must *believe* bankruptcy to be the necessary and unavoidable result of his condition. Here, the evidence shews that Green was doing his utmost to avoid bankruptcy: the fact of his having desired his clerk not to deny him to any creditor, was a strong circumstance to shew that bankruptcy was not his object. [*Bosanquet*, J.—It is a two-edged sword: it rather shews that he *had* the *prospect* of bankruptcy in his mind.] In *Fidgeon* v. *Sharp*, 1 Marsh. 196, 5 Taunt. 539, it was held, that, whether or not a trader in embarrassed circumstances, who delivers goods to a creditor in discharge of his debt, does it in contemplation of bankruptcy, is a question of fact for the jury; and, though he contemplates that his trade must cease, and that he cannot pay his creditors unless they give him time, he does not therefore necessarily contem-

plate bankruptcy. There, A. purchased goods of B. on
the 8th October, for the purpose of exportation; but,
finding that he must stop payment, and that he could not
apply the goods to the purpose for which they were
bought, he returned them to B. on the 16th: on the 17th
he stopped payment; but, expecting remittances from
abroad more than sufficient to pay his debts, he entertained no doubt but that his creditors would give him
time: they, however, refusing, he was made a bankrupt
on the 2nd November. In an action by the assignees
against B. to recover the value of the goods, it was held
that the jury were warranted in finding that the delivery
of the goods to B. was not made in contemplation of bankruptcy. The judgment of Gibbs, C. J., in that case shews
the true principle upon which voluntary payments or de-
liveries of goods are avoided. "It was argued," says his
lordship, "by my Brother Lens, that, if a man is in such
a state that he knows he cannot without the indulgence of
his creditors resume his payments immediately, he cannot
make a payment to a creditor, because he must necessarily
contemplate that bankruptcy will be the consequence. I
cannot go along with him in this conclusion. By the common law, he may pay any one: the general effect of the
statutes on the subject of bankrupts is, that all payments
made before bankruptcy are legal and valid; but a certain
class of cases has arisen in which certain payments have
been supposed to be made in fraud of the bankrupt laws,
and are therefore fraudulent and void. But I find in all
the cases, from *Fordyce's* to the present, the fact found,
that the act was done in fraud of the bankrupt laws: it
must be an act, then, not only that in effect contravenes
the bankrupt laws, but it must be done with intent to con-
travene them, and in contemplation of bankruptcy. The
innocence or guilt of the act *depends,* then, *on the mind of
him who did it; and it cannot be in fraud of the bankrupt
laws, unless the actor meant it should be so.*" And in

Morgan v. *Brundrett*, 5 B. & Ad. 296, 2 N. & M. 280, the court of King's Bench held the question for the jury in such cases to be, whether *bankruptcy* (not mere *insolvency*) was contemplated. Parke, J., there says: "In order to render the deposit void, it was incumbent on the plaintiffs to shew, first, that it was made in contemplation of bankruptcy, and, secondly, that it was voluntary. There was very slight evidence that it was made in contemplation of bankruptcy. The meaning of these words I take to be, that the payment or delivery must be with intent to defeat the general distribution of effects which takes place under a commission of bankrupt. It is not sufficient that it should be made (as may be inferred from some of the late cases) in contemplation of insolvency. These cases I think have gone too far." And this court attorned to the doctrine of that case in *Atkinson* v. *Brindall*, ante, Vol. 2, 369, where it is distinctly laid down, that, in order to constitute a fraudulent preference, so as to avoid a payment made by a trader, it must be a voluntary preference and made in actual contemplation of *bankruptcy:* it is not enough to shew that the party was in such a state of insolvency and embarrassment as to render bankruptcy a *probable* event. [*Tindal*, C. J.—Though I fully accede to the general doctrine of *Morgan* v. *Brundrett*, I cannot go along with Mr. Baron Parke to the full extent. Where a party is in so hopeless a state of insolvency that he cannot reasonably expect to avoid bankruptcy, though he chooses to fight it off as long as possible, I cannot look upon a payment voluntarily made by him to a favoured creditor in any other light than as a payment calculated and intended to defeat the bankrupt laws.] Declarations articulo mortis, to be available, must be made by the party under such circumstances as shew that he contemplated almost immediate death as inevitable. The doctrine of fraudulent preference is in principle precisely the same. The motives and intention of the party, as evidenced by the surrounding circumstances, present a question of fact that it is peculiarly for the jury to determine.

Bompas, Serjeant, *Martin*, and *James*, in support of the rule.—It may be conceded that a contemplation of insolvency alone will not avoid a voluntary payment. The cases of *Morgan* v. *Brundrett* and *Atkinson* v. *Brindall* have definitively established the proper mode of leaving a case of this sort to the jury—whether the payment was *voluntary* and made *in contemplation of bankruptcy*. The question is, what is the true meaning of the expression "in contemplation of bankruptcy." Does it mean anything more than a consciousness in the mind of the party that he is in a state of utter, hopeless insolvency, and liable to be made a bankrupt? The circumstances of this case shew clearly that this was the state of Green at the time of making the payment to the defendant. He might have entertained a strong desire to effect an arrangement with his creditors by means of a composition: that is not at all inconsistent with a contemplation of bankruptcy. Contemplation of bankruptcy does not mean a wish or expectation to be made a bankrupt; but a consciousness that the party's affairs are in such a state that bankruptcy is inevitable. In *Fidgeon* v. *Sharp*, the bankrupts had no idea that bankruptcy was probable at the time of the delivery of the goods. Gibbs, C. J., there says: "With respect to this doctrine of contemplation in cases of bankruptcy, we have nothing either in the common or statute law to shew what it is. The cases in which this doctrine was introduced make it depend upon the quo animo: if a trader thought he should not ultimately have enough to pay all his creditors, it must be presumed, that, if he gives full payment to one, he does it in contemplation of bankruptcy." Here, Green was using endeavours to induce his creditors to accept a composition; well knowing that if he failed in this he must be a bank-

1836.

GIBSON
v.
BOUTTS.

rupt. Under these circumstances, the very day before certain acceptances of his were becoming due, he, in order to serve his friend, parts with nearly his whole substance, without pressure, without request; and thereby effectually puts it out of his own power to carry into effect the proposed composition. It is impossible to conceive a clearer case of contemplation of bankruptcy. In *Gibbins* v. *Phillips*, 2 M. & R. 238, 7 B. & C. 529, Bayley, J., says: "By contemplation of bankruptcy is not meant the expectation of a commission issuing, but that the party is in such a state that bankruptcy is likely to follow, or that it is one of the probable results." And in *Stewart* v. *Moody*, 1 C. M. & R. 777, Parke, B., says: " It has been clearly settled, that, if the necessary consequence of a man's act is to delay his creditors, he must be taken to intend it."

TINDAL, C. J.—This certainly is a case in which I should have felt quite as well satisfied had the verdict been the other way. But, at the same time, in conformity with the general rule laid down by all the courts touching motions for new trials where the question is one purely of fact and has been properly submitted to the jury, I feel great reluctance to send this cause down for a second investigation. It certainly was a case pregnant with suspicion. Contemplation of bankruptcy I take to mean, where the party believes bankruptcy to be the necessary result of his condition, and such belief is operating upon his mind at the time of making the payment.

PARK, J.—I do not pretend to say which way the verdict ought to be in this case: but, upon the whole, I cannot help thinking it would be more satisfactory to have it submitted to a second jury. There cannot now be any difference of opinion as to the law on this subject.

VAUGHAN, J.—I concur with my Brother Park in thinking a second investigation advisable in the present

case: I think justice requires it; though I must confess
myself at all times extremely reluctant to interfere with the
province of the jury in a matter that is peculiarly for them
to decide, where the balance is even. But, where the preponderance of the evidence one way is very great, and
one feels it impossible to relieve the mind from the impression that injustice has been or may have been done;
then a second inquiry becomes imperatively necessary.
Here two questions arose, and were properly presented to
the jury—first, whether the payment was voluntary—
secondly, whether made in contemplation of bankruptcy.
That the payment was voluntary, was plain and palpable,
and in fact was admitted. With respect to the second question—Look at the situation of the party at the time. Every
man may be supposed to contemplate the necessary and
ordinary consequences of his acts. It is so laid down by
Lord Ellenborough in *Newton v. Chantler*, 7 East, 138.
" As a general proposition," says his lordship, " it cannot
be disputed that a conveyance by deed by a trader of all
his property to a particular creditor in prejudice to the
rest is an act of bankruptcy. Every man must be taken
to contemplate the ordinary consequences of his own act
at the time of the act done. Here the necessary effect of
the act done was to turn round all his other creditors, and
prevent them from pursuing their present ordinary remedy
against him for the payment of their demands, leaving them
only to look to him for the future surplus, if any. Being
insolvent within his own knowledge at the time, and two
writs out against him, he must have contemplated bankruptcy by means of arrest and lying in gaol two months;
and under these circumstances he gives the bill of sale to
one of his creditors, conveying all his property. Must he
not then have contemplated the necessary consequence of
his own act? And as such an act must have the effect of
defeating or delaying all his other creditors, by stripping
him of all he had, and disabling him from carrying on his

trade, must I not deduce the inference from it that he meant to defraud all his other creditors ?" I agree that the guilt or innocence of the act depends upon the mind of the actor. What was the situation of Green on the 3rd September, the day he made the payment in question? He had not assets to pay more than one fourth of the acceptances that were arriving at maturity in the course of the month. The knowledge of his insolvency was before him. Under all the circumstances, I think it is due to justice to send this case down for further investigation.

BOSANQUET, J.—I agree with my Brothers Park and Vaughan that it would be more satisfactory if this case were to undergo a second investigation. If a man, believing himself to be in danger of bankruptcy, voluntarily hands over money for the purpose of securing a favoured creditor, that, in my opinion, is a payment made in contemplation of bankruptcy within the meaning of the law as laid down upon the subject of fraudulent preference.

Rule absolute, on payment of costs (a).

(a) See Abbott v. Burbage, ante, Vol. 2, p. 636.

LAYTHOARP v. BRYANT.

A contract of purchase (of leasehold property sold by auction) written on the back of the particulars of sale (which contains the name of the owner of the property), and signed by the *purchaser* only, is a sufficient note or memorandum of the *agreement* between the parties to satisfy the 4th section of the statute of frauds: the *vendor's* signature is not essential.

THIS was an action brought to recover from the defendant a compensation in damages for a loss sustained by the plaintiff upon a re-sale of certain leasehold premises which the defendant had purchased at an auction on the 3rd December, 1833 (b). The particulars of sale stated that the lease and goodwill of the premises, situate in

(b) See the declaration set out in a report of a former trial of this cause, ante, Vol. 1, p. 327.

Stoke Newington, in which the coke, coal, and seed trades had been carried on, would be *peremptorily* sold by auction by Mr. Thomas Ross, at the Auction Mart, on the 3rd December, by order of Mr. W. Laythoarp, the proprietor, retiring from the trade. The defendant was the highest bidder, and the premises were knocked down to him at the price of 441*l.* The contract of purchase was written on the back of the particulars of sale, and signed by the defendant, who was not required to pay any deposit. Shortly after the day of sale, an abstract was sent by the plaintiff's solicitor to the defendant, accompanied by a request that the purchase might be completed without delay. The defendant immediately returned the abstract, making no objection thereto, but stating that he had no intention to become a buyer, but had only bid for the premises at the request of the plaintiff. An assignment was subsequently tendered to the defendant for execution and acceptance. The defendant, however, still insisting that he had not purchased the premises, they were again submitted to the hammer. On the second sale the highest bidding was 194*l.* 5*s.;* whereupon the present action was brought to recover the difference, together with the costs of the first sale. At the trial, before Tindal, C. J., at the sittings in London after last Trinity Term, it was submitted, on the part of the defendant, that there was a want of mutuality on the face of the contract, the *vendor* not being bound by it; and that, although the name of the plaintiff as owner of the premises appeared in the particulars of sale, yet there was no signature by him, or by any agent duly authorized by him, to satisfy the statute of frauds, 29 Car. 2, c. 3, s. 4. For the plaintiff it was contended that no signature by the vendor was necessary, the 4th section of the statute merely requiring the agreement, or some memorandum or note thereof, to be signed *by the party to be charged therewith*—the defendant in the action; and that, if necessary, the letter of the plaintiff's attorney inclosing the assignment shewed a sufficient mutuality to entitle the plaintiff to maintain the action. The jury having found for the plaintiff—damages, 284*l*. 15*s*. 11*d*., with liberty to the defendant to move to enter a nonsuit—

Atcherley, Serjeant, in Michaelmas Term, accordingly obtained a rule nisi.—He cited *Champion* v. *Plummer*, 1 N. R. 252, 5 Esp. 240; and especially relied on *Lawrenson* v. *Butler*, 1 Sch. & Lefr. 13, where Lord Redesdale refused to enforce a specific performance, on the ground that, in the absence of a signature to bind the vendor, there was no mutuality in the contract: saying—" I confess I have no conception that a court of equity ought to decree a specific performance in a case where nothing has been done in pursuance of the agreement, except where both parties had by the agreement a right to compel a specific performance according to the advantages which it might be supposed that they were to derive from it; because otherwise it would follow that the court would decree a specific performance where the party called upon to perform might be in this situation, that, if the agreement was disadvantageous, he would be liable to the performance, and yet, if advantageous to him, he could not compel a performance. This is not equity, as it seems to me. If, indeed, there was a concealment, or an ignorance of the facts on the one part, and that thereby the other party was led into a situation from whence he could not be extricated, then he would have a right to have the agreement executed cy prés; that is, a new agreement is to be made between the parties." And also on *O'Rourke* v. *Perceval*, 2 Ball. & B. 58, where this doctrine of Lord Redesdale was mentioned with approbation by Lord Manners; and *Martin* v. *Mitchell*, 2 Jac. & W. 428, where Sir Thomas Plumer said: " When one party, having entered into a contract that has not been signed by the other party, afterwards repents, and refuses to proceed in it, I should have felt great difficulty in saying that he had not a locus penitentiæ, and was not at liberty to recede until the other had signed or in some manner made it binding upon himself. How can the contract be complete before it is mutual? and how can it be complete as to the one and not as to the other?" [*Tindal*, C. J.—The want of mutuality may have weight in a court of equity: but here the question is, whether, sitting in a court of law, we can say that this contract does not satisfy the statute.] The buyer and seller ought to have reciprocal rights and liabilities (b).

Bompas, Serjeant, and *Steer*, shewed cause.—Before the passing of the 29 Car. 2, c. 3, it was competent to parties to enter into contracts of this description by parol, without writing. The statute requires that they shall be in writing, and signed by the party to be charged: it enacts (s. 4) that "no action shall be brought whereby to charge any executor or administrator upon any special pro-

---

(b) A further point was made. It appeared that at the time of sale the particulars were read by the auctioneer; and that no notice was given to the parties assembled that any person was employed to bid on the part of the vendor, though it was admitted by the auctioneer at the trial that an individual named Allen had been so employed, and had made two or three bids: whereupon it was contended on the part of the defendant that the circumstance not having been disclosed to the company at the time, and the sale being declared to be " peremptory" (which, it was submitted, was equivalent to "without reserve,") the sale was void. The learned

Serjeant cited Bexwell v. Christie, Cowp. 395; Twining v. Morrice, 2 Bro. C. C. 326; Howard v. Castle, 6 T. R. 642; Smith v. Clarke, 12 Ves. 477; Meadows v. Tanner, 5 Madd. 34; Wheeler v. Collier, M. & M. 125; Crowder v. Austin, 11 Moore, 283, 3 Bing. 368, 2 C. & P. 208; and Rex v. Marsh, 3 Y. & J. 331. Contra, Bramley v. Alt, 3 Ves. 624; Connolly v. Parsons, 3 Ves. 625.

The court however held, that, whatever the merits of the abstract question, it did not arise on the facts that appeared on the notes of the Lord Chief Justice: consequently the rule was not granted on this point.

mise to answer damages out of his own estate, or to charge
the defendant upon any special promise to answer for
the debt, default, or miscarriage of another person, or to
charge any person upon any agreement made upon consideration of marriage, or upon any contract or sale of
lands, tenements, or hereditaments, or any interest in or
concerning them, or upon any agreement that is not to be
performed within the space of one year from the making
thereof, unless the agreement upon which such action
shall be brought, or some memorandum or note thereof,
shall be in writing, and signed by the party to be charged
therewith, or some other person thereunto by him lawfully
authorized." Here the contract is perfect in all its parts,
and signed by the defendant, the party to be charged
therewith.   The name of Ross the auctioneer is printed
on the back of the catalogue to which the particulars of
sale are prefixed ; and that, if any signature be necessary
on the part of the vendor, is a sufficient signature by an
agent thereunto by him lawfully authorized, to satisfy the
statute. A promise to answer for the debt, default, or
miscarriage of another, and a promise upon consideration
of marriage, are also required to be in writing, and signed
by the party to be charged therewith: and in neither of
these cases was the contract ever signed by *both* parties.
In *Payne* v. *Cave*, 3 T. R. 148, the court say: " The
auctioneer is the agent of the vendor, and the assent
of both parties is necessary to make the contract binding; that is signified on the part of the vendor by
knocking down the hammer." *Emmerson* v. *Heelis*, 2
Taunt. 38, is to the same effect. In *Palmer* v. *Scott*, 1
Russ. & Mylne, 391, it was held that the written undertaking of one party will be enforced, although the other
party is not mutually bound by writing. In *Allen* v. *Bennet*, 3 Taunt. 169, it was held to be no objection to the
validity of a contract for the sale of goods, signed by the
seller, that the seller cannot enforce the same contract

against the buyer, because the buyer has never signed it.

Sir James Mansfield, in that case, after disposing of one of the points made on the part of the defendant, said: "It was then objected that one party who has not signed is not bound; but the fact was the same in the cases of *Egerton* v. *Mathews*, 6 East, 307, and *Champion* v. *Plummer*, 1 New Rep. 252, and the objection was never taken in either of these cases; but the whole of this case supposes that the plaintiff had agreed: suppose he had not contracted by writing, he has by parol, and he is bound in honor; and it has never yet been decided that an obligation in honor would not be a good consideration. All these cases, *Egerton* v. *Mathews*, *Saunderson* v. *Jackson*, 2 B. & P. 338, and *Champion* v. *Plummer*, suppose a signature by the seller to be sufficient, and every one knows it is the daily practice of the court of Chancery to establish contracts signed by one person only, and yet a court of equity can no more dispense with the statute of frauds than a court of law can." In *Egerton* v. *Mathews*, Lord Ellenborough observed "that the words of the statute were satisfied if there were 'some note or memorandum in writing of the bargain, signed by the parties to be charged by such contract.' And this was a memorandum of the bargain, or at least of so much of it as was sufficient to bind the parties to be charged therewith, and whose signatures to it is all that the statute requires." In *Schneider* v. *Norris*, 2 M. & S. 286, a bill of parcels in which the name of the vendor was printed, and that of the vendee written by the vendor, was held to be a sufficient memorandum of the contract within the statute, to charge the vendor. "Here," says Lord Ellenborough, "there is a signing by the party to be charged, by words recognising the printed name as much as if he had subscribed his mark to it, which is strictly the meaning of signing, and by that the party has incorporated and avowed the thing printed to be his; and it

is the same in substance as if he had written Norris & Co.
with his own hand.   He has by his handwriting in effect
said, I acknowledge what I have written to be for the purpose of exhibiting my recognition of the within contract."
In *Buckhouse* v. *Crosby*, 2 Eq. Cas. Abr. 33, the Lord
Chancellor said " he had often known the objection taken
that a mutual contract in writing ought to appear on both
sides; but that that objection had as often been over-
ruled."   In *Seton* v. *Slade*, 7 Ves. 265, an agreement
signed by one party only (the defendant) was held good
to charge him within the statute of frauds.   Lord Eldon
says, in *Coles* v. *Trecothick*, 9 Ves. 249, where the vendor was held bound by the signature of his agent's clerk:
"The form of the two clauses (ss. 4 and 17) is not the
same : but the terms as to the memorandum in writing are
exactly the same.   Unless some distinction can be pointed
out, the law is very inconvenient as to sales by auction:
particularly if the auctioneer is to be considered the agent
of one only ; and if, putting down the name, and ascertaining the sum, and putting that down upon the conditions of sale, which ascertain all the other terms, it is competent after that to the vendor to say, according *Payne* v.
Cave, that, though the other party is bound in a degree
by knocking down the hammer, he may at that moment revoke the authority.   Upon such terms mankind will not
very readily engage in these transactions.   If the putting
down the name and the sum by the auctioneer is a signing,
that would furnish a new class of cases; that, the effect
being to ascertain the terms of the agreement, it should
be good both in law and equity." *Hatton* v. *Gray*, 2 Cha.
Cas. 164, is an authority to the same effect; "Hatton
sold houses to Gray for 2000*l*.   Note was made by Hatton
of the agreement, signed by Gray, but not by Hatton.   Mr.
Solicitor—The note binds not him who signed it not, for
the statute of frauds and perjuries, &c., and therefore in
equity cannot bind the other party, for, both must be

bound or neither of them in equity. But decreed contrary."
In *Lord Ormond* v. *Anderson*, 2 Ball & B. 370, Lord Manners says: "An objection has been made to the execution of this agreement, on the ground that it has not been
signed by the plaintiff, and that the defendant could not
have enforced it against the plaintiff. I am very well
aware that a doubt has been entertained by a judge in
this court of very high authority, whether courts of equity
would specifically execute an agreement where one party
only was bound. There exists no provision in the statute
of frauds to prevent the execution of such an agreement;
and Sir James Mansfield, who certainly had great experience in courts of equity, lays it down in the case of
Allen v. *Bennet*, that a contract signed by one party
would be enforced in equity against that party, and that
such was the daily practice of that court." And Sir
William Grant, in *Western* v. *Russell*, 2 Ves. & B. 192,
says: "After the cases that have been determined, I
should hardly be at liberty, notwithstanding the considerable doubt thrown upon that point by Lord Redesdale, to
refuse a specific performance upon the ground that there
was no agreement signed by the party seeking a performance." All the authorities at law are uniformly in favour
of the validity of the contract; and with respect to the
cases in equity, the only one that at all favours the argument on the other side is that containing a dictum of Lord
Redesdale: but that has never been expressly recognized
since. Sir E. Sugden, in his treatise of the law of Vendors and Purchasers, 8th edit., p. 78, says: "It is to be
observed that the statute requires the writing to be signed
only by the person to be charged; and therefore if a bill
be brought against a person who signed an agreement,
he will be bound by it, although the other party did not
sign it, as the agreement is signed by the person to be
charged. This point has been established by the concurrent authority of the Lord Keeper North, Lord Keeper

Wright, Lord Hardwicke, Lord C. B. Smith, and Bathurst and Aston, Justices, when Lords Commissioners,
Lord Thurlow, Lord Eldon, and Sir W. Grant.   The
legislature has expressly said that the agreement shall be
binding *if signed by the party to be charged;* and, as
Lord Hardwicke has observed, the word *party* in the
statute is not to be construed *party* as to a deed, but person in general; but there have been instances in which
the want of the signature to the agreement by the party
seeking to enforce it, has been deemed a badge of fraud
(see *O'Rourke* v. *Perceval,* 2 Ball & B. 58); but perhaps
the transaction ought not to be viewed in that light,
unless the other party called on the party who had not
signed to execute it, in which case a refusal to sign might
be held to operate as a repudiation of the contract."—If,
in order to entitle the plaintiff to recover, he was bound
to shew a contract binding on himself, such a contract is
fairly deducible from the letters written by the plaintiff's
attorney on tendering the abstract and the assignment.

Atcherley, Serjeant, and *Busby,* in support of the rule.
In order to constitute a valid contract, there must be a
mutuality—a right on the part of the purchaser to hold
the vendor to his bargain, and an equal right on the part
of the vendor to hold the purchaser to his. In the present
case nothing of the kind appears.   To make the contract
good within the 4th section of the statute of frauds, the
consideration also must appear— *Wain* v. *Warlters, Egerton* v. *Mathews;* and the signature is part of the consideration.   All the cases that have been relied upon on the
other side are either cases in equity or cases determined
on the 17th section of the statute; neither of which classes
of cases applies to the present case.   Courts of equity
differ from courts of law in their mode of dealing with this
statute. Formerly, indeed, the former courts required the
agreement to be signed by both parties; but, in a case of

Cotton v. *Lee*, before the Lords Commissioners, in 1770, it was held sufficient if the party to be charged had signed it—*Whitchurch* v. *Bevis*, 2 Bro. C. C. 564. In equity, indeed, there is an end to the objection as to the want of signature, from the moment the defendant puts in his answer, and thereby acknowledges the agreement—Roberts on Frauds, 106. And with respect to the cases of contracts for the purchase of an interest in land, where a signature by one party has been held sufficient, as in *Seton* v. *Slade*, and the other cases already cited, it is to be observed that the 4th section requires only a note in writing signed by the party; whereas, upon the 17th section, it was essential that the names of both the contracting parties should appear on the contract. In *Charlwood* v. *The Duke of Bedford*, 1 Atk. 497, Lord Chief Baron Comyns says: " It was urged by the plaintiff's counsel, that, if an agreement be made in part, and executed on one side, that this is a foundation for equity to establish the agreement, especially where there has been an expense to one of the parties. But, in all cases where there is a performance only of one side, that is not a dispensation of the statute, but *casus omissus*, against which there is no provision made." *Champion* v. *Plummer*, 1 N. R. 252, is an express authority that, in a court of law, a note or memorandum in writing of a contract for the sale of goods, signed by the seller only, is not a sufficient memorandum within the meaning of the statute. " How," says Sir James Mansfield, " can that be said to be a contract, or memorandum of a contract, which does not state who are the contracting parties? By this note it does not at all appear to whom the goods were sold. It would prove a sale to any other person as well as to the plaintiffs: there cannot be a contract without two parties, and it is customary in the course of business to state the name of the purchaser as well as of the seller in every bill of parcels. This note does not appear to me to amount to any memorandum in

writing of a bargain." [*Tindal*, C. J.—Laythoarp's name
is mentioned; the sale is stated to be made by his order:
will not that suffice?] That does not get rid of the objection as to the want of mutuality. In *Egerton* v. *Mathews*, it is true, the contract was signed by one party only:
but the decision there proceeded upon the ground of the
distinction between the 4th and the 17th clauses of the
act. In order to satisfy the words of the 4th section, there
must be an *agreement*. Can there be an *agreement* without mutuality? In *Wheeler* v. *Collier*, M. & M. 125, on
the sale of an estate by auction, the name of the owner
did not appear in the particulars or conditions of sale, and
the agreement signed by the purchaser did not mention
the owner's name, and was not signed either by him or the
auctioneer: and Lord Tenterden inclined to think that
the seller could not maintain an action for the non-com-
pletion of the contract. "The declaration," says his lordship, "alleges the consideration to be the sale by the
plaintiff; but nothing at all appears to bind him; his name
is not mentioned in the conditions, nor in the agreement.
What a court of equity would do in this, I cannot possibly
say." In *Lees* v. *Whitcomb*, 2 M. & P. 86, 5 Bing. 34,
a written agreement " to remain with A. B. two years, for
the purpose of learning a trade," was held not binding,
for want of an engagement in the same instrument by A. B.
to teach.—The letter inclosing the abstract cannot be
called in aid. It formed no part of the agreement: it was
not intended as a completion of an inchoate contract; but
an enforcing of an already perfect agreement. At all
events, the attorney had no authority to bind his client.

TINDAL, C. J.—This case is brought before the court
upon two objections urged on the part of the defendant to
the plaintiff's right to recover—first, that the contract
(which relates to the sale of land) omits all mention of the
name of one of the contracting parties—secondly, that the

contract of sale was not signed by the vendor. 1. I am
prepared to admit, that, in order to its validity, the agreement must either on the face of it or by necessary reference contain the names of the parties, as well as the subject-matter of the contract, the consideration, and the
promise.   The agreement is written upon the conditions
of sale, whence it sufficiently appears that the property is
sold by Ross, the auctioneer, on behalf of Laythoarp. This
gets rid of the first objection. 2. The second objection is
one of far greater importance—that the agreement is unsigned by the vendor.   In order to see the validity of this
objection, recourse must be had to the terms of the 4th
section of the statute of frauds, 29 Car. 2, c. 3, which
enacts that " no action shall be brought whereby to charge
any executor or administrator upon any special promise to
answer damages out of his own estate, or to charge the
defendant upon any special promise to answer for the
debt, default, or miscarriage of another person, or to
charge any person upon any agreement made upon consideration of marriage, or *upon any contract or sale of
lands, tenements, or hereditaments, or any interest in or
concerning them,* or upon any agreement that is not to be
performed within the space of one year from the making
thereof, unless the *agreement* upon which such action
shall be brought, or some memorandum or note thereof,
shall be in writing, and signed *by the party to be charged
therewith,* or some other person thereunto by him lawfully
authorized."   The object and meaning of the act appear
to me to be, that, unless it is proved at the trial that the
contract or *agreement* is signed by the party to be charged
therewith (the defendant in the action), the action is not
maintainable.   It is said that there is a want of mutuality,
the party charged by this agreement not having the full
benefit of his adversary's liability by the same instrument.
But, whose fault is that?   The defendant might, had he
thought fit, have required the signature of the vendor.

1836.

LAYTHOARP
v.
BRYANT.

First point.

Second point.

What is the object of the statute? According to the preamble, "the prevention of many fraudulent practices which
are commonly endeavoured to be upheld by perjury and
subornation of perjury." The whole object of the act is
completely attained when the agreement appears to bear
the signature of the defendant, "the party to be charged
therewith." Then, it is said, that the word *agreement* imports a signature by both parties; and that, in the absence of
such signature by both, there is a want of mutuality. But
here a little confusion arises between the consideration for
the agreement, and the mutuality of claim or liability from
the signatures of the parties. It is true, the consideration
for the promise must appear on the face of the agreement:
this is effectually decided by *Wain* v. *Warllers*; one express ground of the decision in that case was, that, in the
4th section of the statute of frauds, the word "agreement"
imported something more than the word "bargain" in the
17th section. What is the meaning of the term consideration? It is defined to be any act of the plaintiff from which
the defendant derives a benefit or advantage, or any labour, detriment, or inconvenience sustained by the plaintiff, provided such act is performed or such inconvenience
suffered by the plaintiff, with the consent, either express
or implied, of the defendant—Sel. Ni. Pri. 8th edit. p. 47.
So, if a creditor at the request of a third person consent
to forbear to sue his debtor for a certain time, that is a
sufficient consideration to support a promise by such third
person to pay the debt. But I find no such reason for
saying that the signature forms part of the agreement.
The agreement is in fact completed before either party is
called upon to sign. Apply this doctrine to several of
the cases alluded to in s. 4. I agree that the same construction must be put upon the cases pointed out by that
clause. Is any signature required in any of these cases
other than by the party to be charged? "No action shall
be brought whereby to charge any executor or administra-

tor upon any special promise to answer damages out of his own estate—unless the agreement upon which such action shall be brought, or some memorandum or note thereof, shall be in writing, and signed by the party to be charged therewith, or some other person thereunto by him lawfully authorised." Suppose a letter written by an executor undertaking to be responsible out of his own estate: who ever heard, that, in order to make this promise binding on the executor, the *agreement* or letter should be signed by the party to whom it is addressed? If the letter contain merely an offer, there must undoubtedly be some intimation that the offer is accepted before the party can be sued thereon: but, where it contains a direct promise, founded on a good consideration, the only signature that is required is, the signature of the "party to be charged therewith." Take the next case—a special promise to answer for the debt, default, or miscarriage of another person. It is every day's practice to put in an agreement signed only by the surety. I never yet heard it suggested that the signature of the plaintiff also was requisite. The objection might have been urged in *Wain* v. *Warlters*, and would, if a valid one, have afforded a complete answer to the action. I take it, therefore, that the word "agreement" as used in this 4th section, is satisfied if the memorandum states the contract and the consideration, and bears the signature of the party to be charged by it in the action. Several cases have been referred to in the course of the argument. I shall content myself, however, with noticing two of them, which arose in courts of law—*Emmerson* v. *Heelis*, and *Allen* v. *Bennet*. In the first of these cases it was expressly held that an auctioneer is an agent lawfully authorized by the buyer to sign a contract for him, whether it be for the purchase of an interest in land or goods, and his authority is given by the buyer bidding aloud; and the name of a purchaser of divers lots at an auction being written down on the

sale bill opposite to such lots for which the purchaser
was declared to be the highest bidder, is a note or memorandum in writing sufficient to satisfy the intent of the
statute.   There was no signature by the vendor in that
case, and yet the contract was held valid. *Allen* v. *Bennet*
turned upon the 17th section.   It was there held to be no
objection to the validity of a contract for the sale of goods,
signed by the vendor, that the latter cannot inforce the
same contract against the buyer, because the buyer has
never signed it.   The word *parties* is found in section 17,
party in s. 4: but that difference is not relied on.   The
authority of these cases is fortified by the fact, that, in the
construction of the 17th section, courts of equity have not
in general required the signatures of both parties.   Lord
Redesdale and Sir T. Plumer, it is true, in *Lawrence* v.
Butler and *Martin* v. *Mitchell,* seemed to be of opinion that specific performance ought not to be enforced
where the contract was signed by the vendor only.   Since
that time, however, courts of equity have pursued the
same course of decision as before; and the general rule
can hardly be said to have been broken in upon by these
dicta rather than acta.   *Lees* v. *Whitcomb,* I think, does
not bear out the point for which it was cited: there, the
decision turned upon two grounds—first, the want of consideration for the defendant's promise; and, secondly, a
variance between the contract declared on and that given
in evidence.   I think the rule should be discharged.

PARK, J.—I am of the same opinion.   His lordship
having so fully gone into the case, I shall add but little.
The cases that have arisen in equity may be put out
of the question: but, even there, the preponderance is
greatly in favour of the present plaintiff; for, though
Lord Redesdale and Sir Thomas Plumer, both very
able men, were inclined to think that the contract ought
to be signed by both parties, Lord Manners a ·year or

two afterwards held the contrary on two several occasions; and many cases in equity since have been decided the same way as before. The cases that have arisen on the construction of the 17th section may also be put very much out of the question. The two clauses contain different words: in s. 17 the note of the bargain is required to be "signed by the *parties* to be charged by such contract," &c.; whereas by s. 4, the agreement upon which the action is brought, or some memorandum or note thereof, is required to be "signed by the *party* to be charged therewith," &c. But, even under the 17th section, it has been held not to be necessary that the contract should be signed by the vendor. In *Saunderson* v. *Jackson*, 2 B. & P. 238, 3 Esp. 180, and in *Schneider* v. *Norris*, 2 M. & S. 286, it was held that a bill of parcels in which the name of the vendor was printed and that of the vendee written, delivered to the latter at the time of giving an order for the future delivery of goods, was a sufficient memorandum of the contract, signed by the parties, to charge the vendor. With respect to the 4th section, the wiser course seems to me to be to look at the words of the act, rather than to attempt to discover fanciful distinctions between the conflicting decisions. The words are perfectly plain and intelligible—"No action shall be brought whereby to charge any person upon any contract or sale of lands, tenements, or hereditaments, or any interest in or concerning them, unless the *agreement* upon which such action shall be brought, or some memorandum or note thereof, shall be in writing, and *signed by the party to be charged therewith*, or some other person thereunto by him lawfully authorized." Here, the agreement *is* signed by the party to be charged therewith: the consideration sufficiently appears; and the auctioneer's name as well as that of the plaintiff are stated. I am clearly of opinion that this is a sufficient compliance with the statute. The point did not arise in *Lees* v. *Whitcomb*: the main question there was

whether or not the contract was truly set out in the declaration.   It certainly is no authority for the position for
which it was cited.

VAUGHAN, J.—I am also of opinion that all the essential
requisites of the statute have been fully complied with,
both according to the letter and the spirit.   The longer I
live the more am I satisfied of the impropriety of importing into a statute a latitude of construction.   I believe no
case ever underwent more discussion than did *Wain* v.
Warlters.   It is quite a mistake to suppose that that case
proceeded on the ground of want of mutuality: all that it
decided was, that, by the term "agreement," must be
understood, not merely the promise, but also the consideration; otherwise all the mischief that the statute was designed to prevent would again be let in.   This is the
first case in which the objection now taken has ever been
thought of in a court of law.   In the construction of a
statute, courts of equity are governed by the same rules
as courts of law.   In equity, the opinions of Lords Hardwicke, Thurlow, and Eldon, and of Sir W. Grant, are all
in accordance with the doctrine laid down in *Seton* v. *Slade*,
7 Ves. 275. and *Fowle* v. *Freeman*, 9 Ves. 351, that a signature by the vendee, the party to be charged, is sufficient.   The very point arose and was decided in *Bowen*
v. *Morris*, 2 Taunt. 374, where Sir James Mansfield said:
" In equity, a contract signed by one party would be enforced, and it was not clear that it was different in law."
The question came under consideration in *Egerton* v. *Mathews*, 6 East, 307, 2 Smith, 339, where it was held that a
memorandum signed by the defendants, whereby they
agreed to give so much for goods, takes the case out of
the statute, though not signed by the seller, nor expressing any consideration for the defendant's promise, otherwise than by inference from their own obligation.   And
again in *Allen* v. *Bennet*, 3 Taunt. 169, where it was held

that it is no objection to the validity of a contract for the sale of goods, signed by the seller, that the seller cannot enforce the same contract against the buyer, because the buyer has never signed it. And Sir James Mansfield says: " All these cases, *Egerton* v. *Mathews*, *Saunderson* v. *Jackson*, and *Champion* v. *Plummer*, suppose a signature by the seller to be sufficient, and every one knows it is the daily practice of the court of Chancery to establish contracts signed by one person only; and yet a court of equity can no more dispense with the statute of frauds than a court of law can." With the exception of the dicta of Lord Redesdale and Sir T. Plumer, the stream of decisions in the courts of equity has uniformly flowed in favour of the construction we are putting upon the statute. The language of the act appears to me to admit of no other. Is not this an agreement that excludes the necessity of parol evidence to shew what is the subject-matter of the contract, who are the parties to it, and what the consideration moving from the plaintiff to the defendant? and is it not signed by " the party to be charged therewith?"

BOSANQUET, J.—I am of the same opinion, and I found that opinion upon the 4th section of the statute, contrasting it with the 17th. It is supposed that there has been a difference in the interpretation of the act in the courts of equity from that which has obtained in our courts. But, if it were necessary, there could be no difficulty in shewing that the construction which has been put upon the sections referred to, by the courts of common law, has received the sanction of by far the majority of the judges who have presided in equity. In the courts of law the decisions on the subject are uniformly one way: and even had there been as much fluctuation in them as there appears to have been in equity, resort must at last be had to the statute itself. The 4th section provides that " no action shall be brought whereby to charge any person upon any contract or sale of lands, tenements, or hereditaments, or any interest in or concerning them, unless the agreement upon which such action shall be brought, or some memorandum or note thereof, shall be in writing, and signed by the party to be charged therewith, or some other person thereunto by him lawfully authorized." The statute does not *avoid* the contract; but merely provides that no action shall be maintainable upon it unless the contract be established by a particular mode of proof. The language of the 17th section is much stronger; it absolutely avoids all contracts entered into in a manner different from that pointed out by the act—"No contract for the sale of any goods, wares, or merchandise, for the price of 10*l.* or upwards, shall be allowed to be good, except the buyer shall accept part of the goods so sold, and actually receive the same, or give something in earnest to bind the bargain, or in part payment, or that some note or memorandum in writing of the said bargain be made and signed by the *parties* to be charged by such contract, or their agents thereunto lawfully authorised." Even under this section it has been held that a signature by the vendee alone is sufficient, notwithstanding the word *parties*, in the plural, occurs therein, a circumstance that to me appears to be entitled to some weight. It is said there must be an agreement, and that agreement must be evidenced by signature. To this I accede. But I would ask, is not the memorandum in this case an agreement? It purports to be an agreement. It is written on the particulars of sale, which states who is the vendor and what the subject-matter of the sale, and the price: and the defendant by his signature testifies that such agreement exists. The next question is whether the agreement can be enforced by the party who has not signed it. The statute requires the agreement, or some memorandum or note thereof in writing, to be signed by *the party to be charged therewith.* Here, the defendant is the party to be charged, and the agreement is signed by him. I cannot think it was intended by the legislature to make it incumbent on the plaintiff to prove another paper signed by himself which may be in the hands of the other party. It is not necessary in any case of agreement that both should sign the same identical paper: two parts are commonly interchanged. Such is the case of an assignment inter partes, or of an agreement contained in a correspondence. In the common transactions of life it is often impossible for a party to prove his own letters: and it would be imposing a grievous burthen upon a plaintiff to compel him in all cases to produce an agreement actually signed by himself as well as by the party to be charged therewith. How are we to say in this case that there is not in the defendant's possession a paper containing the terms of the contract and bearing the plaintiff's signature? In *Knight* v. *Crockford*, 1 Esp. 189, an agreement in the handwriting of the party, beginning " I, A. B., agree to sell," though not signed by the vendor, was held sufficient to satisfy the statute (*b*). It is not necessary to observe upon the correspondence between the parties: though, if any difficulty had existed upon the other point, I must say I should have entertained a very strong opinion upon the effect of the letters.

Rule discharged.

1836.

LAYTHOARP
v.
BRYANT.

(*b*) Whether a note written in the third person, " Mr. T. proposes," &c., making an offer to purchase, and accepted, amounted to a contract in writing, signed, within the statute of frauds, was doubted by Lord Eldon in *Morison* v. *Tournour*, 18 Ves. 175. But, in a later case, *Propert* v. *Parker*, 1 Russ. & Mylne, 625, it was expressly held, that, if the defendant himself writes the agreement for the purchase of a leasehold house, and states his own name in the third person, as "Mr. A. B. has agreed;" this is a good contract within the statute, though he does not otherwise sign the agreement.

BEASLEY *v.* CLARKE.

TRESPASS quare clausum fregit. The defendant justified under a right of way over the locus in quo—in his second plea claiming the way as having been used for twenty years without interruption by the occupiers of his farm; and in the third plea (*a*) as having been used for forty years by the occupiers of the same farm, as of right and without interruption. To the second plea, the plaintiff replied, that, when the occupiers of the defendant's farm used the way, they used it with the leave or license, sufferance, or permission of the occupier of the plaintiff's closes; which leave and license the defendant traversed in his rejoinder. To the third plea the plaintiff replied, tra-

was used by stealth, or in the absence of the occupier of the close and without his knowledge, or that it was merely a precarious enjoyment by leave and license, or any other circumstances which negative that it was an user or enjoyment under a claim of right: the words of the 5th section, "not inconsistent with the simple fact of enjoyment," being referable to the fact of enjoyment as before stated in the act, viz. an enjoyment claimed and exercised "as of right."

(*a*) On the 2 & 3 Will. 4, c. 71, s. 2, by which it is enacted, "that no claim which may be lawfully made at the common law, by custom, prescription, or grant, to any way or other easement, or to any watercourse, or the use of any water, to be enjoyed or derived upon, over, or from any land or water of our lord the king, his heirs or successors, or being parcel of the duchy of Lancaster or of the duchy of Cornwall, or being the property of any ecclesiastical or lay person, or body corporate, when such way or other matter as herein last before mentioned shall have been actually enjoyed by any person claiming right thereto without interruption for the full pe-

riod of twenty years, shall be defeated or destroyed by shewing only that such way or other matter was first enjoyed at any time prior to such period of twenty years; but nevertheless such claim may be defeated in any other way by which the same is now liable to be defeated: and where such way or other matter as herein last before mentioned shall have been so enjoyed as aforesaid for the full period of forty years, the right thereto shall be deemed absolute and indefeasible, unless it shall appear that the same was enjoyed by some consent or agreement expressly given or made for that purpose by deed or writing."

versing that the occupiers of the defendant's farm had for
and during the full term of forty years and upwards, as of
right, had and used the way without interruption.

At the trial before Gaselee, J., at the last Summer Assizes at Lincoln, evidence was given on the part of the
defendant to shew that the way in question (along the side
of a public drain from the defendant's farm, called Lambert's, to the river Welland, a navigable stream,) had been
used by the occupiers of his farm for a period of fifty-five
years. For the plaintiff it was proved that the way had
always been called a trespass way, and that applications
had been made for leave to use the way within twenty
years: and a witness named Mary Meyer stated that her
late husband had occupied Rag Marsh farm (the plaintiff's
farm, in which the disputed way was situate), and that
about twenty-nine years since, she recollected one Emmett
(the then occupier of Lambert's farm) coming to pay her
husband an acknowledgment for the use of the way. On
the part of the defendant it was submitted, that this evidence, if admissible at all, was clearly not so under a general traverse of the user for forty years; but that the plaintiff should have replied that the way was used by leave
and license, pursuant to the 5th section of the 2 & 3 Will.
4, c. 71, which enacts, "that, if the other party intends
to rely on any proviso, exception, incapacity, disability,
contract, agreement, or other matter hereinbefore mentioned, or on any cause or matter of fact or of law not inconsistent with the simple fact of enjoyment, the same
shall be specially alleged and set forth in answer to the
allegation of the party claiming, and shall not be received
in evidence on any general traverse or denial of such allegation "—meaning that, where the way has been enjoyed
for forty years or upwards, the right shall be indefeasible
unless it appears to have been enjoyed under a license by
deed in writing; the object of the statute being to shut
out loose testimony like that of Mrs. Meyer in this case.

The learned judge, however, directed the jury to find for the plaintiff upon both the issues, if they believed the evidence of Mrs. Meyer. A verdict was accordingly taken for the plaintiff, damages one shilling.

Goulburn, Serjeant, in Michaelmas Term last, moved for a rule nisi for a new trial on the grounds of misdirection and that the verdict was against the weight of evidence.

Adams, Serjeant, and *Humfrey*, in Hilary Term, shewed cause.—The defendant claiming the way as of right, it was perfectly competent to the plaintiff, under a general traverse of such right, to shew its non-existence : the payment of an acknowledgment for the user of way was the strongest possible evidence of that. The finding for the plaintiff on the issue taken upon the second plea cannot be questioned ; and a finding for the defendant on the issue on the third plea would be a manifest inconsistency : it would in effect be deciding that, though the defendant had used the way by leave and license within *twenty* years, his enjoyment had been by *right* for *forty* years. In *Bright* v. *Walker*, 1 C. M. & R. 211, 4 Tyr. 502, it was held that one claiming a right of way must shew that he had enjoyed the way for the full period of twenty years, and that he had so enjoyed it *as of right and without interruption;* and that such claim might be answered by proof of a license, written or parol, for a limited period, comprising the whole or part of the twenty years. Parke, B., in delivering the judgment of the court, there says : " In order to establish a right of way, and to bring the case within this section, it must be proved that the claimant has enjoyed it for the full period of twenty years, and that he has done so ' as of right,' for that is the form in which, by s. 5, such a claim must be pleaded ; and the like evidence would have been required before the statute to prove a claim by prescription or non-

existing *grant.* Therefore, if the way shall appear to have
been enjoyed by the claimant, not openly and in the manner that a person rightfully entitled would have used it,
but by stealth as a trespasser would have done—if he shall
have occasionally asked the permission of the occupier of
the land—no title would be acquired, because it was not
enjoyed ' as of right.' " And in *The Monmouthshire Canal
Company* v. *Harford,* 1 C. M. & R. 614, 5 Tyr. 68, the
plea stated that the occupiers of the adjoining closes had
for twenty years, *as of right,* and without interruption,
used and been accustomed to use the privilege and easement of passing and repassing &c., and laying down rail-
roads across the plaintiff's rail-road. The replication traversed the claim *as of right.* Upon the issue with regard
to the twenty years' enjoyment of the easement, it was
held that the defendants were bound to shew an uninterrupted enjoyment *as of right* during that period; that the
plaintiffs might, under that issue, prove applications by
the defendants during the twenty years for leave to cross
their rail-road; and that it was not necessary for them
to reply such license specially under the 2 & 3 Will. 4,
c. 71, s. 5.

[*Crowder,* Amicus Curiæ, stated that the precise point
was at the present moment under discussion in the court of
King's Bench in a case of *Tickle* v. *Brown,* 6 N. & M. 230.]

Goulburn, Serjeant, and *Amos,* in support of the rule.—
The points of law said to be now under discussion in the
King's Bench, and mentioned arguendo in the court of
Exchequer in *The Monmouthshire Canal Company* v. *Harford,* as applicable to the facts of this case, were not submitted to the jury: the defendant is therefore entitled to
a new trial. The main object of the statute was, that,
where the way had been used openly and uninterruptedly
for forty years, the right of the party should not be de-

feated by parol evidence of loose conversations depending
upon the memory of old persons.   In *Bright* v. *Walker,*
the question arose upon the declaration; and there is no
similarity between the case there put by Mr. Baron Parke
and the present; for, here, the right of way was shewn to
have been exercised and asserted in the most open possible manner.   Leave from the occupiers of the plaintiff's
farm was clearly a matter of fact not inconsistent with the
simple fact of enjoyment of the way by the defendant and
those who preceded him in the occupation of the farm appendant to which the right of way was claimed, and therefore it should have been replied specially.

Cur. adv. vult.

TINDAL, C. J., delivered the judgment of the court:—
In this case, the defendant justifies the trespasses complained of in the declaration under a right of way over
the closes in which &c.   In his second plea, he claims the
way as having been used for twenty years without interruption by the occupiers of his farm; and, in the last
plea, as having been used for forty years by the occupiers
of the same farm as of right and without interruption.
To the second plea the plaintiff replies, " that, when the
occupiers of the defendant's farm used the way, they used
it with the leave or license, sufferance, or permission of
the occupiers of the plaintiff's closes;" which leave and
license is traversed by the defendant in his rejoinder.   To
the last plea the plaintiff replies by traversing that the occupiers of the defendant's farm have for and during the full
term of forty years and upwards as of right had and used
the way without interruption.   The jury found a verdict
for the plaintiff upon both these pleas; and the question
arises before us on a motion to set aside the verdict as well
upon the ground of misdirection as also that it is against
the weight of the evidence.   The misdirection complained
of is, that the learned judge, upon the issue joined on the

last plea, directed the jury to find a verdict for the plaintiff if they believed the evidence that a former occupier of the defendant's farm had applied for and obtained leave to use the way in question, and that he had paid an acknowledgment for such user. It being contended on the part of the defendant, that, if such evidence was admissible at all under the 5th section of the statute 2 & 3 Will. 4, c. 71, at all events it was not admissible under a traverse of the user for forty years, but that the plaintiff ought to have replied that the way was used by leave and license, as he had done to the plea which claims the way for twenty years. This objection on the part of the defendant rests on the 5th section of the act above referred to, by which it is enacted, " that, if the other party intends to rely on any cause or matter of fact or of law not inconsistent with the simple fact of enjoyment, the same shall be specially alleged and set forth in answer to the allegation of the party claiming, and shall not be received in evidence on any general traverse or denial of such allegation." The question, therefore, turns upon the construction and meaning of this clause—whether by the expression that any matter must be pleaded which is " not inconsistent with the simple fact of enjoyment," the legislature intended to compel the plaintiff to reply in all cases the special facts and circumstances which shew that the way was not used under a claim of right; or whether it only meant to compel the plaintiff to reply all collateral matters which may defeat the right of way. And, whatever might have been our opinion if the matter had been res integra, we think the interpretation which has been put upon this clause by the Court of King's Bench in the recent case of *Tickle* v. *Brown*, may be held to be the construction to be put upon the statute: and, according to that construction, we hold, that, under a replication denying that the defendant had used the way for forty years, as of right and without interruption, the plaintiff is at liberty to shew the character

and description of the user and enjoyment of the way during any part of the time; as, that it was used by stealth,
or in the absence of the occupier of the close and without
his knowledge, or that it was merely a precarious enjoyment by leave and license, or any other circumstances
which negative that it was an user or enjoyment under a
claim of right: the words of the fifth section, "not inconsistent with the simple fact of enjoyment," being referable,
as we understand the statute, to the fact of enjoyment as
before stated in the act, viz. an enjoyment claimed and
exercised "as of right." The case of *The Monmouthshire
Canal Company* v. *Harford*, 5 Tyr. 68, in the court of
Exchequer, is another authority for the same construction
of the act. We therefore think the evidence objected to
was admissible under the traverse of the last plea: and it
would certainly be extremely inconsistent if the defendant
should be allowed to insist upon a verdict in his favour for
the right of way when claimed by him as of right and without interruption for the last *forty* years, whilst upon the
same record the plaintiff should be entitled to retain the
verdict in his favour upon the issue raised on the second
plea, establishing the same way to have been used for the
last twenty years by the leave and license of the plaintiff.

Upon the other ground of objection, that the verdict is
against evidence, we can only observe there was evidence
on both sides for the consideration of the jury, and we
cannot so clearly see that it preponderated in favour of the
defendant as to induce us to disturb the verdict.

Rule discharged (b).

(b) See Wright v. Williams, 1 Meeson & Welsby, 77.

T. HOLLIS and CHARLOTTE, his Wife, Executrix of JOHN
DAVIES, deceased, *v.* PALMER.

Friday,
April 29th.

ASSUMPSIT on a promissory note. The declaration
stated that the defendant, theretofore and in the lifetime of
John Davies, to wit, on the 26th July, 1819, made his
promissory note in writing, and delivered the same to the
said John Davies, and thereby promised to pay to the
said John Davies, or his order, *on demand*, the sum of
127*l.*10*s.*8*d.*, for value received for goods, *with interest
on the same from the day of the date of the said promissory
note;* and the defendant then, in consideration of the
premises, promised the said John Davies in his lifetime
to pay him the amount of the said note according to the
tenor and effect thereof: yet the defendant had disre-
garded his promise, and had not paid the amount of the
said note and interest, or any part thereof, to the said
John Davies in his lifetime, or to the said T. Hollis and
Charlotte, his wife, executrix as aforesaid, or either of
them, since the death of the said John Davies, *except interest on the said note at the rate of 5l. per centum from
the day of the date of the said note up to a certain day
within six years next before the commencement of this
suit,* to wit, the 26th April, 1830, and which interest was
heretofore and within six years next before the commencement of this suit, to wit, on the said last mentioned
day, paid by the defendant to the said John Davies in his
lifetime, &c.

The defendant pleaded—first, that the said cause of
action in the declaration in that behalf mentioned did not
nor did any part thereof accrue at any time within six
years next before the commencement of the suit, in manner and form as the plaintiffs had above thereof complained against him: verification—secondly, that he did

To a declaration
on a promissory
note made in
1819 (about
sixteen years
before the com-
mencement of
the suit), pay-
able on demand,
with interest for
the same from
the day of the
date of the note
—averring that
defendant " did
not pay the
amount of the
note and in-
terest, or any
part thereof,
&c., except in-
terest on the
said note from
the day of the
date of the said
note up to a
certain day
within six years
next before the
commencement
of the suit"—
the defendant
pleaded that the
cause of action
did not nor did
any part there-
of accrue at any
time within six
years next be-
fore the com-
mencement of
the suit:—
Held, on special
demurrer, that
the plea was a
sufficient an-
swer to the ac-
tion; the alle-
gation as to the
payment of in-
terest being pre-
maturely intro-
duced into the
declaration, and
at most amounting to matter of evidence.

not pay the said interest in the declaration in that behalf
mentioned, or any part thereof, heretofore and within six
years next before the commencement of the suit to the
said John Davies in his lifetime, in manner and form as
the plaintiffs had above in that behalf alleged; concluding
to the country.

Demurrer to
first plea.

The plaintiff demurred specially to the first plea, assigning for causes—that the said first plea contained no
answer to the declaration, inasmuch as it admitted that
the defendant had within six years next before the commencement of the suit paid to the said John Davies interest on the said note at the rate of 5l. per centum from
the day of the date of the said note up to a certain day
within six years next before the commencement of the
suit—that the said first plea was argumentative, as it argu-
mentatively denied the payment of such interest within
six years next before the commencement of the suit—that
it ought for that reason to have concluded to the country,
and not with a verification—that the first plea, being entire and perfectly distinct and separate from the second
plea, must be good in itself, and could not be aided by
the denial of payment of such interest contained in the
second plea—and also that the said first plea was in other
respects informal and insufficient, &c.

The defendant joined in demurrer.

Argument for
plaintiff—that
payment of in-
terest within six
years takes the
case out of the
statute of limi-
tations, and that
such payment
of interest is ad-
mitted by the
first plea.

Peacock, in support of the demurrer.—It being admitted upon the face of the record that the promissory
note was payable with interest from the day of its date,
and that interest had been paid within six years before
the commencement of the action, the statute of limitations
does not operate upon the debt at all: and, if it does, still
interest is recoverable; the original debt subsists, though
the remedy for its recovery is barred, and the interest is
a continually accruing demand constituting a distinct debt;
like the case of a lien on goods, which still endures
notwithstanding the demand in respect of which the lien

arises may be barred by the statute of limitations—*Spears* v. *Hartly*, 3 Esp. 81. The case is different where there is no specific contract for the payment of interest: but here the interest forms a debt distinct and separate from the principal. [*Tindal*, C. J.—So that the maker of the note must go on paying interest for ever! The general notion is, that, when the principal ceases to be a debt, the accessory follows it. The case put of a lien is one to which the statute does not apply: what deduction can thence be drawn in arguing a case to which the statute *does* apply? The principle now contended for is perfectly new and unheard of.] In *Higgins* v. *Scott*, 2 B. & Ad. 413, it was held that the statute of limitations bars the remedy only, not the debt; and that therefore, where an attorney for a plaintiff had obtained judgment, and the defendant was afterwards discharged under the lords' act, but at a subsequent period a fi. fa. issued against his goods, upon which the sheriff levied the damages and costs, the attorney (though he had taken no step in the cause, or to recover the amount of his bill of costs, within six years) had still a lien on the judgment for his bill of costs; and the court directed the sheriff to pay him the amount out of the proceeds of the goods. A payment of interest by A. on a joint and several note of A. and B., is evidence of a promise by B., and takes the note out of the statute of limitations, though B. was a mere surety, and the payment was made without his knowledge—*Burleigh* v. *Stott*, 2 M. & R. 93, 8 B. & C. 36; *Pease* v. *Hirst*, 10 B. & C. 122; *Besly* v. *Greenslade*, 2 C. & J. 61. Here the note was payable on demand; and *Gascoigne* v. *Smith*, 1 M'Clel. & Y. 338, is an authority to shew that a note payable on demand, with interest until paid, is not to be considered as payable immediately. The statute of limitations, therefore, clearly is no bar to the action, as pleaded.

Stephen, Serjeant, contrà.—Where the principal debt is barred, the interest, which is merely an accessory, is

Interest is not
stated as the
cause of action,
and that, even
if it is consider-
ed to be as
stated, still the
plea is correct.

equally barred. Were this not so, there would be no
limitation whatever in a case of this description. The
payment of interest within six years is mere matter of evidence, whence the jury might infer a promise to pay so
as to take the case out of the statute. The plaintiff in
this form of declaring improperly and unnecessarily de-
parts from the accustomed course for the purpose of betraying the defendant into an admission of something that
may anticipate his defence, and which it would be difficult
to meet by plea. According to the rules of pleading, a
party is not bound to take notice of an allegation that is
prematurely introduced. This is fully established in *Sir
Ralph Bovey's* case, 1 Vent. 217, and *Harvey* v. *Sir G.
Reynold*, Latch. 200 (a).

Peacock, in reply.—Since the new rules it is usual to
give credit for payments, in order to supersede the necessity
of the defendant's pleading them. In *Barough* v. *White*,
6 D. & R. 379, 4 B. & C. 325, it was held that a note made
payable to the payee, " or order, with interest, on demand," cannot, in the hands of an innocent indorsee for
value, be treated as overdue at the time of indorsement,
without proof of actual presentment and dishonor. Here,
by the payment of interest within the six years, the defendant has treated the note as a continuing security.
Where interest is reserved on the face of the note, it constitutes a debt for which the party may be arrested.

TINDAL, C. J.—The objections in this case arise upon
the first plea, which is a plea of the statute of limitations
in the ordinary form, viz. that the cause of action in the
declaration mentioned did not, nor did any part thereof,
accrue at any time within six years next before the commencement of the suit, modo ac forma. The objections
to this plea are two—first, that, without reference to the
particular mode of stating the case in the declaration, the

(a) See Sir George Reynell's case, Cro. Jac. 657.

plea constitutes no bar; that an action may be maintained
for the interest, notwithstanding the principal debt is
barred by the statute. This branch of the argument proceeds upon the assumption that the contract to pay interest is severable from the contract as to the principal.
It is possible perhaps to suppose a case in which this
might be so: but, generally speaking, interest is always
treated as an accessory to the principal debt; and, where
the right to recover the latter is barred, the former falls
with it. I am therefore of opinion that this argument
ought not to prevail. The next ground of objection is,
that, shaped as the declaration is, the first plea is no bar
to the plaintiff's demand. The declaration does not state
the cause of action in a very usual mode: it states that
the defendant made his promissory note in writing, and
delivered the same to the testator, and thereby promised to
pay to him, or his order, on demand, the sum of 127l. 10s.
8d., with interest for the same from the day of the date thereof; and then alleges by way of breach that the defendant did not pay the amount of the said note and interest,
or any part thereof, except interest thereon from the day
of its date up to a certain day within six years next before
the commencement of the suit: all which is put in a very
vague and uncertain manner. The question is, whether
or not the plea affords an answer to the whole cause of
action: and this leads to another question, viz. what is the
cause of action? It is a debt arising out of a promissory
note. It therefore appears to me that the defendant has
in his first plea properly stated that the real cause of
action accrued more than six years before the commencement of the suit. What is the legal effect of payment of
interest? It is the same since the statute 9 Geo. 4, c. 14, as
before. The 1st section of that act contains a proviso "that
nothing therein contained shall alter or take away or lessen
the effect of any payment of any principal or interest made
by any person whatsoever." It is matter of evidence only,
and may shew that primâ facie there exists a cause of ac-

tion. I am satisfied, however, with the first answer: the claim for interest forms no part of the cause of action. I therefore think the defendant is entitled to judgment.

PARK, J.—The matter introduced by way of averment into the declaration may be very good evidence to take the case out of the statute: but the proviso in the 9 Geo. 4, c. 14, s. 1, shews that it is not conclusive evidence; for it speaks of the effect of the payment of interest. We cannot take notice of such payment by way of bar to a defence on the statute: it would be withdrawing the effect of the evidence from the consideration of the jury. I am of opinion that the plea is a good answer to the cause of action appearing upon the face of the declaration, and that it is not met by the averment therein.

VAUGHAN, J.—I am of the same opinion. We cannot treat the principal and the interest as constituting two distinct and substantive causes of action.

BOSANQUET, J.—The six years are to be reckoned from the time the cause of action accrued: the cause of action quoad the principal debt accrues on a demand being made; and the interest, being an accessory only, follows the principal. It is somewhat singular that no trace is to to be found, from the time of Queen Anne to the present hour, of an action having been brought for the recovery of interest on a debt like this barred primâ facie by the statute, and supported by evidence of the payment of interest within six years. If, notwithstanding the principal debt is barred, interest be recoverable in perpetuity, the payee's claim could only be put at rest by payment of the debt.—With regard to the supposed admission on the face of the declaration that interest has been paid within six years: the allegation, unanswered as it is by the plea, will not have that effect; it is only evidence of a subsequent renewed obligation to pay the note. The proviso in the 9 Geo. 4, c. 14, s. 1, goes no further than to say that nothing therein contained shall alter or take away or lessen the effect of any payment of principal or interest made by any person whatsoever:" not that it shall operate so as to set up the debt again. The allegation, at all events, was prematurely introduced in the declaration, and therefore the defendant was not bound to notice it in pleading.

1836.

HOLLIS
v.
PALMER.

Judgment for the defendant.

DOE d. ROGERS v. PULLEN.

*Wednesday,
May 4th.*

THIS was an action of ejectment to recover possession of certain premises situate in Newgate Market. The cause was tried before Park, J., at the sittings at Guildhall after last Trinity Term, when the following facts appeared in evidence:—One Fisher, the ground landlord of the premises in question, in April, 1829, granted a lease of them to the defendant for twenty-one years. In September, 1831, the defendant being indebted to Rogers, the lessor of the plaintiff, for money borrowed, assigned the lease to him by way of security, Rogers by indenture of the same date granting the defendant an underlease at a rent sufficient to cover the interest. An action of ejectment being afterwards brought by Fisher, for non-payment of rent, and for breach of the covenant to insure the premises, the parties, viz. Fisher, the defendant, and Rogers, met for the purpose of negotiation; and in the result it was verbally agreed that judgment for the plaintiff should be signed in the action of ejectment, and that a new lease of the premises should be granted by Fisher to Rogers, he paying the arrears of rent and the costs of the ejectment. Rogers having accordingly paid the money,

The defendant held premises under lease from one F., and assigned the same by way of mortgage to one R. The lease being forfeited, it was agreed between F., R., and the defendant that a new lease should be granted to R., and that R. should grant an underlease to the defendant. The lease from F. to R. was accordingly executed. The underlease from R. to the defendant was not prepared: but possession was given to the latter, to whom R. said on delivering him the key— "Go on as before; pay me the money as

fast as you can; and when you have paid it you shall have your underlease." No rent was ever paid under the tenancy thus created, though a quarter was demanded:—Held, that the defendant did not thereby become tenant from year to year; but a mere tenant by sufferance.

Fisher executed a lease of the premises to him. At the time of the execution of the last-mentioned lease, the 23rd July, 1834, the Key was delivered to Rogers, who immediately restored the possession to the defendant. No rent was ever paid by the defendant since that period; the first quarter being demanded and not paid, and the mortgage money also remaining unpaid, the lessor of the plaintiff gave him a week's notice to quit, and thereupon brought the present action of ejectment.

On the part of the defendant it was proved, that, at the time the parties met and agreed that a new lease of the premises should be granted to Rogers, it was also agreed (verbally) that Rogers should grant an underlease to the defendant; that this proposed underlease was never executed; but that, when the defendant was put into possession by Rogers, the latter said to him—" Go on as before: pay me the money as fast as you can; and when you have done so you shall have your underlease." It was also proved that the defendant had at the same meeting with the knowledge of Rogers entered into an agreement with one Clarke to underlet to him a portion of the premises for one year certain; and that, at a subsequent time, a person named Gunn having applied to Rogers to purchase his interest in the premises, the latter said, that, if he, Gunn, purchased it, he must engage to grant Pullen an underlease upon the terms on which he then held.

For the plaintiff, it was contended that the defendant was a trespasser, and therefore no regular notice to quit was necessary. On the other hand, it was insisted, that, although no underlease from Rogers to Pullen had ever been executed, nor any agreement in writing to grant such underlease, yet, the defendant having been let into possession upon an arrangement under which rent was payable, he thereby became tenant from year to year, and entitled to the usual notice to quit: and *Clayton* v. *Blakey*, 8 T. R. 3, was relied on. The learned judge told the jury he was of opinion that the conversation proved did not amount to an agreement for a tenancy from year to year, and therefore that the defendant was not entitled to the usual notice to quit. A verdict having accordingly been found for the lessor of the plaintiff—

Atcherley, Serjeant, in Michaelmas Term last, obtained a rule nisi for a new trial, on the grounds of misdirection, and that the verdict was against evidence.

Bompas, Serjeant, and *Erle*, shewed cause.—A mere demand of rent will not constitute a tenancy from year to year: in *Clayton* v. *Blakey*, and all the other cases wherein a party entering under an agreement for a future lease has been held to acquire such an interest, there has been a holding for more than a year, accompanied by the fact of actual payment of rent. In *Doe d. Hollingsworth* v. *Stennet*, 2 Esp. 717, it was ruled by Lord Kenyon, that, if a tenant whose lease is expired be permitted to continue in possession pending a treaty for a further lease, he is not a tenant from year to year, but so strictly a tenant at will that he may be turned out of possession without notice: but that it is otherwise if he has continued in possession for a year, or rent has been received. And in *Doe d. Moore* v. *Lawder*, 1 Stark. 308, where in an agreement for the sale of leasehold premises, to be paid for by instalments, it was stipulated that, in default of payment of the instalments at specified times, the former instalments should be forfeited, and the vendor should not be compellable to convey, upon which the purchaser was let into possession, and made default; it was held that he was from thenceforth a mere tenant upon sufferance. That an agreement for a lease will not per se raise a presumption of a tenancy from year to year, is clear from the cases of *Dunk* v. *Hunter*, 5 B. & A. 322, and *Regnart* v. *Porter*, 5 M. & P. 370, 7 Bing. 451. The agreement to grant the underlease was merely conditional, on payment of the money that had been advanced by the lessor of the plaintiff. As mortgagor in possession, the defendant was a mere occupant by sufferance—*Doe* d. *Price* v. *Price*, 2 M. & Scott, 464, 9 Bing. 356—and this being the state of things anterior to the grant of the new lease, the conversation deposed to by the defendant's witness must be taken to have reference thereto, and not to any intention to create a tenancy from year to year.

Atcherley, Serjeant, and *Barstow*, in support of the rule.—The question is whether the defendant, having received possession of the premises from Rogers upon an understanding that he was to go on *as before*, did not thereby become tenant from year to year, and entitled to the usual notice to quit: it must have been intended that he should go on at the same rent as was reserved by the first lease, not as a mere tenant at will. The relation of landlord and tenant, and not that of vendor and vendee, was in the contemplation of the parties. In *Roe* v. *Lees*, 2 W. Bl. 1173, De Grey, C. J., says—"All leases for uncertain terms are primâ facie leases at will; it is the reservation of an annual rent that turns them into leases from year to year." This is similar to the case of a tenant holding over after the expiration of his term, who becomes thereby tenant from year to year under the terms of the expired lease. Notwithstanding the first section of the statute of frauds, a parol lease for more than three years will create a tenancy from year to year; the intention of the statute being satisfied by its not operating as a term— *Clayton* v *Blakey*: the statute does not destroy the agreement altogether, it merely cuts down the legal interest. In *Doe* d. *Rigge* v. *Bell*, 5 T. R. 471, Lord Kenyon says: "Though the agreement be void by the statute of frauds as to the duration of the lease, it must regulate the terms on which the tenancy subsists in other respects, as to the rent, the time of the year when the tenant is to quit, &c. So, where a tenant holds over after the expiration of his term, without having entered into any new contract, he holds upon the former terms. Now, in this case, it was agreed that the defendant should quit at Candlemas; and, though the agreement is void as to the number of years for which the defendant was to hold, if the lessor choose to determine the tenancy before the expiration of the seven years, he can only put an end to it at Candlemas." A parol agreement to lease lands for four years creates a tenancy at will—*Goodtitle* d. *Galloway* v. *Herbert*, 4 T. R. 680. In *Stomfil* v. *Hicks*, 2 Salk. 413, 1 Ld. Raym. 280, it is said, that, "if A. demise lands to B. for a year, and so from year to year, this is not a lease for two years, and afterwards at will; but it is a lease for every particular year, and, after the year is begun, the defendant cannot determine the lease before the year is ended." Even if a mere tenant at will, the defendant was not liable to be turned out of possession without a regular notice of the determination of the will. The demand of a quarter's rent, however, is totally inconsistent with any other than a yearly holding. The sub-agreement entered into by the defendant with Clarke at the time possession was given to him of the premises, in the presence of Rogers, is strong evidence of the understanding of the parties that a tenancy from year to year (a relation which, as was observed by Lord Eldon in *Daniels* v. *Davison*, 16 Ves. 252, the law favours,) should be created.

TINDAL, C. J.—The question in this case is whether or not the defendant was clothed with the character and interest of a tenant from year to year of the premises. It appears from the evidence reported to us that there had existed a former lease of the premises, and an underlease under which the defendant had occupied; that the lease was forfeited and the defendant ejected; that the parties (the superior landlord, the defendant, and one Rogers, to whom the defendant had assigned his underlease as security for a loan,) met, when it was agreed that a new lease should be granted to Rogers for a term of fourteen years, and that Rogers should grant to the defendant an underlease co-extensive with his interest; that, in pursuance of this arrangement, the lease to Rogers was prepared and executed, and the key delivered to Rogers, who thereupon put the defendant into possession upon an understanding, that, upon his paying the money due to Rogers, he the defendant should have the proposed underlease; and that, after the defendant had occupied the premises for some time (short of a year), no rent having been paid, and the mortgage money remaining unpaid, Rogers gave him a week's notice to quit, and then brought this action of ejectment. Upon these facts, the question arises—whether the occupation by the defendant under this contract amounts to a tenancy from year to year. After the best consideration I am able to bring to the case, it appears to me that it does not. If Rogers had entered into an absolute and unqualified agreement to grant an underlease to the defendant, though such agreement would have been void by the statute of frauds for want of writing, still, according to *Clayton* v. *Blakey*, 8 T. R. 3, *Doe* d. *Rigge* v. *Bell*, 5 T. R. 471, and other cases, it would have been a good agreement for a tenancy from year to year. But the defendant was not let into possession upon any such agreement: no such intention is to be implied from the conversation between the parties. The very object of the arrangement—the compelling the defendant to repay the money—would be defeated by such a construction. I am clearly of opinion that there exists not the slightest ground for presuming an intention to create a tenancy from year to year. It is said that a lessee who holds over after the expiration of his term thereby acquires the interest of a tenant from year to year subject to the terms of the expired lease. Undoubtedly he does; for, in the absence of a new express agreement between the parties, no other terms could be implied. Expressum facit cessare tacitum : we have no right to imply anything contrary to the declared intention of the contracting parties. Suppose, instead of the defendant's being let into possession under this verbal agreement, the terms had been reduced into writing, the defendant might in a court of equity be held entitled to the lease on payment of the money due : but a court of law could not under such an agreement hold him to be tenant from year to year. There is a broad distinction between an executory agreement and one that is executed. The doctrine thrown out by the court in *Doe* d. *Jackson* v. *Ashburner*, 5 T. R. 163, is strictly as applicable to this case as to that. There, the intention of the parties, as evidenced by the agreement, was, to have a future lease : the case would have been the same had the party been let into possession under the agreement. I am of opinion that the facts of this case do not warrant an inference that a tenancy from year to year was contemplated; and therefore that the present action is well maintainable.

VAUGHAN, J.—I am of the same opinion. The question is whether under the circumstances the defendant was not tenant at will to Rogers, the lessor of the plaintiff, and might not after a demand of possession be treated as a trespasser. I am of opinion that he must be so considered. The agreement for the tenancy was made subject to a condition precedent, viz. the payment of the money due to Rogers. On the performance of this condition, the lessor of the plaintiff agreed verbally to grant an underlease to the defendant. The condition never was performed. It is difficult to distinguish this from the ordinary case of vendor and purchaser: the latter, being let into possession, and failing to complete the purchase, may be treated as a trespasser and turned out (a). Such was the case of *Doe* d. *Moore* v. *Lawder*, 1 Stark. 308. There, in an agreement for the sale of leasehold premises, to be paid for by instalments, it was stipulated that in default of payment of the instalments at specified times, the former instalments should be forfeited, and the vendor should not be compellable to convey; upon which the purchaser was let into possession, and made default: and it was held that he was from thenceforth a mere tenant upon sufferance. So, here, the defendant never having performed the condition upon which the proposed tenancy was made to depend, never became clothed with the character and rights of a tenant from year to year.

BOSANQUET, J.—The simple question is, what is the proper construction to be put upon the language used by the lessor of the plaintiff on putting the defendant into possession of the premises. The grant of an underlease to the latter is thereby made prospective and conditional on the payment of the mortgage money. It is perfectly clear that the defendant took no interest at law whatever: and it is equally consistent with law to suppose that the lessor of the plaintiff may have agreed to grant to the defendant an interest in the premises as tenant from year to year in the meantime. Is it a rational construction of the contract to suppose that it was intended that the defendant, though he did not pay the money, should take an interest in the premises for a whole year, or for two years provided the lessor of the plaintiff omitted to give him notice to quit at the end of the first six months of his occupation? It appears to me not. It is said that the words, "Go on as before," shew an intention on the part of Rogers that the defendant should continue to hold on the same terms upon which he had previously held; and that a reservation of rent constitutes a tenancy from year

(a) See Chapman v. Gatcombe, ante, Vol. 2, p. 738.

to year. But, taking the whole conversation together, it amounts to no more than a permission to occupy at the will of Rogers, until the defendant should have put himself into the position of having an equitable right to demand an underlease.

Park, J.—Having tried the cause, I was anxious to hear the opinions of my Lord and my learned Brothers before expressing mine. I entirely concur with them. I told the jury that the defendant was not under the circumstances entitled to a notice to quit as a tenant from year to year: and I do not hear any complaint of misdirection. No rent appeared to have been paid by the defendant; and on that circumstance the finding of the jury mainly turned.

Rule discharged.

Elizabeth Smith v. Margaret Kingsford.

INDEBITATUS assumpsit for work and labor, and for money due upon an account stated. Pleas—first, nonassumpsit, as to all but 2l. 2s.—secondly, as to the said sum of 2l. 2s., a tender of that sum; which was brought into court, and taken out by the plaintiff—thirdly, as to the sum of 1l. 1s., parcel &c., that, before and at the time of her dismissal and discharge thereinafter mentioned, the plaintiff was in the defendant's service in the capacity of a cook, at the yearly wages of 12l. 12s.; that theretofore, and during the first year of such service, and before such dismissal and discharge as aforesaid, to wit, on the 14th January, 1836, the plaintiff conducted

The plaintiff, a domestic servant, entered into the defendant's service on the 19th November. On the 15th January, her mistress caused her to be taken before a magistrate on a charge of stealing some small articles of plate: the magistrate remanded her till the 20th, when she was again brought up, and discharged. On the 22nd, the plaintiff went to demand her clothes and wages, including 1l. 1s. in lieu of a month's warning. The defendant tendered 2l. 2s. for the two months' actual service, but refused to pay the additional guinea:—Held, that, inasmuch as the placing the plaintiff in custody on a charge that was afterwards abandoned was no dissolution of the contract of hiring, the plaintiff was under the circumstances entitled to wages for the third month, which had been entered upon; and that the whole might be recovered under the common count for work and labour.

herself improperly as such domestic servant, in this, to
wit, that the plaintiff, without the defendant's knowledge
or consent, and against her will, wrongfully introduced
into the defendant's dwelling house, in which the plaintiff
was employed, two men and one woman whose names and
persons were unknown to the defendant, and harboured
and entertained such persons, and then wrongfully kept
and harboured the said persons during unreasonable
hours, to wit, from eight o'clock in the evening until
one o'clock the following morning, without the defendant's
knowledge or consent; and that, during the said time the
said persons were so in the said house, twenty-nine silver
tea-spoons, of the value of 10*l.*, of the defendant, were in
that part of the house where the said persons were, and it
was then the duty of the plaintiff to take due care of the
same and prevent the same from being lost or purloined;
yet the plaintiff, during the time the said persons were in
the said house as aforesaid, conducted herself so negligently and improperly, that, on the night aforesaid, six of
the said spoons were feloniously and unlawfully taken from
the said house, and were lost to the defendant, by reason
of such misconduct as aforesaid; and the plaintiff, during
the time of her being in such service, behaved and conducted herself in an improper and negligent manner:
wherefore the defendant, after the said loss of the said
spoons had been discovered, and before the expiration of
the first year of such service, and before such first year's
wages became due, dismissed and discharged the plaintiff
from such service as aforesaid: and the defendant further
said that the said sum of 1*l.* 1*s.* was and is a sum due from
the defendant to the plaintiff in respect of wages for a
portion of the said first year, and which accrued after such
dismissal and discharge, and not otherwise; and that the
plaintiff, from such dismissal, hath continued discharged
from the service of the defendant.

The plaintiff joined issue on the first and second pleas,

and to the last replied that the defendant of her own wrong, and without the cause by her in her said last plea alleged, dismissed and wholly discharged the plaintiff from her said service, and from the said dwelling-house.

At the trial before the under-sheriff of Middlesex, the following facts appeared in evidence:—The plaintiff entered into the service of the defendant on the 19th November, 1835, in the capacity of cook, at yearly wages of 12*l.* 12*s.* On the evening of the 14th January, 1836, without the knowledge of her mistress, the plaintiff, at her mistress's expense, entertained two men and a woman. On the following morning, six silver tea-spoons belonging to the defendant were missed, and, in consequence of what had occurred on the previous evening, the plaintiff was suspected of having stolen them or been accessory to the theft, and was taken before a magistrate, who remanded her for a further examination. After being detained in the house of correction for five days, the plaintiff was (on the 20th January) again brought up, and discharged. The plaintiff on the 22nd demanded of the defendant 2*l.* 2*s.* for two months' wages, and 1*l.* 1*s.* in lieu of a month's warning: the defendant tendered the 2*l.* 2*s.*, but refused to accede to the latter demand; whereupon the plaintiff brought this action. The plaintiff's clothes were taken away by her on the 22nd January.

On the part of the defendant it was contended that she was under the circumstances justified in dismissing the plaintiff without warning; and that the common count for work and labour was insufficient to cover the plaintiff's claim for the period during which no service had been performed—*Archard* v. *Horner*, 3 C. & P. 439, where it was ruled by Lord Tenterden, that, if the contract between master and servant be the usual one for a year, determinable at a month, the servant, if turned away improperly, cannot recover on a count stating the contract to have been for an entire year; and that he cannot, on the common count for wages, recover for any further period than that during which he had served.

A verdict having been found for the defendant on the issue on the second plea, and for the plaintiff on the first and third, damages 1l. 1s.—

C. Jones, on a former day in this term (pursuant to leave), obtained a rule nisi that the general verdict might be entered for the defendant, or that a new trial might be had.

Byles shewed cause.—It stands admitted upon the record that the plaintiff entered the defendant's service under a yearly hiring; and it appeared from the evidence that the service commenced on the 19th November, 1835, and was not finally interrupted until the 22nd January, 1836— for, the placing her in custody under a charge that was afterwards abandoned, was not a dissolution of the contract of hiring. Although, therefore, it is true, that, where the plaintiff claims a compensation for constructive work and labour only, the common count is inapplicable, but, there being no actual service, the declaration must be special: yet here, inasmuch as there has been an actual service for three or four days of the third month, the whole may be recovered under the common count. If it were otherwise, a servant who is absent for a short period on account of sickness, or having a holiday, would be disabled from recovering wages on the common count, by reason of this partial interruption of the actual service. In *Gandall* v. *Pontigny*, 1 Stark. 198, 4 Camp. 375, A., being employed by B. as a clerk at a salary of 200l. per annum, payable quarterly, was discharged in the middle of a quarter, and paid proportionably; and Lord Ellenborough held that he was entitled to recover his salary for the remainder of the quarter under the general count for work and labour. That case was recognized and acted upon by this court in

Collins v. *Price*, 2 M. & P. 233 (*a*). There, the plaintiff kept a day school at which the defendant's daughter was the only boarder. At the end of the first quarter, the plaintiff's charge for schooling was sent to the defendant and discharged. Four days after the commencement of the second quarter, the child was taken ill and sent home, and did not return to school again. It was held that the defendant was liable for the whole quarter, although there was no express contract for a quarter's notice previously to the removal of the child. And Park, J., commenting upon *Gandall* v. *Pontigny*, says: " It was contended for the defendant that the plaintiff was not entitled to recover on the general count for work and labour, since none had been performed subsequently to the period of the discharge, and that, up to that time, the plaintiff had been paid, and the case of *Hulle* v. *Heightman*, 2 East, 145, was cited, and it was urged that the plaintiff ought to have declared specially on the contract: but Lord Ellenborough said, ' If he has done work for any part of the quarter, it is done for the whole. This is an objection of a strict nature, and since no dissolution of the contract has been proved, the plaintiff is entitled to recover for the remainder of the quarter.' That appears to us to be expressly applicable to this case."

C. Jones, in support of his rule.—After the 15th January there was no service either actual or constructive: the placing the plaintiff in custody on a charge of stealing was the strongest possible mode of putting an end to the relation of mistress and servant. The cases cited on the other side suppose the absence of misconduct in the servant, and no reasonable ground of dismissal. [*Bosanquet*, J.—The finding of the jury in this case negatives the

(*a*) And see Beeston v. Collyer, 4 Bing. 309, 12 Moore, 552, 2 C. & P. 607.

1836.

SMITH
v.
KINGSFORD.

charge of misconduct: the dissolution of the contract must
be assented to by both parties.] The conduct of the
plaintiff sufficiently shews her assent to the determination
of the contract: she was discharged from custody on the
20th January, and did not return to the defendant's house
until the 22nd. *Archard* v. *Horner* is a distinct authority
to shew that the form of declaring adopted in this case is
improper.

TINDAL, C. J.—It appears to me that the mere causing
the plaintiff to be sent to prison upon a charge that was
subsequently abandoned, was not a dissolution of the contract of hiring. However little in degree the relation of
mistress and servant between these parties may have been,
still I think the plaintiff entitled to recover for the month.

PARK, J., concurred.

BOSANQUET, J.—I am also of opinion that the contract
in this case was not put an end to until the third month's
service had been entered upon. The sending the plaintiff
to prison was no more a putting an end to the contract
than locking her up in a room of the house would have
been.

Rule discharged (*b*).

(*b*) See Robinson v. Hindman,
3 Esp. 235; Spain v. Arnott, 2
Stark. 256; Sherman v. Bennett,
M. & M. 489; Atkin v. Acton, 4
C. & P. 208; Callo v. Brouncker,
4 C. & P. 518.

———

Friday,
April 29th.

After plaint in
in the county
court, the plain-
tiff (a female)

HOLLIS *v.* FREER and Others.

REPLEVIN.—The defendants prayed judgment of the
original writ issued in this behalf, because they said that

married; the defendant removed the plaint into this court by re. fa. lo., and then pleaded in abatement the plaintiff's marriage:—Held, that the plea was good.

the plaintiff before and at the time of the suing forth of the said original writ in this behalf was and still is married to one John Osborne then and yet her husband, who is still living: and this the defendants were ready to verify: they then proceeded to avow for rent arrear for two half-years under a demise at the yearly rent of 187*l.*

The plaintiff replied that the suit was commenced by plaint and without any writ, in the county court of the sheriff of Stafford, and that after the same was so commenced as aforesaid, and while it was pending in that court, the defendants, for the purpose of removing the same therefrom into this court, issued and prosecuted a certain writ of our lord the king, being the writ in the plea mentioned, called a recordari facias loquelam, to the tenor and effect following, that is say, "William the Fourth &c. to the sheriff of Staffordshire, greeting: We command you, that, in your full county, you cause the plaint to be recorded which is in the same county, without our writ, between Hannah Hollis and William Henry Freer, Francis Cooper, and Henry Hall, of the cattle, goods, and chattels of the said Hannah taken and unjustly detained as it is said," &c. &c.

General demurrer and joinder.

Addison, in support of the demurrer.—The replication is no answer to the plea, and entirely admits the defence therein contained: and the plea itself is unexceptionable—*Milner* v. *Milnes*, 3 T. R. 627. In *Morgan* v. *Painter*, 6 T. R. 265, it was held, that, if the plaintiff take husband after suing out the writ, and before the declaration, the defendant cannot give her coverture in evidence under the general issue, but, if he wishes to take advantage of that circumstance, he must plead it in abatement. Whether the marriage were before or after the commencement of the action is immaterial.

R. V. Richards, contrà.—The plaint was levied by the

1836.

HOLLIS
*.
FREER.

plaintiff in her maiden name; the re. fa. lo. was sued out, not by her, but by the defendants; and the plaintiff's marriage took place after the commencement of the suit in the county court, and before the removal of the plaint to this court by re. fa. lo. The consequence of this demurrer being allowed will be the forfeiture of the replevin bond; for, the suit cannot be continued. The general rule, as laid down in Bac. Abr. *Abatement* (G.), is, that, where the action has been properly commenced, the defendant cannot by a plea in abatement avail herself of her subsequent marriage to defeat the action. It is there said, that, "if an action be brought in an inferior court against a feme sole, and pending the suit she intermarry, and afterwards remove the cause by habeas corpus, and the plaintiff declare against her as a feme sole, she may plead coverture at the time of suing the habeas corpus, because the proceedings here are de novo, and the court takes no notice of what was precedent to the habeas corpus; but, upon motion on the return of the habeas corpus, the court will grant a procedendo; for, although this be a writ of right, yet, where it is to abate a rightful suit, the court may refuse it: and the plaintiff had bail below to this suit, which by this contrivance he is ousted of, and possibly by the same means of the debt." And in *Haddock* v. *Howard*, Barnes, 355, where the defendant, whilst a feme sole, was arrested in the Palace Court, and a day or two after the arrest married, and then removed the plaint by hab. corp. into this court, and pleaded her coverture in abatement; the court set aside the plea. Here, the situation of the plaintiff is altered by the removal of the plaint by the defendants: and the true question is, whether they can be permitted so to alter the situation of the plaintiff as to work a forfeiture of the bond. [*Tindal*, C. J.—Is it not a virtual compliance with the bond?] By the marriage of the plaintiff, the suit is abated: it must be commenced de novo.

PER CURIAM.—This case must be governed by *Morgan* v. *Painter*, where it was held, that, if the plaintiff take husband after suing out the writ and before declaration, the defendant cannot give her coverture in evidence under the general issue, but, if she wish to avail herself of it, must plead it in abatement. When the parties are in court by a writ of re. fa. lo., it is the same as a new cause of action: that writ is subject to all the modes of being abated that any other writ is subject to. It is said that the plaintiff is placed in such a situation by the re. fa. lo. as to work a forfeiture of the replevin bond, inasmuch as the suit cannot now be prosecuted in the county court with effect and without delay, according to the condition. That may be so: but, if it be, it is a consequence which follows from the legal effect of the re. fa. lo., and which we cannot help. The judgment must be for the defendants.

The rest of the court concurring—

Judgment for the defendants.

1836.

HOLLIS
v.
FREER.

GRAHAM *v.* BEAUMONT.

Friday, May 6th.

MARTIN, for the defendant, obtained a rule nisi for costs under the 43 Geo. 3, c. 46, s. 3, on the ground that the defendant had, without reasonable or probable cause, been arrested for 600*l.*, and the plaintiff had only recovered 550*l.* The defendant had paid 500*l.* into court.

Bompas, Serjeant, shewed cause.

The defendant, in person, in support of the rule, objected that the affidavit upon which cause was shewn had been sworn after the day upon which the rule was due.

BOSANQUET, J., referring to a note to the case of *Hoar*

In shewing cause against a rule, affidavits sworn after the day on which the rule is due may in general be used.

On a motion for costs under 43 Geo. 3, c. 46, s. 3, the amount of the verdict is not the criterion by which the discretion of the court is to be guided.

v. Hill, 1 Chit. Rep. 27, where it is said, that, " where no particular time is prescribed for filing the affidavits on which a party shews cause, they may be sworn and filed at any time before shewing cause, though after the day appointed by the rule;" and to *Tilley* v. *Henley,* 1 Chit. Rep. 136, where it was held that affidavits sworn before the time of shewing cause, although after the time mentioned in the rule nisi, may be read, unless by the terms of the rule it be required that they shall be filed by a particular day; and *Braine* v. *Hunt,* 2 Dowl. 391, where it was also held that affidavits on shewing cause are in time if sworn at any time before cause is shewn—the objection was overruled.

The defendant then proceeded to support his rule.— He contended that the amount of the verdict conclusively shewed that the arrest for 600*l.* was an arrest without reasonable and probable cause.

TINDAL, C. J.—The statute 43 Geo. 3, c. 46, s. 3, was not intended to apply to a case where the plaintiff might reasonably be supposed to believe he should be able to establish at the trial that his debtor owes him the sum for which he arrests him. It must not be a mere measuring cast. Neither do I agree that it is by the verdict of the jury that our discretion is to be guided, although some of the cases seem to have gone almost that length (*a*).

The rest of the court concurring—

Rule discharged.

(*a*) See Summers v. Grosvenor, 2 C. & M. 341, 4 Tyr. 222, 2 Dowl. 224; Mantell v. Southall, ante, Vol, 2, p. 132, 2 New Cases, 74; Tipton v. Gardiner, 5 N. & M. 424; Shotwell v. Barlow, 3 Dowl. 709; Smith v. Smith, 2 Dowl. 733; Twiss v. Osborne, 4 Dowl. 107; Nicholas v. Hayter, 4 N. & M. 882, 2 Ad. & E. 348.

1836.

HYDE and Another *v.* JOHNSON.

Monday,
May 9th.

THIS was an action of assumpsit for goods sold and delivered, to which the defendant pleaded non assumpsit and the statute of limitations. At the trial before the undersheriff for the county of Middlesex, the plaintiff, in order to take the case out of the statute, tendered in evidence a letter written by the defendant's wife, at the defendant's request, to the plaintiff, containing an offer to pay the debt by instalments; which letter was transmitted to the plaintiff by the defendant, who it appeared could not write. On the part of the defendant it was objected that this letter was not receivable, the statute 9 Geo. 4, c. 14, s. 1, requiring the writing that is to have the effect of reviving the debt to be signed " *by the party chargeable thereby,*" the signature by the wife, though at her husband's request, was not sufficient to charge him. The evidence, however, was admitted, subject to a motion to enter a nonsuit should this court be of opinion that the letter ought not to have been received.

The written acknowledgment required by the 9 Geo. 4, c. 14, s. 1, to take a case out of the statute of limitations, must bear the actual signature of the party to be charged thereby: the signature of an agent will not suffice.

Chilton, accordingly, in the last term, obtained a rule nisi.—The intention of the 9 Geo. 4, c. 14, s. 1, was, to a certain extent to engraft upon the statute of limitations the provision contained in the statute of frauds 29 Car. 2, c. 3, s. 4, which provides that no action shall be brought whereby to charge the defendant upon any special promise to answer for the debt, default, or miscarriage of another person, unless the agreement upon which such action shall be brought, or some memorandum or note thereof, shall be in writing, and signed by the party to be charged therewith, or *some other person thereunto by him lawfully authorised :* the 9 Geo. 4, c. 14, s. 1, repudiating these latter words. If a memorandum signed by an agent were held to be sufficient to charge a defendant under the last mentioned act, all the mischief would arise that the statute was intended to prevent. That this is the true construction of the act, is clear from the authorities. Thus, in *Willis* v. *Newnham*, 3 Y. & J. 518, it was held that, verbal acknowledgment of the payment of part of a debt within six years is not sufficient within the statute 9 Geo. 4, c. 14, to take the case out of the statute of limitations. Garrow, B., in delivering the judgment of the court, there said : " In the course of the argument the case of an account current was put, in which the party charges himself, and takes credit for payments made by him; and it was said, shall not this be evidence to take the case out of the statute of limitations ? I answer no, because the act says the defendant shall not be charged except by an acknowledgment in writing *signed by him*. It must be a writing with the solemnity of a signature, and nothing short of that can bind the party." In *Whippy* v. *Hillary*, 3 B. & Adol. 399, in order to take the case out of the statute, the plaintiff produced in evidence a letter signed by the defendant, wherein he stated that family arrangements had been making to enable him to discharge the debt; that funds had been appointed for that purpose, of which A. was trustee; and that he (the defendant) had handed the plaintiff's account to A.; that some time must elapse before payment, but that the defendant was authorized by A. to refer the plaintiff to him for further information : and it was held that this letter did not prevent the operation of the statute—the act requiring the writing to be signed by the party whom the instrument itself makes chargeable. " The words of the act", says Lord Tenterden, " are, ' unless such acknowledgment or promise shall be made or contained by or in some writing to be signed by the party *chargeable thereby*.' The defendant himself must be chargeable by the instrument relied upon to bar the statute." *Gibson* v. *Baghott*, 5 C. & P. 211, is precisely in point. There, the defendant had written a letter to T. to make a proposition to the plaintiff respecting a debt he owed him; and in this latter he desired T. to arrange with the whole of his creditors. T. wrote a letter to the plaintiff, offering an acceptance for 7*s.* 6*d.* in the pound on the debt; and it was held to be insufficient to take the case out of the statute of limitations: Parke, J., observing—" There is nothing *signed by the defendant* which acknowledges any debt due to the plaintiff."

Byles shewed cause.—A written acknowledgment signed by an agent is sufficient to charge the principal within the 9 Geo. 4, c. 14, s. 1. Before the passing of that act, a verbal acknowlededement by a wife who had been accustomed to act as the agent of her husband in purchasing goods and managing his business generally was sufficient—*Anderson v. Sanderson,* 2 Stark. 204, Holt, 591. But for the omission (probably accidental) of the words " or some other person thereunto by him lawfully authorized," which are found in the 4th (and to the same effect) other sections of the 29 Car. 2, c. 3, no doubt could have arisen: and the mere omission of those words will not be permitted so to vary the construction of the statute as to evade and destroy the principal object the legislature had in view, viz. to substitute written evidence of the promise for the uncertain oral testimony which before sufficed to take a case out of the statute of limitations. The authority of an agent to bind the party may as reasonably be implied from the words used as that of his executors or administrators. If this question arose upon the record, that is, if the plaintiff, as he might well have done, had replied specially an acknowledgment or promise signed by the defendant within six years, and issue had been taken on the fact of the signature by the defendant, it is perfectly clear that the evidence tendered upon this occasion would have sustained that issue—*Helmsley* v. *Loader,* 2 Camp. 450; *Heys* v. *Heseltine,* 2 Camp. 604. With regard to part payments, the 9 Geo. 4, c. 14, has left the authority of agents precisely where it was before. The same 1st section of the act contains a proviso, that, "where there shall be two or more joint contractors, or executors or administrators of any contractor, no such joint contractor, executor, or administrator, shall lose the benefit of the said enactments or either of them, so as to be chargeable in respect or by reason only of any written acknowledgment or promise made and signed by any other or others of them." (a) This enactment would be superfluous and unnecessary if the prior clauses are to be construed to take away the authority of agents. Where two statutes are made in pari materiâ, they are to receive the same construction, notwithstanding there be some slight variation in the language employed in them—per Abbott, C. J., in delivering the judgment of the court of King's Bench in *Gale* v. *Laurie*, 5 B. & C. 163. The statute of frauds and the act now under discussion are in pari materiâ: the 9 Geo. 4, c. 14, like the 29 Car. 2, c. 3, was intended to take away the temptation to perjury, by substituting the certain evidence of a writing signed by the party (a signature by an authorized agent would have precisely the same effect), instead of the insecure and precarious testimony to be derived from the memory of witnesses. It would be extraordinary to hold that an acknowledgment by an agent will not satisfy the statute, seeing that an agent may draw, accept, or indorse bills, or sign bonds, so as to bind his principal: the consequence of such a doctrine will be that an account made out by a merchant's or a banker's clerk in his principal's name will not enure to prevent the operation of the statute of limitations as against the latter. In *Smith* v. *Forty*, 4 C. & P. 126, an administratrix sued for a debt due to the intestate. It appeared that the debt accrued more than six years before the commencement of

(a) See Martin v. Bridges, 3 C. & P. 83.

the action, but that within six years the defendant and
the agent of the administratrix went through the account together and' struck a balance, which the defendant promised to pay as soon as he could: and it was
ruled that the administratrix was entitled to recover on
a count upon an account stated with her, and that the
statute of limitations was no bar. Vaughan, J., there
says: "I think the plaintiff has shewn a good cause of
action on the count upon an account stated with the administratrix. The plaintiff does not go upon the original
debt at all. I take the statute 9 Geo. 4, c. 14, to apply to
cases where you go for the original debt, and then give
some evidence of an acknowledgment to rebut the presumption raised by the statute of limitations that the debt
has been satisfied in the course of six years since it occurred." It would not be difficult to suggest cases where
an absolute physical impossibility in the party himself to
make any kind of signature might exist. It is true that
mention is made of a signature by an agent in the 7th section of the 9 Geo. 4, c. 14, where the 17th section of the
statute of frauds is recited: and the only reason that can
be suggested for the absence of the word from the clause
now under consideration is that a more concise mode of
expressing the same thing had come into use, and it was
considered that the act of the agent was the act of the
principal. No greater inconvenience could in this case
result from the reception of the evidence tendered than
from admitting *oral* testimony of a *written promise* signed
by the party, as was done in *Haydon* v. *Williams*, 4 M. &
P. 811, 7 Bing. 163. And, in *Whippy* v. *Hillary*, the endeavour was, as was observed by Parke, J., "to raise a
promise on the letter produced, contrary to what the instrument itself implied." If, however, the statute imperatively requires the signature of the party, and of him only,
the evidence in this case established a sufficient signature
by the defendant; the letter was written by his wife, by

whom the business of the house was conducted, and was delivered by the defendant himself to the carrier who conveyed it to the plaintiff: this, by analogy to the sealing of a deed, renders the acknowledgment the act of the party himself. In 2 Bl. Com. 307, it is said—" If another person seals the deed, yet, if the party delivers it himself, he thereby adopts the sealing (Perkins, s. 130), and, by a parity of reason, the signing also, and makes them both his own."

F. Kelly and *Chilton*, in support of the rule.—The only question here is, whether or not there has been, within the words and meaning of the statute 9 Geo. 4, c. 14, s. 1, an acknowledgment or promise "made or contained by or in some writing *signed by the party chargeable thereby.*" *Whippy* v. *Hillary* and *Gibson* v. *Baghott* are decisive authorities to shew that nothing short of an actual signature by the party himself will suffice. *Haydon* v. *Williams* has no bearing whatever on this case. There, the letter containing the promise being lost, secondary evidence of its contents was admitted. In the present case, the plaintiff is compelled to resort to oral testimony to shew an adoption of the act of his supposed agent by the delivery of the letter in question to the carrier for the purpose of its being forwarded to the plaintiff. The passage cited from Blackstone is equally inapplicable: delivery is essential to the validity of a deed, and that cannot be matter of admission. A bill of exchange or a bond, no doubt, may be signed by an agent having competent authority—for the former purpose a parol authority will suffice, for the latter the authority must be under seal. But here the court is called upon to give effect to the words of an act of parliament the language of which is perfectly plain and unambiguous. To hold that oral testimony may be given of the authority of an agent to charge the party by a written promise, would at once be letting in all the mis-

chief the statute designed to exclude. The statute requires two things, an acknowledgment in writing, and a
signature by the party to be charged thereby. The occurrence of the word "agent" in the 7th section affords a
strong argument in favour of the exclusion of this document : it shews that the framer of the act had the statute
of frauds in this view at the time, and advisedly made a
distinction between the language of that statute and of
the one now under discussion. Any mark intimating the
assent of the party would be a sufficient signature to bind
him : and it is morally impossible to conceive a case of
such absolute physical deprivation as would render a man
possessed of his reason wholly incapable of signing an instrument. The 6th section of the statute, which came
under the consideration of the court of Exchequer in the
case of *Lyde* v. *Barnard*, 3 C. M. & R. 101, enacts "that
no action shall be brought to charge any person upon or
by reason of any representation or assurance made or
given concerning or relating to the conduct, credit, ability,
trade, or dealings of any other person, to the intent or
purpose that such other person may obtain credit, money,
or goods upon [money or goods upon credit?], unless
such representation or assurance be made in writing,
signed *by the party to be charged therewith*." Gurney, B.,
thereupon observes : " By this clause the protection is
carried even further than by the statute of frauds. There,
the party might be charged on a writing signed by a person thereunto by the defendant lawfully authorized, which
left him exposed to be charged by the verbal representation of another that he had authority to sign." And Lord
Abinger, taking a general view of the act (9 Geo. 4, c. 14),
says : " The obvious policy of this statute was to prevent
that fraud and perjury which had been found by experience, or was thought probable, to arise from trusting to
evidence of less authority than that of a written document
for fixing upon a defendant the responsibility for the debt

default, or miscarriage for which another person was primarily liable."

                                        Cur. adv. vult.

TINDAL, C. J., now delivered the judgment of the
court:—

The short question in this case is, whether a letter
offering to pay a debt by instalments, written by the defendant's wife to the plaintiff, in her husband's name, and
at his request, and afterwards sent by him to the plaintiff,
is a sufficient acknowledgment or promise " made or contained by or in some writing signed by the party chargeable thereby," within the meaning of the 9 Geo. 4, c. 14,
s. 1. The question turns entirely on the construction of
the statute, and it amounts in other words to this—does
the statute 9 Geo. 4, c. 14, extend to a writing signed by
an agent of the party, or is it confined to a writing signed
by the party himself? Looking at the words of the statute, it is confined in terms to a writing " signed by the
party chargeable thereby:" and, as the effect of that statute is, for the first time, to introduce a legislative exception into the statute 21 Jac. 1, c. 16, and thereby pro tanto
to repeal it, we do not feel ourselves justified in extending
such exception beyond the plain and unambiguous meaning of the words employed therein. The legislature has,
in many statutes, given equal efficacy to written instruments when signed by the parties and when signed by
their agents: but, in all those cases, express words have
been employed for that purpose. The statute of frauds,
in its 3rd section, requires for the purposes of that section
a note in writing to be signed by the parties " or their
agents thereunto lawfully authorised *by writing*:" in the
4th section, a memorandum or note in writing is required,
" signed by the party to be charged therewith, or some
other person thereunto by him lawfully authorised:" in
the 5th section, a devise of lands is required to be made

in writing, to be "signed by the party so devising, or by some other person in his presence and by his express directions:" in the 7th section, a declaration of trusts of any lands shall be in writing, "signed by the party:" and, lastly, the 17th section requires, upon the sale of goods, that there shall be some note or memorandum in writing of the bargain, "signed by the parties to be charged by such contract, or their agents thereunto lawfully authorized." It appears, therefore, that the legislature well knew how to express the distinction, not only between a signature by the party and a signature by his agent; but also to describe the different modes by which agents for different purposes are to be appointed. The same observation arises upon referring to the more recent statutes, 3 & 4 Will. 4, c. 27, s. 42, and c. 42, s. 5. When, therefore, we find in the statute now under consideration that it expressly mentions the signature by the party only, we think it a safer construction to adhere to the precise words of the statute, and that we should be legislating, not interpreting, if we extended its operation to writings signed, not by the party chargeable thereby, but by his agent. And we feel ourselves the more compelled to adopt this construction as we find the 7th section of this same statute recites the 17th section of the statute of frauds; so that the legislature must have had in their view, at the very time of passing this statute, and therefore must have intended, the distinction between writings signed by a party or signed by his agent.

Some inconveniences have in the course of the argument been pressed upon our attention, in cases where a total inability of parties to sign may exist: but the nature of the signature which is necessary to comply with the requisites of the statute, is such as to render it almost impossible to suppose a case in which a party could not make such a signature as would satisfy the statute: and, after all, in construing a statute, we must not look to cases of

1836.

HYDE
v.
JOHNSON.

very rare and singular occurrence, but to those of every day's experience; and, whatever may be the consequence, we must interpret the statute according to the plain import of the language employed in it.

Upon the whole, we think in this case the letter was not a sufficient writing, *signed by the party*, to take the case out of the operation of the enactments of the 21 Jac. 1, c. 16, and therefore direct a nonsuit to be entered.

Rule absolute accordingly.

———◆———

HEWISON and Another, Assignees of GEORGE MICKLE, a Bankrupt, and JOHN MICKLE, v. GUTHRIE.

THIS was an action of trover. The declaration stated, that, after the bankruptcy of George Mickle, to wit, on the 23rd January, 1835, Lawrence Hewison and Charles Smith as assignees of George Mickle, and the plaintiff John Mickle, were lawfully possessed as of the property of them the said Lawrence Hewison and Charles Smith, as such assignees as aforesaid, and the said John Mickle, of a certain policy of insurance whereby Chalmers & Guthrie, agents, as well in their own name as for and in the name and names of all and every other person or persons to

then set up a balance due to him *at the time of the demand and refusal.* The plaintiffs replied that the sum for which the lien was claimed was the price of certain canvass which the defendant had sold to the bankrupt at a credit of twelve months, and which credit had not expired at the time of the conversion; and further, that the defendant had drawn a bill of exchange at twelve months upon the bankrupt, which bill was accepted by him, and was received by the defendant on account of the price of the canvass, *before the time of the conversion.* To this replication the defendant demurred:—Held, that it was not competent to the defendant under this plea to set up a right to retain the property in question for a balance due to him on mutual credit between himself and the bankrupt; and that, even if it were, it did not sufficiently appear upon the record that the mutual credits, upon the result of which the balance was claimed, were given *before the bankruptcy,* so as to make the balance claimed *a balance due at the time of the bankruptcy.*

If a security is taken for a debt for which the party has a lien upon property of the debtor, such security being payable at a distant day, the lien is gone.

whom the same did, might, or should appertain, &c., did make assurance, &c., upon the ship Diadem; and, being so possessed thereof, the plaintiffs afterwards, to wit, on the same day, casually lost the said policy of insurance out of their possession &c. &c., alleging a finding and conversion by the defendant, in the common form.

The defendant pleaded that he, before and at the time when the said George Mickle became bankrupt, and from thence until and at the time of the said supposed conversion in the declaration mentioned, carried on and still carries on the trade and business of a merchant and insurance agent in the city of London, under the style and firm of Guthrie & Chalmers, and that there is an antient and laudable usage and custom of merchants in the said city of London for all insurance agents who shall effect policies of insurance on behalf of others to have a general lien upon such policies of insurance in their possession for their general balance; that, previous to and at the time when the said policy of insurance in the said declaration mentioned was effected by the defendant as thereinafter mentioned, and before and until the said George Mickle became bankrupt, the defendant was accustomed to deal with the said George Mickle on his the said G. Mickle's own and separate account, and not with the said George Mickle and the said plaintiff John Mickle jointly; and that mutual accounts, before and at the time of the said policy of insurance being effected by the defendant for and on account of the said G. Mickle as thereinafter mentioned, existed between the defendant and G. Mickle only, and not between the defendant and the said G. Mickle and the plaintiff John Mickle jointly; that, whilst such mutual dealings and accounts as aforesaid existed between him and the said G. Mickle, and before the said G. Mickle became bankrupt, to wit, on the 22nd April, 1833, the said G. Mickle solely and on his own separate account, and not jointly with the said plaintiff John

Mickle, gave an order to the defendant to effect the said policy of insurance in the declaration mentioned for him the said G. Mickle, and on his account, and without any notice that the plaintiff John Mickle had any concern or interest whatsoever in the said policy of insurance, and the said John Mickle concealed from the defendant that any other person had any concern or interest in the said insurance: and the defendant further said, that he, having so received such order as aforesaid, afterwards, to wit, on the 14th May, 1833, effected the said policy of insurance on the credit and account of the said G. Mickle alone, and not for the said G. Mickle and the plaintiff John Mickle jointly, and without any notice or knowledge that the plaintiff John Mickle was in any manner concerned or interested in the said policy; that, from the time of the said policy of insurance being effected, hitherto, the said policy of insurance had constantly remained in the possession of the defendant; and that, at the time of the request and refusal to deliver the said policy, and the said supposed conversion in the declaration mentioned, the said G. Mickle was indebted to the defendant, on the general balance of accounts between them, in a large amount, to wit, the sum of 201l. 11s. 9d.; that, by the said usage and custom of merchants, the defendant had a lien to the extent of the said debt upon the said policy in the declaration mentioned, and was entitled to retain the same until such lien as aforesaid was satisfied; that, at the time the said policy was so converted as in the declaration mentioned, the defendant gave notice to plaintiffs of his said lien, and refused to deliver the same to the plaintiffs until the same was satisfied, as he lawfully might for the cause aforesaid; yet the plaintiffs wholly refused to pay or satisfy the said lien; whereupon the defendant refused to deliver to the plaintiffs the said policy as in the said declaration was mentioned, which was the said supposed conversion in the said declaration mentioned—verification.

The plaintiffs replied, that the said sum of 201*l.* 11*s.* 9*d.*
in the plea mentioned, was and is the price and value of
certain canvass before then sold and delivered by the defendant to the said G. Mickle at his request, and that the
said canvass was sold and delivered by the defendant to
the said G. Mickle upon a credit of twelve months from
the time of such sale and delivery, and which credit had
not expired at the time of the said conversion; that, at
the time of the said sale and delivery of the said canvass,
to wit, on the 31st January, 1834, the said defendant, for
and on account of the price of the said canvass, made and
drew a certain bill of exchange in writing upon the said
G. Mickle, whereby the defendant requested the said G.
Mickle to pay to him or his order the sum of 204*l.* 10*s.* 6*d.*,
being the price of the said canvass, twelve months after
the date thereof, which period had not elapsed at the
time of the said conversion in the declaration mentioned,
or at the time of the commencement of this suit; which
said bill of exchange the said G. Mickle, before his
bankruptcy, and before the said conversion, to wit, on the
said last-mentioned day, accepted and delivered to the defendant for and on account of the said canvass, and which
the defendant then received and accepted of and from the
said G. Mickle for and on account of the price of the said
canvass—verification.

Demurrer and joinder.

Sir *W. Follett*, in support of the demurrer.—The defendant is entitled to retain the policy in question until
his lien is satisfied: had there been no bankruptcy, his
right would have been indisputable; the fact of the bankruptcy having taken place cannot alter his position. On
the part of the plaintiff the contention will be, that the
debt in respect of which the lien is claimed being for goods
sold and delivered, it is not such a debt as will give the
defendant a right of lien; and, further, that, a bill, which

had not arrived at maturity at the time the policy was demanded, having been given for the debt, there was no existing debt upon which to found the lien. Until the
passing of the 46 Geo. 3, c. 135, the principal statute relating to bankrupts was the 5 Geo. 2, c. 30, the 28th section of which enacts, " that, where it shall appear to the
commissioners, or the major part of them, that there hath
been mutual credit given by the bankrupt and any other
person, or mutual debts between the bankrupt and any other
person, at any time before such person became bankrupt,
the said commissioners, or the major part of them, or the
assignees of such bankrupt's estate, shall state the account
between them, and one debt may be set against another;
and what shall appear to be due on either side on the
balance of such account, and on setting such debts against
one another, and no more, shall be claimed or paid on
either side respectively." In *Ex parte Deeze*, 1 Atk. 228,
the facts of which case very nearly resembled those of
the present, and which is a leading decision on this subject, it was held that a packer may retain goods till he is
paid the price of packing; and that, if he has another debt
due to him from the same person, the goods shall not be
taken from him till he has paid the whole, notwithstanding the debtor is become a bankrupt. And Lord Hardwicke said that the clause in the act of parliament of the
5 Geo. 2, relating to mutual credit, had received a very
liberal construction; and that there had been many cases
in which that clause had been extended to where an action
of account would not lie, nor could the court of Chancery
upon a bill decree an account. And in *Ex parte Ockenden*, 1 Atk. 235, the same learned judge observes: "The
clause in the act of the 5 Geo. 2, relating to mutual credit,
has been carried, to be sure, further, and rightfully, than
a mere matter of account, but I do not know that a court
of equity has gone further than the courts of law in the
cases of a set-off." *Ex parte Deeze* was cited and acted

upon in *French* v. *Fenn*, Cook's B. L. 536, Eden's B. L.
(2nd edit.) 191, and in *Atkinson* v. *Elliott*, 7 T. R. 378.
In *French* v. *Fenn*, three persons joined in an adventure
to buy and sell pearls; one was to advance the money and
to sell the pearls, but the profit and loss were to be divided between the three. One of the parties becoming
bankrupt, the party who was to sell the pearls was allowed
to set off a debt due to him by the bankrupt against the
third share of the pearls belonging to the bankrupt,
although the pearls were not sold nor the produce
received before the bankruptcy. The court observed
that the act of parliament was accurately drawn to
avoid the injustice that would be done if the words were
"mutual debts," and it therefore provides for *mutual
credits;* and that, where there is a *trust* between two men
on each side, that makes a mutual credit. Here is a
mutual *trust* between the parties. In *Atkin on* v. *Elliott*,
A. first purchased one and afterwards another parcel of
goods of B., each at six months' credit; when the first
sum became due, A. lodged in B.'s hands a bill of exchange for a larger amount than the value of the goods
in order to pay for them, B. engaging to return to A. the
overplus when the bill should be paid: B. received the
amount of the bill, and then A. became a bankrupt, not
having paid for the second parcel of goods: in an action
brought by A.'s assignees for the surplus of the bill, it
was held that B. might retain it to satisfy his demand on
A. for the second parcel of goods. "The statute 5 Geo.
2, c. 30, s. 28," said Lord Kenyon, "enacts that where
there are either *mutual credit or mutual debts* between the
bankrupt and any other person, one debt may be set off
against another, and only the balance claimed. Now,
in using those words, the legislature must have intended
something more than would have been expressed by
' mutual debts' only; and the decisions referred to [*Ex
parte Prescott*, 1 Atk. 230, *French* v. *Fenn*, and *Smith* v.

Hodgson, 2 T. R. 411], shew that this construction has been put upon this act." [*Tindal*, C. J.—You are arguing this as a question of set-off. *Bosanquet*, J.—If Mickle had not been bankrupt, and the bill not due, do you contend that it would not have been competent to him to withdraw the policy?] It is not necessary on the present occasion to discuss that : the point for which the defendant is contending arising out of the bankrupt act and out of the circumstance of the action being brought by the assignees. In *Olive* v. *Smith*, 5 Taunt. 56, it was held, that, if a person entrusted with value trusts his creditor with that which may become productive of value, the first becoming bankrupt, the second may retain his debt out of the proceeds of the thing intrusted to him, and only pay the balance. Gibbs, J., in that case, observed, "that, in *Parker* v. *Carter*, it was held, that, after the defendant had been beaten out of both his grounds, of lien and of mutual debts, he might substantiate his demand on the ground of mutual credit. In that case the defendant set up a claim on a policy for the general balance due to him as agent, and he was allowed to retain the policy as a security for the money lent as well as for the premiums." "If the doctrine of *Ex parte Deeze* is to be supported, the doctrine of lien is quite put out of doors in all cases of bankruptcy whatever. For, the doctrine of mutual credit will cover all the cases of lien, and also goes a great deal further. In the case of *French* v. *Fenn*, the court speaks with great approbation of *Ex parte Deeze*, and Buller, J., and afterwards Mansfield, C. J., adopted it as a principle, that, wherever there is a mutual trust, that is, wherever one party, being indebted to another, intrusts that other with goods, it is a case of mutual credit. And this is not an obiter dictum, but made a material ingredient in the judgment in an important case—*French* v. *Fenn*." The only difference between *Olive* v. *Smith* and the present case is, that there a

part of the sum claimed by the defendant was due for
premiums, whereas here the whole is an extrinsic debt.
Gibbs, C. J., is erroneously supposed to have narrowed
the doctrine of that case in *Rose* v. *Hart*, 8 Taunt. 499, 2
Moore. 547. His lordship, citing *French* v. *Fenn*, observed: "*French* v. *Fenn* has been followed by a string of
cases running through a period of more than thirty years,
all professing to depend upon it, some of them containing
the fullest approbation of *Ex parte Deexe* from the bench.
Whatever I might think of the original decision, I could
not persuade myself to break in upon a class of cases so
long established; and, if they could not be supported without carrying the doctrine found in *Ex parte Deexe* to its
fullest extent, speaking for myself, I should be ready to
follow it, rather than overturn all that has been settled
upon this subject for such a length of time. But it is
first to be considered whether these cases may not be
supported by a construction of the statute which will not
go to that extent, and will leave the opinion of Lord
Hardwicke in the case of *Ex parte Ockenden* untouched."
After reading the 28th section of the 5 Geo. 2, c. 30, his
lordship proceeded—"Something more is certainly meant
here by *mutual credits* than the words *mutual debts* import; and yet, upon the final settlement, it is enacted
merely that one debt shall be set against another. We
think this shews that the legislature meant such *credits*
only as must in their nature terminate in *debts*, as, where
a debt is due from one party, and credit given by him on
the other for a sum of money payable at a future day, and
which will then become a debt, or where there is a debt
on one side, and a delivery of property with directions to
turn it into money on the other; in such case the credit
given by the delivery of the property must in its nature
terminate in a debt, the balance will be taken on the two
debts, and the words of the statute will in all respects be
complied with: but, where there is a mere deposit of pro-

perty, without any authority to turn it into money, no debt
can ever arise out of it, and therefore it is not a credit
within the meaning of the statute. This principle will
support all the cases from *French* v. *Fenn* to *Olive* v.
Smith, which is the last case that has occurred." A
similar construction was put upon this statute in the case
of *Easum* v. *Cato*, 5 B. & A. 861, where J. S. being desirous of making a shipment for his own risk and advantage, but not in his own name, represented to the merchants through whom the shipment was to be made, that
the goods were the property of A., and shipped on his
account, and A. accordingly by the desire of J. S. wrote
to those merchants, stating the property to be so, and directing them to insure, and to advance money to J. S. on the
goods, which was done: and it was held that this was a
credit given to A. by J. S., by the delivery of goods, in its
nature likely to terminate in a debt, and that therefore,
J. S. having subsequently become bankrupt, A. was entitled to recover the proceeds of the shipment from the
merchants, and to set off against them a debt due from
the bankrupt to him, it being a case of mutual credit
within the 5 Geo. 2, c. 30, s. 28. Bayley, J., there said:
"I am not sure whether any case in the books goes the
full length of this; but I think that this is a case of mutual
credit within the statute 5 Geo. 2, c. 30, s. 28, which is
now held to be confined to such credits as must in their
nature terminate in debts." So, in the present case, there
is a mutual credit that will eventually terminate in a money
balance. The late case of *Gibson* v. *Bell*, ante, Vol. 1,
712, 1 New Cases, 743, has corrected the decision in *Rose*
v. *Hart*. "It is observable," says Tindal C. J. (ante
Vol. 1, 724), "that, in giving judgment in *Rose* v. *Hart*,
the Lord Chief Justice states the law of set-off to depend
upon the enactment in the 5 Geo. 2, c. 30, s. 28, and lays
great stress upon the circumstance that it *is* enacted
merely in the final words of the clause 'that one *debt*

shall be set against another.' But, in point of fact, the law of set-off at that time was governed, not by the 5 Geo. 2, c. 30, only, but also by the 46 Geo. 3, c. 135, s. 3, by which latter statute it was enacted, that ' one *debt* or *demand* may be set off against another: and it is difficult to see for what purpose such latter word can have been introduced, and have been since continued in the 50th section of the last bankrupt act, except for the purpose of giving a greater latitude than the strict meaning of the word debt would of itself import." In the present case, it appears from the record that insurance brokers are by custom entitled to a lien on policies in their hands for their general balance, and that a sum of money is due from the bankrupt to the defendant for goods, for which a bill has been given payable at a future day. Upon this state of facts, and upon the authorities cited, the defendant is clearly entitled to retain the policy on the ground of a mutual trust between himself and the bankrupt. The fact of the debt in respect of which the lien is claimed not being due, makes no difference. The 50th section of the 6 Geo. 4, c. 16, enacts, " that, where there has been mutual credit given by the bankrupt and any other person, or where there are mutual debts between the bankrupt and any other person, the commissioners shall state the account between them, and one debt or *demand* may be set against another, notwithstanding any prior act of bankruptcy committed by such bankrupt before the credit given to or the debt contracted by him, and what shall appear due on either side on the balance of such account, and no more, shall be claimed or paid on either side respectively; and every debt or demand hereby made provable against the estate of the bankrupt, may also be set off in manner aforesaid against such estate." And the 51st section provides for the proof of debts the credit on which had not expired at the time of the bankruptcy.

Bompas, Serjeant, contrà.—The plea is insufficient.

The defendant has no lien on the policy: for, a lien by custom for a general balance can only have reference to a balance due to the party in the particular business in respect of which the lien is claimed; and such lien is destroyed by a special contract, or by taking security. This was expressly determined in *Cowell* v. *Simpson*, 16 Ves. 275. Lord Eldon there says: "Looking through the general doctrine of lien as applicable to all cases except the purchase of an estate, with reference to which it has in a series of decisions been extended, it may be described as primâ facie a right accompanying the implied contract. In the case of a factor, who has a lien both for his expenditure upon the goods in his possession and his general balance upon former transactions, entering into a special contract for a particular mode of payment, he loses his lien." [*Vaughan*, J.—Do you contend that the taking the bill destroyed the defendant's lien?] Beyond all doubt. In the case of *Houghton* v. *Matthews*, 3 B. & P. 485, A., a factor, having sold goods of B. in his own name to C., the latter, without paying for these goods, sent another parcel of goods to A. to sell for him, never having employed A. as a factor before: C. then became bankrupt, and the assignees claimed the goods sent by him to A., and which still remained unsold, tendering the charges upon those goods. A. refused to deliver them up, claiming a lien upon them for the price of the former goods sold by him to C., there being a balance then due from B. to himself: and it was held that the assignees were entitled to recover. Chambre, J., took a distinction as to whether or not the demand of the party arose out of the dealing in respect of which the lien grew, saying—"The demand of the defendant upon the first goods did not arise out of any course of dealing in the relation of principal and factor, but was as foreign to that relation as if it had arisen upon a legacy or any other species of debt the most remote from that course of dealing. I do not find any authority for saying that a factor has any general lien in respect of debts which arise prior to the time at which his character of factor commences: and if a right to such a lien is not established by express authority, it does not appear to me to fall within the general principle upon which the liens of factors have been allowed. It seems to me that the liens of factors have been allowed for the convenience of trade, and with a view to encourage factors to advance money upon goods in their possession, or which must come to their hands, as factors; but debts which are incurred prior to the existence of the relation of principal and factor, are not contracted upon this principle." The like was held by Lord Kenyon in *Weldon* v. *Gould*, 3 Esp. 268, and by Sir Thomas Plumer in *Worrall* v. *Johnson*, 2 Jac. & W. 214. Here, it no where appears that anything was due from the bankrupt to the defendant in respect of premiums or advances made on account of the policy, or in his character of insurance broker. The only proper meaning attributable to this plea is in reference to the cases, and none are to be found in the books extending the lien beyond the trade of the party setting it up: and if it did extend so far, the facts set forth in the replication, for the reasons already assigned, afford a distinct answer. That the taking a bill, or other special contract, destroys the lien, is clear from *Cowell* v. *Simpson*, *Stevenson* v. *Blakelock*, 1 M. & S. 535, and *Chase* v. *Westmore*, 5 M. & S. 186. Unless it is competent to the defendant to rest his defence upon the doctrine of mutual credit, the plaintiffs are clearly entitled to judgment. Now, this plea is not calculated to raise that question: it expressly asserts a right of lien. Besides, the plea contains no averment that the bankrupt was indebted to the defendant before the bankruptcy; it merely states the supposed debt to have accrued from the bankrupt at the time of the request and refusal to deliver the policy, and of the supposed conversion, which, as appears from the replication, was *after*

1836.

HEWISON
v.
GUTHRIE.

the bankruptcy.—With respect to the cases cited, it is to be observed that the doctrine laid down by Lord Hardwicke in *Ex parte Deeze* is to be taken with the restriction which that learned judge himself applied to it in the subsequent case of *Ex parte Ockenden:* and in the former case the party had at the time of the bankruptcy a right to retain the goods as against the bankrupt. *French* v. *Fenn,* too, is clearly distinguishable from the present case: for, there, the defendant alone had a right to receive the proceeds of the pearls. The general result of all the cases, from *Atkinson* v. *Elliott* down to *Sampson* v. *Burton,* 4 Moore, 516, 2 B. & B. 89, *Rose* v. *Sims,* 1 B. & Ad. 521, and *Gibson* v. *Bell,* is, that, by the term *mutual credits,* the legislature meant such credits only as must in their nature terminate in debts. "From the earliest practice," says Tindal, C. J., in the last mentioned case, "to the latest provision by statute, the object seems to have been that the account should be stated as between merchant and merchant, and that whatever would be in ordinary practice a pecuniary item in such account should be the subject of set-off."

Sir *W. Follett,* in reply.—Taking the whole of the record together it sufficiently appears that the entire transaction took place before the bankruptcy of G. Mickle. Had the bankruptcy not intervened, the replication might have afforded an answer to the plea: but, upon the whole facts, the defendant's right to retain the policy in satisfaction of his lien, sufficiently appears. The result of the argument on the part of the plaintiffs is, that the doctrine of mutual credit can only apply where the whole must necessarily result in a money demand on both sides. In *Ex parte Deeze,* the goods were not intrusted for sale. In *Atkinson* v. *Elliott,* *Rose* v. *Hart,* *Easum* v. *Cato,* *Rose* v. *Sims,* and *Gibson* v. *Bell,* there was no lien: all those cases turned strictly upon the doctrine of mutual credit.

Cur. adv. vult.

TINDAL, C. J., delivered the judgment of the court:— We think the question in this case must be disposed of upon a ground which will make it unnecessary to consider many of the points which have come into discussion before us. The plaintiffs declare in trover for a policy of insurance; and the defendant by his plea alleges an antient custom in the city of London for insurance brokers to retain in their possession all policies effected by them, under a lien for their general balance, and then sets up the balance due to him at the time of the demand and refusal. The plaintiffs, in their replication, state that the sum for which the lien is claimed is the price of some canvass which the defendant had sold at a credit of twelve months, which credit had not expired at the time of the conversion; and further, that the defendant had drawn a bill of exchange at twelve months upon the bankrupt, the purchaser of the canvass, which bill was accepted by him, and was received by the defendant on account of the price of the canvass, before the time of the conversion : to which replication the defendant demurs. Now, it is well established by the authorities cited at the bar, that, if a security is taken for the debt for which the party has a lien upon property of the debtor, such security being payable at a distant day, the lien is gone. The case of *Cowell* v. *Simpson*, 16 Ves. 230, and the authority of Lord Eldon in applying the doctrine there laid down to the case of factors and other traders, is decisive on the point. But, if the defendant has lost by his own act the right to retain as a lien, upon which he relies in his plea, under a particular custom of the city of London, he cannot be allowed to desert his plea, and rest his defence upon another and totally distinct ground, viz. a right to retain the property in question for a balance due to him on mutual credit between himself and the bankrupt. Even if the facts of the case would have warranted such a defence, he was as much bound to plead the particular facts, and bring himself within the clause of the statute relating to mutual credits, as to plead the custom which he has actually set up, and to endeavour to bring himself within such custom. And although it has been argued at the bar that the general balance for which the lien is claimed is virtually and substantially a balance upon mutual credit between the parties, yet it has been answered, and we think satisfactorily answered, that it does not appear on the record that the mutual credits, upon the result of which the balance is claimed, were given before the bankruptcy, so as to make the balance claimed a balance due at the time of the bankruptcy; the only allegation being, that the bankrupt was indebted to the defendant in this general balance " at the time of the request and refusal to deliver the policy, and of the supposed conversion." Even, therefore, admitting the defendant might set up this right to retain the policy for his general balance under a plea of mutual credit, we think the facts pleaded upon the record do not bring the case within the principle. We therefore give judgment for the plaintiffs.

Judgment for the plaintiffs.

END OF EASTER TERM.

IN THE COMMON PLEAS.

TRINITY TERM, 6 WILL. IV.

THE JUDGES WHO SAT IN BANC DURING THIS TERM WERE
TINDAL, C. J., AND PARK, J., GASELEE, J., AND VAUGHAN, J.

STANLEY v. TOWGOOD and Others, Executrix and Executors of EDWARD TOWGOOD, deceased.

1836.

Tuesday,
May 24th.

COVENANT on an indenture of lease whereby the plaintiff demised certain premises to the testator, Edward Towgood, for a term of fourteen years from Michaelmas, 1823. This indenture contained, among others, a covenant that the said Edward Towgood " should and would, during the continuance of the demise, preserve and keep, and at the end or other sooner determination of the said term of fourteen years thereby granted, leave the said demised messuage and other buildings, and all the outhouses, offices, windows, doors, drains, sewers, pipes, and other watercourses, gates, hedges, and fences belonging to, in, or about the said demised premises, in good and tenantable order and repair, all losses and damage by fire or tempest in the meantime excepted." The declaration alleged

A lessee covenanted to preserve and keep, and at the end of the term leave the demised premises in good and tenantable repair:—Held, that this covenant would be satisfied by leaving the premises in such a state as, regard being had to the age of the building at the time of the demise, might be considered tenantable.

The lessee during the term erected a lean-to, with a roof so ill constructed that it did not exclude the weather, and so left it at the end of the term :—Held, that this was a breach of his covenant to repair.

1836.

STANLEY
v.
TOWGOOD.

that the testator, in breach of this covenant, while possessed
of the premises, and thence until the commencement of the
suit, suffered and permitted the demised premises to be,
and the same were for and during all that time ruinous,
prostrate, broken, fallen down, choked, foul, miry, out of
repair, and in great decay for want of needful and necessary maintaining, upholding, supporting, and keeping the
same, although the delapidation was not, nor was any part
thereof, occasioned by fire or tempest, contrary to the form
and effect of the said indenture, and of the covenant of the
said Edward Towgood so by him made as aforesaid.

The defendants pleaded that the said Edward Towgood
in his lifetime and the defendants as executrix and executors since his decease, and each of them, had during the
continuance of the demise preserved and kept the demised premises in good and tenantable order and repair,
according to the form and effect of the said indenture:
whereupon issue was joined.

The cause was tried before Bolland, B. at the last Summer Assizes at Huntingdon. It appeared that at the time
of the demise the premises were old, and it was agreed on
all hands that at the expiration of the term some reparations (especially with reference to certain fences) were
necessary, though the witnesses on either side differed as
to the amount. It further appeared that the lessee
had during the term erected a covered way or lean-to on
part of the premises, but so ill constructed that from the
first the roof was not water-tight. On the part of the defendant it was contended, with respect to the lean-to, that
he was not bound to new roof it (for, it was admitted that
no mere repair would cure the defect), but was justified
in leaving it in the same state in which it had always
been: and, with reference to the general repairs, it was
proposed to call evidence to shew the ruinous condition
of the premises at the time of the demise. The learned
Baron, however, refused to receive such evidence; and

under his direction the jury returned a verdict for the plaintiff, damages 14*l.* 10*s.*, leave being reserved to the defendant to reduce them to 8*l.* 10*s.*, if the court should be of opinion that, under the circumstances, he was not bound to leave the lean-to in such a state as to render it available.

Storks, Serjeant, in Michaelmas Term last, obtained a rule nisi accordingly; and also for a new trial, on the ground of misdirection. He stated the learned Baron to have told the jury, that, in reference to the defendant's covenant, they were at liberty to consider the premises as *new* at the time of the demise; distinguishing it from the case of a tenancy from year to year.

F. Kelly and *Gunning* shewed cause.—Where a lessee enters into an absolute covenant to repair like this, he is bound to perform that covenant whatever the state of the premises at the commencement of the term: the covenant is to *preserve* and *keep*, and, at the expiration of the term, to *leave* the demised premises in "good and tenantable order and repair." The learned Baron did not say that the jury were to construe this covenant as if the premises were perfectly new when the demise was made. The only question for the jury was, what was the state of the premises at the time of bringing the action. It is no defence to say that they were not in a tenantable condition when the party entered; and, if it were so, there is no plea upon this record adapted to meet that state of facts. The tenant was bound to leave the premises in substantial repair—*Harris* v. *Jones*, 1 M. & Rob. 173. With respect to the lean-to, it is no defence to say, that its original construction was so bad that it cannot be put into a state of substantial repair. In Bacon's Abridgment, *Covenant* (F.), it is said: "If a man takes a lease of a house and land, and covenants to leave the demised premises in good re-

pair at the end of the term, and he erects a messuage upon
part of the land, besides what was before, he must keep
or leave this in good repair also—3 Lev. 265, per Curiam:
S. P. adjudged between *Brown* and *Burden*, Skin. 121; for,
it is a continuing covenant; and though the house had no
actual, yet it had a potential being at the time of the
lease." Upon the whole, the simple question for the jury
was, whether or not the premises were left in good and
substantial repair at the expiration of the term: and this
was properly left to them.

Storks, Serjeant, and *B. Andrews*, in support of the
rule.—It was clearly a misdirection to tell the jury that
they were not at liberty to look to the state of the premises at the commencement of the tenancy. The learned
Baron summed up in direct opposition to *Harris* v. *Jones*
and *Gutteridge* v. *Munyard*, 7 C. & P. 129, 1 M. & Rob.
334. In *Harris* v. *Jones*, it was held that a general cove-
venant to repair is satisfied by the lessee keeping the premises in substantial repair (meaning, of course, in reference to their condition at the time of the demise); and
that a literal performance of the covenant is not to be required: and in *Gutteridge* v. *Munyard*, it was held, that,
where a very old house is demised, with the usual covenants to repair, it is not meant that the house should be
restored in an improved state, or that the consequences
of the elements should be averted; but that the law imposes upon the tenant the duty of *keeping the house in the
state in which it was at the time of the demise*, by the
timely expenditure of money and care. The state of the
premises at the time of the demise, therefore, was a material question, and one to which the defendant ought to
have been permitted to produce evidence. In *Ferguson*
v. ———, 2 Esp. 590, it was ruled by Lord Kenyon that
a tenant from year to year is only bound to fair and tenantable repairs, so far as to prevent waste or decay of the

premises, and not to substantial and lasting repairs, such 1836.
as new roofing &c. The jury in the present case should ———
have been directed to consider whether or not, regard be- STANLEY
ing had to the condition of the premises at the date of the TOWGOOD.
demise, the covenant had been substantially performed.
With respect to the lean-to: its erection was a voluntary
act on the part of the lessee: and, from a defect in its
original construction, it appeared that no repair would
make it water-tight. The argument on the other side
would amount to this, that the lessee was bound to erect
the lean-to in the best possible manner. The cases cited
from Bacon's Abridgment, and from Skinner and Levinz,
involve an entirely different principle: in each of those
cases there was a direct violation of the lessee's covenant.
If a lessee choose to erect four walls, without a roof, he
might be liable to an action of waste for incumbering the
land with an useless structure, but he clearly would not
be liable on his covenant to repair. [*Vaughan*, J.—You
give no effect to the words "*tenantable order :*" do they
mean nothing?] "Tenantable order" means neither more
nor less than "tenantable repair."

TINDAL, C. J.—This is an action of covenant upon an
indenture of lease for fourteen years, wherein the lessee
covenanted that he would "during the continuance of the
demise preserve and keep, and at the end or other sooner
determination of the said term of fourteen years thereby
granted, leave the demised premises and other buildings,
and all the outhouses, offices, windows, doors, drains,
sewers, pipes, and other watercourses, gates, hedges, and
fences belonging to, in, or about the said demised premises, in good and tenantable order and repair, all losses
and damages by fire and tempest in the meantime excepted." In answer to the action, the defendant has
pleaded performance modo ac formâ. The question, therefore, for the jury was, whether or not, upon the evidence

before them, it appeared that the defendant's testator
had performed this covenant. I agree, that, in cases of
this description, the true question is whether or not the
premises have been substantially kept in repair; and that,
to entitle the plaintiff to a verdict, he must shew some
real, tangible want of reparation. In the present case, the
jury have found a verdict for the plaintiff for 14*l.* 10*s.*
Two objections have been taken to this verdict: the one,
as to a sum of 8*l.* 10*s.* which the jury awarded as damages
in respect of the breach of the covenant to repair generally; the other as to a sum of 6*l.* given in respect of a
lean-to built by the lessee, which it appeared was originally
so ill constructed that it never could be put into a proper
state of repair. The misdirection complained of was, that
the judge was supposed to have told the jury that they
were not to consider whether the premises were new or
old at the time the covenant was entered into. Undoubtedly,
that circumstance is to a certain extent to be taken into
consideration: and, if this had clearly been made appear
to have been the learned judge's direction, I should have
thought there ought to have been a further investigation.
The learned judge's report, however, does not lead us to
this conclusion; and the counsel in the cause are not
agreed as to what was the point presented to the jury, or
as to the precise terms of the direction. I therefore think,
that, if the expressions imputed to the learned judge did
in reality escape him, they must have been intended as
merely illustrative of the principle which he was laying
down, viz. that the lessee's liability to repair was not to
be measured by the state of the premises at the time of
the demise. From the course the cause appears to have
taken, this must have been so; for, both in the examination
and in the cross-examination of the defendant's witnesses,
questions are put as to the state of repair of the premises
at the time the lease was granted. The question, therefore, resolves itself into a mere question as to the reason-

1836.

ableness of the damages. The witnesses on both sides agree that some repairs were necessary: and, the damages being under 20*l*., we are by the general rule precluded from entertaining the matter upon that ground. If it had been shewn clearly that the learned Baron told the jury that the antiquity of the premises at the time of the demise was to be dismissed entirely from their consideration, I must admit that I should not have been prepared to support his ruling: but, inasmuch as all the witnesses seem to have brought the minds of the jury to the time present, I think it is sufficiently apparent that the substantial question in the cause was left to them. I therefore think the rule must be discharged.

STANLEY
v.
TOWGOOD.

PARK, J., and VAUGHAN, J., concurred.

GASELEE, J., gave no opinion.

Rule discharged.

———◆———

GOODFELLOW *v.* ROLLINGS.

THE defendant having remained in execution for more than twelve months for damages to the amount of 20*l*. recovered against him in an action for criminal conversation with the plaintiff's wife—

Crowder moved that he might be discharged under the statute 48 Geo. 3, c. 123, which enacts that "all persons in execution upon any judgment for any debt or *damages* not exceeding the sum of 20*l*., exclusive of the costs recovered by such judgment, and who shall have lain in prison thereupon for the space of twelve successive calendar months next before the time of their application to be discharged as thereinafter mentioned, shall and may, upon his, her, or their application for that purpose in term time, made to some one of his majesty's superior courts of record at Westminster, to the satisfaction of such court,

Tuesday,
May 24th.

The 48 Geo. 3, c. 123, applies to the case of a prisoner in execution for damages not exceeding 20*l*, recovered against him in an action for criminal conversation with the plaintiff's wife.

1836.

GOODFELLOW
v.
ROLLINGS.

be forthwith (a) discharged out of custody as to such execution by the rule or order of such court." He referred to *Winter* v. *Elliott*, 3 N. & M. 315, 1 Ad. & El. 24, where the statute in question was held to apply to persons in execution for damages in actions of assault (b).

Barstow shewed cause in the first instance.—The statute 48 Geo. 3, c. 123, was obviously not intended to apply to a case like the present. The title and preamble shew that *debts* only were contemplated. That part of the statute which relates to the liability of bail was not adverted to in *Winter* v. *Elliott:* and it may be that the word "damages" was used in reference to debts recovered in the shape of *damages*. It is clear from the 41 Geo. 3, c. 70 (insolvent debtors act), the 41st section of which expressly excludes from the benefit of that act persons charged in execution for damages given in actions of this sort, and from the 53 Geo. 3, c. 102, s. 37, which provides that they shall remain in prison for a period of five years, that such damages were not in the contemplation of the legislature, when passing the 48 Geo. 3, c. 123.

TINDAL, C. J.—I see no reason for withholding our assent to the decision of the court of King's Bench in *Winter* v. *Elliott*, where a more extended signification is applied to the word damages than that which is now contended for on the part of the present plaintiff. It is to be observed that under the 48 Geo. 3, c. 123, a boon is given to the plaintiff: he may, notwithstanding the defendant's discharge, still sue out a fi. fa. against his goods (c). The

(a) See the next case.

(b) One convicted upon an indictment for an assault, who, upon reference to the king's coroner and attorney, was directed by his award to pay so much for costs and compensation to the prosecutor, is entitled to be discharged as an insolvent debtor under the lords' act, 32 Geo. 2, c. 28. Rex v. Wakefield, 13 East, 190.

(c) " Provided always, that, for

legislature may probably have thought a year's imprison- 1836.
ment a sufficient punishment where the damages given by GOODFELLOW
the jury do not exceed 20*l.* v.
ROLLINGS.

The rest of the court concurred; VAUGHAN, J., observing that the act was remedial, and therefore to receive a
liberal construction.

Rule absolute.

and notwithstanding the discharge of any debtor or debtors by virtue of this act, the *judgment* where-upon any such debtor or debtors was or were taken or charged in execution, shall nevertheless remain and continue in full force to all intents and purposes, except as to the taking in execution the person or persons of such debtor or debtors thereupon, as is here-inafter provided; and that it shall and may be lawful for the creditor or creditors at whose suit such debtor or debtors had been, was, or were so taken or charged in execution, to take out all such *execution* or executions on every such judgment, against the lands, tenements, hereditaments, goods and chattels of any debtor or debtors (other than and except the necessary wearing apparel of and for him, her, or them, and for his, her, or their family, and the necessary tools for his, her, or their trade or occupation, not exceeding the value of 10*l.* in the whole), or to bring any such action or actions on any such judgment against such debtor or debtors respectively, or to bring any such action or use any such remedy for the recovery and satisfaction of his, her, or their demand, against any other person or persons liable to satisfy the same, in such and the same manner, but in such and the same manner only, as such creditor or creditors otherwise could or might have done in case such debtor or debtors had never been taken or charged in execution upon such judgment."

DAVIS *v.* CURTIS.

Wednesday, November 9th.

IN Trinity Term, the defendant, a prisoner, was brought
up at the suit of the plaintiff under the compulsory clauses

In Trinity Term the defendant was brought up at the instance

of the plaintiff under the compulsory clauses of the lords' act, and, claiming his sixty days, was remanded. The sixty days expired in June; and in August the defendant had been twelve months
in execution in the action. On the first day of the following term, the defendant applied for his
discharge under the 48 Geo. 3, c. 123, the debt being less than 20*l.* The notice required by the
90th rule of Hilary Term, 2 Will. 4, not having been given, the court granted only a rule nisi. On
the next day the prisoner was brought up at the suit of the creditor under the lords' act. The
prisoner was called upon by the court to deliver in a schedule of his effects in pursuance of the
act; which he declined to do:—Held, that, notwithstanding such refusal, he was entitled to his
discharge under the 48 Geo. 3, c. 123.

1836.

DAVIS
*.
CURTIS.

of the lords' act, 32 Geo. 2, c. 28, ss. 16, 17. The prisoner claimed the sixty days allowed by the statute, and was thereupon remanded. The sixty days expired in June; and, on the first day of Michaelmas Term—

Andrews, Serjeant, moved for the prisoner's discharge under the 48 Geo. 3, c. 123, he having been in custody more than twelve months for a debt not exceeding 20*l.* The year of imprisonment expired in August.

The ten days' notice required by the rule of Hilary Term, 2 Will. 4, s. 90 (*a*), not having been given, the court held that the party had not placed himself in a position to be entitled to his discharge.

On the second day of the same term, the prisoner was brought up at the instance of the plaintiff under the lords' act.

Andrews, Serjeant, on behalf of the prisoner, contended, that, inasmuch as he would have been entitled to his discharge under the 48 Geo. 3, c. 123, on the preceding day, but for the want of the notice which the practice of the court required, he could not now be the subject of any compulsory proceeding under the lords' act; for that, having suffered the imprisonment mentioned in the former statute, and thereby entitled himself to his discharge, he must be considered as if actually discharged, especially with reference to proceedings under an act so highly penal as the lords' act.

(*a*) By which it is provided, that "A rule or order for the discharge of a debtor who has been detained in execution a year for a debt under 20*l.*, may be made absolute in the first instance, on an affidavit of notice given ten days before the intended application, which notice may be given before the year expires.

1836.

DAVIS
v.
CURTIS.

Mansel, contra.—The defendant having been brought up under the lords' act in Trinity Term last, and having claimed the sixty days allowed him by the statute for preparing his schedule, and been remanded, on the expiration of the sixty days (within the twelve-month) he was in default, and became liable to the penalty imposed by the statute. The notice required by the rule of court not having been given, the prisoner is not in a condition now to apply to the court for his discharge under the 48 Geo. 3, c. 123. All therefore that the court has power to do is, to call upon the prisoner to make an assignment of his effects for the benefit of his detaining creditors.

TINDAL, C. J.—In *Langdon v. Rossiter*, M'Clel. 6, 13 Price, 186 (nom *Ex parte Rossiter*), the court of Exchequer held that a person who has lain in prison more than twelve months in execution for damages under 20*l.*, exclusive of costs, is entitled to be discharged out of custody forthwith as to such execution, on an application made under that statute, notwithstanding he had previously been brought up under the compulsory clauses of the lords' act, and then refused to deliver in a schedule of his effects, in consequence of which he had been remanded. The words of the 48 Geo. 3, c. 123, are, that "all persons in execution upon any judgment for any debt or damages not exceeding the sum of 20*l.*, exclusive of the costs recovered by such judgment, and who shall have lain in prison thereupon for the space of twelve successive calendar months next before the time of their application to be discharged, shall and may, upon his, her, or their application for that purpose in term time, made to some one of his majesty's superior courts of record at Westminster [wherein such judgment shall have been obtained], to the satisfaction of such court, *be forthwith discharged out of custody as to such execution, by the rule* *or order of such court.*" The rule of court provides, that, to entitle the party to succeed on such an application, ten days' notice shall be previously given to the detaining creditor. In the present case, had the prisoner complied with this rule, we should have pronounced an order for his discharge yesterday. The question therefore is, whether he is not already virtually discharged. Let there be a rule nisi for the prisoner's discharge under the 48 Geo. 3, c. 123, and the matter may be discussed on a future day.

A rule nisi having been granted accordingly (*b*),

Mansel, on a subsequent day, shewed cause.—In *Langdon* v. *Rossiter*, the twelve months had expired before the expiration of the sixty days; a circumstance which materially distinguishes it from the present case. The practice, before the late rule, with respect to motions under the 48 Geo. 3, c. 123, is thus stated by Mr. Tidd (Prac. 9th edit. 388)—" On a motion for the discharge of an insolvent debtor under the above statute, the rule, in the King's Bench, is absolute in the first instance, after due notice of the application has been given to the plaintiff or his attorney (*Davis* v. *Rogers*, 2 B. & C. 804, 4 D. & R. 361); but, in the Common Pleas, it is in the first instance only a rule nisi"—citing *Ex parte Neilson*, 7 Taunt. 37, and *Magnay* v. *Gilkes*, 7 Taunt. 467. Here, the prisoner was bound within the time prescribed by the lords' act to deliver in upon oath a full account of his estate and effects, and to execute the proper assignment. When brought up on the second day of the term, the course which ought to have been pursued was, for the court to call upon him to comply with the statute, by delivering in such account, and making such assignment (*c*). The circumstance of of time having been granted to him by the court ought not to be permitted to prejudice the plaintiff's right.

(*b*) Moore v. Clay, 4 Dowl. 5.   (*c*) Evan v. James, 1 Dowl. 260.

Andrews, Serjeant, in support of his rule.—*Langdon* v. *Rossiter* is not to be distinguished from the present case. When the prisoner was brought up in Trinity Term, the court had no power to remand him otherwise than generally—*Langdon* v. *Rossiter*, *Ex parte White*, 1 Dowl. 64. The statute 48 Geo. 3, c. 123, is explicit and imperative; and it contains no reservation of the power of the detaining creditors under the 32 Geo. 2, c. 28. The creditor is in no way injured; for, his judgment will remain in force notwithstanding the defendant's discharge, and he may still have execution against his effects.

Cur. adv. vult.

TINDAL, C. J., now said.—Having attentively looked into the acts, and considered the circumstances of this case, we are of opinion that our determination must be the same as it would have been had the defendant placed himself in a situation to call for it on the first day of term. The facts appear to be these:—In Trinity Term last, the defendant was brought up at the suit of the plaintiff under the compulsory clauses of the lords' act, claimed his sixty days, and was remanded. The sixty days expired in the month of June. On the first day of the present term, the defendant applied for his discharge under the 48 Geo. 3, c. 123, he having been in execution upon a judgment obtained against him in this court for a debt not exceeding 20*l.*, and having lain in prison thereupon for the space of twelve successive calendar months. The twelve months were not completed until the month of August. When the last-mentioned application was made to the court, the party had failed in pursuing strictly the practice of the court: no notice of the motion had been given to the detaining creditor, and consequently the prisoner could not then be actually discharged. Qui prior est tempore, potior est jure. The prisoner not having been discharged under the 48 Geo. 3 at the time of the plaintiff's applica-

1836.

DAVIS
v.
CURTIS.

tion (on the second day of this term) under the lords' act, I think we must call upon the prisoner to deliver in his schedule before we dispose of the other rule. But, inasmuch as, by the 48 Geo. 3, he is declared entitled to his discharge on application to the court, I do not see that his refusal to deliver a schedule and make an assignment affords any answer to his motion under that statute. If he has been guilty of any offence he is still liable to be indicted.

The prisoner was then asked by the court if he was prepared to deliver in upon oath a schedule of his estate and effects in the manner required by the statute. He answered in the negative: whereupon the court ordered the rule for his discharge under the 48 Geo. 3, c. 123, to be made—

Absolute.

———◆———

KNIGHT v. WOORE.

Tuesday,
May 24th.

In trespass, the defendant in his third plea justified under an alleged right of way with horses, carts, and carriages, for the purpose of fetching goods and water from a navigable river. The jury affirmed the right set up so far as it related to the fetching of water, but negatived it as to the rest:—The court directed the verdict to be entered distributively (for the plaintiff as to the goods, for the defendant as to the water), under the rules of Hilary Term, 4 Will. 4, *Trespass*, V., ss. 4—6.

THIS was an action of trespass. The defendants in their third plea justified the trespasses complained of under an alleged right in the inhabitants of the town of Monmouth to pass and repass with horses, carts, and carriages, for the purpose of bringing water and goods from the river Wye. The replication denied the alleged right of way. At the trial the jury affirmed the right set up as to the fetching water, but negatived the right set up as to the goods.

Ludlow, Serjeant, in Easter Term last, obtained a rule calling upon the defendant to shew cause why the verdict should not be entered generally for the plaintiff upon the whole record.

Maule and *Whateley* shewed cause.—The defendant is entitled to have the verdict entered for him in respect of that part of the third plea which the jury have found for him. Before the new rules of pleading (Hilary Term, 4 Will. 4), the defendant would have separately pleaded each of the rights of way that are set up by the plea in question: since the promulgation of those rules, the main object of which was the shortening of records, the whole may be contained in one plea. By the fifth division of those rules, s. 4, it is provided, that, "where, in an action of trespass quare clausum fregit, the defendant pleads a right of way with carriages and cattle and on foot in the same plea, and issue is taken thereon, the plea shall be taken distributively; and if a right of way with cattle or on foot only shall be found by the jury, a verdict shall pass for the defendant in respect of such of the trespasses proved as shall be justified by the right of way so found, and for the plaintiff in respect of such of the trespasses as shall not be so justified." "And (s. 5) where, in an action of trespass quare clausum fregit, the defendant pleads a right of common of pasture for divers kinds of cattle, ex. gr., horses, sheep, oxen, and cows, and issue is taken thereon, if a right of common for some particular kind of commonable cattle only be found by the jury, a verdict shall pass for the defendant in respect of such of the trespasses proved as shall be justified by the right of common so found, and for the plaintiff in respect of the trespasses which shall not be so justified." "And (s. 6) in all actions in which such right of way or common as aforesaid, *or other similar right*, is so pleaded that the allegations as to the extent of the right are capable of being construed distributively, they shall be taken distributively." The obvious intention of these rules was, that, if the defendant proved only one part of a plea setting up distinct and divisible rights, he should have the benefit of the verdict for that part as if the several rights had been separately

1836.

KNIGHT
v.
WOORE.

1836.

KNIGHT
v.
WOORE.

pleaded: and such is the construction which the court of Exchequer has put upon them in the late case of *Phythian* v. *White*, 1 M. & W. 216, 4 Dowl. 714.

Ludlow, Serjeant, and *R. V. Richards*, in support of the rule, contended that, the defendant having failed to establish the right set up by the plea in the manner and to the extent therein alleged, the entire verdict must be entered for the plaintiff.

TINDAL, C. J.—I am of opinion that this case falls within the rules to which our attention has been directed. The right of way set up by the defendant in his third plea being negatived as to the carrying of goods, and affirmed as far as it related to the fetching of water from the river Wye, the plaintiff is entitled only to have the verdict upon that plea entered for him in respect of the first right claimed; as to the other, the verdict must be entered for the defendant.

PARK, J.—I am of the same opinion. Were we to decide otherwise, we should go far to defeat one of the most important objects of the late rules. The right here claimed embraces two several things: the jury have negatived one and affirmed the other. The case is clearly within the rules adverted to.

GASELEE, J.—Upon the finding as reported to us, the course suggested is clearly the proper one. If the right pleaded had been a right of way with carriages and cattle and on foot, and the jury had established the right of way *with cattle* or *on foot only*, the verdict would unquestionably have been entered for the defendant in respect of the qualified right so found. In the present case the right is, in the language of the 6th rule, "so pleaded that the allegations as to the extent of the right are capable of being construed distributively," and therefore is to be so taken.

1836.

KNIGHT
v.
WOORE.

VAUGHAN, J., concurred.

Rule accordingly, without costs.

GRISSELL and Another v. ROBINSON.

ASSUMPSIT for money alleged to have been paid by the plaintiffs to the use of the defendant. At the trial before Park, J., at the sittings at Westminster after last Trinity Term, the following facts appeared in evidence:—The plaintiffs were executors of one Peto, who died in September, 1830. In the preceding year, Peto had entered into a verbal agreement with the defendant to grant him a lease for twenty-one years of certain premises then in the defendant's possession, in consideration of 450*l.*; and a sum of 300*l.*, in part of the purchase money, was thereupon paid by the defendant to Peto. After the death of Peto, his property becoming the subject of dispute in the court of Chancery, the defendant sought to obtain a specific performance of his contract. By reason, however, of its not having been reduced to writing, the court of Chancery could not direct that agreement to be carried into effect: but the executors subsequently consented to grant the defendant a lease upon the terms previously settled. This lease was prepared by Mr. Taylor, the solicitor of the executors: and it recited, amongst other things, the former agreement between the testator and the defendant,

*Thursday,
May 26th.*

Pending a negotiation between the defendant and one P. for a lease of certain premises belonging to the latter, P. died. A suit in Chancery was instituted for the purpose of carrying his will into effect. The agreement between the defendant and P. not being in writing, and therefore not capable of being enforced in equity, the plaintiffs, the executors of P., consented to grant the defendant the lease upon the terms originally agreed on by their testator. The lease was accordingly prepared by their solicitor, and executed, but was retained by

him, a part of the purchase money remaining unpaid. The defendant afterwards paid the balance of the purchase money, and demanded the lease, but refused to pay the expenses of preparing the same. The plaintiffs having paid such expenses out of a fund in Chancery belonging to them as executors:—Held, that, on proof of the usual course of business in such cases being for the lessor's solicitor to prepare the lease, and for the lessee to pay the expenses, the plaintiffs were entitled to recover the amount as money paid to the defendant's use; and that they need not sue in their representative character.

the death of the former, the proceedings in Chancery, and that the then lease was granted in pursuance of a proposal by the plaintiffs as thereinafter mentioned. This lease was executed in June, 1835; but, the residue of the purchase money not having been paid at that time, it was left in the hands of Taylor. Taylor's bill of costs was, by order of the court of Chancery, paid out of a certain fund in that court belonging to the plaintiffs. The residue of the purchase money was afterwards paid to the plaintiffs: but, the defendant refusing to repay them the expenses attending the lease, they retained it, and now brought this action to recover the amount. On the part of the plaintiffs, several attornies were called to prove that the usual course on the grant of a lease was, for the lessor's solicitor to prepare it, and the lessee to pay the expenses. A verdict having been found for the plaintiffs—

Talfourd, Serjeant, in Michaelmas Term, obtained a rule nisi to enter a nonsuit, on the grounds—first, that, the money having been paid to Taylor out of funds belonging to the testator, the plaintiffs should have brought the action in their representative character, *Aspinall* v. *Wake*, 3 M. & Scott, 423, 10 Bing. 51—secondly, that the plaintiffs should have declared on the special custom set up at the trial, and not simply for money paid.

Thesiger and *W. H. Watson* now shewed cause.—The first ground of objection to the verdict in this case is, that the money in question was paid in respect of a contract made with the testator in his life-time; and therefore, it is contended, the plaintiffs should have sued in their representative and not in their own individual character. This argument, however, proceeds upon a misapprehension of the facts: the transaction was one entirely between the plaintiffs and the defendant; for, the original contract with the testator was void for want of writing; and the money paid to Taylor being a debt arising out of that transaction, they clearly could not sue for it in any other way than they have done. In *Brassington* v. *Ault*, 9 Moore, 340, 2 Bing. 177, 1 C. & P. 302, where three executors ordered goods to be sold as the property of their testator, and afterwards sued the purchaser for the amount, without describing themselves as executors in the declaration, and without joining a fourth executor who was named in the will; it was held, that, inasmuch as they did not act in their character of executors, and the order for the sale was given by the three alone, the action was well brought. All that was decided in *Aspinall* v. *Wake* was, that, the plaintiffs, as executors, having continued to carry on the business of the testator, and having drawn bills as executors for goods sold to the defendants, several of which bills the defendants accepted and paid, the plaintiffs *might* sue as executors for the price of such goods. It may be taken as a clear proposition, that, wherever the cause of action arises after the death of the testator or intestate, the personal representative *may* and generally *must* sue in his own right.

Then, as to the form of action. It is said that money paid will not lie, under the circumstances of this case; but that the plaintiffs should have declared specially on the implied contract arising out of the custom, or rather the course of business, proved at the trial. In support of this part of the case, *Rigley* v. *Daykin*, 3 Y. & J. 83, will probably be relied on. There, B., being desirous of raising a sum of money upon mortgage, employed an attorney for the purpose, who applied to A., an attorney, telling him at the same time the name of his principal, and A. agreed to advance the money on behalf of a client, but ultimately the negotiation failed from a defect of title: and it was held that A. could not maintain an action against B. for his fees, although it was proved to be the practice for the proposed borrower to pay the expenses of the proposed lender—the course being for the attorney of the latter to send his bill to the attorney of the former, who, if the bill were reasonable, recommended his client to pay it. In that case, however, no custom was established by the evidence: and, giving the largest possible effect to the decision, it only shews that Taylor could not have recovered these expenses from the defendant; the proper form of action was not in question. *Spencer* v. *Parry*, 4 N. & M. 770, is another case of the same sort. There, a tenant agreed with his landlord to pay the rent clear of all rates and taxes, and, after having occupied the premises some time, quitted them, leaving poor-rates and land-tax unpaid; the receiver of the rents was compelled to pay the rates under a local act, and the succeeding tenant the land-tax; which rates and land-tax were repaid to them by the landlord: and it was held that the landlord's remedy was on the special agreement, and that he could not recover those sums from the former tenant as money paid to his use. In that case, it is to be observed that the defendant incurred no liability except that which arose out of the written agreement: the act of parliament threw the burthen in the first instance on the landlord. It is clearly settled, that, where one is compelled to pay money for which another is liable either primarily or ultimately, the former may recover it in an action for money paid to the use of the latter—*Exall* v. *Partridge*, 8 T. R. 308, 3 Esp. 8; *Brown* v. *Hodgson*, 4 Taunt. 189; *Dawson* v. *Linton*, 1 D. & R. 117, 5 B. & A. 521; *Pownal* v. *Ferrand*, 9 D. & R. 603, 6 B. & C. 439: and this although no action has been brought against the former—*Brown* v. *Hodgson*. In the present case, the course of business proved by the plaintiffs' witnesses, uncontradicted by any evidence on the other side, shewed that the defendant was primarily liable to pay the expenses in question: he was not entitled to demand the lease until he had satisfied Taylor's lien thereon. In *Adams* v. *Dansey*, 4 M. & P.

245, 6 Bing. 506, the plaintiff, an occupier of lands, having been sued by the vicar for tithes, gave up the occupation, and quitted the parish during the progress of the suit; upon which the defendant undertook to indemnify him from all costs of the suit, if he would suffer the defendant to defend in his (the plaintiff's) name. The vicar having succeeded in the suit, the plaintiff's attorney paid him the costs incurred before as well as after the defendant's promise of indemnity. The plaintiff afterwards gave his attorney a promissory note for the amount of the costs so paid, but which was not paid at maturity, when he sued the defendant on his promise. It was held that the payment of such costs by the plaintiff's attorney was equivalent to a payment by the plaintiff himself, as the attorney might be considered his agent for the purpose of making such payment. Here, at all events, the sum paid for the stamps was the money of the plaintiffs, and paid to the use of the defendant.

Talfourd, Serjeant, in support of his rule.—The money alleged to have been paid by the plaintiffs to Taylor, was paid out of the fund in the court of Chancery belonging to the testator, and not out of money belonging to the plaintiffs; and the payment was made in respect of a contract entered into with the testator; the undertaking of the defendant, therefore, to repay the money, must be referred to the original agreement; and consequently was properly the subject of an action by the plaintiffs in their representative character. The principle contended for on the other side may be conceded: its applicability to the particular case now before the court is denied. Taylor's demand having been satisfied, he has no right to retain the lease on his own account; and, if he holds it on behalf of the plaintiffs, they cannot sue the defendants as for money paid to his use, except in respect of a special contract arising under the alleged custom. In *Stokes* v. *Lewis*,

1 T. R. 28, it was held that assumpsit for money paid, laid out, and expended, will not lie, where the money has been paid against the express consent of the party for whose use it is supposed to have been paid: therefore, where two parishes had been a long time united, and had jointly paid one sexton, but afterwards one of them, upon claiming a right of electing a separate sexton, gave notice to the other of their intention, and did so elect; it was held that they could not maintain an action for money paid, laid out, and expended to the use of the other parish for their quota of the sexton's salary.

TINDAL, C. J.—The first objection to the maintenance of this action arises from the circumstance of the plaintiffs' having sued in their personal character, and not as executors: and it has been contended, that, inasmuch as the payment in respect of which they sue arose out of a transaction which commenced in the lifetime of the testator, the plaintiffs should have sued in their representative character. But it appears to me, that, as the payment was made after the death of the testator, and upon a state of facts arising altogether after his death, the plaintiffs were *entitled* to sue, if, indeed, they were not *compellable* to sue, in their own right. The struggle has always been the other way; plaintiffs, previously to the passing of the recent statute, 3 & 4 Will. 4, c. 42, frequently attempted to assume the character of executors where they were not warranted in so doing, for the purpose of avoiding the payment of costs if unsuccessful: as in *Ord* v. *Fenwick*, 3 East, 107, where the plaintiff below joined a count on promises to her as executrix to repay money paid by her as executrix to the use of the defendant below, with a count on promises to her testator for money paid by him to the use of the defendant below: and it was asked what right the plaintiff had to join the claim in her capacity of executrix; no one doubting she could sue in her natural character. Apply that doctrine

1836.

GRISSELL
v.
ROBINSON.

to the present case. Here, the testator entered into a parol contract for a lease, which was so far carried into effect that money was lodged by the defendant to pay part of the consideration. The testator then died, and the court of Chancery refused to enforce the contract because there was no memorandum in writing; and by a recital in the lease, it appears to be granted on the proposal of the plaintiffs thereinafter mentioned; that is, a new and distinct proposal after the death of the testator. The payment, therefore, having been made by the plaintiffs after the testator's death, and on a state of facts arising after his death, there is no reason why they should not sue in their personal character.—The second objection is, that the action for money paid does not lie against the defendant under the circumstances; but it is contended that the plaintiffs should have declared on the special contract. I have always understood the distinction as to the obligation to sue on the special contract rather than on the general count, to be, that, if any condition remains to be performed on the part of the plaintiff, the action must be brought upon the special contract; but that, where all has been done on the plaintiff's part, he may throw aside the special contract, and recover under the common count: and, in order to recover on the common count for money paid, the plaintiff must shew an express or implied assent of the defendant to the payment, or that it was made upon compulsion for the use of the defendant. Here, the money was paid by the plaintiffs to Taylor, their attorney, who had prepared the lease of the premises demised to the defendant. The evidence shewed the usual course of dealing in such cases to be for the landlord's attorney to prepare the lease, and for the lessee to pay the expenses. There was no evidence offered on the part of the defendant to contradict this: it must therefore be supposed that he was aware of the practice, and came to an agreement with the plaintiffs to that effect. Such being the position of the parties, in what way could a special contract be stated, which would not ultimately shape itself as money paid. Here, the money has been paid by the plaintiffs to the defendant's use; for, the payment was made in respect of a lease for which the defendant was ultimately bound to pay, and for which the plaintiffs were compellable to pay in the first instance by virtue of the privity between them and Taylor. The payment was made for the benefit of the defendant; and I do not see that anything remained to be done by the plaintiffs to put them in a situation to sue the defendant. Where one of two joint sureties pays the whole sum for which the two are jointly liable, and which either of them may be called on to pay, a special contract by the co-surety to repay him *might* be stated in an extended form; but, in a compressed shape, the moiety is money paid to the use of the co-surety. The same reasoning applies to the present case. Here the money was paid by the plaintiffs, under an implied contract by the defendant to repay them, he being ultimately liable. I therefore think this action maintainable in its present shape.

PARK, J.—I am of the same opinion. The first question is, whether this action should have been brought by the plaintiffs in their personal or in their representative character. The money was paid by the plaintiffs after the death of the testator. It is true that there had been an agreement for a lease in the lifetime of Peto; but that agreement was inoperative; the court of Chancery refused to carry it into effect; and the whole was settled anew after his death. The case seems to me to fall very much within the decision in *Ord* v. *Fenwick*. The other question is one of more importance. The plaintiffs were liable to their own attorney in the first instance; and all the evidence offered at the trial tended to shew that the usual course of business was for the lessee ultimately to pay for the lease. It must therefore be taken that the defendant impliedly assented to the payment made by the plaintiffs; and consequently the action is well brought.

1836.

GRISSELL
v.
ROBINSON.

GASELEE, J.—The case has been so fully discussed by the Lord Chief Justice and by my Brother Park, that I shall content myself with observing, that, upon all contracts for work, to be done in a particular way, or at a particular time, or for goods sold, to be paid for or delivered at a particular time, after the work has been done, or the goods delivered, the plaintiff is at liberty to resort to the general count for work and labour, or for goods sold and delivered.

VAUGHAN, J.—I concur with the rest of the court upon both points. There was no binding contract for a lease in the lifetime of the testator; the real and only operative contract was entered into with the plaintiffs in their own right. The action therefore is properly brought by them in their personal character. Had this action been brought before the late statute, it would probably have been contended that the plaintiffs *must* have sued in the manner they have done. As to the other point—when once it is ascertained that the defendant is ultimately liable to defray the expense of the lease, the money paid by the plaintiffs becomes money paid to his use.

Rule discharged.

The plaintiff, owner of the ship Hero, entered into a charterparty with one J. B. G., a merchant in London, for a voyage from London to Calcutta and back, covenanting, amongst other things, to take in a cargo in London and proceed therewith to Calcutta, receive on board a homeward cargo, and deliver the same agreeably to bills of lading; the ship *to take her regular turn in the East India Docks for the purpose of delivering her cargo;* the freighter to pay a certain sum for every passenger; and all the cabins except one for the use of the cap-

CAMPION *v.* COLVIN and Others.

THIS was a feigned issue, directed by an order of the court of Chancery. The issue recited, that " certain goods, to wit, 511 bales of cotton wool, consigned to the defendants, had been carried and conveyed in and on board of a certain ship or vessel called the Hero, whereof the plaintiff and others were owners, from Calcutta to the port of London;" and the question to be tried was—"whether the said plaintiff and his said co-owners of the said ship or vessel called the Hero, or any of them, had a lien upon the said cotton wool for freight beyond the amount of freight payable in respect of the carriage of the said cotton wool upon the said voyage." The jury found for the plaintiff, viz. the affirmative of that issue, subject to the opinion of the court upon the following case :—

In the year 1816, and from thence until after the completion of the voyage hereinafter mentioned, the plaintiff and others were owners of the ship called the Hero, of London, and a charterparty with a memorandum thereto was then entered into between the plaintiff and one John Burton Gooch, then a merchant carrying on business in the city of London, for a voyage from London to Madeira, Madras, and Calcutta, and back to London; by which it

tain to be at the disposal and for the benefit of the freighter, who was to appoint a supercargo, not only to act as supercargo, but to take upon him the authority of the captain in the stowage of the cargo, which was to be done under his entire direction, but he was not in any other particular to interfere with the duties of the captain. And the freighter, J. B. G., covenanted to load the ship, and to pay for the freight or hire of the ship for the voyage, at the rate of 14*l.* per ton register tonnage, with primage, to be paid as follows—500*l.* in cash at the expiration of six months from the date of the charterparty, a moiety of the remainder by bills at two months after date from *the day of the ship's arrival in the Thames* on her return voyage, and *the residue by bills at four months' date from the same period.* The defendants and C. & Co. of Calcutta, to whom the outward cargo was consigned, were cognizant of this charterparty. The ship sailed with a captain and crew appointed and paid by the owner. Arrived at Calcutta, C. & Co., as agents of J. B. G., received the cargo, and put up the ship as a general ship, but not being able to fill her, they purchased and shipped on account of J. B. G. (but in their own name) 511 bales of cotton wool, which by the bill of lading were made deliverable to the defendants, and the freight for which was in the bill of lading expressed to have been paid by bills on London. It was found as a fact that the cotton wools in question were the property of J. B. G.:—Held, that the owner had a lien upon these goods for the general freight due under the charterparty, the payment of the entire freight being by the charterparty to precede the delivery of the cargo.

was witnessed, that the owners, for the considerations therein mentioned, covenanted with the freighter, that the ship, being then tight, staunch, &c., the commander should immediately take on board the ship, in the port of London, from the freighter, all such goods as he might think fit to load, reserving sufficient room in the forecastle and half-deck of the ship for the stowage of the provisions and cables, the cargo not exceeding what she could reasonably carry beyond her stores, tackle, &c.; and that, having received the same on board, the ship should proceed to Madeira, where she was to receive from the freighter's agents such other goods as they might think fit to load, and then proceed to Madras and Calcutta, and there deliver the outward cargo, and after being refitted should receive on board all such lawful goods as the freighter's agents might think fit to load, and should then proceed to London, and there, after immediate notice to the freighter of her arrival at the port of London and readiness to deliver the cargo, deliver her homeward cargo agreeably to bills of lading, and so complete the voyage.

The charterparty contained the usual covenants, specifying the number of lay days, and stipulating that the ship should take her regular turn in the East India Docks in London for the purpose of delivering her cargo; that the freighter should pay to the owner a given sum for every passenger carried in the ship; that all the cabins of the ship, except one for the use of the captain, should be at the disposal and for the benefit of the freighter; and that a supercargo to be appointed by the freighter should be conveyed out and home, and be found and provided with the ship's provisions. The charterparty then set out covenants from the freighter to load the ship at London, Madeira, and Madras, within the lay days, &c.; and then to pay to the owner for the freight or hire of the ship for the voyage at and after the rate of 14l. sterling per ton upon the ship's registered tonnage, and 2l. 10s. per cent.

primage on the amount of the freight, in lieu of port and pilotage charges; and that the freight and primage should be paid as follows, viz. 500l. in cash at the expiration of six months from the date of the charterparty, a moiety of the remainder by bills at two months after date from the day on which the ship should arrive in the Thames on her return from her homeward voyage, and the residue by bills at four months' date from the same period. There was then a covenant with respect to demurrage; and also a memorandum that the freighter should have liberty to appoint one James Gooch Thompson to proceed out and home in the ship, and not only to act as supercargo, but to take upon him the authority of the captain in the stowage of the cargo, which was to be done under the entire direction of James Gooch Thompson, but he was not in any other particular to interfere with the duties of the captain of the ship. The defendants and Messrs. Colvin & Co. of Calcutta, at the time of the sailing of the vessel and of her arrival at Calcutta, were cognizant of the said charterparty. The said ship under the said charterparty, with a captain and crew appointed and paid by the owners, in or about the month of January, 1817, sailed on her said voyage with a cargo of merchandise belonging to the said J. B. Gooch, which had been shipped on board thereof by the said J. B. Gooch. The cargo was invoiced at 11,488l. 14s. Messrs. Bazett, Farquhar, Crawford, & Co. of London, of which firm the defendants were surviving partners, advanced to J. B. Gooch divers large sums of money to enable him to purchase his outward cargo, and the same was consigned by J. B. Gooch to Messrs. Colvin & Co., then merchants of Calcutta, as his agents, and was by Messrs. Colvin & Co., as agents of J. B. Gooch, received from on board the said ship at Calcutta, who disposed of the same for and on account of the said J. B. Gooch, the said Messrs. Colvin & Co. of Calcutta being at the same time the general agents and correspondents of the defendants,

and Bazett, since deceased, and David Colvin, one of the
defendants, being at the time of making of the said charterparty and arrival of the ship in London, partner, as
well in the house of Bazett & Co. of London, as of Colvin
& Co. of Calcutta.   Messrs. Colvin & Co., according to
the direction of J. B. Gooch, put up the ship as a general
ship at Calcutta, and succeeded in obtaining several ship-
ments on freight; but, not being able to fill the ship on
advantageous terms, they purchased the 511 bales of cotton wool in the issue mentioned, with advances made by
them on account of the said J. B. Gooch, they, Colvin &
Co., having the outward cargo at that time in their possession.   Price, the master or commander of the said ship
Hero, signed the following bill of lading for those and
other goods:—

"Shipped, by the grace of God, in good order and well
conditioned, by Messrs. Colvin, Bazett, & Co., in and upon
the good ship the Hero, whereof is master, under God,
for the present voyage, John Price, and now riding at
anchor in the river Hooghly, and by God's grace bound
for London; that is to say, 53 bales filature raw silk, 511
bales cotton, &c., and being marked and numbered as in
the margin; and are to be delivered in the like good order
and well conditioned at the aforesaid port of London, the
act of God, the king's enemies, fire, and all and every
other dangers and accidents of the seas, rivers, and navigation, of whatever nature and kind soever, excepted,
unto Messrs. Bazett, Farquhar, Crawford, & Co., or to
their assigns; freight for the said goods paid by bills on
London: in witness whereof the master or purser of the
said ship hath affirmed to four bills of lading, all of this
tenor and date, the one of which four bills being accomplished, the other three to stand void.   Dated in Calcutta,
29th of September, 1817. Contents unknown. John Price."

The letters J. B. G., with which the 511 bales of cotton
wool were marked, referred to the initials of the name of

the said John Burton Gooch. It was left to the jury whether those cotton wools so shipped were the goods of the said J. B. Gooch or not, and the jury found that they were the goods of Gooch, which was to be taken as a fact in this case. On the arrival of the vessel in London the cargo was deposited in the warehouses of the East India Company, and the proper notices were given by the plaintiff to preserve his lien under the statute. Before the arrival of the ship in London, J. B. Gooch stopped payment, and afterwards became a bankrupt. For the goods shipped on freight the plaintiff and his co-owners received the amount of such freight, and also a sum equal to the current rate of freight for the said 511 bales was paid to the plaintiff; but adverse claims were put in by the plaintiff and the defendants to the residue of the money produced by the sale of the said bales, the defendants claiming the same under the bill of lading as consignees thereof, and the plaintiff claiming a lien thereon for the sum due to him by J. B. Gooch on the said charterparty. The East India Company thereupon filed their bill of interpleader in the court of Chancery, in which suit this issue was sent.

The question for the opinion of the court was, whether the plaintiff, as owner of the ship Hero, had a lien on the said bales of cotton wool for freight under the charterparty beyond the freight due in respect of the carriage of the said cotton wool upon the said voyage. If the plaintiff had such a lien, the verdict was to stand; but, if the court should be of a contrary opinion, the verdict was to be entered for the defendants.

Cresswell, for the plaintiff.—Under this charterparty, the plaintiff had a lien on all the goods of the freighter, for the entire freight stipulated for. The case of *Saville* v. *Campion*, 2 B. & A. 503, which arrose upon this same charterparty, decides the question: the court of King's Bench there held, that, there being no express words of

demise of the ship itself in the charterparty, the freighter
did not thereby become the owner for the voyage, but
that the possession continued in the owner, *and that he
therefore had a lien upon the cargo for his freight.* That
case was determined not long after *Hutton* v. *Bragg,* 7
Taunt. 14, 2 Marsh. 339, and *The Trinity House* v. *Clark,*
4 M. & S. 228. *Hutton* v. *Bragg* was expressly overruled
in *Christie* v. *Lewis,* 5 Moore, 211, 2 B. & B. 410. There,
the defendant, as owner of a ship, entered into a charterparty with the freighter, by which the former "granted
and to freight let," and the latter "hired and to freight
took," the ship, for a voyage out and home. The owner
covenanted, that, the vessel being well manned and furnished as is usual for vessels in the merchant service, the
master should receive on board at London goods to be
sent alongside her there by the freighter, and deliver them
alongside at Newfoundland to the agents of the freighter,
according to bills of lading; and, such cargo having been
discharged there, should receive other goods in like
manner, and deliver them at Demerara, and, having discharged the same, should receive other goods there, and
deliver them at London, agreeably to bills of lading. The
owner also agreed that the ship's boats should assist in unloading and loading the cargoes when required by the
freighter, provided no impediment was thereby to be
made in carrying on the exclusive duties of the ship; in
consideration whereof the freighter covenanted to send
and take the goods from alongside, and to pay for the
freight and hire of the vessel for the voyage 2600*l.,* with
primage, &c., one quarter part thereof on delivery of
the cargo at Newfoundland, by two bills at sixty days'
sight on London, and the remainder by good bills at two
months' date from the day of the ship's report inwards at
the port of London. The voyage was performed, and
goods of third persons brought from Demerara under
bills of lading deliverable to the consignees on payment of

certain specified freight, which freight the owner received. Bills of exchange for one quarter of the freight were drawn on the freighter at Newfoundland, which were afterwards accepted and dishonoured by him, and no sum or bill for the remaining three fourths of the freight per charterparty was given or tendered to him on the return of the ship. It was held, that, taking the whole of the charterparty into consideration, the possession of the ship did not pass to the freighter, but remained in the owner, notwithstanding the words of grant used in its commencement; and that the mere circumstance of his having entered into an agreement with the charterer as to the mode by which he should be paid freight, did not divest him of his lien on the cargo; and that it made no difference that he had delivered the homeward cargo to the consignees, and received the freight due upon the bills of lading, which was different from that due upon the charterparty. *Tate* v. *Meek*, 2 Moore, 278, is to the same effect: there, the payment of the freight and the delivery of the cargo being concomitant acts, it was held that the owner was entitled to detain the cargo until the freight was paid. In *Faith* v. *The East India Company*, 4 B. & A. 630, the same question arose, and the same parties were the real defendants. There, by charterparty, freight was agreed to be paid for the use or hire of the ship at a certain rate per ton for a voyage out and home, in manner following, viz. a certain sum in advance on the ship's clearing outwards, and the residue, half in cash, and half in approved bills, upon the delivery of the homeward cargo; and the owner appointed a master at the request of the charterer (Gooch, the charterer in the present case), who executed a bond conditioned for the faithful performance of the master's duty; and also instructed the master to be careful to sign all bills of lading with the clause "freight payable as by charterparty;" and the ship was consigned to Colvin & Co. in Calcutta, by whom she was put up for her homeward cargo as a general ship, and different merchants shipped goods by her ; Colvin & Co. taking for homeward freight bills payable sixty days after the delivery of the cargo, and a new master having been appointed by them, in conjunction with the former master, signed bills of lading with the clause " paying freight agreeably to freight bill ;" and the freight bills were made payable in London to B. & Co. (the house of the present defendants), to whom (as in this case) the charterer was indebted for advances on the outward cargo, and who, as well as Colvin & Co., where cognisant of the terms of the charterparty: it was held that the owner of the ship had a lien on the goods to the extent of the homeward freight. Colvin & Co. also put on board the ship goods purchased by them on account of the charterer ; but he being indebted to them and B. & Co. their agents, those goods were by the bill of lading consigned to B. & Co.: and it was held, that, as between the owner of the ship and B. & Co., the goods were to be considered as the goods of the charterer, and liable to the owner's lien on them for the freight due by the charterparty. That case and *Saville* v. *Campion* are direct authorities for the plaintiff. In *Newberry* v *Colvin,* 4 M. & P. 876, 7 Bing. 190, 1 C. & J. 192, 1 Tyr. 55, where the decision of the court of King's Bench in *Colvin* v. *Newberry,* 2 M. & R. 47, 8 B. & C. 168, was reversed, the question was altogether different; and that case leaves *Saville* v. *Campion, Tate* v. *Meek,* and *Faith* v. *The East India Company,* wholly untouched. And see Abbott on Shipping, 5th edit. pp. 19—22.

Taddy, Serjeant, for the defendants.—*Saville* v. *Campion* is the only case directly in point upon this charterparty: and there Lord Chief Justice Abbott cautiously limits his judgment to the consideration of the question as between the parties to that suit—the assignees of Gooch, and the owner. And in *Faith* v. *The East India Company,* Abbott, C. J., says: " I am of opinion, that, as between these parties, these are to be considered as the goods of · Gooch and Saville, and in that case they are liable to the lien of the owner of the ship to the full extent of the freight due on the charterparty. If this had been a question between Gooch and Colvin & Co., the case might have been different." The same distinction is taken by that learned judge in *Colvin* v. *Newberry,* in the House of Lords, 6 Bligh, 189. Here the parties are, the owner, and the consignees of the goods—third parties—under a bill of lading expressing that freight upon the goods therein has been actually paid. The question therefore becomes entirely new. *Faith* v. *The East India Company* did not arise on this charterparty, but upon one the provisions of which were materially different: and there the special verdict was never drawn up, the matter having been compromised. *Hutton* v. *Bragg* certainly is not to be reconciled with *Christie* v. *Lewis:* but in this latter case the judgment of the court was not unanimous. The question is, whether, taking the whole contract together, the owner can be supposed to have intended to part with the possession of the ship. In *Birley* v. *Gladstone,* 3 M. & S. 205, where by charterparty the ship-owners covenanted to receive a full cargo, and the freighter to load the same, and to pay so much for every ton of flax, &c. which should be delivered at the king's beams at L., and so much per diem for demurrage, and the parties mutually bound themselves, especially the ship-owners the ship, her tackle, and appurtenances, and the freighter the goods laden and put on board, in a penal sum, for the performance of every article contained in the charterparty: it was held that the ship-owners had not a lien upon the goods actually brought home to L. for a sum of money claimed to be due in respect of goods which were put on board at the loading port, but afterwards re-

landed and restored to the agent of the freighter under
process of law at the loading port; nor for a sum claimed
for dead freight: nor for a sum claimed for demurrage.
Lord Ellenborough there said: "This is a mutual penalty; but, if we are to consider the clause in the way of
a lien, the remedy will not be mutual; it will stand thus,
that the owner of the ship may detain the goods of the
freighter as a security for the performance of the covenants, but the freighter can never detain the ship, so that
there will be no mutuality of lien between them." And
in *Gladstone* v. *Birley*, 2 Mer. 401, with reference to the
same clause in the same charterparty, the Master of the
Rolls (Sir W. Grant), said: "It was asked what effect
a clause would have if it gave no lien either at law or in
equity. A court of equity is not bound to find an equitable effect for a clause, merely because the construction
which a court of law has put upon it would leave it inoperative. In truth, it has been copied from foreign charter-
parties, with very little consideration of the effect that
might be allowed to it by the law of this country." And
in *Paul* v. *Birch*, 2 Atk. 621, Lord Hardwicke says: "As
to the general law, the cargo is no doubt liable to pay the
freight, or the expense of carrying the goods. What
occasions the difficulty is, that the 48*l.* a month is termed
for the freight of the goods; but improperly, for it is
rather for the hire of the ship." These authorities clearly
shew that there can be no general right of lien in respect
of the hire of a ship. The recognition of the owner's
right to detain arose out of an argument drawn from the
clause respecting the payment of freight: when it could
be inferred from the contract between the parties that the
payment of freight was to precede the delivery of the
goods, the courts held that that virtually amounted to a
stipulation that the owner should have a lien on the cargo
to enforce payment. The question was considered doubtful at the time of the decision of this court in *Hutton* v.

Bragg. Afterwards came a series of cases—*Tate* v. *Meek,*
Yates v. *Railston,* 2 Moore, 294, *Yates* v. *Mennell,* 2
Moore, 297, *Christie* v. *Lewis,* and *Faith* v. *The East India
Company*—all which are founded upon a principle that
is not applicable to the present case. There the payment
of the freight and the delivery of the goods were either
concomitant acts, or the former was by the express con-
vention of the parties to precede the latter. As far as regards the possession of the ship, the question is determined by the judgment of Tindal, C. J., in *Newberry* v.
Colvin. The proposition laid down in Abbott on Shipping, 5th edit. 178, that the owner's lien for freight exists
" even if it do not appear that the payment of the freight
is to precede or accompany the the delivery of the goods,"
is not supportable : to entitle the owner to such lien there
must be an express reservation of it, where the contract is
for the hire of the ship. [*Tindal,* C. J.—The necessary
intendment from the language of the charterparty in the
present case, is, that the payment of the freight was to precede the delivery of the goods.] The freight here, being
a mere tonnage freight, would be equally payable if no
goods at all had been put on board. Undoubtedly, on a
mere contract for the carriage of goods, the carrier would
have a right to detain the particular goods for the carriage or freight due in respect of them. The bill of
lading in the present case creates a material distinction
between this and the case of *Saville* v. *Campion.* Even
supposing the plaintiff's right to detain these particular
goods would exist as between Gooch and the defendants,
the rights of third parties having intervened, it is gone.
The captain having signed a bill of lading whereby he
contracts to deliver the goods to a third person, and freight
being paid, is not the owner bound by that contract?
Whether the goods belong to Gooch or not, makes no
difference. In *Evans* v. *Martlett,* 1 Ld. Raym. 271, 12
Mod. 156, 3 Salk. 290, it was held, that, upon a general

consignment the property vests in the consignee, notwithstanding it appears upon the invoices that he is a
trustee only. Bills of lading, made out to the order of
the shipper or his assigns, are negotiable and transfer-
able by the shipper's indorsement—*Haille* v. *Smith*, 1 B.
& P. 564. The bill of lading here totally alters the aspect
of the case: the fact of the general property in the goods
being in Gooch is not inconsistent or incompatible with
the existence of a qualified property in the defendants.

Cresswell, in reply, was stopped by the court.

TINDAL, C. J.—I am unable to come to a conclusion
different from that at which the court arrived in *Saville* v.
Campion, *Tate* v. *Meek*, *Faith* v. *The East India Company*,
and some other cases, in which it was held, that an owner,
retaining the possession of his ship, has a lien on the cargo
for the hire of the ship due under a charterparty. It has
been contended that these cases are distinguishable from
the present in two important particulars—first, that this
charterparty is not so framed as to leave the owner in
possession of the ship, and therefore he can have no such
possession of the cargo as to entitle him to a lien for the
hire of the ship—secondly, that in none of the cases has
the owner been entitled to enforce his lien, unless where
the payment of the freight for the ship was to be concomitant with or precedent to the delivery of the cargo.
In the general doctrine I agree. The main reliance of
the defendants, who insist that the property in the vessel
here was in Gooch, has been on the case of *Newberry* v.
Colvin. The charterparty, however, in that case seems
to me to be perfectly distinguishable from this in many
respects. This is the simplest case of a charterparty by
which the owner covenants to take on board the ship, in
the port of London, from the freighter, all such goods as
he might think fit to load, not exceeding what she could

reasonably carry beyond her stores, &c., and should proceed therewith to Madeira, there to receive other goods,
and then proceed to Madras and Calcutta, and there deliver the outward cargo, and, after being refitted, should
receive on board all such lawful goods as the freighter's
agents might think fit to load, and then proceed to London, and there deliver the homeward cargo agreeably to
bills of lading.   There is no demise, no parting with the
possession of the ship, either by express words or by necessary inference, as in *Newberry* v. *Colvin*.   In this respect, therefore, the two cases are perfectly distinguishable.   Then, is the freight stipulated for by the charterparty payable before delivery of the goods?   It seems to
me that it is only necessary to advert to the charterparty
itself to ascertain that such is the case.   The freight is
perfectly independent of the quality of the goods; it is to
be paid after a given rate per ton upon the ship's register
tonnage—500*l.* in cash at the expiration of six months
from the date of the charterparty; a moiety of the remainder by bills at two months after date from the day
on which the ship should arrive in the Thames on her
return from her homeward voyage; and the residue by
bills at four months' date from the same period.   By another part of the instrument it is provided that the vessel,
on her arrival, should take her regular turn in the East
India Docks for the purpose of unloading and delivering
her cargo.   This clearly shews it to have been in the contemplation of the parties that the owner should have the
right to insist on the delivery of the bills before the cargo
was delivered.   Another ground upon which it is contended that this case is distinguishable from *Saville* v.
Campion (which otherwise, it is admitted, must, if it be
law, govern the present case), is, that there the action
was brought by the assignees of Gooch, whereas here
the interests of a third party are before the court, viz. a
consignee of goods under a bill of lading signed by the

captain. Let us see whether or not this circumstance in reality furnishes any distinction. In the first place, the outward cargo was consigned to and received by Colvin & Co., of Calcutta, the agents of Gooch: in the next place, the goods in question were purchased by Colvin & Co. with advances made by them on account of Gooch, they having the outward cargo at that time in their possession: and, in the third place, the jury found, and it is expressly stated as a fact in the case, that the goods were the goods of Gooch. I am of opinion that we should be varying the real situation and interests of the parties if we were to attribute to this bill of lading any force beyond an authority to deliver the goods therein mentioned to the real consignor himself, or to his order. We are dealing with the goods of Gooch: and, if we were to hold that the plaintiff had not a lien on these goods for the general freight due under the charterparty, we should be allowing Gooch so to deal with them, in the mode of consignment he has adopted, as to evade the lien which would clearly have attached under the charterparty had they been consigned by him in his own name. Upon the whole, I am of opinion that this case is not in any degree distinguishable from *Saville* v. *Campion*, and therefore that the plaintiff is entitled to a verdict.

PARK, J.—I am of the same opinion. I think it quite idle to re-discuss the cases anterior to *Smith* v. *Campion*, which was well and maturely considered by the court of King's Bench before its ultimate decision: and the question in this case arises upon the same charterparty. It is expressly stipulated that the delivery of the freight bills shall precede the delivery of the cargo: for, the bills are made deliverable the moment the vessel arrives in the river Thames, and the cargo is not to be delivered until she is moored in the proper dock. *Saville* v. *Campion* clearly binds us: the fact of the goods being consigned

1836.

CAMPION

v.

COLVIN.

to a third party, under the circumstances stated in the case, makes no difference.

GASELEE, J.—I am of the same opinion. I do not think the defendants are in this case to be deemed third parties any more than the assignees were in *Saville* v. *Campion*. Colvin & Co., of Calcutta, were the agents of Gooch, the freighter, and acting for his benefit.

VAUGHAN, J.—*Saville* v. *Campion* was determined after grave deliberation, and in my opinion rightly. Upon a proper consideration of this charterparty, I think it is impossible to say that the owner ever parted with the possession of the vessel.

Verdict for the plaintiff.

JAMES SMITH *v.* GEORGE SMITH, Administrator of JAMES SMITH.

Tuesday,
May 31st.

In trover for a watch, the defendant pleaded that it was not the property of the plaintiff. At the trial, the defendant proved that the watch (which had belonged to his father, whose personal representative he was) had been in his, the defendant's, possession for four years previously to the father's death, and then put in evidence letters of administration:—Held, that declarations of the intestate as to the ownership of the watch, were evidence against the defendant.

TROVER for a watch. Pleas—first, not guilty— secondly, that the watch was not the property of the plaintiff; upon which issue was joined.

At the trial, before Vaughan, J., at the sittings at Westminster in last Hilary Term, it appeared that the watch in question had originally belonged to the intestate, the father of the plaintiff and defendant, who died in 1833. The plaintiff proved, that, in 1824, the intestate had given him the watch; but one of the plaintiff's witnesses, on cross examination, proved a declaration by the intestate, in the presence of the plaintiff, that the latter having clandestinely abstracted the watch from the intestate's strong box in 1828, the intestate had given the watch to the defendant. The plaintiff then offered evidence of other declarations by the intestate as to the circumstances under which the watch came into the plaintiff's hands; but the learned judge thought this evidence not admissible, though he offered to receive evidence as to what the father had said at the time he gave the watch.—The defendant then proved that he had been in possession of the watch for four years previously to the death of the intestate; and concluded his case by putting in the letters of administration granted to him of the intestate's effects. A verdict having been found for the defendant—

Bompas, Serjeant, in Hilary Term, obtained a rule nisi for a trial, on the ground that what the father (through whom the defendant, from his putting in the letters of administration, must be deemed to claim,) said at a time anterior to the claim set up by the defendant, was evidence as to his property in the watch. He cited *Ivatt* v. *Finch*, 1 Taunt. 141, where, upon an issue between A. and B., whether C. died possessed of certain property, it was held that evidence might be given of declarations made by C. that she had assigned the property to A.

Byles now shewed cause.—On the second plea, the defendant rested on his possession, not on his title as administrator; and that was sufficient until the plaintiff established a better title. The declarations, therefore, were not admissible as the declarations of a party under whom the defendant claimed. But, even if the defendant did claim as administrator, the declarations were equally inadmissible, as having been made at a time when the intestate was not possessed of the watch. In *Pocock* v. *Billing*, 2 Bing. 269, 9 Moore, 499, 1 C. & P. 230, R. & M. 129, it was held, that, in an action by an indorsee of a bill of exchange against the acceptor, the declarations of a former holder are admissible in evidence, if it can be shewn that he was the holder of the bill at the time, and made such declarations to his own prejudice, and against his own interest: and Best, C. J., said he likened the case to that of declarations made by the owner of an estate during his possession. Neither was the evidence receivable as the declarations of a deceased person, made against his own in-

1836.

SMITH
v.
SMITH.

terest: the transfer to the intestate's son, being in diminu-
tion of the expense of maintenance, cannot be said to have
been adverse to the intestate's interest. If he were still
living, his own declarations would not be evidence for
him; nor, upon the same principle, can they be for his representative. In *Woolway* v. *Rowe*, 1 Ad. & E. 114, declarations respecting the subject-matter of a cause by a person
who at the time of making them had the same interest in
such matter as one of the parties to the cause had at the
time of the action, were held to be admissible in evidence
against that party, though the maker of them was still
alive, and might have been called as a witness. But, in
Glyn v. *The Bank of England*, 2 Ves. 43, where a bill was
brought by executors, on a loss of notes described in a
list in the testator's own handwriting, the list was not admitted as evidence of the property in a court of equity,
but left to a court of law, although the rule of evidence
there was the same as at law. And in *Rex* v. *Debenham*,
2 B. & A. 85, where, on an appeal, the respondents, in
order to prove the fact of the delivery to them of a certificate given by the appellants, acknowledging the pauper
to be their settled inhabitant, produced an old book from
their own parish chest, in which was an entry of that fact
in the handwriting of a former parish officer, it was held,
that such evidence was inadmissible. So, in *Bernasconi* v.
Farebrother, 3 B. & Ad. 372, assignees were not allowed
to avail themselves of the declarations of the bankrupt
under whom they claimed. Declarations of a deceased
person, admitted as made against his own interest, must,
in order to their reception, be made in the course of a
business in hand, and not dropped loosely and sponta-
neously: 1 Stark. Evid. 297. In *Ivatt* v. *Finch* the party
was bound to justify under the deceased, and could make
no case in any other way.

Bompas, Serjeant, and *Chandless*, in support of the

rule.—The defendant having put in the letters of administration, was precluded from afterwards saying that he did not claim the property in his representative character. *Ivatt* v. *Finch* is a distinct authority to shew that the declarations which the learned judge rejected were admissible. In *Davis* v. *Pierce*, 2 T. R. 53, it was held that declarations by tenants are admissible in evidence after their death, to shew that a certain piece of land was parcel of the estate which they occupied: and in *Doe* d. *Brune* v. *Rawlings*, 7 East, 279, 3 Smith, 254, that the entries by A., the tenant for life, in his book, of the receipt of the rent to the amount stated, are evidence of the fact. In this latter case, Lord Ellenborough said: "There are several instances in the books where the declaration of a person having knowledge of a fact, and no interest to falsify it, has been admitted as evidence of it after his death. Thus, the written memorandum of a father as to the time when his child was born, has been received to prove when the infant would come of age, and that he was in fact under age at the time of making his will. And yet the most that can be said for such evidence is, the peculiar means of knowledge of the fact by the father, and the absence of all interest in him at the time of the memorandum or declaration made to falsify the truth in respect of it."

TINDAL, C. J.—The opinion I form in this case arises from its position at the time it was presented to the jury. The issue, it is true, was negative—that the plaintiff had no property in the watch; but that issue might be decided by an affirmative inconsistent with the negative; which, indeed, would be the most satisfactory of all proof. At the close of the defendant's case, the letters of administration granted to him were put in evidence. It might be supposed, from his offering such evidence, that he claimed as administrator; it was open to the jury to draw that inference; and, in answer to that evidence it was competent

1836.

SMITH
v.
SMITH.

to the plaintiff to offer in evidence declarations of the intestate upon the subject of the article in contest. Strictly speaking, the defendant claims under the intestate; and consequently the reason is stronger for the admission of the evidence than in *Ivatt* v. *Finch.* I think, therefore, the rule for a new trial should be made absolute.

PARK, J.—I should have acted as the learned judge at the outset; but, when the letters of administration were put in, the defendant seemed to claim in right of the intestate, and the plaintiff was entitled to give in evidence the intestate's declarations.

The rest of the court concurring—

Rule absolute.

———◆———

THE WARDENS AND COMONALTY OF THE MYSTERY OF GROCERS v. DONNE.

Wednesday,
June 1st.

In order to render commissioners acting in the bonâ fide performance of a public duty liable to an action for an injury to an individual resulting from an act so done by

THIS action was brought by the Grocers' Company against the defendant, as clerk to the commissioners of sewers, under the 42nd section of the 4 Geo. 4, c. 114, to recover damages for an injury occasioned to a house belonging to the plaintiffs, and occupied by Mr. Bicknell, their clerk, bordering upon Princes Street. The house, as was alleged, settled and sank, and was cracked and

them, it must appear that they have been guilty of negligence or want of skill in the conduct of it.

In case against commissioners of sewers for an injury done to the plaintiffs' premises by the construction of an adjoining sewer, the cause was referred to an arbitrator, who found, that there were two modes of making a sewer practised in London, the one by what is called tunnelling, the other by what is called open cutting; that, in this case, a deep sewer could not be made either by the one method or the other without risk of damage to the adjoining buildings; that the amount of risk varied according to the nature of the soil, which here was of a nature to make the risk considerable; that the probability of damage accruing was *in some degree less* where the sewer was made by open cutting than by tunnelling; that the sewer was made by the mode of tunnelling; that the commissioners, in directing it to be made, and in the making of it, were acting bonâ fide in the honest discharge of their duty as commissioners; that the sewer was fit and proper to be made for the convenient drainage of the city of London, and was made in a workmanlike, skilful, and proper manner in all respects, provided that the commissioners were justified in making it by the mode of tunnelling; and that, in consequence of the making of the sewer, the plaintiffs' house was damaged to a certain amount. It did not appear that the plaintiffs had had any notice of the progress of the work or of the mode of doing it:—Held, that the commissioners were not responsible for the injury so occasioned.

damaged. in various places, in consequence of the foundations being disturbed and drawn from under it by the
works connected with the construction of a sewer along
Princes Street. The mode of construction adopted was
by a tunnel carried along the street at a depth of thirty
feet from the surface, and contiguous to the foundation of
the plaintiffs' house; and it was alleged that the excavation for the tunnel caused a subsidence of the soil which
affected the foundation.

The declaration stated, that, before and at the time of
the committing of the grievances thereinafter mentioned,
the plaintiffs were lawfully possessed of a certain antient
messuage and premises situate and being in the parish of
St. Mildred the Virgin, in the city of London, which said
messuage was then used by the plaintiffs for the occupation of a certain servant of the plaintiffs; yet the said
commissioners of sewers of the city of London and liberties thereof, well knowing the premises, but wrongfully
and injuriously intending to injure the plaintiffs in
respect of their said antient messuage and premises with
the appurtenances as aforesaid, to wit, on the 7th August,
1834, wrongfully and injuriously did make, cut, and dig a
certain shaft, sewer, gutter, and ditch, near unto the said
antient messuage and premises so in possession of the
plaintiffs as aforesaid, and did unskilfully, wrongfully, and
improperly, make, cut, and dig the said shaft, sewer, gutter, and ditch, so being near unto the said antient messuage and premises of plaintiffs as aforesaid, and did also
make, cut, and dig, the said shaft, gutter, sewer, and
ditch without shoring up, propping, or duly securing the
said messuage and premises, or the earth and subsoil
supporting the walls of the said antient messuage and
premises of the plaintiffs as aforesaid, in order to prevent
the same from being injured by the said making, cutting,
and digging of the said shaft, sewer, gutter, and ditch as
aforesaid, and without giving due notice to the plaintiffs

of the intention of them the said commissioners to dig, make, and cut the said shaft, sewer, gutter, and ditch, so as to enable the plaintiffs to shore and prop up their said antient messuage and premises: by means of which several premises, the said antient messuage and premises of the plaintiffs became and were and still are greatly injured and weakened, and the walls, partitions, ceilings, floors, and other parts of the said antient messuage and premises of the plaintiffs were damaged, so that the said messuage of the plaintiffs had become and was dangerous to live and reside in ; and the plaintiffs, from the time of committing the aforesaid grievances, hitherto, had been and were hindered and prevented from enjoying their said antient messuage and premises in so ample and beneficial a manner as they might and otherwise would and ought to have done; and had been obliged to expend divers sums of money, amounting to the sum of 500*l.*, in and about the obtaining another residence for the said servant of the plaintiffs, and in and about removing divers articles of furniture and other goods and chattels from and out of their said antient messuage ; and by means of the said several premises, the said messuage and premises had been and were much injured and lessened in value, and thereby the same had become and were of no use or value to the plaintiffs ; and the plaintiffs, by means of the premises, were injured and damnified to a large amount.

Plea, not guilty.

The cause having been referred to arbitration under an order of Nisi Prius, the arbitrator found, that the defendant was clerk to the commissioners of sewers of the city of London and liberties thereof, and that a deep sewer had been lately made by order and under the directions of the said commissioners, in Princes Street in the said city, and within the jurisdiction of the said commissioners, near to the dwelling-house of the plaintiffs in the declaration in this cause mentioned ; that Princes Street

1836.

THE GROCERS'
COMPANY
v.
DONNE.

was a narrow street; and that there were in most parts of it heavy buildings on one or other of the sides, and in some places on both sides of the street, one of which was the said house of the plaintiffs; that there were two modes of making a sewer practised in the city of London—the one by what is called tunnelling, and the other by what is called open cutting; that, in Princes Street, as in most other narrow streets, with heavy buildings adjoining on them, a deep sewer could not be made either by the one method or the other without risk of damage to the adjoining buildings; that the amount of risk varied according to the nature of the soil; that the soil of Princes Street was of a kind to make the risk considerable; and that the nature of the soil was known, or might by due inquiry and proper experiments have been known to the said commissioners before the making of the sewer; that the probability of damage accruing was in some degree less where the sewer was made by open cutting, than by tunnelling; that the sewer in this case was made by the mode of tunnelling; that the commissioners, in directing the sewer to be made, and in the making of it, were acting bonâ fide in the honest discharge of their duty as commissioners; and that the sewer was fit and proper to be made for the convenient drainage of the city of London, and was made in a workmanlike, skilful, and proper manner in all respects, provided that the commissioners were justified in making the sewer by the mode of tunnelling; that, in consequence of the making of the sewer, the house of the plaintiffs was damaged to the amount of 400*l.* Upon the whole matter, therefore, the arbitrator found, that, if the commissioners were authorized to make the sewer by the mode of tunnelling, the verdict ought to be for the defendant. But, if the commissioners were bound to pursue the mode which afforded the utmost possible chance of preventing damage to the adjoining buildings, the verdict ought to be for the plaintiffs, to the amount of 400*l.* And there-

upon the arbitrator awarded that the verdict which had
been taken for the plaintiffs should stand, if the court
should be opinion that the verdict ought to be entered
for the plaintiffs; but, if the court should be of opinion
that the verdict ought to be entered for the defendant,
then he awarded that the verdict already entered should
be set aside, and, instead thereof, that a verdict should be
entered for the defendant.

Spankie, Serjeant (*W. H. Watson* was with him), for
the plaintiffs.—Enough is stated upon the face of this
award to entitle the plaintiffs to a verdict for the sum
therein mentioned. It is not the policy of the law that
the execution of public works should in any case enure to
the private damage of an individual. In the present case
the award states that the commissioners of sewers were
the persons by whose order and under whose direction
the work in question was carried on. In so doing, it was
their duty to guard against damage to the property in the
neighbourhood. They were bound to exclude all perils
which prudence might possibly avoid—not ordinary prudence only: but they were bound to exert the utmost
possible care and discretion. They should have adopted
that course which the arbitrator finds would have been
attended with the smallest risk. The omission to do this
was such a culpable degree of negligence as to render
them responsible for all the consequences. That the duty
of a party under such circumstances is, to use something
more than a reasonable degree of negligence, is clear from
Colvin's Lexicon, "Culpa;" The Digest, Book 9, tit. 2,
law 31, and Book 39, tit. 2, law 24, s. 12; and from Huber,
77, 78. In *Slingsby* v. *Barnard*, 1 Roll. Bep. 430, there
was no allegation of negligence; but a bare statement of
the fact that the defendants dug a cellar under Barnard's
house so near the foundation of the plaintiff's house that
it was undermined, and part fell, was held sufficient to en-

title the plaintiff to recover. In *Roberts* v. *Read*, 16 East, 215, a surveyor of highways was held subject to an action on the case for an injury resulting to an individual, for having in the exercise of his office undermined a wall adjoining a highway, which in consequence fell. In *Wyatt* v. *Harrison*, 3 B. & Adol. 871, it was held that the possessor of a house which is not *antient* could not maintain an action against the owner of adjoining land, for digging away that land so that the house fell in. But, in the subsequent of *Dodd* v. *Holme*, 3 N. & M. 739, 1 Ad. & E. 493, it was held that an action lies against a party who by *carelessness* or *negligence* in excavating his own ground, either causes or accelerates the fall of an adjoining house. That case seems to throw some doubt upon *Wyatt*. v. *Harrison*. The statute 11 Geo. 3, c. 29, s. 117, which regulates the mode of proceeding against commissioners of sewers, amounts to a legislative declaration of their liability to be sued: and there can be no reason why they should be exempted from such liability, seeing that they are indemnified by the public for that which they do in the bonâ fide discharge of their duty. At all events, the commissioners were bound in the present case to give the plaintiffs notice of their proceedings, so as to enable them to adopt measures for their own security. In *Jones* v. *Bird*, 1 D. & R. 407, 5 B. & Ald. 844, where bricklayers, employed by the commissioners of sewers to repair a public sewer, performed the work in such a manner as to occasion a damage to a neighbouring house; it was held that the commissioners were liable to an action, although the work itself appeared to be performed in a skilful manner. And Abbott, C. J., said: " One question arising at the trial was, as to the effect which shoring up would have produced, and I stated that the commissioners of sewers and their agents, when repairing sewers in the neighbourhood of houses, were bound to take all proper precaution for their security;

and that one question for the jury to consider was, whether shoring up was a proper precaution, and whether it had been omitted. I also told them, that, even if they were of opinion that the stack of chimneys could not, by any shoring up whatsoever, have been prevented from falling, still that it was the duty of the defendants, if they thought so, to give specific notice of the danger to the owner; and that, if they did not do so, they were responsible. Here, no such specific notice of the peculiar construction of the stack of chimneys, and of the danger arising from it, was given. On either of these grounds, therefore, the verdict of the jury is sustainable." And Bayley, J., said : " As to the merits of the case, it is contended that the defendants are protected if they acted bonâ fide and to the best of their skill and judgment. But that is not enough; they are bound to conduct themselves in a skilful manner ; and the question was most properly left to the jury to say whether the defendants had done all that any skilful person could reasonably be required to do in such a case."

Sir *W. Follett*, for the defendants.—Where an individual is acting for his own private advantage, he is undoubtedly bound to exercise the greatest possible degree of caution the case will admit of, so as to avoid doing injury to his neighbour. This is all that *Slingsby* v. *Barnard* (which, however, seems to be a very absurd case) decided. But the principle which governs actions against persons acting in the performance of a public duty, is widely different: where the act done is done in the bonâ fide discharge of such public duty, and in a skilful and workmanlike manner, they are not responsible for accidental injuries. The distinction is clearly pointed out in some of the later cases. Thus, in *The Plate Glass Company* v. *Meredith*, 4 T. R. 794, it was held, that, where the acts of commissioners appointed by a paving act occasion a damage to an individual, without any excess of jurisdiction on their part, the commissioners (or the paviors acting under them) are not liable to an action. So, in *Bolton* v. *Crowther,* 4 D. & R. 195, 2 B. & C. 703, where trustees under the general turnpike act, 3 Geo. 4, c. 126, in improving the course of a public road, had effected a consequential injury to a private individual whose estate abutted on the road, it was held that they were not liable to an action; it appearing that they had not exceeded the authority given them by the statute. And in *Sutton* v. *Clarke,* 6 Taunt. 29, 1 Marsh. 429, it is laid down that one who in the exercise of a public function, without emolument, which he is compellable to execute, acting without malice, and according to his best skill and diligence, and obtaining the best information he can, does an act which occasions consequential damage to a subject, is not liable to an action for such damage. Gibbs, C. J., there says: "This case is perfectly unlike that of an individual who, for his own benefit, makes an improvement in his own land according to his best skill and diligence, and not foreseeing it will produce any injury to his neighbour: if he thereby unwittingly injure his neighbour, he is answerable. The resemblance fails in the most important point of comparison, and his act is not done for a public purpose, but for a private emolument. Here the defendant is not a volunteer; he executes a duty imposed on him by the legislature, which he is bound to execute. He exercises his best skill, diligence, and caution in the execution of it; and we are of opinion that he is not liable for an injury which he did not only not foresee, but could not foresee. He has done all that was incumbent on him, having used his best skill and diligence." *Jones* v. *Bird* is an authority for the same position: the defendants were held liable there solely on the ground of negligence in the mode of conducting the work. In the present case the arbitrator has not found that the damage was the result of any negligence or want of skill, that any necessary precaution was omitted, that the accident would not have happened if the sewer had been made by open cutting instead of by tunnelling, or that the plaintiffs had no notice that the work was proceeding. On the contrary, the award finds expressly, that the commissioners in the construction of the sewer were acting bonâ fide in the honest discharge of their duty, and that the sewer was fit and proper to be made for the convenient drainage of the city of London, and was made in a workmanlike, skilful, and proper manner in all respects, provided that the commissioners were justified in making the sewer by the mode of tunnelling. It does not follow from this finding that there were not advantages in the mode of working by tunnelling over the other mode, which would justify the commissioners in adopting it; or that, taking all things into consideration, the same degree of damage might not have resulted in either case. The commissioners were to consider the relative expense of the different modes: and, having employed skilful workmen, and seen that the work was done in a skilful manner, they have done all that the law requires of them.

Spankie, Serjeant, in reply.—The arbitrator not having found that the defendants had notice, it must be assumed that none was in fact given. Considering the nature of the soil, as found by the award, more than ordinary precaution ought to have been used: and the non-adoption of the *best* mode is a want of skill. It being conceded that a private individual would under the circumstances have been responsible, there is no reason either in law or good sense why these commissioners, or the public through them, should not be held responsible for an injury that has resulted from the construction of a work that is for the general benefit.

TINDAL, C. J.—It appears to me that the question is,

1836.

THE GROCERS'
COMPANY
v.
DONNE.

whether the facts found upon this award bring the case within the terms of the declaration. The cause having been referred, and the arbitrator having stated the facts for the opinion of the court, we must see whether or not the facts so found raise the duty set up by the plaintiffs in their declaration. The declaration states that the commissioners wrongfully and injuriously did make, cut, and dig a certain shaft, sewer, gutter, and ditch, near unto an antient messuage and premises in possession of the plaintiffs, and did unskilfully, wrongfully and improperly make, cut, and dig the said shaft, sewer, gutter, and ditch, so being near unto the said antient messuage and premises of the plaintiffs as aforesaid, and did also make, cut, and dig the said shaft, gutter, sewer, and ditch, without shoring up, propping, or duly securing the said messuage and premises, or the earth and subsoil supporting the walls of the said antient messuage and premises of the plaintiffs as aforesaid, in order to prevent the same from being injured by the said making, cutting, and digging of the said shaft, sewer, gutter, and ditch as aforesaid. As to the want of notice, the arbitrator has raised no question. We must then look at the award, and see whether or not the commissioners have conducted themselves in an unskilful, wrongful, and improper manner in the construction of the sewer in question. The allegation of unskilfulness is negatived by the award, for it expressly finds that the work was done in a skilful and proper manner. But the question is, whether the commissioners are to be mulcted in damages by reason of their having proceeded by a process called tunnelling, in preference to open cutting. If the award had found, that, in the judgment of experienced men, no injury would have resulted to the plaintiffs, had the commissioners proceeded by open cutting, the plaintiffs would have been entitled to a verdict. But the arbitrator finds that there was risk in either way, though less in degree from open work than from the other mode: and if the commissioners were bound to pursue that mode which gave the greatest possible chance of escape from injury, the verdict ought to be entered for the plaintiffs. But how are we to say that the commissioners are to be liable in damages, not because they did not perform the work in a skilful, proper, and workmanlike manner, but because they did not adopt that course which afforded the utmost possible chance of averting danger? The court is not to balance possibilities. We are called upon to pronounce a judgment against the commissioners because, had another mode of operation been resorted to, by some remote possibility the damage of which the plaintiffs complain *might* not have accrued. It seems to me that the plaintiffs can only entitle themselves to a verdict by shewing that the injury would not have happened if the sewer had been constructed by open cutting : and consequently the verdict must be entered for the defendant.

PARK, J.—I am of the same opinion. To entitle the plaintiffs to recover in this action, it was undoubtedly necessary for them to shew that the defendants, who are public commissioners, had been guilty of negligence. The award however shews that no mode of proceeding that could have been adopted was wholly unattended with risk. The arbitrator states that the street was narrow; that there were two modes of making a sewer practised in London, the one by tunnelling, the other by open cutting; that in Princes Street (the street in question) a deep sewer could not be made either by the one method or the other without risk of damage to the adjoining buildings ; that the amount of risk varied according to the nature of the soil; that the soil of Princes Street was of a kind to make the risk considerable; and that the probability of damage accruing was in some degree less where the sewer was made by open cutting than by tunnelling. How are we to estimate that? or why hold the commissioners to be responsible for a very slight possible increase of risk? especially as the award finds that "the commissioners, in directing the sewer to be made, and in the making of it, were acting bonâ fide in the honest discharge of their duty as commissioners; and that the sewer was fit and proper to be made for the convenient drainage of the city of London, and was made in a workmanlike, skilful, and proper manner, in all respects, provided that the commissioners were justified in making the sewer by the mode of tunnelling; that, if the commissioners were authorised to make the sewer by the mode of tunnelling, the verdict ought to be for the defendant; but that, if the commissioners were bound to pursue the mode which afforded the *utmost possible chance* of preventing damage to the adjoining buildings, the verdict ought to be for the plaintiffs." I am not aware that it has ever been held that a public officer who acts to the best of his judgment and with proper skill, is responsible for a damage resulting from his omission to adopt that course of proceeding which offers the greatest possible chance of avoiding the injury.

GASELEE, J.—I could have wished that this matter were sent back to the arbitrator; for, upon the facts found by him, I do not feel prepared to give any decided opinion. The award is not so framed as to enable me to form any satisfactory judgment as to whether the commissioners should not have pursued that course which offered something less of probability of risk. But, when it is found by the arbitrator "that the commissioners, in directing the sewer to be made, and in the making of it, were acting bonâ fide in the honest discharge of their duty as commissioners; that the sewer was fit and proper to be made for the convenient drainage of the city of London, and was made in a workmanlike, skilful, and proper manner in all respects, provided that the commissioners were justified in making the sewer by the mode of tunnelling," I am not prepared to say that the commissioners ought to be charged. Upon the whole, however, I must confess myself unable to make up my mind either way.

VAUGHAN, J.—I agree with my Lord Chief Justice and my Brother Park in holding the defendant entitled to judgment upon the facts presented by this award. Looking at the declaration and at the award, it appears to me to be impossible to say that the commissioners are tort-feasors, or that the allegation in the declaration, that they unskilfully, wrongfully, and improperly made the sewer, has been made out. It is not found in the award that the damage of which the plaintiffs complain was occasioned by tunnelling. The question is, whether public officers are not protected in the discharge of a public duty, where it is found that they have acted bonâ fide and in a skilful and proper manner. I think the distinction taken in *Sutton* v. *Clark*, between private persons and public functionaries, is well founded. In the present case, it appears that two modes of proceeding were pointed out to the commissioners. In the exercise of their judgment they have chosen one of those modes; and the arbitrator finds that there was a *possibility* of less damage accruing from the other. This clearly is not enough to render them chargeable.

Verdict for the defendants.

———◆———

WOOD *v.* HURD.

THIS was an action for a breach of promise of marriage. The damages (3500*l.*) and costs (293*l.*) having been paid to the plaintiff's attorney—

of promise of marriage, without a warrant of attorney from the plaintiff, notwithstanding a judge's order had been obtained for the purpose by consent.

Butt moved to enter satisfaction on the judgment roll under a judge's order, obtained by consent of the plaintiff's attorney on record. The secondary (Mr. Cancellor) had objected that a warrant of attorney from the plaintiff was necessary. This, it was submitted, was not the practice of the other courts; and the attorney was the proper person to pay the money to.

Mr. *Cancellor* observed that the order in this court is always drawn up " upon reading the warrant of attorney."

TINDAL, C. J.—We cannot depart from the practice of the court. The warrant of attorney is the only security to the court that the damages have been paid to the plaintiff. How are we to say that the attorney who conducted the suit for the plaintiff is now the attorney upon the record? Getting rid of a judgment of the court is so solemn a thing, that I think we should not be warranted in departing from a practice which appears so consonant with reason and good sense. Via trita via tuta.

The rest of the court concurring—

Rule refused.

————

GOLDSMID, Assignee of F. HIRSCHFIELD, a Bankrupt, *v.* LEWIS.

AN issue having been directed by this court under the interpleader act, 1 & 2 Will. 4, c. 56, to ascertain whether or not an alleged sale of certain candles by Hirschfield, the bankrupt, to the defendant was a bonâ fide transaction, which came on to be tried before Tindal, C. J., at the sittings in London after last Hilary Term, a verdict was found for the plaintiff, damages 31*l.* Before judg-

debtors act, 7 Geo. 4, c. 57, having inserted the amount of the verdict and the supposed amount of costs in his schedule:—Held, that, under the 50th section of the statute, the defendant was discharged from the damages and costs.

B B 2

[right margin:]

1836.

WOOD
v.
HURD.

*Thursday,
June 2nd.*

In trover for goods, the plaintiff recovered a verdict. Before the taxation of costs or the entry of final judgment, the defendant obtained his discharge under the insolvent

1836.

GOLDSMID
v.
LEWIS.

ment was signed, or the costs ascertained, the defendant on the 9th March petitioned the insolvent debtors court for his discharge under the 7 Geo. 4, c. 57. In his schedule filed in that court, the plaintiff appeared as a creditor: the entry was as follows :—

" M. A. Goldsmid, official assignee of F. Hirschfield, candle maker, a bankrupt, 231*l.* and costs.

" In April last, I purchased a quantity of candles from the bankrupt, for which I paid him. The assignees have since brought an action against me in the court of Common Pleas, on the ground that he had committed an act bankruptcy prior to my purchase, and they have recovered a judgment against me for 31*l.*: the remaining 200*l.* inserted as supposed costs."

After the defendant had been discharged under the act, he was taken in execution at the suit of the present plaintiff for the damages and costs in the action.

Bompas, Serjeant, on a former day in this term, obtained a rule calling upon the plaintiff to shew cause why the defendant should not be discharged from this execution. The learned Serjeant referred to the 46th section of the 7 Geo. 4, c. 57, which enacts, " that, after such examination made into the matters of the petition and schedule of any such prisoner as thereinbefore directed, it shall and may be lawful at such hearing or adjourned hearing as aforesaid, for the said court or commissioner or justices, upon such prisoner's swearing to the truth of his or her petition and schedule, and executing such warrant of attorney as is thereinafter directed, to adjudge that such prisoner *shall be discharged* from custody, and entitled to the benefit of the act, at such time as the said court or commissioner or justices shall direct, in pursuance of the provisions thereinafter contained in that behalf, *as to the several debts and sums of money due or claimed to be due at the time of filing such prisoner's pe-*

tition from such prisoner to the several persons named in his or her schedule as creditors or claiming to be creditors for the same respectively, or for which such persons shall have given credit to such prisoner before the time of filing such petition, and which were not then payable, and as to the claims of all other persons not known to such prisoner at the time of such adjudication, who may be indorsees or holders of any negotiable security set forth in such schedule so sworn to as aforesaid." And to the 50th section, which further enacts "that the discharge of any prisoner so adjudicated as aforesaid *shall and may extend to all process issuing from any court,* for any contempt of any court, ecclesiastical or civil, *for non-payment* of money or *of costs or expenses* in any court, ecclesiastical or civil; and that, in such case, the said discharge shall be deemed to extend also to all costs which such prisoner would be liable to pay in consequence or by reason of such contempt, or on purging the same; and *that every discharge so adjudicated as aforesaid as to any debt or damages of any creditor of such prisoner, shall be deemed to extend also to all costs incurred by such creditor before the filing of such prisoner's schedule, in any action or suit brought by such creditor against such prisoner for the recovery of the same;* and that all persons as to whose demands for any such costs, money, or expenses as aforesaid, any such person shall be so adjudged to be discharged, shall be deemed and taken to be creditors of such prisoner in respect thereof, and entitled to the benefit of all the provisions made for creditors by this act, *subject nevertheless to* such ascertaining of the amount of the said demands as may be had by *taxation* or otherwise, and to such examination thereof as is herein provided in respect of all claims to a dividend of such insolvent's estate and effects."

Talfourd, Serjeant, and *Cleasby,* now shewed cause.—
The 46th section of the statute of 7 Geo. 4, c. 57, applies

only to "debts and sums of money due or claimed to be due at the time of filing the prisoner's petition." The damages and costs in this action did not constitute a debt or a sum due, the judgment not having been signed or the costs taxed, until after the filing of the petition. In *Ex parte Todd*, cited in *Goddard* v. *Vander Heyden*, 3 Wils. 270, it was expressly held that costs do not become a debt till judgment, and that the creditor could not prove them under a commission issued before the judgment, notwithstanding the verdict was previous to the bankruptcy. In this respect, costs and damages are placed upon the same footing precisely. In *Ex parte Charles*, 14 East, 197, 16 Ves. 256, 1 Rose, 372, which is a case exactly in point, it was held, that, if a defendant commit an act of bankruptcy between the time of a verdict in case for unliquidated damages, and final judgment, the damages are not a proveable debt. *Ex parte Charles* over-ruled *Longford* v. *Ellis*, 1 H. Bl. 29, n., in which the contrary had been determined. So, in *Buss* v. *Gilbert*, 2 M. & S. 70, 2 Rose, 157, it was held that a debt due on a judgment signed in an action for damages after an act of bankruptcy committed by the defendant, and a commission issued thereon, was not discharged by the certificate, though the verdict was obtained *before* the bankruptcy. And in *Wilmer* v. *White*, 3 M. & P. 671, 6 Bing. 291, it was held that an insolvent is not exonerated from damages unascertained at the time of his discharge, although the action in which they are sought to be recovered was commenced and judgment by default suffered prior to his first imprisonment. Tindal, C. J., there said: "There are no words in the act which can be applied to such a liability under a suit pending at the time of the insolvent's first imprisonment; on the contrary, he is required to insert in his schedule the precise sum due from him to his creditor; a thing impossible where the damages are unascertained." The 50th section applies only to costs as incident to a debt from which the party would be discharged by the preceding provisions of the act. Here, at the time of the filing of the defendant's petition, there was no *debt* due from him to the plaintiff. The statute therefore can have no application.

Bompas, Serjeant, in support of his rule.—The defendant is clearly entitled to his discharge: the damages were ascertained by verdict before the filing of his petition; and the 50th section, the main object of which was to remove an existing difficulty in cases where the costs are not at the time ascertained, provides that the discharge as to debt or damages of any creditor of such prisoner, shall extend to all costs incurred by the creditor before the filing of the prisoner's schedule in any action or suit brought by such creditor against the prisoner for the recovery of the same. The case must be decided solely on the construction of the statute, without reference to the conflicting decisions which took place under the bankrupt acts prior to the passing of this act.

TINDAL, C. J.—If this question had rested on section 46, I should have thought the defendant not entitled to his discharge; for, that section is expressly limited to the several debts and sums of money due or claimed to be due at the time of filing such prisoner's petition from such prisoner to the several persons named in his or her schedule as creditors or claiming to be creditors for the same respectively, or for which such persons shall have given credit to such prisoner before the time of filing such petition, and which was not then payable, and as to the claims of all other persons not known to such prisoner at the time of such adjudication, who may be indorsers or holders of any negotiable security set forth in such schedule so sworn to as aforesaid; and it is perfectly clear that a verdict in an action of tort of itself can create no debt: there must also be a judgment ascertaining the amount of the costs. But the question is, whether the 50th section has not a wider range in favour of a party in execution than the 46th. That section includes not only debts with or without judgment, but process issuing for contempt of court for non-payment of money or of costs or expenses in any court; and provides that in such case the discharge shall be deemed to extend also to all costs which such prisoner would be liable to pay in consequence or by reason of such contempt or on purging the same. There the sense is closed. The sentence then begins again, and declares " that every discharge so adjudicated as aforesaid as to any debt or damages of any creditor of such prisoner, shall be deemed to extend also to all costs incurred by such creditor before the filing of such prisoner's schedule, in any action or suit brought by such creditor against such prisoner for the recovery of the same." That can only refer to the debts provided for by the 46th section. The clause then proceeds to enact, " that all persons as to whose demands for any such costs, damages, or expenses as aforesaid, any such person shall be so adjudged to be discharged, shall be deemed and taken to be creditors of such prisoner in respect thereof, and entitled to the benefit of all the provisions made for creditors by this act ; subject, nevertheless, to such ascertaining of the amount of the said demands as may be had by taxation or otherwise, and to such examination thereof as herein provided in respect of all claims to a dividend of such insolvent's estate and effects." The legislature were clearly contemplating the case of a judgment which had not been signed. It seems to me that this 50th section expressly includes the case of damages ascertained by the verdict of a jury, and of costs unascertained, but capable of being so by taxation. I therefore think this rule must be made absolute.

PARK, J.—I am of the same opinion. The question is

a novel one. Upon mature consideration, and referring
back to section 46, I am clearly of opinion that the 50th
section embraces the present case. The 46th section says
nothing as to costs; it seems to suppose everything completed; and provides for the discharge of the insolvent
from debts: then comes section 50, which, after providing
for the case of costs in respect of attachments and con-
tempts, goes on, " that every discharge so adjudicated as
aforesaid, as to any debt or damages of any creditor of
such prisoner, shall be deemed to extend also to all costs
incurred by such creditor, before the filing of such prisoner's schedule, in any action or suit brought by such
prisoner for the recovery of the same; and that all persons
as to whose demands for any such costs, money, or expenses, as aforesaid, any such person shall be so adjudged
to be discharged, shall be deemed and taken to be creditors of such prisoner in respect thereof, and entitled to
the benefit of all the provisions made for creditors by this
act." That seems to me to have been an after thought,
and to have been designed to include the case of costs incurred before the filing of the petition; the discharge in
respect of the principal debt being already provided for
by the 46th section.

GASELEE, J.—I am of the same opinion. *Wilmer* v.
White turned on the 61st section of the act, which was
held not to apply to unliquidated damages accruing upon
a judgment by default. Now, the 50th section does clearly
apply to unliquidated damages reduced to a certainty by
the verdict.

VAUGHAN, J.—I am of the same opinion. This is a
remedial law, entitled to a favourable construction. The
legislature, having before them the conflicting decisions
as to the proof of debts under commissions of bankrupt,
seem to me to have contemplated, with regard to insolvent

debtors a provision that should exclude all doubt. The 46th section of the 7 Geo. 4, c. 57, taken alone, applies only to debts or damages due at the time of the filing of the petition. The 50th section extends the provision to costs incurred before the filing of the petition, subject to taxation. The clause, from its very language, must of necessity have been intended to apply to a case circumstanced like this: and the 51st section evinces the desire of the legislature to go as far as they could in giving prospective relief; for, it contains a provision for the valuation of annuities for the payment of which the insolvent may be liable.

Rule absolute, without costs—the defendant undertaking to bring no action.

JONES v. PRICE.

In trespass quare clausum fregit, the defendant pleaded an uninterrupted enjoyment, under a claim of right, of common over the locus in quo "for the full period of thirty years before the commencement of the suit:"—Held, sufficient, without alleging the enjoyment to have been for thirty years next before the commencement of the suit.

IN trespass quare clausum fregit, the defendant pleaded that the closes in which &c., at the times when &c., were part and parcel of a certain common, to wit, Dolevan Common; that, before and at the times when &c., the defendant was and still is the occupier of a certain messuage and lands with the appurtenances situate and being at Dolevan aforesaid, and that he and all the other occupiers of the said messuage and lands with the appurtenances, for a full period of thirty years before the commencement of the suit, had actually taken and enjoyed, claiming right thereto, and without interruption, for himself and themselves, occupiers of the said messuage and lands with the appurtenances, common of pasture in respect of the said messuage and lands with the appurtenances, in, upon, and throughout the said closes in which &c., for all his and their commonable cattle levant and couchant in and upon the said messuage and lands with the appurtenances, every year and at all times of the year: wherefore &c.

Special demurrer assigning for cause—that it was not
averred or shewn in or by the said plea that such right of
common as in that plea mentioned was actually exercised
or enjoyed by the defendant and the occupiers of the
messuage and lands in that plea mentioned, uninterruptedly, for the full period of thirty years *next before the
commencement of the suit;* so that, if issue were taken on
the existence and exercise and enjoyment of such right of
common, the defendant would, in manner and form as that
plea was framed and drawn, be at liberty to give in evidence an uninterrupted exercise and enjoyment of such
right of common by the occupiers of the said messuage
and lands in respect of which it was claimed, for any one
continuous period of thirty years before the commencement of the suit, however remote, although such right
might have been subsequently, and for more than thirty
years *next* before the commencement of the suit, extinguished and lost.

The defendant joined in demurrer.

R. V. Richards, in support of the demurrer.—The question arises under the statute 2 & 3, Will. 4, c. 71, ss. 1, 4, and
5 (*a*), whether the defendant should not have pleaded that

1836.

JONES
v.
PRICE.

(*a*) The 1st section enacts, "that
no claim which may be lawfully
made at the common law, by custom, prescription, or grant, to any
right of common or other profit or
benefit to be taken and enjoyed
from or upon any land of our
sovereign lord the king, his heirs
or successors, or any land being
parcel of the duchy of Lancaster,
or of the duchy of Cornwall, or
of any ecclesiastical or lay person, or body corporate, except
such matters and things as are
therein specially provided for,
and except tithes, rents, and services, shall, where such right, profit, or benefit shall have been actually taken and enjoyed by any
person claiming right thereto,
without interruption, for the full
period of thirty years, be defeated
or destroyed by shewing only that
such right, profit, or benefit was
first taken or enjoyed at any time
prior to such period of thirty years,
but nevertheless such claim may
be defeated in any other way by
which the same is now liable to be
defeated; and when such right,

the right claimed by him had been enjoyed for thirty years *next* before the commencement of the suit. Great difficulty would be thrown upon the plaintiff in taking issue on the plea, if it were held sufficient as it now stands; inasmuch as proof of an enjoyment for a period of thirty years at any time, even though the thirty years should have expired more than twenty years before the action commenced, would support the issue on such a plea, and entitle the defendant to a verdict. In *The Monmouthshire Canal Company* v. *Harford*, 1 C. M. & R. 614, the right was claimed as having been enjoyed for twenty years *next* before the commencement of the action. So, in *Wright* v. *Wiliams*, 1 M. & Welsby, 77, the user was alleged for forty years next before the commencement of the suit; and the principal contention there was, that it should have been alleged for forty years next before the act complained of in the declaration.

Maule, contrà, was stopped by the court.

TINDAL, C. J.—It strikes me very strongly that the 4th section of the 2 & 3 Will. 4, c. 71, is nothing more than a mere exposition of the proof required to establish the right.—I think it is but a question of evidence.—If the plaintiff joins in the issue tendered by this plea, the defendant must prove an enjoyment of the right for thirty years *next* before the commencement of the action.

profit, or benefit shall have been so taken and enjoyed as aforesaid for the full period of sixty years, the right thereto shall be deemed absolute and indefeasible, unless it shall appear that the same was taken and enjoyed by some consent or agreement expressly made or given for that purpose by deed or writing."

The 4th section provides "that each of the respective periods of years thereinbefore mentioned shall be deemed and taken to be the period *next before* some suit or action wherein the claim or matter to which such period may relate shall have been or shall be brought in question."

For the 5th section, vide ante, Beasley v. Clarke, 258.

The rest of the court coucurring—

1836.

JONES
(?.
PRICE.

Richards prayed leave to amend, on the usual terms, by withdrawing the demurrer, and replying.

Rule accordingly.

———◆———

YOUNG *v.* MURPHY.

Friday,
June 3rd.

THE plaintiff declared on a promise of marriage made to her by the defendant, and alleged as a breach that the defendant had intermarried with one Elizabeth Sherratt.

The defendant pleaded—first, non assumpsit—secondly, that, after the making the supposed promise and undertaking in the declaration mentioned, and before his intermarriage with the said Elizabeth Sherratt in the declaration mentioned, to wit, on the 31st May, 1834, he discovered, and received information that the plaintiff was an immodest, lewd, unchaste, and immoral person, and, being sole and unmarried, had had carnal intercourse with, and was carnally known by, and committed fornication with, one Henry Penleaze; of which the defendant had no notice, knowledge, or suspicion at the time of making the supposed promise and undertaking in the declaration mentioned: and the defendant further said, that the information he so received and had was true, and that the plaintiff was an immodest, lewd, unchaste, and immoral person, and, being sole and unmarried, had, after the making the said supposed promise and undertaking in the declaration mentioned, and before his (the defendant's) intermarriage with the said Elizabeth Sherratt, carnal intercourse with, and had been carnally known by, and had committed fornication with, the said Henry Pen-

To an action for a breach of promise of marriage, the defendant pleaded—first, that, after the making of the promise, the defendant discovered that the plaintiff was an immodest, lewd, unchaste, and immoral person, and, being sole and unmarried, had had carnal intercourse with one H. P.—and secondly, that, after the making of the promise, the defendant had notice that the plaintiff, being so sole and unmarried, had committed fornication with some person or persons to defendant unknown, and was pregnant with a child likely to be born a bastard (averring the fact to be so), of which he had no notice or knowledge at the time of making the promise :—Held, sufficient.

lease; wherefore the defendant refused to marry the plaintiff, and intermarried with the said Elizabeth Sherratt, as he lawfully might for the cause aforesaid—verification.—Thirdly, that, after the making of the said supposed promise and undertaking in the declaration mentioned, and before his intermarriage with the said Elizabeth Sherratt, he received information and had notice that the plaintiff, being so sole and unmarried, had committed fornication with some person or persons to him the defendant unknown, and was pregnant and with child of a child likely to be born and which was afterwards born a bastard, but of which he had no notice, knowledge, or suspicion at the time of making the said supposed promise and undertaking in the declaration mentioned: and the defendant in fact said that the plaintiff, being sole and unmarried, after the making of the said supposed promise and undertaking in the declaration mentioned, and before the intermarriage of the defendant with the said Elizabeth Sherratt, had committed fornication with some person or persons to the defendant unknown, and had become and was pregnant and with child of a child likely to be born and which was subsequently born a bastard; wherefore he, the defendant, did refuse to marry the plaintiff, and did marry the said Elizabeth Sherratt, as he lawfully might for the cause aforesaid—verification.

To the second and third pleas the plaintiff demurred specially; assigning for causes of demurrer to the second plea—that, although every plea ought to contain but one answer to the declaration, and not to contain several distinct matters of defence, yet the defendant had endeavoured, by his said second plea, to include two answers to the declaration in the same plea, and to include therein two distinct matters of defence to the cause of action mentioned in the declaration, inasmuch as in one part of the said second plea he had alleged that the plaintiff was an immodest, lewd, unchaste, and immoral person, and in an-

other part of the same plea, that she, being sole and unmarried, had had carnal intercourse with, and had been
carnally known by, and committed fornication with, the
said Henry Penleaze; that the said plaintiff could not traverse or confess and avoid either of those distinct answers
and matters of defence without admitting the other of
them, nor could she take or offer any certain issue upon
the said matters of defence; that the said plea tended to
prolixity in pleading, and could not be answered by a
single replication; that the said allegation contained in
the said second plea, by which it was alleged that the
plaintiff was an immodest, lewd, unchaste, and immoral
person, was bad, not sufficiently certain, nor did it give or
convey to the plaintiff any sufficient or certain information
or knowledge as to the manner in which the defendant
intended to impeach her modesty, chastity, or morality,
or upon what immodest, lewd, unchaste, or immoral conduct of the plaintiff the defendant iutended to rely in support of that allegation, nor would the plaintiff, from such
allegation, be in any way prepared to answer the said
charge; that the second plea did not sufficiently state or
allege that the plaintiff was an immodest, lewd, unchaste,
or immoral person, because she had carnal intercourse
with, and been carnally known by, and committed fornication with, the said H. Penleaze, as mentioned in the
plea, or for any other separate and distinct causes or cause;
that the plaintiff was by the said second plea left in uncertainty as to what particular charge of immodesty, lewdness, unchastity, and immorality the defendant meant to
bring against her by the allegation first above mentioned;
that the second plea was in other respects double, uncertain, informal, and tended to prolixity in pleading, and to
several issues, and was against the rules of pleading; and
that the defendant had not stated or alleged in his second
plea at what time or times the plaintiff committed fornication with the said Henry Penleaze, as in the said second

plea mentioned, although that allegation was a material one, and ought to have been stated with certainty of time. And to the third plea—that, although every plea ought to contain but one answer to the declaration, and ought to contain only one matter of defence, yet the defendant had endeavoured by his third plea to include two answers and matters of defence to the declaration in the said third plea, inasmuch as he had alleged in the said plea that the plaintiff had committed fornication with some person or persons to the defendant unknown, and then had gone on to allege in the same plea that the plaintiff had become and was pregnant and with child of a child likely to be born and which was subsequently born a bastard, while a plea containing either of the above allegations would be a sufficient answer to the declaration: that it was not alleged by whom the said plaintiff had become and was pregnant with the said child, or that the persons or person by whom she was so pregnant were unknown to the defendant, or that such pregnancy was the result of the fornication so alleged to have been committed as in the third plea; that the defendant had not alleged in or by the said third plea with sufficient certainty whether he intended to rely on the plaintiff's having committed fornication with one person only, or with more than one, but had stated in the alternative that she committed fornication with some person or persons unknown to him; and that defendant had not stated in his said third plea with sufficient certainty at what time such fornication was committed, or that the time when it was committed was unknown to him, although the committing of such fornication was a material fact, and ought to have been alleged with sufficient certainty as to time.

The defendant joined in demurrer.

Peacock, in support of the demurrer.—The pleas in question are bad both on the ground of duplicity and of want of certainty. The plaintiff could not take issue on

the general charge of want of chastity without admitting
the particular instance specified : and, if she took issue
on the latter, she might be wholly unprepared to meet the
defendant's evidence in respect of the former. In *l'Anson*
v. *Stewart*, 1 T. R. 748, it was held that a justification of
a charge of a person being a swindler must state the particular instances of fraud by which the defendant means
to support it. Ashhurst, J., there says : "When the defendant took upon himself to justify generally the charge
of swindling, he must be prepared with the facts which
constitute the charge, in order to maintain his plea: then
he ought to state those facts specifically to give the plaintiff an opportunity of denying them ; for, the plaintiff cannot come to the trial prepared to justify his whole life." ·
This is laid down as a general rule applicable to all cases,
and is not confined to cases of libel only. So, in *Holmes*
v. *Catesby*, 1 Taunt. 543, it was held that a justification
of a libel must state issuable facts, not general charges of
misconduct. And *Jones* v. *Stevens*, 11 Price, 235, is an
authority to the same effect. The second special plea
states that the plaintiff had committed fornication with
some person or persons to the defendant unknown, and
further that she had become and was pregnant—not alleging such pregnancy to be the result of the general fornication before charged, but leaving it open to be inferred
that it might have been a consequence following a fornication with the defendant himself. [*Tindal*, C. J.—Might
not the whole have been put in issue by the general replication, de injuriâ?] That possibly might only put in issue the excuse; and would not put in issue the question
as to whether or not the defendant was himself the father
of the child of which the plaintiff was alleged to be pregnant.

PER CURIAM.—The cases cited were all cases of libel,
where the defendant is a wrong-doer: here, he is putting

himself upon his defence. The plaintiff may, if she wishes, amend, by taking issue, on the usual terms.

Leave to amend accordingly.

---

*Friday,
June 3rd.*

On demurrer to a replication, the court will not permit the plaintiff to attack the defendant's plea, unless the point has been marked for argument pursuant to the rule of Hilary Term, 4 Will. 4, s. 2.

BAYLEY *v.* HOMAN.

ON a demurrer to the replication in this case coming on for argument—

Gurney, for the defendant, objected that no points had been marked for argument on the part of the plaintiff, pursuant to the rule of this court and of the court of Exchequer of Trinity Term, 11 Geo. 4, 4 M. & P. 621, 6 Bing. 802, and the general rule of Hilary Term, 4 Will. 4, s. 2. He referred to *Brogden* v. *Marriott*, ante, Vol. 2, 708 (*a*).

Stephen, Serjeant, contrà, submitted that the effect of holding him bound by the rule in this case would be to leave upon the record a plea in which there was manifest error.

THE COURT held that the plaintiff was not at liberty to attack the plea: but permitted *Stephen* to offer arguments in support of his replication.

The case was ultimately disposed of by both sides agreeing to amend, without costs.

Rule accordingly.

(*a*) See Grottick v. Phillips, 3 M. & Scott, 135; Darling v. Gurney, 2 Dowl. 101; Ross v. Robinson, 3 Dowl. 779: Lacy v. Umber, 3 Dowl. 732; and Rex v. Woollett, 2 C. M. & R. 256, 3 Dowl. 694.

1836.

GOLDSMID and Another, Assignees of HIRSCHFIELD and WILKINSON, Bankrupts, *v.* RAPHAEL and Another.

Saturday,
June 4th.

CASE, with a count in trover. The action was brought by the plaintiffs as assignees of Hirschfield & Wilkinson, bankrupts, against the late sheriffs of the city of London, for an alleged seizure of goods of the bankrupts after acts of bankruptcy committed by them. At the trial before Tindal, C. J., at the sittings in London after last Hilary Term, evidence was offered on the part of the defendants, not in answer to the action (there being no plea upon the record adapted to such a defence), but in reduction of damages, of certain payments on account of rent and of executions which it was admitted the sheriffs were bound to satisfy This evidence was objected to on the part of the plaintiffs; but received by his lordship conditionally. A verdict was found for the plaintiffs for the entire value of the property, with a reservation of leave to move to reduce the damages by the amount of the payments so proved to have been made, should the court be of opinion that evidence was admissible in the absence of a special plea.

Quære whether, in an action of tort against the sheriff, by the assignees of a bankrupt, for seizing goods of the bankrupt, the defendant may, without specially pleading them, give in evidence payments necessarily made by him out of the proceeds, in reduction of the damages.

Alexander, in Easter Term, obtained a rule nisi according, and also for a new trial upon other grounds.

Talfourd, Serjeant, who shewed cause, likened this to a set-off, which is wholly inapplicable to an action of tort, and of which a defendant is not entitled to give evidence unless it be specially pleaded—*Graham* v. *Partridge,* 1 M. & W. 395.

Alexander and *Butt,* in support of the rule, submitted, that, by analogy to the cases of *Lediard* v. *Boucher,* 7 C. & P. 1, *Cousins* v. *Paddon,* 2 C. M. & R. 547, *Shirley* v. *Jacobs,* ante, Vol. 1, 157, 2 New Cases, 88, and `Palfrey *v. Sill*, ante, Vol. 2, 159, n., the defendants were entitled to give in evidence the payments necessarily made by them out of the proceeds of the goods, in reduction of damages, notwithstanding they had omitted to plead the matter specially. [*Tindal*, C. J.—In the cases cited, the payments were made *to the plaintiff;* he therefore could not be taken by surprise on evidence being offered at the trial under the general plea. Here, the payments are made *to third parties* (a).] That cannot make any difference in principle. The sheriffs were bound to make the payments; the plaintiffs could not prevent them: and it is for the jury to say what amount of damages the defendants are to pay.

It appeared that a notice had been served upon the defendants, by the plaintiffs' attorney, at the time of the demand, specifying the property claimed by them; which notice expressly excepted the sums now in question: whereupon—

TINDAL, C. J., said.—I think the verdict should be reduced by the sums included in the notice served upon the defendants, the plaintiffs having by their own act excepted them out of the demand. It is unnecessary, therefore, on the present occasion, to give any opinion upon the question as to whether or not payments made under the circumstances disclosed in this case can be given in evidence, in reduction of damages, in an action of this description. The question may be considered as still open.

PARK, J.—I am of the same opinion. The question that has been agitated before us, is one of considerable importance: but the point is not now ripe for a decision.

GASELEE, J., concurred.

VAUGHAN, J.—I am of the same opinion. We should

(a) See *Hellings v. Young*, post, Michaelmas Term.

be doing gross injustice to the defendants not to allow them the benefit of the sums which the plaintiffs have themselves excepted out of their demand. With respect to the general question, I do not profess to have formed an opinion.

1836.

GOLDSMID
v.
RAPHAEL.

Rule accordingly.

GREEN and Another, Assignees of LAST & CASEY, Bankrupts, *v.* WHITE and Another.

Saturday,
June 4th.

ASSUMPSIT for money had and received by the defendants to the use of the plaintiffs as assignees. At the trial before Tindal, C. J., at the sittings in London after last Hilary Term, the facts that appeared in evidence were as follows:—Last & Casey, the bankrupts, and the defendants, both silk merchants, had mutual dealings, in the course of which the former, on the 13th November, 1835, deposited with the latter certain silk warrants, by way of security for advances of money made to them. On the 17th November, Last & Casey were in a state of insolvency. On the 22nd, the defendants (knowing that Last & Casey had stopped payment) wrote to them stating that they should hold the silks till the 2nd December, when, if the advances they had made thereon were not repaid, they would sell them. On the 23rd, circulars were issued by them for the purpose of calling a meeting of their creditors for the 30th. On the 27th, the following order, *dated the 13th,* was presented to the defendants by one Waite:—" Please to advance the further sum of 500*l.* upon the silks, and pay same to bearer." No advance was at that time made to Waite: but, on the 6th December the defendants paid him 150*l.* and agreed to set off the remaining 350*l.* against certain acceptances of Waite which

L. & C., silk
merchants, de-
posited silk war-
rants with the
defendants, who
advanced
money to them
thereon ; on the
27th November,
one W. handed
to the defen-
dants an order
(which the jury
found to be a
fraudulent pre-
ference) from L.
& C., directing
the defendants
to make to the
bearer a further
advance of 500*l.*
on the silks; no
money was ad-
vanced on this
order until the
6th December,
when the de-
fendants gave
W. 150*l.* and it
was agreed that
they should re-
tain the remain-
ing 350*l.* to
meet certain
acceptances of
W.'s which
they held, and
which were due
on the 14th De-
cember. On the
3rd December,

L. & C. committed an act of bankruptcy, and on the 5th, a fiat issued against them:—Held, that the payments made by the defendants on the 6th and 14th December were not protected by the 6 Geo. 4, c. 16, s. 82.

they held, and which would become due on the 14th December. A meeting of the creditors of Last & Casey was held on the 30th November, one of the defendants being present. On the 2nd December, Last & Casey offered a composition of 4s. in the pound; on the 3rd, they committed an act of bankruptcy; and, on the 5th, a fiat issued against them, under which they were duly declared bankrupts, and the plaintiffs were appointed assignees. The defendants subsequently sold the silks, and claimed to retain the proceeds as well to cover former advances, as the advances made to Waite under the order of the 27th November.

Upon these facts, it was submitted, on the part of the plaintiffs, that the transaction as between Last & Casey and Waite was a fraudulent preference in contemplation of bankruptcy. On the part of the defendants, it was contended that the order given by the bankrupts to Waite operated as an equitable assignment of the property—*Bailey* v. *Culverwell*, 8 B. & C. 448, 2 M. & R. 564; and also that the payment to Waite was equivalent to a payment *to* the bankrupt, and within the protection of the 82nd section of the 6 Geo. 4, c. 16.

His lordship left it to the jury to say whether or not the transaction as between the bankrupts and Waite was fraudulent; and also whether or not the defendants at the time of making the payments were cognizant of the fraud. The jury returned a verdict for the plaintiffs on the first point, damages 380l. 6s.; upon the second, they were unable to agree.

Crowder, in Easter Term last, obtained a rule nisi for a new trial, on the ground that, assuming the transaction as between the bankrupts and Waite to amount to a fraudulent preference, there being no evidence that the defendants were cognizant of the fraud, the payments made by the defendants on the 6th and 14th December, having relation to the order lodged on the 27th November, were protected by the 82nd section of the 6 Geo. 4, c. 16, as payments made *to the bankrupt* before the date and issuing of the fiat by one having no notice of a prior act of bankruptcy having been committed; and also on the ground that the order given to Waite operated as an equitable assignment.

Storks, Serjeant, and *Turner*, now shewed cause.—The jury having found, that, as between the bankrupts and Waite, the transaction was fraudulent, the payments made in pursuance of the order lodged with the defendants on the 27th November were clearly not protected payments; and it is perfectly immaterial whether the defendants had or had not cognizance of the fraud at the time, for, the payments were made after the issuing of the fiat, which by the 83rd section of the 6 Geo. 4, c. 16, is declared to be notice to all the world of a prior act of bankruptcy having been committed by the bankrupts: and therefore, if the cause were to go down again upon that ground, it would be sending it down to ascertain a fact totally irrelevant to the issue between the parties. The 82nd section protects only payments made to bankrupts in the ordinary course of business, and without notice of an act of bankruptcy. Here, the case is put either as a payment to the bankrupts, or as an equitable assignment. If an equitable assignment, it cannot be a payment *to* the bankrupts, which is quite incompatible with a fraudulent preference. The order given to Waite might have operated as an equitable assignment, provided the bankrupts had at the time dominion and control over their property. But this transaction, being found by the jury to have been fraudulent, was in itself an act of bankruptcy. And the order conferring no right upon Waite, the payments made by the defendants under it were clearly payments made in their own wrong.

Crowder and *Gurney*, in support of the rule.—After the finding of the jury that the transaction as between the bankrupts and Waite was fraudulent, it cannot be contended that it amounted to an equitable assignment. The defendants were, however, no parties to the fraud: and the payments were in effect payments made by the defendants *to* the bankrupt. If the money had been actually advanced on the 27th November, the day the order was lodged, such payment would clearly have been within the protection of the 6 Geo. 4, c. 16, s. 82. That which took place between Waite and the defendants amounted to the same thing: the order bound the money in the hands of the defendants, and the arrangement for the mode of payment was equivalent to actual payment. Waite might have maintained an action against the defendants had they declined to obey the order. [*Tindal*, C. J.—Not after the jury had found the order was obtained by fraud.] Upon the delivery of the order, the defendants held the money, not as the money of the bankrupts, but of Waite. In *Bailey* v. *Culverwell*, A., as broker for B., sold goods which were in A.'s custody to C., to be paid for by the acceptance of D. Upon the insolvency of D., A. obtained from C. an order to sell the goods and apply the proceeds to meet the acceptance; C. becoming bankrupt, A. delivered the goods to B., who subsequently returned them to A., after which they were demanded by the assignees of C.: it was held that the jury, or the court, upon a special case, were at liberty to infer the adoption by B. of the act of A. in obtaining the order; and that neither the delivery of the goods to B., nor the refusal to deliver them to the assignees, amounted to a conversion. And in *Bedford* v. *Perkins*, A., a trader, before any act of bankruptcy, directed his broker, who had authority to distrain for rents due to him, to pay a certain sum to B. in satisfaction of a debt, and the broker bonâ fide agreed with B. to pay him as

soon as he received the rents, and after this A. became
bankrupt: it was held that the assignees of A. could not
recover this sum from the broker; though he did not in
fact pay it over to B. till after the commission issued.
[*Tindal*, C. J.—That was a case of equitable assignment:
the negation of which constitutes the weakness of this
case.]

TINDAL, C. J.—I see no reason for sending this cause
down to a second trial. It appears from the evidence reported to us that the order for the payment of the money
given by the bankrupts was lodged with the defendants
on the 27th November. The order directed the defendants to advance 500*l.* to Waite on the security of goods
of the bankrupts then in the defendants' hands. If the
advance had been actually made on that day, it might have
been treated as a payment to the bankrupts before the
bankruptcy, and therefore protected by the 82nd section
of the 6 Geo. 4, c. 16. No advance, however, was then made
to Waite under the authority of the order: the silks remained in the defendants' hands; and an arrangement was
entered into between the defendants and Waite, under
which 350*l.*, part of the 500*l.* mentioned in the order, was
retained as a set-off against certain acceptances of Waite
in the hands of the defendants, due on the 14th December,
and the residue (150*l.*) was on the 6th December paid to
Waite. If the order of the bankrupts lodged on the 27th
November operated as an equitable assignment of the
goods, the subsequent payment under it would have been
valid: but the jury expressly found that the order was
obtained fraudulently and by way of preference. The
order, therefore, could not affect the property in the
goods: they still remained the goods of the bankrupts,
and unaffected by any lien. On the 3rd December, they
became the property of the assignees; and when converted into money, the proceeds were equally unaffected by

any lien. The payments on the 6th and 14th December, were payments made after an act of bankruptcy, and after the issuing of the fiat, and are not referable to any by-gone transaction binding the property either in the goods or in the money. It seems to me therefore that the defendants were bound to stay their hands; the fiat operating as a notice to all the world: and they would have had a good answer to any claim made by Waite, had they so done; for, if he had brought an action against them for not paying over the money in obedience to the order, the assignees would have given them notice of their claim, and the court would, under the interpleader act, have directed an issue to try whether or not the order had been fraudulently obtained; and, if the jury who tried that issue affirmed the fraud, there would have been an end of the claim of Waite. The question seems to me to stand as if the actual payment had taken place on the 6th December, when it clearly would not be within the protection of the 82nd section of the bankrupt act. The 83rd section makes the commission notice of the bankruptcy to all intents and purposes. It was, therefore, unnecessary to leave it to the jury to say whether or not the defendants were cognizant of the fraud. I think the rule must be discharged.

PARK, J.—I am of the same opinion. If, under the circumstances, it was necessary that the question whether the defendants were cognizant of the fraud or not should have been submitted to the jury, I should have thought it right to send the cause down again. But I am of opinion that it was not necessary to leave the question to the jury. The payments were not made until the 6th and 14th December. The issuing of the fiat (which by the 83rd section of the 6 Geo. 4, c. 16, is declared to be notice of a prior act of bankruptcy) on the 5th December, was a sufficient authority to the defendants to stay their hands. After that they were not bound to comply with the order; and therefore the payments subsequently made by them have been made in their own wrong.

GASELEE, J., concurred.

VAUGHAN, J.—I am of the same opinion. When the defendants' counsel admitted they could not support the transaction as an equitable assignment, it seems to me they conceded the whole case. The payments under the circumstances, are not within the protection of any section of the statute.

Rule discharged.

———

GRAINGER *v.* TAUNTON.

BY the 61st section of the municipal corporation act, 5 & 6 Will. 4, c. 76, it is enacted, " that, in the city of Oxford, in the town of Berwick-upon-Tweed, and in the counties of the cities of Bristol, Canterbury, Chester, Coventry, Exeter, Gloucester, Lichfield, Lincoln, Norwich, Worcester, and York, and in the counties of the towns of Carmarthen, Haverdfordwest, Kington-upon-Hull, Newcastle-upon-Tyne, Nottingham, Poole, and Southampton, the council shall on the 1st of November in every year appoint a fit person to execute the office of sheriff, with the like duties and powers as the sheriff *or the person filling the office of sheriff* in the said town and counties respectively would have had if this act had not passed; and every person who at the time of the passing of this act shall hold the office or execute the duties of sheriff in the said town and counties respectively, shall continue to hold and execute the same until the first appointment of a sheriff therein under the provisions of this act, and no longer."

Before the passing of the above act, there were two local courts in the city of Oxford, and two bailiffs having the

*Saturday,
June 4th.*

The municipal corporation act, 5 & 6 Will. 4, c. 76, s. 61, has effected no change in the mode of executing process from the superior courts in the city of Oxford; they are still to be executed by the sheriff *of the county.*

execution of process there, but not of process issuing out of the superior courts of Westminster, which was always executed by the sheriff of the county. Under the act, a sheriff of the city had been duly elected by the town council. To this officer a writ of testatum ca. sa. sued out in this cause was directed. Conceiving that the sheriff of the county was, as heretofore, the proper person to have the execution of all writs from the superior courts, the sheriff of the city refused to return the writ: and in order to raise the point he was ruled to return it; to set aside which rule—

Henderson obtained a rule nisi, on the ground that it called upon the sheriff of the city to do an act which by law he could not do.

F. Kelly shewed cause.—The simple question here is, whether it is the duty of the sheriff of the city or of the sheriff of the county to execute the process of the superior courts. Before the passing of the late act, that duty, it appears, devolved upon the sheriff of the county. But it appears also that there were certain officers in Oxford who before the act had certain duties to perform in relation to the office of sheriff. In several of the places mentioned in the 61st section, there were sheriffs who before the act did execute process within their several jurisdictions, and some where there were no sheriffs at all eo nomine; but in all, save in Oxford, writs were executed by some officer within the city or town. The object of the enactment was, that each of the places named should have its own proper officer; that the practice should be uniform throughout the kingdom. [*Tindal,* C. J.—There are no words in the act calculated or seemingly intended to take away from the sheriff of the county any jurisdiction he before possessed. The fault here seems to have been in addressing the writ to the wrong person.] The act clearly intended that the new sheriff should do all that the sheriff of the county would before the passing of the act have had to do. Could it have been intended that the new officer should have no greater jurisdiction than the bailiff already had?

Henderson, contra, was stopped by the court.

TINDAL, C. J.—On looking at the 61st section of the act, the construction it is to receive appears to me to be very plain. The clause affects to deal with places which had and with places which had not sheriffs before the passing of the act; it directs that the town council shall on a given day appoint a fit person to execute the office of sheriff, and it goes on to state what shall be the duties of the person so appointed—" the like duties and powers as the sheriff or the person filling the office of sheriff in the said town and counties respectively would have had if this act had not passed." It appears here that the city of Oxford had no sheriff, no person filling the office, no person whose duty it was to receive and return the process of the courts at Westminster. I think the power to execute such process is still limited to the sheriffs of those places which had sheriffs before upon whom that duty devolved. The writ in the present case ought not to have been directed to the sheriff of the city. I cannot help thinking, that, if the legislature had intended to take away from the sheriff of the county any of the powers or authorities he possessed before the passing of the act, they would have expressed themselves in direct terms to that effect, or at least the act would have contained words of direction to the courts. I think the rule must be discharged.

PARK, J.—I am of the same opinion. There is nothing in the act to alter the mode of directing writs. We can only judge of the intention of the legislature from the language they use.

GASELEE, J., concurred.

VAUGHAN, J.—I am also clearly of opinion that there is nothing in the act to warrant a supposition that the legislature intended to detract in any degree from the authority of the sheriffs of counties.

Rule absolute, without costs.

———•———

Monday,
June 6th.

This court cannot exercise a summary jurisdiction over a party who is not one of its own officers, although the matter be pending here.

SHARP v. HAWKER.

HUMPHREY, on a former day, obtained a rule calling upon the plaintiff's attorney to shew cause why he should not pay over to his client a sum of 21l. 17s. 1d., received by him in the course of the cause, together with the costs of the application.

Whitmore shewed cause, upon an affidavit stating that the party against whom the application was directed was not an attorney of this court, but had acted in the name of one who was.—He cited *In re Beck*, 1 H. & W. 417, and *In re Lord*, ante, Vol. 2, p. 131 (a), to shew that the court had no authority over parties not being its officers.

Humphrey, in support of his rule.—The ground of decision in those cases was, that there was *no cause* in court. Unless the motion is made in the court in which the cause is pending, the plaintiff is without remedy. And it cannot be permitted to a party who has assumed to act as an attorney of the court, to turn round and say, when it suits his purpose, that he is not so. Besides, the objection has

(a) In this case the court held that they would not entertain a motion touching the conduct of an attorney, unless it appeared upon affidavit that he was an attorney of the court, or *that the transaction arose in part at least out of a cause before the court*. The present case overrules this latter part of the decision in that case.

been waived.   [*Vaughan*, J.—How can an objection of
this nature be waived ? We cannot deal with the party at
all, unless he is an officer of this court.]

Butt (Amicus Curiæ) referred to *In re Greaves*, 1 C. &
J. 374, n.   There, an action having been commenced in
this court, and judgment obtained, an attorney of the
King's Bench (but not of the Common Pleas), who was attorney for the defendant, verbally agreed to give his two
notes for the debt and costs, in consideration of the plaintiff staying the proceedings; and it was held, that, although the undertaking was void by the statute of frauds,
the court of King's Bench might nevertheless exercise a
summary jurisdiction over one of its own officers, and
compel him to perform it (*b*).

TINDAL, C. J.—The difficulty I feel in this case is, that,
if it should ultimately become necessary to strike this person off the roll, we could not do it. Suppose he were
ordered to pay over the money, and should refuse to obey
such order, what remedy would the client have? It seems
to me that the rule is answered by the fact of the alleged
delinquent being dehors our jurisdiction. The rule must
be discharged, but without costs.

GASELEE, J.—I am of the same opinion. It is highly
desirable that some rule should be made by all the courts
to meet the case of an attorney of one court acting in the
name of an attorney of another court, by making both
equally amenable to the court in which the cause is pending.

The rest of the court concurring—

Rule discharged, without costs (*c*).

(*b*) But see Payne v. Johnson,
1 C. & J. 373, n.
  (*c*) And see Ex parte Higgs, 1
Dowl. 495; In re Bateman, 2
Dowl. 161; In re Chitty, 2 Dowl.
421; Ex parte Bull, 3 Deac. &
Chit. 116.

Tuesday,
June 7th.

NORTON *v.* LORD MELBOURNE.

The court granted a commission for the examination of a witness in an action for criminal conversation with the plaintiff's wife.

BAYLEY, on a former day, on the part of the plaintiff, obtained a rule nisi for a commission for the examination of a witness named Mansell, at present in the service of Lord Mulgrave at Dublin Castle. The affidavit stated, in the usual form, the party named to be a material and necessary witness for the plaintiff, and that the trial was expected to take place on the 16th June.

Sir *John Campbell,* A. G., shewed cause.—This is an application to the discretion of the court: and the question is, whether, in a case of this description (an action for criminal conversation with the plaintiff's wife), the court will permit a witness whose evidence is important and necessary to substantiate the charge to be withdrawn from the jury, upon an affidavit entirely. denuded of any facts to shew that the presence of the witness cannot be procured. By the 45 Geo. 3, c. 92, s. 3, power is given to subpœna witnesses in *criminal* cases, in any part of the kingdom. That provision undoubtedly has no application to civil suits: but it may afford a convenient guide to the court's discretion in the construction of the 1 Will. 4, c. 22, and shews the anxiety of the legislature in all cases to procure the personal attendance of witnesses before the jury. The affidavit should at least shew some endeavours to procure the personal attendance of this witness; it being of infinite importance in a case of this description that all the witnesses should be subjected to examination and cross-examination in open court, and that the jury should have the opportunity to judge from their demeanour the degree of credit to which their evidence may be entitled: whereas here it does not appear that any application has been made to the witness to attend the trial; nor does the affidavit negative the fact of his being in London at the commencement of the action, or state when he left this country.

Bayley, in support of the rule, was stopped by the court.

TINDAL, C. J.—The affidavit upon which this motion is made is framed in the usual manner; and I do not see how we can lay down in this case, which is a civil action, a rule different from that which obtains in all other actions, though in its aspect this certainly is a matter involving a charge somewhat approximating to a criminal character. If the proposed witness should before the trial come within the jurisdiction of the court, the examination under the commission will not be evidence.

PARK, J.—Applications under this statute are usually made at chambers: they are of almost daily occurrence; and I never yet saw an affidavit containing that which the Attorney-General suggests. By the law of England this is an action of a merely civil nature, and to be governed by the same rules as any other civil action.

GASELEE, J., concurred.

VAUGHAN, J.—The act in question was passed to remedy the difficulty that had before been found to exist where witnesses were out of the jurisdiction of the courts at Westminster, and consequently could not be subpœnaed. I am of opinion that the affidavit upon which this motion is founded is sufficient to entitle the plaintiff to make his rule absolute.

Rule absolute.

1836

The Company of Proprietors of the CROSS KEYS BRIDGE *v.*
RAWLINGS and Another.

In case for ne-
gligently navi-
gating a vessel,
whereby the
plaintiffs' bridge
was damaged,
the defendants
pleaded that the
plaintiffs had,
wrongfully,
and without the
knowledge of
the defendants,
contracted and
narrowed the
channel, and
that, in conse-
quence of such
contraction of
the waterway,
and the in-
creased rapidity
of the current
thereby occa-
sioned, and
without the de-
fault of the de-
fendants, the
vessel was
driven against
the bridge;
*without this that
the vessel of the
defendants ran
foul of and
struck against
the bridge by
and through the
carelessness and
negligence of the
defendants as in
the declaration
alleged*—con-
cluding to the
country:—
Held, that, un-
der this plea, it
was competent
to the defen-
dants to offer

THIS was an action on the case for an injury resulting to
the plaintiffs through the negligence and want of skill of
the defendants. The declaration stated, that the Cross
Keys Bridge Company, before the passing of a certain
act of parliament passed in the seventh year of the reign
of Geo. 4, intituled, " An act for constructing a bridge
across Sutton Wash, otherwise called Cross Keys Wash,
between the counties of Lincoln and Norfolk," caused to
be made, built, and erected, a certain bridge and embank-
ment according to the provisions of the said act over the
new cut or channel in the said act named, and at the place
in the said act mentioned ; that the plaintiffs, before and
at the time when &c., were lawfully possessed as of their
own property, by virtue and for the purposes in the said
act specified, of the said bridge (which said bridge was
then so constructed as to admit the centre thereof to open
at the top as a drawbridge for the purpose of permitting
ships and other vessels trading to and from the antient
sea-port town of Wisbech to pass through at all times
without striking any mast), and by virtue of an act of
parliament passed in the 7th and 8th years of the reign
of Geo. 4, and intituled " An act for improving the outfall
of the river Nene, and the drainage of the lands discharging their waters into the Wisbech river, and the
navigation of the said Wisbech river from the upper end
of Kindersley's cut to the sea, and for embanking the salt
marshes and bare sands lying between the said cut and
the sea;" that the defendants, before and at the said

evidence to disprove the carelessness charged in the declaration, notwithstanding they had failed in
establishing the preceding matter, or inducement in the plea, as to the alleged obstruction by the
plaintiffs.

times when &c., were then the owners and lawfully possessed of a certain vessel there navigating and proceeding
in and along the said new cut or channel; that, before
and at the said times when &c., the said bridge was opened
for the purpose of allowing the said vessel of the defendants to pass through the said bridge, and the said vessel
was then about to pass through the said bridge, and might
have passed through the same without damaging or injuring the said bridge; yet the defendants, not regarding
their duty in that behalf, whilst the said bridge of the
plaintiffs was so opened for the purpose of allowing the
said vessel to pass through the same, to wit, on the 7th of
November, 1835, took so little and such bad care by the
persons, the then servants of the defendants, then in
charge and care of the said vessel, in the navigating,
management, and direction of the same vessel, that the
same, by and through the carelessness and negligence,
mismanagement and improper conduct of the persons, the
then servants of the defendants in that behalf then in
charge and care of the said vessel of the defendants, with
great force and violence ran foul of and struck against
the leaf and other parts of the said bridge of the plaintiffs,
and thereby then destroyed, broke down, and greatly
broke, damaged, and injured the same, and the same
thereby and then became and was greatly injured, damaged and destroyed; and also by reason of the premises
the plaintiffs were forced and obliged to pay, lay out, and
expend, and necessarily paid, laid out, and expended a
large sum of money, to wit, the sum of 2000l., in and
about the repairing the said damage so done to the said
bridge; and also by means of the premises the plaintiffs
lost and were deprived of the use of the said bridge for
a long space of time, to wit, from thence hitherto, and
thereby the plaintiffs lost and were deprived of all the
tolls, profits and advantages which during that time they

might and otherwise would have derived and acquired from the use of their said bridge.

The defendants pleaded—first, that the said bridge was not built or erected according to the provisions of the act of parliament in that behalf in the declaration first mentioned, in manner and form as in the declaration alleged —secondly, that, before the time of committing the supposed grievances, the plaintiffs had wrongfully and without the knowledge of the defendants placed divers large quantities of stones, and the same at the committing of the said supposed grievances were near to and round the piles and buttresses of the said bridge, through and between which said butresses vessels navigating the said channel were accustomed and ought to pass, and by means whereof the waterway or passage for vessels between and through the said buttresses was not only greatly contracted and narrowed, but also by means of the premises the rapidity of the current of the said channel through and between the said buttresses was greatly increased, and the navigation and management of vessels near and through the said bridge was thereby rendered difficult and dangerous; and in consequence of the said contraction and narrowness of the said waterway, and the said increased rapidity of the said current occasioned as aforesaid, and without the default of the defendants, the said vessel of the defendants was at the time of the committing of the said supposed grivances driven, compelled, and carried against the said leaf and other parts of the said bridge, *without this that the said vessel of the defendants ran foul of and struck against the said leaf and other parts of the said bridge, by and through the carelessness, negligence, mismanagement, or improper conduct of the persons the then servants of the defendants, in manner and form as in the declaration was alleged*—concluding to the country.

Upon each of these pleas, the plaintiffs took issue.

The cause was tried before Park, J., at the last Spring

Assizes at Norwich. It appeared that the bridge in question, which was erected over a navigable river, was so constructed as to admit ships to sail through; and the injury of which the plaintiffs complained, was, that the defendants, in navigating their vessel through the bridge, ran foul of and carried away one of its gates. The first plea was confessedly negatived by the evidence: and, with respect to the second, the defendants' own witnesses disproved the allegation therein that the channel had been narrowed by the plaintiffs; but the defendants proposed, nevertheless, to shew that they had navigated their vessel without negligence, and according to the ordinary and proper course, and that the damage was occasioned by an accidental failure of wind. On the part of the plaintiffs, it was contended, that, the defendants having failed in establishing the first part of their second plea, they could not be entitled to a verdict even in the event of their proving the traverse of negligence. The learned judge assented to the objection, and declined to receive the proposed evidence. A verdict was thereupon taken for the plaintiffs—the damages being referred.

Storks, Serjeant, in Easter Term last, obtained a rule nisi for a new trial, on the ground that this evidence had been improperly rejected, the denial of the negligence charged in the declaration being the substance of the issue.

F. Kelly, and *B. Andrews*, now shewed cause.—The whole of the plea having been put in issue, the defendants were bound to prove the whole of it. They were bound to prove that the accident happened in the manner stated in the plea: it was not competent to them to treat it as a mere plea of the general issue. In *Tuck* v. *Tooke* (a), 4

(a) Error from this court—see Took v. Tuck, 12 Moore, 435,
4 Bing. 224.

M. & R. 393, 9 B. & C. 437, it was held that a plea stating that the plaintiff and the defendant's other creditors agreed to accept a composition and release their debts, that several creditors, relying upon the agreement, executed a release, and that the plaintiff *afterwards* obtained and accepted the bond in suit for the residue of the plaintiff's debt, by fraud and covin, without the knowledge and consent, and in fraud of the other creditors, was tantamount to an allegation, not of fraud and covin generally, but of fraud and covin effected by the particular means described in the inducement; and, as the facts stated did not shew any stipulation for the giving of the bond contemporaneous with the agreement for the composition, the plaintiff was entitled to judgment non obstante veredicto, after an issue upon the fraud and covin found in favour of the defendant. Here, the plea is in the nature of a special traverse. In Stephen on Pleading, 3rd edit., after stating the form and the general design of a special traverse (pp. 165, et seq.), " which must always consist of an inducement, a denial, and a conclusion to the country" (the latter requisite having been introduced by the rule of Hilary Term, 4 Will. 4, 1, s. 13), the learned author observes (p. 183): " First, it is a rule that the inducement should be such as itself amounts to, a sufficient answer in substance to the last pleading. For, it is the use and object of the inducement to give an explained or qualified denial; that is, to state such circumstances as tend to shew that the last pleading is not true; the absque hoc being added merely to put that denial in a positive form, which had previously been made in an indirect one. Now, an indirect denial amounts in substance to an answer; and it follows, therefore, that an inducement, if properly framed, must always in itself contain, without the aid of the absque hoc, an answer in substance to the last pleading." Here, the plea amounts to a qualified denial of carelessness and negligence under the circumstances before alleged in the plea.

TINDAL, C. J.:—I believe the whole difficulty in this
case has arisen from the omission to call the attention of
the learned judge who presided at the trial to the state of
the record. When that is looked at, the difficulty vanishes.
The new rules in pleading have effected no alteration in
the law with regard to the traverse, except that now, by
the rule of Hilary Term, 4 Will. 1, s. 13, all special traverses, or traverses with an inducement of affirmative
matter, are required to conclude to the country. Suppose
this action had been brought before the new rules, and
the plaintiffs had in their declaration charged the defendants with injuring their bridge through carelessness and
negligence: the defendants would have pleaded that the
plaintiffs by their own wrongful act narrowed the waterway, with an absque hoc denying the imputed carelessness
and negligence, and concluding with a verification: and
the proper issue on that would have gone to the carelessness and negligence. The rule always was, with respect
to a special traverse, that the opposite party has no right
to pass by the traverse, and take issue on the inducement (a), unless the traverse be immaterial or bad. In
Comyns's Digest, *Pleader* (G. 20.), it is said that "a traverse ought to be introduced with a proper title or inducement." And (G. 17.), "if there be a traverse of a
point apt and material to the plaintiff's title, he cannot
refuse it, and tender another traverse." "Yet (G. 18.), if
upon the pleading it appears that the plaintiff's title is
immaterial, the plaintiff may traverse the inducement to
the traverse by the defendant: as, in quare impedit, the
plaintiff declares of a seisin in A., who conveyed to B.,
who conveyed to the plaintiff; the defendant pleads, that,
before the conveyance to the plaintiff, the church became
void, and B. presented him, and traverses the avoidance
after the conveyance to the plaintiff; the plaintiff may say
that the church became void after the conveyance to him,
and that C. presented the defendant, and traverse that the

(a) See Stephen on Pleading, 3rd edit. 186.

1836.

CROSS KEYS
BRIDGE
COMPANY
v.
RAWLINGS.

defendant was in by the presentment of B." "So (G. 19.),
if the first traverse be not to the point of the action, a
traverse on a traverse may be allowed : as, in waste for cutting down and selling trees, the defendant pleads that he
used them for repairs, and traverses the selling, the plaintiff
may waive this, and traverse the using in repairs; for, the
first point was not material to the action, it was surplusage
in the declaration, and ought not to have been traversed,
and the plaintiff might have demurred on the traverse."
I cannot see that the plaintiff is injured by this mode of
pleading; the defendants shew pretty well the course that
will be taken at the trial, for, by the special inducement they
shew that one ground on which they intend to rely is, that
the accident was occasioned by the plaintiffs' own default,
and not, as charged in the declaration, by the carelessness
and negligence of the defendants. That which we are
now called upon to decide is, whether the defendants, not
having proved the whole of the inducement, might still
go on to prove the traverse. I think they were at liberty
so to do; and consequently that the cause must go down
again upon the second issue, the evidence tendered upon
which was rejected. Upon the first issue the verdict
against the defendants will remain, and the rule will be
silent as to costs.

PARK, J., and GASELEE, J., concurred.

VAUGHAN, J.—The gist of the issue was, the negligence
charged in the declaration.

Rule absolute accordingly.

Wednesday,
June 8th.

The court will
permit judg-
ment to be sign-
ed on a sci. fa.

WEATHERHEAD and Another *v.* LANDLES.

A SCIRE FACIAS (to revive a judgment) was lodged
with the sheriff, and notice given to the defendant (who

after eight days from the return (r. 81, H. T. 2 Will. 4), where the defendant resides abroad, he
 ·ving had *reasonable notice of the proceeding.*

resided at Paris) on the 17th May. The writ was returned nihil: and now, on the 8th June—more than eight days since the return of the sci. fa.—

W. H. Watson moved for leave to sign judgment, pursuant to the 81st rule of Hilary Term, 2 Will. 4, which provides that "no judgment shall be signed for non-appearance to a scire facias without leave of the court or a judge, unless the defendant has been *summoned;* but such judgment may be signed by leave after eight days from the return of one scire facias." He submitted that all that was necessary under the circumstances had been done; and cited *Hopcraft* v. *Fermor*, 8 Moore, 424, 1 Bing. 378, where this court ordered an attachment to issue against a party for non-performance of an award although he resided in France, where the copy of the award and rule on which the application was founded were served on him.

PER CURIAM.—It is only necessary to shew that something has been done to convey notice to the party of the proceeding against him.

Fiat.

———◆———

DOE d. JARMAN v. LARDER.

THIS was an action of ejectment by mortgagee against the devisee of the mortgagor, to recover possession of the mortgaged premises. At the trial before Bolland, B., at the last Assizes at Taunton, it appeared that the mortgagor had held the premises in question under a lease for twenty-one years from the governors &c. of Bruton Hospital, at the yearly rent of two shillings, renewable every

On a mortgage of premises held under a corporation on a renewable lease, the sum originally advanced was 130*l.*; in the mortgage deed there was an absolute covenant on the part of the *mortgagor* to renew, and a power to the mortgagee to renew in case of default by the mortgagor, with a proviso that the money paid by the mortgagor for such renewal should not be a charge upon the premises to an amount exceeding 70*l.*; the deed was stamped with a 2*l.* stamp, as a deed for securing a sum not exceeding 200*l.*:—Held, sufficient.

seven years. The mortgage deed was put in, bearing date the 30th June, 1830. By that deed the mortgagor, the father of the defendant, in consideration of 130*l.* advanced to him by the lessor of the plaintiff, assigned to the latter the premises in question, with a proviso for redemption on payment of the 130*l.* and interest on a given day, and trusts for sale in default of payment. The deed also contained a covenant on the part of the mortgagor to procure a renewal of the lease as often as might be necessary; with power to the mortgagee to renew on failure of the mortgagor so to do; and a proviso, that, in the event of the latter renewing, the sum expended by him in so doing should not be secured *upon the premises* by that deed to a greater extent than 70*l.* This deed was stamped with a 2*l.* stamp, which was sufficient to recover the 130*l.* advanced in the first instance, and the 70*l.* which might be advanced under the last-mentioned covenant—55 Geo. 3, c. 184, sched. part 1, tit. " Mortgage "—by which a 2*l.* stamp is imposed " where the deed shall be made as a security for the payment of any definite or certain sum of money advanced or lent at the time, or previously due and owing, or forborne to be paid, being payable, exceeding 100*l.*, and not exceeding 200*l.*" On the part of the defendant, it was objected that this stamp was insufficient; but that, the mortgage deed being made to secure an uncertain sum, and the mortgagor being *personally* bound to procure a renewal of the lease at whatever price the lessors might demand for it, the stamp should have been 25*l.* —55 Geo. 3, c. 184, sched. part 1, tit. " Mortgage "—" And where the same shall be made as a security for the repayment of money to be thereafter lent, advanced, or paid, or which may become due upon an account current, together with any sum already advanced or due, or without, as the case may be (other than and except any sum or sums of money to be advanced for the insurance of any property comprised in such mortgage or security against damage by fire, or to be advanced for the insurance of any life or lives pursuant to any agreement in any deed whereby any annuity shall be granted or secured for such life or lives), if the total amount of the money secured or to be ultimately recoverable thereupon shall be uncertain and without any limit, 25*l.* : but, if the total amount of the money secured or to be ultimately recoverable thereupon shall be limited not to exceed a given sum, the same duty as on a mortgage for such limited sum." In support of the objection *Halse* v. *Peters*, 2 B. & Ad. 807, was relied on. There it was held, that, in order to render the ad valorem duty sufficient, the limit must be one expressed on the face of the deed; and therefore, that a mortgage for 1500*l.*, with covenants for the payment of the yearly premium and other charges of an insurance of 1,000*l.* upon a particular life for seven years, required a 25*l.* stamp.

A verdict having been entered for the plaintiff, with leave to the defendant to move to enter a nonsuit—

Bere, in Easter Term last, obtained a rule nisi accordingly.

Crowder shewed cause.—The stamp is clearly sufficient : the amount to be secured by the deed is expressly limited to 200*l.*, the proviso to that effect having been introduced with the precise view of avoiding this objection. *Doe* d. *Scruton* v. *Snaith*, 1 M. & Scott, 230, 8 Bing. 146, is a distinct authority in favour of the plaintiff: there, it was held that a mortgage deed to secure 3000*l.* and interest, together with all expenses incurred in the execution of the powers of sale, &c. contained in the deed, and interest thereon, does not require a 25*l.* stamp, as a security for an uncertain and indefinite amount. Tindal, C. J., said: "All acts that impose a burthen on the subject must be construed most strictly; and, if there be on the face of them any doubt, the subject should have the benefit of that doubt."

In *Pruessing* v. *Ing*, 4 B. & A. 204, a note for the payment
of 30*l.* at three months after date, with interest from the
date, was held to require only a stamp applicable to a note
not exceeding 30*l.* "The object of the legislature," says
Lord Tenterden, " was, to impose a pro ratâ stamp duty
upon the sum actually due at the time of taking the security, and not upon what might become due in future for
the use of that money." In *Deardon* v. *Binns*, 1 M. & R.
130, it was held that a bond conditioned for the payment
of money and interest, and also for the performance of
collateral acts, requires only the ad valorum stamp appropriated to the principal sum, where that stamp exceeds
the 1*l.* 15*s.* which the collateral matter would require if it
stood alone. *Dickson* v. *Cass*, 4 B. & Ad. 343, cited in
Doe d. *Scruton* v. *Snaith*, is distinguishable for the reasons
given in the latter case. [*Tindal*, C. J.—The safest course
in all these cases is to decide solely and strictly according
to the words of the statute.]

Bere, in support of the rule. The present case is in no
wise distinguishable from *Halse* v. *Peters*, which is not inconsistent with any of the cases cited on the other side.
Here, the mortgage would be an imperfect and valueless
deed without the covenant to renew. The act provides
that the deed shall have a 25*l.* stamp, " if the total amount
of the money secured, or *to be ultimately recoverable
thereupon*, shall be uncertain and without any limit."
The sum secured *on the premises* in this case is limited to
the 70*l.* in addition to the 130*l.* previously advanced: but
there is no limit to the personal responsibility of the mortgagor. Suppose the hospital required 300*l.* for a renewal,
and the mortgagor refused to pay that sum, would not the
mortgagee have a right under this deed to renew, and to
sue the mortgagor thereon? If so the deed is a security to
an uncertain and unlimited extent. The limitation applies
only to the charge on the land : the mortgagee has the per-

sonal security of the mortgagor to an unlimited extent.
[*Tindal*, C. J.—The argument tends to reduce this to a
mere naked covenant, which would not require a mortgage
stamp.]

TINDAL, C. J.—This case presents to my mind no
difficulty. The question is, whether a 2*l.* stamp is sufficient on a mortgage deed given to secure a sum of 130*l.*,
with a power of renewal of the lease by the mortgagee,
on default on the part of the mortgagor so to do, provided such further advance on renewal should not operate
as a charge on the land to an extent exceeding 70*l.*; or
whether the deed should have been stamped with a 25*l.*
stamp, which is the proposition asserted on the part of
the defendant. The 55 Geo. 3, c. 184, sched., part 1, tit.
"Mortgage," imposes a 2*l.* stamp where the deed " shall be
made as a security for the payment of any definite or certain
sum of money advanced or lent at the time, or previously
due and owing, or forborne to be paid, being payable, exceeding 100*l.* and not exceeding 200*l.*" Now, it is clear
that the stamp imposed on a mortgage applies only to a
case where a pledge is given operating as a security, and
not to the case of a dry covenant under the seal of the party.
In the present case, the deed containing a covenant on the
part of the mortgagor to renew the lease, without any limitation as to the fine to be paid for such renewal, it is contended on the part of the defendant, that, inasmuch as
this operates as a further charge to an uncertain and unlimited extent on the person of the mortgagor, in respect
of which an action would lie at the suit of the mortgagee,
the deed enures as a security wherein the total amount *to
be ultimately recoverable thereupon* is uncertain and without limit, and therefore subject to the larger duty of 25*l.*
It appears to me, however, that such a liability is not
within the meaning of the act. The duty of 25*l.* is imposed "where the deed shall be made as a *security* for

the repayment of money to be thereafter lent, advanced, or paid, or which may become due upon an account current, together with any sum already advanced or due, or without, as the case may be"—" if the total amount of the money to be secured, or to be ultimately recoverable thereupon, shall be uncertain and without any limit:" that is, where the land is made to bear an additional burthen of an uncertain extent. The exception—"other than and except any sum or sums of money to be advanced for the insurance of any property comprised in such mortgage or security against damage by fire, or to be advanced for the insurance of any life or lives, pursuant to any agreement in any deed whereby any annuity shall be granted or secured for such life or lives"—shews that such is the true interpretation of the act. Here, no money was to be advanced to the mortgagor beyond the 130l., and the additional sum which the mortgagee might be called on to pay, was to be charged on the premises to an extent only that would, with the former advance, be covered by the 2l. stamp. As for the probability of the mortgagor's personal liability extending beyond the 200l., the same argument would apply to the covenant for quiet enjoyment. I therefore think the rule must be discharged.

PARK, J.—I am of the same opinion. Where an act of parliament imposes a burthen on the subject, it must always be continued strictly, lest it work injustice. It seems to me that it would be unjust as well as absurd to call this deed a mortgage security for an uncertain and unlimited sum.

GASELEE, J.—I am also of opinion that a 2l. stamp, which is sufficient to cover the 130l. originally advanced, and the 70l. to which the further advance on the security of the premises is expressly limited, is sufficient.

VAUGHAN, J.—I am of the same opinion. Before we

hold the larger stamp requisite, we must be clearly satisfied that the deed is one upon which the legislature intended to impose such stamp. I entirely subscribe to the
doctrine laid down by this court in the case of *Doe* d.
Scruton v. *Snaith.*

Rule discharged (a).

(a) See Doe d. Bartley v. Gray, 4 N. & M. 719, 3 Ad. & E. 89.

1836.

Doe
d.
Jarman
v.
Larder.

GAUNT *v.* WAINMAN.

DOWER unde nihil habet. The tenant pleaded that
the demandant ought not to have her dower of the messuages, houses, lands, tenements, and premises aforesaid
of the endowment of the said William Gaunt, heretofore
her husband, because he said that the said William
Gaunt, heretofore her husband, was not either on the
day on which he married the said demandant, or ever
after, seised of the appurtenances aforesaid, whereof &c.,
that he could endow the said demandant thereof: and of
this he put himself upon the country: whereupon issue
was joined. At the trial before Lord Denman, C. J., at
the last York Assizes, it appeared that, in 1607, the premises in question were demised for a term of 1000 years
by Sir John Saville to one Richard Walker; that, after
several mesne assignments, the assignees of one Swires, a
bankrupt, became in 1796 entitled to the residue of the
term, and assigned the same to one Thomas Rushforth,
by way of mortgage, subject to redemption by John
Gaunt, the real purchaser (the father of William Gaunt,
the demandant's late husband), on payment to Rushforth
of 160*l.*; that John Gaunt continued in possession of the
term down to the time of his death in 1814, when he
devised to his son William Gaunt "the lower moiety or
half part of all that close of land situate in Armley, called

Tuesday,
June 7th.

W. purchased
from the assig-
nees of G. lands
which had been
devised to G. as
freehold, and
which were
described as
freehold in the
conveyance to
W. :—Held,
that W. was
not estopped
by the deed,
as against the
widow of G.,
from shewing
that the lands
were not free-
hold, and con-
sequently not
chargeable with
dower.

the near bank, with the dwelling-house and out-buildings lately erected, and all other the appurtenances thereto belonging, which are valued at 485*l.*, to hold to him the said William Gaunt, his heirs and assigns, for ever;" and that, in 1824, William Gaunt having become bankrupt, the premises were conveyed by his assignees to the defendant, under the description of "all that messuage or dwelling-house, and all such plot, piece or parcel, or part or parts, as is or are of the nature or tenure of *freehold* of and in that close commonly called or known by the name of the near bank, situate &c." On the part of the plaintiff, it was submitted that the defendant, having accepted a conveyance of the property as freehold, was estopped from shewing that he took under it a more limited estate. On the other hand, it was insisted, that, although the parties conveying would be estopped from offering evidence to falsify their deed, such estoppel could not operate upon the defendant. Lord Denman, however, yielded to the objection, and directed a verdict to be entered for the demandant.

Wightman, in Easter Term, in pursuance of leave, obtained a rule nisi to enter the verdict for the defendant, or for a new trial.

Cresswell and *Hoggins* shewed cause.—The land having been conveyed to the defendant, and taken by him as a fee, he is estopped from denying the truth of the recitals in the deed upon which alone his title rests. In Comyns's Digest, *Estoppel,* (A. 2), it is said that " a party executing a deed is stopped by the recital of a particular fact in that deed to deny such fact"—citing *Shelley* v. *Wright,* Willes's Rep. 9, *Cossens* v. *Cossens,* Willes, 25. And see Shephard's Touchstone, p. 53. In an action on a bond, appearing upon oyer to be conditioned for the payment of the rent of certain premises recited in the

condition to be demised by indenture at a certain specific
rent, as by the said indenture &c., the defendant cannot
plead that the indenture mentioned in the condition was
an indenture by which a certain rent, less in amount than
the rent mentioned in the condition, was reserved, and
that such less rent has been paid—*Lainson* v. *Tremere*,
1 Ad. & E. 792, 3 Nev. & Man. 603.   Lord Denman, in
delivering the judgment of the court, there says: " It
appears upon these pleadings that the condition of the
bond is to pay the rent of 170*l.* at certain times mentioned in the condition, and to perform and observe the
covenants, conditions, and agreements in the lease, and
then, as the lease, when set out, shews the rent to be
140*l.*, the question is whether the payment of 140*l.* constitutes a performance of this part of the condition, or
whether the defendant is estopped from shewing that the
rent is different from the 170*l.* mentioned in the condition.   The first point to be considered is, whether, upon
this bond, the defendant would be estopped from saying
there is no such lease as is mentioned in the condition.
In 1 Rolle's Abridgment, *Estoppel* (P.), pl. 1, it is said:
' If the condition contains a generality to be done, the
party shall not be estopped to say there was not any such
thing.   But, in all cases where the condition of a bond
has referred to any particular thing, the obligor shall be
estopped to say that there is no such thing'—Ibid. pl. 7.
The same rule as to generalities and particularities is laid
down in *Strowd* v. *Willis*, Cro. Eliz. 362, and *Shelley* v.
Wright, Willes, 9, and urged in argument in *Hosier* v.
Searle, 2 B. & P. 299, and *Hill* v. *The Proprietors of
the Manchester and Salford Waterworks*, 2 B. & Ad.
549.   A great number of instances are given in Rolle's
Abridgment, and in several other books, of these generalities and particularities.   And, amongst them, as more
nearly applicable to the present case, if a condition be to
perform the covenants of an indenture, the obligor is

estopped to say there is no such indenture—1 Rol. Abr. 872, *Estoppel* (P.), pl. 3. So also in *Jewell's* case, 1 Rol. Rep. 408, *Halloway's* case, 1 Mod. 15, and *Hosier v. Searle.* In the present case, the condition is as to a particular thing, as it gives the date and all the particulars of the lease. And, by parity of reason, the defendant would be estopped from saying that there is no such indenture." [*Tindal*, C. J.—As between the parties to the original conveyance, there might be an estoppel : but the estoppel would rather be set up by the defendant. Here, it is set up as against a stranger to the deed, a purchaser from the assignees of the husband.] The defendant purchased the land as freehold, and subject to dower; and he cannot now be permitted to deny the contract he made, not with the husband alone, but also in effect with the wife. [*Tindal* C. J.—Suppose the tenant had purchased the premises in question as leasehold, would the demandant have been estopped from saying that they were freehold ?] She would not.

Wightman, in support of his rule.—The concession that, if the premises had been bought as leasehold, the demandant would not have been estopped from shewing them to be freehold, disposes of the question; for, it is perfectly clear that estoppels must be reciprocal. It would, indeed, be a great hardship on a party to say that he is estopped from alleging that he has a less estate than he bargained for.

TINDAL, C. J.—It appears to me, that, as against the present demandant, who is not bound by the same estoppel, the tenant is not estopped from shewing that his estate is not such as to be chargeable with dower. In Co. Litt. 352. a., it is said that " every estoppel ought to be reciprocal, that is, to bind both parties; and this is the reason that, regularly, a stranger shall neither take advantage nor be-bound by the estoppel: privies in blood, as, the heir; privies in estate, as, the feoffee, lessee, &c.; privies in law, as, the lords by escheat, tenant by curtesie, tenant in dower, the incumbent of a benefice, and others that come under by act in law, or in the post, shall be bound and take advantage of estoppels." It would be a great hardship on the one party to be held bound by an estoppel which did not bind the other. If a party to a deed of purchase is bound, his heir is bound also. Suppose an action brought against the heir on the bond of his ancestor, in respect of his possession of lands whence he was evicted after the decease of the ancestor by title paramount: it would be very hard to say that the heir would be estopped from shewing that the land in respect of which he was charged was not the freehold of his ancestor. The rule must be made absolute for a new trial, unless, on speaking to the learned judge, we find that he reserved leave (as to which the counsel are not agreed) to enter a verdict for the tenant.

1836.

GAUNT
v.
WAINMAN.

Rule absolute.

₁NAPIER *v.* DANIELL and WELCH.

*Thursday,
June 9th.*

THIS was an action on the case for a libel published by the defendants in a newspaper called The Bath Herald, of the 9th January last, in the form of a letter supposed to be addressed to the editor by a parishioner of the parish of Freshford.

The declaration stated that the plaintiff, before and at the time of composing and publishing of the false, scandalous, malicious, and defamatory libel thereinafter mentioned and set forth, was and still is an officer, holding a commission of high rank in his majesty's service, to wit, a colonel in his majesty's army, always carrying and con-

A plea of justification in an action for a libel contained three material allegations, as to one of which the jury in the course of the summing up expressed themselves satisfied that the proof failed. The judge, told them, that, to warrant a finding in favour of the defendant, they must be after two hours'

satisfied that all three of the allegations were substantially made out The jury, after two hours' deliberation, returned a verdict for the defendant upon that plea:—The court refused to set it aside.

ducting himself as a gentleman and a soldier, and as a man of honor, veracity, courage, and humanity, and, until the committing of the several grievances by the defendants as thereinafter mentioned, was always so reputed, deemed, and accepted to be by and amongst all his neighbours and other good and worthy subjects of this realm to whom he was in any wise known; yet the defendants, well knowing the premises, but wickedly and maliciously intending to injure the plaintiff in his said credit, rank, and character, and to bring him into public scandal, infamy, and disgrace, with and amongst all his neighbours and other good and worthy subjects of this realm, and to cause it to be suspected and believed by them and other his majesty's subjects that the plaintiff had been guilty of committing a gross and unmanly assault on one T. Newth, thereinafter mentioned, and had conducted himself on that occasion in a dastardly, ungentlemanly, and unsoldierlike manner, and that he had afterwards caused to be paid to the said T. Newth a certain sum of money to compromise the matter with the said T. Newth, and to prevent the said T. Newth from following up legal proceedings against him the plaintiff for committing the said assault; and also that the plaintiff had been guilty of wilfully publishing a false statement with respect and in relation to the matter aforesaid; and further that the plaintiff had behaved and conducted himself in a harsh, oppressive, and arbitrary manner towards certain parish officers mentioned in the said libel, to wit, by wantonly and unnecessarily being concerned in instituting and following up certain legal proceedings against them, and that in the prosecution of such proceedings he had illegally tampered with certain witnesses called to give legal testimony in such proceedings, and that he had gained unfair and undue advantage over such parish officers in such proceedings, and that he otherwise and in the matter aforesaid behaved and conducted himself in a manner highly unbecoming an honorable man, a gentleman, and a soldier;—theretofore, to wit, on &c., in a certain newspaper called the Bath Herald, and in the form of a letter addressed to the editor of the said newspaper, falsely, wickedly, and maliciously did compose and publish and cause and procure to be composed and published, of and concerning the plaintiff, a certain false, scandalous, malicious, and defamatory libel, containing amongst other things the false, scandalous, malicious, defamatory, and libellous matter following, of and concerning the plaintiff, that is to say:—

"Sir—I trust you will excuse the liberty I have taken in requesting the favour of you to insert in your paper the following remarks on the observations made by Colonel Napier on a paragraph which appeared in the Herald of the 1st instant, which observations were addressed to the editor of the Bath Guardian, and published in the same of the 2nd instant, wherein it was stated that coals to the value of 5l. were distributed by the Rev. Mr. Bythesea to the poor of the parish of Freshford, being the amount given to Thomas Newth, gamekeeper to P. Borthwick, Esq., of Claverton Park, to stop legal proceedings on his part for an assault committed on him by Colonel Napier in the course of last summer. Colonel Napier, in his observations on the paragraph in question, has thought proper to deny in the most unequivocal terms that any money has at any time been given or promised to be given by himself or any other person on his behalf to or for the use of the said T. Newth, to induce him to stay legal proceedings against him, or that he ever connived at any other person's doing so. Now, if that gentleman's statement be true, I cannot conceive the object the donor of the 5l. could have in view in thus disguising the charitable act; but, as the extraordinary nature of the circumstance, as well as common report, led me to believe that Colonel Napier's statement was incorrect as respects the payment of the 5l., I have made a most strict

inquiry; and you, Sir, shall now have my gleanings, which
are as follow:—In the summer of last year, Thomas Newth,
in the performance of his duty, unintentionally offended
Colonel Napier, by forbidding his son (whom he did not
then know) to sport on his master's manor. The Colonel,
on hearing of this circumstance, started off, taking Captain Penruddock with him, to Newth's house. On inquiry, they were told that he was not at home: but Newth,
who was at no great distance, hearing that two gentlemen had been inquiring for him, immediately went in
search of them, and, on coming up with the colonel and
his friend, the colonel, without saying a word to Newth,
commenced a most brutal attack on his person, by beat-
ing him with a large stick which he held in his hand, and
then ran away as fast as his legs could carry him, without
sounding a retreat, so as to afford his friend an opportunity of escaping also, or giving his enemy time to return a
blow. Newth, who was determined such a dastardly retreat should not avail him, commenced a spirited pursuit;
but, considering such base and unmanly treatment unworthy of manly chastisement, and thus to end, he resolved on making him atone for his unconstitutional conduct in a different way; which he did, by giving directions
to his solicitor, Mr. R. Savage, to commence an action
against the gallant colonel: and it was to stay the proceedings that Newth was promised and did receive 5l.; and
he, with an almost unparalleled generosity, came to the
resolution that the money should be laid out in coals and
given to the poor of the village of Freshford, and desired
one of the officers of that parish to inform his rector, Mr.
Bythesea, of his intention, and that, if he, Mr. Bythesea,
would call at his (Newth's) house, he should receive the
5l. Mr. Bythesea called accordingly and received the
money, and disposed of it in coals agreeably to Newth's
desire.

"Now, Sir, I will leave you and your readers to judge

if the paragraph in question be 'a mere silly impertinence' or not; and I must beg your further indulgence to permit me to make a few observations on Colonel Napier's re-commendation that (to use his own words) 'some of the persons should settle their own law proceedings, and not meddle with mine.' Does Colonel Napier mean the two officers of Freshford, Messrs. Watts and Dike? It is true one of the officers did assist Mr. Bythesea to distribute the coals given by Mr. Newth; but surely he cannot be so illiberal, after the spirit displayed, in forcing up legal pro-ceedings, and hurling them on the heads of those two in-dividuals, of whom I will defy any being who possesses a spark of principle or the least regard for truth to say one word against; surely I say he cannot recommend that those two men should settle their law proceedings. If so, let him not deceive himself; but think for a moment, and then say whether the law proceedings are his or theirs: let him reflect on the manner in which those law proceedings were got up against these two poor men (I call them poor, although they are respectable farmers, because they de-pend on their personal exertions to maintain their families), and then say whether such conduct accords with the senti-ment which he so emphatically expressed, and wished to be so clearly understood as entertained by him, when, at the public dinner given at Bath on the 9th November last, speaking of overseers, he said: 'Is it no injury at all to send a poor man to jail and his wife to a workhouse?' I say, then, knowing as I do a great deal of the management of this affair, that there is a vast discrepancy between the speech and the conduct of the gallant colonel; for, the law proceedings in question were got up in a way dis-reputable from the very commencement. But, to say nothing of the manner in which the witnesses who were brought against these two men were tampered with (in which, I am sorry to say, a neighbouring magistrate was concerned), did not the colonel and his party take those witnesses before a grand jury, and did not they (meaning the said grand jury) patiently examine those witnesses for the space of nearly, or quite, four hours, and yet could find no charge against them? Yes, that was the case, and the colonel was so exasperated at not being able to carry his measure before the grand jury, that, after inveighing bitterly against those gentlemen, he started for London to confer with his constitutional friend on what was to be done. And, what was done? Why, many barristers were consulted, and three counsel's opinion taken. As to the manner in which the cases submitted to those counsel were got up, those that know Colonel Napier best may conjecture. Those opinions, I understand, were reserved with the greatest secrecy until the following Quarter Sessions, when, with one or two of the witnesses before examined by the grand jury at the Assizes, they were exhibited before a jury composed of men very different in character and education from those who had previously examined the witnesses (upwards of twenty in number), and who, as might be expected, could not stand the glare of so much parchment shooting forth so many legal opinions. They accordingly (hoodwinked, like owls in noon-day,) contented themselves with half examining one of the witnesses, and then found a true bill. And now, Sir, perhaps even you will be astonished, who are more cognizant of the casualties of human life than most other men, when I state that Colonel Napier is not at one farthing expense in all these law proceedings. Then, who is? you will say. Why, the expenses are to be paid from the public purse. But I am sorry to say the colonel, in this instance, has been unmindful of the character of the British Soldier, who disdains an unequal combat; he having arranged with his parliamentary friend Mr. Roebuck, so as to conduct the affair with the Right Hon. Mr. Goulburn and others in such a way that all the expenses incurred by the colonel in this affair (even should the charges prove groundless) are to be paid by the public, whilst the expenses incurred by the two officers in defending their characters and persons from so foul an attack, should their innocence be established (of which there is no doubt), must be borne by themselves; and, if not paid, a prison must be their doom, and their families left destitute. But I sincerely hope that a liberal and discerning public, as they become more acquainted with the case of these two individuals, will feel that degree of sympathy towards them to which they are so eminently entitled."

By means of the committing of which said several grievances by the defendants as aforesaid, the plaintiff had been and was greatly injured in his said good name, fame, and credit, rank and character, and brought into public scandal, infamy, and disgrace with and amongst all his neighbours and other good and worthy subjects of this realm.

The defendant Daniell pleaded not guilty: the other defendant, Welch, pleaded—first, not guilty—secondly, a justification as to the first paragraph of the libel, averring that, before the composing and publishing of the said supposed libellous matter in the introductory part of that plea and in the declaration mentioned, to wit, on the 2nd January, 1836, a certain paragraph appeared in the newspaper called the Bath Herald, wherein it was stated that coals to the value of 5*l.* were distributed by the Rev. Mr. Bythesea to the poor of the village of Freshford, being the amount given to Thomas Newth, gamekeeper to P. Borthwick, Esq., of Claverton Park, to stop legal proceedings on his part for an assault committed on him by Colonel Napier in the course of last Summer; that certain observations on the same paragraph were afterwards, and before the publishing and composing of the same supposed libellous matter in the introductory part of the plea and in the declaration mentioned, to wit, on the same 2nd January,

1836, addressed by the plaintiff to the editor of a certain
newspaper called the Bath Guardian, and then published
therein; in which said observations the plaintiff did deny
in the most unequivocal terms that any money had at any
time been given or promised to be given by himself or any
other person on his behalf to and for the use of the said
T. Newth, to stay legal proceedings against him, or that
he, the plaintiff, ever connived at any other person's doing
so; that the extraordinary nature of the circumstance in
the said supposed libellous matter referred to, as well as
common report respecting the same, did then lead him the
defendant Welch to believe, and he did in fact then
believe, that the plaintiff's statement above mentioned in
the said observations published as aforesaid in the said
Bath Guardian newspaper, was incorrect as regarded the
payment of the said sum of 5l., and the said statement
was in fact in that respect incorrect, &c. [The plea
reiterated the facts stated in the alleged libel as to the
supposed brutal attack made by the plaintiff on Newth,
and his then running away as fast as he could, and as to
the proceedings instituted against the plaintiff by Newth
for the assault; and then proceeded to aver] that a certain person, to wit, one Falconer, did then on behalf of
the plaintiff promise Newth 5l. to induce him to stay proceedings, and that the proceedings were then stayed, and
Newth did receive from Falconer, on behalf of the plaintiff, the sum of 5l. for staying the said proceedings, &c. &c.

Thirdly, a justification of the rest of the alleged libel,
setting forth the proceedings had upon the bill of indictment alluded to in that paragraph, and averring that the
plaintiff did on that occasion tamper with the witnesses,
&c. &c.

The plaintiff replied de injuriâ.

At the trial before Bolland, B., at the last Assizes for
the county of Somerset, the defendant Welch, in support
of his first plea of justification, called Newth, who stated,

that, when the assault mentioned in the alleged libel was committed, the plaintiff was accompanied by Captain Penruddock, the plaintiff's son, and young Falconer ; that the plaintiff seized him by the neckcloth and beat him violently with a stick, whilst the three individuals above mentioned held him ; and that, when he attempted to strike the plaintiff, the latter ran away to a distance of about fifteen yards, and Captain Penruddock and the others held him until he promised not to strike the plaintiff.   On the part of the plaintiff, Captain Penruddock and young Napier and Falconer were called.   They admitted that the plaintiff struck Newth with his stick ; but denied that the latter was held by any of the party, or that the plaintiff attempted to run away.

In the course of the learned Baron's summing up, the foreman of the jury (which was a special one) intimated that they were satisfied with Newth's evidence as to the assault : whereupon the plaintiff's counsel called the learned Baron's attention to that part of the justification which applied to the alleged running away.   His lordship then read the evidence of the plaintiff's witnesses as to this fact : and the foreman stated that the jury were satisfied that the plaintiff made the attack, but that *he did not run away ; that they had mistaken the issue when they before observed that they were satisfied with Newth's evidence ; they only meant as to the attack of the plaintiff.*   The learned Baron having concluded his summing up, and told the jury, that, as the first plea of justification (upon which alone any question arose) contained three material and substantive allegations, all of which must be found affirmatively to support the plea, viz. the assault, the running away, and the subsequent payment of the 5*l.* to compromise proceedings on the part of Newth, they must find for the plaintiff, unless they were satisfied that these three allegations were established in proof.   The jury retired for about two hours, and then returned a verdict generally for the defendant Welch on the first justification; and for the plaintiff as to the rest of the record, damages 5*l.*

Wilde, Serjeant, in Easter Term last, obtained a rule nisi that the verdict might be entered for the plaintiff on the second issue, or for a new trial. He submitted that the statement made by the foreman of the jury in the course of the summing up, taken in connection with the general verdict afterwards delivered, negativing a material allegation in the plea, amounted in effect to a verdict for the plaintiff.

Bompas, Serjeant, *Crowder*, and *Rowe*, shewed cause.— They contended that the statement made by the foreman in the course of the learned Baron's summing up constituted no part of the verdict; and that the verdict was sustainable if there was any evidence which in substance proved the three material allegations in the plea.

Fraser, Bingham, and *Butt*, in support of the rule.— The plea in question contains three material allegations— the assault, the running away, and the payment of the 5*l.;* and the jury by the mouth of their foreman declare that the allegation as to the running away (which was the only one that was material to the character of the plaintiff as a gentleman and a soldier) was not supported by the evidence. This therefore in substance amounted to a special verdict, which the court will enter according to its legal effect—Comyns's Digest, *Amendment* (P.), *Verdict*, Bacon's Abridgment, *Verdict* (D).

TINDAL, C. J.—The court is called upon in this case to alter the verdict found upon one of the issues after it it has been recorded, in consequence of an opinion expressed by the jury before the close of the learned Baron's summing up. I think it would be in a high degree dan-

gerous to listen to such an application. It is perfectly
clear that what fell from the foreman was not a verdict;
for, a verdict is a finding of the jury upon the whole issue:
but, at most, this amounted only to an expression of opinion
as to the weight of a certain piece of evidence. Until the
verdict is actually recorded, the jury are at liberty to withdraw it and to tender a new verdict. It is so laid down in
Co. Litt. 227. b.—"After the verdict recorded, the jury
cannot vary from it; but before it is recorded they may vary
from the first offer of their verdict, and that verdict which
is recorded shall stand." It appears here, that, whilst
the judge was proceeding to sum up the evidence, the
jury interposed, and said they were satisfied that one of
the allegations in the defendant Welch's second plea, viz.
that Colonel Napier ran away after having committed the
assault, was not proved. The judge continued to sum up,
and at the end the jury retired, and continued two hours
in deliberation, and then returned a general verdict for
the defendant. It would be dangerous in the extreme to
hold, that, because the jury express an opinion one way
in the course of the summing up, their subsequent deli-
berate verdict is to be thereby affected. I think the proper course under the circumstances would have been for
the plaintiff's counsel to have insisted at the time that the
whole issue was substantially determined by this interlocutory finding of the jury, and that it might be recorded.
That course not having been pursued, I think we have
now no authority to alter the verdict that has been recorded.

PARK, J.—I quite agree that this application is totally
unprecedented, and ought not to be entertained. It is
not suggested that the learned Baron did not fully explain
to the jury the law applicable to the case they had to consider: and we must assume that, as they deliberated so
long, the evidence was duly discussed by them. As

1836.

NAPIER
v.
DANIELL.

the point which the plaintiff's counsel aver not to have been proved was essential to the defendant's justification, and the jury have found a general verdict establishing that justification, it must now be taken to have been actually and substantially proved to the satisfaction of the jury.

GASELEE, J., expressed his entire concurrence.

VAUGHAN, J.—We should be seriously invading the province of the jury if we entertained this application. The argument on the part of the plaintiff assumes that this was in fact a special verdict: and the court is called upon to enter it according to its legal effect. It appears that, in the course of the summing up, the foreman (and we may take it that he expressed the sense of the whole jury) stated that the jury were satisfied that Colonel Napier did not run away: whereupon the learned Baron told them, that, inasmuch as the defendant's first plea of justification contained three distinct allegations that were material, viz. that the plaintiff assaulted Newth, that he ran away, and that money was paid on his behalf to avert the threatened proceedings, they must, before they could hold the justification proved, be satisfied that all these allegations had been substantially made out by the evidence. The jury, after having been absent two hours, delivered a general verdict upon the plea in question for the defendant. No misdirection is imputed to the learned Baron. There is therefore no pretence for disturbing the verdict.

Rule discharged.

1836.

Saturday,
June 11th.

ROBERT GILL RANSON, RICHARD CRAWLEY, and HENRY
HAKEN *v.* DUNDAS and KELLY, Esqrs.

THIS was an action of debt upon the statute 9 Geo. 4,
c. 22, s. 63. The declaration stated that the defendants,
on &c., were indebted to the plaintiffs, under and by
virtue of a certain act of parliament made and passed in
the ninth year of the reign of his late Majesty, King
George the Fourth, to consolidate and amend the laws
relating to the trial of controverted elections to serve in
parliament, in the sum of 4694*l.* 15*s.* 7*d.*, for the costs and
expenses incurred by the plaintiffs in prosecuting a certain
petition of the said plaintiffs, complaining of an undue
election and return of the said defendants as burgesses to
serve in parliament for the borough of Ipswich, and which
said sum was to be paid by the defendants to the plaintiffs
on request; whereby &c.

The circumstances out of which the proceedings arose
were as follow :—In the month of January, 1835, the two
defendants were returned as members for the borough

A petition pre-
sented to the
house of com-
mons, complain-
ing of an undue
return, and
charging the
sitting mem-
bers with having
been guilty of
bribery by
themselves and
their agents,
incidentally
complained also
of misconduct
and partiality
in the returning
officers; but,
in its prayer,
the petition
merely called
upon the house
to determine
the validity of
the election, and
was altogether
silent as to any
claim for re-
dress against
the returning officers on the ground of their alleged misconduct :—Held, that the returning officers,
notwithstanding they appeared before the committee in opposition to the petition, were not to be
considered as *parties* entitled to assist in striking the committee, under the 9 Geo. 4, c. 22, s. 36—
the necessary construction of that clause being, that it does not comprehend the case where the
sitting members are called upon to appear, do actually appear at the bar of the house, and are the
parties opposing the petition; and, consequently, that the want of a notice to the returning officers,
and an order upon them to attend the house at the striking of the committee, did not invalidate
the appointment of such committee.

The petition was subscribed by three individuals *in the same interest*, and the recognizance
taken in pursuance of the 5th section of the statute, and in the form given in the schedule, was
entered into by *one* of them only, and was conditioned for payment of the costs of witnesses summoned on his behalf (being altogether silent as to the other two petitioners), and also for the costs
and expenses of the party who should appear *before the house* in opposition to the petition, in the
event of its being unsuccessful :—Held, sufficient.

The report of the committee failing to decide anything with respect to the charge, or the opposition to the charge, made against the returning officers, being frivolous or vexatious :—Held, that
it was not therefore void as against the sitting members.

The committee having reported the opposition of the sitting members to the petition to be frivolous and vexatious, a request was made to the speaker to refer the bill of costs of the petitioners
to taxation. The speaker thereupon directed two examiners appointed by him to tax the costs,
and the examiners reported that the costs and expenses allowed by them on such taxation amounted
to a certain sum, and that the sitting members, whose opposition to the petition appeared to the
committee to be frivolous and vexatious, were liable to pay the same :—Held, that the speaker's
certificate being, by the 60th section of the statute, declared to be conclusive evidence of the
amount of the demand, in all cases and for all purposes whatsoever, the court had no power to try
the propriety of the examiners' allowance of costs, or the principle upon which it was conducted.

of Ipswich ; the unsuccessful candidates being Messrs. Wason and Morrison. On the 25th of February following, a petition complaining of their return was presented to the house of commons by the plaintiffs, Robert Gill Ranson, Richard Crawley, and Henry Haken. The petition alleged that the petitioners were entitled to vote, and did vote, at the last election of members to serve in parliament for the borough of Ipswich, and that Robert Adam Dundas, Esq., and Fitzroy Kelly, Esq., the defendants, and James Morrison, Esq., and Rigby Wason, Esq., were candidates to represent that borough : that the bailiffs of the said borough are the returning officers, and that John Chevalier Cobbold, attorney-at-law, and Henry Gallant Bristo, spirit dealer, were such bailiffs and re-

Unregistered and disqualified persons admitted to vote.

turning officers at the said election : That divers persons were admitted to vote, and did vote, at the said election, for the defendants, who were not duly registered as electors to vote at the said election, and who were not entitled to vote at the said election : That divers persons were admitted to vote, and did vote, at the said election, for the defendants, or one of them, who had not, at the time they so voted, the same qualification for which their names had been originally inserted in the register of voters then in force for the borough of Ipswich aforesaid : That divers persons who were registered as electors for the said borough, became disqualified to vote as electors at such election subsequently to the period of the list of electors being revised and signed for the purpose of such registry, and previously to their so voting, by receiving alms or parish relief, or by not residing within the said borough, or within seven miles thereof, or any part thereof, or by other legal or personal disqualifications and incapacities, and they and divers other persons who had no legal right to vote were nevertheless admitted to vote, and did vote, at the said election, for the defendants, or one of them : That divers persons were admitted to vote, and did vote, at the said election, for the defendants, who were disabled or disqualified from or incapable of voting at the said election, by reason of their being or having been within twelve months previously to such election concerned or employed in the charging, collecting, levying, and managing duties of excise, customs, or other duties or revenues, or in some other office or employment: That divers persons were admitted to vote, and did vote, at the said election, for the defendants, who were or had been, either during such election, or within six calendar months previous to such election, or within fourteen days after it was completed, employed at such election as counsel, agent, attorney, poll-clerk, flagman, or in some other capacity for the purposes of such election, and had either before, during, or after such election accepted or taken from the said candidates, or some or one of them, or from some other person, for or in consideration of or with reference to such employment, a sum or sums of money, or a retaining fee, office, place, or employment, or a promise or security for a sum or sums of money, or a retaining fee, office, place, or employment: That divers persons were admitted to vote, and did vote, at the said election, for the defendants, who had asked, received, and taken money or other reward by way of gift, loan, or other device, or had agreed or contracted for money, gift, office, employment, or other reward, to give their votes to the defendants, or one of them, and to refuse or forbear to give their votes to the said James Morrison and Rigby Wason, or either of them; and divers persons were admitted to vote, and did vote, at the said election, who by themselves or persons employed by them did by gifts or rewards, or by promises, agreements, or securities for gifts or rewards, corrupt or procure, or attempt to corrupt or procure persons to give their votes for the defendants, or one of them, or to forbear to give their votes to the said James Morrison and Rigby Wason, or either of them: That all such persons who were so admitted to vote and did vote

1836.

RANSON
v.
DUNDAS.

Qualified persons excluded from voting.

Charge of partiality in returning officers, and improper rejection of votes.

as aforesaid, and divers other persons who voted at the said election for the defendants, or one of them, were disabled or disqualified from voting, or incapable, or unqualified, or incompetent to vote at the said election: That divers persons who were duly registered as electors at the said election, and who were entitled to vote at such election, claimed to vote thereat for the said James Morrison and Rigby Wason, or one of them, at the proper polling places, and were illegally and improperly excluded from voting, by the returning officers: That the said Henry Gallant Bristo, after receiving the writ for the said election, and previously to and during such election, and particularly in respect to the taking the poll at such election, was guilty of great and undue partiality in favour of the defendants; and, as well before as after the receipt of such writ, canvassed many of the electors in company with or on behalf of the defendants, or one of them, and solicited and recommended several electors to vote for them or one of them, and prevailed upon several electors to vote for the defendants, or one of them, or to forbear to vote for the said James Morrison and Rigby Wason, or either of them; and otherwise improperly interfered with the freedom of election: That the said returning officers rejected as false and illegal divers votes which were tendered at the said election for the defendants and for the said James Morrison and Rigby Wason, or some or one of them; and that the said Henry Gallant Bristo, finding at the close of the poll that more votes had been so tendered for the said defendants than for the said James Morrison and Rigby Wason, did admit and place such votes upon, or add such votes to, or cause the same to be placed upon, or added to, the poll, after the close of such poll, or after the legal and proper time for closing the same had expired; and did also improperly and illegally insert or cause to be inserted upon the said poll, without the concurrence and contrary to the desire of the said John Chevalier Cobbold, several votes which ought not to have been so inserted thereon;

and did otherwise illegally and improperly alter the said
poll; and the said returning officers did, in casting up the
said votes on the said poll, knowingly and wilfully reckon
many votes so illegally and improperly placed on the poll,
and did not declare the true and real state of the poll as
it stood at the final close thereof: That, after the place in
parliament to be supplied by such election became vacant,
and as well before as after the teste or issuing out of the
writ for the said election, and at and during the said election, the defendants did, by themselves, and by their agents,
friends, and partisans, by divers ways and means, at their
and each or one of their charge and behalf, directly and
indirectly, give, present, and allow to persons having votes,
at such election, money, meat, drink, lodging, entertainment, provision, and reward, and did make presents, gifts,
rewards, and promises, agreements, and obligations and
engagements to give money, meat, drink, provision, presents, reward, and entertainment to and for persons having votes as aforesaid, and to and for the use, advantage,
benefit, employment, profit, and preferment of such persons, in order that they, the defendants, might be elected,
and for being elected to serve in parliament for the said
borough: That, before and at and during the said election, the defendants were, or one of them was, by themselves and by their agents, guilty of divers acts of bribery
and corruption, in order to corrupt and procure, and did,
by themselves and by their agents, friends, managers, and
other persons employed in their behalf, by gifts, presents,
money, rewards, and promises and agreements and securities for money, gifts, and rewards, and by threats, inti-
midations, promises, undue influence, and other corrupt,
illegal, and improper practices, acts, and means, corrupt
and procure divers persons having or claiming to have
votes at such election, to give their vote in favour of the
defendants, and to forbear to give them in favour of the
said James Morrison and Rigby Wason: That the defen-

dants, by the said corrupt and illegal practices, were and
are, and each of them was and is, wholly disabled and in-
capacitated and ineligible to serve in this present parliament for the said borough of Ipswich; and the return of
the defendants was and is wholly null and void; and that
the said returning officers had notice of, and were informed
and well knew of, such corrupt and illegal conduct and
practices, which were also well known to the electors, and
notorious in the said borough: That, by the several illegal
ways and means aforesaid, the defendants obtained a colorable majority of votes over the said James Morrison and
Rigby Wason, and procured themselves to be returned to
serve for the said borough; whereas the said James Morrison and Rigby Wason, and each of them, had a legal
majority of votes at the said election, and were duly elected, and ought to have been returned to serve in this parliament for the said borough:—The petitioners therefore
prayed the house to take the premises into consideration,
and to declare the election and return of the defendants
wholly null and void, and that they were not nor ought to
be deemed members to serve in that parliament for the
said borough of Ipswich; and that the names of the defendants might be erased from the said return; and that
the said James Morrison and Rigby Wason might be declared duly elected to serve in that parliament for the said
borough; and that the names of the said James Morrison
and Rigby Wason might be substituted in the said return; and that the house would grant to the petitioners
such relief as to the house might seem meet.

This petition was ordered to be taken into consideration on the 26th of March; and the usual notices thereof,
and orders to attend, pursuant to the 9 Geo. 4, c. 22, s. 2,
were served upon Messrs. Kelly and Dundas, *but not upon
either of the returning officers.* On the 4th of March,
however, the returning officers were served with the usual
speaker's summons to appear at the bar of the house with

the poll-books and other documents on the 26th of March, and receive such further orders as the house or the committee then to be appointed should make.

The speaker, on the 25th of February, by writing under his hand, nominated and appointed John Rickman, Esq., clerk assistant of the house of commons, and Francis Cross, Esq., one of the masters of the high court of Chancery, " to examine into the sufficiency of the sureties named or to be named in the recognizance *entered into by one or more of the persons* subscribing the said petition," pursuant to the 9 Geo. 4, c. 22, and to report to him their judgment upon the sufficiency of such sureties.

On the 7th of March, the petitioner Robert Gill Ranson entered into the following recognizance :—

" Be it remembered, that, on the 7th day of March, in the year of our lord, 1835, before me, The Right Honourable James Abercromby, speaker of the house of commons, came Robert Gill Ranson, and acknowledged himself to owe to our sovereign lord the king the following sum, that is to say, the sum of 1000*l.*, to be levied on his goods and chattels, lands and tenements, to the use of our said sovereign lord the king, his heirs and successors, in case the said Robert Gill Ranson shall fail in performing the condition hereunto annexed :

" The condition of this recognizance is, that, if the said Robert Gill Ranson shall well and truly pay all costs and expenses and fees which shall be *due and payable from the said Robert Gill Ranson to any witness who shall be summoned to give evidence in his behalf,* or to any clerk or officer of the house of commons, upon the trial of the petition signed by the said Robert Gill Ranson complaining of an undue election or return for the borough of Ipswich; and if *the said Robert Gill Ranson shall also well and truly pay the costs and expenses of the party who shall appear before the house in opposition to the said petition,* in case the said Robert Gill Ranson shall fail to

appear before the house at such time or times as shall be
fixed by the house for taking such petition into consideration; or in case the said Robert Gill Ranson shall withdraw his said petition by the permission of the house; or
in case the select committee appointed by the house to
try the matter of the said petition shall report to the
house that the said petition appears to them to be frivolous or vexatious: Then this recognizance to be void,
otherwise to be of full force and effect."

Sureties.   On the same day, his sureties, Jeremiah Head and William May, entered into a recognizance with the same condition; and on the 9th of March the examiners appointed by
the speaker certified in writing that Head and May were
sufficient sureties in that behalf.

Committee ap-   On the 26th of March a committee was appointed to
pointed.   examine into the allegations of the petition, who sat on
the 27th, and evidence was heard in support of it from
day to day till the 16th of April, when the committee adjourned till the 18th of May; they then re-assembled, and,
after hearing further evidence, made the following report
to the house on the 10th of June:—

Report of the   "That Robert Adam Dundas and Fitzroy Kelly, Esqrs.,
committee.   are not duly elected burgesses to serve in this present parliament for the borough of Ipswich: That the last election
for burgesses to serve in this present parliament for the
borough of Ipswich is a void election: That the petition
of Robert Gill Ranson, Richard Crawley, and Henry
Haken, does not appear to the said committee to be frivolous or vexatious: That the opposition to the said petition
by the said Robert A. Dundas and Fitzroy Kelly, Esqrs.,
does appear to the said committee to be frivolous and vexatious: That the committee have altered the poll by striking out the names of Richard Bantoft, Horatio Beckham,
John Cox, Thomas Etherington, James Hayward, Her-
man Gullen, Abbott Lord, Samuel Osborn, Lawrence
Squire, Robert Smith, Jeptha Waller, Abraham Wolsey,

and Robert Barber, who were put upon the poll after the termination of the election; and also the names of Frederick Hewes and James Martin Howard, who were employed at such election by the sitting members; and also the names of John Brown, King Garnham, George Horatio Coe, Arthur Bott Cooke, Edward Bolton Finch, and William Coe Abbott, who were proved to have been guilty of bribery at such election."

The house was also informed that the select committee had come to the following resolutions :—" That it appears to this committee that Robert Adam Dundas and Fitzroy Kelly, Esqrs., were by their friends and agents guilty of bribery and corruption at the late election for the borough of Ipswich; and that Arthur Bott Cooke, John Bury Dasent, Esq., John Pilgrim, and others, were guilty of bribery at the said election: That it appears to this committee that John Bury Dasent, Esq., John Bond, Arthur Bott Cooke, Robert B. Clamp, and John Pilgrim, were guilty of absconding, to avoid being served with the speaker's warrant; and that John Eddowes Sparrow and John Clipperton, the avowed agents of the sitting members, and Peter Frederick O'Malley, Esq., one of the counsel employed by the sitting members, aided and abetted them in keeping out of the way to avoid giving their evidence before this committee: That it appears to this committee that the said John Pilgrim, having at length being served with the chairman's warrant, was prevented attending this committee by being arrested on a charge of embezzlement made against him by Messrs. Sewell, Blake, Keith, & Blake, under very suspicious circumstances: That it appears to this committee that the conduct of the magistrates, Samuel Bignold and Edward Temple Booth, Esqrs., before whom the said John Pilgrim was charged, was a breach of the privileges of this house."

No report was made concerning the returning officers.

On the 11th of August, Messrs. Ashurst & Gainsford,

Application to
the speaker to
refer the bill
of costs for
taxation.

the petitioners' agents, addressed the following requisition
to the speaker:—

" Ipswich Election Petition.

" Sir—In consequence of the committee to whom the
matters of this petition were referred having declared
the opposition thereto frivolous and vexatious, we take
the liberty of sending to your secretary herewith the bill
of costs of the petitioners, and request you will be pleased
to order that the same may be referred to the proper officers for taxation, as provided by the statute 9 Geo. 4, c.
22, s. 60."

On the the same day, the following order was issued by
the speaker:—

Order thereon.

" By virtue of the powers given to the speaker of the
house of commons by the act referred to in the requisition
hereunto annexed—I do hereby direct John Rickman,
Esq., clerk assistant of the house of commons, and George
Boone Roupell, Esq., one of the masters of the high court
of Chancery, to examine and tax the costs and expenses
mentioned in the said requisition; and the said John Rickman and George Boone Roupell, Esqrs., are to report to
me the amount thereof. Given under my hand, the 11th
day of August, 1835.

(Signed) " J. Abercromby, Speaker."

On the 1st of October the examiners reported as follows:—

" Ipswich Election.

Examiners'
report.

" In pursuance of the within-mentioned order of the
right honourable the speaker of the house of commons
dated the 11th day of August last—We, the examiners
thereby appointed, do certify, that, in obedience thereto,
we have examined and taxed the costs and expenses mentioned in the said order: And we do hereby report to the
right honourable the speaker of the house of commons
that the costs and expenses allowed by us on such tax-

ation amount to the sum of 4694*l*. 15*s*. 7*d*. : And we further report, that Robert Adam Dundas, and Fitzroy Kelly, Esqrs., whose opposition to the petition of Robert Gill Ranson, Richard Crawley, and Henry Haken, appeared to the select committee appointed to try and determine the merits of the said petition to be frivolous and vexatious, are liable to pay the same. Given under our hands the 1st day of October, 1835.

(Signed) "G. B. Roupell.
" John Rickman."

The speaker therefore signed the following certificate:—"Whereas John Rickman, Esq., clerk assistant of the house of commons, and George Boone Roupell, Esq., one of the masters of the high court of Chancery, who were duly authorized and directed by me, in pursuance of an act passed in the ninth year of the reign of his late majesty, King George the Fourth, intituled 'An act to consolidate and amend the laws relating to the trial of controverted elections or returns of members to serve in parliament,' to examine and tax the costs and expenses incurred by John Gill Ranson, Richard Crawley, and Henry Haken, the persons who signed a petition complaining of an undue election and return for the borough of Ipswich, have reported to me the amount thereof: I do hereby certify that the costs and expenses allowed in the said report amount to the sum of 4694*l*. 15*s*. 7*d*.: And I do further certify that Robert Adam Dundas, and Fitzroy Kelly, Esqrs., whose opposition to the said petition was declared by the select committee appointed to try and determine the merits of the said petition to be frivolous and vexatious, are liable to pay the same. Given under my hand the 27th day of October, 1835.

(Signed) " J. Abercromby, Speaker."

Talfourd, Serjeant, in Michaelmas Term, 1835, on the part of the plaintiffs, obtained a rule nisi to enter up

Marginal notes: 1836. RANSON *v.* DUNDAS. Speaker's certificate. Rule for entering up judgment thereon.

Affidavits in
support of the
rule.

final judgment on the above certificate, *for the sum there-in mentioned*, in pursuance of the statute 9 Geo. 4, c. 22, s. 63. The rule was drawn up on reading the certificate and the following (amongst other) affidavits :—

By Mr. E. B. E. Gainsford, the plaintiff's agent, which, after reciting the speaker's certificate, stated, that, by a deed-poll or letter of attorney, dated the 2nd day of November, 1835, under the hands and seals of the plaintiffs in this cause, the plaintiffs appointed W. H. Ashurst and the deponent, jointly and severally the attornies and attorney of the plaintiffs, to ask, demand, recover, and receive of and from the defendants in this cause the said sum of 4694*l.* 15*s.* 7*d.*, and to give and sign all necessary receipts, releases, and discharges for the same ; whereupon, on the 5th of November, 1835, deponent, as such constituted attorney of the plaintiffs, did personally serve the said defendants with copies of the said certificate, and also with copies of the said deed-poll or letter of attorney, and an affidavit of the due execution thereof ; and did at the same time, as such constituted attorney of the plaintiffs, personally demand payment from the defendants respectively of the said sum of 4694*l.* 15*s.* 7*d.*, being the sum to which they were certified to be liable as aforesaid ; but that the defendants did not nor did either of them then pay the said sum of 4694*l.* 15*s.* 7*d.*, or any part thereof, &c.

And also by one Harris, Gainsford's clerk, stating that writs of summons in an action of debt had been issued out of this court against the defendants ; that they had been served with true copies ; that appearances thereto had been entered for the defendants ; and that a declaration had been filed on the 20th of November, pursuant to the 9 Geo. 4, c. 22, s. 63, of which the defendants had notice.

Against this rule, cause was shewn in Hilary Term,

1836, by *The Attorney-General, Wilde,* Serjeant, Sir *W.*
Follett, Humfrey, and *Wrangham* (a).—Where application

1836.

RANSOM
v.
DUNDAS.

(a) The following is the substance of the affidavits used in opposition to the
rule:—An affidavit of Clipperton, the defendants' agent, which stated, that, on
or about the 25th February, 1835, a petition was presented to the House of
Commons, signed by the plaintiffs, complaining of the election and return of the
defendants for the borough of Ipswich; that the petitioners proceeded to support
the several allegations and parts of the said petition, and that the petitioners did
accordingly produce evidence in support of that part of the petition which charged
the defendants with having personally been guilty of various acts of bribery, and
also of that part of the petition which alleged that James Morrison, Esq., and
Rigby Wason, Esq., had polled a majority of legal votes at the said election, and
ought to have been returned as duly elected, and which prayed that the return
might be amended by striking out the names of the defendants, and inserting
therein instead the names of the said James Morrison and Rigby Wason as duly
returned to serve in parliament for the said borough, which last-mentioned part
of the petition required a scrutiny of the votes given at the said election, and in
prosecution of which scrutiny the said evidence was produced and examined;
and also in support of that part of the said petition which charged the returning
officers or one of them with partial and corrupt conduct at the said election, and
in the making the return of the persons elected: that the charge of undue conduct and partiality against the said returning officers, or one of them, was, after
the hearing of evidence tendered in support of it on the part of the petitioners,
expressly negatived by the committee; and that the committee accordingly, on
the 15th April last, agreed to the following resolution—" That it was the opinion
of the committee that no animus of an improper nature had been proved against
the returning officers:" that, on the 10th day of June last [which was the last
day of their sitting], the committee presented to the house, through their chairman, their report, and also informed the house that they had come to the following among other resolutions—" That it appears to this committee that Robert
Adam Dundas and Fizroy Kelly, Esqrs., were by their friends and agents guilty
of bribery and corruption at the late election for the borough of Ipswich, and
that Arthur Bott Cooke, John Bury Dasent, Esq., John Pilgrim, and others, were
guilty of bribery at the said election:" that the committee did not make any
other report to the house than the report above mentioned: that, previous to,
during, and after the sittings of the said committee, deponent was retained and
employed by and on the behalf of the defendants as their agent: that the committee, on the 27th March last past, actually met and proceeded upon the said
petition during about thirty-nine or forty days; and that several days were
occupied in investigating and trying the said charges contained in the said petition, of personal bribery by the said defendants; and the said committee was also
occupied about a fortnight of the said time in the scrutiny of votes, in order to
determine whether Messrs. Morrison and Wason had the legal majority, and
ought to have been returned, as alleged in the said petition; but, although about
one hundred votes for the late members were objected to by the petitioners, their
counsel finally gave up that part of the case, leaving both the defendants with a
majority, and without calling upon the defendants to disqualify any of the votes

Marginal notes:

Affidavits filed
in opposition to
the rule.

Charge of par-
tiality in the re-
turning officers
negatived by the
committee.

Resolution as to
bribery by
agents.

Proceedings be-
fore the commit-
tee as to person-
al bribery.

Scrutiny.

is made to a court of law, under the statute now in question, to give force and effect to the speaker's certificate,

Opposition of
returning offi-
cers made by
counsel on their
behalf only.

for Messrs. Morrison and Wason to which they the defendants had objected:
that the committee also proceeded in investigating and trying the charge in the
said petition of undue and partial conduct in the said returning officers, or one of
them: that the returning officers' opposition to the said charge and their defence
thereto, was made and conducted on their behalf before the committee by their
own counsel, acting on their particular and express behalf, and was so recognised
by the said committee, nor was that part of the petition relating to the returning
officers opposed by the defendants, nor were the defendants' counsel heard upon
it; and the committee resolved, as aforesaid, that the charge was unfounded:
that, after ten days and upwards had been occupied in the proceedings upon the
scrutiny of the votes, the petitioners, by their counsel, informed the committee
that they abandoned that part of the petition which alleged that the said James
Morrison and Rigby Wason had a majority of legal votes, and which prayed for
their return: that, on or about the 15th day of August last, deponent received a
notice to attend the taxation of the petitioners' bill of costs from the agents of
the petitioners: that the agents of the petitioners at the same time caused to be
delivered at the office of deponent a certain paper writing or bill of costs purporting to be the bill of costs mentioned in the requisition hereinafter next mentioned, and which amounted to upwards of 5,000l.: that deponent had been informed and verily believed, that, on or about the 11th August last, the agent to
the said petitioners transmitted to the speaker of the house of commons the
letter or requisition set forth ante, p. 438, together with the said bill of costs; and
that, on or about the said last-mentioned day, the speaker did make his order of
reference, referring the said bill for taxation to John Rickman and George Boone

That a large
portion of the
costs was incur-
red by the peti-
tioners in refe-
rence to those
allegations in
the petition
which were
abandoned by
themselves or
negatived by the
committee.

Roupell, Esqrs., as examiners: that a very large portion of the amount of the said
bill, amounting, as deponent verily believed, to 3,000l. and upwards, was charged
therein for and in respect of monies, costs, charges, and expenses purporting to
have been incurred by the petitioners in respect of the allegations contained in
the said petition, of improper conduct in the returning officers, of personal
bribery by the said defendants, and that Messrs. Morrison and Wason had a
legal majority of votes at the said election: that, in pursuance of the said notice,
deponent attended from time to time before the examiners, on behalf of the defendants, for the purpose of taxing the said bill, and that previously to proceeding upon such taxation deponent protested against the authority or jurisdiction
of the said examiners to tax the said bill at all as against the defendants, and
further protested against such parts being allowed or taxed as were charged in
the said bill in relation to the prosecution of the several last-mentioned parts of
the said petition which the petitioners had themselves abandoned, and also
against those parts of the bill being taxed or allowed, which the committee had
either expressly negatived, or had not reported to have been established; that is
to say—first, the charge of personal bribery against the defendants—secondly,
the allegation that Morrison and Wason had a legal majority of votes at the said
election, and ought therefore to have been returned instead of the defendants—
thirdly, the charge of undue and partial conduct in the returning officers of the
said borough, or one of them, at the said election: that, on subsequent occasions,

founded upon the resolutions of a committee of the house of commons for the trial of controverted elections, which

and during the taxation of the bill, deponent by himself, and through counsel, on behalf of the defendants, repeated such protest: that the said examiners nevertheless did tax, as against the defendants, the several costs and charges alleged to have been incurred by the said petitioners in supporting the three last-mentioned allegations:

That the said bill of costs contained charges of 5l. 5s. a day during twenty-five days, or thereabouts, for the alleged attendance of Mr. Young as a solicitor for the petitioners; that Mr. Young was a partner in the late firm of Young & Stafford; that the deponent, well knowing that Mr. Stafford had died before the committee met, and that Mr. Young had not attended before the committee, and that no other solicitor attended in his stead, but that Mr. Wason himself alone attended to conduct the proceedings, and did the business usually done by a solicitor on such occasions, therefore protested before the examiners against the said charge; that Mr. Young himself appeared before the examiners, and stated and admitted, that, in consequence of the death of his late partner, Mr. Stafford, who was alone acquainted with the business, he, Mr. Young, had informed Mr. Wason that he could not attend to it, and therefore should not appear, or make any charge; that the deponent thereupon objected that the examiners had no jurisdiction to allow or admit to taxation the said charge contained in the bill for the attendance of Mr. Young before the committee; that the examiners nevertheless admitted the charge to taxation as against the defendants, and allowed a considerable part thereof: that a vast number of charges contained in the bill, between the 26th March and the 26th May, both inclusive, were charges for the transacting of a solicitor's business; whereas no solicitor actually appeared as agent for the petitioners from the day of the first sitting of the committee till on or about the 39th May, when Mr. Ashurst first appeared before the committee as the agent for the petitioners, the whole of the business before the committee usually transacted by the solicitor having been during that interval discharged by Mr. Wason (who was a barrister): that a charge of upwards of 40l. was contained in the bill for the attendance of one R. Taylor as a witness before the committee for the space of twenty-one days; whereas Taylor, after being examined on the sixth day of his attendance, was permitted to remain in the room where the committee sat for the purpose of taking notes of the evidence (he being a newspaper reporter), which was objected to by the counsel for the defendants, and was not conceded by the committee until the counsel for the petitioners declared that his examination was concluded, and that they had no further use for him as a witness; and that Taylor did attend from that time in the committee-room, under such permission and indulgence, in order to take notes, and not as a witness, but on the express ground that he was no longer and should not be a witness: that, although the deponent objected thereto, the examiners allowed the charge on account of Taylor for thirteen days subsequent to such declaration of the petitioners' counsel, and although Taylor was not, and, according to the rules of parliamentary committees, could not have been, called or examined as a witness after he had been so permitted to remain and had remained in the committee-room during the proceedings of the committee: that

Objections to specific charges contained in the bill of costs.

Allowance to Mr. Young as agent to the petitioners.

Allowance to Taylor, a witness.

Fees to Mr.
Rose on taxa-
tion before him,
and costs of at-
tendances
thereon.

Expenses of
witnesses not
summoned:

of witnesses not
examined.

Supplemental
bill.

is a statutable tribunal of limited authority, to the validity
of whose proceedings a strict observance of the conditions

Taylor did on the day after he was so permitted to remain as aforesaid, identify
a paper which he had delivered in on the preceding day, and, with that exception,
remained solely to take notes as aforesaid:

That the deponent further objected before the examiners to the allowance of a
charge of 40l. and upwards alleged to have been paid to Mr. Rose, clerk of the
recognizances attached to the house of commons, for taxing the expenses of
ninety-four witnesses, and to other sums constituting a charge of 30l. for the
alleged attendances of Mr. Ashurst, the petitioners' agent, before Mr. Rose on
the alleged taxation of the last-mentioned expenses, which taxation was alleged
to have taken place on or about the 6th and 7th August, 1835, and long subsequently to the report of the committee; Ashurst attending the same taxation
before Mr. Rose on behalf of the petitioners, and one George Christopherson, a
tradesman residing at Ipswich, on behalf of the ninety-four witnesses who were
alleged to have attended the committee on behalf of the petitioners; that neither
the defendants nor the deponent, nor any other person on behalf of the defendants, attended the alleged transaction before Mr. Rose, or received any notice
that any such taxation was about to be entered upon; that the amount of the
bills of the said ninety-four witnesses after such taxation before Mr. Rose
amounted to 1700l. and upwards; that the examiners disallowed and taxed off
400l. and upwards from the sum allowed in respect of those ninety-four bills by
Mr. Rose, over and above the sum already disallowed by him upon his alleged
taxation; but, while they thus treated the proceeding before Rose as altogether
a nullity, they yet allowed the above-mentioned sums of 40l. and upwards for
Rose's fees upon such alleged taxation, and 30l. and upwards for the two days'
attendance upon it by the agent of the petitioners; and the two last-mentioned
sums were accordingly included in and formed part of the sum mentioned in the
certificate of the speaker, and for which this action was brought:

That a claim was made before the examiners, and objected to by the deponent,
for the expenses of a great number of witnesses who were not proved to have
been summoned either by the warrant of the speaker or of the chairman of the
committee, but appeared to have attended merely by the direction of the agent
or other person on behalf of the petitioners; which objection was overruled by
the examiners, and such costs and charges respectively were allowed in full or in
part, and formed part of the sum mentioned in the speaker's certificate, and for
which this action was brought: that, although the examiners decided that no
costs should be allowed in any case where the witness had not been either summoned as last aforesaid or examined, yet they allowed the expenses of several
witnesses who had been neither summoned nor examined, on the ground that
such expenses had been already passed over in the course of the taxation,
although the deponent was not, at the time of the said witnesses' expenses being
so taxed, aware of the fact that they had been neither summoned nor examined
as aforesaid, but, on the contrary, was led to believe at the time of such taxation
that they had been duly summoned as such witnesses:

That, on or about the 29th September last, the solicitor for the petitioners
presented an entire new bill of costs, containing charges amounting to above

attached to the exercise of such authority is essential, the court will inquire whether or not that tribunal has acted

1836.

RANSON v. DUNDAS.

200*l.* for business done or alleged to have been done on and between the 20th August and the end of September or beginning of October, 1835, both inclusive, in relation to the taxation of the first-mentioned bill of costs, and prayed the examiners to tax such last-mentioned bill, and add such amount as they might think fit to allow in respect thereof to the amount allowed in respect of the first-mentioned bill of costs; whereupon the deponent objected and protested against the examiners' having any jurisdiction to tax or allow any of the items in the said last-mentioned bill. that the examiners, notwithstanding the said protest, proceeded to tax and examine the several items of the said supplemental bill, and eventually did tax off 50*l.* and upwards, and did allow the residue of such bill, amounting to 100*l.* and upwards, and thereupon added the last-mentioned sum so allowed to the amount of the said first-mentioned bill of costs, by inserting the gross amount of such supplemental bill under an item left in blank in the original bill, in the following words—" Attending to tax"—and inserting in the margin thereof the sum taxed off or disallowed as aforesaid; the said sums so allowed not being in truth for attending to tax, but only a very small part thereof being really and truly for attending to tax, and the residue being for other and different charges, incurred between the 25th August and the beginning of October, consisting of attendances to procure affidavits, or preparing and obtaining affidavits of facts to support the charges contained in the first-mentioned bill of costs, and of letters and correspondence in relation thereto ; and the examiners included the sum so allowed, and the same is now included in and forms part of the sum mentioned in the speaker's certificate, and to recover which this action is brought:

That a certain sum of upwards of 50*l.* is inserted and allowed under the item— " Paid fees thereon"—meaning, on taxing, and also is included in and forms part of the sum mentioned in the speaker's certificate, and for which this action is brought ; and that the said sum is made up of examiners' and their clerks' fees, the speaker's secretary's fee, and copying bill of costs, and drawing report of examiners, and fair copy.

Examiners' fees, &c.

John Chevallier Cobbold and Henry Gallant Bristo also deposed that they were the bailiffs and returning officers for the borough of Ipswich at the general election in January, 1835, and were the persons whose conduct was complained of in and by the petition of the plaintiffs against the return of the defendants; that they never did, nor did either of them, receive or hear or know of any notice by or from the speaker of the house of commons, or any person or persons on his behalf, of the day and hour appointed by the house for taking the said petition into consideration, except the paper or notice hereunto annexed, or any other order to them or either of them to attend the house at the time appointed, by themselves, their counsel, or agents ; that they did never, nor did either of them, receive or hear or know of any notice in writing, order, warrant, or other document to them as to the hearing of the said petition, save and except the speaker's warrant to attend before the committee, a copy of which is hereunto annexed; that, having understood that they, as returning officers, were charged by the said petition with having illegally and improperly excluded divers persons

Affidavit of the returning officers, negativing their having any notice or order to attend the house.

within the scope of its jurisdiction. It is open to the parties sought to be affected by the decisions of that tribunal to rebut the presumption that omne rite actum, and to shew a defect or an excess in the exercise of the powers given to it by the statute. And before this court will lend

from voting at the said election, and other misconduct, and knowing themselves to have been wholly innocent of the same, they appeared before the committee by their counsel, on or about the 15th April, 1835, when such charges against them were proceeded with, and witnesses called to establish them on the part of the petitioners; and that the committee resolved to the effect that there was no ground whatsoever for such charges, or any of them, against them, and so resolved without calling upon their counsel for any defence whatsoever.

Speaker's warrant.

The speaker's warrant, referred to in the above affidavit, was as follows:—

"Whereas, by an order of the house of commons, the matter of the petition of Robert Gill Ranson and others, complaining of an undue election and return for the borough of Ipswich, is appointed to be taken into consideration by the said house upon Thursday the 26th March instant, at three o'clock in the afternoon:

"These are therefore to require you, Henry Gallant Bristo and John Chevallier Cobbold, and each of you, to bring in your custody the poll-books containing the names of those who polled at the last election for members to serve in parliament for the borough of Ipswich, and also the list of voters for the said borough, signed by the barrister appointed to revise the same, and in force at the last election; and also the contracts or estimates and original drawings or plans furnished to you or either of you by the architect or any other person employed by you in the erection of polling booths for the purpose of taking the poll at the said election; and also the original bills delivered to you by the several tradesmen employed by you or either of you in the erection of such polling booths; and also the receipts for any monies paid by you to any person on account thereof; and also that you, Henry Gallant Bristo, do bring in your custody a certain letter addressed to you, and written by F. Kelly, Esq., bearing date the 26th January, in this present year, and received by you on the following day; and therewith to be and appear at the bar of the house of commons upon the 26th day of March as aforesaid, to receive and obey such further order as the house, or the select committee then to be appointed to try the matter of the said petition, shall make concerning the same, &c. Dated March 4, 1835.

(Signed)   " J. Abercromby, Speaker."

Further affidavit of Mr. Clipperton.

Mr. Clipperton, in a second affidavit, deposed, that he had searched the official records of orders made in regard to election petitions, to ascertain what orders were made by the house of commons before the nomination and appointment of the committee upon or in relation to the petition by the plaintiffs against the return of the defendants; that the only orders made prior to the nomination and appointment of such committee for or relating to the house taking the matters of the petition into consideration, or for or relating to the attendance of parties thereon, were made on the 25th February last, when an order was made directing the sitting members and the petitioners to attend the house at the time apits authority to enforce the decree, it will look with caution to see that the provisions of the statute have been strictly complied with. The speaker's certificate is conclusive evidence of the *amount* of the demand, but of nothing else. If it shall appear that the house had under the circumstances no right to strike the committee, or that the committee was irregularly or improperly struck, or, the certificate being for one joint sum, if a single shilling is included therein which could not legally be included, then the certificate will be void, and this court will not interfere to enforce it. In Viner's Abridgment, *Authority*, pl. 4, it is said: " All authorities, whether judicial or ministerial, or privately from one person to another, must be pursued; for, when one has no right to do a thing but by a deriva-

1836.

RANSON
v.
DUNDAS.

As to the jurisdiction of the select committee.

pointed for taking the petition into consideration; that the following are copies of the entries of such orders:—

Date of Order.	No.	Subject Matter.	Date of Delivery.	Messengers to whom delivered.
26th February.	25	Ipswich Election.—Sitting Members.	27th February.	W. Cook.
	26	Do. do.—Petitioners.		

That, at the time such last-mentioned orders were made, an order was also made for the attendance of witnesses, and the entry of the said order was as follows:—

" Ipswich Election Committee, 25° Februarii.

" Ordered—

" That Mr. Speaker do issue his warrant or warrants for such persons, papers, and records as shall be thought necessary by the several parties on the hearing of the matters of the said petition."

Order for the attendance of witnesses.

That John Chevallier Cobbold and Henry Gallant Bristo, the returning officers mentioned in the petition, and many other persons, were served with the usual speaker's summons served on witnesses required to give evidence upon the matters of the petition [see the form, ante, p. 446, note], which is in the usual form of summons obtained by parties to petitions, to serve upon such witnesses as the parties respectively may require to attend; and that, in pursuance of the said order, the petition was taken into consideration by the house of commons on the 26th March, and a committee was then appointed to try the matter of the petition, and which committee afterwards made the report referred to in the former affidavit of this deponent sworn in this cause.

There was also an affidavit by one Impey, a clerk to Messrs. Brutton & Clipperton, verifying the copies of the recognisances respectively entered into by Ranson and his sureties, as set forth ante, p. 435.

Affidavit verifying recognisance.

tive power, he must shew he has pursued his power; and especially, if the thing to be done be entire, and more is done than is warranted by the power, all is void." When it is said (9 Geo. 4, c. 22, s. 63), that the certificate of the speaker shall have the force and effect of a warrant to confess judgment, that is to be understood of a certificate signed in accordance with the provisions of the statute: and, when asked to issue its process upon such certificate, this court may properly inquire whether or not the certificate was given under the circumstances on which alone the act authorizes it to be given. Notwithstanding the provision in the statute that judgment *shall* be given for the amount claimed, upon the production of the speaker's certificate, the court is at liberty to inquire into the circumstances upon affidavit; and, if any of the requisites of the act have not been complied with, so as to give complete legal validity to such certificate, and the proceedings upon which it is founded are in accordance with those principles of justice which are binding on all jurisdictions, the court will refuse to give effect to it by entering up judgment. For this there are numerous authorities. Thus, in *Strachey* v. *Turley*, 7 East, 507, the court of King's Bench took notice that the speaker's certificate was not conformable to the 28 Geo. 3, c. 52, although by the 23rd section of that statute it was declared that the speaker's certificate of the amount of costs (with an examined copy of the entries in the journals of the resolutions of the select committee) should be deemed " full and sufficient evidence in support of such action." And upon a case stated in a second action, on a new certificate by the speaker of a subsequent parliament, the court inquired into the validity of that certificate, and held it to be good— 11 East, 194. So, in *Magrane* v. *White*, 2 M. & R. 440, 8 B. & C. 412, where the speaker of the house of commons certified that a certain sum was due to A. B., " a witness summoned by and on the behalf of C. D., one of the sitting members for Dublin, to give evidence before an election committee," the court of King's Bench ordered judgment to be entered up against C. D. for that sum as upon a warrant of attorney, the certificate being held conclusive as to the fact of the witness having been summoned : the authority, however, of the speaker to certify for costs in the particular case, was discussed and determined by the court. Again, in *Trueman* v. *Lambert*, 4 M. & S. 234, the court of King's Bench examined as to whether or not the plaintiff was a party opposing the petition, within the meaning of the 28 Geo. 3, c. 52, s. 23. In *Ex parte Williams*, 8 Price, 3, the court of Exchequer vacated the recognizance, on the ground that there had been no default. And in *Gurney* v. *Gordon*, 2 M. & Scott, 187, 9 Bing. 37, 2 C. & J. 614, 3 Tyr. 616, the Exchequer Chamber decided, upon the construction of the 9 Geo. 4, c. 22, that the speaker's certificate might be directed against one of several petitioners. The last case upon the subject is that of *Bruyeres* v. *Halcomb*, 5 N. & M. 149, 3 Ad. & E. 381, where it was expressly determined that the court will not allow judgment to be entered up, under the 9 Geo. 4, c. 22, on a certificate of the speaker of the house of commons for the costs of opposing an election petition, where it appears upon affidavit that the certificate was founded upon the report of a select committee for trying the merits of the petition, which was not duly appointed according to the provisions of that act. It appeared that the defendant, in 1830, was a candidate to represent the town of Dover in parliament, and that Sir John Rae Reid was declared duly elected. The defendant petitioned against the return ; and the house of commons ordered that the petition should be taken into consideration on the 8th March, 1831, at three o'clock in the afternoon ; but neither the defendant nor any person on his behalf attended the house at that time or within one hour after the time appointed for calling on the parties to proceed to the appointment of a

select committee to try the merits of the petition, according to the statute. The house, however, balloted for and
appointed a select committee to try the petition, neither
the defendant nor his counsel or agent being present or
having an opportunity of striking out eleven names from
the list of members to be chosen by ballot; nor did the
defendant know by whom the eleven names were struck
out on his behalf. On the 9th, the committee met to
try the merits of the petition, the defendant not attending to support it, either in person or by his counsel or
agent; and it was decided that Sir John Rae Reid was
duly elected, that the petition was frivolous and vexatious, and that the opposition to it was not frivolous or
vexatious. The costs of the plaintiff as returning officer,
in opposing the petition, were taxed, and the speaker
made his certificate, pursuant to the statute. On a motion
to enter up judgment under the 63rd section of the statute,
it was contended, on the part of the defendant, that, there
being under the circumstances no power to appoint a
committee (s. 3), the certificate was irregular, and could
not be enforced. On the other hand, it was contended
that the speaker's certificate was final, and the court was
not at liberty to inquire into the grounds upon which it
was given. Lord Denman, in delivering the judgment of
the court (himself, and Littledale, Patteson, and Coleridge, Js.), said:—"It was objected at the bar, that none
of the courts in Westminster Hall are at liberty to inquire
into the legality of proceedings by the house of commons,
nor can do so consistently with the respect due to the
privileges of that body. It is unnecessary to enter upon
that general question in the present case, for, in this instance at least, we are bound to institute the inquiry, as
our assistance is prayed to give effect to the speaker's
certificate; and we should be unwarranted in issuing our
process to that end, unless we saw that his certificate was
founded on a proceeding legal by the act of parliament,

and in compliance with those general principles of justice which are binding on all jurisdictions. The certificate by itself possesses no authority to issue process; recourse must be had to the act for that purpose; and obviously that can only be in cases where the act applies. If this were otherwise, the speaker's certificate that A. owed B. a sum of money, without more, would authorize, nay, compel, the court to issue execution against B., to seize his goods, and throw him into prison. But the speaker's certificate here produced plainly refers to the 60th section of the statute, for, it recites a report of examiners appointed under its provisions, and by them empowered to tax the costs of prosecuting or opposing any petition presented under the provisions of that act. But these costs become due by the 57th section, already cited, the words of which, it is true, apply to 'any committee appointed to try the merits;' but we think they must be confined to committees *duly* appointed under the act, and possessing the powers it confers. The house of commons does not, by virtue of this act, lose its power to appoint an unsworn committee to try the merits of an election, by the examination of witnesses not upon oath; many cases may be supposed in which this ought to be done ; but, though the decision of such a committee should be that a petition was frivolous and vexatious, it is clear that the liability to pay costs would not ensue, nor, if they should be awarded, could payment be enforced in a court of law. The 30th section has also been supposed to give validity to any committee de facto appointed, and supersede all inquiry into the process actually pursued in appointing it. The words are, ' The said eleven members shall be sworn at the table well and truly to try the matter of the petition referred to them, and a true judgment to give according to the evidence, and *shall be deemed and taken* to be a select committee *legally* appointed to try and determine the merits of the return or election appointed by the house to be by them taken into consideration, from and after the time of any such select committee having been sworn at the table.' And these words may possibly have been introduced with the intention of dispensing with the necessity of proof of the facts which must concur to give a committee jurisdiction, though they are not very well selected for the purpose. But they do not exclude proof that the preliminary facts never took place, nor prevent the consequence that the jurisdiction never was created. The proof in the present instance is, that the committee was appointed in such a state of things that the statute positively required that it should not be appointed: it therefore had no power over the petitioner: their report that his petition was frivolous and vexatious, they had no right under the statute to make: the speaker could not lawfully put the examiners in motion to tax the costs; their report was an unauthorized statement of an immaterial fact; and the speaker's certificate of its being made could give it no authority." So, here, the report of the examiners must be equally considered an unauthorised statement of an immaterial fact; the speaker's certificate can give it no authority; and this rule must meet the same fate as the rule in that case, and be discharged with costs.

The facts are these :—At the general election in 1835, four candidates offered themselves for the borough of Ipswich—Messrs. Dundas and Kelly, and Messrs. Morrison and Wason. The two former were returned; and their return was petitioned against by Ranson, Crawley, and Haken, three of the electors. The petition contained four charges—1. of bribery by the sitting members —2. of bribery by avowed agents—3. that Messrs. Morrison and Wason, the rejected candidates, had a majority of legal votes, and ought to have been returned—4. of misconduct in the returning officers, alleging that they had been guilty of partiality and corruption, and had made a false return. The returning officers, therefore, were made parties to the proceedings, and consequently were entitled to notice of them, and ought to have been duly served with the speaker's order to attend the house. They had material privileges, not on their own account only, but also on account of the sitting members: and in their absence the committee could not be properly constituted. The committee were then balloted for, without the recognizance having been entered into which the statute requires—viz., a recognizance by the person or persons subscribing the petition, or some one or more of them, in 1000*l.*, with two sufficient sureties in 500*l.* each, or four in 250*l.* each. The committee then proceeded to examine the merits of the petition, and continued sitting during forty days. The first charge entered upon was that of personal bribery, which entirely failed. Then, came the scrutiny, which occupied about fourteen days, at the expiration of which that charge was abandoned, and the sitting members were not called upon to attack any of the votes given for Messrs. Morrison and Wason; the committee notwithstanding came to the resolution that the last-named gentlemen had a majority of legal votes. The committee then proceeded to the investigation of the charges against the returning officers, who attended by counsel. In this investigation the sitting members, not being interested, took no part; and the committee decided that the charges were wholly unsupported. Thus, on three several grounds, the petitioners entirely failed. With respect to the last charge—bribery by avowed agents—the committee came to a resolution "that Robert Adam Dundas and Fitzroy Kelly, Esqrs., were by their friends and agents guilty of bribery and corruption at the late election for the borough of Ipswich, and that Arthur Bott Cooke, John Bury Dasent, Esq., John Pilgrim, and others, were guilty of bribery at the said election." The report of the committee is altogether silent as to the returning officers; and therefore is so defective that it could not legally be made the foundation for any charge against the sitting members.   On the subsequent taxation of costs, which the sitting members attended under a protest as to the irregularity of the proceedings, costs were allowed, and included in the examiners' report, which had been incurred by the petitioners subsequently to the report of the committee, and subsequently to the reference to the examiners, and of a nature for which the sitting members could in no event be liable—amongst the rest, costs of an unauthorized taxation before Mr. Rose of the expenses of several witnesses, as between those witnesses and the petitioners for whom they appeared. This was a proceeding altogether nugatory; and was so held by the examiners on their taxation, and yet they allowed the costs of that supposed taxation.   The examiners' report also included the costs of certain affidavits taken during the progress of the taxation, their own fees for attending the taxation, and all the costs incurred by the petitioners in their attendance before the committee in support of those charges which they failed to substantiate.

Objections.

The objections arising out of this state of facts, are— First, That no notice in writing was given by the speaker to the returning officers of the time appointed for taking the petition into consideration, accompanied with an order to them to attend the house, as required by the 9 Geo. 4, c. 22, s. 2, they being parties affected by the petition.— Secondly, That no sufficient recognizance was entered into under s. 5, and that consequently the committee was improperly constituted.—Thirdly, That the report of the committee was defective, in omitting to state whether or not the opposition of the returning officers to the petition, as far as it related to them, was frivolous or vexatious.— Fourthly, That the examiners' report and the speaker's certificate included costs incurred subsequently to the report of the select committee.—Fifthly, That the certificate embraced the costs attending the taxation before the examiners.—Sixthly, That it included also costs allowed to witnesses who had never been summoned to attend before the committee.—Seventhly, That the certificate included all the costs incurred in the prosecution of the scrutiny, and of the abandoned or negatived charges of personal bribery by the sitting members, and of partiality and corruption in the returning officers.

1. The returning officers were entitled to notice of the day and hour appointed by the house for taking the petition into consideration, and should have been served with a speaker's order to attend. The 9 Geo. 4, c. 22, s. 2, enacts, "that, whenever a petition complaining of an undue election or return of a member or members to serve in parliament (or complaining that no return has been made to any writ issued for the election of any member or members to serve in parliament on or before the day on which such writ is made returnable, or, if such writ be issued during any session or prorogation of parliament, that no return has been made to the same within fifty-two days after the day on which such writ bears date, or that any return is not according to the requisition of the writ, or complaining of the special matters contained in any such return), shall be presented to the house of commons within such time as shall be from time to time limited by the house, a day and hour shall be appointed by the said house for taking the same into consideration, and *notice thereof in writing shall be forthwith given by the speaker* to all parties so petitioning, and to the sitting members, and to any parties who may have petitioned to be permitted to defend any such election or return, and *where* no such return has been made, or *the conduct of any returning officer is complained of, to the returning officer or officers, accompanied with an order to the parties to attend the house at the time appointed,* by themselves, their counsel, or agent." The third section enacts "that the

house may alter the day and hour so appointed for taking any such petition into consideration, and appoint some subsequent day and hour for the same, as occasion shall require, *giving to the respective parties the like notice* of such alteration, accompanied with an order to attend on such subsequent day and hour as aforesaid." The 18th, 30th, 32nd, 33rd, 34th, 35th, and 36th sections, regulate the mode of striking the committee for the trial of election petitions; and shew that the returning officers, as *parties complained of* by this petition, were entitled to assist in the striking : s. 36 enacting, that, if the returning officer or officers by whom any return ought to have been made, or has been made, shall attend the house when any petition complaining of any undue election or return, or omission to make a return, is ordered to be taken into consideration, in consequence of such order and notice as is thereinbefore described ; and in case there shall be more petitions than one, presented on distinct interests, or complaining upon different grounds, the house shall determine, from the nature of the case, whether the returning officer or officers, his or their counsel or agents, shall, together with such petitioners, be entitled to strike off from the list of members drawn by lot, in the manner thereinbefore directed in cases where there shall be more than two parties before the house, or whether such list shall be reduced by the parties severally presenting such petitions only; and, if such officer or officers cannot be found, to be served with such notice or order, or, being served, shall not appear, by himself or themselves, his or their counsel or agents, at the day and time appointed for taking such petition into consideration, the house may permit or authorize any person to appear in the stead of him or them, and in like manner shall decide whether the person so nominated or appointed to appear in the place of such returning officer or officers shall be entitled to strike off from the said list of thirty-three members so drawn by lot as

aforesaid, as it might do in case the returning officer or.
officers had appeared." The attendance of *all the parties*
affected by the petition upon the speaker's notice and
order, is a condition precedent to the valid and effective
constitution of the select committee: the notice and order
are essential; and a *voluntary* attendance of a party would
not entitle him to the privilege of assisting in striking the
committee. That the returning officer is a party within
the meaning of the 28 Geo. 3, c. 52, s. 23, so as to be entitled to his costs on a resolution of the committee that
the petition was frivolous and vexatious, was decided in
Trueman v. *Lambert*, 4 M. & Sel. 234: and it is equally
clear that the returning officer is now a *party* chargeable
with costs under the 9 Geo. 4, c. 22, s. 58, where his opposition to the petition is reported to be frivolous and
vexatious. Here, no notice or order to attend having
been served on the returning officers, the house had no
authority to proceed to a ballot for the committee; for,
the returning officers had no opportunity to appear and
claim the privileges the statute gave them. The committee therefore was an improperly constituted court: and
the proceedings were coram non judice. The fact of the
returning officers having actually appeared by their counsel, in opposition to the petition, makes no difference; for,
where there is a defect of jurisdiction, the appearance and
submission of a party cannot cure that defect, and confer
a jurisdiction which the law had not contemplated. Thus,
in *Holt* v. *Meadowcroft*, 4 Mau. & Sel. 467, where a
common jury panel was returned, together with a special
jury panel, and, no special jurymen appearing, the cause
was tried by a common jury, the trial was set aside, notwithstanding the defendant had appeared and offered a defence; Lord Ellenborough observing—" If you drag him to
the stake, he has a right to make the best of it when there."
The sitting members, too, were damnified by the want of
notice to the returning officers; for, if these latter had

assisted in the striking of the committee, the committee might, and in all probability would, have been differently constituted. The returning officers, also, might have called upon the committee to declare the petition as against them to be frivolous and vexatious, and then their costs would have been payable to them by the petitioners, instead of the latter claiming theirs from the sitting members: or, the returning officers might in another event have been liable to pay to the petitioners the costs occasioned by that part of the proceedings which affected them, when the sitting members would have been relieved from that part of the burthen. The 60th section, which requires the examiners to report to the speaker the amount of the costs, "together with the name of the party liable to pay the same," shews that the legislature contemplated an apportionment of costs among the different parties. The committee, therefore, and the examiners, should have separately reported as to each of the parties petitioned against. If the report of the committee had been properly framed, the examiners never would have taxed the costs in the manner they have done. [*Tindal*, C. J.—Is it usual to make an order on the sitting member, and also upon the returning officer?] *The Attorney-General.*—Yes; the practice is thus: The petition goes to the journal office. It is the duty of the clerk there to certify the fact to the speaker when a charge is brought against the returning officer. In the present case, that was omitted: no intimation to that effect was given to the speaker, and therefore no order to attend the house was addressed to the returning officers. If the returning officers would, in any case where they are inculpated by the petition, be entitled to assist in the striking of the committee, they ought to have been served with an order to attend the house. There is no obligation upon the house to refer the consideration of the personal delinquency of a returning officer to the committee. He may appear by counsel at the bar of the house, and obtain the discharge of that part of the petition which relates to him, before the reference of the matters to the committee. In the present case, the returning officers not having been served with the speaker's order, they lost the opportunity of being heard in this manner. By the 36th section, it is in the discretion of the house to permit the returning officer, when petitioned against, to assist in striking the committee. In order to be able to avail himself of the privilege, he should be ordered to attend the house: and a committee struck in his absence and in the absence of such order, is clearly not legally and properly constituted. [*Tindal*, C. J.—You contend that there *might have been* three distinct striking parties; and that, consequently, the committee might have consisted of persons different from those who in fact comprised it?] Precisely so. And it is perfectly immaterial, for the purpose of this argument, whether or not the house would, under the circumstances, have allowed the returning officers to assist in striking.

2. No recognizance having been entered into in pursuance of the provisions of the statute, the house had no right to proceed, and order the committee to be struck. The 5th section enacts "that *no proceeding shall be had upon any such petition, unless the person or persons subscribing the same, or some one or more of them, shall,* within fourteen days after the same shall have been presented to the house, or within such further time as shall be limited by the house, *personally enter into a recognizance* to our sovereign lord the king, *according to the form thereunto annexed,* in the sum of 1000*l.*, with two sufficient sureties in the sum of 500*l.* each, or four sufficient sureties in the sum of 250*l.* each, for the payment of all costs, expenses, and fees which shall become due to any witness summoned in behalf of the person so subscribing such petition, or to any clerk the house upon the trial of such petition, or

2. No sufficient recognizance pursuant to the statute.

1836.

RANSON
v.
DUNDAS.

who shall appear before the house or any committee of the
house, in opposition to such petition, in case such person
or persons shall fail to appear before the house at such
time or times as shall be fixed by the house for taking
such petition into consideration; or in case such petition
shall be withdrawn by the permission of the house; or in
case such committee shall report to the house that such
petition appears to them to be frivolous or vexatious; and
if at the expiration of the said fourteen days such recognizance shall not have been entered into, or shall not have
been received by the speaker of the house of commons,
or the time for entering into or receiving such recognizance shall not previously have been enlarged, the
speaker shall report the same to the house, and the order
for taking such petition into consideration shall thereupon
be discharged, unless upon special report of the examiners
into the sufficiency of the sureties, or upon matter specially stated and verified upon oath to the satisfaction of
the house, the house shall see cause either to enlarge the
time for entering into such recognizance, or to allow the
names of any such sureties to be changed; and whenever
such time shall be so enlarged, or the name of any such
surety shall be changed, the order for taking such petition
into consideration shall, if necessary, be postponed, so
that no such petition shall be taken into consideration till
after such recognizance shall have been entered into and
received by the speaker: provided always that the time
for entering into such recognizance shall not be enlarged
more than once, or for any number of days exceeding
thirty, nor the name of any proposed surety be more than
once changed." *Bruyeres* v. *Halcomb* is an authority to
shew that the want of a recognizance vitiates the proceedings: and it is precisely the same whether there has
been a total omission to enter into the required recognizance, or an omission to enter into it in the required form.
The recognizance contemplated by the statute is to secure

two things—the expenses of witnesses summoned in behalf of *the person or persons subscribing the petition*, and also the costs due to any party who shall appear before the house or the committee in opposition to the petition, in case of default in the petitioners, or the petition being declared by the committee to be frivolous or vexatious: whereas, here, the recognizance is entered into by *one* of the petitioners only, and is conditioned merely for the payment of costs and expenses due from *him* to any witness summoned on *his* behalf, and for payment by *him*, in case the petition should be withdrawn or be declared frivolous or vexatious, of the costs and expenses of the party who should appear *before the house* in opposition to the petition—making no provision whatever either for the expenses of witnesses called in behalf of the other two petitioners, or of parties appearing *before the select committee* in opposition to the petition. Suppose Ranson, after having entered into the recognizance, and pending the proceedings upon the petition, became insane or died, and the petition were proceeded with by the other petitioners, Crawley and Haken, could it be said that the witnesses summoned by them under such circumstances were witnesses called on behalf of Ranson? or could any action be maintained by the witnesses so summoned, upon this recognizance, against the representatives of Ranson? In the case of an indictment or an action for a tort by three plaintiffs, the suit would not abate by the death of one of them; but the witnesses called by the survivors could not sue the representatives of the deceased for their expenses. The recognizance entered into in the present case gives no remedy either to the witnesses summoned before the *committee* or to the returning officers, who, though they appeared before the *committee*, cannot be said to have appeared before *the house*, they not having been duly summoned; although, by ss. 10 and 12, parties not before the house may be admitted to appear as parties before the committee, and, by s. 40, the committee are directed to report to the house " with respect to every party who shall have appeared *before them* in opposition to such petition," &c., and by ss. 57 and 58, the committee are authorised to inflict or award costs upon or to parties so attending *before them*. This recognizance, therefore, would give no remedy for their costs either to the returning officers or to witnesses or parties attending before the committee under the circumstances above supposed. It is true the 5th section requires the recognizance to be given " according to the form thereunto annexed :" but the form given in the schedule is applicable to the case of a single petitioner only. The purpose of the schedule is, not to control or repeal the enacting parts of the statute, but simply to explain and operate as a guide to the parties. Numerous authorities have decided, that, although the words of a conviction follow the form given in a schedule, such form does not dispense with a strict compliance with the common and ordinary rules of law, or with the express words of the enacting part of the statute. The form given in a schedule is in no case to be blindly and implicitly followed. In *Rex* v. *Loxdale*, 1 Burr. 447, Lord Mansfield says: " There is a known distinction between circumstances which are of the *essence* of a thing required to be done by an act of parliament, and clauses *merely directory*." Here, the clause in question is not merely directory; it is of the essence of the things required by the act to be done. In *Rex* v. *Jarvis*, 1 Burr. 154, Denison, J., observes: " It is said that it is sufficient to lay the offence [gaming—5 Ann. c. 14,] in the words of the act of parliament. But that is not always sufficient: it may be necessary to go further. P. 28 Geo. 2, B. R., *Rex* v. *Chapman*, about robbing an orchard, was a case where the mere pursuing the words of the statute was *not* sufficient." In *Rex* v. *James*, Cald. 458, a conviction in the very terms of the lottery act, 22 Geo. 3, c. 47, was quashed for insufficiency. Buller, J., there said: "It is not true, that, in framing a conviction, it is sufficient to follow the words of the statute in all cases. In some, indeed, it may; as, where the statute gives a particular description of the offence; but it is otherwise where a particular offence is included under a general description. Where a particular act constitutes the offence, it may be enough to describe it in the words of the legislature; but, where the legislature speak in general terms, the conviction must state what act in particular was done by the party offending, to enable him to meet the charge." In *Rex* v. *Dimpsey*, 2 T. R. 96, a conviction following the precise form given by the statute 35 Geo. 3, c. 6, was quashed, the statute requiring the justice to distribute the penalty on conviction among certain persons according to their discretion, and the justices having in strictly pursuing the form given omitted to adjudge what the several proportions should be. *Rex* v. *Priest*, 6 T. R. 538, is an authority to the same effect. Lord Kenyon there says: "When a form of conviction is prescribed by a statute, it is most safe in general to adopt the very words used: but, taking the whole of this act of parliament together, the legislature could not intend that there should be a literal adherence to the form prescribed." There are numerous other cases to be found, where the form of conviction given by a schedule has been strictly and closely followed, and yet the conviction has been held bad because the form was not precisely adapted to the particular case—*Fleming* v. *Bailey*, 5 East. 313, *Doe* d. *Bywater* v. *Brandling*, 1 Man. & Ryl. 605. And in *Morgan* v. *Brown*, 6 Nev. & M. 57, where the plaintiff and one Parker were convicted before the defendants, two magistrates, under the 9 Geo. 4, c. 31, the conviction pursuing the precise words of the form given in a schedule to the act, which was applicable to one person only, the court held that the defendants could not justify the imprisonment of the plaintiff under it. The decision of the house of commons in the *Leicester* case, during the present session, shews the spirit in which they themselves construe the clause in question. By the 7th section of the act, it is provided that seven clear days shall intervene between the day on which the names of the sureties shall have been delivered in and entered in a book kept in the office of the clerk of the house of commons, and the day on which the sufficiency of the sureties shall be examined into. In that case, a mistake having been made in the christian name of one of the sureties, notice thereof was given on the 25th March, the day appointed for the examination being the 31st ; consequently there were not seven days intervening, as required by the act. The order for taking the petition into consideration was discharged, and the house refused to extend the time for putting in the security, holding that the act must be strictly pursued.

3. As to the omission of the committee to report on the opposition of the returning officers.

3. The report of the committee is altogether silent as to whether or not the opposition of the returning officers, or the petition in relation to them, was frivolous or vexatious, as required by the 40th section. That section provides that the committee " at the same time that they inform the house of their final determination on the merits of the petition which they were sworn to try, shall also report to the house whether such petition did or did not appear to them to be frivolous or vexatious ; and in like manner report *with respect to every party who shall have appeared before them in opposition to such petition,* whether the opposition of such party did or did not appear to them to be frivolous or vexatious." The report of the committee on the present occasion has not complied with the act of parliament in this respect, and therefore is not capable of being made the foundation of any ulterior proceedings. The petition embraces several distinct matters. The report thereon is confined to that part of the petition

which affects the sitting members, and is altogether silent as to the opposition by the returning officers. If several distinct parties are called into action by the allegations contained in the petition, and, the committee reporting the opposition by one party to be frivolous and vexatious, the petitioners are entitled to receive from that one party the whole costs of the proceedings on their parts as against all who appeared in opposition to the petition, it is of the highest importance that the report of the committee should embrace all the parties. Grievous injustice will be done by allowing a partial report. Suppose a petition presented complaining of the return of the four members of the city of London, and of the conduct of the returning officer in relation thereto, charging A. with bribery, B. with treating, that C. was without qualification, and D. a minor, and that E. (the returning officer) had been guilty of corruption; and it should turn out on the report of the committee that there is no charge against A. or B., that C. proves a qualification, that D. *is* a minor, and his opposition to the petition was frivolous and vexatious, and that the charge against E. was unfounded—the report being in favour of four of the parties and against one only, would the petitioners be entitled to recover from that one the entire costs of the unfounded attempt to charge the other four? There is no pretence for saying that they would: and that is precisely this case. If, in the present case, the opposition of the returning officers had been reported to be not frivolous and vexatious, the petitioners clearly would not have been entitled to the costs of the proceedings against them; or, if the petition as against them had been reported frivolous and vexatious, they would have been entitled to receive their costs from the petitioners. If the report had been silent as to the opposition of the sitting members, and the opposition of the returning officers been declared to be frivolous and vexatious, would the latter have been fixed with the entire costs? In the case of a special limited

1836.

RANSON
v.
DUNDAS.

jurisdiction, the effect of an omission to determine as to one of several matters affecting the consequences of the points that are decided, is well ascertained by the cases of *Mitchell* v. *Staveley*, 16 East, 58, *Simmonds* v. *Swaine*, 1 Taunt. 549, *Winter* v. *Munton*, 2 Moore, 723, and the authorities cited in 1 Wms. Saund. 32 *a*, n.

4. Costs included in the certificate that arose after the report of the committee.

4. The certificate including costs unauthorised by the act, and arising after the report of the committee, is void. The 58th section enacts, that, where an opposition is frivolous and vexatious, the petitioner shall be entitled to recover from such parties the full costs which he shall have incurred *in prosecuting his petition*. The costs to which this objection applies are costs attending the sham taxation before Mr. Rose, the clerk of the recognizances in the house of commons, and the costs incurred subsequently to the reference to the examiners, the whole of which are included in the examiners' report and in the speaker's certificate. These clearly were not legitimately costs incurred in the prosecution of the petition.

5. Costs of taxation included in the certificate.

5. The speaker's certificate includes also the costs of the taxation before the examiners, which the act nowhere authorizes; and also the new bill presented to the examiners on the 29th September, after the close of their taxation, and after the authority of the speaker to refer them to taxation was at an end, embracing charges for affidavits, journies, and attendances at various times between the 20th August and the day of the delivery of such last-mentioned bill, none of which are contemplated by the act. Had the legislature intended to give the costs of taxation, they would have expressed themselves to that effect.

6. Costs of witnesses not summoned.

6. A further objection to the certificate arises from the circumstance of its including the expenses of witnesses not *summoned* either by the speaker or by the chairman of the committee. In *Magrane* v. *White*, 2 M. & R. 440, 8 B. & C. 412, where the speaker of the house of commons certified that a certain sum was due to A. B., "a witness *summoned*

by and on the behalf of C. D., one of the sitting members
for Dublin, to give evidence before an election committee,"
the court ordered judgment to be entered up against C. D.
for that sum, as upon a warrant of attorney, the certificate
being (until the contrary appeared) conclusive as to the
fact of the witness having been summoned.

7. In the speaker's certificate was also included the
expenses attendant upon the scrutiny, and of that part of
the petition which charged the sitting members with personal bribery; in both of which the petitioners failed,
these charges being, the one wholly unfounded, and the
other abandoned. That there cannot be a joint taxation
of costs where there are two petitions, was decided by
Strachey v. *Turley*, 7 East, 507. There, the speaker having first certified a joint taxation of costs for a certain sum
against all the petitioners, and having afterwards by an
amended certificate apportioned how much of the first-
mentioned sum taxed was incurred by the sitting members
in opposing the two petitions *jointly*, and how much was
so incurred by them in opposing each *separately*, the plaintiffs, by the advice of the court, submitted to enter non-
suits as well in two several actions prosecuted against the
respective petitioners for the separate costs certified against
each, as also in a joint action against all to recover the
taxation certified against them all *jointly*. There cannot
in principle be any difference between the case of two
separate petitions, and a single petition on two distinct and
specific grounds. It is impossible to say that a certificate
like this, declaring the sitting members liable for costs incurred in the prosecution of charges that have turned out
to be altogether unfounded, is a certificate made in pursuance of the authority conferred by the act.

Talfourd, Serjeant, *M. D. Hill*, and *Austin*, in support
of the rule.—If it be competent to the defendants to bring
before this court upon affidavit all the objections that

(margin notes:)
1836.

RANSON
v.
DUNDAS.

7. Costs of the scrutiny and of the abandoned or negatived charges both against the sitting members and the return-ing officers.

might suggest themselves in the course of the proceedings before the house and before the committee, in what a difficult position are placed the parties seeking to put in force the speaker's certificate. The plaintiffs have no opportunity to answer the defendants' affidavits, presenting their own view of their own case. This affords a strong presumption against the right of parties to raise any question at all upon the certificate. Besides, it is perfectly consistent with the allegation that the returning officers received no notice to attend at the striking of the committee, that they were actually present by themselves or their counsel, as they afterwards were before the committee. It is also consistent with Mr. Clipperton's affidavit, that the charge of bribery should have been first entered upon, and that the petitioners should have failed to bring home the charge to either principals or agents, in consequence of the absence of those witnesses who absconded in order to avoid giving their evidence, and who are reported by the committee to have been abetted therein by Mr. Clipperton himself; that the scrutiny should then have been proceeded with; that, pending the scrutiny, one of the witnesses should have been discovered and brought before the committee; that the committee should then have reverted to the charge of bribery, and should have found the sitting members, by their agents, guilty of bribery; and that, the seats being avoided, and only one of the witnesses returned, the petitioners should have preferred a new election to a continuation of the scrutiny: and so, the petitioners having been driven to the scrutiny by the misconduct of the defendants' agents, and the absconding of the witnesses who might have established the personal bribery, there is no injustice in calling on the defendants to pay the expenses incurred in support of those charges. But, assuming that the affidavits are properly admitted, it is impossible for the court to sanction or sustain the objections they present. By the 58th section of

the 9 Geo. 4, c. 22, it is enacted "that, whenever the
committee shall report to the house, with respect to the
opposition made to the petition by any party or parties
who shall have appeared before them, that such opposition appeared to be frivolous or vexatious, the person
or persons who shall have signed such petition shall be
entitled to recover from such party or parties, or any of
them, with respect to whom such report shall be made,
the full costs and expenses which such petitioner or petitioners shall respectively have incurred in prosecuting
their petition, such costs and expenses to be ascertained
in the manner thereinafter directed." And the 60th section enacts, "that the costs and expenses of prosecuting
or opposing any petition presented under the provisions
of this act, and the costs, expenses, and fees which shall
be due and payable to any witness summoned to attend
before such committee, or to any clerk or officer of the
house of commons, upon the trial of such petition, shall
be ascertained in manner following, (that is to say), that,
on application made to the speaker of the house of commons within three months after the determination of the
merits of such petition, by any such petitioner, party,
witness, or officer as before mentioned, for ascertaining
such costs, expenses, or fees, the speaker shall direct the
same to be taxed by two persons, of whom the clerk or
one of the clerks assistant of the house shall be one, and
one of the following officers, not being a member of the
house, shall be the other, (that is to say), masters in the
high court of Chancery, clerks in the court of King's
Bench, prothonotaries in the court of Common Pleas, and
clerks in the court of Exchequer; and the persons so
authorised and directed to tax such costs, expenses, and
fees, shall, and they are hereby required to examine the
same, and to report the amount thereof, together with
the name of the party liable to pay the same, to the
speaker of the said house, who shall, upon application

made to him, deliver to the party or parties a certificate signed by himself, expressing the amount of the costs, expenses, and fees allowed in such report, together with the name of the party liable to pay the same; and the persons so appointed to tax such costs, expenses, and fees, and report the amount thereof, are hereby authorised to demand and receive for such taxation and report such fees as shall be from time to time fixed by any resolution of the house; *and such certificate,* so signed by the speaker, *shall be conclusive evidence of the amount of such demands, in all cases and for all purposes whatsoever;* and the witness, officer, or party claiming under the same, shall, upon payment thereof, give a receipt at the foot of such certificate, which shall be a sufficient discharge for the same." Before the case of *Bruyeres* v. *Halcomb,* there existed no authority for contending that the court whose assistance was asked to render the speaker's certificate available, could do more than see that the certificate was properly framed, and the demand of the amount therein mentioned duly made. In *Strachey* v. *Turley,* the objection presented itself on the face of the certificate. In *Ex parte Williams,* 8 Price, 3, the court of Exchequer, having an equitable jurisdiction over recognizances under the 33 Hen. 8, c. 39, independently of the statute now under consideration, exercised that jurisdiction by discharging the recognizance given in that case, upon information laid before them on affidavit, of which the committee could not be apprized. But, what were the circumstances of *Bruyeres* v. *Halcomb?* The petitioner made default; and the house, notwithstanding, proceeded to strike a committee; whereas the proper course was, to discharge the order of the day for taking the petition into consideration—9 Geo. 4, c. 22, s. 3. The proceedings therefore were an entire nullity. Where, however, no irregularity appears on the face of the certificate, the jurisdiction of the court is merely collateral and ancillary to the higher jurisdiction created by the statute. The mere act of applying to this court to lend its aid to the enforcing the certificate, does not give it a jurisdiction to inquire into all the proceedings anterior to the grant of such certificate. The speaker's certificate is to have the force and effect of a warrant to confess judgment —s. 63. All that this court is authorized to do is, to execute that judgment, not to question the propriety of the grounds upon which or the means by which it has been obtained. There is no analogy between the judgment of a select committee of the house of commons, and that of a court of inferior jurisdiction, whose proceedings are regulated and controlled by the superior courts. By the 9th article of the Bill of Rights, it is expressly declared that no court shall interfere with the authority of parliament, which is superior to that of the courts—1 Bl. Com. 163, 4 Inst. 15; *Regina* v. *Paty*, 1 Lord Raym. 1105. And in *Trueman* v. *Lambert*, 4 M. & Sel. 234, Lord Ellenborough said that the committee were upon this subject a court not only of competent but of exclusive jurisdiction. If the matter be within the jurisdiction of the house, therefore, there is no appeal from their decision; for, that would place the court in direct collision with the house. In the case of foreign judgments, where the judgment appears to have been pronounced by a competent tribunal, and upon a subject within its jurisdiction, the courts of this country, where it is sought to be enforced here, will accredit the judgment of the foreign court, and will presume that it has proceeded according to its jurisdiction. In every case the law must repose confidence somewhere: and where with such propriety as in the speaker of the house of commons?

The objections urged on the part of the defendants in effect resolve themselves into these four—1. That the returning officers, as *parties* within the meaning of the statute, were entitled to notice of the time appointed for taking the petition into consideration, and an order to attend at the bar of the house; and that the omission of that ceremony destroys the very constitution of the committee, and renders void all the subsequent proceedings.—2. That the recognizance entered into by one of the petitioners and his sureties was not a compliance with the act.—3. That the report of the committee was essentially vicious, inasmuch as it omitted to adjudicate upon that part of the petition which related to the conduct of the returning officers.—4. That costs have been taxed by the examiners for which the statute imposes upon the present defendants no liability.

The answer to these objections is three-fold—First, that all the provisions contained in the statute, with reference to the proceedings before the house and before the committee, are directory only, and are not conditions precedent, the nonperformance or malperformance of which will operate in avoidance of the speaker's certificate.—Secondly, that all these directions have in substance been complied with.—Thirdly, that, if these provisions either do constitute conditions precedent, or have been insufficiently complied with, the objections cannot be urged at this stage of the proceedings, but should have been taken either before the house or before the committee.

1. The provisions of the act directory only.

1. If a failure strictly to observe, in the proceedings before an election committee, the course pointed out by the act in any one particular, would have the effect contended for on the part of the defendants, to what absurd and mischievous consequences would it not lead? A variety of acts are required to be done anterior to the striking of the committee: an inquiry into the manner in which these have been performed would be endless. By the 2nd section of the 9 Geo. 4, c. 22, it is provided that a day *and hour* shall be appointed by the house for taking the petition into consideration: suppose a day appointed, but no hour specified, could it be contended that all the subsequent proceedings on the petition were therefore void,

notwithstanding all the parties had been actually in attendance? The 6th section requires the names of the sureties, together with their additions and usual places of residence, to be delivered to the cleɪk of the house of commons: would an incorrect description of one of the sureties vitiate the recognizance? The 8th section provides, that, where the parties to enter into the recognizance or their sureties reside at a greater distance than forty miles from London, the recognizance may be taken before · a justice of the peace: would it be competent to a party at this stage of the proceedings to produce affidavits to shew that one of the sureties so entering into the recognizance resided within the prescribed distance? By the 17th section, the serjeant-at-arms is directed, at the time appointed for taking the petition into consideration, to go with the mace to the places adjacent, to require the attendance of the members: would an omission to perform that ceremony invalidate the appointment of the committee? By the same section, the speaker is required to count the house, and, in the event of the number of members present falling short of one hundred, the order of the day for taking the petition into consideration is to be adjourned: would it be competent to this or any other court, on a motion like the present, to receive affidavits to shew that the speaker had miscounted? By s. 21, members are under certain circumstances disqualified from serving on committees: would the presence of a disqualified person render void all the acts of that committee?

2. The directions of the statute have been substantially complied with. The returning officers were not parties to the proceedings within the meaning of the act, or entitled to notice: the petition was directed against the sitting members, praying for inquiry into the validity of their return; it is true, it incidentally noticed the misconduct of the returning officers; but that does not make them *parties*. The 10 Geo. 3, c. 16, and the 11 Geo. 3, c. 42, s. 6, apply only to the case of petitioners and sitting

1836.

RANSON
v.
DUNDAS.

2. The directions of the act have in substance been complied with.

members. The 25 Geo. 3, c. 84, ss. 10, 11, and 12, provide for the case of a returning officer making no return in proper time, or a return of special facts, instead of a return of members: neither of these cases applies to the present. The 9 Geo. 4, c. 22, s. 2, provides for the case where no return is made in due time, or no return according to the requisition of the writ, or where the special matter in the return is complained of. The 36th section only applies to the conduct of the returning officer where there is more than one petition, or where he is the only person petitioned against. It provides " that, if the returning officer or officers by whom any return ought to have been made, or has been made, shall attend the house when any petition complaining of any undue election or return, or omission to make a return, is ordered to be taken into consideration, in consequence of such order and notice as is hereinbefore described; and in case there shall be more petitions than one presented on distinct interests, or complaining upon different grounds; *the house shall determine, from the nature of the case, whether the returning officer or officers, his or their counsel or agents, shall, together with such petitioners, be entitled to strike off from the list of members drawn by lot, in the manner hereinbefore directed in cases where there shall be more than two parties before the house, or whether such list shall be reduced by the parties severally presenting such petitions only ;* and, if such officer or officers cannot be found to be served with such notice or order, or, being served, shall not appear, by himself or themselves, his or their counsel or agents, at the day and time appointed for taking such petition into consideration, the house may permit or authorize any person to appear in the stead of him or them, and in like manner shall decide whether the person so nominated or appointed to appear in the place of such returning officer or officers shall be entitled to strike off from the said list of thirty-three members so drawn by lot as aforesaid, as it might do in case the return ing officer or officers had appeared." It is *in the discretion* *of the house*, under the circumstances mentioned in that section, to allow the returning officers to assist in striking the committee: it does not follow that they would have been allowed. The *Colchester case*, 1 Peckwell, 504, and the *Nottingham case*, Id. 150, shew that the returning officers here could, under no circumstances, interfere in the striking of the committee. The objection, therefore, as to the want of notice to them, entirely fails. The advantage of the mode that was pursued was all on the side of the defendants; for, they had the right to strike half the number, instead of a third—unless, indeed, they were colluding with the returning officers. Besides, the issuing of the order was the speaker's duty : a breach of duty on his part could never be permitted to prejudice the rights of the petitioners.

Then, as to the recognizance. It may be conceded, that, if the recognizance, or if a conviction under any statute which provides a form, pursues the form literally, and fails substantially in complying with the requisitions of the act itself, it will be bad. In the present case, however, there has been both a substantial and a literal compliance with the 5th section. All that the defendants or any other parties would be entitled to under the act, is secured to them by the recognizance in its present form. They are only entitled to the security of some one or more of the petitioners and the sureties. The three petitioners were in one interest; the witnesses called by any one of them, would be called in behalf of all. The sitting members and the returning officers were the only persons who could appear in opposition to the petition either before the house or before the committee : and for costs incurred by them the recognizance is an ample indemnity.

The omission of the committee to report upon the charge against the returning officers cannot be complained of by the defendants; they were in no respect damnified by it. The objection, indeed, assumes either that the notice which

1836.

RANSON
v.
DUNDAS.

As to the form
of the recog-
nizance.

As to the omis-
sion of the com-
mittee to report
upon the charge
against the re-
turning officers.

it is contended was required to render the returning officers parties was in fact not necessary, or that the speaker's certificate is conclusive evidence that such notice was given.

As to the costs included in the certificate.

With respect to the costs—this court has no power to interfere with the amount: as to that the speaker's certificate is conclusive. The committee having reported that the opposition of the defendants was frivolous and vexatious, it was in the discretion of the examiners to determine what costs had been incurred through the misconduct of the parties reported against.

3. Objections urged at too late a stage of the proceedings.

3. Whatever weight be intrinsically due to any of the objections, the defendants have waived them by not taking them at the proper time, before the house, when the order of the day was called on, or at least before the committee. After verdict and judgment, it is not competent to the defendant to take an exception to the validity of the bail-bond, or to the appearance. Had the defendants objected to the recognizance at the proper period, the petitioners might (if it were defective) have come in within fourteen days with an amended recognizance. In *Brunskill* v. *Giles*, 2 M. & Scott, 45, 9 Bing. 13, after a trial had been had, the court refused to grant a venire de novo, on an allegation that the jury had been convened by the partner of the plaintiff's attorney. In *Hill* v. *Yates*, 12 East, 229, it was held that the son of a juryman summoned and returned, having answered to his father's name when called on the panel, and served as one of the jury on the trial of a cause, was not of itself a sufficient ground for setting aside the verdict as for a mistrial. In *Dovey* v. *Hobson*, 6 Taunt. 460, 2 Marsh. 154, the irregularity being noticed before verdict, this court awarded a venire de novo. But in *Rex* v. *Hunt*, 4 B. & Ald. 430, where, upon the trial of an information for a libel, only ten special jurymen appeared, and two talesmen were sworn on the jury, it was held to be no ground for a new trial, that two of the non-attending special jurymen named in the panel had not been

summoned, though it appeared that that fact was unknown to the defendant until after the trial. *In the Matter of the London and Greenwich Railway Company* and *The Sheriff of Surrey*, 4 Nev. & M. 458, the court said that the applicant ought to have objected at the time to the oversight in respect of the jury. In *Rex* v. *Stone*, 1 East, 649, the appearance of the party, though in a criminal case, was held to cure the want of a summons. In cases of treason, although the statute which entitles the prisoner to a copy of the indictment before trial, is imperative, and not merely directory, yet it has been held too late to object after plea pleaded that a prisoner has not had the whole of the indictment—*Rookwood's* case, Holt, 604, 13 Howell's State Trials, 154, 155, 156, *Cook's* case, 13 Howell's State Trials, 330. So, in *Watson's* case, 2 Stark. 158, 32 Howell's State Trials, 496, where a witness was described as *Hayward* instead of Hey*wood*, and as of a wrong profession, it was held that the objection under the statute of Anne should have been taken in the first instance. Holroyd, J., there says: "Objections to disqualify a witness, such as questions of interest or description, should be taken in the first instance." By the civil law, objections to the jurisdiction are the first to be taken—Cujatius, e. 83, Potier, Code de Procedure, art. 1029, 1030. The like rule obtains in the law of Scotland.

Cur a dv. vult.

TINDAL C. J.—The question before us in this case arises upon an action of debt brought upon the sixty-third section of the statute 9 Geo. 4, c. 22, to recover the costs and expenses occasioned by the trial of a petition before a select committee of the house of commons, complaining of the undue election and return of members for the borough of Ipswich. The plaintiffs under the section above referred to obtained a rule drawn up on reading the certificate signed by the speaker, and affidavits of the demand of the costs, and refusal, which called on the defendants to shew cause why the plaintiffs should not be at liberty to sign and enter up final judgment against the defendants for the sum specified in such certificate. On shewing cause against this rule, the defendants have urged various objections against the certificate, and have contended, that, upon the authority of the case of *Bruyeres* v. *Halcomb*, 5 N. & M. 149, 3 Ad. & E. 386, the certificate of the speaker in the present case ought to be held by us as altogether void. In that case the court of King's Bench held that the committee appointed for the trial of the petition was appointed in a state of things which required that the committee should *not* have been appointed; that it was a committee which had no authority over the petitioner; and that the report of such a committee, which was the sole foundation upon which the speaker's certificate rested, was a report which they had no power to make. In the judgment of the court upon the facts before them, we entirely concur. A select committee appointed in the mode required by the statute, is the court which is to exercise the jurisdiction given by the statute : and, if the appointment of the committee takes place under circumstances where the statute does not allow the appointment to be made (which was the state of facts before the court of King's Bench), or in a manner contrary to or inconsistent with the essential requisites prescribed by the statute, there is no court at all. The whole of the proceedings take place coram non judice; the jurisdiction fails altogether; and, with the jurisdiction, the whole of the superstructure built upon it by the statute falls to the ground also : Debile fundamentum, fallit opus. The question, therefore, in the present case will be, whether any of the objections urged in argument before us are objections which essentially touch the constitution of the court or the legality of its proceedings; or whether, at most, they extend any further than to the non-

observance of certain directions to be found in the statute
as to the course of its proceedings: for, whilst in the one
case, as well upon the necessary construction of the statute,
as in conformity with the decision of the court of King's
Bench, we should be bound to hold the certificate absolutely void; in the other, notwithstanding a failure in
the observance of matters, not essential, but directory
only, we should be equally bound to uphold it, and to
give it effect. That the plaintiffs made out a primâ facie
case by their affidavits, setting forth the certificate of the
speaker, the demand of the costs, and the refusal to pay,
was admitted in the course of the argument. But it is
contended that the facts disclosed in the affidavits filed
on the part of the defendants, form an answer to the
application; and more particularly, that, upon four distinct grounds of objection, the certificate of the speaker
must be held altogether void.

The first objection which has been urged before us,
goes to the legality of the appointment of the select committee. It has been contended that the returning officers
were *parties* within the meaning of the statute, and, as
such, entitled to notice in writing of the time of taking the
petition into consideration, and to an order of the house
to attend at the bar, and to be present at and assist in
striking the committee; and that, by reason of the omission of such notice and order, and of the returning officers
not attending as parties, in the present case, the constitution of the committee was defective from its very foundation. In the next place, it has been objected that the
recognisance entered into for the petitioners was essentially defective, and that, by reason of such defect, all the
subsequent proceedings became void. In the third place,
that the report of the committee is void, inasmuch as it
contains no finding upon the charge made against the
returning officers, nor upon the opposition to such charge,
whether the same were respectively frivolous and vexa-

1836.

RANSON
v.
DUNDAS.

First point—
As to the ap-
pointment of
the select com-
mittee.

tious, or the reverse. And lastly, that costs are included within the certificate which are unauthorized by the statute, and some even which have accrued at a time subsequent to the report itself.

I. Now, as to the first objection, we are not prepared to say that, if, under the circumstances existing at the time, the house had no authority by the statute to constitute the court, the appearance of the defendants before such court, and their acquiescence in its subsequent proceedings from the commencement of such proceedings down to their termination, could have the effect of setting up a jurisdiction which was in its original formation null and void; although at the same time we cannot but observe the inconvenient consequences which must follow if an objection to the jurisdiction, known at the time to exist, and which in ordinary cases is always held to come too late if not made in the very first instance, should in this case be allowed to prevail, after the termination of the contest is known to be adverse to the parties who now stand on the objection: a consideration which should at least induce us to pause, and to weigh scrupulously the grounds upon which the original objection is founded, and to require it to be made out clearly and distinctly that the proceedings are absolutely void, before we can be justified in refusing to give them their full effect. And this observation comes with greater force, when the objection is made on the part of the sitting members, not on the part of the returning officers—of the sitting members, who were at the bar of the house, and present at all the proceedings; who made no objection to the course pursued by the house, and indeed received a benefit, not an injury, by the mode adopted in striking the committee, inasmuch as they had a greater advantage in reducing the number of the committee, than they would have been entitled to, if the returning officers had been allowed to assist therein. The whole strength of the first objection appears to us to depend on one single inquiry, viz. whether the returning officers, upon the proper construction of the statute, are to be considered as a *party* having power to assist in striking the committee. If they were a party having such power, and by the course taken were not allowed to exercise it, then the committee must be held to have been improperly constituted: if they had no such power, the whole weight of the objection falls to the ground; for, as to the mere want of notice from the speaker, or of an order on the returning officers to attend at the bar of the house, if they had no power of interfering when there with the choice of the committee, such omission can be considered as an omission to comply with a matter directory only, and not essential to the legal constitution of the court. The petition in this case, which was signed by the three plaintiffs, claiming on behalf of themselves and others a right to vote for members for the borough of Ipswich, prayed only "that the house would declare the election and return of the sitting members wholly null and void, and that they are not nor ought to be deemed to be members to serve in parliament for the borough of Ipswich, and that the names of the said sitting members may be erased from the return, and the two other candidates declared duly elected, and their names substituted in the said return." The petition, in the course of its statements, complained incidentally of misconduct and partiality in the returning officers of the borough; but in its prayer is silent altogether as to any claim for redress against them on the ground of misconduct. It is, therefore, in fact, a petition complaining of the undue election and return of members in parliament, and of nothing else. That it was so treated by the house of commons itself, is evident from the form of the order of the house for taking the petition into consideration; such order distinctly mentioning the sitting members and petitioners only as the subjects of the petition; and again the service of such notice and of the order of the house being made upon them alone. First, therefore, looking at the form of the petition in question, we think the returning officers were not called upon as original parties to the petition to appear before the house; and that, even if they are held to be included within the petition as parties petitioned against, yet, upon the proper construction of the act (upon which the real question before us turns), they had no power whatever to interfere in striking the committee. In order to arrive at a just conclusion upon this point, on which the whole strength of the first objection rests, let us consider, first, how the case stood as to returning officers before the present act, and next, what alteration with respect to them has been effected by the statute now under consideration.

The original act, 10 Geo. 3, c. 16, commonly called the Grenville act, the first which established the tribunal for the trial of controverted election returns, provides for the case of two parties only—the petitioners and the sitting members. This is obvious from a simple reference to the act itself. The statute 11 Geo. 3, c. 42, s. 6, provides for the case of two parties before the house, where they petition on distinct interests, or complain on different grounds. But, as to returning officers, both these acts are altogether silent. It is the 25 Geo. 3, c. 84, which for the first time mentions returning officers, and provides, in sections 10, 11, and 12, for two cases, viz. the case of no return made by the returning officer in proper time, and of a return made, not of members, but of special facts only; in both which cases, and in no other, the statute appears to put the returning officers in the place of the party petitioned against in the former acts, as to the notice to be served upon them, the order of the house for attending at the appointment of the committee, and the power of striking the committee; the twelfth section expressly providing, that, if there shall be more petitions than one presented,

1836.

RANSON
v.
DUNDAS.

complaining of such return or omission of such return, upon distinct interests or upon different grounds, the house shall determine from the nature of the case whether the returning officer shall together with the petitioners be entitled to strike off from the list of members drawn by lot, or whether the list shall be reduced by the parties severally presenting the said petitions only. Under the acts, therefore, above referred to, if they had still remained in force, it would seem that the returning officers would not have been entitled to strike off from the list of members drawn by lot, upon a petition against them for partiality or misconduct; or, more properly, that the case of partiality or misconduct did not fall within the scope of the 25 Geo. 3, and would not have been necessarily tried before a select committee of the house appointed under that act ; but that the house would have disposed of such a petition against the returning officers, of their own authority, and according to the customs, course of proceeding, and privileges of the house. The question therefore is, whether the 9 Geo. 4, c. 22, has made any difference in this respect, and given any right to the returning officers which they had not before of striking the committee in the case of a petition charging them with partiality or misconduct. The 2nd and the 36th are the only clauses which seem to apply to the case of returning officers. The 2nd section, so far as it relates to returning officers, appears in its commencement to be confined to three cases of complaint—where no return is made in due time, or no return according to the requisition of the writ, or there is complaint of the special matters contained in such return : it is altogether silent as to misconduct. But, as the enacting part of that section directs, that, " where no return has been made, or the special matter of the return, or the *conduct of the returning officer* is complained of," notice in writing of the time appointed for taking the petition into consideration shall be forthwith given by the speaker to the returning officer or officers, accompanied with an order *to the parties* to attend the house at the time appointed, by themselves, their counsel, or agent, it may be too narrow a construction to hold the clause to be limited to the precise instances mentioned in the beginning of it, or to exclude from its operation any petition against the returning officers for misconduct, in the wider sense of that word. But, whatever may be the scope and intention of the 2nd section, and whether it includes within it a petition against the returning officers for partiality or misconduct, or is confined to the cases before adverted to, it is the 36th section, and that alone, which carries out the intention of the statute, and shews the power given to the returning officers in respect of striking the committee. Now, before we come to the consideration of that section, it is to be observed that the statute has provided for all the cases of petitions in which the sitting members are parties before the house, in three distinct sections, the 30th, the 33rd, and the 34th. The first of these sections provides for reducing the numbers of the committee in the case where there are before the house, the petitioners, the sitting members, or any party who has been admitted to defend the return or right of election : the second provides for the case where there are more than *two* parties before the house on distinct interests, or complaining or complained of upon distinct grounds; still, however, " parties whose right to be elected or returned may be affected by the determination of any such committee :" and the last provides for the case where no parties appear before the house to oppose the petition. All which sections do by their frame manifestly apply to the cases where the sitting members, or those who appear to defend the return, are the parties; and have no application whatever to cases where the returning officers are parties before the house upon any ground of complaint against them. The cases of sitting members and parties whose rights to the return and election are in question having been thus provided for, the statute proceeds in the 36th section to make provision for the case of petitions against returning officers. This section is so worded as to make it in some degree doubtful whether it provides for the case where there is *one* petition only against the returning officers. It begins by referring to the case where there is one such petition only, and also to the case where there are more than one; but is silent altogether as to the course of proceeding where there is only one, whilst it gives clear and precise directions " where there shall be more petitions than one presented on distinct interests, or complaining on different grounds." It is unnecessary to say, that, if such clause does not comprise the case of a single petition against the returning officers, the case now under consideration is altogether unaffected by it. But, assuming the case of a single petition against the returning officer to be necessarily within the intention of the clause, and that, by analogy to the other provisions of the act, the same mode of striking the committee shall take place as where there is one petition only in the case of sitting members, we think it clear the clause cannot apply to any case where the petition is not a petition against the returning officers alone, but is also, as in the present case, a petition against the sitting members, who appear at the bar, and are made parties to defend their return before the house—first, because the case of the petition where the sitting members are parties is already clearly and expressly provided for, and there can be no reason to infer any intention that their rights in striking the committee, which have already been defined by the act, should be altered or affected by any complaint against the returning officers—next, because the provision in this section is one which would exclude the sitting members altogether from assisting in striking the committee. The section provides expressly " that the house shall determine whether the officer shall *together with such petitioners* be entitled to strike off the list in the manner hereinbefore directed, or whether such list shall be reduced by *the parties severally presenting such petitions only*"—a provision which would exclude the sitting members altogether from assisting in striking the committee, and which therefore is necessarily incompatible with the case of a petition in which they are included as parties.—Again, if this section could be held to relate to the case of a petition against the sitting members and the returning officers jointly, and it should be held that both had the power of striking, in what order or in what proportion are they to strike off the members? We cannot suppose that a clause intended to comprehend such a case would have been altogether silent upon the only point necessary to give it any operation. Now, this is the only clause in the act which gives the returning officers a power to interfere in striking the committee; if the case is not brought within this clause, it cannot be held to come within the act. Without relying upon the objections to which we have before adverted, that it is not a petition against the returning officers at all for such ground of complaint as the statute had in view, or that it is not a case in which there are more petitions than one on distinct interests or different grounds of complaint; we hold it to be the necessary construction of the clause that it does not comprehend the case where the sitting members are called upon to appear, do actually appear at the bar of the house, and are the parties opposing the petition. And it cannot but suggest itself as an observation, that, in such a case, there is no necessity to hold the returning officers within the clause; for, where the petition is against the sitting members, and complaint is incidentally made of the misconduct of the returning officers, there is no reason, upon general principles, why the committee struck by the petitioners and the sitting members should not be supposed, à priori, an adequate tribunal to sit in judgment with the strictest impartiality upon the conduct of the returning officers, if the house think proper to depute their authority as to the returning officers to such committee. It appears, therefore, to us, that, in the present instance, the court was composed of the very same identical persons as those who would have constituted it had the returning officers received notice from the speaker of the time of taking the petition into consideration, and had they attended at the bar of the house in pursuance of the order to that effect: for, in such case, they would have had no authority to alter a single name.

The second and following objections will, we think, require less consideration.

II. It is objected, in the second place, that the recognisance entered into for the petitioners is not the recognisance required or even sanctioned by the act; and that, as the language of the 5th section is *in the negative*, " that *no* proceedings shall be had upon any such petition, *unless* the person or persons subscribing the same, or some one or more of them," shall enter into the recognisance directed in and by that section, the entering into the proper recognisance forms a condition precedent to the validity of all the subsequent proceedings, and that the condition of the present recognisance, not providing for all the events, nor agreeing with all the requisites contained in that section, the recognisance itself is altogether void, and the case stands precisely in the same position as if there had been no recognisance at all. But we are of opinion, upon the best consideration we can bring to the question, that the recognisance entered into upon the present occasion, although subject to some exception in point of form, is not open to any objection which affects it in substance or legal operation. The recognisance, it is to be observed, follows the form given in the schedule: and, though such form, if it varies from the requisites of the act in any important or essential particular, cannot be taken to overrule the enactments of the statute itself; yet it is obvious that if the schedule can be made consistent with the act, upon any sound and legal principles of construction, it is our duty so to construe the schedule. The 5th section expressly directs the recognisance to be entered into "according to the form hereunto annexed:" so far, therefore, as the intention of the legislature was concerned, there can be no doubt but that they intended that the form given in the schedule should embody in it the different requisites expressed in the act itself, and that they thought it sufficient for that purpose; otherwise the form would only operate as a false light, to mislead instead of affording assistance to those who are endeavouring to follow the directions of the act. The question therefore is, whether the discrepancies which have been pointed out between the 5th section and the form in the schedule are real and essential, or formal only; for, in the one case, the recognisance which has been given must be held to be void, in the other, good.

1. That the petition is subscribed by three, and the recognisance entered into by one only.

1. Now, the objections which have been urged against the validity of the recognisance are in effect two. First, that, whereas the petition is subscribed by three persons, yet the recognisance is not only entered into by one only of the petitioners, but is altogether silent about the other two: so that (it is argued) it makes Ranson liable only for the costs of the witnesses summoned to give evidence in *his behalf;* whereas, it is said, witnesses might be summoned, and the trial carried on, by the other petitioners, in case Ranson died, or refused or became incapable to go on with the trial before the committee. The objection is not merely that the recognisance is given by one only of the three petitioners; for, to such objection it would be a sufficient answer, which was given at the bar, that, by the 5th section, it is expressly provided that the recognisance shall be entered into "by the person or persons signing the petition, *some one or more of them;*" so that

It was the manifest intention of the legislature that the responsibility of one only of the petitioners should be held sufficient: but the strength of the objection consists in that there is not any mention in the recognisance of the acts of the other petitioners. As an answer, however, to this objection, it is to be remembered that the three petitioners were petitioners upon one and the same interest; that is, as electors of the borough; so that there was one petition only, not several, upon distinct interests or different grounds of complaint. When, therefore, the condition of the recognisance is so framed that Ranson shall pay " all costs, expenses, and fees which shall be due and payable *from him* to any witness who shall be summoned to give evidence *in his behalf*, it necessarily means, summoned to give evidence *on the behalf of that interest* which he represents; that is, generally *in support of the petition.* Again, the condition is not, as it has been argued, confined in its terms to witnesses *summoned by him.* Under the terms used in the condition, they may be summoned indiscriminately by any of the three petitioners; for, witnesses so summoned would equally be " summoned to give evidence on *his* behalf." And, after all, comparing the words actually used in the recognisance with the words employed in the 5th section, viz. that the recognisance shall be entered into by some one or more of the petitioners " for the payment of all costs &c. which shall become due to any witness summoned on behalf of the person or persons so subscribing such petition," we think the meaning of both substantially the same, namely, that each provides a security for the costs and expenses of all witnesses summoned in the course of the investigation in support of the petition.

2. The second objection urged against the recognisance, is this; that it provides only for the payment of the " costs and expenses of the party who shall appear before the *house* in opposition to the petition;" whereas the 5th section directs security to be given for the payment of the

costs and expenses " to any party who shall appear before the house, or *any committee* of the house, in opposition to such petition." And it is argued, that new parties may and often do come in and are allowed to appear before the committee after the petition is pending before them, who were not originally before the house ; and that in this very case the returning officers appeared before the committee, the charges against them were entertained by the committee, and the returning officers were allowed to defend themselves, and did defend themselves against such charges. The question therefore that arises is, what is the meaning of the expression used in the 5th section, "a party who appears before the house, or any committee of the house." It is manifest, by referring to the various parts of the statute, that the statute itself makes provision only for parties to be admitted parties by the house: it nowhere makes any provision for parties to be admitted by the committee to appear before them. The 10th and the 12th sections establish that point ; in which provision is made for allowing parties not originally petitioned against to appear—in the one case, where the application is made within fourteen days after the petition has been presented—in the other, where a similar application is made within thirty days after the notice in the gazette therein referred to. But, in both those cases, the application is directed to be made to the *house*, not to the committee: and power is given to the house, not to the committee, to admit them. When, therefore, parties are said to appear before the committee, in opposition to appearing before the house, it is not in pursuance of any power given, or any provision made, by this act, but under the power which committees have, by long and invariable usage, been known to possess, viz. that, when sitting on the trial of elections, they have taken cognisance of incidental charges against the returning officers, and have allowed them a hearing and a defence, more as a matter of indulgence than a matter of

strict right. For, unless the returning officers are made
parties to the investigation by the house itself, under the
powers given by the act, the house are not bound by the
finding of the committee; but the right to call upon the
returning officers, and to investigate any charge against
them, and punish them for misconduct when established
by proof, still remains with the house itself. The first
observation therefore is, that the recognisance, in its present shape, provides for all the costs when the party
appears before the only tribunal at which his appearance
is directed by the statute itself; that is, before the house.
But it is said the 5th section comprises within its meaning,
not only the costs and expenses of the parties appearing
before the house under the provisions of the act, but of
parties afterwards appearing before the committee under
the usage and practice of election committees. Now, it is
manifest that the objection which has been made in this
case must apply to every election petition presented to the
house; for, it never can be known at the time when the recognisance is entered into whether there will or will not be
parties appearing before the committee. It is not a question therefore (as represented in the course of the argument) of varying the form in order to make it suit the
particular case: the form must be altered in every instance
by adding to the recognisance " the appearance of the
parties before the committee." Whilst, therefore, the
5th section directs that the party *shall* enter into the recognisance according to the formed annexed, we must, if
we yield to the objection, adopt the conclusion that the
party shall not, in any case, enter into the recognisance in
that form; but that the recognisance must in every case be
held void, unless it is first altered in the manner contended
for. But we think so harsh and unreasonable a conclusion
ought not to be resorted to, where the section and the form
given in the schedule can, by any fair intendment, be reconciled together. And we are of opinion that such is

the case; and that, construing the 5th section and the form in the schedule together, the words used in the form, viz. " the party who shall appear before the house in opposition to the said petition," must be taken to comprise those parties who should appear generally in opposition to the petition, either at the bar of the house at an earlier period, or in a more advanced stage of the proceeding, before the committee appointed to inquire and report its decision to the house; and that it is by no means improbable that the words relating to the appearance before the committee have been introduced into the 5th section for no other purpose than that of removing any doubt whether costs and expenses before the committee were intended to be included within the terms of the form of the recognisance. One argument used in support of the objection now under consideration, was, that the form of the recognisance given by the schedule is subject to the same consequences as the form of a conviction or a declaration, given for the recovery of a penalty; in which latter case, if the form is defective in stating a legal ground for the conviction or the demand, the whole proceedings fall to the ground. But, in that case, the conviction or declaration forms the basis or ground-work upon which the whole of the subsequent proceedings rest; which if void, the whole must fall together: but here, the proceedings in the suit before us are perfectly regular; the objection arises upon the form of a recognisance which is wholly collateral to the proceedings in the suit, and does not appear, nor does it form any part whatever of the proceedings in the action before us. And it is impossible here not to advert to the marked difference between this case and the case referred to, wherein Mr. Halcomb was the petitioner. There, the petitioner did all he could to withdraw himself from the trial. He did not, after the committee was struck by the officer of the house, appear before the house, or before the committee. Nothing,

therefore, was done by him which could be construed into
a waiver of the irregularity of the proceedings, or an admission of the jurisdiction of the court. Here, on the
contrary, the sitting members, with full knowledge of the
form in which the recognizance was given, instead of
treating it as a nullity, and insisting that the course should
be pursued which is marked out by the 5th section, where
no recognizance is given, raise no objection to its form,
but attend the committee throughout, and contest the petition down to the final close of the trial. Without, however, resting in any manner upon the effect of such a
waiver, we think the objections made to the recognizance
are substantially answered by the construction of the
statute itself.

The third objection is made against the report of the
committee, which it is contended is altogether void, inasmuch as it decides nothing with respect to the charge, or
the opposition to the charge, made against the returning
officers, being frivolous or vexatious. And upon this
head it is insisted that the 40th section marks out the line
of duty of the committee, by requiring them to make such
report: and that, they having failed in reporting on any
one point submitted to their judgment, the whole of the
report is void, and with it all the subsequent proceedings
are also avoided. That clause directs, that every such
committee, at the same time that they inform the house
of their final determination on the merits of the petition
which they were sworn to try, shall also report to the
house whether such petition did or did not appear to them
to be frivolous or vexatious; [this is complied with in the
present case]; and in like manner report, with respect to
every *party* who shall have appeared before them in
opposition to such petition, whether the opposition of
such *party* did or did not appear to them to be frivolous
or vexatious: this also has been complied with, so far as
relates to the sitting members; but the contention is, that,

1836.

RANSOM
v.
DUNDAS.

III. Conse-
quence of the
silence of the
report as to the
charge against
the returning
officers.

as no report is made as to the opposition of the returning officers, whether frivolous and vexatious or the reverse, therefore the whole of the report, upon which alone the certificate for costs depends, is void. Now, admitting, after the decision of the court of King's Bench in the case of *Trueman* v. *Lambert*, 4 M. & S. 234, that the returning officers in this case, upon a petition shaped in its prayer as is the present, might have been considered a party appearing before the committee in opposition to the petition, and therefore entitled to recover their costs as such party if the committee had reported in their favour; still we see no provision in this act which can be construed to make the report altogether void as against the sitting members, because it is silent as to the petition against the returning officer or the opposition made thereto. This question turns upon the 40th and the 57th and 58th sections. The 40th section directs that the committee, at the time they inform the house as to their final determination on the matters of the petition, shall also report to the house whether the petition did or did not appear to them to be frivolous or vexatious; and in like manner report, with respect to every party who shall have appeared before them in opposition to such petition, whether such opposition appeared to them to be frivolous or vexatious. The 57th and 58th sections shew the consequences which follow from such report, viz. that, in one case, the parties who appeared before the committee in opposition to the petition shall be entitled to their costs; in the other case, the petitioners. Now, the report in this case is, that the opposition to the petition by the sitting members appears to the committee to be frivolous and vexatious; and the consequence immediately follows under the 58th section, that the petitioners are entitled to their costs, to be taxed in the manner pointed out. There are no words in the 40th section which make the report of the committee as to the opposition of all the parties who have appeared before them, a condition precedent to the validity of the report as to those who are adjudicated upon in the report. The returning officers may have cause to complain that they have no remedy for their costs, by a report made in their favour. But it can make no difference to the parties against whom the report is actually made, that it is silent as to others against whom the committee might have reported. The measure of costs payable by any party reported against must be precisely the same, if properly estimated, whether the report extends to others or not. We see no ground, therefore, for holding that the want of the adjudication for or against the returning officers, supposing it to have become necessary under the circumstances before the committee, can upon any clause in this statute be held to avoid the whole report.

The last ground of objection relates to the mode in which the taxation of costs is conducted. It is alleged that it included costs not strictly and properly occasioned by the opposition of the sitting members against the petition; such as costs occasioned by the charge against the returning officers, and other charges not authorised by the statute. The costs to which the sitting members were liable under the report of the committee, were undoubtedly confined by the act to those only which were strictly and properly occasioned by their own opposition, and by the taxation ought certainly to be confined to those alone. The course pursued appears to have been this:— The committee reported the opposition to be frivolous and vexatious; in consequence of which, a request was made to the speaker to refer the bill of costs of the petitioners to taxation; the speaker thereupon directed the two examiners appointed by him to tax the costs and expenses mentioned in the requisition; and the examiners afterwards report that the costs and expenses allowed by them on taxation amount to a certain sum, and that the sitting members,

IV. As to the
taxation of the
costs.

whose opposition to the petition appeared to the committee to be frivolous and vexatious, are liable to pay the
same. Looking, therefore, only at the course of proceeding which took place, it appears to be strictly in conformity with the directions of the act; and there is nothing
in the course of proceeding which can lead to the inference that the examining officers in taxing the costs,
or the speaker in granting this certificate, did any thing
beyond their strict duty, by allowing any other costs than
those occasioned by the opposition to the petition by
the sitting members; and the only question is, whether,
in this stage of the proceedings, this court has any power
to try the propriety of this allowance, or the principle
upon which it was conducted, after the certificate thereon
has been granted by the speaker. And we are decidedly
of opinion that we have no such authority; but that the
terms of the 60th section, "that the certificate signed by
the speaker shall be conclusive evidence of the amount of
such demands in all cases, and for all purposes whatsoever," are at once so clear and so precise, that we should
be taking upon us a jurisdiction not granted or intended
by the statute, if we interfered in any manner on the
subject. It is obvious that any such interference would
be altogether useless; for, if upon the discussion before
us it appeared to us that any mistake was made, we have
no means of rectifying it by sending the matter back
to the examiners, or to any other officer; and the consequence would therefore be, that, if the smallest mistake
in the amount was discovered as to a single item (as
indeed was avowed in the course of the argument), the
petitioners must lose the whole of their costs: a conclusion at once so unjust and unreasonable, that, if there
was any doubt upon the words of the act, it would go
strongly to shew that we could not have the power contended for. We, therefore, think the certificate must be

treated as conclusive evidence before us as to the amount for which the verdict is to be entered up.

Upon consideration, therefore, of the several objections which have been argued before us, we think them answered by a reference to the act itself, and that the judgment must be entered for the plaintiffs as prayed.

Rule absolute.

SAME v. SAME.

THE ATTORNEY GENERAL moved for leave to enter upon the record a suggestion of the grounds upon which the court had pronounced judgment for the plaintiffs.—Wherever a judgment for a plaintiff is given, as in this case, under the supposed authority of an act of parliament, against the course of the common law, though upon motion, there ought to be a suggestion upon the roll shewing facts authorizing the judgment. Under the courts of conscience acts, such suggestion is invariably entered, though the statute itself contains no direction on the subject—Tidd's Pr., 9th edit. 516, 961, Appendix, c. xxxix. s. 32, 33: so, of a judgment for treble costs in an action against commissioners, on the property tax act—Ibid. s. 28. So, on the 42 Geo. 3, c. 46, s. 3, to entitle the defendant to costs, where the plaintiff recovers less than the sum for which the defendant was held to bail—Tidd's Pr. 982, 3, Appendix, c. xxxix. s. 34. Without such suggestion, the proceedings would clearly be erroneous. By the Welsh judicature act, 5 Geo. 4, c. 106, it is provided, that, in case for words, debt, trespass on the case, assault and battery, or other *personal* action, and all transitory actions, brought in any court of record out of the principality of Wales, where the debt or damages found by the jury shall not amount to 50*l.*, and it shall appear on the trial that the cause of action arose in Wales,

Monday,
June 13*th.*

Judgment having been given for the plaintiffs in an action of debt upon the speaker's certificate, under the 9 Geo, 4, c. 22, s. 63, for the costs therein mentioned, the court refused to allow a suggestion to be entered on the record of the circumstances upon which the judgment was founded.

and that the defendant was resident there at the time of the service of the process, *on such facts being suggested on the record or judgment roll*, a judgment of nonsuit shall be entered thereon against the plaintiff. So, under the 14 Geo. 2, c. 17, which enacts that, "where any issue is or shall be joined in any action or suit at law in any of his majesty's courts of record at Westminster, &c., and the plaintiff or plaintiffs in any such action or suit hath or have neglected, or shall neglect, to bring such issue on to be tried *according to the course and practice of the said courts respectively*, it shall and may be lawful for the judge or judges of the said courts respectively, at any time after such neglect, upon motion made in open court (due notice having been given thereof), to give the like judgment for the defendant or defendants in every such action or suit, as in cases of nonsuit; unless &c.; and that the defendant or defendants shall, upon such judgment, be awarded his, her, or their costs in any action or suit where he, she, or they would upon nonsuit be entitled to the same"—the course is to enter a suggestion—Tidd's Appendix, c. xxxix. s. 26. The foundation of the judgment in such case is the suggestion of the plaintiff's default. By analogy to these cases, a suggestion must be equally necessary here, to shew that the court had jurisdiction over the subject matter. The judgment by nil dicit is contrary to the fact: and where such a judgment is entered under a statute, the circumstances authorizing the court to pronounce the judgment ought to be suggested, and the absence of a suggestion would make the record erroneous. Even supposing the declaration in this case would be sufficient without a suggestion, and its omission would not constitute error; yet, inasmuch as it is only by virtue of the statute that the court has authority to pronounce judgment, the facts which give rise to that authority ought to appear by suggestion on the record. [*Tindal*, C. J.— Suppose the plaintiffs traverse the suggestion, what machinery have we for raising the question before a jury? The act gives none; and a proceeding by consent would not do. Suppose a case of perjury?] This may be casus omissus. But, unless the act of parliament *deprives* the defendants of the right to enter a suggestion, they are clearly entitled to it. In *Farr* v. *Denn*, 1 Burr. 362, it was held, that, if an ejectment be against two, and one die after issue joined but before trial, the death must be suggested on the roll; and in *Kemp* v. *Potter*, 6 Taunt. 549, it was held, that, where the plaintiff, in an action against a bankrupt, makes his election to proceed under the commission, the defendant is entitled to have some entry or suggestion, recording the election, put on the record.

TINDAL, C. J.—We should be most happy if we could put the facts of this case upon the record so as to enable the parties to bring our judgment under the review of a higher tribunal. But I am unable to satisfy myself that we have any power so to do. The act upon which these proceedings are founded is express. The 9 Geo. 4, c. 22, s. 63, provides "That it shall and may be lawful for the party or parties entitled to such costs or expenses, or for his, her, or their executors or administrators, to demand the whole amount thereof so certified as above from any one or more of the persons respectively who are hereinbefore made liable to the payment thereof in the several cases thereinbefore mentioned, and, in case of nonpayment thereof, to recover the same by action of debt in any of his majesty's courts of record at Westminster, in which action it shall be sufficient for the plaintiff or plaintiffs to declare that the defendant or defendants is or are indebted to him or them in the sum to which the costs and expenses, ascertained in manner aforesaid, shall amount, by virtue of this act; and the certificate of such amount, so signed as aforesaid by the speaker, shall have the force and effect of a warrant to confess judgment; and the court in which such action shall be commenced shall, upon motion, and on the production of such certificate, enter up judgment in favour of the plaintiff or plaintiffs named in such certificate, for the sum specified therein to be due from the defendant or defendants in such action, in like manner as if the said defendant or defendants had signed a warrant to confess judgment in the said action to that amount." We must, therefore, consider the speaker's certificate as of equal force with a warrant to confess judgment; and we must look upon this as an application, in the ordinary course, to set aside the warrant. All, therefore, we have to do is, to inquire into the genuineness of the certificate, and the circumstances under which it is sought to enforce it. Nobody ever heard of such facts being suggested on the roll after the validity of the warrant has been contested upon motion. It appears to me that it would be not only idle and inoperative, but injurious to the rights and interests of the plaintiffs, to put upon the record that the only effect of which would be to create delay.

PARK, J.—The attempt is quite novel; and, I think, wholly unwarranted.

GASELEE, J., was ill, and VAUGHAN, J., the ex-judge when the principal case was argued in Hilary Term: both therefore declined taking any decided part in this judgment, but generally expressed themselves of opinion that the application was not authorized either by the statute or the practice of the court.

                                        Rule refused.

Talfourd, Serjeant, who, with *Hill* and *Austin*, was instructed to shew cause in the first instance, now applied for leave to enter up the judgment as of Hilary Term last, one of the plaintiffs having died since that period.

THE COURT, however, suggesting that the death would not have the effect of making the record erroneous, declined to interfere.

Refused.

1836.

RANSON
v.
DUNDAS.

1837.

Tuesday,
Jan. 24th,

SAME v. SAME.

The judgment was entered up for the amount mentioned in the speaker's certificate, and also *for the costs of the motion*, including those of appearing to shew cause in the first instance against the application for leave to enter a suggestion, as follows:—

"In the Common Pleas.

"On the 20th of November, 1835.

"London (to wit) Robert Gill Ranson, Richard Crawley, and Henry Haken (the plaintiffs in this suit), by W. H. Ashurst, their attorney, complain of Robert Adam Dundas, Esq., and Fitzroy Kelly, Esq., (the defendants in this suit), who have been summoned to answer the plaintiffs in an action of debt—For that whereas the defendants, on the 2nd November, 1835, were indebted to the plaintiffs, under and by virtue of a certain act of parliament made and passed in the 9th year of the reign of his late majesty, George the Fourth, to consolidate and amend the laws relating to the trial of contested elections or returns of members to serve in parliament, in the sum of 4694*l.* 15*s.* 7*d.*, for costs and expenses incurred by the plaintiffs in prosecuting a certain petition of the plaintiffs complaining of an undue election and return of the said defendants as burgesses to serve in parliament for the borough of Ipswich, and which said sum was to be paid by the defendants to the plaintiffs on request; whereby and by reason of the nonpayment thereof, and by virtue of the said act, an action had accrued to the plaintiffs to demand and have of and from the defendants the sum of 4694*l.* 15*s.* 7*d.* : yet the defendants had not paid the said sum, or any part

The judgment
entered up on
the speaker's
certificate for
costs under the
9 Geo. 4, c. 22,
s. 63, can only
be for the sum
mentioned in
such certificate,
and not for the
costs of the
motion for leave
to enter up the
judgment
thereon.

thereof—to the damage of the plaintiffs of 10*l.*, and therefore they bring their suit, &c.

" And the said defendants, by the said W. H. Ashurst, attorney for the said plaintiffs, who appears for the said defendants according to the form of the statute in such case made and provided, come and defend the wrong and injury when &c., but say nothing in bar or preclusion of the said action of the said plaintiffs, whereby the said plaintiffs remain undefended against the said defendants; and afterwards, to wit, on the 11th June, 1836, come here the said Robert Gill Ranson and Henry Haken, by their attorney aforesaid, and the said Richard Crawley comes not; and hereupon the said Robert Gill Ranson and Henry Haken give the justices here to understand and be informed, that, after the commencement of this suit, and before this day, to wit, on the 10th February, in the year last aforesaid, the said Richard Crawley died, and the said Robert Gill Ranson and Henry Haken survived him, which the said defendants do not deny, but admit the same to be true; therefore let no further proceedings be had in this cause at the suit of the said Richard Crawley: and the said Robert Gill Ranson and Henry Haken also give the justices here to understand and be informed, that, after the commencement of this suit, and before this day, to wit, on the 25th January, in the year last aforesaid, the said Robert Adam Dundas took upon himself the name of Robert Adam Christopher, by virtue of his majesty's license and authority in that behalf, and hath ever since been and now is called and known by the said name of Robert Adam Christopher, which is also not denied: therefore it is considered that the said Robert Gill Ranson and Henry Haken do recover against the said Robert Adam Christopher and Fitzroy Kelly their said debt, and 295*l.* for their damages which they have sustained as well on occasion of the detention of the said debt as for their costs and charges by them about their suit in this behalf expended, by the justices here adjudged to the said Robert

Gill Ranson and Henry Haken, and with their assent:
and the said Robert Adam Christopher and Fitzroy Kelly
in mercy &c."

Wilde, Serjeant, in Michaelmas Term, obtained a rule
nisi to set aside the judgment or that it might be amended
by striking out so much thereof as related to the award
of costs, or for a review of the taxation—the former, on
the ground that the judgment was neither in accordance
with the prayer of the rule nor with the statute, the rule
not asking and the statute not giving costs, and, by the
general practice of the courts, costs not being recoverable
on a warrant of attorney to confess judgment for a given
sum without any mention of costs—the latter, on the ground
that the prothonotary had improperly allowed a sum of
20*l.* for the plaintiffs' costs of appearing in the first instance
to oppose the motion for leave to enter on the record a
suggestion of the grounds of the judgment.

Talfourd, Serjeant, *M. D. Hill,* and *Austin,* in the course
of the term, shewed cause.—By the statute of Gloucester,
6 Edw. 1, c. 1, in all cases where a plaintiff recovers damages, he is entitled to costs; and this though the damages
are given by any statute made after that parliament—
Jackson v. *Calesworth,* 1 T. R. 71, *Creswell* v. *Houghton,*
6 T. R. 355. This, therefore, being an action in which
damages are recoverable, costs follow of course; and, unless expressly deprived of them by some provision in the
9 Geo. 4, c. 22, the plaintiffs are clearly entitled to costs in
this case. In *Tyte* v. *Glode,* 7 T. R. 268, the court said
" that the rule was well established in a variety of cases,
William v. *Hill, Jackson* v. *The Inhabitants of Calesworth,*
Ward v. *Snell,* 1 H. Bl. 10, and *Creswell* v. *Houghton,* that,
where by any act since the statute of Gloucester, an action is
given to the *party grieved,* he is entitled to costs if he succeed, though he had no remedy before such act." In 3 Bl.
Com. 399, it is said that costs are a necessary appendage to

a judgment—" It being now as well the maxim of ours as of the civil law, that. ' victus victori in expensis condemnandus est.'" In *North* v. *Wingate*, it was resolved by the court (Cro. Car. 560), that, " when a statute gives a penalty certain, and gives an action of debt, there, if the defendant doth not pay it upon demand, but enforceth the party into a suit, and he recovers by action of debt, ex consequenti he shall recover his damages, because he did not pay the duty due by the statute upon demand; and he shall also recover costs, for otherwise he should be at a loss, to expend more than he recovers, which the statute never intended." In *Witham* v. *Hill,* 2 Wils. 91, 2 Lord Ken. 474, it was held that the plaintiff was entitled to costs in actions both on the riot act, Geo. 1, c. 5, and on the statute of hue and cry. By the 10 Hen. 8, it is enacted that no person shall practise the faculty of physic within the city of London, or seven miles thereof, unless licensed by the president, college, and commonalty of physic, under the penalty of 5l. for every month he shall exercise the same faculty without being so licensed : in an action of debt brought to recover penalties incurred under this act, it was held that the plaintiffs would be entitled to costs if they succeeded, because, where a right is vested in an individual or corporation, the withholding, and thereby compelling a party to sue for it, is an injury for which damages may be recovered; and consequently, that, under the 4 Jac. 1, c. 3, the defendant, having succeeded, was entitled to costs— *College of Physicians* v. *Harrison,* 9 B. & C. 524. The 28 Geo. 3, c. 52, s. 23, the 53 Geo. 3, c. 71, s. 13, and the 9 Geo. 4, c. 22, s. 63, taken together, clearly shew the intention of the legislature to be that the successful party should be fully and completely indemnified against costs: and the court will advance the remedy to the full extent of that intention. The 61st section of the existing act, which directs the taxation of the costs in parliament as between attorney and client, strongly denotes the anxiety of the legislature that the successful party should not be at all out of pocket in consequence of the frivolous and vexatious opposition of the sitting members. The plaintiffs were bound to proceed for the recovery of their costs according to the course pointed out by the 68rd section. The action of debt existed before. [*Tindal*, C. J.—Not simply on the speaker's certificate.] On the certificate coupled with the report of the committee. The certificate merely ascertains the amount: both together give the party in whose favour the certificate is granted, a liquidated right in pounds, shillings, and pence. Under the Grenville act, the plaintiff brought his action, and the certificate of the speaker was conclusive evidence as to the amount of the demand. The mode of proceeding out by the 9 Geo. 4, c. 22, s. 63, is in lieu of a trial: the court is interposed for the jury: but this effects no alteration in the incidents of the judgment.

The statute declares that the speaker's certificate shall have the force and effect of a warant to confess judgment. No form of a warrant of attorney is given: the legislature refers to an instrument of a known and common form, which impowers an attorney of the court to enter up judgment for a certain sum besides cost of suit. Suppose the statute had directed a warrant of attorney to be set out on the record, would not the court require it to be done according to the common and ordinary form?

With respect to the costs of the motion for entering up judgment, the plaintiffs are clearly entitled to them. In Hullock on costs, 2nd edit., p. 625, the rule is thus laid down—" Where nothing is said about costs in the rule, or by the court in making it absolute or discharging it, they are considered as costs in the cause, and must be paid to the party ultimately prevailing, if the rule be made *before* judgment: but, if it be not made till *after* judgment, the costs depend entirely on the rule: and, if it be silent concerning them, each party must pay his own costs." The motion for entering up judgment is rendered necessary by the altered mode of proceeding. It would be unreasonable to hold that a party, a witness, for example, must come to the court at an expense possibly exceeding the amount of costs he seeks to recover under the speaker's certificate, and has no means of recouping himself. In *Magrane* v. *White*, the applicant (a witness) sought by the rule to recover costs to the amount of 50*l*; the costs of obtaining the rule in that case were 18*l*: and there the rule was drawn up and the judgment entered in precisely the same manner as has been done here—that the plaintiff recover " debt, damages, and costs." So, in *Gurney* v. *Gordon*, 2 M. & Scott, 187, 9 Bing. 37, 2 C. & J. 614, 3 Tyr. 616, the judgment included damages and costs.

As a general principle, it is true, where cause is shewn in the first instance, neither party is entitled to costs— *Weldron* v. *Norris*, 2 W. Bl. 769, *Rex* v. *Long*, 1 M. & R. 189, *Gerrard* v. *Gaskill*, 2 Chit. 401, *Warn* v. *Bichford*, 9 Price, 14. But this case does not come before the court under ordinary circumstances. Generally speaking, where there is no rule, there is nothing to tax upon: but here, the costs being costs in the cause, and no judgment having been signed at the time, the matter was one entirely for the discretion of the prothonotary.

Wilde, Serjeant, *Sir W. Follett*, and *R. V. Richards*, on a former day in this term, were heard in support of the rule.—The application on the part of the plaintiffs was that judgment might be entered for them for the sum mentioned in the speaker's certificate : nothing was said about costs in the rule ; and the court has no power under the statute to give costs, even had costs been asked for. It has been contended on the other side, that the 28 Geo. 3, c. 52, which gave an action of debt for the recovery of the costs certified by the speaker, entitled the plaintiff to costs in that action ; and that there is nothing in any of the subsequent acts to take away that right. It is not denied, that, if the plaintiffs had proceeded by an action of debt in the ordinary way, costs would have been recoverable. It has been further contended that the acts referred to on the subject are all remedial; and that the court will adopt such a construction as will best advance the remedy. What is or is not a remedial statute is frequently a matter of considerable doubt. Generally speaking, all acts which give costs are held to be penal, and are to be construed strictly. It is then said that the warrant to confess judgment is given but as a mode of obtaining the judgment of the court; and that it was not a voluntary proceeding on the part of the plaintiffs, but was the only mode which it was competent to them to pursue. That, however, is not so. Where different remedies are given, the last does not deprive the party of the right to use the former. In *Rex* v. *Jackson*, Cowp. 297, it was held that subsequent statutes which only add accumulative penalties, do not repeal former statutes: and in *Sharp* v. *Warren*, 6 Price, 131, it was held that an act of parliament giving a summary remedy, though in terms apparently prescribing such remedy, is cumulative, and does not take away a previous right to sue by action at law. *Ward* v. *Bird*, 2 Chit. 582, is to the same effect. The words " shall and may" are only imperative where the clause in a statute is for the public benefit—*Rex* v. *The Commissioners of the Flockwood Inclosure*, 2 Chit. 251. By the 54 Geo. 3, c. 84, it is enacted that the Michaelmas quarter sessions *shall* be holden in the week after the 11th of October: in *Rex* v. *Leicester*, 9 D. & R. 772, 7 B. & C. 6, it was held that this enactment is merely directory, and that those sessions may be legally holden at another time. [*Bosanquet*, J.—The statute 8 & 9 Will. 3, c. 11, s. 8, provides, that, "in all actions upon any bond or bonds, or on any penal sum, for nonperformance of any covenants or agreements in any indenture, deed, or writing contained, if judgment shall be given for the plaintiff on a demurrer, or by confession or nil dicit, the plaintiff upon the roll *may suggest* as many breaches of the covenants and agreements as he shall think fit," &c. : and this is held to be imperative—*Drage* v. *Brand,* 2 Wils. 377, *Hurst* v. *Jennings,* 5 B. & C. 650, 8 D. & R. 424, Tidd's Practice, 9th edit., 584.] The course prescribed by the 9 Geo. 4, c. 22, s. 63, for enforcing the payment of the parliamentary costs of the successful party, gives him a great boon. The defendant is thereby deprived of all right of appeal; and this is an advantage for which the plaintiff can hardly be said to pay too large a price in the loss of the costs incurred by him in entering up his judgment. Besides, these particular costs are incident to the new mode of proceeding pointed out by the statute ; and could not have been incurred had the plaintiffs pursued the ordinary remedy by action of debt. A warrant of attorney to confess judgment for a given sum, clearly does not authorize the entering up a judgment for that sum *and costs* : the authority given by it must be strictly pursued. The ordinary form, as found in Tidd's Appendix, 181, is " for the said sum of ——*l.,* besides costs of suit." [*Bosanquet,* J.—It is not an unfrequent, though a reprehensible practice, to include the costs in the gross sum for which the warrant of attorney is given; in which case the costs are not taxable.] The legislature authorize the court, " upon motion, and on the production of such certificate, to enter up judgment in favour of the plaintiff or plaintiffs named in such certificate *for the sum specified therein* to be due from the defendant or defendants in such action." Can anything be less ambiguous than this? The clause goes on—" in like manner as if the said defendant or defendants had signed a warrant to confess judgment *to that amount.*" If the defendants in the present case had confessed judgment for 4694*l.* 15*s.* 7*d.,* what would have been the authority of the court? clearly to enter up judgment for that sum, and

no more. In *Delane* v. *Mott*, 2 Chit. 423, where the
plaintiff brought an action upon an annuity deed, and
afterwards took a warrant of attorney for the sum due,
with a provision that, if within a certain time the annuity
was not paid, he should be at liberty to take out execution
for the sum specified, together with all costs incurred for
or by reason of the nonpayment of the annuity: it was
held that he was not at liberty to take out execution for
the costs of the action. It no where appears from the reports of *Magrane* v. *White*, that the costs of the application were either obtained or asked for: and in *Gurney* v.
Gordon, the point was not raised; the only question there
was, whether or not the action could be maintained against
one petitioner.

1836.

RANSON
v.
DUNDAS.

Cur. adv. vult.

TINDAL, C. J.—The rule in this case calls upon the
plaintiffs to shew cause, why the judgment entered up by
them should not be set aside for irregularity; or why it
should not be amended by striking out so much thereof
as relates to the award of costs ; or why the prothonotary
should not review his taxation of the costs in the cause,
and the judgment be reduced in regard to the costs to
such amount as should be allowed on such review. And
upon shewing cause before us, the argument on both
sides has been principally confined to the question, in
fact the real question between the parties, whether the
plaintiffs who have signed their judgment in an action of
debt under the 63rd section of the 9 Geo. 4, c. 22, are
entitled to sign judgment for costs in such action, or are
limited simply to the amount of the sum mentioned in the
speaker's certificate.

The 63rd section of the last mentioned statute is borrowed from the 13th section of the 53 Geo. 3, c. 71, with
which it agrees in substance; before which last mentioned
statute, the remedy for costs and expenses certified by

the speaker, was governed by the 23rd section of the 28 Geo. 3, c. 52, and directed to be by action of debt in any of his majesty's courts of record at Westminster; in which action it was provided that it should be sufficient for the plaintiff to declare that the defendant was indebted to him (in the sum to which the costs and expenses ascertained in manner aforesaid should amount) by virtue of that act: and it was provided that the certificate of the speaker under his signature of the amount of such costs and expenses, together with an examined copy of the entries of the journals of the house of the resolution of the select committee, should be deemed full and sufficient evidence in support of such action of debt. And an express provision follows, that no wager of law, or more than one imparlance, should be allowed, "and that the party in whose favour judgment should be given in any such action should recover his costs."

It is obvious therefore, that a trial of the action of debt by a jury, was contemplated by the legislature, for provision is made to take away the trial by wager of law: and although a form of declaration is given by the statute, so as to relieve the plaintiff from all difficulty in that particular, yet, under the general issue of nil debet, or by means of special pleading, very great impediments might have been thrown in the way of the plaintiff's recovery, and points raised as to the regularity or legality of the proceedings in parliament, either by the production of evidence before the jury, or by means of bills of exceptions, or by pleading to the action. It is further obvious that the legislature thought it necessary to provide for costs by a special enactment, and that the enactment is so framed as not only to give costs to the plaintiff, but to the defendant also, in case the plaintiff failed in recovering his debt.

The statutes therefore of the 53 Geo. 3 and 9 Geo. 4 introduced an entirely new remedy, and conferred a new and a very great benefit on the plaintiff. For, after these statutes, the defendant's plea was taken from him: he could neither have any trial of the fact before a jury, nor raise any point of law upon the record; the certificate of the amount of costs and expenses by the speaker, is directed to have the force and effect of a warrant to confess judgment; and the court is directed, upon motion, and on the production of such certificate, to enter up judgment in favour of the plaintiff named in such certificate for the sum specified therein to be due from the defendant, " in like manner as if the defendant had signed a warrant to confess judgment in the said action to that amount.

If the question, therefore, had rested merely on this comparison between the new and the former provision, the inference would appear to us to be strong, that, under the latter, there was no intention in the legislature to allow costs to the plaintiff upon his judgment. The costs, in all cases, under the new provision, would be small when compared with those upon a trial before a jury; in all ordinary cases, very trifling indeed: and when it is observed, that, by the first statute, the costs are expressly given to the party who succeeded in obtaining the judgment, which might be either the plaintiff or the defendant; and that, by the present statute, the judgment, if entered up, can only be entered up for one party, viz. the plaintiff; and that the statute omits any mention whatever of costs: we think it a reasonable inference, that, under the new mode of recovering the amount, it was intended the plaintiff should forego his claim to costs, as the price for the greater facility and certainty of obtaining his demand. And we think, even if such inference is not to be drawn, the silence of the new statute as to costs makes that subject a casus omissus, and that we have no authority to supply it.

But, on another and perfectly distinct ground, we think we have no power to give judgment for costs. This is a statutary power given to the court to enter up a judgment;

and the terms of such power must be strictly followed. The certificate by the speaker is declared to have "the force and effect of a warrant to confess judgment;" and the court is directed to enter up judgment in favour of the plaintiff " for the sum specified therein to be due from the defendant." This gives an authority expressly to enter up judgment for the very sum mentioned as the amount of the debt, and no more. But the clause directs the judgment to be entered up " in like manner as if the defendant had signed a warrant to confess judgment in the said action to that amount." Now, the statute cannot be more safely construed than by considering what would be the course of proceeding if the defendant had actually signed a formal warrant of attorney to confess judgment in the action to the amount of the sum mentioned in the speaker's certificate, and the plaintiff had entered up his judgment under such warrant of attorney. In that case, it is the well known course and practice of the court, that, the warrant of attorney being silent as to costs, the judgment would have been entered up for the sum specified as the debt, and for no more.

It has been urged in the course of argument that it would be unjust that the plaintiff should suffer by a vexatious and expensive opposition to his entering up judgment. But, in answer to this, it should be recollected that there is nothing in the statute which deprives the court of its inherent authority to fix the defendant with the payment of costs on a vexatious opposition to a rule for entering up the judgment; such costs, however, not forming part of the judgment itself, but being one of the terms on which the rule is made absolute.

We think, therefore, that so much of the rule which has been obtained must be made absolute as relates to the amending of the judgment by striking out the award of costs, and the residue of the rule must be discharged.

                                   Rule accordingly.

1836.

MELLIN v. TAYLOR.

Monday,
June 13th.

THIS was an action brought by the plaintiff, an affluent manufacturer residing near Wakefield, in Yorkshire, against the defendant, an attorney of apparently high respectability, resident in the same neighbourhood, to recover a compensation in damages for alleged criminal conversation by the latter with the wife of the former. At the trial, before Lord Denman, at the last Spring Assizes at York, a great number of witnesses were produced on the part of the plaintiff. They proved beyond question many stealthy interviews between the parties, and several distinct acts of adultery under circumstances of peculiar grossness—on one occasion, on a stile in a public and much frequented footpath; on another, in the library of the plaintiff's house, with the door unfastened: and further, that, during the plaintiff's absence from home, the defendant came one night to the plaintiff's house after all the servants were supposed to be in bed, and was admitted by the plaintiff's wife, the defendant taking off his boots in the garden and walking into the house with them in his hand, and retiring in the same manner at two o'clock in the morning. On the part of the defendant, several witnesses were called principally with a view of casting discredit upon the testimony, or doubt upon the characters, of some of the plaintiff's witnesses. To this also, as well as to the improbability of persons in the station which the plaintiff's wife and the defendant occupied in society recting with the coarse and disgraceful sensuality and lewdness ascribed to them by the witnesses, the observations of the defendant's counsel were chiefly directed. Some further witnesses were called on the part of the defendant, for the purpose of shewing the felicitous terms upon which *he* lived with his own family. This evidence, not being objected to, was received. In the course of his summing up, Lord Den-

In an action for crim. con., evidence was offered on the part of the *defendant* to shew the affectionate terms upon which he lived with his own wife and family, which, being unobjected to, was admitted, and was observed upon by the judge in his summing up as affording an inference in the defendant's favour:—Held, that this was no misdirection.

The jury having found for the defendant, and it appearing from the report of the learned judge who tried the cause that there was a manifest preponderance of evidence the other way, and that he himself was not satisfied with the verdict—the Court granted a new trial, on payment of costs.

man observed that the evidence last adverted to was irrelevant to the issue before them; but that, as no objection had been made to its reception, he thought it presented a serious obstacle to the plaintiff's recovery: and he left it to the jury to say whether, taking all the evidence into consideration, they believed that the parties had been guilty of the acts imputed to them. The jury (a special jury) having found for the defendant—

Wilde, Serjeant, in Easter Term last, moved for a rule nisi for a new trial, on the grounds of misdirection, and that the verdict was against the weight of evidence.—He submitted that too much effect had been given by the learned judge, in leaving the case to the jury, to the evidence produced on the part of the defendant to shew the terms on which he lived with his wife and family, which, though unobjected to, was clearly irrelevant, and should have been put out of consideration altogether. He further contended, that, the evidence given on the part of the plaintiff not having been impeached in any material particular, the jury were not warranted in discrediting their testimony; and that, although no instance could be adduced of a new trial having been granted in a case of this description, where the jury had found a verdict for the *defendant,* yet that the court had authority to grant it, by virtue of the general jurisdiction assumed by them, on the disuse of the writ of attaint, to set aside the verdict of the jury when palpably wrong.

TINDAL, C. J.—I see no reason to object to the summing up. The observations alleged to have been made by the learned judge to the jury certainly do not amount to a misdirection in point of law. But I think the rule should be granted for a new trial, on the ground of the verdict being against the weight of evidence, upon the usual terms.

PARK, J.—The evidence offered as to the terms on which the defendant stood with his own family certainly was exceptionable, and probably would not have been received if objected to. But still I cannot discover any misdirection.—With respect to the evidence, if it were at all doubtful which way it preponderated, I for one should not feel disposed to grant a rule : but, as at present advised, it seems to me that the weight of evidence was clearly against the finding of the jury.

VAUGHAN, J., concurred.

BOSANQUET, J.—I agree that the rule should only go for a new trial on the ground of the verdict being against evidence. The piece of evidence in question having been admitted without objection, I think it was properly a subject of comment by the judge in his summing up.

The rule was therefore granted upon the second ground only, on payment of costs. Lord Denman reported that he was dissatisfied with the verdict. In the course of the present term—

Cresswell, Alexander, Cowling, and *Wortley* shewed cause.—It is a clear and settled rule, that, where the facts are properly left to the jury, and the case involves no matter of law, it is no part of the duty of the court to interfere with their decision. It is admitted that this is the first time that a new trial has been asked for in a case of this description, where the jury have found for the defendant, merely on the ground that the verdict is against. evidence: and this affords a strong presumption, that, as this is not a sort of action in which the jury are likely to be prejudiced in favour of the defendant, so it is not one in which the court would on light grounds overstep the natural bounds of their jurisdiction, and set aside the

1836.

MELLIN
v.
TAYLOR.

verdict. It is said that the privilege of moving for a new trial
is given in substitution for the antient writ of attaint: but
that is not so; that was merely a privilege the suitor had,
where he conceived the jury had misconducted themselves
by corruptly giving a false verdict, to have the matter re-
tried *upon the same evidence* before a jury of twenty-four.
The cases where new trials have been refused, when asked
for on the ground of the verdict being against the weight
of evidence, are numerous and distinctly applicable here.
In *Anonymous*, 1 Wils. 22, where there was evidence on
both sides, a new trial was refused, although the verdict
was against the opinion of the judge who tried the cause.
So, in *Swain* v. *Hall*, 3 Wils. 45, a new trial was refused,
though the Chief Justice reported that the strength of the
evidence was against the verdict. In *Ashley* v. *Ashley*,
2 Str. 1142, and *Smith* v. *Huggins*, 2 Str. 1142, the like
doctrine is laid down and acted upon. In *Carstairs* v.
Stein, 4 M. & S. 192, Lord Ellenborough enters into a
very elaborate discussion of the question. In delivering
the judgment of the court (the other judges being Le
Blanc, Bayley, and Dampier), he says : " The question
before us is not whether the verdict given in this case is
such as we should ourselves have given ; but whether,
having been given by a jury, to whom the whole case was
fully left in point of fact, and to whom the law upon the
subject was distinctly stated, it ought, upon the grounds
of argument suggested to us, to be now set aside and a
new trial granted.   We cannot discover any question of
law upon which the jury were misdirected, or (being directed
as they were) upon which they have come to an erroneous
conclusion.   All the questions which this case presented
for their immediate consideration, were questions properly
of fact, upon which, and upon the credit due to the several
witnesses by whom the testimony was given, it was their
peculiar province to decide.   As far as in the evidence
which has been reported any contradiction is to be found,

the jury must (in this as in all other cases) be presumed to
have given credit to such of the witnesses as were best
entitled to belief, unless the contrary should distinctly
appear to have been the case; and, as to their deduction
from the whole of the testimony, it ought in general to
have effect given to it, unless it appears clear that the jury
have drawn an erroneous conclusion. The court, in granting new trials, does not interfere, unless *to remedy some
manifest abuse,* or *to correct some manifest error in
law or fact.* That there are circumstances in this case
strongly pregnant of suspicion, and which lead to a
conclusion different from that which the jury have
drawn, cannot be denied. But this was a question
for the consideration of the jury, and to their consideration it was fully left, with a strong intimation of
opinion on the part of the judge that the transaction
was colourable, and the commission of course usurious.
The jury have drawn a different conclusion, and which
conclusion, upon the view they might entertain of the
facts, they were at liberty to draw; and, they having done
so, for the reasons already stated, we do not feel ourselves,
as a court of law, and acting according to the rules by
which courts of law are usually governed in similar cases,
at liberty to set aside that verdict, and grant a new trial."
In *Belcher* v. *Prittie*, 10 Bing. 408, 4 M. & Scott, 295,
it was held that it was no ground for a new trial for
misdirection, that the judge expresses a strong opinion
upon the facts either way; the whole being left to the
discretion of the jury, and the question one peculiarly
for their consideration. Tindal, C. J., in that case
lays down the rule in terms very similar to that recognized by Lord Ellenborough in *Carstairs* v. *Stein.*—
"The question for the consideration of the court," he
says, "is, not whether we are *satisfied* with the verdict, but whether, upon the evidence adduced at the
trial, assisted by the arguments of the learned counsel,

we can see with sufficient clearness that the jury have
come to a wrong conclusion in finding a verdict for the defendants : for, where the case involves mere matter of fact,
and it has been properly submitted to that tribunal which
the law has appointed to determine upon questions of fact,
we are not at liberty capriciously to interfere to deprive
the successful party of the right which he had acquired by
the verdict of a jury, notwithstanding we may entertain a
doubt as to the correctness of the conclusion at which
they have arrived : we ought to be clearly satisfied that
the verdict is against the weight of evidence before we
put the parties to the expense and anxiety of a further investigation." The like result was arrived at in three un-
reported cases lately decided. *Horne* v. *Bramwell*, in the
court of King's Bench, and *Chattock* v. *Shaw* and *Tanner*
v. *Downie*, in the Exchequer. In criminal cases (and
this is in the nature of a criminal charge), the court invariably refuses to grant new trials—*Norris* v. *Tyler*, Cowp.
37. In *Francis* v. *Baker*, Bac. Abr. Trial (L), 3, Pratt,
C. J., before whom the cause was tried, after reporting
the evidence specially, expressed himself to this effect :—
" If I had been upon the jury, and had known no more of
the witnesses than I did when this cause was tried, I
should have thought the verdict ought to have been for
the defendant; but I do not choose to declare myself dissatisfied with the verdict, because, where there is a con-
trariety of evidence as to the principal matter in issue, and
the characters of the witnesses on both sides stand un-
impeached, the weight of evidence does not depend
altogether upon the number of witnesses; for, it is the
province of the jury, who may know them all, to determine which of the witnesses they will give credit to; and
no judge has in my opinion a right to blame a jury for
exercising their power of determining in such a case :" and
he concluded with leaving the matter to the other justices.
A new trial was refused. Clive, J., said : " The granting

of a new trial in this case would be taking away that power which is by the constitution vested in the jury." And Bathurst, J.—"As there was in this case strong evidence for the plaintiff, a new trial ought not to be granted; although the weight of evidence was, in my Lord Chief Justice's opinion, with the defendant." In the present case, there was nothing calculated in the slightest degree to embarrass or mislead the minds of the jury. They deliberated long. They had means of judging from their appearance and demeanour, of the degree of credit due to the witnesses on either side, which the court has not. And, they having exercised their judgment upon the whole case fairly and dispassionately, the court has no right to overturn the verdict: if they did so, it would be vain for the defendant to hope for an impartial trial on the second occasion.

Wilde, Serjeant, in support of his rule.—If by any reasonable intendment the verdict of the jury may be consistent with justice, undoubtedly the court will not grant a new trial. But, if the arguments urged on the part of the defendant were well founded, there never could in any case be a new trial, as for a verdict against evidence. That new trials can be and are frequently granted in cases similar to this, is beyond doubt. Thus, new trials have been granted in actions for giving false characters of serants and tradesmen, in actions for fraudulent preference, and the like, which do not necessarily involve any question of law. Here, the whole tenor of the evidence as reported by the learned judge was such that no rational view of the case could possibly justify the conclusion to which the jury have thought fit to come.

Cur. adv. vult.

TINDAL, C. J., delivered the opinion of the court:— We agree, that, in every case in which the verdict has turned upon a question of fact that has been submitted to a jury, and there is no objection to the verdict, except that it is found, in the opinion of the court, against the weight of the evidence, the court ought to exercise, not merely a cautious, but a strict and sure judgment, before they send the case to a second jury. The general rule, under such circumstances, is, that the verdict once found shall stand: the setting it aside is the exception, and ought to be an exception of rare and almost singular occurrence. The argument before us has gone the length of contending, that, if we send this case to a second trial, we invade the province of the jury, and, in the particular instance before us, almost insure a verdict against the defendant. I cannot conceive how the benefit of trial by jury can be in any way impaired by a cautious and prudent application of the corrective which is now applied for: on the contrary, I think, that, without some power of this nature residing in the breast of the court, the trial by jury would, in particular cases, be productive of injustice, and the institution itself would suffer in the opinion of the public. And with respect to this particular case, I can never persuade myself, that, in the cautious manner in which we express ourselves as to the former verdict, a second jury will not exercise their judgment upon the facts brought before them with as perfect freedom, and with as little bias, as if the investigation was for the first time brought before that tribunal. Strong observations have been made, that we cannot have the opportunity of giving an opinion on the demeanour of the witnesses at the trial. It is an observation which would apply to every case of a motion to the court, as to some of the judges, if not as to all. But, in this case, the learned judge who presided at the trial had that opportunity; and he has reported to us that he is not satisfied with the verdict; a course which has in it no novelty whatever, but has been the constant practice from the earliest time at which new trials have been granted, and is acted upon every day. I shall, therefore, content myself with saying that the present case appears to us, in some of its circumstances, of a very extraordinary character and nature; and that, as the evidence now stands, the verdict appears to us so much against the weight of the evidence, that, before we can feel satisfied in giving the judgment of the court for the defendant upon the verdict which he has obtained, we think the facts of this case ought to be considered by a second jury.

Rule absolute for a new trial, on payment of costs (a).

1836.

MELLIN
v.
TAYLOR.

(a) Upon the second trial, the plaintiff had a verdict, with 1000l. damages. A third trial was moved for, but was refused.

LEUCKART v. COOPER and Another.

TROVER for wools. Pleas—first, not guilty—secondly, as to certain parts of the goods and chattels in the declaration mentioned, to wit, eleven bales of wools, parcel of the said bales of wool therein mentioned, that, long before and at the time of the committing of the grievances in the declaration mentioned, the defendants were public warehousekeepers, and the trade or business of public warehousekeepers as aforesaid during all the time aforesaid exercised and carried on in the city of London; that, in the course of exercising and carrying on their said trade or business of public warehousekeepers as aforesaid, they the defendants were retained and employed by merchants and other persons to enter at the Custom-House at and for the port of London goods consigned to them from abroad, and afterwards to land such goods and house the same at and in the warehouses of the said

Monday,
June 13th.

In trover the defendants justified the retaining of the goods under an antient custom from time immemorial used in the trade of public warehousekeepers in London, for all such public warehousekeepers to have a general lien upon all goods from time to time housed or remaining in their warehouses, *for and in the name of* the merchants or other persons by whom such public warehousekeepers are retained or employed, for

all monies, or any balance thereof, due from such merchants or other persons to such public warehousekeepers for or on account of advances or expenses which such public warehousekeepers should have made or been put to in or about the payment of duties or of customs on goods consigned to them from abroad, or the payment of freight and other charges for the conveyance of such goods to the port of London, or the entering, landing, and warehousing such goods:—Held, that such custom was unreasonable and unjust, and could not be supported in law.

defendants for and in the name of such merchants or
other persons, subject to their order, for certain reasonable reward to the defendants in that behalf, they the defendants paying, if required so to do by such merchants
or other persons, the duties and customs by law imposed
and charged upon such goods consigned from abroad to
London, and also paying, if required so to do by the said
merchants or other persons, the freight and other charges
payable in respect of the conveyance of such goods to the
port of London aforesaid; that there is now, and from time
whereof the memory of man runneth not to the contrary
hath been, and still is a certain antient and laudable usage
and custom in the trade of public warehousekeepers in the
city of London, for all such public warehousekeepers to
have and be entitled to a general lien upon all goods from
time to time housed or remaining in the warehouses of
such public warehousekeepers for and in the name of the
merchants or other persons by whom such public warehousekeepers were retained and employed as aforesaid,
for all monies or any balance thereof remaining due from
such merchants and other persons to such public warehousekeepers for or on account of any advances or expenses which such public warehousekeepers should have
made or been put to in and about the paying of the duties
and customs by law charged and imposed on any goods
consigned to such merchants or other persons from abroad,
if required so to do as aforesaid, and in and about the
paying, if required to do so by the said merchants or
other persons, the freight and other charges for the conveyance of such goods to the port of London aforesaid,
and also for and on account of all and every other advances, charges, and claims which such public warehousekeepers should have made or been put to, or to which
they might be entitled for and in respect of the entering,
landing, and warehousing such goods at and in the warehouses of the said public warehousekeepers; that there-

tofore, and whilst the defendants were such public warehousekeepers as aforesaid, to wit, on the 1st January, 1833,
and on divers times and occasions between that day and
the 10th October, 1834, the defendants were retained
and employed by one Edward Heilbronn, of the city of
London, merchant, as such public warehousekeepers as
aforesaid, to enter at the Custom-House at and for the
port of London, divers, to wit, two hundred bales of wool
(of which the said eleven bales of wool in the introductory
part of this plea referred to were part and parcel,) consigned to the said Heilbronn from abroad as aforesaid,
and afterwards to land and house the same wools at and
in the warehouses of the defendants for and in the name
of the said Heilbronn, subject to his order, for certain
reasonable reward to the defendants in that behalf, and
were by the said Heilbronn required to pay the duties
and customs by law charged and imposed upon such wools;
and the said Heilbronn on the said several times and occasions last aforesaid then required the defendants to pay
the freight and other charges for the conveyance of the
last-mentioned wools to the port of London aforesaid;
that, in pursuance of such retainer and employment, they,
the defendants, as such public warehousekeepers as aforesaid, did, on the several times and occasions last aforesaid, accordingly enter at the Custom-House at and for
the port of London the said last-mentioned wools, and
did pay the duties and customs by law charged and imposed on the same wools, and did also, on the several times
and occasions last aforesaid, pay the freight and other
charges for conveyance of such wools to the port of London aforesaid, and on the said several times and occasions
aforesaid did land the said last-mentioned wools, and did
house the same for and in the name of Heilbronn, subject
to his order, at and in the warehouses of the defendants;
that the duties and customs, freight, and other charges so
advanced and paid by the defendants for and in respect

of the said last-mentioned wools so entered, landed, and housed as aforesaid, and all other the advances, charges, and claims which the defendants as such public ware-housekeepers as aforesaid had made, been put to, and were entitled to, for and in respect of the entering, landing, and housing the said wools as aforesaid amounted in the whole to a large sum of money, to wit, the sum of 2000*l.*, and that a great part thereof, to wit, the sum of 1030*l.* 13*s.* 5*d.*, before the time of the committing the said grievances, was due and owing from Heilbronn to the defendants, and still is due and unpaid to the defendants; that the defendants, as such public warehousekeepers as aforesaid, on divers times and occasions during the time last aforesaid, did deliver the greater part of the said two hundred bales of wool to the order of Heilbronn, according to the usage and custom of trade in that behalf, and that the residue of the said last-mentioned bales of wool, to wit, eleven bales thereof, being the eleven bales of wool in the intro-ductory part of this plea referred to, and parcel of the said bales of wool in the declaration mentioned, before and at the time of the committing of the said grivances, were and still are lying, being, and remaining in the warehouses of the defendants; that the defendants, as such public warehousekeepers as aforesaid, by virtue of and according to the usage and custom of the trade of public warehouse-keepers in the city of London aforesaid, before and at the time of the committing of the said grievances, retained and held, and still do retain and hold, the said eleven bales of wool, parcel &c., as and by way of a general lien for a large sum, to wit, the said sum of 1030*l.* 13*s.* 5*d.* so due and owing from Heilbronn, and still unpaid to the defendants as aforesaid; which is the said conversion of the said eleven bales of wool, parcel &c., in the intro-ductory part of this plea referred to: And this, &c.

To this plea, the plaintiffs replied—that there is not now, nor from time whereof the memory of man runneth

not to the contrary hath there been, nor is there still, the
said supposed antient and laudable usage and custom in
the trade of public warehousekeepers in the city of London, for all such public warehousekeepers to have and be
entitled to a general lien upon all goods from time to time
housed or remaining in the warehouses of such public
warehousekeepers for and in the name of the merchants
or other persons by whom such public warehousekeepers
were retained and employed as aforeaid, for all monies or
any balance thereof remaining due from such merchants
and other persons to such public warehousekeepers for
or on account of any advances or expenses which such
public warehousekeepers should have made and been put
to in and about the paying of the duties and customs by
law charged and imposed on any goods consigned to such
merchants or other persons from abroad, if required so to
do as aforesaid, and in and about the paying, if required
to do so by the said merchants or other persons, the freight
and other charges for the conveyance of such goods to
the port of London aforesaid, and also for and on account of all and every other advances, charges, and claims
which such public warehousekeepers should have made
or have been put to, or to which they might be entitled for
and in respect of the entering, landing, and warehousing
such goods at and in the warehouses of the said public
warehousekeepers, in manner and form as the defendants
had in their said second plea above alleged.

At the trial before Tindal, C. J., at the sittings in London after Trinity Term, 1835, it appeared that the plaintiff, who resided in Saxony, was in the habit of consigning
wools to Heilbronn in this country, with directions to hand
them over to a third person, for sale on commission; that
Heilbronn also acted as agent for other foreign merchants,
and was in the habit of depositing the goods consigned to
him in the warehouses of the defendants, they paying all
charges; that, in September, 1834, twenty bales of wool

arrived in this country by consignment from the plaintiff to Heilbronn, and were by the latter deposited with the defendants; that shortly afterwards nine of these bales were transferred to a third person, and, Heilbronn dying, the defendants claimed to hold the remaining eleven bales, under the custom alleged in the second plea, for a sum of 1030*l.* 13*s.* 5*d.*—900*l.* for money lent, and the residue for charges upon these eleven bales and also for charges in respect of other goods belonging to other persons that had been deposited with the defendants by Heilbronn under the same custom. The jury found that the charges due upon these particular goods had been tendered. The custom as alleged in the second plea was proved, and a verdict was thereupon found for the defendants.

Wilde, Serjeant, in the following Michaelmas Term, moved for a new trial, on the ground that the evidence did not support the custom as alleged; or that judgment might be entered for the plaintiff non obstante veredicto on the issue taken on the second plea, on the ground that the custom relied on was unreasonable, and not sustainable in point of law. By the custom set up, the defendants claim a lien, not merely upon goods that are the property of the individual by whom they are deposited with the warehousekeeper, but upon all goods so deposited in the name of the depositor, whether they are his property or not. At the trial, the principle reliance of the defendants was upon the decisions establishing the lien of a wharfinger—*Nayler* v. *Mangles,* 1 Esp. 109, and *Spears* v. *Hartley,* 3 Esp. 81. The case of a wharfinger, however, is in many respects materially distinguishable from that of a mere warehousekeeper. The public legal quays are appointed by the crown—*Stephen* v. *Coster,* 3 Burr. 1408, 1 W. Bl. 413, 423: and the wharfinger's general lien is allowed as against the owner of the goods only. In *Rushforth* v. *Hadfield,* 6 East, 519, 2 Smith, 624, it was held that the lien of a common carrier for his general balance, to be inferred from a general usage of trade, must be proved by clear and satisfactory instances, sufficiently numerous and general to warrant so extensive a conclusion affecting the custom of the realm, and is not to be favoured, nor can it be supported by a few recent instances of detention of goods by four or five carriers for their general balance. And, a jury having negatived such a general usage, though proved to have been frequently exercised by the defendant and various other common carriers throughout the north for ten or twelve years before, and in one instance so far back as thirty years, though not opposed by other evidence, the court refused to grant a new trial—7 East, 224, 3 Smith, 221. And in *Oppenheim* v. *Russell*, 3 B. & P. 42, it was held that an usage for carriers to retain goods as a lien for a general balance of account between them and the consignees, cannot affect the right of the consignor to stop the goods in transitu. *Butler* v. *Woolcott*, 2 B. & P. 64, and *Richardson* v. *Goss*, 3 B. & P. 119, are to the same effect. In *Holderness* v. *Collinson*, 1 M. & R. 55, 7 B. & C. 212, it was held that a wharfinger has not a general lien in respect of labourage and warehouseroom. And in *Wright* v. *Snell*, 5 B. & A. 350, where a carrier had given notice that all goods would be subject to a lien, not only for the freight of the particular articles, but also for any general balance due from their respective owners, and goods were sent by the carrier addressed to the order of J. S., who was merely a factor; it was held that the carrier had not any lien, as against the real owner, for a balance due from J. S. A claim of lien generally fails from its own weakness, and not by evidence of a negative character, which in most cases is wholly impracticable.

The Court thought that, the evidence being all one way, there was no ground for a new trial: but granted a rule nisi to enter judgment for the plaintiffs non obstante veredicto on the second plea.

Cresswell and *R. V. Richards,* in the course of the last term, shewed cause.—The jury have found the custom proved as alleged ; and the presumption is that it is a reasonable and convenient custom, for otherwise it never would have obtained. It is for the party who impugns it to shew that it is unreasonable—1 Inst. 62, not for the party who relies upon it to shew it reasonable. In *Hix* v. *Gardiner,* 2 Bulstr. 196, Croke, C. J., says: You cannot imagine the reason of a custom; the custom of Borough English and Gavelkind are no reasonable customs; the reason to be shewed of the beginning of them is impossible." The custom is not alleged to exist where the goods are known to belong to a third person, and not to the depositor. Heilbronn here appeared and acted as the true owner. A general lien, it is admitted, exists in favour of wharfingers. *Oppenheim* v. *Russell* and *Richardson* v. *Goss* are wholly distinguishable: in each of these cases the question arose before the goods came to the hands of the consignee—whether the carrier's lien as against the consignee · could defeat the consignor's right of stoppage in transitu, a right to be exercised before the goods come to the hands of the consignee. In *Rushforth* v. *Hadfield,* the custom attempted to be set up was much more extensive than that now under consideration, and yet there was no suggestion that it was illegal or unreasonable. At common law, the subject has a right to have his goods carried by a common carrier, paying the reasonable charges on them only. Here, the consignee, Heilbronn, had the absolute dominion over the goods ; and therefore, for the purposes of this lien, the defendants were entitled to consider him the real owner. In *George* v. *Claggett,* 7 T. R. 359, 2 Esp. 557, Peake's Add. Cas. 131, it was held, that, if a factor who sells under a del credere commission, sells goods as his

own, and the buyer knows nothing of any principal, the
buyer may set off any demand he may have on the factor
against the demand for the goods made by the principal.
What rule of law can be stronger against the foreign principal than that? or, in what is the custom here set up
more inconvenient? The foreign merchant is bound by
the usages of trade here. The plaintiff must be supposed
to be conversant with the custom and course of dealing
here: he must have known that Heilbronn must of necessity warehouse the wools; he gives him a right to pledge
them at all events to a certain extent. In *Forster* v. *Pearson*, 1 C. & M. 849, Parke, B., in summing up, told the
jury that the principle laid down in *Haynes* v. *Forster*,
2 C. M. & R. 237 (that a bill broker who receives a bill
from a customer to procure it to be discounted, has no
right to mix it with bills of other customers, and to pledge
the whole mass as a security for an advance of money to
himself; and that still less has he a right to deposit such
bill as a security or part security for money previously due
from him), was to be taken by them as the general law;
but that, notwithstanding such general rule of law, the
parties might contract as they thought proper: and he
left it to them to say whether the usage set up by the
defendants, as to the course of dealing in such cases, was
established to their satisfaction, and, if so, whether they
thought that the plaintiff, who was a bill broker himself, had
contracted with reference to that usage. The jury having
found for the defendants, the court refused to disturb the
verdict.

Atcherley, Serjeant, and *W. H. Watson*, in support of
the rule.—The custom set up in this case is, not for a lien
for advances on the particular goods, but in respect of any
goods whatever deposited by the same individual. This
is clearly unreasonable. In none of the cases has a lien
ever been established except as against the *owner* of the

goods or some person acting or claiming under him. A
wharfinger stands in a different situation from a mere warehousekeeper : he has certain known duties cast upon him
by law : and it has been held that even he has no lien for
warehouse-room or rent. His lien does not extend to render
the goods of a consignor liable for the debt of a middle man.
In *Stephen* v. *Coster*, the rights and liabilities of wharfingers are clearly and ably defined.   In *Maanss* v. *Henderson*, 1 East, 337, Lord Kenyon said : " If the agent disclose his principal at the time, it is clear that he cannot
pledge the property of such principal to another with
whom he is dealing for his own private debt." The precise difference between the principle in this case and in
that of *George* v. *Claggett*, is shewn in *Wright* v. *Snell* :
Abbott, C. J., there says : "Where goods are consigned
to A. B. or order, the carrier has a right to consider A. B.
as the owner of the goods for the purpose of delivery,
but not for the collateral purpose of creating a lien on the
goods, as against the owner, in respect of a general balance
due from the consignee; nor will any prejudice arise to
the carrier from our holding this to be the law, for he need
not deliver the goods in any case till the price of the carriage is paid for them." Bayley, J., said : " There was
nothing in the manner in which these goods were consigned
to Robinson to induce the carrier to believe that they were
consigned to him on his own account, and as his own property, rather than in his character of factor ; and if they
were consigned to him in that character, it would be most
unjust to allow the carrier this lien." And Holroyd, J.,
said : " The mere act of consigning goods to another
cannot give to a third person any right to retain the goods
of the consignor until the payment of the debt of the
consignee. *George* v. *Claggett* differs materially from
the present ; there, the goods were consigned to a factor,
who carried on business also on his own account, and he
sold, acting under the authority given to him, but *in his*

own name ; and it was held that the purchaser of the goods

had a right to set off, in an action brought by the prin-
cipal, the debt due from the factor." All customs are to
be construed strictly. Here, Heilbronn was the plaintiff's
agent for a certain purpose, viz. to receive the goods and
hand them over to a third person for sale ; not for the collateral purpose of giving any one a general lien upon them.
He had no authority under the factors' act 6 Geo. 4, c. 94,
to pledge them.

Cur. adv. vult.

TINDAL, C. J., delivered the judgment of the court:—
The jury having found a verdict in this case for the defendants upon the issue raised upon the second plea, the
plaintiff has moved for judgment non obstante veredicto.
The question therefore is, whether the custom stated in
that plea is a custom that can be supported in law. The
plea justified the retaining and holding of eleven bales of
wool, parcel of the quantity claimed in the declaration,
under an antient custom from time immemorial used in
the trade of public warehousekeepers in the city of London, for all such public warehousekeepers to have and be
entitled to a general lien upon all goods from time to time
housed or remaining in their warehouses, *for and in the*
name of the merchants or other persons by whom such
public warehousekeepers are retained or employed, for all
monies, or any balance thereof, due from such merchants
or other persons to such public warehousekeepers, for or
on account of advances or expenses which such public
warehousekeepers should have made or been put to in or
about the paying of duties or of customs on goods consigned to them from abroad, or the payment of freight
and other charges for the conveyance of such goods to
the port of London, or entering, landing, and warehousing such goods. So that the general lien claimed is not
confined to goods the property of the person who employed or retained the warehousekeeper, but extends to

all goods which are put by him in his own name into the hands of the warehousekeeper, whether his property or not.   The custom set up in the plea, if supportable, would make the goods of a foreign merchant, which have been consigned to a London factor for sale, and by him put into the warehouse of the warehousekeeper for safe custody, liable to a private debt of the factor for expenses incurred in respect of other goods of third persons which had been in his hands at former times, for charges contracted upon such goods during any antecedent period of time, and that to an unlimited extent.   It appears to us that such a custom is at once unreasonable and unjust, and therefore bad in law.   It is a custom which is obviously prejudicial in a direct manner and in a very high degree to foreign trade; for, no foreign merchant would be content to consign his goods to this country for sale, if they could be made liable, whilst warehoused for the purpose of custody, to satisfy a debt already due from the factor to the warehousekeeper in respect of other goods. No authority whatever has been cited in support of this custom; and, as far as any analogy can be drawn from decided cases, it is against its validity.   The case of *Oppenheim* v. *Russell*, 3 Bos. & Pull. 42, establishes the principle, that, although a common carrier may have acquired by usage or special agreement a lien for a general balance of account between him and a consignee, this lien shall not affect the right of a consignor to stop in transitu: that is, in effect, that this right of lien shall not operate upon or against the rights of third persons.   And the doctrine laid down in *Wright* v. *Snell*, 5 B. & Ad. 350, bears still more closely upon the point now under discussion; a general lien being held not sustainable by a carrier against the true owner of the goods for the general balance due from the factor to whom the goods were consigned for sale.   That case, in effect, decides the present; for, no sound distinction can be taken in this respect between a public warehousekeeper and a public carrier, except indeed that the latter stands in a position more favoured by the law in respect to lien than the former; the carrier being obliged by law to receive and carry the goods, whilst the warehousekeeper's claim arises out of a voluntary contract. And the present case appears to us to differ from that of *George* v. *Claggett*, 7 T. R. 359, principally relied on by the defendants. In that case the owner put his goods into the hands of his factor to sell as his own; the factor sold them as his own; and the defendant had no knowledge that the factor was not the real owner of the goods: in such case the set-off of the debt due from the factor to the purchaser followed as a necessary consequence from the sale by him as of his own goods. In this case there was no sale by the factor; but the proposition contended for is, that the goods became, by the operation of the custom, *pledged for the factor's debt*, though the factor was not authorized by law so to pledge them directly. And although the factor may now, under some circumstances, pledge, the facts of the present case do not bring it within the operation of the statute 6 Geo. 4, c. 94.

It is unnecessary, as a further objection to the custom set up by this plea, to observe that it is pleaded so largely as to comprehend all goods put into the hands of a ware-housekeeper by a factor in his own name, whether or not the warehousekeeper has knowledge or notice that they are not the property of the factor, but of the foreign merchants. But, without relying on this objection, we think the custom unreasonable, and consequently bad, upon the more general ground above stated, and therefore give our judgment for the plaintiff non obstante veredicto.

Judgment for the plaintiff accordingly.

Monday,
June 13th.

It is not essential to the validity of an alias or pluries that the writ of summons or capias should be previously returned, except where the object is to save the statute of limitations, or where the capias is made the foundation of proceedings to outlawry.

GREGORY *v.* DES ANGES, Knight.

BOMPAS, Serjeant, on a former day in this term, obtained a rule calling upon the plaintiff to shew cause why the proceedings on the bail-bond given in this cause should not be set aside, on the ground of irregularity. The principal irregularity insisted upon was, that the writ of capias, which had issued on the 12th December, 1835, had not been returned when the alias capias issued (22nd April, 1836) under which the defendant was arrested. The learned Serjeant contended that a return to the first writ was essential to the validity of the alias—2 Will. 4, c. 39, s. 10, which enacts " that no writ issued by authority of this act shall be in force for more than four calendar months from the day of the date thereof, including the day of such date; but every writ of summons and capias may be continued by alias and pluries, as the case may require, if any defendant therein named may not have been arrested thereon or served therewith : provided always that no first writ shall be available to prevent the operation of any statute whereby the time for the commencement of the action may be limited, unless the defendant shall be arrested thereon or served therewith, or proceedings to or toward outlawry shall be had thereupon, or unless such writ, and every writ (if any) issued in continuation of a preceding writ, shall be returned non est inventus and entered of record within one calendar month next after the expiration thereof, including the day of such expiration, and unless every writ issued in continuation of a preceding writ shall be issued within one such calendar month after the expiration of the preceding writ, and shall contain a memorandum indorsed thereon or subscribed thereto, specifying the day of the date of the first writ."

Adams, Serjeant, and *R. V. Richards,* shewed cause, contending that the clause above cited only required the capias to be returned before the issuing of the alias in those cases where the capias is issued for the purpose of saving the statute of limitations.

Bompas, Serjeant, in support of his rule.—In order to justify the issuing of an alias, the capias must be returned; and, unless the capias be returned within one month after the four months during which the act provides that it shall remain in force, it cannot be returned at all. The statute intended the alias to be a continuation of a previous writ, which it cannot be if that writ has lost its efficacy.

TINDAL, C. J.—Upon reference to the 10th section of the 2 Will. 4, c. 39, I do not find that the return of the capias is made necessary to the issuing of the alias. On the contrary, I am led to infer that it was not necessary, or that it might be made, in ordinary cases, at any time afterwards. Were it not so, great inconvenience would oftentimes result: the sheriff might during the long vacation neglect to make his return, when he could not be ruled to return the writ probably until long after (supposing the defendant's argument is to prevail) the writ had ceased to be an efficient writ. The capias is to be in force four months; but it " may be continued by alias and pluries, as the case may require, if any defendant therein named may not have been arrested thereon or served therewith"— making the issuing of the alias or pluries depend, not on the return of the preceding writ, but on the service or non-service. Then follows a proviso which is applicable only to those cases where it is sought to prevent the operation of the statute of limitations, making a return of the first writ essential for this purpose. It is clear from the 5th section that the legislature were aware of the difference between the expiration and the return of a writ: that section makes the return of non est inventus to the writ of

1836.

GREGORY
*
DES ANGES.

capias, and of non est inventus and nulla bona to the distringas, essential to the proceeding to outlawry. With respect to the clause now more immediately under consideration, I think we are not at liberty to insert therein as a necessary preliminary that the capias shall in all cases be returned before an alias can issue.

PARK, J.—I am of the same opinion. If the intention of the legislature was that the capias should be returned before the issuing of the alias or pluries, they have not been successful in expressing it. The proviso in the 10th section, where the return is required, applies only to the case of writs issued for the purpose of saving the statute of limitations. It seems to me that there has been no irregularity in this case.

The rest of the court concurring—

Rule discharged, with costs.

———◆———

Monday,
June 13th.

By an award the defendants were directed to pay a certain sum to the plaintiffs and to sign a memorandum containing an engagement on the part of the defendants to abstain for a certain time from pirating the plaintiffs' patterns:—
Held, that the signature of this memorandum by both defendants was a sufficient recognition of the arbitrator's authority, to dispense with proof of a formal submission by both.
Quære whether such an engagement amounts to a contract in restraint of trade?

STUART and Others v. NICHOLSON and Another.

THE plaintiffs declared, that, before and at the time of the making of the promise and the committing of the breaches thereinafter mentioned, and thence hitherto, the plaintiffs carried on the trade and business of manufacturers of stove grates and fenders, under and by the name, style, and firm of Messrs. Stuart, Smith, & Co., and in the prosecution and exercise of their said trade and business during all that time laid out large sums of money in and about the inventing, designing, making, and producing, and causing to be invented, designed, and made, and in and about the purchasing and procuring divers new and original patterns and models for the said stove and fender manufactories, in their said business as aforesaid, to wit, at Sheffield, in the county of York; and the defendants during all the time aforesaid were also manufacturers of stoves and fenders, to wit, at Sheffield aforesaid; that, before and at the time of the making of the promise thereinafter mentioned, the said patterns of the plaintiffs, invented, produced, and purchased by them from time to time, had been frequently pirated, and the models thereof abstracted from the premises of the plaintiffs for clandestine and surreptitious imitation, use, and copy of the said patterns; whereby the plaintiffs were greatly injured, harrassed, oppressed, and impoverished in the exercise of their said trade and business; that, before and at the time of the making of the promise of the defendants thereinafter mentioned, to wit, on the 18th of October, 1831, one of the said patterns of the plaintiffs had been and was found on the premises of the defendants, and divers disputes and differences and certain legal proceedings thereon arose touching the same between the plaintiffs and defendants; that thereupon, on the day and year aforesaid, in order then to settle the said disputes and differences, and put an end to the said legal proceedings, and to ascertain, define, and regulate the conditions, terms, and agreement on which the plaintiffs and defendants should thereafter carry on their said business respectively, touching the patterns of the said plaintiffs in their said trade and business, it was then agreed to refer the whole matter to and leave it in the hands of mutual friends of the plaintiffs and defendants for their direction, finding, award, and determination touching and concerning the same: and thereupon, on the day and year aforesaid, in consideration of the premises, and that the plaintiffs would consent to refer the said disputes to certain mutual friends, to wit, Messrs. J. L., G. R., and R. S., and leave the whole matter aforesaid, and the said dis-

putes, differences, and legal proceedings, in their hands,
for their award, direction, end, and determination, and
would agree and faithfully promise the defendants to abide
by, perform, and keep their award, finding, direction, and
determination in the same, the defendants then agreed to
refer the whole matters aforesaid, and the said disputes,
differences, and legal proceedings, to the said J. L., G. R.,
and R. S., and faithfully promised the plaintiffs to abide
by, perform, and keep their award, finding, direction, and
determination in the same; that the plaintiffs and defendants then referred the whole matters aforesaid, and the
said disputes, differences, and legal proceedings, to the
said J. L., G. R., and R. S., for their award, direction,
end, and determination, of which the defendants then had
notice; and the said J. L., G. R., and R. S. afterwards
thereupon, on the day and year aforesaid, entered into and
upon the whole matters of the said disputes, differences,
and legal proceedings, and afterwards, on the 19th of
October, 1831, awarded, found, directed, and determined
in the same, that the defendants should pay a certain large
sum of money, to wit, the sum of 200*l.* (in the premises
aforesaid so referred)-to the plaintiffs, and that they the
defendants should make, and sign, and perform, and keep,
the matters on the defendants' part and behalf to be performed and kept of and in a certain memorandum in writing
to the effect and form following; (that is to say), " that
they the defendants thereby acknowledged having received
the patterns of the plaintiffs surreptitiously and clandestinely, and that one was found on the defendants' premises
on the 12th day of October, 1831, for which the defendants were sorry, and then bound themselves from that
day, to wit, from the 19th of October, 1831, not to use
directly or indirectly any patterns of the plaintiffs' on any
account whatever until the patterns should have been out
a clear twelvemonth from the time the said plaintiffs should
have had any one pattern in the market; and that thereby

it should be mutually agreed that the said document, then
so signed by the defendants as aforesaid, should not be
printed in any newspaper or otherwise, and that only two
written copies should ever be in circulation." The plaintiffs then said that they, relying on the said promise and
undertaking of the defendants in that behalf, had always
abided by, performed, and kept the award, finding, direction, and determination of the said J. L., G. R., and R. S.,
in the said matter, and in the said disputes, differences,
and legal proceedings; and afterwards, on the said 19th
of October, 1831, received of the defendants the said sum
of money, to wit, 200*l.*, pursuant to and upon the said
finding, award, determination, and direction of the said
J. L., G. R., and R. S., and had not printed the said document, or caused the same to be printed in any newspaper
or otherwise, and did not circulate or cause to be circulated
more than two written copies of the said document. And
the plaintiffs further said, that, although the defendants,
on the said 19th of October, 1831, paid the sum of money,
to wit, 200*l.*, to the plaintiffs, pursuant to and under and
upon the said award, finding, determination, and direction
of the said J. L., G. R., and R. S., and also then made
and signed the said memorandum in writing to the effect
and form before mentioned, and delivered the same to the
plaintiffs; and although the said disputes, differences, and
legal proceedings upon and by virtue of the said award,
finding, direction, and determination of the said J. L.,
G. R., and R. S., then wholly ceased, determined, and
were put an end to; nevertheless the defendants, from the
making and signing of the said memorandum, wholly refused and neglected to perform or keep the said memorandum in writing and the matters thereof on the defendants'
part and behalf to be performed and kept, or any part
thereof, but, on the contrary thereof, broke their said promise to the plaintiffs. The plaintiffs then averred, that,
after the making and signing of the said memorandum, to

wit, on the 20th of October, 1831, and on divers other
days and times from that day to the commencement of this
suit, they expended large sums of money and labour in
and about the inventing, designing. and producing, and
causing to be invented, designed, and produced, and in
and about purchasing and procuring divers new patterns
and models in the prosecution and exercise of the business
and trade of the plaintiffs as aforesaid; and in so doing
the plaintiffs, after the making and signing of the said
memorandum in writing, to wit, on the 1st of August, 1835,
at Sheffield aforesaid, invented and designed a certain pattern, to wit, of a certain fender, at considerable cost and
labour to them, the plaintiffs, from the use whereof, and
from the sale of fenders from the said pattern, large profits
and gains would have arisen to them the plaintiffs within
and during twelve months from the invention and design
thereof, and from the time the said plaintiffs had the same
in the market, but for the breach of promise and misconduct of the defendants thereinafter next mentioned: yet
the defendants, well knowing the premises, and not regarding their said promise to the plaintiffs, but contriving
and intending to defraud the plaintiffs in that behalf, afterwards, and after the said plaintiffs had had the same in
the market, and long before the expiration of twelve
months from the time of the said invention and design of
the said fender, and the time when the said plaintiffs
first had the same in the market, to wit, on the 1st of
August, 1835, and on divers days between that time and
twelve months next following the time when the plaintiffs
first had the same in the market, did use directly and indirectly the said pattern of the said fender of the plaintiffs,
and then made divers, to wit, two thousand fenders from
the use direct and indirect of the said pattern, and in imitation and copy thereof, and then sold divers, to wit, two
thousand fenders from the use direct and indirect of the
said pattern, and in imitation and copy thereof, and after

and according to the said pattern of the said fender; by
reason whereof the plaintiffs sustained great injury and
damage in the market, and were unable to sell and dispose of fenders to the same extent as they would have
done of the said pattern: and the plaintiffs further said,
that the defendants did not incur the like or any expenses in and about the making and working fenders of
the said pattern, and were thereby enabled to sell, and
did in fact sell, within a year of the time when the pattern
of the said fender of the plaintiffs first came into the market, divers, to wit, ten thousand fenders as aforesaid, so
made by use direct and indirect of the said pattern of the
plaintiffs, below the price at which the plaintiffs were able
or could reasonably be expected to sell, or did sell the
same; and divers persons, to wit, one T. P., one E. G.,
one J. H., one J. B., one J. E., Messrs. B. & H., Messrs.
B. & Sons, and others, who before that time had been
and usually were customers of the plaintiffs, and would
have bought divers, to wit, two thousand fenders of the
said pattern of and from the plaintiffs, but for the piracy
and breach of promise of the defendants as aforesaid, for
a long space of time, within a year of the time when the
pattern of the said fender of the plaintiffs first came into
the market, bought and purchased of the defendants
divers, to wit, two thousand fenders, so made by the defendants in direct and indirect use of the said pattern of
the said fender of the plaintiffs; and divers other persons,
to wit, the said several persons aforesaid respectively, and
divers others, refused to buy or take the said fenders of
the said pattern of or from the plaintiffs: of all which
premises the defendants had notice: and by reason of the
said several premises the plaintiffs lost divers great gains
and profits which they otherwise would have made of and
from the sale and use of the said pattern of the said
fender invented and belonging to the plaintiffs as aforesaid: and the plaintiffs said, that, by reason of the pre-

mises, and of the defendants' selling and offering the
fenders of the said pattern in the market at a much less
price than the plaintiffs could afford to do—they, the
plaintiffs, having incurred cost and labour in producing,
inventing, and designing the same, which the defendants
did not incur—divers persons, to wit, Messrs. M. & L.,
and divers others, refused to do further business with the
plaintiffs, unless the plaintiffs would sell and let them have
the fenders of the said pattern at the said reduced price
at which the same were offered in the market by the defendants.

In the second count, after stating the circumstances which
led to the arbitration, the award, and the signature and
delivery by the defendants of a memorandum " to the
effect and form before mentioned," the plaintiffs alleged,
that, in consideration of the said premises, and that the
plaintiffs would abide by, perform, and keep the said award
on the part of the plaintiffs to be performed and kept, the
defendants faithfully promised the plaintiffs not to use,
directly or indirectly, thereafter, any patterns of the plaintiffs on any account whatever, until the patterns had been
out a twelvemonth from the time the plaintiffs should have
had any one pattern in the market, according to the said
memorandum of agreement, and the award and direction
of the said arbitrators. Averment, that the plaintiffs,
confiding in the said promise, invented and produced a
pattern of a fender in the market, of which defendants had
notice: breach, as before.

The defendants pleaded—first, that they did not promise
in manner and form as the declaration alleged—secondly,
that the plaintiffs did not invent the fenders—thirdly, that
the defendants did not use or sell fenders in imitation of
the plaintiffs'; upon all which pleas issue was joined.

At the trial before Lord Denman, at the last Spring
Assizes for the county of York, the plaintiffs, amongst
other evidence, produced the memorandum stated in the

declaration, signed by both the defendants. There was no proof, beyond the fact of his having signed this memorandum, that the defendant Hoole was a party to the submission, nor was the signature of the memorandum in any direct manner shewn to be connected with the preliminary circumstances. It was thereupon objected, on the part of the defendants, that the plaintiffs ought to be nonsuited. His lordship was of opinion that Hoole's signature to the memorandum was a sufficient recognition of the authority of the arbitrators : but he reserved to the defendants leave to move to enter a nonsuit, should the court think the objection well founded.

Maule, accordingly, in Easter Term, obtained a rule *nisi* to enter a nonsuit, on the above ground ; and also for a new trial, on the ground that there was no evidence to connect the promise with the consideration alleged in the declaration, and that, under the general issue, the plaintiffs were bound to shew that the promise was founded on the consideration alleged ; and also in arrest of judgment, on the ground that the memorandum or agreement entered into by the defendants was in restraint of trade, and therefore void.

Cresswell and *Hoggins*, on a former day in this term, shewed cause.—The evidence was that Nicholson signed the submission, and that Hoole recognised and acted upon it; for, the signature by the latter of the memorandum directed by the arbitrators, was a recognition of their authority, and was as effective for the purpose of charging him as a formal submission. At the trial no objection was taken to the sufficiency of the consideration ; and therefore it is too late now to urge it. But a sufficient consideration for the defendants' promise does appear on the face of the declaration. The defendants, having pirated the plaintiffs' patterns, were liable to an action. It is clearly

1836.

STUART
v.
NICHOLSON.

N N 2

a sufficient consideration for a defendant's agreeing to a reference, that disputes and differences exist between the plaintiff and himself, which will be determined by the reference. In *Sykes* v. *Sykes,* 5 D. & R. 292, 3 B. & C. 541, the declaration alleged that the defendants sold goods as and for goods manufactured by the plaintiff; the evidence was, that the persons to whom the defendant sold the goods knew that they were not manufactured by the plaintiff, but that the defendant copied the plaintiff's mark, and sold the goods so marked, in order that the purchasers might re-sell them as and for goods manufactured by the plaintiff, and which they did: it was held that this was no variance. The agreement to abstain from pirating the plaintiffs' patterns for the space of twelve months after their first appearance in the market, is clearly not in restraint of trade. A covenant to restrain a person from exercising a trade is not illegal if it be not to the prejudice of the public, and the consideration be reasonable—*Horner* v. *Ashford,* 11 Moore, 91, 3 Bing. 322. There is no want of mutuality: the plaintiffs, having claims against the defendants, agree to refer them to arbitration, and the parties enter into mutual engagements to abide by the award. The award, too, is sufficiently final; it decides all that was in dispute between the parties.

Maule, Alexander, and *Wightman,* in support of the rule.—*Sykes* v. *Sykes* was a clear case of fraud. There was no evidence whatever given in this case to shew that Hoole ever heard of the submission. It was essential for the plaintiff, under the new rules of Hilary Term, 4 Will. 4, to prove, not only that the promise was made as alleged, but also with reference to the alleged consideration; for, that is put in issue by non assumpsit. In *Passenger* v. *Brooks,* 7 C. & P. 110, 1 Scott, 560, 1 New Cases, 587, the special contract declared on was produced and proved. In *Wallace* v. *Broadbent,* the court of King's Bench held that the plaintiff was bound, under non assumpsit, to prove the promise with reference to the alleged consideration. If this be an express promise, none was proved; if a promise is to be implied, it clearly can only be implied from proving all the preliminary matters. The memorandum itself imports no consideration.—Then, as to the arrest of judgment. The award is neither mutual nor final: and, if the award be bad, there is an entire absence of consideration for the promise to do the thing awarded; for, a promise to abide by a void award, is a void promise. The award directs the defendants to pay a certain sum, and to bind themselves to abstain from doing that which they had a perfectly good common law right to do. The plaintiffs are to do nothing. The award is not final; for, it does not profess to put an end to the disputes and differences between the parties. It is for the party relying on a contract which on the face of it appears to be in restraint of trade, to shew that it does not go beyond the justice of the case. In *Horner* v. *Greaves*, 7 Bing. 735, 5 M. & P. 768, an agreement that the defendant, a moderately skilled dentist, would abstain from practising over a district two hundred miles in diameter, in consideration of receiving instructions and a salary from the plaintiff, determinable at three months' notice, was held to be unreasonable and void, being a restraint of trade, not founded on an adequate consideration. And in a late case—*Hitchcock* v. *Cohen*—the court of King's Bench held a contract not to carry on the trade of a druggist within three miles of the plaintiff's shop, to be void, as being in restraint of trade. On this ground also the award is therefore bad.

Cur. adv. vult.

Tindal, C. J.—There have been two objections urged on the part of the defendants under this rule: one against

1836.

Stuart
v.
Nicholson.

the verdict which has been found for the plaintiffs, the other in arrest of judgment.

The principal objection which was urged at the trial against the plaintiffs' right to recover, and upon which the learned judge who tried the cause was strongly pressed to nonsuit the plaintiff, was, that there was no evidence of the submission of the two defendants to the reference, the award under which forms the groundwork of the action. But we think the signature of the memorandum of agreement by both the defendants, which agreement was directed by the arbitrators, after the investigation of the case, to be given by the defendants, was a sufficient recognition of the authority of the arbitrators, to supply the place of a more regular and formal submission.

In the argument before the court, another objection has been taken and strongly urged upon our attention, viz. that there is no evidence whatever to connect the promise with the consideration alleged in the declaration, and that, under the plea of non assumpsit, the plaintiff is bound to shew that the promise which he alleges to have been made was grounded on the previous consideration or state of facts alleged by him as its groundwork and support. Without giving any opinion whatever on that abstract question, we think the objection cannot, in any event, be allowed in this case: first, because the objection was not taken at the trial, which, if taken at that time, might have been removed by further evidence; and, secondly, because we are unable to see upon the evidence any state of facts other than and different from those alleged in the declaration, to which the promise can by possibility apply. The several facts stated in the declaration were proved, and the promise was proved in writing by the signature of the parties. We see no other circumstances than those that preceded which could form the consideration.

As to the motion in arrest of judgment, we think the point raised, that the agreement was in restraint of trade,

is far too doubtful upon the allegations in this declaration
to justify us in arresting the judgment. The objection
appears upon the record, if the defendants shall be advised
further to insist upon it, and we give our judgment for the
plaintiffs.

1836.

STUART
v.
NICHOLSON.

Judgment for the plaintiffs.

——◆——

ARNALL v. ARNALL.

Monday,
June 13th.

ASSUMPSIT for money lent &c.—Plea, non assumpsit.
The writ issued on the 20th February, 1836; the declaration, which stated the cause of action to have accrued
on the 27th February, was filed on the 8th March. After
verdict for the plaintiff—

Newman moved in arrest of judgment, on the ground
that the cause of action appeared on the face of the record to have accrued after the commencement of the
action. [*Tindal*, C. J.—In assumpsit, the day on which
the promise is laid is immaterial. It is not to be assumed
that evidence was received on the trial of any thing that
took place after the issuing of the writ.] In *Ward* v.
Rich, 1 Vent. 103, where an action was brought for taking
away the plaintiff's wife and keeping her from him until
such a day (which was some time after the exhibiting of
the bill), after verdict for the plaintiff, the judgment was
arrested, because the jury must be intended to have given
damages for the *whole* time mentioned in the declaration.
And in *Brasfield* v. *Lee*, 1 Lord Raym. 329, where the
plaintiff declared that the defendant imprisoned him on
the 1st October, 9 Will. 3, and detained him in prison
four months; after verdict for the plaintiff, and entire
damages, judgment was arrested, because the declaration
being of Michaelmas Term, 9 Will. 3, and the damages

In indebitatus
assumpsit the
day of the pro-
mise alleged in
the declaration
is immaterial;
and therefore
it is no ground
for arresting
the judgment,
that the pro-
mise is stated
to have been
made at a day
subsequent to
the issuing of
the writ; other-
wise, where
the day is ma-
terial.

being entire, and given for the imprisonment of four months from the 1st October, it appeared that the damages were given for an imprisonment after the commencement of the action. After citing these and other cases, among the rest *Baker* v. *Bache*, 2 Lord Raym. 1382, and *Hanburgh* v. *Ireland*, Cro. Jac. 618, which are to the same effect, Mr. Serjeant Williams says (2 Wms. Saund. 171 *b*): "These cases seem to establish this principle, that, where it is positively and expressly averred in the declaration that the plaintiff has sustained damages from a cause subsequent to the commencement of action, or previous to the plaintiff's having any right of action, and the jury give entire damages, judgment will be arrested: but, where the cause of action is properly laid, and the other matter either comes under a scilicet, or is void, insensible, or impossible, and therefore it cannot be intended that the jury ever had it under their consideration, the plaintiff will be entitled to his judgment." [*Vaughan*, J., referred to *Dickinson* v. *Plaisted*, 7 T. R. 474, where it was held that the court will give leave to amend a record by inserting a special memorandum of the day when the plaintiff's bill was filed, after error brought, notwithstanding an objection by the defendant that the application was made too late.] Formerly, the practice was so in the King's Bench: but, since the passing of the uniformity of process act, 2 Will. 4, c. 39, the issuing of the process is in all the courts for all purposes the commencement of the action—*Alston* v. *Underhill*, 1 C. & M. 492, 3 Tyr. 447, 2 Dowl. P. C. 26. In Comyns's Digest, "*Pleader*" (C. 19), it is said: "The time of a matter charged in the declaration ought to be certainly alleged; and therefore, in assumpsit, if the plaintiff omits the day when the promise was made, it is bad." And see the authorities collected in Com. Dig. "*Pleader*," (3 M. 5). After verdict the court will suppose every thing to be right, *unless the contrary appear on the record*—*Bull* v. *Steward*, 1 Wils. 255. Here the contrary does appear on the record. In *Acton* v. *Eels*, Salk. 662, which was an action for an assault and battery, after verdict for the plaintiff, it was moved in arrest of judgment that the time laid in the declaration was not yet come. The court said : " Then it is a time impossible, and the jury must be supposed to give damages for another trespass; and it is as if no time had been alleged." So, in *Champion* v. *Skipweth*, 1 Sid. 307, in covenant the breach was alleged to have been committed after the issuing of the writ; and the defendant had judgment. The statute of Jeofails, 16 & 17 Car. 2, c. 8, enacts that, after verdict, the judgment shall not be stayed or arrested for a mistake of time, where the day has been once truly alleged: here it has nowhere been truly alleged. [*Tindal*, C. J.—Unless the new rules affect the question, I think there is nothing in the objection. *Matthews* v. *Spicer*, Str. 806, seems to approach very nearly to this case. There, the plaintiff declared in assumpsit upon a promise made the 26th March, 12 Geo. 1. The defendant pleaded, that, after the promise, and before the bill filed, viz. the 2nd of April, he tendered the money. The plaintiff replied, that, after making the promise, scilicet, 12th February, he filed his bill &c., and, upon demurrer, it was objected, that, by the plaintiff's own shewing, he had brought his action before the cause of action accrued ; for, the promise he declared on was on the 26th March, and his bill was filed on the 12th February before. Sed per curiam—as the plaintiff would not in evidence have been confined to the day in his declaration, there is no reason he should be more confined in pleading. Indeed, if this was a note, the day would be material and an essential part of the agreement, from which he could not vary ; but, in the case of a common assumpsit, the day is alleged only for form, and therefore the defendant cannot confine the plaintiff to the day alleged in the declaration. The statute of Jeofails is nothing to the purpose.] The objection, though perhaps not sustainable as a ground of demurrer—*Ring* v. *Rox-*

brough, 2 C. & J. 418—is nevertheless a good one in arrest of judgment. A rule nisi having been granted—

Bompas, Serjeant, now shewed cause.—The cases relied on are all cases where the day has been material. In assumpsit, however, except on bills of exchange and promissory notes, the day is not material. The plaintiff could not have succeeded at the trial, except on proof of a promise before the commencement of the action. In *Steward v. Layton,* 3 Dowl. P. C. 430, the record in an action for slander stated that the writ issued on the 4th June, and that the words were spoken on the 27th : and it was held that this discrepancy on the record was no ground for arresting the judgment.

Newman was heard in support of his rule.—The only additional authority to which he adverted was Rolle's Abridgment, p. 792, pl. 12, where it is said: " En un action de debt en un inferior court sur un bill obligatory, si le plea soit enter devant le debt devient due per le bill, scilicet, devant le temps de payment, et defendant plede al issue, et ceo trove pur plaintiffe, et judgment done accordant, uncore ceo est error. M. 11 Caroli, B. R., enter *Holden & Collett,* adjudge: En brief d' error sur un judgment en Nottingham, et le judgment revers accordant: Intratur, H. 10 Caroli, Rotulo 762; H. 11 Caroli, B. R., enter *Walker & Wigfall,* adjudge: En case de trespas sur judgment en Chesterfield, et enter *Marshall & Wigfield;* Intratur, Trin. 11 Caroli."

TINDAL, C. J.—It appears to me that no ground has been laid for arresting the judgment in this case. The statute 16 & 17 Car. 2, c. 8, applies only to cases where there is a mistake in the day, the day being material. In the present case, the day is perfectly immaterial. The statute therefore has no application. In *Cole v. Hawkins,* Str. 21, it was held, on demurrer, that the alleging a dif-

ferent day in the replication from that mentioned in the
declaration was no departure, the day not being material.
That case and *Matthews* v. *Spicer*, before cited, go on the
broad distinction between a verbal promise and a promissory note or bill of exchange.   In the case of bills and
notes the day is material: proof of a bill of a date different from that declared on would constitute a variance.
In indebitatus assumpsit the day is perfectly immaterial;
and we cannot assume that the jury have given damages in
respect of a cause of action accruing since the issuing of
the writ.   There is not therefore that discrepancy on the
face of the record which the law requires before the judgment can be arrested.   The late case in the Exchequer,
Steward v. *Layton*, is decisive on the point.

1836.

ARNALL
v.
ARNALL.

The rest of the court concurring—

Rule discharged.

———————

FURNIVAL *v.* STRINGER.

Monday,
June 13th.

THE plaintiff, being in the custody of the Warden of
the Fleet under an execution at the suit of a third person,
was brought up by writ of habeas corpus ad satisfaciendum issued at the instance of the defendant in this action,
and charged in execution for the taxed costs of a judgment of nonsuit herein.

In order to ren-
der a party
liable to be
brought up by
writ of habeas
corpus ad satis-
faciendum to be
charged in exe-
cution, it is not
necessary that
he should be in
custody *in the*

Goulburn, Serjeant, on a former day, obtained a rule
nisi for the plaintiff's discharge as to this action, on three
grounds—first, that the rule of court of 1654 did not
authorize the issuing of a habeas corpus to charge a
plaintiff in execution, but only to charge the *defendant*,
when already in custody *in the same suit*—secondly, that
the writ had been sued out without any affidavit to inform

particular suit:
and such writ
may issue at the
suit of a defen-
dant to charge
the plaintiff in
execution for
costs of a non-
suit.

No affidavit
is necessary to
authorise the
issuing of the

writ: nor need the number roll of the judgment be indorsed thereon.

the court of the ground for the detention of the plaintiff—thirdly, that the number roll of the judgment was not indorsed upon the writ. He cited *Smith* v. *Sandys*, 5 N. & M. 59, where it was held that a defendant in custody of the marshal cannot be charged in execution by a plaintiff in another suit by a side-bar rule to the marshal to acknowledge him in custody; and that a proceeding to charge a defendant in custody by a side-bar rule, where he is not in custody in the particular suit, is not merely irregular, but is wholly void and inoperative, and cannot be waived by lapse of time.

Spankie, Serjeant, shewed cause.—The party has been regularly brought up. The rule referred to provides " that a habeas corpus ad satisfaciendum may be granted to the warden of the Fleet, or &c., returnable on a day certain; the number roll of the judgment to be indorsed upon the writ by the attorney who sues it out; and such writs to be a cause of detainer." That rule has been duly complied with, except in respect to the indorsement of the number roll of the judgment, which is now no longer required. In the case cited, the objection was that the party was sought to be charged by a side-bar rule: it was assumed that, had he been brought up by writ of habeas corpus, the proceeding would have been regular. If the remedy under the rule of 1654, were confined to the case of a defendant, and to one already in custody in the particular suit, the plaintiff in an action of tort would have no other remedy for his costs than by bringing an action upon the judgment for them. With respect to the want of an affidavit to inform the court as to the cause of the detainer; that by the practice of the courts never has been required: nor is it reasonable that it should be; for, the party may, when brought up, shew that he is improperly charged.

Goulburn, Serjeant, in support of his rule.—The ques-

tion is, whether or not the defendant had of his own mere
motion, without shewing any ground, by affidavit or otherwise, a right to sue out this writ in order to bring up the
plaintiff and charge him in execution for the costs of the
nonsuit. There is no precedent to warrant it; and the
case is wholly untouched by the rule of 1654. Unless in
custody in the particular suit, the party cannot be brought
up by such means: the proper course would have been for
the defendant to have filed a declaration against the
plaintiff under the 4 & 5 William & Mary, c. 21, s. 2, a
statute that was passed for the very purpose: the declaration then would have operated as a detainer. In the
King's Bench, it appears, the practice is to do this by a
side-bar rule; and that only where the party is already in
custody in the particular cause. In *Smith* v. *Sandys*,
Lord Denman says: "The proceeding by side-bar rule
does not operate to charge a prisoner in execution, *unless
he be at the time in custody in the particular suit.*"

TINDAL, C. J.—The question in this case is whether
or not the rule of court which has been acted upon from
1654 down to the present time, has been complied with.
The rule provides "that a habeas corpus ad satisfaciendum may be granted to the warden of the Fleet, or &c.,
returnable on a day certain; the number roll of the judgment to be indorsed upon the writ by the attorney who
sues it out; and such writs to be a cause of detainer."
The first objection urged on the part of the defendant, is,
that, in this instance the writ of habeas corpus was obtained, not against the defendant, but against *the plaintiff;*
and it has been strenuously contended that the above rule
applies exclusively to the case of *a defendant, in custody
in the cause.* I see nothing in the rule to limit its operation to the case of a defendant; and, in the case of a
plaintiff, it is impossible to assume that he is *in custody in
the cause.* The only interpretation I am capable of putting

upon the rule is, that it applies as well to a plaintiff sought to be charged with costs where he is in custody at another's suit, as to a defendant.—It is then said that a writ of habeas corpus should in no case be issued without an affidavit to inform the court of the circumstances under which the aid of its process is sought. The usual course on a habeas corpus ad respondendum or habeas corpus ad satisfaciendum is thus—the party is taken before a judge, who indorses his fiat on the writ. If the judge saw reason to call for any further information, he would do so. When he comes before the court, the party may shew cause against his recommitment. The secondary marks the writ, and, before he does so, he sees the postea, with the prothonotary's allocatur thereon indorsed for the sum claimed for costs, and in general also a judgment paper. It seems to me, therefore, that every possible precaution is taken for the benefit of the prisoner. It is then said that the defendant might have brought an action for his costs, instead of charging the plaintiff in execution. This, however, would be a very circuitous and expensive mode of proceeding, and is never resorted to except where the judgment is more than a year and a day old, or under very particular circumstances. A further objection taken is, that the number roll of the judgment is not indorsed upon the writ. That, however, since the new rules is no longer necessary. The case of *Smith* v. *Sandys* appears to me to go very far to shew that all that was necessary has been done in the present case.

GASELEE, J.—The writ itself states the object for which it was sued out.

The rest of the court concurring—

Rule discharged.

1836.

Monday,
June 13th.

WORTHINGTON, and Mary, his Wife v. WIGLEY.

DEBT on a bond dated the 24th June, 1831, conditioned for the payment, by one Grierson and the defendant, or either of them, on the 31st January, 1832, of 552*l.*
19*s.*, and interest.

The defendant craved oyer of the bond and condition,
and pleaded—first, as to the sum of 276*l.* 13*s.*, parcel of
the said sum of 552*l.* 19*s.* and interest in the said condition mentioned, that, *after the said 31st January,* 1832,
and whilst the said Mary was sole and unmarried, and before the commencement of this suit, to wit, on the 18th
March, 1833, the said Mary, for and on account of the
said sum of 276*l.* 13*s.*, parcel &c., and the cause of action
in respect thereof, made and drew her three several bills
of exchange in writing, respectively bearing date the day
and year last aforesaid, and by each of the said bills respectively required the defendant, at the respective periods of four, five, and six years respectively after the
dates of the said bills (neither of which periods had elapsed
at the time of the commencement of this suit), to pay to
the order of the said Mary the respective sums of 30*l.*
each, amounting together to the sum of 90*l.*, part and
parcel of the said sum of 276*l.* 13*s.*, parcel &c., and also
a certain other bill of exchange in writing, bearing date the
day and year last aforesaid, whereby the said Mary required
the defendant to pay to the said Mary the sum of 186*l.*
13*s.* (being the residue of the said sum of 276*l.* 13*s.*), in manner following, that is to say, the sum of 30*l.* on the 18th
March, 1840, and the further sum of 40*l.* on the 18th March
in every succeeding year, until the full sum of 186*l.* 13*s.*
be fully paid and satisfied, neither of which last mentioned
days had elapsed at the time of the commencement of this
suit; and the defendant then accepted the said four several
last mentioned bills respectively so drawn as aforesaid, and

After verdict
for the plaintiff
in debt on bond
(the defendant
not appearing at
the trial), the
court granted a
new trial on the
ground that in
the issue deli-
vered the pleas
were not dated,
pursuant to the
rule of Hilary
Term, 4 Will. 4.

delivered the same to the said Mary, and she then took
the same for and on account of the said sum of 276*l.* 13*s.*,
parcel &c., and the causes of action in respect thereof—
verification.   Secondly—as to the residue of the said sum
of 552*l.* 19*s.*, parcel &c., and interest, in the said condition
mentioned—that, after the said 31st January, 1832, in the
said condition mentioned, and whilst the said Mary was
sole and unmarried, and before the commencement of this
suit, to wit, on the 1st January, 1835, the defendant and
his co-obligor paid to the said Mary; and, after the said
marriage, and before the commencement of this suit, to
wit, on the 1st January, 1836, the defendant and his co-
obligee paid to the plaintiffs and the said Mary whilst unmarried, and the plaintiffs after their marriage respectively
accepted and received from the defendant and his co-obligee
divers monies, to wit, to the amount of the residue of the
said sum of 552*l.* 19*s.* in the said condition mentioned, and
all interest then due thereon, in full satisfaction and discharge of the said residue of the sum of 552*l.* 19*s.* and interest, and all the causes of action in respect thereof—
verification.

At the trial, no person appearing on the part of the defendant, the plaintiff had a verdict, in the usual way, for
the penalty of the bond, and 1*s.* damages for the detention.

Miller, for the defendant, on a former day, obtained a
rule for a new trial, upon an affidavit stating that the issue
had been delivered with the pleas not dated; and therefore
the defendant, conceiving the proceedings to be a nullity, did
not appear to make his defence.   He referred to the rule of
Hilary Term, 4 Will. 4, First general rules and regulations,
s. 1, which provides that " Every pleading, as well as the
declaration, shall be intitled of the day of the month and
year when the same was pleaded, and shall bear no other
time. or date: and every declaration and other pleading

shall also be entered on the record made up for trial, and on the judgment-roll, under the date of the day of the month and year when the same respectively took place, and without reference to any other time or date, unless otherwise specially ordered by the court or a judge."

Atcherley, Serjeant, shewed cause.—The want of a date is perfectly immaterial in this case: or, if irregular, the irregularity should have been pointed out sooner. [*Tindal,* C. J.—Why did not the plaintiff amend at the trial? The date of the plea may in some cases be material.] The rule referred to defines what is intended to be required. The date is to be entered on the record, and upon the judgment roll : it is not in terms required to be on the issue delivered. The only object of the date is, to give information to the opposite party. The defendant knows when he pleads. [*Tindal,* C. J.—The defendant knows *what* he pleads: as well might it be said that the issue delivered need not for that reason contain the pleas at all.] The simple question is, whether or not the mere omission to transcribe the date of the pleas into the issue delivered, is such an irregularity as to render its delivery a mere nullity. At all events, it is no ground for a motion for a new trial: the defendant should have returned the issue.

Miller, in support of his rule, was stopped by the court.

TINDAL, C. J.—The simple question here is whether or not there is such a variance between the issue delivered and the record itself as the defendant has a right to stand on. The issue should doubtless be a faithful transcript of the pleadings. The rule requires all pleadings to be intitled of the day and year when pleaded, and to be so entered of record. The omission, therefore, of the date

1836.

WORTHINGTON
*.
WIGLEY.

of these pleas was an evident irregularity, of which the defendant might avail himself at any time, if the imperfection were in the record. The issue is all that is communicated to the defendant before the trial. Although the objection is certainly one of extreme subtilty, yet, inasmuch as the rule declares that which has been omitted to be essential, and the plaintiff has not thought fit to amend when he might have done so, I think the defendant has a right to stand upon the rule.

The rest of the court concurring—

> Rule absolute—the defendant undertaking to accept short notice of trial.

1837.

Friday,
Jan. 20th,

A plea of part payment, or the delivery of bills, in satisfaction of a bond, after the day on which the money was by the condition made payable, is bad on general demurrer.

The plaintiffs afterwards delivered a general demurrer to the pleas—on the ground that the giving of the bills, as stated in the first plea, could not satisfy or extinguish the plaintiffs' claim on the bond, or suspend their right to sue thereon; and, as to the second plea, that payment of a part of the sum mentioned in the condition after the day thereby appointed for payment, was no bar to the action.

Swann, in support of the demurrer.—The action is brought on a bond conditioned for the payment of 552*l.* 19*s.* and interest on the 31st January, 1832. The first plea, as to part of that sum, sets up by way of answer the delivery of certain bills of exchange, and the second, payment of part of the sum mentioned in the condition, *after the bond became absolute,* in satisfaction of the bond. *Davis* v. *Gyde,* 2 Ad. & E. 624, is a distinct authority to shew that these pleas afford no answer to the action. There, to an avowry for rent, the plaintiff pleaded in bar, as to 10*l.,* part of the rent, that he made his promissory note for that amount, payable to the defendant, at two months, which had not expired at the time when &c., and delivered the same to the defendant, who received the note for and on account of the said sum, and at the said time when &c. held the note for that sum ; and it was held that the plea was no answer as to the 10*l.*, rent being a debt of a higher degree than a debt by simple contract. Lord Denman said —" *Gage* v. *Acton*, 1 Salk. 325, 1 Com. R. 67, 1 Lord Raym. 515, Freem. 512, 515, Carth. 511, Lord Holt, 309, 12 Mod. 290, decided that a debt due upon a bond may be set off against rent, because the latter is a debt of equal degree with the former. Here, the promissory note being a debt of an *inferior* degree to the rent, the receipt of the note can have created no extinguishment of the rent:" and Littledale, J., says : " In *Hayford* v. *Andrews*, Cro. Eliz. 697, it was determined, that, to debt on bond conditioned for payment on a certain day, a plea that the plaintiff gave a longer day of payment, was bad." In Comyns's Digest, " *Pleader*," (2 W. 46), it is laid down that to debt by bill, by the statute 4 & 5 Anne, c. 16, the defendant may plead payment : but he cannot plead *another bond given in satisfaction* to debt on bond ; nor an agreement by *parol* to give a longer day of payment (a). So, in *Doe d. Gregson* v. *Harrison*, 2 T. R. 425, it was held that a parol license was no discharge of a condition in a lease not to underlet without leave in writing. The second plea in substance amounts to a plea of *part* payment after the day mentioned in the condition, which is clearly no bar to the action.

Miller, in support of the pleas.—Taken together the pleas amount to a plea of solvit post diem, which would be an answer to the action ; for, it is not to be assumed that the bills will not be paid when due. There is nothing to

---

(a) A specialty security is not waived by a promissory note taken for the balance of the amount of interest—Curtis v. Rush, 2 Ves. & B. 416. And see Balston v. Baxter, Cro. Eliz. 304.

prevent a party from accepting bills in satisfaction of a bond debt.

PER CURIAM.—The pleas are addressed to the condition of the bond, and attempt to shew a performance of it. The bond, however, having become absolute, the penalty is the debt. Consequently both pleas are bad.

Judgment for the plaintiff.

END OF TRINITY TERM.

IN THE HOUSE OF LORDS.

The Bishop of MEATH, and JAMES ALEXANDER, Clerk,
v. The Marquess of WINCHESTER.

[Error from Exch. Ch., Ireland.]

1836.

Wednesday,
July 6th.

THIS was an action of quare impedit brought by the
Marquess of Winchester, the plaintiff below, in the court

In quare impedit to recover the presentation to the church of K. the advowson whereof was claimed to be part of the temporalities of the Bishop of Meath, a case dated the 28th February, 1695, purporting to be a case stated for the opinion of counsel on the part of Anthony Dopping, then Bishop of Meath, wherein it was, among other things, stated, "that, in the year 1637, Ulick, Earle of Clanricarde, granted to Dr. Donnellan, incumbent of Rathweir, his executors and administrators, the next presentation to the rectory and vicarage of Rathweir, dated the 28th March, 1637 ; that, in 1642, both rectory and vicarage being void by the death of Dr. Donnellan, his widow and executrix presented pro hac vice tantum William Barry to both, who was instituted by the Bishop June 13th, 1642, but not inducted till the 27th of February, 1660 ; and that by a mandate from the bishop's successor, the bishop that instituted being dead before William Barry's induction." This case was produced by a descendant of Anthony Dopping, into whose possession it had come from the family mansion of the Doppings, where it was found among other papers, the house being occupied by a member of the Dopping family:—Held, that the case, being found in a place in which and under the care of persons with whom papers of Bishop Dopping might naturally and reasonably be expected to be found, was properly receivable in evidence against the bishop's successors:—Held, also, that the grant referred to in the case, being found in the same place and under precisely the same circumstances, was also admissible.

By letters patent, dated at Drogheda, the 5th January in the 9th year of his reign, King Edward the Fourth granted to William Sherwood, Bishop of Meath, and his successors, the advowson as well of the rectory as of the vicarage of the parish church of Rathweir, county of Meath. By an act passed in a parliament held at Drogheda in the 10 Hen. 7, it was enacted "that there be resumed, seized, and taken into the king our sovereign lord's hands all manors, lordships, &c., *advowsons of churches, free chapels,* &c., and all other manner of profits, hereditaments, and commodities whereof our said sovereign lord, or any of his noble progenitors, kings of England, was at any time seised in fee simple or fee tail from the last day of the reign of King Edward 2 to this present act:—Held, that this grant of Edward 4 fell within the operation of the above statute of Henry 7, and was avoided thereby ; although it was contended—first, that the statute revoked no grants made by any kings except those who were the progenitors of Henry 7 in the strict sense of that word, and that Edward 4 was not a progenitor of that king—secondly,

of Common Pleas in Ireland, in Easter Term, 1829,
against the Lord Bishop of Meath and the Rev. James
Alexander, to recover the advowson of the parish church
of Killucan, otherwise Rathweir, in the diocese of Meath,
and county of Westmeath, in Ireland. The questions
arose only on the fifth count, and the pleadings and evidence relating to that count. The fifth count began by
setting out from the year 1544 to the year 1626 the pedi-
gree of the earls of Clanricarde, which the defendants

that the statute did not extend to grants of which such progenitors were seised jure privato only,
and that Edward 4 *was* seised jure privato of the advowson in question—thirdly, that it did not
extend to revoke grants to corporations, whether sole or aggregate—and lastly, that it did not
extend to any grants but those under the great seal either in England or Ireland, and that the
grant of the advowson in question was made under neither.

Held, also, that the effect of the resumption of the grant of Edward 4 by the statute of Henry
7, was, to re-append the advowson to the manor of Rathweir.

In quare impedit, the plaintiff, in his fifth count, alleged that Richard, fourth Earl of Clanricarde, was in 1626 seised in fee of the manor of Rathweir, to which the advowson of the church
of Killucan, otherwise Rathweir, was then appendant ; and, after deducing title through the successive earls, averred that one H. P. W. and himself became possessed of the advowson in gross
for a term of five hundred years; and that, in 1810, H. P. W. died, leaving the plaintiff him surviving, who thereupon "became and was possessed of the advowson for the residue of the term;"
that the church became vacant; and that it then belonged to him to present. The bishop in his
fifth plea (averring that he, as Bishop of Meath, was seised of the advowson in gross in right of
his see), and the clerk in his eighth plea, traversed this allegation in these terms—" without this
that the plaintiff is possessed of the said advowson of the said church of Killucan, otherwise Rathweir, in manner and form as the said plaintiff hath in his said fifth count alleged. The clerk
concluded his fifth plea with a special traverse that Michael, the fifth earl, was seised ; and his
seventh plea with a special traverse that it now belonged to the plaintiff to present:—Held, that
a fine stated to have been levied in Trinity Term, 1 Jac. 2, by William, seventh Earl of Clann-
carde, and Hester, his wife, to John Brown, Gerard Dillon, and Anthony Mulledy, and the
heirs of the said John Brown, of the manors of Rathweir and Killucan, with the appurtenances,
and also of the advowson and right of patronage of the parish of Killucan, was not admissible in
evidence under the above issues—the traverse being, by the fair and natural import of the plaintiff's allegation, confined to the possession of the plaintiff by reason of the term for years, and of
his surviving his co-joint-tenant in the term: and that, admitting that the averment in the declaration would amount to an allegation, that, by reason of all the various steps in the title of the
plaintiff which were set out in the fifth count, the plaintiff was possessed of the right to the advowson, and admitting the traverse to be equally extensive, and to put all those steps of the title
in issue, still, by analogy to the rules of pleading, the utmost effect that could be given to such a
traverse is, that it is a simple denial of the different allegations of the descent and of the other
steps of the title, so as thereby to put the plaintiff to the proof of his whole declaration ; but that
the traverse would not admit of new affirmative evidence on the part of the defendant, taking
the title out of the plaintiff, and vesting it in another person.

Held, also, that the legal effect of such fine as a bar to the action of quare impedit, was a matter of law merely, and not of fact ; and therefore, if the fine were received in evidence, it ought
not to be left to the jury to say whether or not it operated as a bar to the action.

Held, also, that the fine did not, if properly received in evidence, absolutely of itself bar the
action; not on the ground of estoppel, because the parties to the suit did not both claim respectively
under the parties to the fine ; nor as a conveyance, there being ground for presuming that it was
a conveyance by way of mortgage and that the mortgage had been paid off, and there being no
evidence of any dealing with the advowson or presentation by the conusees of the fine, or any one
claiming under them.

below admitted. It then alleged that Richard, fourth
Earl of Clanricarde, was in 1626 seised in fee of the
manor of Rathweir, to which the advowson of the church
of Killucan, otherwise Rathweir, was then appendant; that
the church became vacant, and that Richard, the fourth
earl, presented one Edward Donnellan, his clerk, who
was admitted, instituted, and inducted; that, in 1635,
Richard the fourth earl died seised, leaving Ulick de
Burgh his only issue male, who became fifth earl, and to
whom the manor to which the advowson of the church
was appendant descended as heir-at-law; that, in 1641,
the Irish rebellion broke out against King Charles the
First; that, in 1652, the manor to which the advowson was
appendant was, on account of the rebellion, sequestered
to the use of King Charles the Second; that, in 1657, the
manor continuing sequestered, Ulick, the fifth earl (called
Marquis Clanricarde) died without issue male, leaving
Richard his heir at-law (whose descent was set out in the
declaration, and admitted by the defendants below), who
became sixth earl; that, by letters patent bearing date
the 8th April, 14 Car. 2, that King granted to Richard,
sixth earl (inter alia), the manor of Rathweir, with the
advowson which was then appendant thereto, to the use
of Richard, sixth earl, in tail male, with remainders over;
that the Irish act of parliament 14 & 15 Car. 2, confirmed
the letters patent, saving the rights of persons claiming
paramount the crown: that, in 1666, Richard, sixth earl,
died without issue male, leaving William, his brother, him
surviving, who became seventh earl, and, being entitled
under the uses limited by the letters patent, became
seised of the manor to which the advowson was appendant, in tail male, with remainders over; that, in 1670,
William, seventh earl, by lease and release with warranty,
conveyed the manor (excepting the advowson) to Sir
Patrick Mulledy in fee; that William, seventh earl, then
became seised in tail of the advowson in gross, with re-

mainders over; that, in 1687, William, seventh earl, died
so seised, leaving his eldest son Richard, who became
eighth earl, and was seised in tail of the advowson; that,
by the act 2 Ann. c. 26, advowsons held by persons professing the Roman Catholic religion were vested in the
crown, according to the estate of the patron, till abju-
ration; that, in 1708, Richard, eighth earl, died seised
without issue, leaving his brother John, ninth earl, who
being entitled in tail under the uses limited, but professing
the Roman Catholic religion, the advowson vested under
the act of 2 Ann. in Queen Anne, and afterwards in King
George the First; that, in 1722, John, ninth earl, died,
leaving his son Michael, tenth earl, who abjuring and
conforming, the estate of the crown in the advowson
determined, and Michael, tenth earl, became seised in
tail; that, in 1726, Michael, tenth earl, died seised, leaving John Smith, his son, eleventh earl, to whom the advowson descended, and who became seised in tail; that,
in 1745, John Smith, eleventh earl, granted the advowson
to Eaton Stannard and Robert French, and their heirs, to
the use of John Smith, eleventh earl, for life, with remainders over; that, by an English act of parliament, 10
Geo. 3, the advowson was vested in Sir Francis Vincent
and William Talbot, in fee, discharged of the uses of the
deed of 1745, to the use of John Smith, eleventh earl, for
life, remainder to his eldest son, Lord Dunkellyn, for life,
with remainders over, and with a power to Lord Dunkellyn
to create a term for securing a jointure; that, thereupon,
in 1770, John Smith, eleventh earl, became seised of the
advowson for life, with remainders over; that, in 1782,
John Smith, eleventh earl, died seised for life, leaving
Henry, Lord Dunkellyn, his eldest son, him surviving, who
became twelfth earl, and seised for life of the advowson,
with remainders over; that, in 1785, Henry, twelfth earl,
by a marriage settlement, in exercise of the power given to
him by the said act of 10 Geo. 3, demised the advowson for

securing a jointure, to Henry Penruddock Wyndham and the plaintiff below, for a term of five hundred years, to commence from the death of himself the said Henry, twelfth earl; that Henry, twelfth earl, married, and in 1797 died, leaving his wife him surviving and still living; that thereby Henry Penruddock Wyndham and the plaintiff below became possessed of the advowson in gross for the said term; that, in 1810, Henry Penruddock Wyndham died, leaving the plaintiff below him surviving, who thereupon became and was possessed of the advowson for the residue of the term; that, in 1828, by the death of the Rev. Henry Wynne, the late incumbent, the church became vacant; that it then belonged to the plaintiff below to present; and that the defendants below disturbed him therein.

To this count the bishop pleaded thirteen pleas; the clerk, eight. The sixth, seventh, eighth, ninth, tenth, and eleventh pleas of the bishop, and the sixth plea of the clerk, were not material to the questions raised on the record.

The bishop's first plea, alleging, by way of inducement, that he was seised of the advowson in gross in right of his see, concluded with a special traverse of the appendancy of the advowson to the manor of Rathweir. The second, after the same inducement, specially traversed that Richard, fourth earl, was seised of the manor with the advowson appendant. The third, after alleging, by way of inducement, that he, the bishop, was seised of the advowson in gross in right of his see, and that Anthony Dopping, one of his predecessors, collated Edward Donnellan, concluded with a traverse, that Edward Donnellan was admitted and instituted on the presentation of Richard, fourth earl. The fourth, after the like inducement as in the first plea, traversed that the manor with the advowson appendant was seised and sequestered to the use of Charles the Second. The fifth, after the like inducement, traversed that Charles the Second granted to Richard, sixth earl, the manor with the advowson appendant. The twelfth, after the like inducement, traversed that the plaintiff below was possessed of the advowson. The thirteenth after pleading, by way of inducement, a grant by Edward the Fourth of the advowson in gross to the see of Meath, and that Anthony, bishop, collated the Rev. Edward Donnellan, concluded with a special traverse that Edward Donnellan was admitted and instituted on the presentation of Richard, fourth earl.

The clerk's
pleas.

The clerk's first plea, alleging, by way of inducement, that he was parson canonically imparsonate on the collation of the defendant below, the Bishop of Meath, and that the bishop and his predecessors were seised in fee of the advowson in gross, in right of the bishoprick; that the church became vacant, and that he, the clerk, defendant below, was collated by the bishop, the defendant below; concluded, like the bishop's first plea, with a special traverse of the appendancy of the advowson. The second, third, and fourth pleas, after inducements the same as that in the clerk's first plea, severally concluded with the same special traverse as the bishop's second, third, and fourth pleas respectively. The fifth plea, after the same inducement as in the first, concluded with a special traverse that Earl Michael was seised. The seventh plea, after the same inducement as in the first, concluded with a special traverse that it now belonged to the plaintiff below to present a fit person to the church. The eighth plea, after the same inducement, concluded, like the bishop's twelfth plea, with a special traverse that the plaintiff was possessed of the advowson.

On all these pleas, issues were joined.

At the trial of the cause, the plaintiff below relied on the title of the Earls of Clanricarde, who derived the property from John King, to whom it had been granted by James the First. In support of this title, the plaintiff

below produced, among other evidence, two documents—
one, a parchment deed, bearing date the 28th March,
1637, purporting to be a grant of Ulick, fifth Earl of Clanricarde, to Dr. Edward Donnellan, of the then next
avoidance of the rectory and vicarage of Rathweir, otherwise Killucan—the other, dated the 28th February, 1695,
purporting to be a case stated for the opinion of counsel
on the part of Anthony Dopping, Bishop of Meath,
wherein it was, among other things, stated, on the part of
the said bishop, "that, in the year 1637, Ulick, Earl of
Clanricarde, granted to Dr. Donnellan, incumbent of
Rathweir, his executors and administrators, the next presentation to the rectory and vicarage of Rathweir, dated
the 28th March, 1637; that, in 1642, both rectory and
vicarage being void by the death of Dr. Donnellan, his
widow and executrix presented pro hac vice tantum William Barry to both, who was instituted by the bishop June
13th, 1642, but not inducted till the 27th February, 1660;
and that by a mandate from the bishop's successor, the
bishop that instituted being dead before William Barry's
induction."

The circumstances under which these documents were
found, were stated as follows upon a bill of exceptions:—
Anthony Dopping, being examined on oath as a witness
on the part of the plaintiff, deposed that he was a descendant of Anthony Dopping, formerly bishop of Meath,
and that he had in his possession several papers, which
were handed to him as coming from Lowton House,
where the Dopping family papers were kept; that Lowton
House was the family mansion of the Doppings; that the
papers in his possession were handed to him by John
Darcy of High Park, a relation of the Dopping family;
that the two documents produced by him (the documents
in question) were handed to him among the said papers
by the said John Darcy at a Major Sirr's; and that he
never saw the said two documents, or any of them, at

1836.

The Bishop of
MEATH
v.
The Marq. of
WINCHESTER.

Grant of Ulick,
fifth Earl of
Clanricarde,
dated 1637, and
case stated for
counsel's opi-
nion in 1695.

Circumstances
under which the
above grant and
case were found.

Lowton House. John Darcy deposed, that he handed a
parcel of papers to Anthony Dopping, the last witness;
that he got the said parcel of papers from one Sir William
Betham; and that there was a paper round them. Sir
William Betham deposed, that he found a parcel of papers
at Lowton House among other papers, and that the Rev.
Mr. Sirr was with him; that he found the said parcel of
papers in a room with other papers, and that he handed
the said parcel of papers to the said Mr. Sirr on or about
the 28th of October, 1828; that Lowton House belonged
to or was inhabited by a Mrs. Dopping, a middle-aged
lady; that he put no mark on the said parcel of papers,
but that he took copies of them; that, at the time of finding the said parcel of papers, he found several visitation
books of the diocese of Meath, particularly one of the year
1616, by George Bishop of Meath; that there were in
the same room several other papers relating to the see of
Meath, several of which were in the same parcel which he
brought away, and that the said two documents produced
by the said Anthony Dopping above mentioned were in
the said parcel of papers; that he was at Lowton House
from two o'clock on Monday till two o'clock on the following day; that he went there on the part of the said Mr.
Sirr and John Darcy, and that he never informed the said
Bishop of Meath that the said papers or books, or any of
them, were at Lowton, but that he shewed copies of some
of them to the plaintiff's agent, and told him the said papers
and books were at Lowton. George Brabazon deposed, that
he was registrar in the registry office of the diocese of
Meath, at Navan; that there was no register of ecclesiastical or other records, except one roll, anterior to the
year 1717; that the said registry office was the proper
place where the visitation books of the diocese, and entry
of all presentations, admissions, institutions, and collations
to ecclesiastical benefices within the diocese, and various
other papers and records relative to the said diocese, and

the several ecclesiastical benefices within the same, should be kept; but that such were not to be found, and were not preserved in the said registry office relating to a period anterior to 1717, the reason of which circumstance he was unable to explain.

Among various documents which tended to shew that the property originally belonged to the crown, the plaintiff below produced an attested and compared copy of an original inquisition, taken before the barons of the Exchequer of Ireland, at Dublin, in the twenty-third year of the reign of King Henry the Eighth, whereby it was found that King Edward the Fourth was seised in his demesne as of fee, the day on which he died, of the manor of Rathweir in the county of Meath, with all its appurtenances, and had issue Elizabeth, Anna, Cecilia, and Bridget, his four daughters; that, being so seised, he died on the 9th April, in the twenty-third year of his reign; that, after his death, the said manor, with all its appurtenances, descended to his said daughters in right of heirship; and that afterwards King Henry the Seventh, in the first year of his reign, took to wife Elizabeth, one the said daughters, by virtue of which King Henry the Seventh and Elizabeth, the queen, his wife, as in right and title of the same queen, entered into the same manor, with all its appurtenances, and were thereof seised in their demesne as of fee, as in right of the said Elizabeth, the queen: and it was thereby further found that the said King Henry the Seventh and Elizabeth his queen had issue King Henry the Eighth, and that the said Anna, Cecilia, and Bridget, died without heirs of their bodies lawfully begotten, in the lifetime of the said queen Elizabeth; that afterwards the said queen Elizabeth died, viz. on the 18th February, in the eighteenth year of the reign of Henry the Seventh; after whose death the said King Henry the Seventh continued in possession of the said manor, with all its appurtenances, during his lifetime, and

1836.

The Bishop of
MEATH
v.
The Marq. of
WINCHESTER.

Inquisition of
23 Hen. 8.

1836.

The Bishop of
MEATH
v.
The Marq. of
WINCHESTER.

Letters patent
of 9 Edw. 4.

died so seised, viz. on 21st April, in the twenty-fourth
year of his reign; after whose death, the said manor, with
all its appurtenances, descended, and ought to descend,
to the said Henry the Eighth as son and heir of the said
Elizabeth his mother: and further, that one William
Darcy, of Plattyn, knight, upon the possession of the said
King Henry the Eighth, in the manor aforesaid, with all
its appurtenances, entered, intruded, and had ingress on
the 1st January, in the first year of the reign of King
Henry the Eighth, and the rents and profits of the said
manor arising and growing, from the said first January to
that time, took and levied, in contempt of the said King
Henry the Eighth.

The defendants below relied chiefly on an attested and
compared copy of letters patent of King Edward the
Fourth, dated at Drogheda, on the 5th January, in the
ninth year of his reign, to William Sherwood, Bishop of
Meath, and his successors, of the advowson as well of the
rectory as of the vicarage of the parish church of Rathweir,
county of Meath, in the following words:—"To all to
whom the present letters shall come, health. Know ye
that we of our special grace, with the assent of our very
dear cousin, John, Earl of Wigram, deputy of our very
dear brother George, Duke of Clarence, and locum tenens
of our Lord, have given and granted to the venerable
father in Christ, William, Bishop of Meath, advowson as
well of the rectory as of the vicarage of the parish church
of Rathweir, in the county of Meath, to have and to hold
the advowson of the rectory and vicarage of the church
aforesaid to the aforesaid bishop and his successors for
ever, any statute, act, or ordinance to the contrary made,
edited, or ordained, notwithstanding: in testimony of which
we have caused these our letters to be made. Witness the
aforesaid deputy, at Drogheda, the ninth day of January,
in the ninth year of our reign: Eustace."

This document was in the same form as one produced

by the plantiff below, purporting to be letters patent whereby Edward the Third had granted the manor of Rathweir, with all advowsons thereto belonging, to John D'Arcy and Johanna his wife, in tail male.

The defendants below also produced an attested copy of a fine sur conusance de droit come ceo &c., bearing date the Morrow of the Holy Trinity, in the first year of the reign of James the Second, with proclamations, and levied by William, seventh Earl of Clanricarde, and Hester, Countess of Clanricarde, his wife, to John Brown, Gerard Dillon, and Anthony Mulledy, Esqrs., of, among other things, the disposition and right of patronage of the parish church of Killucan, for the consideration of 6,200*l.* therein named, and with a warranty by the said earl and countess. It had appeared, however, on the evidence of the plaintiff below, that Richard the eighth earl had conveyed the advowson, in 1699, to John Morgan; and that, in 1744, John Morgan reconveyed it to John Smith, eleventh earl. The defendants below produced also an entry in the visitation book of the diocese of Armagh, of the collation to the rectory and vicarage of Killucan of the Rev. Anthony Dopping, by his father, Anthony Dopping, Bishop of Meath, in 1695, upon the death of W. Barry, the preceding incumbent.

Fine levied by
William, se-
venth Earl of
Clanricarde,
Trinity Term, 1
Jac. 2.

For the plaintiff below, it was contended that no issue had been raised on the pleadings under which the fine levied by William, the seventh earl, was admissible in evidence: and, in answer to the grant of the advowson by Edward IV to the see of Meath, he relied on an attested copy of an act of parliament passed in a parliament held at Drogheda, in the tenth year of Henry VII, in the words following:—" Item, prayen the Commons, in consideration of the great and divers robberies, murders, burnings, ravishing of wives and maidens, the universal and damnable extortion as to coign lyve and pay, had, used, and continued within the poor land of Ireland, with many other

intolerable oppressions and extortions over the poor innocent and true subjects, the which cannot be reformed and
punished without the king's great and royal provision for
the repressing of the same, which cannot be done without
great costs and charges; and, forasmuch as his noble
grace intendeth by the grace of Almighty God to order
and reduce the said land to his whole and perfect obei-
sance; and the great part of his revenues of the said land
being adiminished and granted to divers persons, *such as
for the most part do full little service for the commonweal,*
for lack of said revenues the land could not be defended
for the destruction of the Irish enemies : therefore be it
ordained, enacted, and established by authority of this
present parliament, that there be resumed, seized, and
taken into the king our sovereign lord's hands all manors,
lordships, castles, garrisons, fortresses, *advowsons of
churches,* free chapels, messuages, lands, tenements, rents,
services, moors, meadows, pastures, woods, rivers, waters, mills, dove-cotes, parks, forests, warrens, customs,
cocketts, fees, fee-farms, and all other manner of profits,
hereditaments, and commodities whereof our said sovereign lord, or any of his noble progenitors, kings of England, was at any time seised in fee-simple or fee-tail, from
the last day of the reign of Edward II to this present act;
and, by the same authority, all manner of feoffments, gifts
in tail, grants, leases for term of life or term of years,
releases, confirmations, annuities, fees, pensions, escheats,
wrecks, waifs, reversions of all and every of the aforesaid
honors, manors, lordships, and of all others as before it
is specified, or of any parcel of them, as well by authority
of parliament as by any letters patent made under the
great seal of England or of Ireland, to any person or persons, by whatsoever name or names they be named, jointly
or severally, from the said day be resumed, revoked, annulled, and deemed void and of none effect in law." In
a parchment writing attached to the above act, there was

a saving to William Darcy of Rathweir, and his heirs male, of a grant made in the ninth year of the reign of Edward III, to John Darcy and Johanna his wife, of the manor of Rathweir, with its appurtenances, and a saving of all grants to the Archbishop of Dublin, the Bailiff of Dundalk, and others. As to the presentation by the Bishop of Meath, it appeared that the suit of quare impedit had been brought on the collation of Anthony Dopping, in 1695, but that it terminated in a compromise on an allegation of popery in the then Earl of Clanricarde.

The defendants below contended that the alleged act of 10 Hen. 7 did not revoke the grant by Edward IV to the see of Meath, among other reasons, because the alleged act only avoided grants made jure coronæ, and the evidence shewed Edward IV to have been seised of the property and to have made the grant as of his private estate, and not jure coronæ. The evidence from which the defendants below drew this inference was in substance as follows:—That, after the conquest of Ireland, Henry II granted the land of Meath to Hugh de Lacy in fee; that, by the forfeiture of the De Lacys, the manor of Rathweir, with the advowson, vested in the crown, and was granted by Edward II to Roger Mortimer, Earl of March; that the said Roger Mortimer, on his attainder, forfeited to Edward III; that that attainder was reversed, and the manor revested in Roger Mortimer, grandson of the attainted Earl; that certain liberties and privileges were confirmed to Roger, son of the preceding, by Henry V; that the last-mentioned Roger Mortimer had issue Edmond Mortimer, Ann, and Ellynor; that Edmond and Ellynor dying without issue, Ann was married to Richard, Earl of Cambridge (son of Edmnod Langley, Duke of York, fifth son of Edward III), who had issue Richard Plantagenet, Duke of York, father of Edward IV; that Edward IV dying seised of the manor, it descended in coparcenery to his four daughters, Elizabeth, Anna, Cecilia, and Bridget the three latter of whom dying without issue in the lifetime of Elizabeth, and Henry VII having married Elizabeth, that monarch became seised of the manor in right of the queen, from whom it descended to Henry VIII in right of his mother, as appeared by the inquisition put in on the part of the plaintiff below.

A verdict was found for the plaintiff below on the above issues.

Exceptions.

Both the plaintiff and the defendants below excepted to the opinion of the learned judge at the trial—the former, to the admission of the fine as evidence for the defendants below—the latter, to the admission of the parchment writing and case found at Lowton House, and to the direction of the judge on the effect of the Irish act, 10 Hen. 7, and of the fine.

The court of Common Pleas in Ireland gave judgment for the plaintiff below, which being affirmed on error to the court of Exchequer Chamber in Ireland, the defendants below brought their writ of error returnable in parliament, assigning for errors, besides the common errors,

Assignment of
errors.

that the said parchment writing purporting to be a grant by Ulick, fifth earl, to Dr. Edward Donnellan, of the next avoidance, was improperly admitted in evidence; that the said paper writing purporting to be a case stated in 1695 on behalf of Anthony Dopping, Bishop of Meath, for the opinion of counsel, was also improperly admitted in evidence; that the jury were misdirected as to the operation of the alleged act of 10 Hen. 7 on the grant of the advowson by Edward IV to the see of Meath; and that the jury were misdirected as to the effect of the fine of Trinity Term, 1 Jac. 2.

The exceptions were argued by Sir *J. Campbell*, Sir *W. Follett*, and *Byles*, for the defendants below; and by Sir *F. Pollock* and *Miller* for the plaintiff below.

Lord Chief Justice TINDAL now delivered the opinion of the judges as follows:—

The opinion of the judges was requested by the House on the following questions:—

1836.

The Bishop of
MEATH
v.
The Marq. of
WINCHESTER.
First question.

1. The attention of the judges was directed to an act of parliament passed at a parliament held at Drogheda, in the 10th year of the reign of Henry VII (set out in the appendix to the bill of exceptions, to which their lordships were referred), and to a certain grant of the advowson of K. by Edward IV, whereof he was seised in the same right as of the advowson of Rathweir in the said appendix mentioned, which grant was made to the Bishop of M., and was assumed to be in the same terms as that which was contained in the said appendix; and upon these latter documents, the two following questions were proposed by the House—first, did the act of Henry VII avoid the grant of Edward IV?—secondly, did the same statute re-append the advowson to the said manor whereto it was appendant before the grant?

2. In quære impedit to recover the prensentation to the church of K., the advowson whereof is claimed to be part of the temporalities of the Bishop of M., a deed was offered in evidence purporting to be brought from the custody particularly described in the bill of exceptions*; and also a case, purporting to be a case stated for the opinion of counsel on the part of a former Bishop of M., and brought from the same custody: were such deed and such case respectively admissible in evidence against the successors to the Bishop of M. in that see?

With your lordships' permission we shall reverse the order of considering the two questions proposed to us, and give our answer, first, to the question whether the case was admissible in evidence; for, as the deed and the case were found at the same time, by the same persons, at the same place, and indeed in the very same parcel of papers, the question of admissibility, so far as it depends on the custody, is precisely the same with respect to both. But a difficulty which might exist with respect to the

deed, but which forms no ingredient in the consideration
of the admissibility of the case, will be avoided if the case
should be held to be receivable in evidence; and upon the
question whether the case stated for the opinion of counsel is admissible, the judges who have heard the arguments of counsel on this point are of opinion that it would
be admissible in evidence on the trial of the quære impedit above supposed to be brought: for, although two of
my learned brethren, Mr. Justice Park and Mr. Justice
Coleridge, did at one time feel doubts as to the propriety
of admitting such evidence, I am authorized by them to
state, that, upon further consideration, those doubts are
removed, and that they agree in opinion with the rest of
the judges.

As to whether
the bishop could
have been com-
pelled to pro-
duce, or the
counsel or attor-
ney who drew it
to disclose the
statements con-
tained in, the
case—quære.

It is not necessary to determine on the present occasion
whether the supposed plaintiff in the quare impedit could
have compelled the bishop, the supposed defendant, to
produce in evidence the case which had been stated for
the opinion of counsel by his predecessor, either by any
proceedings in a court of equity or otherwise; or whether
the counsel or attorney who drew up the statements contained in that case could have been compelled to disclose
such statements, either as against their client or as against
the successor of their client. The present inquiry stands
unembarrassed with the consideration of that question;
for, the case stated for counsel has actually come into the
possession of the plaintiff in the quare impedit, and the
plaintiff himself produces it at the trial of the cause as
part of his evidence; and the question is the same as if
a case with the opinion of counsel, which one party was not
bound to produce, had found its way by accident or otherwise into the hands of the other party. Upon this view
of the subject, it appears to us that the only considerations
that arise upon the production of the case are two—first,
whether the custody in which it was found is such as to
stamp it with authenticity as a genuine document—se-

condly, if it is to be taken to be genuine, whether the
statements of the facts contained in it are admissible
against the interests of the successor of the former bishop
who made or caused to be made the statements contained
in the case. The first and indeed the principal question
is, whether this document was found in such custody and
under such circumstances attending the finding of it as to
give it authenticity, as being a case really stated by the
authority and on the behalf of a former bishop of the same
see. Now, before we consider the facts relating to the
finding of the case, as stated in the bill of exceptions to
which we are referred, we cannot but observe that the
statement itself in the bill of exceptions is very loose and
inaccurate. But we think, in construing the statement
contained in a bill of exceptions, we are to consider ourselves placed in a situation analogous to that of a jury;
and that, like a jury, we are bound to make every legal
presumption from the facts stated, and every reasonable
inference which those facts will bear. Supposing facts,
therefore, are stated by the plaintiff's witnesses in an uncertain or ambiguous manner, as the defendant's counsel
have neglected by cross-examination, of which they had
the opportunity, to render the statement more clear and
certain, and to remove any ambiguity of expression, it is
not competent for the defendant below in this advanced
stage of the proceedings to make his stand upon the loose-
ness and ambiguity of the testimony of which he is to a
considerable extent himself the cause. In such case the
judges can only, as judges of the fact, and with the eyes
of common men, endeavour to discover the truth through
the vagueness and uncertainty of the statement, and then
only to act upon it where they can feel a solid foundation
on which they can rely. This observation will dispose of
much of the objection which has been made in the course
of the argument against the testimony of the witnesses
who depose to the time, place, and manner of the finding
of the case and of the grant; and, looking at the state-

1836.

The Bishop of
MEATH
v.
The Marq. of
WINCHESTER.

As to the custo-
dy in which the
document was
found.

ments in the bill of exceptions, we think the fair result
of the evidence is, that both the documents to which exceptions have been taken were found tied up together with
other papers relating to the see, in a house called Lowton
House, which was the family mansion-house of the Doppings, that is, the mansion-house of the family of which
Anthony Dopping, formerly Bishop of Meath, was one
member, and of which the witness who gave the testimony
was another; that this house was occupied by a member
of the Dopping family at the time the papers were found
there; and, lastly, that it was the house in which the
Dopping family papers were kept. There is not one of
these facts, vague as they appear at present, which might
not have been cleared from all ambiguity by a very little
cross-examination if they are founded in truth; and, on
the other hand, not one which would have stood the test
of such cross-examination if untrue. Other parts of the
bill of exceptions corroborate and confirm the result of
the evidence as above stated. That there was an Anthony
Dopping who had been Bishop of Meath, that he had
some family, and that he had collated his son to the living
now in dispute, is proved by documentary evidence set
forth in the bill of exceptions, which documentary evidence was contemporaneous with the fact, and cannot mislead. Again, as the original documents do not appear
before the judges on a bill of exceptions, but the transcript
only is set out upon the record, it is the proper and
necessary intendment that there is nothing upon the face
or in the condition of the documents themselves which
excites suspicion as to their genuineness; for, in this stage
of the proceedings, credit must be given to the court
below, that they would not have allowed the documents to
be read if they had borne upon their face or in their condition any evidence against their admissibility. The
result of the evidence, upon the bill of exceptions, we
think is this—that these documents were found in a place
in which, and under the care of persons with whom,

papers of Bishop Dopping might naturally and reasonably be expected to be found : and that is precisely the custody which gives authenticity to documents found within it; for, it is not necessary that they should be found in the best and most proper place of deposit. If documents continue in such custody there never would be any question as to their authenticity; but it is when documents are found in other than the proper place of deposit, that the investigation commences whether it was reasonable and natural, under the circumstances in the particular case, to expect that they should have been in the place where they are actually found; for, it is obvious, that, whilst there can be only one place of deposit strictly and absolutely proper, there may be various and many that are reasonable and probable, though differing in degree ; some being more so, some less : and in those cases the proposition to be determined is, whether the actual custody is so reasonably and probably to be accounted for that it impresses the mind with the conviction that the instrument found in such custody must be genuine. That such is the character and description of the custody which is held sufficiently genuine to render a document admissible, appears from all the cases. On the one hand, old grants to abbeys have been rejected as evidence of private rights, where the possession of them has appeared altogether unconnected with the persons who had any interest in the estate. Thus, a manuscript found in the Herald's Office enumerating the possessions of the dissolved monastery of Tutbury—*Lygon* v. *Strutt*, 2 Anstr. 601, a manuscript found in the Bodleian Library, Oxford—*Michell* v. *Rabitts*, cited in 3 Taunt, 91, an old grant to a priory brought from the Cottonian MSS. in the British Museum—*Swinnerton* v. *Marquis of Stafford*, 3 Taunt. 91—were held to be inadmissible, the possession of the documents being unconnected with the interest in the property. On the other hand, an old chartulary of the dissolved abbey of Glastonbury was held to be admissible, because found in

the possession of the owner of part of the abbey lands;
though not of the principal proprietor. . This was
not the proper custody, which, as Lord Redesdale
observed, would have been the augmentation office (4
Dow, 321); and, as between the different proprietors of
the abbey land, it might have been more reasonably
expected to have been deposited with the largest; but
it was, as the court argued, a place of custody where it
might be reasonably expected to be found—*Bullen* v.
Mitchell, 2 Price, 413.   So also, in the case of *Jones* v.
Waller, 2 Gwill. 346, the collector's book would have
been as well authenticated if produced from the custody
of the executor of the incumbent, or his successor, as
from the hands of the successor of the collector.   See
also to the same effect the case of *Bertie* v. *Beaumont*, 2
Price, 307.   Upon this principle, we think the case stated
for the opinion of counsel, purporting to be stated on the
part of Bishop Dopping, and found in the place and in
the custody before described, was admissible in evidence.
It was a document which related to the private interests of
the bishop at the time it was stated, for it bears date in
1695, about which time it appears from other facts found,
that Barry, the late incumbent, was dead, and that,
before 1697, Bishop Dopping collated his own son.   It
related, therefore, to a real transaction which took place
at the time, and although it might be said to have related
in some degree to the see, for the right of collation was
claimed as of an advowson granted to the see, yet it is
manifest this case had been stated with reference to the
private interests of the bishop in the particular avoidance,
and that it was more reasonable to expect it to be preserved with his private papers and family documents than
in the public registry of the diocese.   But, even considered as a document belonging to the see, it was not
unreasonable that it should have been found in the
bishop's mansion-house; for, upon the evidence, there is
only one single ecclesiastical record preserved in the

registry of the diocese of Meath of an earlier date than 1717: and, on the other hand, the case and grant are found in the same parcel with several papers relating to the see of Meath; and in the same room were several visitation books of the diocese, and other papers relating to the same see. It is objected in argument, that it does not appear by legal evidence what these papers were. But it seems a sufficient answer to that objection, that the papers themselves were not called for at the trial, which they might have been; neither is their non-production made the ground of any exception to the judge's direction at the trial. The case for counsel, therefore, so found, and the reasonableness of its custody being corroborated by so many concomitant circumstances, we think it was properly admitted in evidence.

But it is objected, secondly, that, though it might have been admissible against the bishop, for whom it was stated, it cannot be so against his successor, because the facts stated in the case took place long before the bishop had any interest, and before he can be supposed to have had any knowledge of the see. The case, indeed, is dated in 1695. The grant which is set out in it is dated in 1635, the presentation under the grant in 1642, and the induction in 1660. Undoubtedly, if by knowledge is meant a personal knowledge of the facts, it must be held to have been wanting in the present case. But the facts stated were all facts that are evidenced by written documents. The grant itself accompanied the case, being bound up in the same parcel: the presentation and induction are only to be proved by written entries, which were peculiarly within his reach. With such, the best means of knowledge, therefore, we think the statement by him or by his attorney of a fact in the case directly against his own interest at the time the case was stated, was not only an admission against him, but against his successors who stood in the same situation. So much having been said about the

1836.

The Bishop of
MEATH
v.
The Marq. of
WINCHESTER.

Statements in
the case evi-
dence not only
against the bi-
shop on whose
behalf the case
was prepared,
but also against
his successors in
the see.

1836.

The Bishop of
MEATH
v.
The Marq. of
WINCHESTER.
Grant admissi-
ble on the same
grounds.

case, it is scarcely necessary to refer to the grant. It is
set forth in the case, and thereby authenticated; and this
alone would make it producible. But it is in itself a grant
of great antiquity, and we are bound to assume, without
any apparent infirmity or defect on the face of it, to
render it unworthy of credit. Upon the whole, therefore, our opinion is, that both the one document and the
other were admissible.

First question—
As to the effect
of the statute 10
Hen. 7 (Irish)
on the grant of
Edw. 4.
Upon the first question, we are of opinion that the
statute of Henry VII did avoid the said grant of Edward IV; and that it did also re-append the advowson
to the said manor. Several objections have been urged
against holding the grant to fall within the operation of
the statute—first, it is said that the statute revokes no
grants made by any kings except those who were the progenitors of Henry VII in the strict sense of that word;
and that Edward IV was not a progenitor of that king;
secondly, that the statute does not extend to grants of
which such progenitors were seised jure privato only, and
that Edward IV was seised jure privato of the advowson
in question; thirdly, that it does not extend to revoke
grants to corporations, whether sole or aggregate: and,
lastly, that it does not extend to any grants but those
under the great seal, either in England or Ireland, and
that the grant of the advowson in question is made under
neither.

Upon these several objections we shall observe in their
order. As to the first objection, if the term progenitors
is to be understood in its literal sense, then the only king
of England who since the last year of Edward II was a
progenitor of Henry VII, would be Edward III: for,
Henry VI was no progenitor in the strict sense of the
word: but, as he is expressly named in the preamble to
the statute 19 Hen. 7, c. 18, he was the uncle of the king.
As, however, the term used in the act is the plural term,
progenitors, more than one king must have been intended,

and it seems not possible to extend it beyond one without allowing it to be synonymous with the word predecessors —a word with which it is often put in apposition in statutes of the same reign—see 11 Hen. 7, cc. 4 and 8, and again, the statute referred to by the counsel for the plaintiff in error, as set out in Plowden's Reports, 226, wherein Henry IV, Henry V, and Henry VI, are called the king's noble progenitors, affords itself a proof that the word is used in a wider sense, for those kings were his predecessors, but not his progenitors. Again, the word must either comprise all his predecessors, kings of England, or his predecessors who were of the house of Lancaster only: but it would lead to an unreasonable result if the word is confined to the latter only; for, in that case, all the grants made by the house of Lancaster to their friends would be annulled, and those made by the house of York to the enemies of the house of Lancaster would be confirmed. And, when the object of the statute is considered, which was that of bringing money into the king's coffers by the annulling of all former improvident grants of the crown, there can be no reason to doubt· that it was intended to comprise within it the grants made by former kings of England, whether of the one house or of the other.

As to the objection secondly above urged, that the statute extends to grants only of such property whereof the crown was seised jure coronæ, no such distinction appears upon the face of the statute itself. The king (Edward IV) was equally seised in fee, whether the advowson belonged to him jure privato or jure coronæ. "Advowsons of churches" are within the express words of the statute; independently of which, the sale of the next presentation, or the sale of the advowsons themselves, made them the possible source of profit to the crown. And, whether the advowson in question, supposing there had been no grant by Edward IV, would have devolved upon

1836.

The Bishop of MEATH v. The Marq. of WINCHESTER.

"Progenitors" and "predecessors," in some cases synonymous.

The statute 10 Hen. 7 (Irish) not confined to grants of property of which the crown was seised jure coronæ;

Henry VII, as parcel of the possessions of the crown, or whether he would have taken it in right of his wife by descent to her and his marriage, in either case, the advowson would have been valuable to him, though perhaps to a different extent upon the two suppositions. It seems, therefore, to become unnecessary to determine whether, on the facts stated in the bill of exceptions, this advowson is the property of Edward IV in right of his crown or not. But it appears to follow from the decision of the case of the *Duchy of Lancaster*, Plowden, 213, and by what is said by Holt, C. J., in the *Banker's case*, Skinner's Rep. 603, that whatever belonged to Edward IV before he came to the throne, on his accession to the crown, belonged to him jure coronæ, in his politic capacity, and not in his private; and as such it would descend to Edward V, be transferred to Richard III, on his accession to the crown, and in like manner devolve on Henry VII. In this respect, therefore, the earldom of March, and all the lands and tenements belonging to it, would be precisely on the same footing as the Duchy of Lancaster would have been but for the charter of Henry IV confirmed by parliament, which, according to the doctrine laid down by the judges, would otherwise have been annexed to the crown—Plowden's Rep. 204.

nor to grants to
private persons;

As to the third objection, that the statute extends only to the case of grants to private persons, and does not include those to corporations, either sole or aggregate, we think it sufficient to observe that the words are large enough to extend to both: the very expression "any person or persons by whatever name or names they may be named," pointing as well, or rather more expressly, to a body politic, which is known only by name, than to persons in their individual capacity; and, if this were left in doubt, the exception annexed to the act of the grant to the Archbishop of Dublin, and to the corporation of the bailiffs of Dundalk, shews, that, if not specially excepted, bodies corporate, both sole and aggregate, were understood to be included in the operation of the act.

1836.

The Bishop of
MEATH
v.
The Marq. of
WINCHESTER.

nor to grants
under the great
seal of England
or Ireland.

The only remaining objection is that which limits the operation of the statute to grants under the great seal of England or Ireland. Upon this head of inquiry, the plaintiffs in error object that the grant in question does not appear to have been made under the great seal, either of the one or of the other kingdom. The argument appears to stand thus—that, from the facts stated in the bill of exceptions, Edward IV must be taken to have been seised of his property as Earl of March; that, by the title deduced in the inquisition, 23 Hen. 8, it appears that the March property was always kept by Edward IV distinct from property held jure coronæ, a course of descent being in that inquisition traced from him to Henry VIII quite inconsistent with that of crown land. It is inferred therefore, à priori, that Edward IV, granting in the right of his earldom of March, would grant under some seal belonging to him as such; at all events, neither by the great seal, nor by act of parliament; that nothing appears on the face of the grant to contradict this presumption, the letters not being stated to be patent, nor any seal now appearing, nor any circumstance from which it can be argued that the grant was originally under the great seal in either country. It is further alleged, that, by 4 Hen. 7, c. 14 (English act), it is expressly recited, that, in Edward the Fourth's time, all grants of property parcel of the earldom of March were made under a special seal, called "Seal of the Marches;" and that, for redress of mischiefs ensuing thereupon, it is by that statute enacted, that, for the future, all such grants shall be made under the great seal. Now, looking at and examining the grant in question, it appears upon the face of it to relate to a subject-matter which the king held as lord of Ireland, and granted as such. No allusion is made to any individual or particular character, but the

king grants with the assent substantially of the lord lieu-
tenant, who, as such, would have nothing to do but with
the property of the king held jure coronæ.   Further, the
grant is made with a non obstante of any statute, act, or
ordinance, to the contrary; a clause which the king,
granting merely as Earl of March, never would assume to
have power to add.   The teste also is from the year of
the reign, a circumstance which would rather indicate
the grant to have been made by the king jure coronæ than
the contrary.   This inference, arising upon the face of
the grant itself, is confirmed by the acknowledged principle of law, that, upon the accession of Edward IV to the
crown, his possessions as Earl of March would become
annexed, in point of government and administration at
least, to the possessions of the crown.   The authority of
the judges in the case of the *Duchy of Lancaster*, Plowden 213, is precisely to the point.   Speaking of the mode
of passing land held by the king jure coronæ, by letters
patent only, without livery of seisin, they add—"So it
has been the practice with regard to the lands which descended to the king from the Duke of York, the Earl of
March, and others of the king's ancestors who never
were kings."   The land, therefore, of the earldom would
properly be passable by such form of grant only as would be
used by the king in conveying property held jure coronæ.
This is a well-known consequence, resulting, not from the
title of the property, but the dignity of the holder, in
whom the body politic absorbs the body natural.   Whether, therefore, the property of the Earl of March were
annexed to the crown at the date of the grant in question
or not, seems not very material; for, being at all events
in the hands of the king for the time being, the legal presumption is, that it would for that time be granted as if it
were held jure coronæ.   The argument, therefore, deduced from the title and course of descent traced by the
inquisition relating to the manor of Rathweir, with its appurtenances, fails in its application, even if we would

attach much weight, upon a question of fact, to a document which is manifestly inaccurate upon the bare inspection of it, omitting, as it does, all mention of the two
sons of Edward IV, from the eldest of whom Edward V,
and not from the father, the daughters must have inhe-
rited. But the difficulty still remains as to the recital in
the English statute 4 Hen. 7, c. 14. If this had been an
inquiry as to property in England, that recital would undoubtedly have presented a difficulty almost insurmounta-
ble; for, a fact is stated therein, and a mischief resulting
from it, for redress of which the statute is made. Whatever legal presumptions there may be to the contrary, the
recital affords stronger evidence that the irregular practice
complained of in the statute had actually taken place.
The weight, however, of this evidence, and even its applicability to the subject under discussion, is answered by
the consideration that we are now dealing with property
in Ireland. The remedy was certainly intended only to apply, and at the time was applicable only, to England and
Wales: for, Poyning's Law had not then passed. There
is no ground for presuming that the English legislature
took notice of any matter passing in Ireland; and the seal
spoken of in the statute, "the Seal of the Marches,"
seems in terms rather to apply to the border property in
England and Wales, than to patrimonial domains in Ireland; and there is de facto an improbability that grants
in Ireland should have passed under a seal used for and
permanently kept in England or Wales. It is further to
be observed, that the bill of exceptions expressly states
the document in question to be letters patent of Edward
IV—a description which primâ facie would imply that it
was under the great seal; and, still further, that the description is in the very same terms with that given of the
letters patent of Edward III, by which he granted the
manor and advowson to John Darcy and Johanna his wife,
in tail male, which letters patent must have been under
the great seal, as the property was then vested in the

1836.

The Bishop of
MEATH
v.
The Marq. of
WINCHESTER.
As to the recital
in the 4 Hen. 7,
c. 14.

crown jure coronæ, under the escheat from Roger Mortimer, Earl of March. If, therefore, the letters patent are
under the great seal in one case, why are we to intend
otherwise in the second instance, which is now under discussion? Upon examination, therefore, of this question,
by the light afforded by the bill of exceptions, and by
such legal presumptions as the facts therein stated afford,
we think this grant of Edward IV did fall within the operation of the statute of Henry VII, and that it was avoided
by that statute.

As to whether,
by the resump-
tion of the grant
of Edward 4,
the advowson
became re-
appended to the
manor.

Upon the question next proposed to us—whether, by
the effect of such resumption of the grant, the advowson
became re-appended to the manor, which still remained
in the hands of the crown—we think the words of the statute itself give the answer without entering into the discussion of the various authorities which have been cited
in the argument before your lordships. Nothing but the
grant of Edward IV had disappended the advowson from
the manor. The resumption act " annuls and makes void
and of none effect in the law" the grant itself. This is not
the case of a parliamentary reconveyance, but the cause
of disappendancy ceases from the time of passing the act,
as if it had never been; and with it all effect of the grant
from that time must necessarily also cease. It was urged
at your lordships' bar, that the consequences would be
monstrous if the grant were to be held altogether void;
that it would avoid and render illegal all intermediate acts
founded on a grant legal in itself when made. But we are
far from thinking the consequences above stated would
follow. A grant which is to be deemed void in law and as
if it had never been, from a certain day, may yet be regarded as having had existence at a former period for
the purpose only of preventing parties who have dealt
with the property from being treated as trespassers or
wrongdoers, and protecting acts done at an intermediate
time.

For the reasons, therefore, above given we think the

advowson became re-appended to the manor by the legal operation of the statute above referred to.

Your lordships lastly refer to the pleadings upon the fifth count of a quare impedit brought by C. against the Bishop of M., and to the issues joined on those pleas; and, after premising that on these issues a fine is tendered in evidence, levied by B., whose estate C. hath, which fine is set forth in the pleadings to which we are referred, your lordships propose the three following questions; viz.—First, whether such fine was admissible in evidence under any of the said issues—Secondly, whether, if received, it ought to be left to the jury to say whether it barred the action of quare impedit—Thirdly, whether the fine did bar the action of quare impedit.

The fine in question is stated to have been levied in Trinity Term, 1 James 2, by William, seventh Earl of Clanricarde, and Hester his wife, to John Brown, Gerard Dillon, and Anthony Mulledy, and the heirs of the said John Brown, of the manors of Rathweir and Killucan, with the appurtenances, and divers quantities of land therein specified, and also of the advowson and right of patronage of the parish of Killucan; and, in answer to the first of the questions proposed by your lordships, we are of opinion that the fine, upon the state of pleadings on the record, was not admissible in evidence under any of the issues joined therein. There are only these issues upon which there can be any ground whatever to contend that the fine was admissible—the issue taken upon the traverse by the bishop in his twelfth plea (which is precisely the same in terms as the issue taken by the clerk in his eighth plea), and the issue taken upon the traverse by the clerk in his fifth and seventh pleas: all the remaining issues being raised on single points quite unconnected with, and altogether unaffected by, the fine. The traverse of the bishop is in these terms—"without this that the plaintiff below is possessed of the said advowson of the

Margin:

1836.

The Bishop of MEATH
v.
The Marq. of WINCHESTER.

As to the admissibility of the fine of Trinity Term, 1 Jac. 2.

said church of Killucan, otherwise Rathweir, in manner and form as the said plaintiff hath in his said fifth count alleged." That this traverse would have been held bad upon special demurrer, there can be no doubt. But it is contended, that, as the plaintiff has, instead of demurring, taken issue upon this traverse, he has waived any objection to it, and must be contented to admit under it all such evidence as by law it is calculated to receive. We must consider the point, therefore, as if this had been the only issue upon the record; and, whether it would have been competent in that case to the defendants to give in evidence the fine by William, the seventh Earl, and Hester his wife, is the question before us. No authority can be found in the books which will throw any light on the question; for, no instance can be brought forward where any parties in a quare impedit have proceeded to trial on such an issue. If the precedents given in Malony on Quare Impedit, and the more numerous precedents to which he has referred from the best books of entries, are consulted, it will be found that, with scarcely an exception, all of them contain at the conclusion of the count the allegation which is found in this, viz. " whereby the plaintiff became possessed of the advowson," or " of the right to present;" and yet in no single instance is there any traverse of that allegation. What evidence, therefore, may or may not be admitted under the traverse, must depend upon principle and analogy to other cases, and cannot be governed by any direct authority. The first inquiry is, to what allegation does the traverse relate. The plaintiff having in his fifth count distinctly alleged the death of Mr. Wyndham, who had been shewn to be joint tenant with the plaintiff of a certain term of years in this advowson, proceeds to allege " whereupon and whereby the plaintiff became and still is possessed of the said advowson as of an advowson in gross for the remainder of the said term so theretofore granted." This is the allegation, and the only allegation, in the count, to which the traverse can

possibly apply. And, as the traverse is taken upon the
precise terms of this allegation, one ground upon which
the fine may be held to be inadmissible, is, that the traverse is confined to the possession of the plaintiff by reason
of the term for years, and of his surviving his co-joint-
tenant in the term; such being the fair and natural import
of the allegation made by the plaintiff. It is unnecessary
to say, that, if such be the proper construction of the traverse, the fine is altogether inadmissible. But, admitting,
for the purpose of the argument, that the averment in the
declaration takes a wider range, and that it amounts to
an allegation that, by reason of all the various steps in
the title of the plaintiff which are set out in the fifth
count of the declaration, the plaintiff is possessed of the
right to the advowson; and admitting the traverse to be
equally extensive, and to put all those steps of the title in
issue; still, we think, by analogy to the rules of pleading,
the utmost effect that can be given to such a traverse is,
that it is a simple denial of the different allegations of
the descent and of the other steps of the title, so as
thereby to put the plaintiff to the proof of his whole declaration; but that the traverse will not admit of new and
affirmative evidence on the part of the defendant, taking
the title out of the plaintiff, and vesting it in another
person. The general principle of pleading is, that the
defendant must either deny or he must confess and avoid
the charge in the declaration: the same plea cannot do
both. But, supposing this traverse to have the effect
of a general denial of each link in the chain of the title,
if, besides compelling the plaintiff to prove them, and
bringing his own witnesses to contest the truth of their
existence, he might prove affirmatively a title in another
person, what is that in effect but giving to this anomalous and unheard of traverse the double force of a
denial of all the steps of the title, and at the same time
a confession of the existence of the title, but an avoidance

1836.

The Bishop of
MEATH
v.
The Marq. of
WINCHESTER.

Q Q 2

of its effect?   In the present case, there is only one allegation in the count to which the fine could by possibility
apply, and that is the allegation which, after stating William, the seventh earl, to have been seised in fee-tail of
the advowson in gross, by virtue of letters patent and of
an act of parliament, and that he continued so seised,
avers that " upon his death the advowson descended upon
Richard, the eighth earl, as his son and heir in tail male."
And we hold, admitting the traverse to amount to a denial
of the steps by which Earl William's title in fee-tail is deduced, it will not allow the defendant to prove, by the fine,
that such title ceased before his death: for, if the title in
fee, or fee-tail, is once admitted or proved in any person,
it must be intended to continue in that person, without any
allegation that it does, until the contrary is shewn—1
Lutw. 357, Plowd. 431 : and the cesser of that estate, by
conveyance or otherwise, is affirmative matter, which
ought to be shewn by a special plea on the other side.
We, therefore, think ourselves well warranted in the conclusion that the fine was not admissible under the issue
above considered.

With respect to the traverse taken by the clerk in his
seventh plea, it is in these terms, " that it doth not belong to the plaintiff to present a fit person to the church,
in manner and form" &c.   This is no more than a precise
denial taken by the defendant of the last words in the
plaintiff's declaration, viz. "and for that reason it now
belongs to the said plaintiff to present a fit person to the
said last-mentioned church."   It is a mere inference of law,
resulting from all the facts stated in the count, and altogether unlike the traverse in the case of *The Grocers'
Company* v. *The Archbishop of Canterbury*, 3 Wilson,
214, which included a matter of fact material to the right.
But, taking it to be a traverse of all the steps by which
the title to the advowson is deduced to the plaintiff from
Richard, the fourth earl, who is averred to have been first
seised in fee, the same objection applies to the admissibi-

lity of the fine in evidence under this traverse, as under that to the bishop's twelfth plea ; and the same observation may also be made with respect to the issue on the fifth plea as to the seisin of Michael the tenth earl : and besides, there is another reason why, under the traverses in the fifth, seventh, and eighth of the clerk's pleas, the evidence of the fine should not be admitted, though the same reason does not exist as to the traverse in the twelfth plea of the bishop, in which he claims to present as patron. It is clearly established that neither the clerk nor ordinary, in that character, could counterplead the plaintiff's title at common law, for neither of them had any interest in the patronage. And, under the statute 25 Ed. 3, st. 3, c. 7, the incumbent (as possessor when presented and instituted) could not counterplead the plaintiff's title, without maintaining his own title, and that of his patron, on which his own depends. This is distinctly laid down by Lord Hobart in the case of *Elvis* v. *The Archbishop of Canterbury*, Hob. 315 ; for, the statute only allows the possessor " to have his answer, and shew and defend his right upon the matter." The plea, therefore, which sets out the title of the patron, ought, in order to maintain it, to traverse the plaintiff's title so far as it is inconsistent with that of his own patron, and so far only ; and, in that sense, the traverse in the fifth, seventh, and eighth pleas must be understood, if the pleas are good in substance ; that is, it must be taken that the clerk means not to set up the title of a stranger to both the litigant parties, which would cut down the title both of himself and of his patron, which the law does not permit him to do, but to affirm that the title to the advowson was in the Bishops of Meath, or some one under whom they claim, and not in Earl Michael or the plaintiff, at the times respectively mentioned in the fifth count, and referred to in the traverses contained in the fifth, seventh, and eighth pleas of the clerk. In this mode of construing the traverses, it is clear that the fine, which shewed the title to be in third persons, was not admissible in evidence under any of the issues joined on this record.

The Bishop of
MEATH
v.
The Marq. of
WINCHESTER.

The legal effect
of the fine, a
question of law,
and not of fact
for the jury.

If properly
receivable in
evidence, the
fine no bar to
the action.

With respect to the second question lastly above proposed to us, viz. whether, if the fine were received in evidence, it ought to be left to the jury to say whether it barred the action of quare impedit, we all think that the legal effect of such fine as a bar to the action of quare impedit is a matter of law merely, and not in any way a matter of fact; and consequently the judge who tried the cause should state to the jury whether in point of law the fine had that effect, or what other effect, on the rights of the litigant parties, upon the general and acknowledged principle, "ad questionem juris non respondent juratores."

In answer to the last question proposed to us, we all agree in opinion that the fine did not, if properly received in evidence, absolutely of itself bar the action of quare impedit. It could not do so on the ground of estoppel, because the parties to this suit did not both claim respectively under the parties to the fine, and the fine is an estoppel only between parties and privies: and, though it operates as a conveyance from Earl William, the seventh earl, to Brown, Dillon, and Mulledy, for a valuable consideration, it is possible that this was a conveyance by way of mortgage, which has been paid off, or that these parties might have re-conveyed the advowson to Earl William, or some subsequent earl: and there is even some evidence stated in the bill of exceptions to raise a presumption that it was so; for, in 1699 Earl Richard conveyed to John Morgan, and in 1744 John Morgan re-conveyed the advowson to Earl John Smith; and there is no evidence of any dealing with the advowson or presentation by the conusees of the fine, or any one claiming under them.

It cannot therefore be said that the fine alone, if it had been admissible, was an absolute bar to the action, which is the last question proposed by your lordships.

The judgment of the court below was—

Affirmed.

IN THE COMMON PLEAS.

MICHAELMAS TERM, 7 WILL. IV.

THE JUDGES WHO SAT IN BANC DURING THIS TERM WERE
TINDAL, C J, AND GASELEE, J, VAUGHAN, J, AND BOSANQUET, J

WRIGHT v. NEWTON.

1836.

*Wednesday,
Nov. 2nd.*

THIS was an action of assumpsit against an attorney for an alleged breach of duty, in taking insufficient security for an advance of money on behalf of the plaintiff, a client. A summons had been taken out by the defendant, and heard before Bosanquet, J., at chambers, for leave to plead the following pleas—1. non assumpsit—2. a denial of the retainer in the terms alleged in the declaration—3. a denial of the advance of the money under such retainer as alleged—4. a denial of the negligence imputed—5. a denial of the alleged insufficiency of the security—6. *a denial of the allegation that the plaintiff had been prevented from enforcing payment of the money advanced.* The learned judge gave the defendant leave to plead the first *or* the second, and the third, fourth, and fifth, but refused to allow the sixth. These pleas having been pleaded—

In an action against an attorney for negligence in procuring insufficient security upon an advance of money, per quod the plaintiff lost the money—the court allowed the defendant to plead, in addition to non assumpsit and several other pleas, that the loss was not the result of the alleged negligence.

Wilde, Serjeant, now moved for leave to withdraw them, and to plead them again with the addition of those that had been disallowed, viz. the second and sixth.—If by pleading non assumpsit merely, the defendant admits the consideration, he is entitled to have the second plea put upon the record: if, on the other hand, non assumpsit puts in issue the consideration, which seems doubtful—*Passenger* v. *Brooks*, 1 Scott, 560—then the second plea would be unnecessary. [*Bosanquet*, J.—*Passenger* v. *Brooks* was the case of an express promise. In an action for goods sold and delivered, the delivery of the goods is the consideration for the promise, and that is not traversed (a). *Vaughan*, J.—The consideration is a matter of fact from which the promise is implied by law.] If there be an implied contract, to entitle the plaintiff to maintain the action, some special damage much be proved. In *Smith* v. *Thomas*, 2 Scott, 546, where a plea negativing the special damage alleged in the declaration, was held bad, on demurrer, the action was slander for words actionable per se, and therefore the law would imply some damage. The present case, however, stands upon a different footing.

PER CURIAM.—The plea denying the special damage as alleged, may be added. But, with respect to the traverse of the consideration, non assumpsit will suffice.

No cause being shewn, the sixth plea was accordingly added.

(a) See Alexander v. Gardner, 1 Scott, 281, where it was held, that, under non assumpsit to a count for goods bargained and sold, evidence may be given that the contract was made subject to conditions which had not been complied with on the part of the vendor.

DAY *v.* BONNIN.

BY an order of reference, it was directed that " *the cause* and *all matters in dispute between the parties* be referred to the award, order, arbitrament, final end, and determination" of the arbitrator, a surveyor. At the time of making the order, the issuing of the writ of summons was the only step that had been taken in the cause. The arbitrator by his award, dated the 6th August, 1836, reciting the order of reference, and "having taken upon himself the burthen of the said arbitrament, and having heard, examined, and considered the allegations, proofs, and answers of both the said parties *touching the matters in difference between them*, and having thoroughly considered of the same," did "award, adjudge, and determine that all further proceedings *in the said cause* should from thenceforth cease and be no further prosecuted, and that the defendant should, on the 12th September then next ensuing, well and truly pay or cause to be paid unto the plaintiff or his attorney the sum of 11*l.* 5*s. in full of all demands in the said cause.*"

The cause and all matters in dispute between the parties were referred to arbitration. The arbitrator, reciting that he had heard "the allegations and proofs and answers of the parties touching the matters in difference between them," awarded, "concerning the same," that the defendant should on a given day pay the plaintiff a certain sum "in full of all demands *in the cause* :—Held, that this award was a sufficiently final adjudication upon the matters in difference.

Hurlstone, upon an affidavit that two claims were set up before the arbitrator, one of which was disputed, and the other admitted, moved to set aside the award, on the ground that it did not sufficiently determine the matters in difference between the parties. He submitted, that, inasmuch as it in no way appeared for what cause of action the writ had been sued out, and as the arbitrator had omitted to determine by his award the other matters in dispute between the parties, the defendant would not be in a condition to plead the award in bar to a second action for the same demand. He cited *Gyde* v. *Boucher,* 5 Dowl. P. C. 127, where a cause and all matters in difference being referred to an arbitrator, and he by his award merely directing a verdict to be entered in favour of the plaintiff for one entire sum, the award was held not final, and therefore bad.

TINDAL, C. J.—I think it appears with sufficient certainty on the face of this award that the arbitrator has taken into consideration all the matters in dispute submitted to him, and has disposed of them. Although he has not by his award expressly negatived that there were other matters in difference between the parties, we cannot help seeing that he intended to do so. The cause and all matters in dispute between the parties were referred. The arbitrator, " having heard, examined, and considered the allegations, proofs, and answers of both the said parties *touching the matters in difference between them*, and having thoroughly considered the same," proceeds to award that " that all further proceedings in the said cause should from thenceforth cease and be no further prosecuted, and that the defendant should on a given day pay to the plaintiff or his attorney a certain sum, in full of all demands in the said cause. The conclusion I come to from reading this award, is, that there were no other matters in dispute between the parties besides the cause. In *Gyde* v. *Boucher*, there *were* other matters which were left undisposed of by the award. I must confess I do not perceive that the difficulty suggested has any existence. This award would operate as a conclusive bar to any demand set up by the plaintiff down to its date, viz. the 6th August. To get rid of the supposed difficulty, all that the defendant would have to do would be, to prove that the subject matter of the second action was in dispute at a period anterior to the 6th August.

GASELEE, J.—If the affidavit had stated that the arbitrator had refused to enter upon the consideration of any matter in dispute, that would be a good ground for applying to set aside the award. But this award expressly states that the arbitrator had "heard, examined, and considered the allegations, proofs, and answers of both the said parties touching *the matters in difference between them*," and had "thoroughly considered *of the same*." It in effect finds that there was no matter in dispute besides the cause.

VAUGHAN, J.—The fair construction of this award appears to me to be that it is an adjudication upon all the matters in difference between the parties that the attention of the arbitrator was directed to.

BOSANQUET, J.—I am of the same opinion. The judgment of Lord Tenterden in *Pearse* v. *Pearse*, 9 B. & C. 484, seems to me to be very closely applicable to the present case. There, by an order of Nisi Prius, an action at law, and all matters between the parties at law and in equity, including a Chancery suit, were referred to an arbitrator, who by his award ordered that a sum of money should be paid to the plaintiff in the action, and that the bill in Chancery should be dismissed, and that all proceedings therein should utterly cease and determine: and it was held that the suit in equity, and all matters in difference in that suit, and all matters in difference between the parties, were thereby finally determined, although one of the matters in dispute in the Chancery suit was brought before the arbitrator as a matter in difference between the parties, and was not otherwise disposed of than by the ending of the Chancery suit. "There was in this case," says Lord Tenterden, "a submission of an action at law, a suit in equity, and of all matters in difference between the parties or either of them. The arbitrator has adjudicated upon the action at law, by ordering the defendants to pay the plaintiff a sum of money: he has adjudicated upon the suit in equity, by ordering the bill to be dis-

missed, and each party to pay his own costs. It does not
appear that there was any matter in difference between
the defendants in the action and T. Browne not included
in the suit in equity. The question whether the 500l. was
a gift or a loan, was a matter included in the suit in equity.
Then, if there were no matters in difference between the
parties besides those included in the action at law and the
suit in equity, the arbitrator, by his award, has decided
upon these matters. The award therefore is good." So,
here, the arbitrator has in effect decided that there were
no matters in dispute between the parties other than those
included in the cause.

                                           Rule refused.

———◆———

DICAS v. SMITH, a Prisoner.

Where the
regular notice
of bail has
been given, the
Court will,
under special
circumstances,
allow time for
inquiry into
their sufficiency,
on payment of
costs.

THE regular notice of bail required by the practice of
the court having been given in this case, and the bail now
appearing to justify—

John Jervis, upon an affidavit stating circumstances to
shew the absolute impossibility, by reason of the shortness
of the notice, of making any inquiry as to the sufficiency
of the bail, applied for time.

Andrews, Serjeant, contra, submitted that the notice
required by the rule of court having been given, the plaintiff was not entitled to further time, in the absence of any
suggestion that the bail were not good bail.

GASELEE, J. (the only judge in court), doubting whether or not the court had authority to grant time, consulted the other judges; and afterwards stated, that, inasmuch as it was not possible under the circumstances for
the plaintiff to inquire into the sufficiency of the bail, the

court thought he might have time for that purpose, on payment of costs, and putting the defendant in the same situation as if the bail had duly justified.

The plaintiff declining to accede to these terms—

Bail justified.

———◆———

PROLE and Another, Administrators of W. S. ANDREWS, Deceased, *v.* WIGGINS.

DEBT on a bond for 200*l.*, dated 23rd March,1829, given by the defendant to one W. S. Andrews in his life time.

The defendant pleaded, amongst other pleas, fourthly, that the said W. S. Andrews, before and at the time of making the said writing obligatory in the first count mentioned, used, exercised, and carried on the art, mystery, and profession of a surgeon, apothecary, and man-midwife, and the said W. S. Andrews so using, exercising, and carrying on the said art, mystery, and profession of a surgeon, apothecary, and man-midwife as aforesaid, theretofore and before the making of the said supposed writing obligatory in the said first count mentioned (to wit) on the 10th July, 1828, at &c. aforesaid, it was unlawfully and corruptly agreed by and between the said W. S. Andrews, and the defendant, that the said W. S. Andrews would take G. H. Wiggins, son of the defendant, as his apprentice, to learn the art, mystery, or profession of a surgeon, apothecary, and man-midwife, *for the term of two years only ;* but that in and by certain articles of agreement of apprenticeship to be made and entered into by and between the said W. S. Andrews, and the defendant and his son the said G. H. Wiggins, it should be stated and be made to appear therein that it had been agreed by and between the said parties thereto, that the

To debt on bond the defendant pleaded, that the bond was given in pursuance of a corrupt and illegal agreement between the obligee and obligor that the obligee should take the obligor's son as his apprentice to learn the art, mystery, and profession of a surgeon *apothecary* and man-midwife, *for the term of two years only,* but that in the articles it should be made to appear that the son had been articled for the full term of five years—in order that by such corrupt contrivance the parties might fraudulently and illegally procure the obligor's son to be admitted

to examination for the purpose of practising as an *apothecary* upon serving an apprenticeship for two years, instead of an apprenticeship for five years, as required by the 55 Geo. 3, c. 194, s. 15:— Held, that the bond was void, and the plea a sufficient answer to the action.

said G. H. Wiggins had been and was articled to the said W. S. Andrews, for the term of five years as his apprentice, and for that purpose that such articles of agreement should be antedated, in order that by such corrupt contrivance the said parties to the said agreement should fraudulently and illegally procure the said G. H. Wiggins to be admitted to examination for the purpose of practising as an apothecary, upon serving an apprenticeship for two years, instead of an apprenticeship for five years, as required by the statute in such case made and provided; and it was also then agreed between the parties aforesaid, that the defendant should pay to the said W. S. Andrews the sum of 200l. at the end of two years from the time the son should go to the said W. S. Andrews, together with interest for the same from the day the said G. H. Wiggins should actually go into the service of the said W. S. Andrews, and which said sum of 200l. and interest should be secured by the said bond or obligation in the said first count mentioned: and the defendant further said, that, in pursuance of such corrupt contract and unlawful agreement so made as aforesaid, the said G. H. Wiggins, afterwards, to wit, on the 15th July, 1828, aforesaid, at London aforesaid, entered into the service of the said W. S. Andrews as his apprentice as aforesaid, and for the purpose aforesaid, and continued in such service for the space of two years from the day and year last aforesaid: and the defendant further said, that, in pursuance and in consideration of such unlawful and corrupt contract and agreement so made as aforesaid on the 23rd March, 1829, aforesaid, the said bond or writing obligatory in the said first count mentioned was executed and delivered by the defendant to the said W. S. Andrews, and certain articles of agreement were then, to wit, on the day and year last aforesaid, also made by and between the defendant of the first part, the said G. H. Wiggins of the second part, and the said W. S. Andrews of the third part, and the same were antedated the 15th July,

1825, (which said articles of agreement, sealed with the respective seals of the defendant, the said G. H. Wiggins, and the said W. S. Andrews, were had, taken, and kept by the said W. S. Andrews, and therefore could not be produced by the defendant); and in and by the said articles of agreement it was falsely and fraudulently recited, whereas it had been agreed between the several parties thereto that the said G. H. Wiggins should be articled to the said W. S. Andrews for the term of five years as an apprentice; and in and by the said articles of agreement it was also (amongst other things) falsely, unlawfully, and corruptly witnessed that the said W. S. Andrews should and would for and during the term of five years teach and instruct or cause to be taught and instructed the said G. H. Wiggins in the art, mystery, or profession of a surgeon, apothecary, and man-midwife, and at the end of said term do all such acts as might and should be needful for the facilitating the said G. H. Wiggins being duly admitted as a regular and qualified surgeon, and as in such cases were usual; and further in the said articles of agreement it is made to appear that the said G. H. Wiggins consented and agreed to become and be, and did thereby bind himself duly to serve the said W. S. Andrews as his apprentice in the said art, mystery, or profession aforesaid, from the day of the date thereof, for the said term of five years, whereas in truth and in fact the said articles of agreement were not made or executed by the said several parties thereto on the said 15th July, 1825, but were really and actually made and executed by them respectively with such object and in pursuance of such corrupt agreement as aforesaid at a subsequent time, to wit, on the 23rd of March, 1829, wherefore the said supposed writing obligatory in the said first count mentioned became and was wholly void in law: and this, &c., verification.

To this plea, the plaintiff replied that the said writing Replication. obligatory was executed and delivered by the defendant to the said W. S. Andrews for a good and valuable consideration, and not in pursuance or in consideration of the supposed unlawful and corrupt contract and agreement in the said fourth plea mentioned, modo ac forma, &c.

At the trial before Tindal, C. J., at the sittings at Guildhall after the last term, a verdict was found for the defendant on the general issue and on the issue taken on the fourth plea, and the jury were discharged as to the other issues.

Storks, Serjeant, on a former day, moved for a rule calling on the defendant to shew cause why judgment should not be entered for the plaintiff non obstante veredicto on the fourth plea. [*Tindal*, C. J.—The intestate was a surgeon and apothecary. The defendant's son was bound to him as an apprentice to serve for the space of two years only, the indenture being fraudulently antedated so as to make it appear that there had been a service for the regular period. And the question was whether or not the bond, which was given to secure a premium for such illegal service, was void.] From the articles of agreement it appeared that the plaintiff contracted to "do all such acts as might and should be needful for the facilitating the said G. H. Wiggins (the defendant's son) being duly admitted as *a regular and qualified surgeon*." To entitle a party to be duly admitted as a surgeon, no period of service is necessary: the statute 55 Geo. 3, c. 194, applying only to apothecaries. [*Tindal*, C. J.—All the evidence tended to shew an intention that the young man should be qualified to act as an *apothecary*.] Suppose the object was to enable the party to be admitted as a surgeon, apothecary, and man-midwife; the former being the principal subject-matter of the contract, and the two latter branches ancillary only, the plaintiff is still entitled to recover upon this bond. [*Tindal*, C. J.—The bond was

given in a gross sum for the performance of a certain contract: to entitle the plaintiff to recover, he must shew a
performance in omnibus.]   Even if the contract on which
the bond was given were illegal, the plaintiff, who was a
party to it, is not at liberty to set up such illegality as a
defence.   A person executing a deed for the purpose of
defrauding the law, cannot come into a court of equity for
the purpose of setting it aside, even though the instrument
has never been made use of; and, therefore, if A. convey
an estate to B. as a qualification to kill game, equity will
not compel a re-conveyance—*Roberts* v. *Roberts*, 1 Daniel,
143 : and, as against the parties to the deed, it is valid, and
sufficient to support an ejectment for the premises—*Doe
d. Roberts* v. *Roberts*, 2 B. & A. 367, 2 Chit. 272.
Armstrong v. *Lewis*, 4 M. & Scott, 1, seems to lean the
other way: it was there said that a contract made between
two or more persons to enter into a partnership in contravention of the law, is void, and confers no rights upon
either party.   But the principal decision there is favourable to the present argument :—A. & B. carried on the
business of a pawnbroker in partnership under a deed,
the business being conducted solely by A., and his name
alone appearing over the shop-door and upon the printed
tickets and duplicates used by persons in that trade, and
the licenses containing the name of A. only: the court inclined to think, that, although the parties might by that
contract have rendered themselves liable to penalties imposed by the statute 39 & 40 Geo. 3, c. 99, yet that, there
being no actual agreement for an infraction of the law,
the contract was not void.   In *Hawes* v. *Leader*, Cro.
Jac. 270, a voluntary deed was held good as between the
parties, though, by the statute 13 Eliz. c. 5, void as
against creditors.   So, in *Smith* v. *Garland*, 2 Meriv. 123,
a voluntary settlement, as between the parties, was upheld.
In the present case, there being no actual agreement for an
infraction of the law, the contract is valid, and the bond

may be enforced. [*Bosanquet*, J.—A security given for the performance of an illegal contract must itself be illegal.] Lord Mansfield, in *Montefiori* v. *Montefiori*, 1 W. Blac. 363, held that no man shall be permitted to set up his own iniquity as a defence any more than as a cause of action. If there be anything illegal in this contract, therefore, it is not competent to the defendant, who was himself a party to it, to avail himself of such illegality as a ground of defence.

Cur. adv. vult.

TINDAL, C. J., now said:—We desired time to look into the pleadings in this case, to see whether or not they contained any specific allegation that the object of the parties in entering into the agreement set out in the fourth plea, was, to evade the provisions of the statute 55 Geo. 3, c. 194, s. 15. The plea does state distinctly that it was unlawfully and corruptly agreed by and between W. S. Andrews and the defendant, that the said W. S. Andrews should take the defendant's son as his apprentice to learn the art, mystery, or profession of surgeon, *apothecary*, and man-midwife, for the term and space of two years only; but that, in the articles, it should be stated and be made to appear that the youth had been articled for the full term of five years—"in order that by such corrupt contrivance the said parties to the said agreement might fraudulently and illegally procure the said G. H. Wiggins (the defendant's son) to be admitted to examination for the purpose of practising as an *apothecary* upon serving an apprenticeship for two years, instead of an apprenticeship for five years, as required by the statute in such case made and provided." The bond declared on was given to secure the premium on such apprenticeship. It is true, that, after thus stating the real agreement between the parties, the plea goes on to allege that the intestate was to do all such acts as might and should be needful for facilitating G. H. Wiggins being duly admitted as a regular and qualified *surgeon*: but that does not

1836.

PROLE
v.
WIGGINS.

destroy the former part of the plea, which distinctly avers the object of the parties to be the evasion of a very useful statute. As, therefore, the finding of the jury upon this plea is wholly unobjectionable, we think there is no ground for giving judgment for the plaintiffs non obstante veredicto. In *Collins* v. *Blantern*, 2 Wils. 341, it is laid down broadly, that, where a bond is void in its inception, it has no legal existence: a bond given by way of indemnity to one who had given his note for 350*l.* to a prosecutor on an indictment for perjury, to induce him to withhold his evidence, was held to be void ab initio, and the facts pleadable specially. In *Doe* d. *Roberts* v. *Roberts*, the defence attempted to be set up was inconsistent with the deed of the party himself. Here the plea shews that the bond never was a legally binding instrument at all; like a bond given to secure the performance of a simoniacal contract, which is altogether void.

Rule refused.

Saturday,
Nov. 12th.

Storks, Serjeant, afterwards moved for a rule calling upon the defendant to shew cause why the plaintiff should not be exempted from costs, pursuant to the 3 & 4 Will. 4, c. 42, s. 31.

TINDAL, C. J.—If the plaintiffs knew of the latent defect in the bond before they put it in suit, they clearly ought not to be excused from paying costs. If the affidavit upon which the application is founded distinctly negatived such knowledge, there might be some pretence for asking this indulgence. But even then I think we should not be justified in granting a rule; for, the plaintiffs were by the plea made acquainted with the illegality of the transaction; and they should then have abandoned the action. The statute never intended that such a case as this should be fought at the expense of the defendant.

Rule refused.

In an action by administrators on a bond given to their intestate, a verdict having been found for the defendant on the ground of an illegality in the contract upon which the bond had been given, and which illegality was fully disclosed by the plea—The Court refused to exempt the plaintiffs from costs under the 3 & 4 Will. 4, c. 42, s. 31.

Tuesday,
Nov. 8th.

The defendants made and delivered to the plaintiffs a promissory note in payment for goods. Before the note became due, and before the plaintiffs had indorsed it, it was stolen by a clerk of the plaintiffs', who forged their indorsement thereon, and presented the note with such forged indorsement at the defendants' bankers, who paid the amount, and in the usual course handed the note over to the defendants. The plaintiffs did not discover the felony till six weeks after the note had arrived at maturity and been paid. Upon a special case stating these facts, and containing no allegation of negligence on the part of the plaintiffs:— Held, that the plaintiffs were entitled to recover the value of the note from the defendants, in an action of trover.

JOHNSON and Another *v.* WINDLE and Another.

THIS was an action of trover to recover the value of a promissory note, of which the following is a copy:—

"Milford Wharf, London, 30th March, 1835.

"Sixty days after date, we promise to pay C. Johnson & Sons, or order, 30*l.*, value received in coals ex ship Two Brothers, at Messrs. Gosling & Sharpe's.

"W. & C. Windle."

The declaration was in the usual form, and alleged that the plaintiffs were lawfully possessed of the note as of their own property. The defendants pleaded—first, not guilty—secondly, that the plaintiffs were not lawfully possessed as of their own property of the promissory note in manner and form as in the declaration alleged. Upon these pleas issues were joined.

By order of a judge and consent of the parties, the following facts were stated in a special case for the opinion of the court:—

The defendants were the makers of the promissory note above set forth, and the plaintiffs were the payees therein mentioned. The note in question was made and drawn by the defendants on the day of its date, and delivered by them to the plaintiffs in the usual course of business, in part payment for part of a cargo of coals ex ship the Two Brothers. The note was afterwards stolen from the plaintiffs; and at the time it was so stolen there was no indorsement upon it. On the day when it became due, Messrs. Wilkins were holders of the said note for value, and the same was presented by a clerk of Messrs. Glynn & Co., bankers in London, on account of the said Messrs. Wilkins, to Messrs. Gosling & Sharpe, for payment, who, as the defendants' bankers, paid the note, and debited the defendants' account with the sum paid. The note was afterwards handed over to the defendants, in whose possession it still remained.   Upon the delivery of the note to the defendants by Messrs. Gosling & Sharpe, and whilst it remained in the defendants' possession, and before the commencement of this suit, the plaintiffs demanded the note of the defendants, but they refused to give it up. Afterwards the present action was commenced.

The promissory note was never indorsed by the plaintiffs or by their authority, nor was any person ever authorized by them to receive the amount thereof.   At the time when the note was handed over to the defendants, the following indorsements appeared upon the back of it:— " By C. Johnson & Sons to Mr. John Atkin—John Atkin— George Wright."   All the indorsements on the note were forgeries, in the handwriting of one George Wryghte, who at the time the note was made and delivered to the plaintiffs, and for some time afterwards, was a clerk in their employ.   The note was stolen from the plaintiffs by the said G. Wryghte whilst he was in their service.   The defendants had no notice that the indorsement of " C. Johnson & Sons" was a forgery at the time their bankers, Messrs. Gosling & Sharpe, paid the note, nor till six weeks afterwards, when notice was given to the defendants of that fact, upon the plaintiffs' first discovering that the note had been stolen.

If the court, upon the circumstances above stated, should be of opinion that the plaintiffs were entitled to the property and to the possession of the note when the same was demanded as aforesaid, and that there was sufficient evidence of a conversion by the defendants, the pleas were to be withdrawn, and judgment was to be entered for the plaintiffs by confession, damages 30*l.* and interest, together with their costs and charges of this suit. But, if the court should be of opinion that the plaintiffs were not so entitled; or that there was not sufficient evidence of a conversion, then judgment of nolle prosequi was to be entered.

Channell, for the plaintiffs.—To entitle them to maintain this action, all that it was incumbent on the plaintiffs to shew was, that they had property in the note, that such property had not been divested, and that the defendants had converted it: all these sufficiently appear upon the case. In many cases of this description, a question has arisen whether the plaintiff has been guilty of such a degree of negligence as to bar his right of action: but in all of them the instrument has been of a negotiable character, passing by delivery—a bill payable to bearer, or indorsed in blank, or the like. In *Smith* v. *Shepperd*, cited in Chitty on Bills, 8th edit. 429, n., it is laid down by Lord Mansfield that, " If a bill, &c., be lost or stolen, &c., payment to the finder, or thief, or swindler, will be good, and will protect the party paying, even as regards the owner, if the instrument were, at the time it was lost &c., negotiable without the indorsement of the owner, that is, by delivery only, and the payer took up the bill bonâ fide, in the usual course of business, without notice of the holder's want of title, and without having cause to suspect it. But, if the instrument were not, when lost &c., transferrable by delivery only—if it required the owner's indorsement—a *forged* indorsement will be unavailing to protect a payment, even to a bonâ fide holder, under circumstances shewing there was no knowledge of the forgery or ground for suspicion, &c. In this case the real owner's title shall prevail." The like doctrine was laid down in *Cheap* v. *Harley*, cited in *Allen* v. *Dundas*, 3 T. R. 127, *Mead* v. *Young*, 4 T. R. 28, and *Forster* v. *Clements*, 2 Camp. 17. From these and many other authorities that might be cited, it is perfectly clear that a party can take no legal interest in a bill or note under a forged indorsement. Nothing but payment could divest the plaintiff's property in the note; and the defendants were clearly guilty of a conversion in retaining after demand the property of another.

Bayley, contrà.—The defendants, by the hands of their bankers, have paid the bill to a holder for value; and that, under the circumstances, affords an answer to the action. Two questions present themselves for the consideration of the court—first, whether the payment is valid as against the plaintiffs—secondly, whether it is so wholly invalid as to entitle them to throw the loss upon the defendants: and it will be important to bear in mind the distinction that exists between securities for money and the ordinary currency of the realm, a distinction that was taken by this court in *Lang* v. *Smith*, 7 Bing. 284, 5 M. & P. 78. The facts of that case were these:—The Neapolitan government raised money upon certain certificats de rente, or bonds. With each certificate or bond was delivered a document called a bordereau, annexed to which were a series of coupons, or receipts, for successive half-yearly payments of the rentes or dividends. When the coupons attached to the bordereau were all made use of, the holder of the certificat and remaining bordereau was entitled to receive from the Neopolitan government a new bordereau, with a new set of coupons; both these instruments referred to the certificat, and they were never sold in the London market without being accompanied by the certificat. The plaintiff, being possessed of certain of these certificats and bordereaux, deposited the latter with his broker, for the purpose of his procuring from the Neapolitan government new bordereaux, retaining the certificats in his own hands. The broker, having procured new bordereaux with coupons, fraudulently pledged them with the defendant. In detinue by the original owner, it was left to the jury to say—first, whether the bordereaux and coupons (unaccompanied by the certificats) were negotiable securities, passing by delivery in the same manner as banknotes, exchequer-bills, and the like instruments—secondly, whether the defendant had exercised due caution in receiving them from the broker, without inquiring for the certificats to which they referred. On a motion for a new trial, the court held this direction right, and declined to disturb a verdict found for the plaintiff. Tindal, C. J., there says : " It is a rule of law, that, if a person trusts or confides his property to an agent, who misapplies it, or disposes of it without the authority of his principal, he may, in case he be enabled to identify it, recover it back from the party holding it, in whatever hands it may be found. There is, however, an exception to this rule, in favour of the ordinary currency of the country, which rests on the ground that the rule would be highly inconvenient if it had the effect of preventing intercourse between merchants, or frustrating mercantile transactions." That case recognises the general rule of law to be, that negligence in the plaintiffs will deprive them of the right to cast the loss upon an innocent defendant. It may be conceded, that, were both parties equally blameless, the defendants in this case must bear the loss. The facts, however, exhibit gross negligence on the part of the plaintiffs. The note, it appears, was stolen by a clerk in their employ; and the theft was not discovered until six weeks after the note had been in due course paid. It was the plaintiffs' duty to keep the note in a place of security, to present it when due, and, in the event of its being lost in the meantime, to give proper notice of such loss. Ordinary care and diligence might have prevented the theft or caused the forgery to be detected, or, at all events, might have enabled the plaintiffs to discover the loss of the note before it became due. [*Tindal*, C. J.—Gross negligence is not found in the case, and we are not at liberty to presume it. Merchants must place a certain degree of confidence in those whom they employ. The plaintiffs, it appears, gave notice of the forgery on the very day on which they discovered it. They took the best care they could of the note, by withholding their indorsement.] In *Morrison* v. *Buchanan*, 6 C. & P. 18, the negligence imputed to the plaintiff was much slighter in degree than

that found here, and yet it was held to be a sufficient
answer to the action. It appearing there to be the regular
and usual course of business in commercial transactions to
deliver out bills of exchange left for acceptance to any
person who mentions the amount and describes any private
mark upon them—it was ruled, by Littledale, J., that, if
the clerk of a party leaving a bill by his conduct enables a
stranger to discover the mark or number, in consequence
of which the bill is delivered out to him, the party leaving
it cannot maintain trover for it against the party who so
delivered it out.

Channell, in reply, was stopped by the court.

TINDAL, C. J.—It would lead to the most dangerous
consequences if we were, by pronouncing judgment for the
defendants in this case, to give validity to a forged indorsement of a bill of exchange or promissory note. The
general rule is, that no title to a bill or note can be acquired through a forged indorsement. Here it appears
that all the indorsements on this note were forgeries. The
answer attempted to be set up is, that the plaintiffs have
been guilty of such gross negligence as to take this case
out of the general rule, and to deprive them of all right
of action against the defendants for the alleged conversion.
The case, however, leaves us entirely in doubt as to the
degree of caution or carelessness to be imputed to the
plaintiffs. If they intended to rely upon the supposed
negligence of the plaintiffs, the defendants should have
inserted in the case a precise statement to that effect.

GASELEE, J.—The difference between *Morrison* v.
Buchanan and the present case is, that there is here no
question, as there was before the jury in that case, as to
negligence in the plaintiffs. Upon the facts stated I think
the plaintiffs are entitled to judgment.

VAUGHAN, J.—The case on the part of the plaintiffs exhibits all that is requisite to entitle them to maintain the action—property in the note in them, an entire absence of anything to shew that that property was ever divested, and a conversion by the defendants: and nothing appears on the face of the case whence we can infer negligence on the part of the plaintiffs. In *Morrison* v. *Buchanan*, both negligence in the plaintiff and the exercise of due caution by the defendant were affirmed by the jury. In Bayley on Bills, 4th edit., p. 107, the rule is thus stated: " A transfer by indorsement will convey no title, except against the person making it, unless it is made by him who has a right to make the transfer: a transfer by delivery may. Therefore, in case of a loss by theft or accident, if the bill or note be assignable by mere delivery, the thief or finder may confer a title by transferring it; if it be assignable by indorsement only, he cannot."

BOSANQUET, J.—The note in question was originally marked as the property of the plaintiffs. The indorsement, being forged, was a nullity; it is the same as if it had not been there at all: consequently, no property passed by it.

Judgment for the plaintiffs.

———◆———

TAYLOR *v.* BLACKLOW.

Tuesday,
Nov. 8th.
The defendant
was retained as
an attorney to
raise money
for the plaintiff
by way of
mortgage.

CASE against an attorney for an alleged breach of duty. The declaration stated, that, before and at the several times thereinafter mentioned, the defendant was an attor-

In the course of his employment on this retainer, the defendant discovered that the legal estate in certain of the property intended to be comprised in the mortgage was in the plaintiff's brother, J. H. T., whose attorney the defendant was. The defendant communicated the discovery to J. H. T., who thereupon instituted proceedings for the recovery of the premises, whereby the plaintiff was put to expense, delayed in procuring the advance he required, and ultimately compelled to pay a higher rate of interest:—Held, that this was such a breach of duty on the part of the defendant as to render him liable to an action.

ney, to wit, an attorney of the court of Common Pleas, at
Westminster; and the plaintiff then claimed to be lawfully
entitled to and interested in a certain estate, to wit, in
certain messuages, buildings, lands, tenements, and premises, with the appurtenances, in the county of Kent, and
before and at the time of the committing of the grievance
by the defendant as thereinafter mentioned, was desirous
to borrow and obtain an advance of money, to wit, the sum
of 4,000l., by way of mortgage of and security upon the
said estate and premises, whereof the defendant, before
and at the time of the committing of the grievance by him
committed as thereinafter stated, had notice: and thereupon, theretofore, to wit, on the 2nd March, 1833, the defendant, so being such attorney as aforesaid, represented
to the plaintiff that he had a client who would advance the
said sum of 4,000l., on sufficient security and at a moderate
rate of interest, to wit, at the rate of 4l. per cent. per
annum for interest upon the same; and the plaintiff, at the
request of the defendant, retained and employed the defendant as such attorney to use due endeavours to obtain
and procure the said sum of 4,000l. on such mortgage for
the plaintiff, for reasonable reward to the defendant in
that behalf; and the plaintiff, at the request of the defendant, then delivered to the defendant, as such attorney,
and in pursuance of the said retainer, divers, to wit, six
abstracts of and relating to the title of the plaintiff of, in,
and to the said estate and premises, and certain other
documents also relating to the same, to wit, a statement of
the number of acres of which the said estate consisted,
and the names of the tenants and occupiers of the same;
and thereupon and by means of the premises the defendant afterwards, and before the committing of the grievance
by the defendant as thereinafter mentioned, to wit, on &c.;
as such attorney of and for the plaintiff as aforesaid, discovered and ascertained that there was a certain defect in
and objection to the legal right and title of the plaintiff to
the said estate and premises, to wit, that in two of the

title deeds of and relating to the said estate and premises,
a part of the said estate and premises, to wit, sixty acres
thereof, and certain messuages, buildings, and improve-
ments thereon, had not been sufficiently conveyed to or
for the use or benefit of the plaintiff; and that, by reason
and on account thereof, a certain other person, to wit,
John Henry Taylor, the brother of the plaintiff, then had
in point of law a legal right to such part of the said estate
and premises, and to recover the possession of the same,
although in justice and equity the beneficial interest in the
whole of the said estate and premises then belonged to
the plaintiff: and by reason of the premises, and under
and by virtue of the said retainer and employment, it
then became and was the duty of the defendant not voluntarily or unnecessarily to divulge and communicate the
said defect in and objection to the legal right and title of
the plaintiff to the said estate and premises to the said
John Henry Taylor, or to any other person, and not to
instigate or cause or procure to be commenced or prosecuted any action or proceeding for the recovery of the
said estate and premises, or any part thereof, from the
plaintiff, for or by reason or on account of such discovery of the defendant by the means aforesaid; nevertheless the defendant, so being such attorney as aforesaid,
but not regarding his duty as such attorney, nor his duty
in the premises under and by virtue of his said retainer
and employment; but contriving and craftily and subtilly
intending to injure and annoy the plaintiff, and to cause
and procure a great part of the said estate and premises,
to wit, the said sixty acres thereof, and the said messuages,
buildings, and improvements thereon, to be recovered
from him by unjust, vexatious, and improper proceedings,
theretofore, to wit, on &c., dishonourably, wrongfully, and
unjustly, and for the sake of fees and unjust reward in
that behalf, in violation of his duty as such attorney, and
contrary to his said duty in the premises, and in violation
of good faith, voluntarily and unnecessarily divulged and

communicated the said defect in and objection to the legal
right and title of the plaintiff to the said estate and premises, to the said John Henry Taylor, and then wrongfully, maliciously, dishonourably, and oppressively, contriving and intending as aforesaid, instigated and caused
and procured divers, to wit, four actions of ejectment respectively on the demise of the said John Henry Taylor,
to be commenced against divers, to wit, twelve tenants of
the now plaintiff, of certain parts of the said estate and
premises of the now plaintiff; and the said now plaintiff
having as landlord duly appeared and defended the said
actions of ejectment, the now defendant prosecuted the
same, and also wrongfully, maliciously, unjustly, and oppressively caused and procured a certain other action, by
and in the name of the said John Henry Taylor against
the now plaintiff, to be commenced and prosecuted for a
certain pretended cause of action, to wit, for cutting down
and converting certain timber before then growing on the
said estate and premises of the now plaintiff: and the now
defendant, further contriving and intending as aforesaid,
also then wrongfully and maliciously, unjustly, and oppressively instigated and caused and procured to be commenced and prosecuted, in the name of the said John
Henry Taylor against the now plaintiff, divers, to wit, four
other actions for the recovery of certain sums of money
claimed to be due from the now plaintiff, which, but for
such instigation and causing and procuring of the now defendant, would not have been so commenced or prosecuted: and the now defendant, further contriving as aforesaid, then falsely and maliciously instigated and persuaded,
and caused and procured the said John Henry Taylor to
commence and prosecute against the now plaintiff a certain untenable suit in the Exchequer for setting aside the
conveyance to the now plaintiff of his said estate of and
in the said premises, and which was afterwards, to wit, on
the 9th July, 1834, according to equity and justice, dis-

1836.

TAYLOR
v.
BLACKLOW.

Special damage.

missed with costs to be paid by the said John Henry Taylor: and the now plaintiff, in order to obtain relief in the premises, was theretofore, in Hilary Term, 4 Will. 4, forced and obliged to file and did file and prosecute his certain bill of complaint against the said John Henry Taylor in the court of Exchequer for relief in the premises, and in order to obtain an injunction against the prosecution of the said actions of ejectment; and was also then forced and obliged to apply to the said court of Exchequer for relief against the said now defendant: By means of which said breach of duty, and of the said false, deceptive, fraudulent, and malicious conduct of the now defendant in the premises, the now plaintiff was forced and obliged to incur, and did incur great trouble of mind and body, and great expense of his monies, to wit, to the amount of 2,000l., in defending and resisting the said unjust and vexatious proceedings, and in obtaining and enforcing, and in endeavouring to obtain and enforce, by due and lawful ways and means. relief against the same, and other unlawful, oppressive, and unjust proceedings of the now defendant in the premises; and by means and in consequence of the said John Henry Taylor having become and being insolvent and unable to pay the costs of the said vexatious proceedings so instigated and caused and procured by the now defendant to be instituted and prosecuted in his name as aforesaid, the now plaintiff was unable to recover or obtain payment or satisfaction of or from the said John Henry Taylor of the said costs, and he was wholly unable to pay or satisfy the same; and the now plaintiff was, by means of the said malicious, unjust, vexatious, and improper conduct of the now defendant, greatly harassed, oppressed, vexed, and impoverished, and otherwise greatly injured; and also by means of the premises the now plaintiff was hindered and prevented from raising and procuring the said money or other money on mortgage of the said estate and premises for a long time, to wit, from thence until the 20th January,

1836, and was then by reason of the premises forced and obliged to raise and procure on mortgage and security of the said estate and premises a much larger sum of money than the said sum of 4,000*l.*, to wit, the sum of 6,000*l.*, and at a greater rate of interest than at and after such rate of 4*l.* per cent. per annum, to wit, at the rate of 4*l.* 10*s.* per cent. per annum for each and every 100*l.* thereof: to the damage of the now plaintiff of 2,000*l.*

The defendant pleaded—that, before and at the time *Plea.* when the defendant represented to the said plaintiff that he the defendant had a client who would advance the said sum of 4,000*l.* in the declaration mentioned on sufficient security and at interest, and before and at the time when the plaintiff delivered to him the defendant the said abstracts and other documents relating to the said estate and premises, and before and at the time when the defendant discovered and ascertained that there was a certain defect in and objection to the legal right and title of the plaintiff to the said estate and premises, and before and at the time when the defendant divulged and communicated the said defect in and objection to the legal right and title of the plaintiff to the said estate and premises to the said John Henry Taylor, the defendant was the attorney and solicitor to the said John Henry Taylor, and had been and was retained and employed by him as such attorney and solicitor generally and in relation to his affairs, whereof the plaintiff had notice ; and thereupon it became and was the duty of the defendant, as such attorney and solicitor of and for the said John Henry Taylor, to divulge and communicate the said defect in and objection to the legal right and title of the plaintiff to the said estate and premises to the said John Henry Taylor, and he did on that account, and without malice or any violation of good faith, at the said time when &c., divulge and communicate the said defect in and objection to the legal right and title of the plaintiff to the said estate and premises to the said John

Henry Taylor, with a view and in order that he might claim
and recover the said estate and premises from the plaintiff if
lawfully entitled thereto, as he then appeared and was believed by the defendant to be; and that thereupon the
said John Henry Taylor did then retain and employ the
defendant as such attorney, to take due and proper proceedings to try and investigate the said right and claim of
the said John Henry Taylor, and to recover the said
estate and premises for him, and to bring and prosecute
the said actions and suits in the declaration mentioned respectively; whereupon the defendant did, as such attorney, and under the said retainer, and without malice to
the plaintiff, advise the said John Henry Taylor to bring
and prosecute, and the defendant, as such attorney, under
the said retainer, did bring and prosecute the said several
actions and suits in the declaration mentioned in that behalf—verification.

Special demur-
rer.

To this plea the plaintiff demurred specially, assigning
for causes—that, although the defendant in and by his
said plea confessed and admitted that he was retained and
employed by the plaintiff to act for him as his attorney in
the premises, and that, under and by virtue of that retainer
and employment, the defendant discovered and ascertained
the said defect in and objection to the legal right and title
of the plaintiff to the said estate and premises, but that
in justice and equity the beneficial interest in the whole of
the said estate and premises then belonged to the plaintiff;
and although the defendant had in and by his said plea
confessed and admitted that it was his duty, under and by
virtue of the said retainer and employment, not voluntarily
or unnecessarily to divulge or communicate the said defect
and objection to the said John Henry Taylor, or to any
other person, nor to instigate or cause or procure to be commenced and prosecuted any action or proceeding for the
recovery of the said estate, or any part thereof; yet the defendant had attempted to defend and justify his said illegal

conduct upon and under colour of a wholly untenable
ground and pretence—and also that, although the said
plea was pleaded in bar to the whole declaration, yet the
said plea did not state or shew any defence or legal or sufficient justification or excuse of or for the said statement
or cause of action against the defendant for or in respect of
his having so wrongfully, maliciously, and dishonourably
instigated and caused and procured the said actions of
ejectment to be commenced and prosecuted, and the said
other actions to be commenced and prosecuted for the
said pretended cause of action, to wit, the cutting down
and converting the said timber, or of or for the defendant
having so wrongfully and maliciously, unjustly, and oppressively instigated and caused and procured to be commenced and prosecuted for the said pretended cause of
action, to wit, the cutting down and converting the said
timber, or of or for the defendant having so wrongfully
and maliciously, unjustly, and oppressively instigated and
caused and procured to be commenced and prosecuted in
the name of the said John Henry Taylor against the
plaintiff the said other actions, and having falsely and maliciously instigated and persuaded and caused and procured the said John Henry Taylor to commence and prosecute against the plaintiff the said untenable suit in the
Exchequer, &c.

F. Kelly, in support of the demurrer.—The question is
whether or not the plaintiff can, under the circumstances
disclosed in the pleadings, maintain an action against the
defendant for a very gross breach of duty, attended by a
pecuniary loss to the plaintiff. The circumstances are
these—the defendant was retained as an attorney to procure for the plaintiff an advance of money upon mortgage.
In the course of that employment he discovered that the
legal estate in part of the premises was outstanding in
another, though the plaintiff, his client, was equitably and

justly entitled. Betraying his employer, he instigated the
party in whom the legal estate was, to take legal proceedings to oust the plaintiff. There is no case to be found the
facts of which are precisely the same as these; but no
precedent can be needed to shew that an action will lie
against an attorney for a breach of duty. When he accepts the retainer of a client for hire and reward, the law
imposes upon him a duty to conduct the business intrusted
to him with integrity and fidelity: he is as much bound to
conduct his client's affairs with fidelity and secrecy, as to
employ therein a reasonable degree of diligence and skill.
In Comyns's Digest, " *Action on the Case for Deceit,*"
(A 5), it is laid down that an action of this sort lies, " if a
man, being intrusted in his profession, deceive him who
intrusted him; or, if a man retained of counsel, become
afterward of counsel with the other party in the same
cause, or discover the evidence or secrets of the cause.
So, *if an attorney act deceptive to the prejudice of his
client;* as, if by collusion with the demandant he make
default in a real action, whereby the land is lost." Lord
Lyndhurst, on a motion before him in this matter, in
the court of Chancery, stigmatised the defendant's conduct as "a gross breach of professional duty." The
ground-work of this action is, that breach of duty. No
precedent can be adduced, because, happily, the defendant's conduct is unprecedented. In *Lord Cholmondeley* v.
Lord Clinton, Coop. C. C. 80, 18 Ves. 273, 19 Ves. 261,
an injunction was granted, to restrain an attorney from
giving up his client (on a change of firms) and acting for
the opposite party in the suit. The damage alleged in the
declaration, viz. that the plaintiff was hindered and prevented from raising the money from the time of the alleged
communication to a certain other time, is sufficiently specific.

John Jervis, for the defendant.—The circumstances
stated in this declaration do not disclose any such duty as

that which has been assumed in argument on the part of
the plaintiff. The facts disclosed by the defendant in this
case were of such a nature as would not have entitled him
to withhold the disclosure of them in a court of justice;
and, if so, he cannot be liable to this action. The privilege of withholding that which is communicated to one in
his character of professional adviser, is not the privilege
of the attorney, but of the client; and it is confined to
cases where a suit is either already commenced or contemplated, or with reference to a matter in difference in which
the party is employed professionally as an attorney, and
does not extend to the case of a money scrivener or con-
veyancer (a). In *Wilson* v. *Rastall,* 4 T. R. 753, it was

1836.

Taylor
v.
Blacklow.

(a) In Turquand v. Knight, 2 M.
& Welsby, 98, the attorney for the
bankrupt, whose assignees were
the plaintiffs, was called to prove
the fact of a lease (for which the
action was brought) having been
in the bankrupt's possession on a
certain day, and that the bankrupt
had then applied to him to raise
money upon it, in order to shew
that it had been deposited with the
defendant after the act of bankruptcy was committed. It was objected that the witness, having
been the bankrupt's attorney at the
time of the communication to him,
was confidential, and he therefore
could not be allowed to answer
the question. Lord Abinger rejected the evidence, and the court
refused to grant a rule for a new
trial. In the course of the argument it was urged, that, where an
attorney is employed merely to
raise money, that is not such an
employment as brings him within
the rule as to confidential and pri-

vileged communications; and that
here he was acting in the character of a scrivener only. Lord
Abinger, in his judgment, referred
to Wheatley v. Williams, 1 M &
Welsby, 533, where an attorney
was not allowed to prove that an
instrument was unstamped at the
time it bore date, it having been
shewn to him as a matter of business, for which he made a charge;
and also to the case of Harvey v.
Clayton, 2 Swans. 221, n., where
Lord Nottingham laid it down that
he would not compel a scrivener
to disclose the communications
made to him. And Alderson, B.,
held that the rule was correlative
with that which governs the summary jurisdiction of the court over
attornies; and referred to the
terms in which that rule was
couched in Ex parte Aitken, 4 B.
& Ald. 49 :—" Where an attorne
is employed in a matter wholly
unconnected with his professional
character, the court will not inter-

held that this privilege is confined to counsel, solicitors, and attornies, when acting in their respective characters. And Buller, J., said : " The nature of this kind of privilege is, that the attorney shall not be permitted to disclose *in any action* that which has been confidentially communicated to him." In *Cobden* v. *Kendrick*, 4 T. R. 431, it was held that an attorney is not restrained by any rule of law from giving evidence of a conversation between himself and his client, touching the justice of his suit, after a writ of inquiry executed on an interlocutory judgment, and a compromise thereupon; for, the purpose of the suit having been obtained, the communication could not be said to have been made by way of instruction for conducting his cause. In Buller's Nisi Prius, p. 284, it is said that there are some exceptions to this privilege—First, as to what such persons knew before the retainer; for, as to such matters, they are clearly in the same situation as any other person : secondly, to a fact of his own knowledge, and of which he might have had knowledge without being counsel or attorney in the cause ; as, suppose him witness to a deed produced in a cause, he shall be examined to the true time of execution." In *Walker* v. *Wildman*, 6 Madd. 47, it was held that the privilege did not extend to the case of an employment in matters not professional. In *Wadsworth* v. *Hamshaw*, 4 Moore, 358, n., 2 B. & B. 5, n., where the defendant's attorney was called as a witness by the plaintiff, to prove the partnership of his clients, his knowledge of which was acquired in a strictly professional capacity, he having been previously consulted by them respecting a dissolution of partnership, Abbott, C. J., was of opinion that this was not a privileged com-

fere in a summary way to compel him to execute faithfully the trust reposed in him. But, where the employment is so connected with his professional character as to afford a presumption that his character formed the ground of his employment by his client, there the court will exercise this jurisdiction."

munication; holding that the protection extended to those cases only which relate to a cause existing at the time of such communication, or then about to be commenced. In *Williams* v. *Mundie*, R. & M. 34, 1 C. & P. 158, the same learned judge observed: "I have invariably laid down that what is communicated for the purpose of bringing an action or suit, or relating to an action or suit existing at the time of the communication, is confidential and privileged: but *what an attorney learns otherwise than for the purpose of a cause or suit, he is bound to communicate* (*b*)." And in *Clark* v. *Clark*, 2 M. & M. 3, Lord Tenterden extends the privilege to all cases where the communication was made to the attorney in his professional capacity concern-in *a matter then in dispute*, although no cause was in existence with respect to it. In *Bramwell* v. *Lucas*, 4 D. & R. 367, 2 B. & C. 745, it was held that a communication made by a client to his attorney to obtain information as to a matter of fact, and not for the purpose of asking him his legal advice, is not privileged: and therefore, where a trader, at the suggestion of his attorney, called a meeting of his creditors, to be held at a given time and place, and on the morning of that day went to the attorney's office, and inquired of him whether he could safely attend the meeting without being arrested for debt, and the attorney having advised him to remain at the office until it was ascertained whether the creditors would engage to give him a safe-conduct, the trader remained at the office accordingly for upwards of two hours to avoid being arrested by some or one of his creditors, until after the attorney had attended at and returned from the meeting; it was held that what passed between the attorney and the trader was admissible in evidence, and might be disclosed by the attorney, on his being called as a witness in a cause where

(*b*) See Broad v. Pill, 1 M. & M. 234, where Best, C. J. was of opinion that it was sufficient to make the communication privileged if any legal proceeding was either instituted or *apprehended*.

the question was whether the trader had committed an act of bankruptcy on that occasion. Abbott, C. J., in delivering the judgment of the court, there says: "Whether the privilege extends to all confidential communications between attorney and client or not, there is no doubt that it is confined to communications, and to communications to the attorney in his character of attorney. A question *for legal advice* may come within the description of a confidential communication, because it is a part of the attorney's duty, as attorney, to give legal advice; but a question for information *as to matters of fact* as to a communication the attorney has made to others, where the communication might have been made by any other person as well as an attorney, and where the character or office of attorney has not been called into action, has never been held within the protection, and is not within the principle on which the privilege is founded. Was this a question for legal advice put to the attorney in his character of attorney, or was it not a question for information as to matter of fact in which his professional character as attorney was not considered? It can hardly be supposed that a man could ask as matter of law whether he could be free from arrest while attending a voluntary meeting of his creditors; but he might well ask as matter of fact from the person at whose suggestion the creditors had been convened, whether any arrangements had been made with the creditors to prevent an arrest: and the attorney's answer implies that the question was put with the latter view. He gives no legal advice; his answer implies that no arrangement had been made, but that he would see at the meeting whether any could be effected: and he recommends the client, not as a legal adviser, but as any agent or any friend might have recommended, to stay where he was till that matter of fact was ascertained (c)." These

(c) See Moore v. Terrell, 1 N. & M. 559, 4 B. & Ad. 870. And see Doe d. Peter v. Watkins, 3 New Cases, 421, post, Vol. 4.

1836.

TAYLOR
v.
BLACKLOW.

authorities fully establish that the communication in question was not within the protection of the privilege adverted to; and, it follows as a necessary consequence, not the subject of an action for damages.

There are many cases wherein applications have been made to restrain attornies from acting adversely to parties a knowledge of whose cause they have obtained whilst acting professionally for them. In *Robinson* v. *Mullett*, 4 Price, 353, it was held that a solicitor who had acted to a certain extent only for parties defendants in an amicable suit in Chancery, would not be restrained from acting in a cause by bill filed by some of those defendants, on behalf of themselves, against others of them; the solicitor making affidavit that he was not confidentially possessed of any secrets which might be used to the prejudice of such other defendants, or had knowledge of any facts unknown to his present clients. In *Beer* v. *Ward*, 1 Jac. 77, on a motion to restrain a solicitor from giving evidence of confidential matters, the Lord Chancellor refused to interfere; leaving the propriety of his examination to the consideration of the court before which he might appear as a witness. In *Bricheno* v. *Thorp*, 1 Jac. 300, where it was held that a clerk to a solicitor, commencing practice for himself, is not to be restrained from acting as solicitor for parties against whom his master was employed, upon general allegations of his having, in his former service, acquired information likely to be prejudicial to the clients of his master, Lord Eldon materially qualifies the rule laid down in the case of *Lord Cholmondeley* v. *Lord Clinton*. In *Grissell* v. *Peto*, 2 M. & Scott, 2, 9 Bing. 1, this court refused to restrain the defendant's attornies from acting for him in the cause, on the alleged ground that they had, in the character of solicitors for the defendant and others interested (jointly with the plaintiffs) in a Chancery suit, in attendance upon a master, obtained a knowledge of the plaintiffs' case, and of the evidence upon which it was to be supported; the defendant's attornies deposing that they in that suit acted also for the defendants, and had not thereby obtained any further knowledge of the plaintiff's case than would be disclosed by a particular of demand. In *Johnson* v. *Marriott*, 2 C. & M. 183, 2 Dowl. 343, 4 Tyr. 78, it was held, that, where an attorney has been employed in a cause, and is afterwards discharged by his client, not on the ground of misconduct, the court will not restrain him from acting for the opposite party, unless it clearly and distinctly appears that he has obtained information in his former character which it was necessary to conceal, and which it would be prejudicial to the cause of his former client to communicate. In none of these cases, however, was it even suggested that an action would lie against the attorney as for a breach of an implied duty. In *Bolton* v. *The Corporation of Liverpool*, 1 Mylne & K. 88, the Lord Chancellor was of opinion that cases laid before counsel in the progress of a cause, and prepared in contemplation of, and with reference to an action or suit, cannot be ordered to be produced for the purposes of that action or suit. This, however, is very different from the legal liability attempted in the present case to be fastened upon the defendant for an alleged breach of duty. Besides, here, the defendant was not the attorney of the plaintiff; but of the proposed lender: and to him he was bound to disclose the precise state of the title. The defendant, being the attorney of John Henry Taylor before his retainer by the plaintiff, was placed in a situation of difficulty. It is true he might be bound to keep the plaintiff's secrets: but it was equally his duty to communicate to John Henry Taylor anything he became acquainted with that might tend to *his* benefit (*d*).

(*d*) In Greenough v. Gaskell, 1 M. & K. 101, Lord Brougham thus lays down the rule—"The question relates to a solicitor who is called upon to produce the entries he had made in his accounts, and letters received and written by him in his character or situa-

F. Kelly, in reply.—The communication which this de-

fendant is charged with having made, was not one which
he could have been compelled to make in a court of law if
examined as a witness: and, even if it were so, that would
afford no argument in answer to the action; for, it may
very well be that a party would be held excused for a disclosure made under compulsion of law, which it would be
a breach of duty to make voluntarily. In *Cromack* v.
Heathcote, 4 Moore, 357, 2 B. & B. 4, where an attorney,
being requested to draw an assignment of property, refused, and the deed was afterwards drawn by another, the
validity of the deed being afterwards questioned, on the
ground of fraud, in an action against the sheriff, in which
the attorney first applied to was not employed, it was held
that the communication made to that attorney was privi-

tion of confidential solicitor to the party; and I am of opinion that he cannot be compelled to disclose papers delivered or communications made to him, or letters or entries made by him, in that capacity. No authority sanctions such a situation of professional confidence as would be involved in compelling counsel or solicitors to disclose matters committed to them in their professional capacity, and which, but for their employment as professional men, they would not have become possessed of. As regards them, it does not appear that the protection is qualified by any reference to proceedings pending or in contemplation. If, touching matters that come within the ordinary scope of professional employment, they receive a communication in their professional capacity, either from a client or on his account and for his benefit in the transaction of his business, or, which amounts to the same thing, if they commit to paper in the course of their employment in his behalf matters which they know only through their professional relation to their client, they are not only *justified* in withholding such matters, but *bound* to withhold them, and will not be compelled to disclose the information or produce the papers in any court of law or equity, either as party or as witness. If this protection were confined to cases where proceedings had commenced, the rule would exclude the most confidential, and, it may be, the most important of all communications—those made with a view of being prepared either for instituting or defending a suit up to the instant that the process of the court issued."

leged, and that evidence of the fraud, proposed to be given through him, was properly rejected. [*Vaughan*, J.— In *Doe* d. *Shellard* v. *Harris*, 5 C. & P. 592, Mr. Baron Parke held that the protection of communications made by a client to his attorney applies to all cases in which the relation of attorney and client subsists, and to all cases where the client applies to the attorney in his professional capacity.] *Moore* v. *Terrell*, in effect decides the question. That was an action for a libel charging an attorney with " disgraceful conduct" in having, at an election, disclosed confidential communications which he had acquired professionally. The defendant pleaded that the plaintiff had, on the occasion alluded to, disclosed details professionally and confidentially made known to him, relating to three transactions (which were specified); two of them being instances in which he had been employed by mortgagors to manage mortgages, and a third, where, in his employment as an attorney, he had become acquainted with the nature of his client's title, and his right to grant freehold leases. At the trial it appeared, that, as to the mortgages, the defendant had acted as attorney both for the mortgagors and mortgagees: it was held that the question for the jury was, whether the matters disclosed by the plaintiff were confidential communications acquired by him professionally, and not whether they were such as he would not be compellable to disclose, if called as a witness in a court of justice. Parke, J., in the course of the argument, observed : " In *Greenough* v. *Gaskell*, 1 M. & K. 98, the Lord Chancellor consulted with Tindal, C. J., Lord Lyndhurst, and myself, and we all thought the client's privilege extended much beyond communications in respect of a suit." The general doctrine laid down in that case (*Greenough* v. *Gaskell*) was, that a solicitor cannot be compelled, at the instance of a third party, to disclose matters which have come to his knowledge in the conduct of professional business for a client, even though such business had no reference to legal proceedings either existing or in contemplation. A court of equity, as appears from the cases cited on the part of the defendant, though it will not interpose upon mere general allegations of fraud or misconduct, will restrain a solicitor from making an undue use of information acquired by him in his professional character, where any specific matter of complaint or injury is alleged. The fact of the plaintiff being aware that the defendant was also the attorney of John Henry Taylor, affords no justification for the defendant's breach of confidence.

TINDAL, C. J.—This case has been argued before us principally with reference to the cause of action disclosed on the face of the declaration. I am of opinion that the plaintiff is entitled to maintain his action; and consequently that, as to this plea, there must be judgment for him. Many cases have been cited and fully discussed on the part of the defendant in order to shew that the disclosure for the making of which this action is brought was one that the defendant, if called as a witness in a court of law, would not be permitted to withhold by reason of the character he filled or the circumstances under which that disclosure was made to him. It is not necessary for us now to consider that question: if it were so, the cases of *Cromack* v. *Heathcote* and *Moore* v. *Terrell* seem to me to be decisive on the point. The complaint here is, that the defendant, being retained as an attorney to procure an advance of money for the plaintiff, dishonourably, wrongfully, and unjustly, and for the sake of fees and unjust reward in that behalf, in violation of his duty as such attorney, and in violation of good faith, voluntarily and unnecessarily divulged and communicated to a third party a defect which he discovered in the plaintiff's title. This case, therefore, stands clear of the questions that arose in the cases cited. No one can doubt that it was the defendant's duty to keep sacred anything that might come to his knowledge respecting the plaintiff's title in the course of his professional employment. When the plaintiff's deeds were put into his hands for the purpose of negotiating the proposed loan, it was clearly the thing the most remote from his duty to disclose the defect to the very person who was to benefit by the disclosure. It is said that the fact of the defendant being at the time the general attorney of the party to whom and for whose benefit the communication was made, not only justified the disclosure, but rendered it the defendant's duty to make it. There may, it is true, be persons who are not possessed of sufficient discretion and firmness to adopt decided measures under such circumstances. But, it appears to me, that, if the defendant felt he had conflicting duties cast upon him, his course was a safe and easy one: he should have restored the deeds to his employer, and sealed his lips with the sacred and solemn seal of silence; he would then have performed his duty. But instead of adopting this, the only safe and honourable course, he thought fit, not only to disclose the defects in the plaintiff's title to a third person, but instigated that individual to avail himself of the information thus dishonourably obtained. It appears, that, in consequence of the discoveries made by the defendant, in breach of his professional duty, the plaintiff has sustained a temporal injury, in being put to costs in defending certain actions, and in being compelled to pay a larger rate of interest on the money obtained on the mortgage of the premises: and I see no reason why an action should not lie for that breach of duty. The passages cited on the part of the plaintiff from Comyns's Digest seem to me to apply very closely to the present case. It is there laid down that an action on the case for deceit lies "if a man, being intrusted in his profession, deceive him who intrusted him; or, if a man retained of counsel become afterward of counsel with the other party in the same cause, or discover the evidence or secrets of the cause. So, if an attorney act deceptive to the prejudice of his client; or, if by collusion with the demandant he make default in a real action, whereby the land is lost." It is said that this action is not maintainable, because the communication was not made with a malicious intent, but was made to another client of the defendant's, to whom he owed an equal duty. I do not perceive how that fact could operate at all as an answer to the action, unless the plaintiff's knowledge of the defendant's being his brother's attorney can be construed to amount to a waiver of his right to complain of any communication made in that quarter. But it appears to me that that circumstance in no degree excuses the defendant, and that the plea is no answer to the declaration.

GASELEE, J.—If it were necessary to determine whether or not the communication in question was, under the circumstances, of a nature which the defendant would have been compellable to divulge if called as a witness in a court of law, I should wish for time to look into the numerous cases upon the subject. That point, however, it is not at all necessary to consider here. The disclosure made by the defendant was not the result of any compulsion legal or moral; it was purely voluntary. The first duty of a professional man is to keep inviolate his clients' secrets. There would be an end of all professional confidence if this were not so. No authority can be wanted for so evident a position: if it were, Comyns's Digest, in the passages already cited, supplies it. If the defendant felt it to be inconsistent with the duty he owed his former client, the defendant's brother, to proceed on the plaintiff's retainer, he should have withdrawn from it, and have preserved a discreet silence on the subject of the discovery the confidence reposed in him had enabled him to make.

VAUGHAN, J.—There cannot I think be two opinions on the defendant's conduct in this transaction. He has been guilty of a gross breach of a great moral duty: and I think the law is never better employed than in punishing breaches of moral duties. I am inclined to think that this was strictly a case of privileged communication.

BOSANQUET, J.—I forbear to enter into a consideration of the question presented by the argument urged on the part of the defendant; it is unnecessary for us now to decide whether the communication were privileged or not. When the defendant undertook to negotiate the loan for the plaintiff, it unquestionably became his duty not to disclose the secrets of his client; and I am clearly of opinion that for the breach of this duty he is liable to an action.

Judgment for the plaintiff.

———————

PHYPERS *v.* EBURN.

A devisee in fee of a copyhold tenement, on his admittance, paid the lord the full fine due by the custom of the manor. He afterwards made a surrender of the premises to the use of himself and his assigns for life, with divers remainders over; and, on being admitted tenant for life of the surrendered premises, he paid a fine of 1*s.* to the lord:—Held, that, in the absence of a custom within the manor to sanction it, no fine was payable on the admission of the remainder-man—the admission of the tenant for life being the admission of the remainder-man.

THIS action was brought against the defendant for trespassing upon certain closes named or described by metes and bounds in the declaration; to which the defendant pleaded—First, that the right of possession of the closes in which &c., was not in the plaintiff—secondly, a special plea of justification, that the defendant, as bailiff, and under a warrant from the steward of the manor of Crowlands, in the county of Cambridge, seized the closes in which &c. quosque, viz. in the mean time and until some person or persons should appear and make good his or their claims to be admitted tenant thereto, at a court of the lord of the manor of Crowlands.

The plaintiff replied, that one John Purchas was admitted to the closes in question as tenant for life, with remainders over; and that one Frances Ann Purchas was seised in remainder under that admittance.

The parties, having joined issue, agreed to submit the following case for the opinion of the court:—

The plaintiff, before the committing the trespasses by the defendant in the closes in which &c., was and still is the tenant and occupier of the lands in question, as tenant to John Purchas, deceased, hereinafter mentioned, and since his decease to Frances Ann Purchas, hereinafter mentioned, daughter of the said John Purchas. The lands in question were copyhold of the manor of Crowlands, in the parish of Dry Drayton, in the county of Cambridge. The fine payable according to the custom of the manor was two years' improved annual value on admission of a tenant of copyhold lands as heir, devisee, or surrenderee.

Customary fine.

At a court held for the said manor on the 26th January, 1789, the homage presented the death of John Purchas, the father of the said John Purchas, a customary tenant of the said manor, who held to him and his heirs divers lands and tenements of the lord of the said manor by copy of court roll; that he died seised thereof; and that, before his death, he duly made and published his last will and testament in writing, bearing date the 23rd February, 1786, having duly surrendered the said premises to the uses thereof, whereby the testator gave and devised unto his son the said John Purchas all and singular his copyhold estates whatsoever and wheresoever, to hold unto the said John Purchas, the son, his heirs and assigns, for ever, upon trust, as soon as conveniently might be, after the testator's decease, to sell and dispose of all his said real estate, and to pay the money arising therefrom in such manner as in such will was particularly mentioned: which said John Purchas, the son, being present in court, desired

Admittance of
tenant.

of the lord of the said manor to be admitted tenant agreeably to the tenor of the said will to the said premises, being
the said closes in which &c. (with other hereditaments);
to whom the lord granted seisin of the said premises by
the rod, to hold the same to the said John Purchas, his
heirs and assigns, agreeably to the tenor of the said will,
of the lord of the said manor, at his will, and according to
the custom of the said manor.

The trust for sale in the above will was never exercised,
the object of the trust being to raise 5,000l. for the testator's youngest son, and to pay debts; but the legacy and
debts were paid and satisfied by the said John Purchas,
the devisee, out of his own monies, and the lord and steward of the manor had no other notice thereof than from
the court books, which were in the terms above specified.

Payment of fine. On the said admittance the said John Purchas paid a full
fine of two years' improved value to the lord of the said
manor.

Surrender of te-
nant.

On the 23rd January, 1790, the said John Purchas did
out of court surrender into the hands of the lord of the
said manor (amongst other hereditaments) the said closes
in which &c., with their appurtenances, by the rod, according to the custom of the manor, by the hands and acceptance of two customary tenants of the said manor, to the
use and behoof of himself, the said John Purchas, and his
heirs, until a marriage then intended between him and one
Sarah Frances Barwick should be had and solemnized;
and from and after the solemnization thereof, to the use
of himself, the said John Purchas, and his assigns, for and
during the term of his natural life; and from and immediately after his decease, to the use and behoof of the said
S. F. Barwick, and her assigns, for and during the term of
her natural life, in augmentation of her jointure; and from
and immediately after the decease of the survivor of them,
the said John Purchas, and S. F. Barwick, his said intended
wife, subject and liable to the several powers, provisos,

conditions, limitations, and agreements mentioned, expressed, and declared in a certain indenture of release of four parts bearing even date therewith, to the use of the eldest or only son of the body of the said John Purchas on the body of the said S. F. Barwick, his said intended wife, to be begotten, and to the heirs of such eldest or only son for ever: and, in case there should be no such eldest or only son, then to the use of the eldest or only daughter of the body of the said John Purchas on the body of the said S. F. Barwick, his said intended wife, to be begotten, and to the heirs of such eldest or only daughter for ever: and, in default of issue of such marriage, to the use and behoof of the right heirs of the said John Purchas for ever, according to the custom of the said manor.

Afterwards, on the 30th May, 1796, at a general court baron of the lord of the said manor, holden before the deputy steward of the court of the said manor, the homage of that court presented the said surrender. And at that court the said John Purchas prayed to be admitted tenant to the said surrendered premises, according to the form and effect of the said surrender; to whom the said lord of the said manor, by the said deputy steward, granted seisin thereof by the rod, to hold the same unto the said John Purchas, and his assigns, for and during the term of his natural life, of the lord of the said manor and at his will, according to the custom of the said manor. And the said John Purchas was thereupon admitted tenant of the said surrendered premises, with the appurtenances, for the term of his natural life, and paid a fine of 1*s.* on such admission.

The marriage between the said John Purchas and S. F. Barwick took place in 1790; and the only issue of the said marriage was Frances Ann Purchas, who is now living, and was of full age at the time of the decease of the said John Purchas.

The said S. F. Purchas (formerly Barwick) died in 1811,

Re-admittance to estate for life.

Fine thereon.

Death of tenant for life.

Proclamations
for the heir.

Warrant of
seizure quous-
que.

Seizure there-
under.

in the lifetime of the said John Purchas; and the said John Purchas died in November, 1833.

On the 10th January, 1834, at a general court baron of the lord of the said manor, holden for the said manor before the steward thereof, the first proclamation was duly made for the heir or heirs at law, or other person or persons entitled to the premises whereof the said John Purchas had then lately died seised within the said manor, to come into court and take admission to the same, for that otherwise the same would be seised into the hands of the said lord of the manor for want of a tenant. A similar proclamation was made on the 5th March and 9th May, 1834.

On the 17th May, 1834, the steward of the said manor, according to the custom of the manor, duly issued a warrant under his hand and seal, directed to the defendant, Francis Eburn, the bailiff of the court of the said manor, reciting that proclamation had been duly made at the usual general court baron holden for the said manor on the 10th January, 1834, the 5th March, 1834, and the 9th May then instant, for any person or persons claiming title to the customary or copyhold lands and hereditaments lying within and holden of the same manor, of which John Purchas lately died seised, to come into court and be admitted thereto; and, forasmuch as no one came to take up and be admitted to the said lands and hereditaments, it was thereby commanded and ordered that he, the said Francis Eburn, should seize, and he was thereby authorised to seize, into the hands of the lord of the said manor, all the said customary or copyhold lands and hereditaments of which the said John Purchas died seised, in the meantime and until some person or persons should appear and make good his or their claim to be admitted thereto. The defendant, under that warrant, entered upon the closes in question, then in the occupation of the plaintiff as tenant to the said Frances Ann Purchas. The said F. A. Purchas was or claimed to be then seised of the said premises in question at the will of the said lord of the manor, according to the custom, under the surrender of the 23rd January, 1790, and the admittance of the 30th May, 1796.

1836.

PHYPERS
v.
EBURN.

The question for the opinion of the court was—Whether the said F. A. Purchas, who claimed as tenant in remainder under that surrender and admittance, was bound to come in to be admitted at the lord's court, and to pay to the lord of the said manor a fine on such admittance.

Question.

The case now came on for argument.

W. H. Watson, for the plaintiff.—It is a general principle of copyhold law, that the admittance of tenant for life is the admittance of him in remainder, except where the lord is entitled by custom to a second fine: and, as it does not appear that there is any custom in this manor for a remainderman to pay a second fine, Frances Anne Purchas was not bound, on the death of the tenant for life in this case to come in and be admitted and pay a fine; and consequently the seizure quousque was wholly unwarranted. *Barnes* v. *Corke*, 3 Lev. 398, is precisely in point (a). There, the father of the defendant, being seised of copyhold land, surrendered it to the use of himself and his wife for their lives, remainder to the defendant in tail; the husband and wife were admitted, and paid a fine; on the defendant claiming to be admitted to his remainder, the lord demanded another fine. And "it was held by Powell and Rokesby, the only judges in court, that no fine was in this case due, except there be a special custom for it; but the admittance to the particular estates was also an admittance to the remainder; and that which is said in 4 Rep. 22, 23. b., that it shall not be to the prejudice of the lord in respect of his fine, is to be intended where a fine is due by custom for an admittance of the remainder;

(a) And see Church v. Mundy, 12 Ves. 422.

but without a special custom none is due." In *Gyppen* v. *Gunney*, Cro. Eliz. 504, Popham, J., says: "Tenant for life and he in remainder have but one estate in law; and therefore the admittance of the one shall serve the other as a livery or attornement. The reason which is objected against it is, because the lord should then lose his fine of him in remainder. But it seemeth to me that there is only one fine due upon this surrender, which the tenant for life shall pay before his admittance; as, where the Queen's tenant in capite aliens for life, remainder over, there is but one fine due for this alienation; so here, unless there be a special custom that two fines shall be due." In *Doe* d. *Whitbread* v. *Jenney*, 5 East, 522, 2 Smith, 116, where a copyholder in fee, who had paid a fine on his original admittance, surrendered to the use of himself for life, remainder to his wife for life, remainder over; on which surrender and readmittance *no new fine was paid;* and, *by the custom,* a remainder-man coming into possession on the death of tenant for life must be admitted and pay a fine— it was held that such a custom was good. That case is no authority against the position here contended for: no such custom is alleged here. Lord Ellenborough, in his judgment in that case, cites all the older authorities upon the subject. [*Tindal*, C. J.—You treat the 1s. paid here on the admittance of the tenant for life as a real fine?] The lord had then a right to a fine: having neglected to claim it on the admittance of the tenant for life, he cannot claim it now. Neither can he apportion it. Apportionment is for the benefit of the tenant for life; and must be made at the time of his admittance, though the portion of the fine that is demandable from the remainder-man is not payable by him until the death of the tenant for life. [*Tindal*, C. J.—The lord in this case had no means of compelling the tenant for life to be re-admitted: and, if he had not come in, the lord would have been entitled to all he now seeks.] The plaintiff stands upon the strict letter

of the law. Supposing the remainder-man were under the
circumstances of this case bound by the custom of this
particular manor to pay a fine, the lord has mistaken his
remedy: he should have brought assumpsit; he has
already a tenant upon the roll from whom to claim the fine.
The fine here was assessed, not in respect of the particular estate, but generally. In *Blackborn* v. *Greaves*, 2 Lev.
107 (also reported in 1 Mod. 102, 120, 1 Vent. 260, 3 Keb.
263), it was held that the admittance to a copyhold of the
particular tenant, is the admittance of him in remainder.
In *The Dean of Ely* v. *Caldecott*, 1 M. & Scott, 633, 8
Bing. 489, it was held that the lord of a manor, having
taken a full fine on the admittance of a tenant for life, is
not entitled to another full fine upon the admittance of the
remainder-man as tenant in fee, unless the imposition of
such latter fine is authorized by a special custom of the
manor; and it requires strong evidence to establish such a
custom. So, in Lord *Kensington* v. *Mansell*, 3 Ves. 240,
Lord Eldon says: " When the tenant for life comes on
behalf of himself and all in remainder and reversion, if the
lord does not take the fine, he cannot afterwards insist
upon the fine from those in remainder. The lord may
apportion the fine among the different parcels of the inheritance; but it is impossible to say the tenant for life
shall pay nothing, and those in remainder shall pay the
whole." From these authorities, it is perfectly clear that
the admittance of the tenant for life is the admittance of
the remainder-man; that, if in such a case as this the fine
could have been apportioned, the apportionment should
have been made at the time of the admittance of the tenant
for life; and that the lord's remedy, if under the circumstances entitled to any fine, was by action of assumpsit,
and not by seizure.

F. Kelly, for the defendant.—It is not necessary for the
defendant in this case to contend that the lord is entitled to

1836.

PHYPERS
v.
EBURN.

a full fine: it is enough to shew that he is entitled to half, or any fair proportion of a full fine. It is said that the lord might have taken a full fine on the admittance of the tenant for life. [*Tindal*, C. J.—He should have apportioned.] He *might* have apportioned, no doubt: but the question is, was he *bound* to apportion. " The admittance of a tenant for life is the admittance of him in remainder to vest the estate in him, but shall not bar the lord of his fine"—*Browne's* case, 4 Rep. 22. The judgment of Tindal, C. J., in *The Dean of Ely* v. *Caldecott*, shews the true meaning of that principle. Wherever a fine is due at all, it must be by custom. [*Tindal*, C. J.—The case does not find any custom authorising the lord to claim a fine from the remainder-man on the death of the tenant for life.] It was not necessary so to state: the defendant did not claim as did the lord in *Doe* d. *Whitbread* v. *Jenney*. [*Tindal*, C. J.—There no fine was paid to the lord on the surrender and re-admittance of the surrenderor as tenant for life; and a custom for the remainder-man to pay a fine upon coming into possession, was proved. That case very closely resembles the present.] It is neither necessary nor usual for the lord to assess the full fine on the admittance of the tenant for life. The dictum of Lord Eldon in *Lord Kensington* v. *Mansell* was extrajudicial. " It was said by Lord Mansfield, in the case of *Roe* d. *Noden* v. *Griffith*, 4 Bur. 1952, according to Sir James Burrow, that, if a copyholder in fee (to which estate he had been regularly admitted) surrender to the use of himself for life or in tail, with remainders over, and the ultimate limitation to himself and his heirs, he need not be admitted on such surrender, for he was tenant already; and consequently would not be subject to a fine. But this position is open to much observation"—Watkins on Copyholds, 288. "As to the fine, indeed, much may be urged; for, though a fine cannot be due without an admission, an admission may be without a fine. However, as a new estate is limited, it should seem that a fine would be due, though I believe it is seldom taken *as to the estate of the surrenderor* in cases like these"—Id. 292. " If, on the admission of the particular tenant, the *whole* fine be actually paid, no portion can be due on the accession of the remainder-man. But it should seem from the case of *Barnes* v. *Corke*, that a fine may be taken by *special custom* on the accession of a remainder-man. If, indeed, a part of the fine only be imposed on the particular tenant, the residue may be assessed on the person in remainder: and the best and most equitable mode is, to assess the fine on the admission of the particular tenant, and to proportion it to the interests of the several claimants, who may pay their shares on acceding to the possession, when they are called in to swear fealty"—Id. 296. " When a person is admitted to an estate in remainder, the fine is usually one half"—Id. 311. *The Earl of Bath* v. *Abney*, 1 Burr. 212, is an authority to shew that a proportional part of the fine is demandable from the remainder-man, where a full fine has not already been paid by the tenant for life. It cannot be said that a shilling was a full fine in the present case. Indeed, the case finds that the full fine payable according to the custom of the manor, is, two years' improved annual value. A shilling might be the fair proportion of the fine payable by the tenant for life on his re-admittance. The consequence of holding that no fine is payable by the remainder-man in such a case as this, will be, to enable in every case at least two admittances to be obtained for one fine.

W. H. Watson, in reply, was stopped by the court.

TINDAL, C. J.—This case comes before us on a question whether or not a warrant by the lord of a manor for a seizure quosque, to enforce the payment of a fine, is valid under the circumstances stated in the case. The fine is claimed in respect of the interest of a remainder-man after the death of the tenant for life ; and, unless the

lord had a right to compel the remainder-man to come in
and be admitted, the warrant must be held bad.   It appears to me that the tenant in remainder is already in by
the admittance of the tenant for life.   The only question
therefore is, whether, by the custom of this manor, a fine
was demandable in this case: for, if so, though the admittance of the tenant for life is for general purposes the admittance of those in remainder, it is not so for the purpose of barring the lord of his fine.   In the first place, it
is to be observed that no custom to that effect is stated in
the special case.   The point therefore presents itself precisely as it arose in the earlier cases to which our attention has been called in the course of the argument, where
it is laid down that the admittance of tenant for life is the
admittance of him in remainder, but not so as to bar the
lord of his fine; which the later cases have interpreted,
where a fine is due by the custom of the manor.   The
case of *Doe* d. *Whitbread* v. *Jenney*, in effect, disposes of
the present; it agrees in all respects with this case, except
that there the fine was due by the custom of the manor.
There, a copyholder in fee, who had paid a fine on his
original admittance, surrendered to the use of himself for
life, remainder to his wife for life, remainder over: on
the admittance of the surrenderor to the new estate, no
fine was paid; but, by the custom of the manor, a remainder-man coming into possession on the death of a
tenant for life, was bound to be admitted and pay a fine:
it was held that such a custom was good; and that, on the
death of the tenant for life, the next in remainder not
coming in to be admitted and pay her fine, after proclamations made, and presentment by the homage, the lord
was entitled to seize quosque, and might maintain ejectment to recover the possession in the meantime.   The
ground of that decision was the custom found by the jury.
In the absence of such a custom here, I do not see how
we can hold the remainder-man liable to be called on to

pay a fine. The settlor, by the settlement, created in
himself a new estate for life, to which he was admitted, and
paid a fine—a nominal one, it is true; but that was the
lord's own fault. It is said, that, if we hold the fine now
claimed not to be payable, we shall be putting it in the
power of any copyhold tenant in fee to cheat the lord, by
in all cases obtaining at least two admittances for one fine.
The answer to that argument is, that, whether or not such
a consequence shall follow, must depend upon the lord
himself. When the tenant for life in this case claimed to
be admitted to his new estate, the lord might have refused
to admit him except upon payment of a full fine for the
whole estate, or a fine fairly apportioned; and then the
remainder-man's proportion might have been made the
subject of an action or a seizure quosque. The warrant
under which the seizure in this case has been made, not
appearing to be sanctioned by any custom within the
manor, has issued improperly; and therefore the plaintiff
is entitled to judgment.

GASELEE, J.—In *Doe* d. *Whitbread* v. *Jenney*, the rule
is laid down in conformity with all the previous authorities,
and I think that case governs the present.

VAUGHAN, J.—I am of the same opinion. It would be
impossible to give judgment for the defendant without
contravening one of the first principles of copyhold law,
viz. that the admittance of tenant for life is the admittance of the remainder-man. The lord having taken a
fine on the admittance of the tenant for life, and there
being no custom to warrant his demanding a second fine
on the accession of the remainder-man to his estate, the
latter was not bound to come in.

BOSANQUET, J.—I am of the same opinion. The general
rule is, that the admittance of the tenant for life is the

1836.

PHYPERS
v.
EBURN.

admittance of the remainder-man: he is already a tenant on the roll. *Doe* d. *Whitbread* v. *Jenney* leads to the conclusion, that, even where no fine has been received from the tenant for life, none is demandable from the remainder-man, unless by virtue of a special custom. Here, a fine (though a nominal one) has been taken. Under the circumstances stated in this case, it seems to me to be perfectly clear, that, the tenant for life having been admitted, and paid a fine, the lord was not entitled to compel the remainder-man also to come in, in order to take a second fine.

Judgment for the plaintiff.

In assumpsit on a bill of exchange drawn in London, the venue was laid in Surrey for the purpose of obtaining speedier execution: the parties and witnesses all residing in London, the prothonotary, on a verdict for the plaintiff, refused to allow him larger costs than he would have been entitled to had the cause been tried in London:—The court directed a review of the taxation.

VERE v. WOOD.

ASSUMPSIT on a bill of exchange drawn in London, where the parties and the plaintiff's witnesses resided. The venue was laid in Surrey. At the trial at the last assizes at Guildford, the defendant not appearing, the plaintiff had a verdict, and the judge certified under the 1 Will. 4, c. 7, that execution ought to issue forthwith; whereupon judgment was signed, and the costs taxed. The prothonotary, on the taxation, refused to allow the plaintiff greater costs than he would have been entitled to had the cause been tried in London.

Thesiger, on a former day, moved for a rule calling upon the defendant to shew cause why the taxation should not be reviewed. He submitted that the plaintiff, having a right to lay the venue where he pleased, ought not to be deprived of the ordinary costs, for having merely in order to obtain more speedy execution, and not for any purpose of vexation, laid his venue in a neighbouring county.

Wilde, Serjeant, shewed cause in the first instance.— The prothonotary has properly exercised his discretion as to the scale of costs applicable to this case. The plaintiff should have proceeded with his action according to the ordinary course. There was nothing to warrant his laying the venue in Surrey. He had no right to speculate upon obtaining a more speedy judgment by such means. If a plaintiff chuse, in order to suit his purposes, to lay the venue in a circuit county, the defendant ought not to be made to pay for it. [*Bosanquet*, J.—This would lead to a very inconvenient discussion in every case before the prothonotary, as to whether or not the venue was properly laid. *Vaughan*, J.—The defendant in this case could not have moved to change the venue: why, then, should he be allowed collaterally to attain all the advantage that would accrue from a change of the venue?] The inconvenience of leaving the matter to the prothonotary's discretion will be infinitely less than that of making parties come to the court to review the prothonotary's decision.

[Mr. Prothonotary *Watlington* stated that it had for many years been the uniform practice in the office to disallow the larger scale of costs in cases like the present: and he mentioned a case that occurred before Mr. Prothonotary Ray on the preceding day, where that officer had in like manner reduced the plaintiff's costs to the amount he would have been entitled to claim had the trial been had in the place where the cause of action arose.— *Tindal*, C. J., asked whether the like practice prevailed in the courts of King's Bench and Exchequer: but the officers were unable to inform his lordship.—*Taddy*, Serjeant, amicus curiæ, observed that it had been a common practice some years since, for the sake of greater expedition, to try insurance causes at Kingston; and therefore the point must have occurred repeatedly in the King's Bench.]

Thesiger, in support of his rule.—The question is one of considerable practical importance, inasmuch as it will form a precedent by which such taxations will in future be governed. The matter is of too great moment to be left altogether to the discretion of the prothonotary.

TINDAL, C. J.—This is certainly a question of considerable importance. I feel great difficulty in supposing that the prothonotary has the power he has assumed to exercise in the present case, inasmuch as the plaintiff had an undoubted right to lay his venue where he pleased. We will therefore take an opportunity of inquiring into the practice of the other courts before we pronounce the rule.

Cur. adv. vult.

TINDAL, C. J., now said.—We think the rule for reviewing the taxation in this case must be made absolute. We have inquired as to what was the practice in similar cases in the courts of King's Bench and Exchequer; and we find that it does not sanction the course pursued here. It is desirable that the practice of the three courts in this respect should be uniform. A case where the venue is for the purpose of vexation laid in a distant county, might be held to be an exception, and might be made the subject of a motion.

Rule absolute.

———

YEATES *v.* CHAPMAN.

A defect in the copy delivered to a defendant at the time of execution of process under the 2 Will. 4, c. 39, s. 4, is not an irregularity that can be taken advantage of on a summons or motion to set aside the bail-bond for irregularity.

THE defendant was arrested on the 2nd September, 1836, and on the 8th gave a bail-bond to the sheriff of Lincolnshire. On the 9th the defendant took out a summons to shew cause before a judge at chambers on the 10th why the bail-bond should not be delivered up to be cancelled for irregularity. There being no judge then in town, the summons was not heard on that day. The plaintiff afterwards took an assignment, and proceeded on the bond; and on the 20th September a second summons was taken out by the defendant, to shew cause on the 22nd why the proceedings on the bail-bond should not be set aside for irregularity. This second summons was obtained upon an affidavit that the assignment of the bail-bond, and proceedings thereon, had been taken pending the first summons, and in defiance of an agreement between the respective attornies that the hearing of that summons should be adjourned till the 22nd. The parties went before Mr. Justice Vaughan on the last mentioned day, when the only objection urged on the part of the defendant was, that the copy of the process served on him at the time of the arrest was defective, the sum for which bail was to be taken not being indorsed thereon: the defendant offered to enter an appearance. The learned judge ordered the bail-bond to be delivered up to be cancelled, and also ordered the proceedings on the bail-bond to be set aside.

Archbold, on a former day, on the part of the plaintiff, obtained a rule nisi to set aside these two orders.—He submitted, that, the irregularity in the bail-bond being the only one pointed at by the summons, it was not competent to the defendant afterwards to abandon that ground, and set up another totally distinct from and unconnected with it—*Hesker* v. *Jarmaine*, 1 C. & M. 408, 3 Tyr. 381, *Smith* v. *Clarke*, 2 Dowl. 218. He also contended that the application was too late; it having been made after the bail-bond was assigned.

Ball shewed cause, upon an affidavit wherein it was positively sworn that the plaintiff's attorney had consented to an adjournment of the first summons to the 22nd September, and to a stay of proceedings on the bond in the interim.—By the 4th section of the 2 Will. 4, c. 39, it is enacted, that, in all cases wherein it is intended to arrest and hold any person to special bail, &c., so many copies of the process, "together with every memoradum or notice subscribed thereto, and *all indorsements thereon*, as there may be persons intended to be arrested thereon or served therewith, shall be delivered therewith to the sheriff or other officer or person to whom the same may be directed, or who may have the execution or return thereof, and who shall, upon or forthwith after the execution of such process, cause one such copy to be delivered to every person upon whom such process shall be executed by him, whether by service or arrest." In the present case, a true copy of the process was not delivered to the defendant. [*Tindal*, C. J.—That is an irregularity in the execution of the process: but, how does it affect the bail-bond?] The object of the delivery to the defendant on his arrest of a copy of the process, with the sum for which bail is to be taken indorsed thereon, is, that he may be thereby facilitated in obtaining bail. The irregularity is in a proceeding ancillary to the bail-bond: the process must support the bond; and, the copy being bad, the process is bad. [*Tindal*, C. J.—The first summons should have been to set aside the service of the copy, and the subsequent proceedings.]

Archbold, in support of his rule.—The application at chambers was, not to set aside the process, or the service of the copy, but to cancel the bail-bond. It is not competent to the defendant now to turn round and say that the bail-bond is regular, and the service of the copy informal: it was expressly so decided in *Hesker* v. *Jarmaine* and *Smith* v. *Clarke*. The writ being a good writ until set aside, the bail-bond cannot be irregular. By the 10th rule of Michaelmas Term, 3 Will. 4, it is provided, that,

" if the plaintiff or his attorney shall omit to indorse on any writ or copy thereof any of the matters required by the act to be indorsed thereon, *such writ or copy shall not be void*, but may be set aside for irregularity."

TINDAL, C. J.—I think the order of my Brother Vaughan, for setting aside the proceedings on the bail-bond, must stand: those proceedings appear to have been taken in defiance of a solemn agreement between the attornies for the respective parties. With respect to the order for cancelling the bail-bond, I think the rule, as far as it relates to the rescinding of that order, must be made absolute. The question as to that is, whether it was competent to the defendant, on a summons taken out expressly on the ground of an alleged irregularity in the bail-bond, to take advantage of an irregularity in the service or execution of the process, of which he had given the plaintiff no previous intimation. I think it clearly was not. According to the 10th rule of Michaelmas Term, 3 Will. 4, the irregularity in the copy did not render the process void, but only entitled the defendant to move to set aside the proceedings thereon. That would have been the correct course. So far therefore the rule must be made absolute; the defendant having a week's time to put in bail.

GASELEE, J., concurred.

VAUGHAN, J.—I am not disposed to differ from the rest of the court: but, when this case was before me at chambers, my impression was that the plaintiff had no right to proceed upon the irregular process, and take a bail-bond; and I must confess I felt extremely anxious on any legal ground to defeat the plaintiff, thinking he had acted very irregularly and improperly in taking an assignment of the bail-bond under the circumstances. I agree, however, with the rest of the court, that the proper course would have been to move to set aside the service and subsequent proceedings. It is better that these rules of practice should be adhered to strictly.

BOSANQUET, J.—The only doubt I have entertained was, whether the delivery of a true copy of the process at the time of its execution was not a condition precedent to the plaintiff's right to take a bail-bond—by analogy to the case of an affidavit to hold to bail. But there is this difference between the two cases: if the affidavit to hold to bail be insufficient, the bond is absolutely void; it is as if there were no affidavit at all; the arrest is altogether unwarranted. But, by the rule referred to, the omission to deliver a copy of the process at the time of the arrest, is a mere irregularity: the process is not thereby avoided.

Rule absolute accordingly.

———◆———

LANE v. PARSONS.

THE declaration in this case was delivered on the 28th October, with notice to plead in four days. On the 29th a summons was taken out for *further* time to plead, returnable on the 31st. A consent for *"four days' time to plead"* was indorsed on the summons, and an order was accordingly so drawn up upon and dated the 29th. By this order, the defendant was put under terms to plead issuably, to rejoin gratis, and to take short notice of trial for the first Sitting in the term—the 8th November. On the 3rd November, shortly before the defendant delivered his pleas, the plaintiff signed judgment.

Roberts, on a former day, upon an affidavit of these facts, obtained a rule calling on the plaintiff to shew cause why

the judgment should not be set aside for irregularity. He
relied on *Aspinall* v. *Smyth*, 8 Taunt. 592, 2 Moore, 655,
where it was held, that, where time to plead is given under a
judge's order, such time is to be reckoned from the expiration of the rule to plead, and not from the date of the order.

John Jervis shewed cause.—The judgment was regularly
signed. In *Simpson* v. *Cooper*, 2 Scott, 840, the declaration was delivered on the 12th January, with notice to
plead in four days; on the 13th, the defendants obtained
a judge's order for seven days' time to plead, undertaking
to plead issuably, and to accept short notice of trial for the
last Sitting in the term, which was the 26th; and the court
held that the seven days were to be reckoned from the
date of the order, and not from the expiration of the four.
days. That case is precisely in point.

Roberts, in support of his rule.—*Simpson* v. *Cooper*
turned upon the meaning of the agreement between the
parties: unless the court had interpreted it as they did, the
object the plaintiff had in view, viz. to go to trial at the
last Sitting, which it was the manifest intention of both
parties that he should be in a condition to do, would have
been frustrated.

TINDAL, C. J.—I do not think the present case is to be
distinguished from *Simpson* v. *Cooper*. The rule there
adopted seems to be reasonable. If the parties had intended that the four days given by the order should be
superadded to the time the defendant already had for
pleading, the order would have stated that "further" time
was meant. The rule may therefore be made absolute on
the usual terms, but not on the ground of irregularity.

The rest of the court concurring—

Rule accordingly (*a*).

(*a*) Time to plead under a judge's　day of the date of the order, but
order is reckoned inclusive of the　exclusive of the day on which it

Where the
plaintiff de-
clares only on
a bill of ex-
change, the de-
fendant is not,
except under
very special
circumstances,
entitled to
particulars of
demand.

BROOKS *v.* FARLAR.

ASSUMPSIT on a bill of exchange for 200*l.*, by indorsee against drawer. The declaration as at first delivered,
in addition to a count upon the bill, contained a count for
money paid, and an account stated; and the plaintiff delivered a particular of demand for 94*l.* 9*s.*, part of the consideration of the bill. The plaintiff subsequently amended
his declaration by striking out the second and last counts.
The defendant took out a summons for further particulars:
but the judge before whom it came on to be heard refused
to make an order.

Bompas, Serjeant, thereupon obtained a rule nisi for
further particulars.—The affidavit upon which the motion
was founded, amongst other things, stated that the bill in
question had been delivered by the defendant to the plaintiff to cover a debt of 22*l.* 17*s.* 6*d.* due for goods purchased
by the former of the latter; that other goods were subsequently sold and delivered by the plaintiff to the defendant to the amount of 70*l.* or thereabouts, but the plaintiff
refused to deliver any more; that no invoice had ever been
delivered; and that the defendant had tendered a sum
sufficient to cover the amount due for the goods; but that
the plaintiff had refused to accept it.

Semble that an
affidavit made
by a defendant
in a cause should
contain the ad-
dition of the
deponent, pur-
suant to the
rule of Hilary
Term, 2 Will. 4,
s. 5.

Stephen, Serjeant, before shewing cause, objected that
the affidavit upon which the motion was founded (made by
the defendant) did not state the deponent's addition, pursuant to the rule of Hilary Term, 2 Will. 4, s. 5, which

expires—Kay v. Whitehead, 2 H.
Blac. 35. But, in an order to enlarge the time for pleading, the
first and the last days are both
reckoned inclusively — Freeman

v. Jackson, 1 Bos. & Pull. 479.
    The rule laid down by this court
in Aspinall v. Smyth was never
adopted by the other courts.

requires that " the addition of *every person* making an
affidavit shall be inserted therein." In *Lawson* v. *Case*,
1 C. & M. 481, 3 Tyr. 489, 2 Dowl. 40, it was expressly
decided that an affidavit made by a defendant in a cause,
cannot be read, unless his addition is inserted. [*Gaselee,*
J., referred to *Jackson* v. *Chard*, 2 Dowl. 469, where it was
held, that, where a defendant makes an affidavit in a cause,
his addition need not be given : and to *Sharp* v. *Johnson*,
2 Scott, 407, 2 New Cases, 246, 4 Dowl. 324, where it was
held by this court that a prisoner defendant need not
comply with the rule, by stating his residence in the affidavit.] *Jackson* v. *Chard* was before a single judge, whose
attention does not appear to have been called to the previous decision of the Exchequer in banc ; and *Sharp* v.
Johnson went solely upon the ground that the residence of
the party deponent sufficiently appeared from his description of himself as a prisoner in the Fleet.

THE COURT entertained considerable doubt as to whether the addition of the deponent ought not to have appeared : but they intimated, that, if the objection were
pressed, they would allow the affidavit to be amended.
The objection was thereupon waived.

Stephen, Serjeant, proceeded to shew cause, upon an
affidavit wherein it was sworn that invoices had been delivered ; that the non-delivery of the residue of the goods
was occasioned by the defendant's own default ; and that
no tender had been made, as alleged.—The defendant is
not entitled to particulars where the declaration contains
only a count on a bill of exchange. His right to particulars
is by the rule of Trinity Term, 1 Will. 4, r. 6, confined to
those cases where the declaration contains counts in indebitatus assumpsit or debt on simple contract. In *Cooper*
v. *Amos*, 2 C. & P. 267, it was held, that, if the declaration
is on a bill of exchange and for goods sold, and a particular

of demand is obtained under a judge's order, the plaintiff may recover on the bill, though it is not mentioned in his particular of demand (a). The defendant ought to have shewn by his affidavit that he did not know for what the plaintiff was proceeding—*Snelling* v. *Chennells*, 5 Dowl. 80. He has not done so: on the contrary, his affidavit shews that he is fully acquainted with every particular of the plaintiff's cause of action.

Bompas, Serjeant, in support of his rule.—The plaintiff can only recover to the extent of the value of the goods he has actually delivered. Without knowing the value of those goods, the defendant cannot safely shape his defence. [*Vaughan*, J.—Do you mean to contend that you are entitled to particulars more minute than the proof that would entitle the plaintiff to a verdict at the trial?] In many cases the defendant is so entitled; for instance, in those where the defendant is entitled to an assignment of breaches under the 8 & 9 Will. 3, c. 11, s. 8.

TINDAL, C. J.—Had we known when this motion was made that the declaration consisted of only a single count on the bill, the rule would not have been granted. A defendant is not in such a case entitled to particulars unless under very special circumstances. It appears from the affidavits here that the defendant has already obtained information as to the limit of the plaintiff's claim, and that he is within a very slight difference likewise acquainted with the precise items. I therefore think the rule must be discharged with costs.

GASELEE, J.—The general rule is that particulars are never given where the action is brought solely on a bill of exchange.

The rest of the court concurring—

　　　　　　　　　Rule discharged, with costs.

(a) See Wade v. Beasley, 4 Esp. 7, and Duncan v. Hill, 5 Moore, 657, 2 B. & B. 682.

1836.

Tuesday,
Nov. 15th.

In re ANN SCHOLEFIELD.

BY the 2nd section of the rules of Hilary Term, 4 Will. 4, relating to acknowledgments of married women under the 3 & 4 Will. 4, c. 74, the act for the abolition of fines and recoveries, it is ordered, " that, where any acknowledgment shall be made by any married woman of any deed under and by virtue of the said act before commissioners appointed under the said act, *one at least of the said commissioners shall be a person who is not* in any manner interested in the transaction giving occasion for such acknowledgment, or *concerned therein as attorney, solicitor, or agent,* or as clerk to any attorney, solicitor, or agent so interested or concerned."

The affidavit of the due taking of the acknowledgment of a married woman under the statute 3 & 4 Will 4, c. 74, may be made by one of the commissioners before whom it was taken, notwithstanding he is the attorney concerned in the transaction.

The next section, which refers to the inquiries to be made of the married woman by the commissioners, directs, " that, before the commissioners shall receive such acknowledgment, they, or, in case one of them shall be interested or *concerned as aforesaid,* then such one of them as shall not be so interested or concerned, do inquire of every married woman, *separately and apart* from her husband and *from the attorney or solicitor concerned in the transaction,* whether she intends to give up her interest in the estate to be passed by such deed, without having any provision made for her in lieu of or in return for or in consequence of her so giving up her interest," &c. &c.

The 4th section directs, " that *the affidavit verifying the certificate* to be made pursuant to the said act, and which certificate shall be in the form contained in the said act, *shall be made by some practising attorney* or solicitor of one of the courts at Westminster, &c.; *and that, in all cases, it shall be deposed,* in addition to the verification of the said certificate, that the deponent, or, if more than one person join in the affidavit, that one or more of the deponents knew the person or persons making such acknowledgment; and that, at the time of making such acknowledgment, the person or persons making the same was or were of full age and competent understanding; and *that one at least of the commissioners taking such acknowledgment*, to the best of his, deponent's, knowledge or belief, *is not in any manner* interested in the transaction giving occasion for the taking of the acknowledgment, or *concerned therein as attorney, solicitor, or agent*, or as clerk to any attorney, solicitor, or agent so interested or concerned," &c.

By the 6th section it is ordered, " that the affidavit shall be in the form thereunto annexed, subject to such variation as the circumstances of the case shall render necessary; or *such affidavit may be made, where it is found convenient, by one of the said commissioners*, with such variation in the form thereof as shall be necessary in that behalf."

And by the Reg. Gen., Trinity Term, 4 Will. 4, it is provided, that, where such parts of the affidavit verifying the certificate of acknowledgment as state the deponent's knowledge of the party making the affidavit, and her being of full age, cannot be deposed to *by a commissioner*, or by an attorney or solicitor, the same may be deposed to by some other person whom the person before whom the affidavit shall be made shall consider competent so to do.

In the present case, the affirmation verifying the acknowledgment was made by one of the commissioners by whom the acknowledgment was taken and certified, and who was a practising attorney, and the solicitor concerned in the transaction for Mrs. Scholefield. The other commissioner was not professionally concerned, nor was either of the commissioners interested in the transaction giving occasion for the acknowledgment. The affirmation complied with the above rules in every respect.

Mr. *Sherwood*, the clerk of the inrolments under the act, objected to receive the affirmation, on the ground that the affirmant was the attorney concerned in the transaction and also one of the commissioners taking the acknowledgment.

Wilde, Serjeant, now moved that the officer might be directed to receive the affirmation.—The course prescribed by the rules of court has been strictly and properly pursued. That the commissioner was the solicitor conducting the transaction, is clearly no objection: it is enough that *one* of the commissioners is unconcerned. The 4th section of the rules of Hilary Term, 4 Will. 4, recognizes the fact that the attorney concerned in the transaction may be one of the commissioners. And in the rule requiring an affidavit of verification, is contained not a syllable to prohibit the attorney making it from being the solicitor conducting the business. To require the introduction of a third person, who must necessarily be a practising attorney, would in all cases be productive of expense and highly inconvenient, and in many almost impracticable. The 6th section of the rules above referred to expressly states that *the affidavit may be made*, where it is found convenient, *by one of the commissioners*: and the subsequent rule of Trinity Term, 4 Will. 4, shews beyond question that the court contemplated one of the commissioners being the party making the affidavit. The commissioner not concerned in the transaction is to make the necessary inquiries separate and apart from the other commissioner; and that this is properly done, the court are satisfied of by the certificate.

Mr. *Sherwood* stated that he had declined to record the affirmation, not deeming it correct or consistent with the rules of court that the affirmant should at the same time be one of the commissioners and also the attorney conducting the transaction.

TINDAL, C. J.—There can be little doubt but that the primary intention of the rules was, that the married woman should have the triple security of the two commissioners and another professional man. It was at first contemplated that the commissioners should make affidavit of the due taking of the acknowledgment: but many solicitors of eminence being of opinion that full credence ought to be given to the commissioners' certificate, their suggestion was attended to. Some inconvenience being found to arise from a third party being required to make the affidavit, it was afterwards thought better, that, where convenient, the affidavit should be allowed to be made by one of the commissioners. It was with this view that the 6th clause in the rule of Hilary Term, 4 Will. 4, was framed. I cannot read that rule without coming to the conclusion that the commissioner in this case was duly authorized to make the affirmation, and that we cannot refuse to receive it.

The rest of the court concurring—

The officer was directed to record the affirmation (a).

(a) The effect of this decision is, that, although the 3rd section of the rules of Hilary Term, 4 Will. 4, directs that the examination of the married woman shall take place before the disinterested and unconcerned commissioner "separately and apart from *the solicitor concerned* in the transaction;" yet, where the person who makes the affidavit is (as it seems he now may be) both one of the commissioners and the solicitor concerned for the lady, she must also go through the ceremony of examination before *him*, to enable him to make the required affidavit. The 6th section of the same rules, which permits the affidavit to be made by one of the commissioners, allows " *necessary variations* to be made in the form thereof:" but there is nothing to warrant a deviation *in any case* from the course of examination prescribed by the 3rd section.

One difficulty that seems to arise from this course is, that, inasmuch as the certificate is not required to state that the inquiries mentioned in the affidavit have been duly made of the married woman

1836.

Saturday,
Nov. 19th.

MONCK *v.* SHENSTONE.

Semble, that
no rule to plead
several matters
is necessary
in the case of
pleas added
under a judge's
order.

THE defendant, after having delivered a plea of the general issue, obtained a judge's order for leave to amend by adding a plea of the statute of limitations. The amended pleas having been delivered without a rule to plead several matters, the plaintiff, conceiving them therefore to be a nullity, signed judgment.

Wilde, Serjeant, on a former day, obtained a rule nisi to set aside the judgment for irregularity.

Adams, Serjeant, shewed cause.—He submitted that the judgment was regular; relying upon the rule of Hilary Term, 2 Will. 4, r. 34, which provides, that, " if a party plead several pleas, avowries, or cognizances, without a rule for that purpose, the opposite party shall be at liberty to sign judgment."

Wilde, Serjeant, in support of his rule.—The judgment is clearly irregular. There is already a plea of the general issue properly placed upon the record. The only consequence of the defendant's neglect to obtain a rule to plead several matters, is, that he has not placed himself in a situation to make the amendment which the order authorized him to make. [*Gaselee,* J.— Is it clear that a rule to plead several matters was necessary under the circumstances?] Probably not: but,

prior to the taking of her acknowledgment, there is nothing *upon oath* to satisfy the court that those inquiries have been made, except the statement of the commissioner who is concerned as the party's solicitor; the very person who is so studiously excluded from the examination.

See the very able remarks of Mr. Hayes upon this subject, in the 5th part of his Introduction to Conveyancing, 3rd edit. 538—573.

1836.

MONCK
v.
SHENSTONE.

even if it were necessary, the judgment is clearly irregular.

TINDAL, C. J.—I think the judgment signed in this case must be set aside without costs. If it were necessary to decide the point, I should not feel much hesitation in saying that the present case is not within the rule relied on by my brother Adams. I should incline to think that that rule applied to the pleas originally delivered; and not to the case of a plea added under the sanction of a judge's order.

The rest of the court concurring—

Rule absolute.

———◆———

In re ABRAHAM GARCIA.

Monday,
Nov. 21st.

A bankrupt detained in the Fleet Prison in several actions, not answering to the satisfaction of the commissioners certain questions which they had put to him, they issued their warrant, addressed "to the keeper of Newgate, or whom else it might concern," authorising the detention of the bankrupt until he

ABRAHAM GARCIA, a bankrupt, and in the custody of the Warden of the Fleet, having been brought up for examination before a subdivision court in bankruptcy, the commissioners, being dissatisfied with his account of the disposal of a sum of 400*l.* or 500*l.*, which he said had been stolen from his breeches pocket whilst riding in an omnibus, sent him back to the Fleet prison charged with a warrant.

Atcherley, Serjeant, on a former day moved for a habeas corpus to bring the bankrupt up to be discharged from this warrant, on the ground that the commissioners had exceeded their jurisdiction. He submitted, that, to

should make answer to their satisfaction. This warrant was delivered to the Warden of the Fleet. To a writ of habeas corpus issued at the instance of the prisoner, the Warden returned that he held him by virtue of the detainers in the civil suits; and added that, on a certain day, the above warrant was left with him:—Held, that, the warrant not being a cause of the prisoner's detainer in the Fleet, it was not necessary to set it forth in the return; and that, under the circumstances, the court could not inquire into the validity of the warrant.

On the return to a habeas corpus being read, the proper course is, for the prisoner's counsel to begin and shew the grounds upon which he claims to be entitled to his discharge from custody.

justify the issuing of the warrant, it was not enough that the commissioners felt dissatisfied with the answers of the party; but it must appear that his answers were such as they might and ought reasonably to hold to be unsatisfactory—*Crowley's* case, 2 Swanst. 75, Buck, 264, *Ex parte Nowlan*, 6 T. R. 118, *Norris's* case, 2 Jac. & W. 437, *Ex parte Oliver*, 2 Ves. & B. 244, 1 Rose, 407, *Taylor's* case, 7 Ves. 328.

THE COURT now called on *Wilde*, Serjeant, to support the warrant. He, however, suggested that the proper course was, for the party applying for his discharge from custody to state the grounds upon which he rested his right to it.

Atcherley, Serjeant, referred to *Rex* v. *Kenworthy*, 3 D. & R. 173, 1 B. & C. 711, and *Rex* v. *Pedley*, 1 Leach, C. C. 365.

THE COURT directed one of the Secondaries to read the writ and return, and the commissioners' warrant—see 6 Geo. 4, c. 16, s. 36.

The return stated that Garcia was in the custody of the Warden by virtue of detainers in five several actions; and that, on the 15th June, a warrant under the hands of three commissioners of bankrupt was delivered to him, by which warrant it was ordered that Garcia be committed to the custody of the keeper of Newgate, there to remain until he should answer certain questions put to him by the commissioners touching his property, to their satisfaction. The warrant, which was addressed to the keeper of Newgate, or whom else it might concern, was appended to the Warden's return to the habeas corpus. The questions put by the commissioners to Garcia, and his answers thereto, were set forth in the warrant.

Atcherley, Serjeant, contended that the prisoner was entitled to his discharge—first, on the ground that no warrant for his detention was set out in the Warden's return. The return, he submitted, should have embodied the commissioners' warrant, and also the examination, to shew that the imprisonment was legal; and that it was perfectly consistent with the return, as at present framed, that the warrant was a nullity. The learned Serjeant then proposed to shew that Garcia's answers to the questions propounded to him were such as the commissioners ought reasonably to have been satisfied with, and were not of a nature to warrant the exercise of the extreme power they had thought fit to put in force; when—

Wilde, Serjeant, objected that the court could not now go into the inquiry.—There being a good cause of legal detainer stated in the return, the court can only re-commit the prisoner. The warrant of the commissioners is not directed to the Warden; nor does he return it as a cause of detainer. The prisoner is not in fact detained under the authority of the warrant. When he is discharged from the actions under which he is detained, the keeper of Newgate will be ready to receive him under the warrant.

Atcherley, Serjeant.—The prisoner's right to a habeas corpus, then, is a mere mockery; for, when addressed to the Warden, his answer is that he does not hold him; and, if addressed to the keeper of Newgate, the return would be, that he has him not. The warrant is directed "to all whom it may concern." It does concern the Warden; for he is already in his custody. [*Tindal*, C. J.—The 6 Geo. 4, c. 16, s. 36, authorizes the commissioners, "if the bankrupt shall refuse to be sworn, or shall refuse to answer any questions put to him by the commissioners touching any of the matters aforesaid, or shall not fully answer to the satisfaction of the commissioners any such questions, or shall refuse to sign and subscribe his examination," &c., " by warrant under their hands to commit him to such prison as they shall think fit," &c.   Here, Garcia is committed to Newgate: the warrant, therefore, can only be addressed to the officers of that gaol.]   The prisoner is detained by the Warden on his road to Newgate. [*Vaughan*, J.—The keeper of Newgate has a reversionary interest in his body, expectant on the determination of the Warden's estate in it.]   The Court may, at all events, as the parties are now before them, hear the matter upon its merits.

TINDAL, C. J.—The prisoner is not in a condition to ask for his discharge.   It would be useless to discuss the validity of the warrant, the party not yet being in custody under it.   It appears from the Warden's return that he detains him by virtue of process issued out of this court in five several actions: and he also informs us that a certain warrant has been lodged with him, not that Garcia is detained by virtue of that warrant.   It appears therefore that this writ improvidè emanavit: we should not have granted it had it appeared to us that the party was not in custody under it.   All that we can do is to remand him to the custody whence he has been brought.

The rest of the court concurring—

The prisoner was accordingly remanded.

1836.

*Monday,
Nov. 21st.*

LAMONT, Vouchee.

In a recovery,
the court will
not allow the
Christian names
of the vouchee
(erroneously
transposed in
the warrant of
attorney) to
be made right,
amendments
never being
allowed in that
instrument.

THE name of the vouchee in this recovery was William
Robert Alexander Lamont; but, in the warrant of attorney and deed to make a tenant to the præcipe, and in all
the subsequent proceedings, his Christian names had been
accidentally transposed, thus—Robert William Alexander
Lamont.

Scriven, Serjeant, now moved that the names might be
correctly inserted in all the proceedings except in the deed
to make a tenant to the præcipe.—He submitted, that,
though the court would not interfere in a case where the
defect is cured by the 3 & 4 Will. 4, c. 74, s. 7 (*Locking-
ton*, Dem., *Shipley*, Conusor, 1 New Cases, 355, 1 Scott,
263), yet, under section 9, the jurisdiction of the court to
amend in cases not provided for by the act (one of which,
he submitted, the present was,) was reserved.

TINDAL, C. J.—According to the old practice, the court
invariably refused to allow amendments in the warrant of
attorney (a): with that therefore we clearly cannot interfere.   And, with respect to the deed to make the tenant
to the præcipe, the vouchee is estopped by his execution
of it from objecting to the misnomer.   Why not procure
an acknowledgment under the statute?

The rest of the court concurring—

Scriven took nothing by his motion.

(a) In *James*, dem., *Williams*,   warrant of attorney was allowed
ten., *James*, vouchee, 7 Taunt. 434,   to be amended, it *not being an in-*
1 Moore, 130, the *caption* of the   *tegral part of the instrument.*

GALE *v.* WINKES.

THE plaintiff being unable to serve the defendant with the writ of summons in this case, his attorney's clerk left at his house a note to the following effect:—" I beg to inform you that I have called to serve you with copy of process at the suit of C. Gale; and if you do not call on Messrs. T. & G., his attorneys, before two o'clock on Saturday, I shall call again on Saturday evening at nine." This note was left at the defendant's place of abode, with a female relative who attended to his business. The defendant not paying any attention to it, the writer called at the time mentioned, when he was informed by the person with whom he had left the note, that the defendant was from home, but that she had given him the note; and, after waiting some time, the clerk went away, leaving with the same person a second note inclosing the writ of summons. Upon an affidavit of these facts, Park, J., at chambers, directed a distringas to issue. The distringas was accordingly issued, returnable on the 12th instant, and a levy made under it on the 1st.

A distringas to compel appearance, under the 2 Will. 4, c. 39, s. 3, must be indorsed with the amount of the debt and costs.

The court refused to set aside an order made by a judge at chambers for the issuing of a distringas, though the affidavit on which the order was obtained did not shew that three calls and two appointments had been previously made for the purpose of serving the writ of summons.

Archbold, on the 9th, moved for a rule nisi to set aside the judge's order on the ground that the practice requiring three calls and two appointments before the issuing of a writ of distringas, had not been complied with; and also to set aside the distringas, on the ground that the amount of the debt was not indorsed thereon, pursuant to rule II. of Hilary Term, 2 Will. 4, which provides, " that, upon every bailable writ and warrant, and upon the copy of any process served for the payment of any debt, the amount of the debt shall be stated, and the amount of what the attorney claims for the costs of such writ or process, arrest, or copy and service, and attendance to receive debt and costs;" which rule is by a subsequent rule (Michael-

mas Term, 3 Will. 4, s. 5,) declared to be applicable to all
writs of summons, *distringas*, capias, and detainer, issued
under the authority of the 2 Will. 4, c. 39, and to the copy
of every such writ.

A rule nisi having been granted—

Wilde, Serjeant, now shewed cause.—By the 2 Will. 4,
c. 39, s. 3, it is enacted, "that, in case it shall be made appear, by affidavit, to the satisfaction of the court out of
which the process issued, or, in vacation, of any judge of
either of the said courts, that any defendant has not been
personally served with any such writ of summons as hereinbefore mentioned, and has not, according to the exigency
thereof, appeared to the action, and cannot be compelled
so to do without some more efficacious process, then and
in any such case it shall be lawful for such court or judge
to order a writ of distringas to be issued, directed to the
sheriff of the county," &c. &c. The rule generally adopted *by the courts* undoubtedly has been, in close conformity
with the practice that prevailed with respect to the distringas under the 7 & 8 Geo. 4, c. 71 (see Tidd's Practice,
9th edit. 115), to require three calls and two appointments,
a copy of the writ of summons being left at the last time
of calling. But the discretion of a judge sitting at chambers is fettered by no such rule. He is to exercise his
judgment upon the facts that are brought before him.
Here, the learned judge having, in exercise of the discretion given him by the statute, thought fit under the circumstances to direct the issue of a distringas, the court
cannot and ought not to interfere. The facts were reasonably sufficient to satisfy the learned judge that the defendant was keeping out of the way to avoid the service
of the process: and even now he has not ventured to swear
that the writ has not come to his possession; nor does he
in the slightest degree attempt to controvert or deny the
inference drawn by the learned judge. With respect to

the want of indorsement on the distringas of the amount of the debt and costs—the rules referred to can scarcely have been intended to apply to a distringas issued for the purpose of compelling an appearance to the writ of summons, which already bears the indorsement of the sum claimed for debt and costs. The rule of Michaelmas Term, 3 Will. 4, s. 5, may more reasonably be referred to the writs of distringas issued into the counties palatine of Lancaster and Durham.

Archbold, in support of his rule.—The distringas at all events must be set aside for irregularity : the rules are imperative, and admit of no doubt. With respect to the order of the learned judge, it ought not under the circumstances to have been made. [*Tindal*, C. J.—It is certainly extremely desirable and convenient that the general rule sanctioned by the practice of all the courts should be strictly adhered to. But, the matter having undergone discussion before a judge, I think the defendant should at least shew that he is injured by the course adopted.] There can be no reason why a different practice should prevail at chambers from that which prevails in court.

TINDAL, C. J.—I think the rule must be made absolute for setting aside the distringas and subsequent proceedings, for want of the proper indorsement: but, as to the other part of the motion, I am not satisfied that we ought to interfere, the statute having left it to the discretion of a judge at chambers, in vacation, to order the issue of the distringas where he is satisfied that the circumstances of the case require it. I am far from saying, the general understanding of the courts being that there should be at least three calls and two appointments before a distringas is issued, that I should under the circumstances have made the order: for, I think it better that a known and intelligible rule should in these cases be adhered to

x x 2

strictly. But, rebus sic stantibus, the question is, whether there was not enough in the case to satisfy the learned judge that " some more efficacious process" was requisite to compel the defendant's appearance. The affidavit upon which the order was made states that the clerk called at the defendant's place of abode, and left a letter for him desiring him to call at his employers' office, and, in default of his so doing, appointing to be again at the defendant's house at a certain day and hour, and that the clerk called at the time appointed, but could not see the defendant, though he was informed by the person with whom he left the letter that it had been delivered to the defendant. I think there was at all events enough to require the defendant, when he calls upon the court to relieve him from the distringas, to shew that the letter in question has never come to his hands.

GASELEE, J.—I think my Brother Park was, under the circumstances, fully justified in making the order.

VAUGHAN, J.—I agree that the rule must be made absolute as far as regards the writ of distringas. But I am of opinion that the order of my Brother Park should remain untouched. It is true, that the courts have usually required three calls and two appointments to be shewn before allowing a distringas to issue: but there is no express *rule* upon the subject. The act of parliament leaves it to the discretion of the court in term time, and of a judge at chambers in vacation. Exercising his matured judgment in the matter, my Brother Park thought it right to make the order: and, though perhaps some of us would not have acceded to the application, that is not a sufficient ground for setting aside his order; particularly as the defendant does not now aver that the writ of summons has not reached him. He is not entitled to any favour.

`Bosanquet, J.—I am also of opinion that the distringas and levy should be set aside; but not the order. The rule in general adopted by the courts certainly is as stated by my Lord Chief Justice and my Brother Vaughan: but that rule must yield to special circumstances.

1836.

GALE
v.
WINKES.

Rule absolute accordingly.

Ex parte GROVE.

*Tuesday,
Nov. 22nd.*

*H*UMFREY, on a former day, obtained a rule calling upon Charles Roberts, an attorney of this court, and one of the perpetual commissioners for taking acknowledgments by married women of deeds to be executed by them pursuant to the statute 3 & 4 Will. 4, c. 74, to shew cause why he should not deliver up certain deeds which had been acknowledged before himself and one Collis, another commissioner, together with their certificates of the due taking thereof, and the affidavits verifying the same. The facts presented by the affidavit upon which the motion was founded, were as follow:—The acknowledgments having been taken, the clerk to the solicitor concerned in the transaction called upon Roberts to ascertain whether the affidavits of verification were made, and was told by that gentleman that he must first see the deeds. The deeds were accordingly sent to him; and, when the attorney demanded them, Roberts refused to deliver them up until *his* fees had been paid. The amount claimed by him for his fees being sent to him, he stated that the deeds were in Mr. Collis's hands, and would be detained until his, Collis's, fees also had been paid.

A commissioner for taking acknowledgments by married women under the 3 & 4 Will. 4, c. 74, has a right to detain the deeds as a security for his own individual fees; and also for those of his co-commissioner, provided he be authorised by him to do so.

Whateley shewed cause, upon an affidavit stating that Roberts had authority from Collis to demand his fees on his behalf.—Mr. Roberts was perfectly justified in his proceeding. The deeds were lawfully in his possession, and he had a clear right to detain them as well for his own fees as for those of his co-commissioner: the fees were due to them jointly. In *Hollis* v. *Claridge*, 4 Taunt. 807, it was held that every one has by law a lien upon a specific deed or paper delivered to him to do any work thereon: and in *Blackbourn* v. *Brown*, 8 Moore, 229, 1 Bing. 277, that the clerk of the warrants might refuse to pass a fine until the attorney employed by the parties had paid the amount of his termage fees. At the time the application was made, the party making it was aware that the deeds were in the hands of Collis; the motion therefore should have been against him, and not against Roberts.

Humfrey, in support of his rule.—At the time the deeds were first demanded, they were in the hands of Roberts. It is true, he was authorized by Collis to demand the fees due to him, but not to detain the deeds: that was an authority Collis could not give him. A lien is a mere personal right, incapable of being transferred.

TINDAL, C. J.—It seems to me to be clear that the commissioners have a lien upon all deeds in their joint possession for the fees due to them for taking an acknowledgment; and that, where the deeds are (as they must be, being indivisible,) in the hands of one of the commissioners, and he is duly authorized by the other to detain them as a lien for his fees, he has a right to do so. Were it not so, the commissioners would be left without any practicable remedy for the recovery of these small demands. In the present case, however, there is a point of time that is uncovered by Roberts's affidavit. It does not appear that he had any authority from Collis to detain the deeds for him, until after the attorney had paid his fees and demanded the deeds. I therefore think the rule must be made absolute, but without costs.

The rest of the court concurring—

Rule absolute, without costs.

1836.

*Thursday,
Nov. 24th.*

BENNETT *v.* SMITH.

THIS was a country cause. The declaration was filed on the 26th October, together with a rule to plead in eight days. The notice of declaration was not served upon the defendant until the 28th. On the 4th November, the plaintiff signed judgment for want of a plea.

Sewell, on a former day, obtained a rule nisi to set aside the judgment for irregularity, on the ground that the time for pleading had not expired, the eight days being to be reckoned from the time of service of the notice of declaration.

Crowder, contra, submitted that the days for pleading were to be reckoned from the time of filing the declaration, where the rule to plead is left at the office at the same time: otherwise, in country causes, the plaintiff must always wait until he has ascertained that the defendant has been served with a notice of declaration before he can file a rule to plead, which would in some cases give the defendant double the number of days for pleading allowed by the practice of the courts.

Sewell, in support of his rule.—" If the declaration be *filed,* and notice thereof given to the defendant or his attorney, it is deemed to be a good declaration from the time of such notice only; and therefore a rule to plead in such case, given before notice of declaration, is irregular"— Tidd's Practice, 9th edit. 456; Archbold's Practice, 3rd edit. 242; citing Reg. Gen. Trinity, 1 Geo. 2, and Trinity, 2 Geo. 2, K. B.; Easter, 49 Geo. 3, and Michaelmas, 1 Geo. 2, C. P.; *Beach* v. *Hobbs,* 8 Mod. 379; *Earl of Hindford* v. *Charteris,* 2 Ld. Raym. 1407; *Hutchinson* v.

Where a declaration is filed, the rule to plead must not be left at the office until notice of the filing of the declaration has been duly served: the time for pleading only beginning to reckon from the time of service of the notice of declaration.

Brown, 7 T. R. 298; *Weddle* v. *Brazier*, 1 C. & M. 69, 1 Dowl. 639; Prac. Reg. 131; *Grey* v. *Saunders*, Cas. Pr. C. P. 111, Barnes, 248.

Cur. adv. vult.

TINDAL, C. J., now said.—We have inquired into the practice of the other courts ; and we find that the rule to plead should not be left in the office until after notice of the filing of the declaration has been served. The prothonotaries inform us that such has also been the practice of this court. The judgment, therefore, in the present case has been irregularly signed.

Rule absolute, without costs (*a*).

(*a*) Whatever the understanding of the prothonotaries may have been, it is well known that no objection has ever been made at the Secondaries' Office to receive the rule to plead, whether in a town or a country cause, at the time of filing the declaration.

EVELEIGH *v.* SALSBURY.

*Thursday,
Nov. 24th.*

Practice under the interpleader act, where the parties called upon by a rule obtained on behalf of the sheriff decline to appear.

A fieri facias was directed to the sheriff of Cambridgeshire, indorsed to levy 100*l*. 17*s*., besides &c., in an action of debt at the suit of the plaintiff against " James Salsbury, the elder, Rose Crescent, Cambridge." The sheriff accordingly, on the 17th October, seized certain goods in the defendant's house. On the 20th October, James Salsbury, the younger, asserting that the goods seized were his property, threatened the sheriff with an action. The sheriff called upon the plaintiff to indemnify him, but he refused.

W. H. Watson, on the part of the sheriff, on a former day in this term, obtained a rule calling upon the plaintiff and James Salsbury the younger to shew cause why, upon delivery up by the sheriff, in such manner as the court should direct, of the goods and chattels of the defendant seized by the sheriff under and by virtue of the writ of fi. fa. issued in this cause, and now in the possession of the sheriff, all further proceedings in the cause against the sheriff should not be stayed ; and why the said plaintiff and James Salsbury the younger should not appear and state the nature and particulars of their respective claims to the said goods and chattels, and maintain or relinquish such claims, pursuant to the statute in that case lately made and provided, &c.—1 & 2 Will. 4, c. 58.

The above rule having been served upon the respective parties, but none of them appearing—

W. H. Watson now prayed the court to pronounce such rule as should appear to them to be just, according to the circumstances of the case. The goods, it appeared, had not been sold.

THE COURT pronounced the following rule :—" That the sheriff be at liberty forthwith to proceed to a sale of so much of the goods and chattels of the defendant seized by the sheriff under and by virtue of the writ of fi. fa. issued in this cause as shall be sufficient to pay the sheriff's poundage and expenses of keeping possession, the amount thereof to be ascertained by one of the prothonotaries of this court, upon reference to him for that purpose ; that the sheriff be at liberty to withdraw from the possession of the remainder of such goods and chattels; that the plaintiff, and also the said James Salsbury the younger, be for ever barred from proceeding against the sheriff; and that the sheriff be discharged."

1836.

Thursday,
Nov. 24th.

In trespass for
an assault,
battery, and
imprisonment
of the plaintiff's
wife, the defen-
dant pleaded—
first, not guilty
—secondly, that
the individual
was not the
plaintiff's wife
—thirdly, a
justification
under process
issued against
her. A verdict
was found for
the plaintiff
on the first and
second pleas,
with a farthing
damages, and
for the defen-
dants on the
third:—Held,
that it was
competent to
the judge to
certify under
the 43 Eliz.
c. 6, s. 2, to
deprive the
plaintiffs of
costs, notwith-

WILLIAM WILSON and ESTHER, his Wife, v. LAINSON and SOLOMONS.

TRESPASS for an assault, battery, and imprisonment of the plaintiff's wife. The defendant pleaded—first, not guilty—secondly, that the plaintiff Esther was not the wife of William Wilson—thirdly, as to the assaulting and imprisoning the female plaintiff, a justification under process at the suit of one Thomas Upton against Ann Wilson, with an averment that Anne Wilson and Esther Wilson were one and the same person. At the trial before Bosanquet, J., a verdict was found for the plaintiffs on the first and second pleas, damages one farthing, and for the defendants on the third. The learned judge thereupon certified, under the statute 43 Eliz. c. 6, s. 2 (a), to deprive the plaintiffs of costs.

S. Martin, on a former day, obtained a rule calling upon the defendants to shew cause why this certificate should not be discharged, and why the prothonotary should not tax the plaintiffs' costs of the action. In *Bone v. Dawe,* 5 N. & M. 230, 3 Ad. & E. 711, in trespass for assault and false imprisonment and tearing the plaintiff's

standing that, on the issue joined on the plea of not guilty, the postea had been entered up generally for the plaintiffs; there being no necessary admission of a battery on the face of the record.

(a) Which enacts, " that, if, upon any action personal to be brought in any her Majesty's courts at Westminster, not being for any title or interest of lands, nor concerning the freehold or inheritance of any lands, *nor for any battery,* it shall appear to the judges for the same court, and so signified or set down by the justices before whom the same shall be tried, that the debt or damages to be recovered therein in the same court shall not amount to the sum of forty shillings or above, that, in every such case, the judges and justices before whom any such action shall be pursued shall not award for costs to the party plaintiff any greater or more costs than the sum of the debt or damages so recovered shall amount unto, but less at their discretion."

clothes, there was an issue upon a new assignment to a plea of son assault demesne; the jury found a verdict for the plaintiff with one shilling damages: and it was held that the judge had no power to certify under the 43 Eliz. c. 6, to deprive the plaintiff of costs; and the court granted a rule for taxation notwithstanding the certificate. Here, on the issue joined on the plea of not guilty, the postea has been entered up generally for the plaintiffs; and, as the declaration charges a battery, and there is no exception of it in the finding of the jury, it must be taken, as against the defendants, that a battery was proved at the trial. Besides, the defendants have put upon the record a plea (the second) that admits the battery. By the 22 & 23 Car. 2, c. 9, s. 136, it is enacted, that, "in all actions of trespass, assault, and battery, and other personal actions, wherein the judge at the trial of the cause shall not find and certify under his hand, upon the back of the record, that an assault and battery was sufficiently proved by the plaintiff against the defendant, or that the freehold or title of the land mentioned in the plaintiff's declaration was chiefly in question, the plaintiff, in case the jury shall find the damages to be under the value of forty shillings, shall not recover or obtain more costs of suit than the damages so found shall amount unto." Under this statute, it was held, in *Smith* v. *Edge*, 6 T. R. 562, that where, to an action for an assault and battery, the defendant pleads the general issue and a justification to the whole, and the plaintiff obtains a verdict with damages under forty shillings, he is still entitled to full costs. So, in *Johnson* v. *Northwood*, 1 Moore, 420, 7 Taunt. 689, where, to a declaration stating that the defendant made an assault on the plaintiff, and beat, bruised, wounded, and ill-treated him, the defendant pleaded the general issue, and a justification as to the assaulting and ill-treating only, by a plea of moliter manus imposuit; this court held that the plaintiff was entitled to full costs, although he had obtained a ver-

1836.

WILSON
v.
LAINSON.

dict for one shilling damages only, and the judge had not certified at the trial. And in *Hughes* v. *Hughes*, 2 C. M. & R. 663, 4 Dowl. 532, 1 Tr. & G. 4, where a plaintiff recovered thirteen shillings damages in an action of trespass quare clausum fregit, to which only the general issue was pleaded, it was held that he was entitled to his full costs, as, under that plea, as restricted by the rules of pleading of Hilary Term, 4 Will. 4, the freehold could not come in question. All the cases on the subject are collected in note (*f*) to the case of *Greene* v. *Jones*, 1 Wms. Saund. 300.

Talfourd, Serjeant, and *Ball*, shewed cause.—There is no battery admitted upon the record, unless imprisonment includes a battery. In *Emmet* v. *Lyne*, 1 New Rep. 255, it was held that a certificate may be granted under the 43 Eliz. c. 6, in an action of assault, battery, and false imprisonment, if no actual battery be proved: and, even if a battery be proved, it will not prevent the judge from certifying with respect to the imprisonment; and, though he cannot certify as to the battery, yet the plaintiff will not be entitled to full costs for that, unless the judge certify under the 22 & 23 Car. 2, c. 9—*Wiffin* v. *Kincaird*, 2 New Rep. 471. In *Briggs* v. *Bowgin*, 2 Bing. 333, 9 Moore, 628, in an action of assault and battery, with a separate count for false imprisonment, where the verdict was for one shilling damages, and the judge certified under the 43 Eliz., this court refused to allow the plaintiff his costs. In *Smith* v. *Edge* and *Bone* v. *Dawe*, a battery was admitted on the face of the record; and in *Hughes* v. *Hughes* the freehold indisputably came in question. In *Page* v. *Creed*, 3 T. R. 391, it was held, that, where, in trespass for an assault and battery, the defendant justifies the assault only, and the plaintiff obtains damages under forty shillings, and the judge does not certify under the 22 & 23 Car. 2, c. 9, the plaintiff is entitled to no more costs than damages. In Hullock on Costs, p. 23, the rule is thus laid down:—" If in an action for an assault, battery, and false imprisonment, the plaintiff obtain a verdict for less than forty shillings damages, the judge may certify, under the 43 Eliz. c. 6, that the damage did not amount to forty shillings, by which certificate the plaintiff will be deprived of full costs, *although a battery were proved at the trial*, unless indeed in the case of an actual battery there should be a certificate under the 22 & 23 Car. 2, c. 9: for, whether there be evidence of a battery or not, it would not prevent the judge from certifying with respect to the imprisonment under the 43 Eliz., and the plaintiff is not entitled to full costs for the assault and battery without a certificate under the 22 & 23 Car. 2, c. 9." The admission of one of several distinct and divisible grounds of action, is not necessarily an admission of the whole.

Martin, in support of his rule.—The declaration charges an assault, battery, and false imprisonment. Upon the first plea, not guilty, to the whole declaration, a verdict is entered on the postea for the plaintiff: that is a finding that the defendant was guilty of a battery. The second plea, also found for the plaintiff, was pleaded to the whole declaration—that Esther Williams was not the wife of the plaintiff William Williams: that plea amounts to a confession of all the other material facts alleged in the declaration. In *Smith* v. *Edge*, Lord Kenyon puts it expressly on the ground of the plea admitting a battery. In *Smith* v. *Edwards*, 4 Dowl. 621, it was held, that, although, in trespass quare clausum fregit, the plaintiff obtaining less than forty shillings damages, the plea of not guilty, since the new rules of pleading, being a special plea, takes the case out of the 22 & 23 Car. 2, c. 9, s. 136, yet the judge may, notwithstanding, grant a certificate under the 43 Eliz. c. 6, s. 2, to deprive the plaintiff of

1836.

WILSON
v.
LAINSON.

costs, the whole record and evidence at the trial being properly taken into consideration. Here, the battery, being neither traversed nor justified, must be taken to have been admitted. *Hughes* v. *Hughes* and *Smith* v. *Edwards* are conclusive of the question.

Cur. adv. vult.

TINDAL, C. J., now delivered the judgment of the court:—The question in this case is, whether, notwithstanding the judge's certificate under the statute 43 Eliz. c. 6, s. 2, the plaintiff is entitled to his full costs; and this depends on another question, whether a battery appears to be confessed upon the record; for, actions for *battery* being expressly excepted out of the statute, if it appears judicially to us that this was an action for *battery*, the statute does not apply. The plaintiffs contend that such admission appears on the record upon two grounds—first, because on the issue joined on the plea of not guilty the postea has been entered up generally for them; and they insist, that, as they have declared for a battery, and there is no exception of it in the finding of the jury, it must be taken, as against the defendants, that a battery was proved at the trial. But to this the answer appears obvious, that the question as to the evidence must be considered now as it was at the time the certificate was given, and at that time there had been no postea formally drawn up; and if the facts were such as that the judge had the power to certify at the moment the cause was decided, the defendants cannot be deprived of the benefit of such certificate by the subsequent voluntary act of the plaintiffs themselves. The other ground on which the plaintiffs rely, is, that the second plea, taking issue only on a single fact alleged in the declaration, must be taken to be an admission of the battery. But we think, taking the whole of the record together, there is no necessary confession of the battery on this record. The plea of not guilty expressly denies it; the last plea, which is a plea in confession and avoidance, excludes the battery. The question therefore arises on the second plea alone. Now, this is not in its form a plea of confession and avoidance; it is a plea of traverse or denial of a particular collateral fact alleged in the declaration: and, if this plea had been pleaded alone, although the plaintiffs might contend that *a* cause of action was admitted by the defendants, yet they never could have contended that *the whole* of their ground of action was admitted: for, their cause of action in this case is several and divisible. Their action is maintainable either for the assault, or the battery, or for the imprisonment: either of those grounds of action would support it. The admission, therefore, of a ground of action that is divisible, we consider no necessary admission of the whole, but that the plaintiffs must still prove at the trial what part of their gravamen they rely on. Holding, therefore, that there is no necessary admission of a battery on this record, we think that the certificate of the judge certifying under the statute of Elizabeth deprived the plaintiffs of full costs.

Rule discharged.

VIVIAN v. BLOMBERG.

THE following case was submitted by the Vice-Chancellor, for the opinion of this court :—

The vicarage of the parish and parish church of St. Giles Without Cripplegate, is a benefice with cure of souls, in the city of London : and the several messuages or tenements hereinafter particularly mentioned (not being the capital messuage or dwelling-house used for the habitation of the vicar, nor having ground to the same belong-

capital messuage or dwelling-house used for the habitation of the vicar, nor having ground to the same belonging above the quantity of ten acres, is a valid lease, notwithstanding the restraining statutes of Elizabeth.

ing above the quantity of ten acres,) are parcel of the possessions of the said vicarage, and are situate and being within the said city, and have been accustomed to be demised by the vicars of the said parish for the time being, for the term of forty years in possession, at the yearly rent of 3*l.*

Lease for forty years from Michaelmas, 1793.

By indenture of lease bearing date the 30th October, 1793, and made between the Rev. George Watson Hand, since deceased, then vicar of the parish church of St. Giles Without Cripplegate aforesaid, of the one part, and Thomas Smith and others of the other part, for the consideration therein expressed, the said G. W. Hand did demise unto the said other persons, parties thereto, the messuages or tenements and other hereditaments hereinafter particularly mentioned, parcel of or belonging to the vicarage of St. Giles Without Cripplegate aforesaid, with the appurtenances: to hold the same unto the aforesaid lessees, their executors, administrators, and assigns, from the 29th September then last past, for the term of forty years, yielding and paying therefor yearly during the said term unto the said G. W. Hand and his successors, vicars for the time being of the said parish church, the yearly rent of 3*l.*, payable quarterly, on the four most usual feasts; the lessees being charged with the reparations, and subject to the covenants and agreements therein expressed and contained: and which said lease was duly confirmed by the patron and ordinary.

The said G. W. Hand departed this life many years since: after his decease the Rev. William Holmes was duly presented and instituted to and inducted into the vicarage of the parish and parish church of St. Giles Without Cripplegate aforesaid.

Lease for twenty-one years, dated Oct. 1830.

In the month of October, 1830, there were less than three years unexpired of the said term of forty years so granted as aforesaid, and the said William Holmes, being then such vicar as aforesaid, duly executed another indenture of lease, bearing date the 8th October, 1830, and made or expressed to be made between him Wm. Holmes as such vicar as aforesaid, of the one part, and James W. Vivian and Christoper Hodgson of the other part, whereby, for the considerations therein expressed, the said William Holmes did demise unto the said J. W. Vivian and C. Hodgson, all that messuage, house, or building, situate and being in Fore Street, in the parish of St. Giles Without Cripplegate, London, called the quest house, and used by the inhabitants of the said parish as a vestry house, and the rooms and other appurtenances thereto adjoining and belonging, and therewith used and enjoyed; and also all and every the messuages, tenements, shops, and buildings therein and hereinafter particularly mentioned, that is to say, all those four messuages or tenements situate, standing, and being in Fore Street, in the said parish of St. Giles Without Cripplegate, London, then or late in the several tenures or occupations of W.W. &c.; and also all that piece or parcel of ground on which stood a building theretofore called Pratt's Buildings, and on which then or late stood the back part or parcel of three messuages or tenements and outbuildings, situate in Fore Street aforesaid, formerly in the tenure or occupation of I. R., &c., and then or late of J. W. &c., together with the small piece or parcel of ground thereunto adjoining, and then laid into the yard or backsides of the said three messuages; and also all that small house or shop in Fore Street aforesaid, formerly in the tenure or occupation of A. S. &c., and then or late of M. D.; and also the ground on the north side of the said church, on which stood a wall and palisadoes; together with all the appurtenances to the said quest house and premises belonging, as the same premises were more particularly described in the plan drawn in the margin of the same indenture: to hold the same unto the said J.W. Vivian and C. Hodgson, their executors, administrators, and assigns, from the making of the said indenture, for the term of twenty-one years thence next ensuing (subject nevertheless to the aforesaid existing lease of the same premises, bearing date the 30th October, 1793, as hereinbefore particularly mentioned); yielding and paying therefor yearly, during the said term of twenty-one years, unto the said W. Holmes and his successors, vicars as aforesaid, the rent or sum of 3*l.*, payable quarterly, on the four most usual feasts, by equal portions; the first payment to be made on the feast day of the birth of our Lord Christ then next ensuing : the lessees being charged with the reparations, and subject to the covenants and agreements on the lessees' part therein contained: which last-mentioned lease was duly confirmed by the patron and ordinary. The said W. Holmes departed this life in the month of June, 1833.

The question for the opinion of the Court was—Whether the said last-mentioned indenture of lease was a valid and effectual lease, and binding upon the successor of the said W. Holmes in the said vicarage, for the remainder of the said term of twenty-one years expressed to be thereby granted.

The case was argued in Trinity Term last.

The point marked for argument on the part of the plaintiff was—that the lease of the 8th October, 1830, was a valid lease, notwithstanding the provisions of the statutes of 13 Eliz. c. 10, 14 Eliz. c. 11, and 18 Eliz. c. 11.

For the defendant—that the lease of the 8th October, 1830, did not bind the defendant, the present vicar, the lease being a lease of houses in London, not comprising the capital dwelling-house nor having land to the same belonging above the quantity of ten acres, and there having been, at the time when such lease was granted, a prior lease for forty years subsisting, but whereof there were less than three years then unexpired.

Maule, for the plaintiff.—The lease in question, having been duly confirmed by the patron and ordinary, was a valid lease, and binding on the lessor's successors. It was clearly a valid demise at common law; for, a lease by patron or ordinary might be for any period. The question is whether the lessor was restrained by any statute from granting the lease. The only statutes applicable to the case are those of 13 Eliz. c. 10, 14 Eliz. c. 11, and 18 Eliz. c. 11. The preamble of the 13 Eliz. c. 10, states, that, "Where divers and sundry ecclesiastical persons of this realm, being endowed and possessed of antient palaces, mansion-houses, and other edifices and buildings, belonging to their ecclesiastical benefices or livings, have of late years not only suffered the same, for want of due reparations, partly to run to great ruin and decay, and in some part utterly to fall down to the ground, converting the timber, lead, and stones to their own benefit and commodity; but also have made deeds of gifts, colourable alienations, and other conveyances of like effect, of their goods and chattels in their lives-time, to the intent and of purpose after their deaths to defeat and defraud their successors of such just actions and remedies as otherwise they might and should have had for the same against their executors or administrators of their goods by the laws ecclesiastical of this realm, to the great defacing of the state ecclesiastical, and intolerable charges of their successors, and evil precedent and example for others, if speedy remedy be not provided." The 3rd section, after reciting "that long and unreasonable leases made by colleges, deans and chapters, parsons, vicars, and other having spiritual promotions, be the chiefest causes of the dilapidations and the decay of all spiritual livings and hospitality, and the utter impoverishing of all successors, incumbents in the same," enacts "that all leases, gifts, grants, feoffments, conveyances, or estates, to be made, had, done, or suffered by any master and fellows of any college, dean and chapter of any cathedral

1836.

VIVIAN
v.
BLOMBERG.

Y Y 2

or collegiate church, master or guardian of any hospital, parson, vicar, or any other having any spiritual or ecclesiastical living, or any houses, lands, tithes, tenements, or hereditaments, being any parcel of the possessions of any such college, cathedral church, chapter, hospital, parsonage, vicarage, or other spiritual promotion, or any ways appertaining or belonging to the same, or any of them, to any person or persons, bodies politic or corporate (other than for the term of one and twenty years, or three lives, from the time as any such lease or grant shall be made or granted, whereupon the accustomed yearly rent or more shall be reserved and payable yearly during the said term), shall be utterly void and of none effect, to all intents, constructions, and purposes, any law, custom, or usage to the contrary any ways notwithstanding." This clause prohibits and avoids a certain class of leases; but it leaves untouched one like the lease now in question. The next statute is the 14 Eliz. c. 11. The 17th section, after reciting that there is in the last-mentioned statute " one branch to avoid certain leases to be made by masters and fellows of colleges, deans and chapters of cathedral and collegiate churches, masters or guardians of any hospital, or by any parson, vicar, or any other having any spiritual or ecclesiastical living," it is enacted, " that the said branch, nor any thing therein contained, shall not extend to any grant, assurance, or lease of any houses belonging to any the persons or bodies politic or corporate aforesaid, nor to any grounds to such houses appertaining, which houses be situate in any city, borough, town corporate, or market town, or the suburbs of any of them; but that all such houses and grounds may be granted, demised, and assured, as by the laws of this realm and the several statutes of the said colleges, cathedral churches, and hospitals, they lawfully might have been before the making of the said statute, or lawfully might be if the said statute were not; so always that such house be not the capital or dwelling-house used for the habitation of the persons abovesaid, nor have ground to the same belonging above the quantity of ten acres; any thing in the said act to the contrary notwithstanding:" and, by section 19, it is provided "that no lease shall be permitted to be made *by force of this act*, in reversion, nor without reserving the accustomed yearly rent at the least, nor without charging the lessee with the reparations, nor for longer term than forty years at the most." The 18 Eliz. c. 11, recites, in s. 1, the 13 Eliz. c. 10, and then proceeds, s. 2: "Sithence the making of which said estatute, divers of the said ecclesiastical and spiritual persons and others having spiritual or ecclesiastical livings, have from time to time made leases for the term of twenty-one years, or three lives, long before the expiration of the former years, contrary to the true meaning and intent of the said statute; be it therefore enacted by this present parliament, that all leases hereafter to be made by any of the said ecclesiastical, spiritual, or collegiate persons, or others, of any their said ecclesiastical, spiritual, or collegiate lands, tenements, or hereditaments, whereof any former lease for years is in being, not to be expired, surrendered, or ended within three years next after the making of any such new lease, shall be void, frustrate, and of none effect; any law, usage, or custom to the contrary notwithstanding." That enactment applies only where three years of the former lease remain unexpired: here, less than three years remained. It will probably be said that this lease is prohibited by the 14 Eliz. c. 11. That, however, is an enabling statute to some extent: it removes upon certain conditions certain disabilities imposed by the 13 Eliz. c. 10; and, this being a good lease at common law, and not a lease made by force of the statute 14 Eliz. c. 11, does not fall within the prohibition of that statute against leases in reversion. In *The Dean and*

1836.

VIVIAN
v.
BLOMBERG.

Chapter of Westminster's case, Carter, 9 (a), where an ecclesiastical lease of town houses for forty years was to begin presently, seventeen years of a former lease remaining unexpired, Tirrell, J., said: "I shall pass by how things were at common law amongst corporations; only I observe this, at common law, dean and chapter had an unlimited power over their possessions till the statute 18th of the Queen, c. 10. Now, the reason of the statute 13th of the Queen was, because long and unreasonable leases made by ecclesiastical persons were the causes of dilapidations; then that enacts that leases made other than for the term of twenty-one years or three lives from the time of the making such lease, shall be void. Then, in the act of 14th of the Queen, c. 11, an act made for the continuing of several statutes, it is enacted that the statute of 13 Eliz. shall not extend to leases made of houses in cities, boroughs, towns corporate, or market towns, but that such houses may be demised as they might have been before the making of that statute; provided always that such house be not the capital or dwelling-house of the said ecclesiastical persons: Provided always and be it enacted that no lease shall be permitted to be made by force of this act in reversion, nor without reserving the accustomed rent, nor for longer term than forty years at the most. Then the statute 18 Eliz. recites the 13th, and enacts that all leases made by ecclesiastical persons whereof any former lease for years is in being, not to be expired, surrendered, or ended within three years next after the making of any such new lease, shall be void. And what alteration these acts have made at the common law, and what one with another, shall be our first consideration. That of the 13th of Eliz. is a disabling act as to corporations ecclesiastical aggregate, for whereas dean and chapter before might have

(a) "I do not know that Carter, nor will allow that report for any authority."—Per Holt,
C. J., in Pennoyer & Brace's case, Comb. 442.

made what leases and grants they would, by that they are now restrained to one and twenty years, or three lives; but, because by the words of that act concurrent leases were devised, and to make a lease before the one and twenty years were out was against the intent of the statute of 13th, though within the letter of it : therefore the statute of 14th of Eliz. is shuffled into an act for continuance of statutes, as my Lord Hobart well expresseth it in *Crane & Taylor's* case, Hob. 269, and therein is some alteration made as to the statute of decimo tertio: and well might it be said to be shuffled in, when there is such inconsistency in the act, which enacts that every clause in the said acts should continue until the end of the next parliament, which it had repealed. Now, to examine whether such leases of houses are totally exempt by the 14th out of the 13th or not; so that, if the qualifications of the 14th be not observed, they fall back to the 13th ; or whether houses in cities are exempt out of the 13th by the 14th sub modo. I hold they are not exempt but sub modo. If you question whether, if a dean and chapter do make a lease for forty years of their dwelling-houses within a city, it be good or not, I think not : and why not? why, because the act saith so always that the said house be no dwelling-house ; that clause is a disabling clause of itself. *Proviso* and *ita quod* are words equally conditional one as well as the other—Litt. sect. 329. If the demise of such an house is gone because of the ita quod in decimo quarto ; by the same reason a reversion is void by the same act of decimo quarto. I do not say every proviso in an act of parliament is a condition ; nor in a deed neither : but this I say, that, where a proviso in a deed makes a condition, it will do so in an act of parliament. If this be then so, that decimo quarto doth not exempt houses in cities totally, but sub modo, and, if the modus be not observed, they fall back into decimo tertio as if decimo quarto had never been made ; our work must be now to prove that the lease made

1836.

VIVIAN
v.
BLOMBERG.

to Sir R. Winn seventeen years before the lease in being was expired be a lease within the statute of decimo quarto, and within the proviso; and I conceive it is. If a man hath power to make a lease in reversion, he may make a lease to commence after a former lease. If a man be restrained to make a lease in reversion, he shall be restrained to make a lease that doth commence after the expiration of another. But the word *reversion* supposes both—*Whitlock's* case, 8 Rep. 69. Now, the dean and chapter being restrained to let after a former lease, they can make no concurrent lease, for that savours more of a reversion. It is all one to say you shall not let anything but what is in possession, as to say you shall not make any lease in reversion. As by the statute of decimo tertio concurrent leases were good, unless of houses, till decimo octavo of the Queen; so are concurrent leases made by bishops at this day, if confirmed by dean and chapter; for, no statute alters 32 Hen. 8 as to that. Upon this ground stands the difference between concurrent leases made by bishops and by dean and chapter." But Bridgman, C. J., said: " I do hold that this is a lease in reversion, and not warranted by decimo quarto of the Queen. Now, the statute of 14th of the Queen prohibiting leases to be made in reversion, whether or not this be a concurrent lease or a future interest, this is all one. But I shall tell you where I differ from my brother that held the same opinion with me. I do hold, that, if a lease be not made according to the proviso of the 14th, it falls back into the 13th; and if it be within the 13th, it falls under the 18th: the words in the statute of decimo quarto are not, that no lease shall be permitted to be made *by virtue of this act*: so that this act leaves us where we were before; but, if it be not within decimo quarto, we are not left at common law, but are within decimo tertio." [*Tindal*, C. J.—Should the three statutes not be construed as one act?] In *Bayly* v. *Murin*, 1 Vent. 244 (*Baily* v. *Man*, 3 Keb. 193, *Bayly* v. *Munday*,

2 Lev. 61), the lease was not per verba de præsenti, but to commence at the following Michaelmas. Twisden, J., thought that the lease had been void even if made to commence presently: but Hale, C. J., inclined to think (3 Keb. 246) that " the lease had been good if it had been made to commence presently, there being less than three years to come of the former lease. First, because the 14 of Eliz. is a kind of an appendix to the 13th of Eliz., and does not repeal it, but sub modo a little enlarging it as to houses in market towns: wherefore the 18th of Eliz., reciting the 13th, does by consequence recite the 14th also. Secondly, there is such a connection betwixt all the statutes concerning leases of ecclesiastical persons, that they have been taken into the construction of one another. The statute of 32 of Hen. 8 is not recited, neither in the 1st or the 13th Eliz.; yet a lease is not warranted upon those statutes, unless it hath the qualifications required by the 32 of Hen. 8. And this course is usual in the construction of statutes made in pari materiâ. Thirdly, it would make a great rummage in leases, as he conceived, if a lease should be void when there was never so little of a former lease unexpired. Fourthly, there is no authority to the contrary. In *Hunt* v. *Singleton*, Cro. Eliz. 564, there was ten years of the former lease in being; and upon that lay the weight of the opinion. *Crane* v. *Taylor*, Hob. 269, is concerning covenants only; and the reason that it doth not extend to the 1st of Eliz. is, because the 18th of Eliz. begins with inferior ecclesiastical persons, and therefore cannot include bishops."

The lease in question, therefore, is clearly a good and valid lease, not being within the prohibition of the 13 Eliz. c. 10, nor requiring any aid from the relaxation of that statute found in the 14 Eliz. c. 11, and the 18 Eliz. c. 11. It might, if necessary, also be contended that this is not a lease in reversion within the 14 Eliz. c. 11, s. 19, but a concurrent lease.

1836.

VIVIAN
v.
BLOMBERG.

Stephen, Serjeant, contra.—This is a lease in reversion, and void under the proviso in the 14 Eliz. c. 11, s. 19. The 13 Eliz. c. 10. was passed to restrain the power of making leases at common law. The 14 Eliz. c. 11. s. 17, excepts certain kinds of property from the operation of 13 Eliz., and in section 19, applies to such property a new law, that no lease shall be permitted to be made by force of the act, in reversion. This has always been the understanding and practice on this head, as appears by Bac. Abr. *Leases* (E), Rule 3, and Watson's Clerg. Law, 437. *Bayly* v. *Murin*, taken in connection with *Hunt* v. *Singleton*, Cro. Eliz. 564, is decisive of the question. In *Bayly* v. *Murin* all the court agreed that the lease (which was in all respects like the present, except that it was to commence at a future period) was void; that it was made by force of the 14 Eliz. c. 11, and void under that statute: the only distinction is the point speculatively taken by Hale, C. J., as to whether or not it would be otherwise if the lease had been made per verba de præsenti. In *Hunt* v. *Singleton*, however, the lease was per verba de præsenti, yet, there being an existing lease with more than three years unexpired, the new lease was held a lease in reversion, and not warranted by the 14 Eliz. c. 11, s. 19. That case therefore removes the distinction taken by Hale, C. J., in *Bayly* v. *Murin*. The like doctrine was held by Bridgman, J., and by Tirrell, J., in *The Dean and Chapter of Westminster's* case. It is clear, therefore, that in *Bayly* v. *Murin*, Hale, C. J., was wrong, or has been wronged by his reporters. *The Bishop of Salisbury's* case, 10 Rep. 59, 60, is a confirmation of *Hunt* v. *Singleton*.

All leases in reversion are prohibited by the 14 Eliz. c. 11. There are three sorts of leases in reversion—one, where the lease is to commence at a future day—another, where it commences presently, another lease being in existence—a third, to commence after the expiration of an existing term. The cases already cited shew that each of these is properly a lease in reversion. There is this peculiarity in concurrent leases, viz. that they are good where made by a bishop: it was so held, under the 1 Eliz. c. 19, in *Fox* v. *Collier*, Moore, 107. But it has never been held that concurrent leases are good under the 14 Eliz. c. 11; for the same reasoning does not apply. It is said that the lease in reversion in this case is made at common law, and not by force of the statute 14 Eliz. c. 11. That, however, is the only statute that applies to leases of property in towns; every lease therefore of such property is a lease made by force of the statute. In *Crane* v. *Taylor*, Hob. 269, the court said: "Though the statute 13 Eliz. c. 10 be general against all leases and grants, other than for twenty-one years, and [or] three lives, of all the possessions of deans and chapters, &c., yet there is a statute of 14 Eliz. c. 11, which is shuffled into an act of continuance of statutes, that enacts that that statute of 13 Eliz. (naming it) shall not extend to any houses in cities, towns, &c., but that the same may be granted, demised, or assured, as they might lawfully have been before, and as if that statute had not been made: so that statute sets all loose touching such houses in cities, as against the statute of 13 Eliz.; and therefore that statute of 14 Eliz. c. 11 makes a new law of itself for them, that no lease shall be made of them in reversion, which was not restrained by the 13 Eliz., as appears by the statute of 18 Eliz., which provides for that mischief, as not provided for before." This, therefore, is clearly a lease under 14 Eliz. c. 11; and it is a lease in reversion in the broadest sense of the words; for, the lessee is to hold from the making of the indenture, subject to an existing lease of the same premises; and, whether a lease is to commence at the Lady-day ensuing, or at the expiration of a prior lease which determines at the Lady-day ensuing, can make no difference. The recital of the existing lease precludes any claim against the lessor by estoppel. In *Wilson* v. *Sewell*, 2 W. Blac. 626, Yates, J., says: "The lease 'in being' is only that in possession. A concurrent lease is not a lease in esse. It operates only by estoppel.

It passes no interest during the former lease. The statute 18 Eliz. meant to restrain leases in *reversion*. Therefore, by lease in being, the legislature meant a lease in possession." Estoppel is the true basis of concurrent leases. In Co. Lit. 352. b. it is laid down, that, "where the verity is apparent in the same record, there the adverse party shall not be estopped to take advantage of the truth, for he cannot be estopped to allege the truth, when the truth appeareth of record. An impropriation is made, after the death of an incumbent, to a bishop and his successors: the bishop by indenture demiseth the parsonage for forty years, to begin after the death of the incumbent; the dean and chapter confirmeth it, the incumbent dieth; this demise shall not conclude, for that it appeareth he had nothing in the impropriation till after the death of the incumbent." The same doctrine is to be found in *Chedington's* case, 1 Rep. 255: " In this case Thomas cannot take advantage of any conclusion, for a conclusion is to estop one to speak the truth, but here the whole truth appears in one and the same indenture: as in 7 Eliz., Dy. 244. a., King Edward the Sixth granted to the Bishop of Coventry and his successors the advowson of a church, and that after the death of the present incumbent he should keep it in proprios usus. The bishop by indenture made a lease to commence after the death of the incumbent, which was confirmed, and the incumbent died; and it was adjudged that the lease was void, and that it should not take effect by estoppel, because it appears in the indenture itself that the lessor had nothing at the time of the lease made." The doctrine of estoppel does not apply here because the existing lease is expressly mentioned in the same indenture; the second lease is made subject to the first.

Maule, in reply—This is clearly a concurrent lease, and not a lease in reversion. And, as to the argument attempted to be derived from the doctrine of estoppel, the only case in which a man can grant by estoppel alone, is, where he has no interest at all in the property granted; but, if he has any interest, the estoppel is fed, and he may grant by the ordinary means such interest as he has. One who has nothing in the land may grant a future fee by estoppel; but, if he grant the fee, having an interest for a year, the interest for a year only passes. Here, the lessor having a reversion, subject to an existing lease, the doctrine of estoppel has no application. And though a lease to commence in futuro may be a lease in reversion, a concurrent lease is not a lease in reversion within the meaning of 14 Eliz. c. 11, s. 19. *Hunt* v. *Singleton,* was the case of a lease of lands in a town, ten years of the preceding lease remaining unexpired. The court held the lease to be void by the 13 Eliz., and not warranted by the 14 Eliz. *Crane* v. *Taylor* is not satisfactorily reported; the nature of the lease does not appear, nor what the covenant was.

Cur. adv. vult.

1836.

VIVIAN
v.
BLOMBERG.

TINDAL, C. J.—As the question which has been sent for our consideration by his Honor, the Vice-Chancellor, has been long considered as vexata questio in the law, it may be more satisfactory that we should explain the grounds upon which our certificate in answer to that question is founded.

The case states a lease by a vicar for twenty-one years from its date, made at the time when a former lease for forty years of the same premises was still in being, but was within three years of its expiration. The subject-matter of the lease consists of certain messuages in the city of London, of which the capital messuage or dwelling-house used for the habitation of the vicar forms no part, and the ground demised is of less extent than ten acres: so that the subject-matter of the demise clearly falls within the statute 14 Eliz. c. 11, s. 17: and the question is, whether such lease is void under any of the restraining statutes of Elizabeth. There are three statutes, and three only, which it will be necessary to consider as bearing on the present question, viz. the 13 Eliz. c. 10, the 14 Eliz. c. 11, ss. 17 and 19, and the 18 Eliz. c. 11, s. 2. Now, the lease in question cannot be held to be made void either by the *first* or *last* of the above-mentioned statutes; not by the first, because it is a lease for twenty-one years only from the date, and complies with all the other requisites of that restraining act. It is indeed a lease in reversion: but there is nothing in that act to make leases in reversion void. And, although the act lastly above named, the 18 Eliz. c. 11, s. 2, after pointing out the mischief of granting leases authorized by the former statute, in reversion, declares the same to be void; yet in its terms it only comprehends those leases in reversion which are made when the former lease for years is in being, " not to be expired or ended within three years next after the making of any such new lease." But, as the lease in question was made when the former lease for forty years was within three years of its expiration by efflux of time, it is not a lease in reversion made void by the operative words of that statute. So far, therefore, as relates to the first and last of the statutes above referred to, this lease does not become void by either; that is, neither of those statutes appears to us to apply to the case. It only remains, therefore, to consider whether in the statute of 14 Eliz. c. 11, there is any enactment which avoids this lease. And indeed the argument on the part of the defendant has been put entirely on that statute; it being contended that the case of leases of houses in cities, of the description therein contained, is taken entirely out of the first restraining statute, and are made subject to a new law created by the statute of the 14 Eliz.; and that, as the 19th section enacts " that no lease shall be permitted to be made by force of this act, in reversion," so the present lease, being a lease in reversion of houses described in the act, is void by the necessary construction of the statute. The first observation that arises on the statute 14

Eliz., is, that it does not contain within it, from beginning to end, any terms importing the avoidance of any lease whatever; on the contrary, it is a statute which excepts from the operation of the former avoiding statute leases of property therein described. It enacts, in section 17, " that the branch of the former statute, nor any thing therein contained, shall extend to any houses, &c. (therein described), but that the same may be demised as by the laws of this realm, and the statutes of the colleges, &c., they lawfully might have been before the making of the said statute, or lawfully might be if the said statute were not." No words can be more large and explicit to exempt such leases from the whole of the effect of the restraining statute, 13 Eliz.: and, although the 19th section goes on to enact " that no lease shall be permitted to be made *by force of this act* in reversion," there are no words added to declare leases made contrary to such permission void : and, taking this statute alone, and by itself, it would be a much stronger construction than we feel ourselves warranted to put upon it, to hold that such words can defeat and avoid an estate, when they may be fully satisfied by allowing them to give a right of action to the successor.

But, in truth, this statute is not to be construed alone, but with reference to the statute 13 Eliz., and the succeeding statute, 18 Eliz. c. 11: not only are all the acts made in pari materia, but the 13 Eliz. c. 11 is expressly intituled " An act for the continuation, explanation, perfecting, and enlarging of (amongst others) the former statute;" and the 18 Eliz. c. 11 is intitutled " An act for the explanation of the statutes against defeating of dilapidations, &c." The three statutes therefore are to be read together as forming one law on the same subject-matter; and it may consequently be well held, that, where leases of houses &c. which are exempted out of the 13 Eliz. by the next statute, the 14 Eliz., do not observe the provisions of the latter statute, they fall within the general enactments of the first statute, and are made void thereby: in other words, a lease not warranted by the 14 Eliz. remains restrained by the 13 Eliz., which makes leases against that act void. But the lease in question, considered as a lease in reversion, is not, as is above stated, void by the 13 Eliz., and is expressly sanctioned by the 18 Eliz.

No decided case has been brought before us by the authority of which the present lease is to be declared void. In the case of *Bayly* v. *Murin*, the lease was clearly void under the statute 13 Eliz., being a lease to begin at a future day, and not at the time of granting the lease. And in that case Hale, C. J., appears to have thought the lease would have been good, " if it had been to commence presently, there being less than three years to come of the former lease." In *Hunt* v. *Singleton*, Cro. Eliz. 546, the lease of a house for forty years by the Dean and Chapter of St. Paul's was held not warranted by the 14 Eliz., there being at the time of granting the lease ten years unexpired of the former lease. The case of *The Dean and Chapter of Westminster*, Carter's Rep. 9, decides that the lease in reversion of a house in the city of Westminster for forty years, by the Dean and Chapter of Westminster, was void, there being at the time of granting the lease seventeen years unexpired of the former lease. And in this latter case the judgment of Bridgman, C. J., is strong to shew that a lease made under the circumstances of the present would be held good—See the judgment more at large in Bridgman's Rep. 122. And the case of *Crane* v. *Taylor*, Hob. 269, does not afford an authority that a lease for twenty-one years in reversion, there being only two years to come of the existing lease, would be void: it is an authority for no more than that a covenant to make a lease is not void under the statute 18 Eliz., being made concerning a house in London.

Upon the whole, therefore, we think this lease is not void, and send our certificate accordingly to the Vice-Chancellor.

The following certificate was afterwards sent :—

" We have heard this case argued by counsel, and are of opinion that the lease therein mentioned of the 8th October, 1830, is a valid and effectual lease, and binding upon the successor of the said William Holmes in the said vicarage, for the remainder of the said term of twenty-one years expressed to be thereby granted.

1836.

VIVIAN
v.
BLOMBERG.

> " N. C. TINDAL,   J. A. PARK,
>   S. GASELEE,   J. VAUGHAN."

TROWER and Others v. CHADWICK.

Thursday,
Nov. 25th.

THE first count of the declaration stated that the plaintiffs, before and at the times of the committing of the grievances thereinafter mentioned, were lawfully possessed of a certain vault or cellar situate in the city of London, ing certain other vaults and walls of the defendant, and which in part rested upon and was of right in part supported by parts of those adjoining vaults and walls; that the plaintiffs were of right entitled that their vault should be so supported in part by the said parts of the said adjoining vaults and walls without the hindrance or disturbance of any person; and that there were certain foundations belonging to and supporting the said vault which the plaintiffs ought to enjoy: yet that the defendant wrongfully took down and removed the said vaults and walls so adjoining the plaintiffs' vault, without shoring up or otherwise securing, or taking other reasonable or proper precautions to support or secure the plaintiffs' said vault, so as to prevent the same from giving way or being weakened or destroyed; and wrongfully dug the earth and disturbed the foundations, without taking due and proper precautions to prevent the said foundations from being weakened and giving way; and by reason thereof the said foundations became and were injured, loosened, and weakened, and also by reason of certain timber &c. falling upon the plaintiffs' vault (which by reason of the acts complained of was unable to bear the weight of the timber &c.), the vault fell in and its contents were injured:—Held, that the count contained a clear and substantial ground of action, viz. that of negligence and carelessness in the exercise of the defendant's rights, by reason whereof the plaintiffs' rights were injured.

The second count stated, that the plaintiffs were possessed of a vault; that the defendant was about to pull down and remove and did pull down and remove certain other vaults and walls next adjoining the plaintiffs' vault; and thereupon it became and was the duty of the defendant, in the event of his not shoring up or protecting the plaintiffs' vault, to give due and reasonable notice to the plaintiffs of his intention to pull down and remove the said vaults and walls so adjoining the plaintiffs' vault, before he pulled down the same, so as to enable the plaintiffs to protect themselves; and also to use due care and skill, and take due, reasonable, and proper precautions in and about the pulling down and removing his vaults and walls, so that for want of such care, skill, and precaution, the plaintiffs' vault and its contents might not be damaged or destroyed:— Held, that the using due care, skill, and precaution in removing his own vaults and walls, so as to prevent injury resulting to the plaintiffs from the absence of such care, skill, and precaution, was a duty clearly imposed upon the defendant by law; that a breach alleging that he conducted himself so carelessly, negligently, and unskilfully in pulling down his vaults and walls as by reason thereof to injure the plaintiffs' vault, was well assigned; and that this allegation of duty being severable from the former (as to the defendant's duty to give notice), the count disclosed a good ground of action.

The first count of the declara-
tion stated that the plaintiffs were possessed of a certain vault adjoin-

and used and occupied the same in and for the purpose of carrying on their trade or business of wine merchants, and that the plaintiffs kept and had in their said vault or cellar divers large quantities of wine, to wit, 30,000 bottles of wine, and divers, to wit, 30,000 bottles, of the plaintiffs, of great value, to wit, of the value of 2,000*l.* ; that, before and at the times of the committing of the grievances by the defendant as thereinafter next mentioned, the plaintiffs' said vault or cellar adjoined certain other vaults, and certain walls there, and in part rested upon and was of right in part supported by parts of the said adjoining vaults and of the said walls, and the plaintiffs, before and at and during those times, were of right entitled that their said vault or cellar should be so supported in part by the said parts of the said adjoining vaults and walls, without the hindrance or disturbance of any person; that, before and at the times of the committing the grievances thereinafter

Quære, whether any obligation on the part of the defendant to give the plaintiffs notice of his intention to pull down his own vaults, if he did not himself shore up their vault, resulted as an inference of law from the mere juxta-position of the respective premises.

To the first count the defendant pleaded—as to the not shoring or propping up the walls, or taking other reasonable or proper precautions to support or secure the plaintiffs' vault, so as to prevent the same from being weakened—that he was not bound by law or otherwise, nor was there any duty, obligation, or liability imposed upon him by law or otherwise to shore up or secure, or take means to secure the plaintiffs' vault : and—as to so much of the count as related to the defendant's not having taken due and proper precautions to prevent the foundations of the plaintiffs' vault from being injured and giving way—that the defendant was not bound by law or otherwise, nor was there any duty, obligation, or liability imposed upon him by law or otherwise to take any precautions to prevent the foundations of the plaintiffs' vault from being weakened and injured :—Held, that both these pleas were bad, the traverses therein respectively not being the traverse of any allegation to be found in the count; and that they raised an issue in law for the consideration of the jury, viz. as to whether or not a duty was cast upon the defendant by law or otherwise.

The defendant further pleaded that the falling of the timber &c. upon the plaintiffs' vault was not occasioned by any act, default, &c. of the defendant, or the breach or neglect of any duty, obligation, or liability imposed upon him by law or otherwise. The count stating the inability of the plaintiffs' vault to bear the weight of the timber &c. to have arisen solely from the wrongful act of the defendant:—Held, that he was the proximate cause of the damage thereby occasioned, and responsible for it; and therefore that the plea was bad, inasmuch as it confessed without avoiding that part of the charge in the count to which it professed to be an answer:—Held, also, that the plea was bad, as being pleaded to part of the special damage alleged in the count; and also on the ground that it traversed an obligation in law (and one not even alleged in the count), thereby tendering an issue improper to be tried by a jury.

Another plea, professing to be an answer to the whole of the first count, omitted to give any answer as to the digging the earth and disturbing the foundations of the plaintiffs' vault:—Held, bad.

Pleas to the second count—that the defendant was not bound by law to shore up the plaintiffs' vault, or, in the event of his not doing so, to give the plaintiffs notice of his intention to pull down his own vaults—and that it was not the defendant's duty to use due and proper or any precautions in and about the pulling down his vaults and walls, so that the plaintiffs' vault might not be damaged :—Held bad, as raising issues of law, instead of issues of fact for the jury.

mentioned, there were certain foundations belonging to
and supporting the said vault or cellar of the plaintiffs,
and that they of right had enjoyed and still of right ought
to enjoy such foundations and the benefit and advantage
thereof, for the support of their said vault or cellar, without the hindrance or disturbance of any person: yet the
defendant, well knowing the premises, but contriving and
intending to injure the plaintiffs, theretofore, to wit, on the
1st October, 1835, and on divers other days and times afterwards and before the commencement of this suit, wrongfully and injuriously took down, pulled down, and removed,
and caused and procured to be taken down and removed,
the said vaults and walls so adjoining the said vault or cellar of the plaintiffs, by which the said last-mentioned vault
or cellar was so in part supported as aforesaid, without
shoring up, propping up, or otherwise securing or taking
other reasonable and proper precautions to support or secure or shore up the said vault or cellar of the plaintiffs,
so as to prevent the same from giving way or being weakened or damaged or destroyed on that occasion; and also
then and there wrongfully and injuriously dug and made,
and caused and procured to be dug and made, divers excavations in the earth near to the said foundations of
said vault or cellar of the plaintiffs, and loosened, weakened, and disturbed such foundations, without taking
due and proper precautions to prevent the said foundations from being weakened and injured and giving way;
and by reason thereof the said foundations then became
and were injured, loosened, and weakened, and the said
vault or cellar of the plaintiffs became and was greatly injured and weakened; and by reason of the said several
premises, and also by reason of certain timber, wood,
bricks and mortar, and other things, afterwards, to wit,
on &c., falling upon the said vault or cellar of plaintiffs
(and which vault or cellar, by reason of the same having
been so weakened and injured as aforesaid, and on no

other account, was then unable to bear or resist the force, weight, and pressure of the said timber, wood, bricks and mortar, and other things, as the same otherwise might and would have done), the same vault or cellar of the plaintiffs, then, to wit, on &c., gave way and fell in, and became and was greatly injured and destroyed ; and by reason of the several premises a great part, to wit, one half of the said wine became wasted, lost, spoiled, and destroyed, and the residue thereof became and was and still is injured and deteriorated in value, and the said bottles were damaged and destroyed ; and thereby also the plaintiffs from thence hitherto lost and became deprived of the use of their said vault or cellar, and of the profits, benefits, and advantages which they otherwise might and would have acquired from the possession and use thereof, and the same became of no use or value to the plaintiffs ; and thereby the plaintiffs were greatly prejudiced and injured in their said trade and business, and necessarily incurred divers expenses, to wit, to the amount of 2,000l., in having their said vault or cellar examined and surveyed, and the nature and extent of the said damages, injuries, and losses ascertained and repaired, and in and about the removal of the ruins of the said vault or cellar, and of such of the said wines as were not wholly lost or destroyed, and in and about the removal of the said wine and bottles and pieces thereof, and the procuring the said vault or cellar and the ruins thereof, and the said wine and bottles, to be watched and taken care of during the times aforesaid, and otherwise in relation to the several premises and matters last aforesaid ; and were otherwise injured.

The second count stated, that, before and at the times of committing the grievances thereinafter mentioned, the plaintiffs were possessed of a certain other vault situate in London aforesaid, and used and occupied the same in and for the purpose of carrying on their said trade and busi-

ness of wine merchants, and kept and had in their said
vault divers large quantities of wine, to wit, &c., and bottles, of the plaintiff's, of great value, to wit, of the value
of 2,000l.; that, at the time of the committing of the
grievances thereinafter mentioned, the defendant was
about to pull down and prostrate and remove, and did pull
down and prostrate certain other vaults and buildings
and walls next adjoining the last-mentioned vault of the
plaintiffs; and thereupon it became and was the duty
of the defendant, in the event of his not shoring up or
protecting the plaintiffs' last-mentioned vault in that behalf, to give due and reasonable notice to the plaintiffs of
his, the defendant's, intention to pull down, prostrate, and
remove the said vaults, buildings, and walls so adjoining
the plaintiffs' last-mentioned vault, before the defendant
prostrated and removed the same, so as to enable the
plaintiffs to protect themselves in that behalf, and also to
use due care and skill, and take due, reasonable, and
proper precautions in and about the pulling down and
prostrating and removing the said vaults, buildings, and
walls so adjoining the plaintiffs' last-mentioned vault, so
that for want of such care, skill, and precaution, the last-
mentioned vault of the plaintiffs, and the contents thereof,
might not be damaged or destroyed on that occasion, or
the plaintiffs injured in respect thereof: yet the defendant,
not regarding his duty in that behalf, but contriving and
intending to injure the plaintiffs, theretofore, to wit, on &c.,
and on divers other days and times afterwards and before
the commencement of this suit, wrongfully and injuriously
pulled down, prostrated, and destroyed the said vaults,
buildings, and walls so adjoining the last-mentioned vault
of the plaintiffs, without giving the plaintiffs or either of
them due or reasonable or other notice of his, the defendant's, intention so to do, according to his said duty in
that behalf, although the defendant did not shore up or
protect the plaintiffs' said last-mentioned vault; and the

defendant did not nor would use due care or skill, or take
due, reasonable, or proper precautions, in or about the
pulling down or prostrating or removing the said vaults,
buildings, and walls so adjoining the last-mentioned vault
of the plaintiffs, upon the said last-mentioned occasion,
according to his said duty; and the defendant, contriving
and intending to injure the plaintiffs, theretofore, to wit,
on &c., and on the said other days and times after that
day and before the commencement of this suit, wrongfully
and injuriously pulled down and prostrated divers parts of
the said vaults, buildings, and walls so adjoining the last-
mentioned vault of the plaintiffs, upon the last-mentioned
occasion, in a careless, unskilful, and improper manner,
and behaved and conducted himself carelessly, unskilfully, and improperly in that behalf; and by reason of the
several premises in this count mentioned, the last-mentioned vault of the plaintiffs became and was greatly
shaken and weakened and injured; and by reason of the
several premises in this count before mentioned, and also
by reason of certain timber, wood, bricks and mortar, and
other things, afterwards, to wit, on &c., falling upon the
said last-mentioned vault of the plantiffs (and which vault
by reason of the same having been so shaken, weakened,
and injured as aforesaid, and on no other account, was
then unable to bear or resist the force, weight, and pressure of the last-mentioned timber, wood, bricks and mortar, and other things, as the same otherwise might and
would have done), the last-mentioned vault of the plaintiffs then, to wit, on &c., was damaged, &c. &c., as in the
first count.

The defendant pleaded—first, not guilty—secondly, that
the said vault or cellar of the plaintiffs in the first count
mentioned did not rest upon nor was of right in part supported by parts of the said adjoining vaults and of the
said walls in that count mentioned, in manner and form as
the plaintiffs had in that count alleged—concluding to the
country.

Thirdly—That the plaintiffs were not before and at and during the times in the said first count in that behalf mentioned, or at any of those times, of right entitled that their said vault or cellar should be supported by the said parts of the said adjoining vaults and walls in that count mentioned, in manner and form as the plaintiffs had in that count alleged—concluding to the country.

Fourthly—As to so much of the first count as related to the defendant not shoring up, propping up, or otherwise securing or taking other reasonable or proper precautions to support, or secure, or shore up the said vault or cellar of the plaintiffs in that count mentioned, so as to prevent the same from being weakened or damaged or destroyed on the occasion in the said first count mentioned —that the defendant was not, on the occasion in that count mentioned, or otherwise, bound by law or otherwise, nor was there any duty, obligation, or liability imposed or cast by law or otherwise upon him to shore up, prop up, or otherwise secure, or to take other reasonable or proper or any means to support or secure or shore up the said vault or cellar of the plaintiffs for the purposes in that count mentioned or otherwise—verification.

Fifthly—As to so much of the said first count as related to the defendant not having taken due and proper precaution to prevent the said foundations of the said cellar of the plaintiffs from being weakened, injured, and giving way, as in that count mentioned—that the defendant was not on the occasion in that count mentioned, or otherwise, bound by law or otherwise, nor was there any duty, obligation, or liability cast or imposed by law or otherwise upon him the defendant, to take due and proper or any precautions to prevent the said foundations of the said vault or cellar of the plaintiffs in that count mentioned from being weakened and injured—verification.

Sixthly—As to such of the said first count as related to the falling of the said timber, wood, bricks and mortar, and other things, upon the said vault or cellar—that the said falling of the said timber, wood, bricks and mortar, and other things, upon the said vault or cellar, was not, nor was the falling of any of them, or any part of them, caused or occasioned by any act, default, neglect, or omission of the defendant, or the breach or neglect of any duty, obligation, or liability, imposed or cast upon him by law or otherwise—verification.

Seventh plea.

Seventhly—That the defendant had good, lawful, and sufficient right, title, power, and authority to pull down, prostrate, and remove, the said vaults and walls in the said first count mentioned, and upon part of which the vault of the plaintiffs was in and by that count alleged to have rested and been supported; that the digging and making the said excavations in the earth in that count mentioned were necessary and proper works for that purpose; and that, if the said foundations of the said vault or cellar in that count·mentioned were loosened, weakened, or disturbed, they were so loosened, weakened, and disturbed by and by reason of such necessary and proper works as aforesaid, for the purpose aforesaid; and further, that the plaintiffs, before any damage or·injury was or could be done or caused to be done to them or their said vault, or the contents thereof, and in sufficient time to guard and protect themselves and· their said vault or cellar and its contents against the consequences of the defendant's pulling down, prostrating, and removing the said vaults, and the necessary and proper works for that purpose, had notice of his intention to pull down, prostrate, and remove the said vaults and walls, and if they were minded and desirous to protect themselves or their property in the premises against the consequences of the defendant's so pulling down the said vaults and walls, it was their duty to have properly shored up and supported their vault or cellar, or to take due and proper precautions to protect themselves and their said vault or cellar and the property therein against the consequences of the exercise by the defendant of the said lawful right of the defendant to pull down, prostrate, and remove the said vaults and walls on which the vault of the plaintiffs in that count mentioned was alleged in part to have rested and to have been supported; and, had they done their duty in that behalf, their said vault or cellar and its contents would have been saved and protected from the alleged damage and injuries in the said first count mentioned; but they wholly neglected and omitted so to do: And the defendant further said, that, in pulling down, prostrating, and removing the vaults and walls, he was not guilty of any unlawful or wrongful act, neglect, default, or breach of any duty imposed upon him by law or otherwise, but exercised his said lawful right in the manner he had lawful right to exercise the same, and not otherwise; and, if any injury or damage happened or was occasioned to the plaintiffs or their said vault or the contents thereof, the same happened and was occasioned by the default of the plaintiffs themselves in not properly shoring up and supporting their said vault and taking due and proper precautions to protect themselves and their said vault or cellar and its contents from the consequences of the exercise by the defendant of his said lawful right to pull down, prostrate, and remove, and in pulling down, prostrating, and removing the said vaults and walls, and not by or through any unlawful or wrongful act of the defendant, or any default or omission of the defendant of any duty or obligation imposed on him by law or otherwise, in the pulling down, prostrating, and removing the vaults and walls—verification.

Eighthly—As to so much of the last count as related Eighth plea. to the defendant not having given the plaintiffs due and reasonable notice of his intention to pull down, prostrate and remove the said vaults, buildings, and walls in that count mentioned—that the defendant was not bound by law or otherwise, nor was there any duty, obligation, or

liability imposed or cast on him by law or otherwise, to
shore up or protect the said last-mentioned vaults of the
plaintiffs, on the occasion in that count mentioned, or
otherwise, nor was it his duty, in the event of not shoring
up or protecting the said last mentioned vault of the plaintiffs, to give due or reasonable or any notice of his the defendant's intention to pull down, prostrate, and remove
the said vaults, buildings, and walls adjoining the vault
of the plaintiffs in that count mentioned, in manner and
form as the plaintiffs had in that count alleged—concluding to the country.

Eleventh plea.

Eleventhly—As to so much of the said last count as
charged it to have been the duty of the defendant to have
taken due and reasonable precautions in and about the
pulling down and prostrating and removing the said vaults,
walls, and buildings in that count mentioned, so that the
said last-mentioned vault of the plaintiffs, and the contents
thereof, might not be damaged or destroyed, or the plaintiffs injured in respect thereof—that it was not his duty to
have used due and proper or any precautions in that behalf, as the plaintiffs had in that count alleged—concluding to the country.

Twelfth plea.

Twelfthly—As to so much of the said last count as related to the falling of the said timber, wood, bricks and
mortar, and other things, upon the said vault of the plaintiffs—that the said falling of the said timber, wood, bricks
and mortar, and other things, upon the said vault of the
plaintiffs in that count mentioned, was not, nor was the
falling of any of them, or any part of them, caused or occasioned by any act, default, omission, or neglect of the
defendant, or the breach or neglect of any duty, obligation, or liability imposed or cast upon him by law or otherwise—verification.

Thirteenth plea.

Thirteenthly—As to the last count of the declaration—
that the defendant had good and lawful and sufficient
right, title, power, and authority to pull down, prostrate,

and remove the said vaults, walls, and buildings in the said last count mentioned, and therein stated to have been pulled down, prostrated, and removed by him; and that the plaintiffs had notice of his intention so to do before any damage or injury was or could be done or caused to be done to their said vault or cellar, and the contents thereof, or any part of such contents, in sufficient time to have enabled them to guard and protect themselves against the consequences thereof, if they had been minded or desirous so to do; and, if they had been so minded or desirous, it was their duty to have shored up and supported their said vault in that count mentioned, or to have taken other due and proper precautions to have protected themselves and their last-mentioned vault and its contents against the consequences of the exercise by the defendant of his said right and authority to pull down, prostrate, and remove, and in and about the pulling down, prostrating, and removing the said vaults, walls, and buildings in that count mentioned; and, had they done their duty in that behalf, their said last-mentioned vault and its contents would have been saved and protected from the alleged damage and injuries in the last count mentioned; but they wholly neglected and omitted so to do: And the defendant further said, that, in pulling down, prostrating, and removing the vaults, walls, and cellars in that count mentioned, he was not guilty of any unlawful or wrongful act, or neglect or default of any duty imposed on him by law or otherwise, but exercised his said right and authority in the manner he had right and authority to exercise the same; and, if any damage or injury happened or was occasioned to the plaintiffs or their said vault or its contents in that count mentioned, the same happened and was occasioned by the default of the plaintiffs themselves, in not properly shoring up or supporting their said last-mentioned vault, or taking due and proper precautions to protect themselves and their said last-mentioned vault and its

contents against the consequences of the exercise by the
defendant of his said right and authority to pull down,
prostrate, and remove, and in and about the pulling
down, prostrating, and removing the vaults, walls, and
buildings in that count mentioned, and not by or through
any unlawful or wrongful act of the defendant, or any
neglect or omission of the defendant of any duty or obligation imposed upon him by law or otherwise in and about
the pulling down, prostrating, and removing the said
vaults, buildings, and walls in the said last count mentioned — verification.

The plaintiffs joined issue on the first, second, third,
and tenth pleas, traversed the ninth, and demurred to the
fourth, fifth, sixth, seventh, eighth, eleventh, twelfth, and

last pleas, assigning the following causes : — That the
fourth plea traversed matter of law, namely, whether it
was the defendant's duty to shore up the plaintiffs' vault,
that it offered an immaterial issue in so doing, and was an

informal traverse. The causes of demurrer to the fifth
plea were similar to those to the fourth plea as applied to

the foundations of the plaintiffs' vaults. The causes of
demurrer to the sixth plea were chiefly that it traversed
mere matter of law, that it offered an immaterial issue,

and that it should have concluded to the country. The
causes of demurrer to the seventh plea were chiefly, that
the plea did not traverse the plaintiffs' right, but set up
that they were bound to support their vault, the same not
being matter material to the cause of action, or proper to
be referred to a jury, that the plea traversed mere matter
of law, that the traverses were uncertain, and that the

plea did not answer all it professed to answer. The causes
of demurrer to the eighth plea were similar to those to the

fourth. The objections to the eleventh plea, were chiefly
that it offered to refer to a jury mere matter of law,
namely, whether the defendant was bound to use the precautions stated, and that no grounds of excuse for not

using such precautions were alleged. The objections to
the twelfth plea were similar to those urged as to the
fourth and fifth pleas—chiefly, that a mere question of
law was attempted to be traversed, and that an immaterial
issue (whether the defendant caused the timber &c. to fall
on the vault) was proffered. The causes of demurrer to
the last plea were, chiefly, that matter of law was thereby
traversed, and an immaterial issue attempted to be raised,
that the traverse was argumentative and informal, and that
the plea did not deny, or confess and avoid.

The case was argued in Trinity Term last.

1836.

TROWER
v.
CHADWICK.

Demurrer to
the twelfth plea.

Demurrer to
the thirteenth
plea.

R. V. Richards (*W. H. Watson* was with him), in support of the demurrers.—The general question in this case
is whether or not the defendant acted carelessly, negligently, and unskilfully in the exercise of his rights, and
thereby occasioned injury to the plaintiffs. If by his pleas
the defendant admits that he has done so, they clearly
afford no answer the action. If one be possessed of a
close adjoining the land of another, the former cannot by
building or otherwise to the confines of his land obstruct
the enjoyment of or inflict injury upon the latter. And it
is enough to allege possession in the declaration. In the
present case the plaintiffs claim as of right the support of
the defendant's vault whereon to rest the foundations of
their own. [*Tindal*, C. J.—Does not the declaration
usually allege a possession by the plaintiff, by reason
whereof he was entitled?] That would apply to a case
where the right claimed was not to be exercised upon the
land. Besides that is not pointed out here as a cause of
demurrer. In *Wyatt* v. *Harrison*, 3 B. & Ad. 871, and in
Dodd v. *Holme*, 1 Ad. & E. 493, the declaration stated
the mere possession by the plaintiff of a dwelling-house
adjoining to a dwelling-house of the defendant: and in the
former there was no allegation that the plaintiff had a right
to the support of his neighbour's wall or soil. In *Dodd* v.

Holme, the plaintiff and defendant having adjacent lands, the former built a house at the extremity of his land; the latter afterwards excavated his own soil near to but without touching the ground so built upon. The declaration alleged that the defendant so negligently, unskilfully, and improperly dug his own soil that the plaintiff's house was thereby injured. Bolland, B., in his summing up, said— "If I have a building on my own land, which I leave in the same state, and my neighbour digs in his land adjacent, so as to pull down my wall, he is liable to an action." The jury having found that the injury to the house was the consequence of the defendant's negligence, the court refused to disturb the verdict. In *Peyton v. The Mayor of London*, 9 B. & C. 725, which was an action on the case by a reversioner of a house in Cheapside against the owners of the adjoining house for pulling it down without shoring up the plaintiff's house, in consequence whereof it was impaired and in part fell down; it was held, that, upon this declaration, the plaintiff could not recover on the ground of the defendant's not having given notice that he was about to pull down his house, that not being alleged as a cause of the injury; and that, as the plaintiff had not alleged or proved any right to have his house supported by the defendant's house, he was bound to protect himself by shoring, and could not complain that the defendant had neglected to do it. Lord Tenterden, in delivering the judgment of the court, said: "The declaration in this case does not allege as a fact that the plaintiffs were entitled to have their house supported by the defendant's house, nor does it in our opinion contain any allegation from which a title to such support can be inferred as a matter of law. The complaint also in both counts relates to the fact of taking down the defendant's house, and the manner in which that was done. The first count is evidently framed upon a supposition that it was the duty of the defendants to use the necessary means to sustain the plaintiff's house

when they took down their own; the second count is more
general, but it does not charge the want of notice of taking
down the defendant's house, in order that the plaintiffs
might themselves use the necessary means to sustain their
own property, as the injury complained of: and therefore,
in our opinion, the action cannot be maintained upon the
want of such notice, supposing that, as a matter of law,
the defendants were bound to give notice beforehand."
The declaration in the present case stands clear of both
these objections. In *Jones* v. *Bird*, 5 B. & Ald. 837, it was
held that commissioners of sewers and persons working by
their order in the course of the necessary repair of a sewer
in the neighbourhood of houses, are bound to take all such
proper precautions for securing them, and to shore them
up if necessary, as skilful persons would do; and that they
were bound to give specific notice to the owner of the
house to which the stack of chimnies belonged (the falling
of which occasioned the damage to the plaintiff's house),
of their construction, and of the danger arising therefrom,
and that a general notice to him to take proper means to
secure his house, was not sufficient. Bayley, J., says:—
" The defendants worked under a stack of chimnies, without either properly securing them or giving notice of their
danger to the owner, in order that he might take them
down; this was improperly and negligently working the
sewer; for, if a party does an act which is improper unless
certain previous precautions are taken, he may fairly be
said to do that act improperly." In *Brown* v. *Windsor*,
1 C. & J. 20, it appeared that the plaintiff's house was
built, in the year 1803, against the pine end wall of the
defendant's house, by permission; and that the defendant,
in 1829, made an excavation in a careless and unskilful
manner in his own land, near to his pine end wall, by which
he weakened his pine end wall and injured the plaintiff's
house: and it was held that an action on the case was
maintainable for this injury. And Garrow, B., observed:

"It is said, that, by the principles of the common law, and adjudged cases, a party may deal as he pleases with his own property; but I must add to that proposition, that he must so deal with it as that he work no injury to his neighbour. If, after acquiescing twenty-seven years in such an easement as the present, the defendant makes a trench so as to injure his own pine end wall, and consequently his neighbour's property, I am of opinion that he is liable for such injury. There may be cases where a man, altering his own premises, cannot support his neighbour's, and the support if necessary must be supplied elsewhere. In such case he must give notice ; and then, if any injury occur, it would not be occasioned by the party pulling down, but by the other neglecting to take due precaution." In every case it must be a question for the jury whether or not the thing complained of has been done carelessly, negligently, and improperly. The plaintiffs here allege that they were lawfully possessed of a certain vault or cellar adjoining the defendant's vaults and walls; that the plaintiffs' vault in part rested upon and was of right in part supported by such adjoining vaults and walls; and that the defendant wrongfully and injuriously pulled down his said vaults without shoring up or otherwise securing or taking reasonable and proper precautions to support or secure the plaintiffs' vault, in consequence of which their

Fourth plea.

vault gave way. The defendant in his fourth plea says that he was not bound by law or otherwise, nor was there any duty, obligation, or liability imposed or cast by law or otherwise upon him to shore up, prop up, or otherwise secure, or to take other reasonable or proper or any means to support or secure or shore up the said vault or cellar of the plaintiffs. That plea traverses a duty nowhere alleged in the declaration : the plaintiffs, in their first count, do not rely on any duty or obligation by law imposed upon the defendant, but on their own right to the support of the defendant's walls. That right, as well as that the defendant did the act complained of carelessly, negligently, and improperly, is admitted by the plea. The fourth plea, therefore, is clearly bad, as well on the ground above stated, as on the ground that it tenders an issue in law for the consideration of the jury. The same observations apply to the 5th plea, which is bad for the same reasons. The sixth plea neither confesses and avoids nor traverses that part of the charge in the declaration to which it professes to be an answer: it is in fact no more than a plea to part of the special damage. It is also objectionable on the ground that it puts in issue a legal obligation not alleged in the count. The seventh plea professes to be an answer to the whole declaration, but in fact leaves unanswered the alleged wrongful act of the defendant in digging the earth and disturbing the foundations of the vault or cellar of the plaintiffs. The eighth and eleventh pleas are bad inasmuch as they traverse a mere matter of law, viz. the defendant's obligation to shore up &c. the plaintiffs' vault. And the twelfth and thirteenth pleas are objectionable on the same grounds as the sixth and seventh.

Wightman (*Hoggins* was with him), contrà.—Admitting the pleas demurred to to be bad, the plaintiff has not properly declared. It is uncertain, upon the face of the declaration, whether the proximate cause of the injury of which the plaintiffs complain was the act of the defendant or the act of a third person. The direct and immediate cause of the damage appears to have been the throwing down the timber, &c.: and for that the defendant is not liable. In *Flower* v. *Adam,* 2 Taunt. 314, it was held, that, if the proximate cause of the damage be the plaintiff's unskilfulness, although the primary cause be the misfeazance of the defendant, the plaintiff cannot recover; at least, if the mischief be in part occasioned by the misfeazance of a third person not sued. There, A. placed

1836.

TROWER
v.
CHADWICK.

Fifth plea.

Sixth plea.

Seventh plea.

Eighth and
eleventh pleas.

Twelfth and
thirteenth pleas.

lime and rubbish in the highway ; the dust blown from it frightened the horse of B., and nearly carried him into contact with a passing waggon, in avoiding which he unskilfully drove over other rubbish placed in the road by C., and was overthrown and hurt: and it was held, that, upon a count stating these facts, B. could not recover against A. [*Tindal*, C. J.—There, the injury the plaintiff complained of was in part the consequence of his own act. Here, the defendant takes issue upon that which is matter of evidence for the jury. At all events, if this be any objection to the declaration, it is cured by pleading over.] Charging the defendant with too large a liability, with the wrongful acts of a third party, is the subject of a general demurrer, and therefore open to him to object now. The declaration merely alleges that the plaintiffs were possessed of a vault adjoining the defendant's vaults, and that their vault in part rested upon and was *of right* in part supported by the defendant's vaults. That is clearly bad. The plaintiffs should have shewn the precise nature and foundation of the right they claimed—whether they claimed it in respect of the antiquity of their vault, or a twenty years' enjoyment, or by virtue of a license. It is no where alleged how or why the defendant was bound to shore up the plaintiffs' vault. [*Tindal*, C. J.—The plaintiffs allege that the defendant was bound, in pulling down his own vaults, so to proceed as to prevent their vault from falling down.] The plaintiffs might be entitled to the support of the defendant's walls whilst standing: but that is not enough to cast upon the defendant the duty of propping up their vault. The plaintiffs should either have shewn such right in their declaration, or they should have replied the ground upon which they found their claim to compel the defendant to prop up their vault. Enough does not appear upon the record as at present framed, according to *Wyatt* v. *Harrison* and *Peyton* v. *The Mayor of London*, to cast upon the defendant any such duty as that supposed. No such obligation results, as an inference of law, from the mere circumstance of the juxta position of the respective premises of the parties. Supposing the declaration to be good, the sixth plea affords a good answer to so much of the first count as charges the defendant with the damage resulting from the falling of the timber, &c. The seventh plea, which in substance avers the injury complained of to have resulted from the plaintiffs' own neglect to take proper precautions to secure their vault, is also unexceptionable. The issues tendered by those two pleas are such as can only be determined by a jury. The second count rests in part upon a supposed obligation on the defendant to give notice of his intention to pull down his walls: but it shews no foundation for any such duty. The defendant, undoubtedly, was bound to avoid negligence: but, was he bound to use any precaution? to do any thing?

Richards, in reply. [The court desired him to confine his observations to the objections to the second count.]— The second count alleges that it was the defendant's duty in the event of his not shoring up or protecting the plaintiffs' vault, to give due and reasonable notice to the plaintiffs of his intention to pull down the adjoining walls; and also to use due care and skill, and take due, reasonable, and proper precautions in and about the pulling down such adjoining walls, that the plaintiffs' vault and its contents might not, for want of such care, skill, and precaution, be injured. All the cases shew that a party cannot remove his walls without using due and reasonable and proper precautions to prevent injury to his neighbour's house. If this duty be laid too largely, the count is not therefore so radically bad as to be objectionable after the defendant has pleaded over. If the whole count goes to the jury, they may be told to confine the damages to the defendant's default in not giving due notice.

Cur. adv. vult,

A A A 2

TINDAL, C. J., now delivered the judgment of the Court :—This is an action on the case, the declaration in which contains two counts, in the first of which the plaintiffs allege their possession of a certain vault or cellar adjoining to certain other vaults and walls, and which in part rested upon and was of right supported in part by parts of the adjoining vaults and walls ; and that the plaintiffs were of right entitled that their vault or cellar should be so supported in part ; and that there are certain foundations belonging to and supporting the said vault or cellar, which the plaintiffs ought to enjoy : yet that the defendant wrongfully took down and removed the said vaults and walls so adjoining to the vault or cellar of the plaintiffs, without shoring or propping up, or taking other reasonable or proper precautions to support or secure it, so as to prevent its being weakened or destroyed, and wrongfully dug the earth and disturbed the foundations, without taking due and proper precautions to prevent the said foundations from being weakened and giving way : and the declaration then states the injury which the plaintiffs sustained, and the special damage which followed thereon. The second count states that the defendant was about to pull down the adjoining vaults and walls, and alleges it to have been the duty of the defendant, in the event of his not shoring up the walls, to give notice to the plaintiffs of his intention to pull down, and also his duty to use due care and skill, and to take due, reasonable, and proper precaution about the pulling down his vaults and walls ; and then alleges a breach of such duty.

To this declaration the defendant pleads thirteen pleas, of which the first seven are pleaded to the first count either in part or in whole ; and the eighth and subsequent pleas are pleaded in like manner to the second count of the declaration.

The plaintiffs demur to the fourth, fifth, sixth, seventh,

eighth, eleventh, twelfth, and last pleas, assigning certain causes of special demurrer to each; and, the defendant having joined in demurrer, the first question arises on the validity of those pleas.

The fourth plea, which is pleaded only to "the not shoring or propping up the walls, or taking other reasonable or proper precautions to support or secure the vault or cellar of the plaintiffs, so as to prevent the same from being weakened," we hold to be bad, on two grounds. In the first place, the traverse contained in that plea is not the traverse of any allegation to be found in the first count of the declaration. The ground of action on which the plaintiffs rely in that count, is, their right to the foundations on which their vault rested; not any duty or obligation of the defendant to prop or shore up the plaintiffs' vault, or to take due and proper precautions in pulling down his vault. When, therefore, the defendant traverses the existence of such duty or obligation, he traverses that which is not alleged by the plaintiffs; who only mention the want of propping and shoring up, and the want of proper precaution by the defendant, as the description of the mode or means by which the injury to them was occasioned. And the second objection to this plea appears to us to be this—that it raises an issue of law, and nothing else, for the consideration of the jury, viz. whether any duty or obligation was cast upon the defendant by law or otherwise. A jury might, indeed, try whether there was any duty of that nature arising from usage or contract; for, the existence of any such duty is a mere question of fact; but they cannot try whether there is any such duty or obligation cast upon him by law, for that is a question to be determined only by the court, and not by the jury.

On the same grounds, and for the same reasons, we hold the fifth plea to be bad in law.

As to the sixth plea of the defendant, it appears to us to be bad also upon two grounds: first, it is a plea which confesses without avoiding that part of the charge in the first count to which it professes to be an answer. This plea is pleaded, not as any answer to the right claimed in the declaration, but to that which is alleged in the first count as a necessary and immediate consequence from the wrongful act of the defendant; that is, it is pleaded to part of the special damage alleged to have followed from the weakening of the plaintiffs' vault or cellar. But, if the vault or cellar of the plaintiffs has been weakened in its walls or foundations by the wrongful act of the defendant, it is no avoidance of the plaintiffs' right of action, as it appears to us, that the timber, bricks, or materials that fell upon the vault or cellar in its weakened state, were not the property of the defendant, or were not thrown there by his carelessness or negligence; but that the defendant is equally liable to answer for the injury, in whomsoever the property of those materials may be, and whether they were placed there by the act of the defendant or of any other person. The plaintiffs have alleged in their declaration, that, but for the wrongful act of the defendant, and the weakened state of the walls, "and on no other account," was the vault unable to bear or resist the weight and pressure of the timber &c. The defendant therefore is the proximate cause of this damage, and appears to us to be answerable for it. And we think this plea is further bad, because it denies an obligation in law, and, still further, an obligation which has not even been alleged in the declaration.

The seventh plea is pleaded to the whole of the first count of the declaration. If, therefore, proposing to give an answer to the whole, it omits any material part, it is bad. Now, the first count of the declaration is founded on the alleged wrongful act of the defendant, not only in pulling down the vaults and walls of the defendant, but also in digging the earth and disturbing the foundations of the vault or cellar of the plaintiffs; and to this cause of action;

though confessed by the plea, there is no matter of avoidance pleaded in bar.

The remaining pleas to which the plaintiffs have demurred apply themselves to the last count of the declaration. And of these we think the eighth plea cannot be supported, inasmuch as it traverses a matter of law. It is pleaded as to so much of the last count as relates to the defendant not having given the plaintiffs due and reasonable notice of his intention to pull down his walls. The allegation in this plea, that he was not bound by law or otherwise, nor was there any duty, liability, or obligation imposed on him by law or otherwise to give any notice of his intention to the plaintiffs, appears to us to raise a direct question of law upon an issue joined on that plea.

As to the eighth plea.

The eleventh plea, which is pleaded to so much of the second count as alleges it to have been the duty of the defendant to have taken due and reasonable precautions about the pulling down his walls, we hold to be bad for the same reason as the last, viz. that it raises an issue of law, instead of an issue of fact, for the jury.

As to the eleventh plea.

The twelfth plea falls altogether within the same consideration as the sixth, and is bad for the same reason.

As to the twelfth plea.

The last plea, to the second count of the declaration, is bad for the same reason as the seventh plea, which is pleaded to a similar part of the first count, and sets up precisely the same defence.

As to the thirteenth plea.

But the defendant contends, that, admitting the pleas to be bad, the plaintiffs have shewn no sufficient ground of action, either in the first or second count of their declaration.

The first count rests upon a precise and distinct allegation that the vault or cellar of the plaintiffs was of right supported by parts of the adjoining walls, and that the plaintiffs were of right entitled to have them so supported, and that there were certain foundations for supporting those vaults, which the plaintiffs ought to enjoy:

As to the first count of the declaration.

and the count then proceeds to allege, as part of the gravamen, that the defendant wrongfully dug the earth and
disturbed the foundations, without taking due and proper
precautions to prevent the foundations from being weakened.   And we think, without entering into the examination of the several cases cited by the plaintiffs, this count
contains a clear and substantive ground of action, viz. that
of negligence and carelessness in the exercise of the defendant's rights, by means whereof the plaintiffs' rights
were injured ; and that, if the defendant meant to object
that the plaintiffs' right and title was not alleged with sufficient certainty, he ought to have demurred specially to
the declaration, instead of pleading over.

With respect to the second count of the declaration,
the right of action, as stated in that count, appears in one
respect more doubtful.   There is no allegation in this
count of any right of easement in alieno solo, which
forms the ground of the plaintiffs' action in the first count.
And, as to the allegation that it was the duty of the defendant to give notice to the plaintiffs of his intention to
pull down his wall, if he did not shore it up himself, it is
objected, and we think with considerable weight, that no
such obligation results, as an inference of law, from the
mere circumstance of the juxta-position of the walls of the
defendant and the plaintiffs.   But we think ourselves not
called upon, on the present occasion, to decide this question : for, the count goes on to allege that it was also the
duty of the defendant to use due care and skill, and take
due, reasonable, and proper precautions, in pulling down
his walls adjoining to the plaintiffs' vault, so that, for want
of *such* care, skill, and precaution, the plaintiffs' vault
might not be injured ; and we think that duty is clearly
imposed by law; and that a breach which alleges that the
defendant conducted himself so carelessly, negligently,
and unskilfully, in pulling down his walls, as by reason
thereof to injure the plaintiffs' wall, is well assigned ; and

that, inasmuch as this latter allegation of duty is severable from the former, it states a good ground of action.

Upon the whole, therefore, we think the plaintiffs are
entitled to judgment on the demurrers filed to the several
pleas of the defendant.

Judgment for the plaintiffs.

1836.

TROWER
v.
CHADWICK.

MALACHY v. SOPER and Another.

THIS was an action on the case against the defendants
for the publication of a libel prejudicial to his title to certain shares in a mine.

The declaration stated that the plaintiff, before and at
the time of the committing of the grievances by the defendants as thereinafter mentioned, was possessed of and
interested in divers, to wit, 1,600 shares or parts, the
whole into divers, to wit, 5,000 shares or parts to be divided, of and in a certain mine commonly known and
called by the name of the Wheal Brothers, situate, lying,
and being in the parish of Calstock, in the county of Cornwall, such shares being of great value, to wit, of the value
of 100,000l.; that, before and at the time of the committing the grievances by the defendants as thereinafter mentioned, the said mine had been worked and used and was
then being worked and used for and on the behalf of the
plaintiff and others the holders of shares and interests in
the said mine, to the great benefit, profit, and advantage

Friday,
Nov. 25th.

An action for
slander of title
is not properly
an action for
words spoken
or for a libel
written and
published, but
an action on
the case for
special damage
sustained by
reason of the
speaking or
publication of
the slander of
the plaintiff's
title.

Therefore, an
action to re-
cover damages
by reason of
the publication
of a paragraph
in a newspaper,
stating that
" the petition
in a bill filed
in the court of
Chancery
against the

plaintiff and certain other persons as shareholders in a certain mine, for an account and an injunction, had been granted by the Vice-Chancellor, and that persons duly authorised had arrived
on the workings," cannot be maintained without an allegation of special damage.

And, held, that an allegation " that the plaintiff was injured in his rights, and the shares so
possessed by him and in which he was interested had been and were much depreciated and lessened
in value, and divers persons had believed and still did believe that he had little or no right to the
shares, and that the mine could not be lawfully worked or used for his benefit, and that he had
been hindered and prevented from selling or disposing of his said shares in the said mine, and
from working and using the same in so ample and beneficial a manner as he otherwise would have
done, and was prevented from gaining divers profits which otherwise would have accrued to him"—
was not a sufficient allegation of special damage.

Held, also, that the publication was not a libel on the plaintiff in his business, but a mere slander
of his title to the shares.

of the plaintiff, and to the great increase of the value of his
said shares; that also, before and at the time of the committing of the grievances by the defendants as thereinafter
mentioned, one Horatio Nelson Tollervey had exhibited his
certain bill of complaint in writing against Robert Malachy,
the plaintiff, and others, in the high court of Chancery of
our lord the king, and in and by the said bill of complaint
the said H. N. Tollervey claimed to be a holder of and interested in divers shares in the said mine, and disputed the
plaintiff's right to the whole of the said shares, and
claimed in himself the said H. N. Tollervey a right in and
to a part of the same; and the said H. N. Tollervey did
in and by his said bill of complaint pray that the said
Robert Malachy, the plaintiff, and others, might answer
the premises therein mentioned, and make a full and true
disclosure and discovery of all and singular the matters
therein mentioned, and that H. N. Tollervey might be declared to be entitled to 18/8th parts or shares of and in the
said mine, or to such other part or share thereof as the
said court should be of opinion that he was entitled to,
and that a proper legal assignment and transfer thereof
might be made to him by all necessary parties; that the
said Robert Malachy, the plaintiff, and others, might be
compelled to come to an account with the said H. N. Tollervey for so much of the profits which had been made in
the said mine as, under the circumstances in the said bill
mentioned, the said H. N. Tollervey had been entitled to
receive in respect of his shares, and so far as such profits
had been divided among the shareholders, and to pay to
the said H. N. Tollervey what should be due to him on
such account; and also to pay to the said H. N. Tollervey
from time to time his share of the profits of the said mine,
which should be divided and paid in respect of such shares
as therein mentioned; and that the said H. N. Tollervey
might also be declared to be entitled to the like share and
interest in the further term therein mentioned to have been

granted in the said mine and premises as he was entitled
to in the therein mentioned lease of the 29th September,
1833; and that he might have the benefit thereof secured
to him accordingly; and that the said Robert Malachy,
the plaintiff, and others, might be restrained by the order
and injunction of the said court from selling or disposing
of or transferring the said H. N. Tollervey's share and interest in the said mine, or any other shares or interests in
the said mine, to the prejudice of the said H. N. Tollervey's therein mentioned rights and interest therein; and
that some proper person might be appointed by the said
court receiver of the said mine and premises, with all usual
and proper directions for carrying on the same under the
direction of the said court, to the end that the said H. N.
Tollervey's shares of the profits thereof might be properly
secured for his benefit; or else that some proper person
might be appointed by the said court as receiver of fifth
parts of the profits of the said mine, with all usual and
necessary directions; and that the said Robert Malachy,
the plaintiff, and others, might be restrained by the injunction of the said court from retaining to their own use,
or appropriating in any other manner, the said H. N. Tollervey's share of the said profit: and such proceedings
were had in the said court, that, before and at the time of
the committing of the grievance by the defendants as
thereinafter mentioned, the said Robert Malachy, the plaintiff, and the others, had demurred to the said bill of complaint, and they demanded the judgment of the said court
of Chancery whether they should be compelled to make
any further or other answer to the said bill or any of the
matters therein contained, and they prayed that the same
might be thenceforth dismissed: that also, before and at
the time of the committing of the grievance by the defendants as thereinafter mentioned, one Richard Deadman
Hayward had exhibited his certain bill of complaint in
writing against Robert Malachy, the plaintiff, and one

Samuel Lyle, in the high court of Chancery of our lord
the king, and the said R. D. Hayward in and by his said
bill of complaint claimed to be entitled to be a holder of
and interested in divers shares in the said mine, and disputed the plaintiff's right to the whole of the said shares,
and claimed in himself, the said R. D. Hayward, a right in
and to a part of the same; and the said R. D. Hayward
did in and by the said last-mentioned bill of complaint pray
that the said Robert Malachy, the plaintiff, and S. Lyle
might make a full and true disclosure and discovery of all
and singular the matters in that bill before mentioned, and
that it might be declared, that, as against the said Robert
Malachy, the plaintiff, and S. Lyle, the said R. D. Hayward was entitled, not only to the two shares in the said
bill mentioned in the said mine, and the said property and
effects belonging thereto, for which shares he had such
certificate as in the said bill mentioned, but also to five
other 500th shares therein, and to all the profits thereof
from the 22nd February, 1834; and that the said Robert
Malachy, the plaintiff, and S. Lyle, might be compelled to
sign and deliver to the said R. D. Hayward certificates of
his title to such five shares, or that the said Robert Malachy, the plaintiff, and S. Lyle, might be compelled to
procure and deliver to the said R. D. Hayward such
certificates; and that he might be decreed to pay the
costs of that suit, or the costs thereof so far as the same
had been made necessary by his conduct; and that the
said Robert Malachy, the plaintiff, and S. Lyle, might be
compelled to account with the said R. D. Hayward for the
profits which had been already declared and divided in
respect of the said mine, and to pay to the said R. D.
Hayward five-th parts of such profits, and also to pay to
the said R. D. Hayward for the time to come what the
said R. D. Hayward should be entitled to receive in respect of such shares as aforesaid of the profits and proceeds thereafter to be divided amongst the owners of the

said mine: and that the said Robert Malachy, the plaintiff, and S. Lyle, might be restrained by the injunction of the said court from selling or disposing of their or either of their shares and interest in the said mine, without first giving to the said R. D. Hayward a proper transfer of such five shares as aforesaid; and that the said Robert Malachy, the plaintiff, and S. Lyle, might in like manner be restrained from making any assignment of the said leases therein mentioned, or either of them; and that the said R. D. Hayward might be protected in the enjoyment of his said therein-mentioned shares of the said mine and the profits and the produce thereof; and, if it should be necessary, then that some proper person or persons might be appointed by the said court as a manager or managers of the said mine, to manage and conduct the same, and to sell and dispose of the produce thereof, with all usual and necessary directions; and that all proper and necessary directions might be given for taking the said accounts and effectuating the several purposes aforesaid: and such proceedings were had in the said last-mentioned suit, that, before and at the time of the committing of the grievance by the defendants as thereafter mentioned, the said S. Lyle had demurred to the said last-mentioned bill of complaint, and had demanded the judgment of the said court of Chancery whether he should be compelled to make any further or other answer to the said last-mentioned bill, or any of the matters therein contained, and prayed the same to be thence dismissed, with the reasonable costs in that behalf sustained: yet the defendants, well knowing the premises, but greatly envying the happy state and condition of the plaintiff, and contriving, and wickedly, and maliciously intending to injure the plaintiff in his said rights, and to cause it to be suspected and believed that the said shares of the plaintiff were of little or no value, and that the plaintiff had no right to use or work the said mine as aforesaid, and to hinder and

prevent the plaintiff from selling or disposing of his said
shares, and from deriving or acquiring from the said mine
any more profits, emoluments, or advantages whatever,
and also to vex, harrass, oppress, impoverish, and wholly
ruin the plaintiff, to wit, on the 2nd January, 1836, wrongfully and unjustly did publish, and cause and procure to
be published, a certain false, malicious, and unfounded
libel in a certain public newspaper, of and concerning the
plaintiff and his said shares, and the said using and working of the said mine, and of and concerning the aforesaid

Libel.   suits, bills, and demurrers, that is to say—" Wheal
Brothers Silver Mine (meaning the said mine). *Tollervey* v. *Malachi* (meaning the said first-mentioned suit),
and *Hayward* v. *Malachi* (meaning the said second mentioned suit).   In these cases (meaning the said two suits,)
which arose out of disputes relating to the celebrated silver mine, Wheal Brothers, in the parish of Calstock
(meaning the said mine), and which have been brought
into the court of the Vice-Chancellor, the learned judge,
after hearing long arguments, and a multitude of affidavits,
has set aside the demurrers (meaning the said demurrers),
and granted the prayer of the petition (meaning the said
prayer of the petition in each of the said bills as aforesaid,
for an account and an injunction); and persons duly authorised have arrived on the workings" (meaning the workings of the said mine): thereby then meaning that the
said several demurrers had been set aside by the said
court, and that the prayer of the said petition in each of
the said bills, for an account and an injunction, had been
granted by the said court, and that persons duly authorised by the same court had arrived on the workings of
the said mine, and were hindering and preventing the
said mine from being used and worked as it before the
committing of the grievance had been, and as the same
would have continued to have been, in so ample and beneficial a manner for the plaintiff and others the holders of

shares in the said mine; whereas, in truth and in fact, at
the time of the committing of the said grievance, the said
demurrers had not nor had either of them been set aside
by the court, nor had the prayer of the said petition in
each of the said bills, for an account and injunction, been
granted by the said court; and whereas, in truth and in fact,
at the time of the committing of the grievance, no person
or persons duly authorized by the said court had arrived
on the workings of the said mine, nor was nor were any
person or persons hindering or preventing the said mine
from being used and worked as it before the committing
of the said grievance had been, and as the same would
have continued to have been, in so ample and beneficial
a manner for the plaintiff and others the holders of shares
in the said mine: By means of which said several pre- Damage.
mises the plaintiff had been and was greatly injured in his
said rights; and the said shares so possessed by him and
in which he was interested as aforesaid had been and
were much depreciated and lessened in value, to wit, in
the value of 50*l.*, on and in respect of each of such shares,
and divers persons had believed and still did believe that
the plaintiff had little or no right to the said shares, and
that the said mine could not lawfully be worked or used
for the benefit of the plaintiff; and the plaintiff had been
hindered and prevented from selling or disposing of his
said shares in the said mine, and from working and using
the same in so ample and beneficial a manner as he otherwise would have done; and the plaintiff had been otherwise hindered and prevented from gaining, acquiring, or
deriving divers profits, emoluments, benefits, and advantages which otherwise would have arisen and accrued to
him from the same; and also, by reason of the premises
aforesaid, the plaintiff had been and was otherwise much
damnified and injured: To the damage &c.

At the trial, before Littledale, J., at the last Spring
Assizes at Exeter, a verdict was found for the plaintiff,
damages 5*l.*

Talfourd, Serjeant, in Easter Term last, obtained a rule nisi to arrest the judgment, on the ground that the action was not maintainable in the absence of an averment and proof of special damage resulting to the plaintiff from the publication of the libellous matter in question.—He cited *Lowe* v. *Harwood*, Sir W. Jones, 196, Cro. Car. 140, *Bois* v. *Bois*, 1 Lev. 134, *Rowe* v. *Roach*, 1 M. & S. 304, and Selwyn's Nisi Prius, 8th edit. 1266. It was also contended that the innuendo was larger than the words of the libel warranted.

Bompas, Serjeant, *Erle*, *Crowder*, and *Butt*, shewed cause.—The objection on the other side assumes that this is an action of slander: it not so, however; it is strictly an action for a libel; and therefore no special damage was necessary. The distinction in this respect between verbal and written slander is well ascertained: and there can be no reason why the like rule should not be held to be applicable to slander of title when it assumes the more injurious and offensive form. There are many cases where words not actionable in themselves if merely spoken, become so when written; writing being permanent; the mere utterance of offensive or vituperative language, on the other hand, being fleeting and transitory—*Thorley* v. *Lord Kerry*, 4 Taunt. 355. In *Bell* v. *Stone*, 1 B. & P. 331, a letter written to a third person, calling the plaintiff "a villain," was held actionable, without proof of special damage. So, in *J'Anson* v. *Stuart*, 1 T. R. 748, it was held to be actionable to print of a man that he is "a swindler." The argument seems to apply with increased force to the case of slander of title. Where the complaint is of words spoken, the individuals to whom they were spoken may be called; but, where the matter complained of is published in a newspaper, who can say into whose hands it may have fallen, or how injurious its effects? It may be well to require the damage to be specifically

alleged where its consequences may be traced. In *Bois v.*
Bois, 1 Lev. 134, the libel had reference to the plaintiff's
estate: the declaration contained no allegation of special
damage; but it was held to be enough that the libel might
have the effect of depriving the party of her estate. That
was an action on the case against the defendant for falsely
and maliciously calling a widow, who held an estate while
sole and chaste, *whore,* with intent to oust her of her estate, and saying he would oust her thereof; and at another time calling her *whore:* after verdict for the plaintiff
on not guilty, it was moved in arrest of judgment, that,
no special damages being laid, the words were not actionable. But, by the court: "They import damage by themselves in this case, in respect of her estate; as, for calling
a man a *thief,* an action lies without special damage, because the words import it in themselves. But, for the last
words spoken at another time, which are not actionable
in themselves, and the damages being entire, the judgment was therefore arrested till the matter be examined,
whether the damages were given entire or not. So, in *Pen-*
nyman v. Rabanks, Cro. Eliz. 427, in an action on the case
for slandering the plaintiff's title to J. S., who was in
speech to buy the plaintiff's land, the words, "I know one
that hath two leases of his land, who will not part with
them at any reasonable rate," were held actionable; though
no special damage appears to have been alleged. And in
Bold v. Bacon, Cro. Eliz. 346, it was alleged, that, by
reason of the words spoken by the defendant, none would
buy the plaintiff's land; and no special damage was alleged. In none of the cases is special damage alleged in the
form in which it is said it should have been alleged here.
The very extent of the slander may be the cause of preventing the possibility of the plaintiff's specifically pointing in-
dividually to one who therefore refused to become a purchaser. In *Hartley v. Herring,* 8 T. R. 130, in an action

for consequential damage from slander imputing incontinence to the plaintiff, it was held enough to state that he was employed to preach to a dissenting congregation at a certain licensed chapel, that he derived considerable profit from his preaching, and that, by reason of the scandal, "persons frequenting the chapel had refused to permit him to preach there, and had discontinued giving him the profits which they usually had and otherwise would have given," without saying who those persons were, or by what authority they excluded him, or that he was a preacher duly qualified according to the 10 Anne, c. 2. *Hargrave* v. *Le Breton*, 4 Burr. 2422, merely decided that there must be malice, express or implied, to maintain an action for slander of title. In *Rowe* v. *Roach*, 1 M. & S. 304, it is true, there was an allegation of special damage: but that affords no argument to shew the necessity of alleging it; and in *Millman* v. *Pratt*, 3 D. & R. 728, 2 B. & C. 486, which was an action for slander of title, no special damage was alleged, and no objection was taken to the want of it. The injury in the present case is much more direct and immediate than that which formed the ground of action in *Rowe* v. *Roach*, for, here, the libel states that an injunction *has* been granted. It was impossible, from the nature of this case, that the plaintiff could aver special damage in any other way than he has done. It was enough to shew that the price of the shares had fallen in the market; and the jury by their verdict have expressed their opinion that the natural and necessary tendency and effect of the libel was to deteriorate and lessen the value of the shares. It would be impossible for the plaintiff to say who, in consequence of the libel, declined to purchase shares in the market: and the law does not require that which is unreasonable. [*Bosanquet*, J.—Do you contend that each individual shareholder would have a right of action?] Undoubtedly: numbers make no difference in law. [*Tindal*, C. J.—The case of *Lowe* v. *Harewood*, as reported in Sir

W. Jones, 196, goes far to shew that special damage must be alleged in such a case as this.] That is the only authority that really presses: the report of the same case in Cro. Eliz. 140, assumes a rather different complexion; and it may be doubtful at this day what was the legal meaning of " special prejudice" at that period.

Besides, this is not simply a case of slander of title: it is a libel on a man in his business, to the maintenance of which no special damage is necessary. The declaration alleges that the plaintiff by means of the publication of the libellous matter was injured in his rights; that the shares so possessed by him, and in which he was interested, had been and were much depreciated and lessened in value; that divers persons had believed and did believe that he had little or no right to the shares, and that the mine could not be lawfully worked or used for his benefit; and that he had been hindred and prevented from selling or disposing of his said shares in the said mine, and from working and using the same in so ample and beneficial a manner as he otherwise would have done, and was prevented from gaining divers profits which otherwise would have accrued to him. The libel alleges that a receiver had been appointed, and that persons duly authorized had arrived on the workings and taken possession of the mine: which is precisely the same in effect as to say of a tradesman that a bailiff had been put in possession of his stock in trade. There can be no doubt that a party who derives his means of living from the working of a mine is entitled to equal protection with any other description of adventurer or trader. Words spoken or written of a man in any lawful employment or office of profit, having a natural tendency to occasion the loss of such office, are actionable—*Lumley v. Allday*, 1 Tyr. 217, 1 C. & J. 301. The rule is not confined to a trade. Here, the libel is alleged to have been published of and concerning the plaintiff and his said shares, and the said using and working of the said mine:

1836.

MALACHY
v.
SOPER.

and the innuendo is not, as is contended on the other side larger than the natural sense of the words warrants.

Talfourd, Serjeant, *Barstow*, and *Rowe*, in support of the rule.—This, being an action for slander of title, is only sustainable in respect of special damage. This is clearly laid down in *Lowe* v. *Harewood*, Sir W. Jones, 196—" Of slander of title the plaintiff shall not maintain action, unless it was reverâ a damage, scil. that he was hindered in sale of his land ; so there the particular damage ought to be alleged." So, in *Tasborough* v. *Day*, Cro. Jac. 484, it was held, that, in such an action, it must be averred that the plaintiff was in actual treaty for the sale of the estate, and that he received special damage. *Manning* v. *Avery*, 1 Keb. 153, and *Gerrard* v. *Dickenson*, Cro. Eliz. 197, are to the same effect. In the present case there is no averment that the plaintiff had ever offered to sell, or entertained any intention to sell his shares. *Millman* v. *Pratt*, which is the only case to be found of an action of slander of title without a distinct allegation of special damage, is widely different in its circumstances from the present case : it was there alleged that the property was actually put up to sale, and persons who were desirous of purchasing had in consequence of the alleged slander been deterred from bidding : the decision turned solely on the ground of a variance between the declaration and the proof. The distinction between oral and written slander is wholly inapplicable to an action of this description, which is properly speaking an action on the case for damage resulting to the plaintiff from the speaking or writing of the slanderous or libellous matter in reference to his title. Nor is the argument at all aided by the suggestion that this is a libel upon the plaintiff in relation to his trade. The libel attaches, not to the trade, but to the individual—to the individual in reference to his trade. Words spoken of a man in trade are not actionable unless spoken of him in the way of his trade. In *Savage* v. *Roberts*, 1 Salk. 694, the plaintiff declared that he was a trader, and that the defendant said of him, "you are a cheat, and have been a cheat for divers years:" upon the first motion, Holt, C. J., held, that the words must be understood of his way of living, and that it needed no colloquium.   But, Pasch. 10 Will. 3, mutatâ opinione, judgment was arrested.   In *Bois* v. *Bois*, the actionable quality was imported to the words by their reference to the plaintiff's enjoyment of her estate. [*Tindal*, C. J.—The declaration avers that the libel was published of and concerning the plaintiff and his shares and the using and working of the mine.]   All that the alleged libel amounts to is this, that disputes in Chancery subsisted in relation to certain shares in the mine, that the Vice Chancellor had granted the prayer of the petition for an account and injunction, and that persons duly authorized had arrived on the workings.   The injunction was, not to restrain the working of the mine, but the sale of the shares. The innuendo goes further, and states that the persons who were alleged to have arrived on the workings were hindering and preventing the mine from being used and worked as it was before the committing of the grievance, and as the same would have continued to have been, in so ample and beneficial a manner for the plaintiff and others the holders of shares in the mine.   This is altogether unwarranted by the words of the libel, and wholly inapplicable to the carrying on of a trade.

Cur. adv. vult.

TINDAL, C. J., delivered the judgment of the court :— In this case, a verdict having been found for the plaintiff at the trial of the cause, with 5*l.* damages, a motion has been made to arrest the judgment on the ground that the declaration does not state any legal cause of action.   And we are of opinion that this objection is well founded ; and that the judgment must be arrested.   This is not an ordinary action for defamation of the person by the pub-

1836.
MALACHY
v.
SOPER.

lication of slander either oral or written; in which form of action no special damage need either be alleged or proved; the law presuming that the uttering of the slanderous words, or the publishing of the libel, have of themselves a natural and necessary tendency to injure the plaintiff. But this is an action to recover damages by reason of the publication of a paragraph in a newspaper, which contains no other charge than "that the petition in a bill filed in the court of Chancery against the plaintiff and certain other persons, as shareowners in a certain mine, for an account and an injunction, had been granted by the Vice-Chancellor, and that persons duly authorized had arrived on the workings." The publication, therefore, is one which slanders not the person or character of the plaintiff, but his title as one of the shareholders to the undisputed possession and enjoyment of his shares of the mine. And the objection taken is, that the plaintiff, in order to maintain this action, must shew a special damage to have happened from the publication, and that this declaration shews none. The first question, therefore, is—does the law require in such an action an allegation of special damage? And, looking at the authorities, we think they all point the same way. The law is clearly so laid down in *Lowe* v. *Harewood*, Sir W. Jones, 196—"Of slander of title the plaintiff shall not maintain action, unless it was reverâ a damage." And, in addition to the cases cited at the bar, viz. *Sir John Tasborough* v. *Day*, Cro. Jac. 484, *Manning* v. *Avery*, 3 Keb. 153, the case of *Cane* v. *Goulding*, Style, 169, 176, furnishes a strong authority. That was an action on the case for slandering the plaintiff's title by speaking these words—"His right and title thereunto is naught, and I have a better title than he." The words were alleged to be spoken falso et malitiosè, and that the plaintiff was likely to sell, and was injured by the words; and that, by reason of speaking the words, he could not recover his tithes. After verdict for the plaintiff, there was a motion in arrest of judgment; and Rolle, C. J., said "there ought to be a scandal and a particular damage set forth, and there is not so here." And, upon its being moved again, and argued by the judges, Rolle, C. J., held "That the action did not lie, although it was alleged that the words were spoken falso et malitiosè, for the plaintiff ought to have a special cause. But that the verdict might supply. But the plaintiff ought also to have shewed a special damage, which he hath not done; and this the verdict cannot supply. The declaration here is too general, and upon which no good issue can be joined; and he ought to have alleged that there was a communication had before the words spoken touching the sale of the lands whereof the title was slandered, and that by speaking of them the sale was hindered." We hold, therefore, on the authority of these cases, that an action for slander of title is not properly an action for words spoken, or for a libel written and published, but an action on the case for special damage sustained by reason of the speaking or publication of the slander of the plaintiff's title. This action is ranged under that divisions of actions in the Digests, and by other writers on the text law, and such we feel bound to hold it to remain at the present day.

The next question is—has there been such a special damage alleged in this case as will satisfy the rule laid down by the authorities above referred to? The doctrine of the older cases is, that the plaintiff ought to aver, that, by reason of the speaking, he could not sell or lease—*Gerrard* v. *Dickenson*, Cro. Eliz. 196, *Lawe* v. *Harwood*, Cro. Car. 140; and that it will not be sufficient to say only that he had an intent to sell, without alleging a communication for a sale—R. 1 Roll. 244. Admitting, however, that these may be put as instances only, and that there may be many more cases in which a particular damage may be equally apparent, without such allegation; they establish at least this, that, in the action for slander of title, there must be an express allegation of some particular damage resulting to the plaintiff from such slander. Now, the allegation upon this record is only this, " that the plaintiff is injured in his rights, and the shares so possessed by him, and in which he is interested, have been and are much depreciated and lessened in value, and divers persons have believed and do believe that he has little or no right to the shares, and that the mine cannot be lawfully worked or used for his benefit; and that he hath been hindered and prevented from selling or disposing of his said shares in the said mine, and from working and using the same in so ample and beneficial a manner as he otherwise would have done." And we are of opinion that this is not such an allegation of special damage as the authorities above referred to require, where the action is not founded on the words spoken or written, but upon the special damage sustained.

It has been argued, in support of the present action, that it is not so much an action for slander of title, as an action for a libel on the plaintiff in the course of his business, and in the way of gaining his livelihood; and that such an action is strictly and properly an action for defamation, and so classed and held by all the authorities. But we think it sufficient to advert to the declaration to be convinced that the publication complained of was really and strictly a slander of the plaintiff's title to his shares, and nothing else. The bill in Chancery, out of which the publication arose, is filed by Tollervey, who disputed the plaintiff's right to the whole of the shares, and claimed in himself a right to part of the same, and prayed that he might be declared to be entitled to some of them; and the only mention made as to the working of the mines, was, with reference to the appointment of a receiver of the profits thereof. And we think it would be doing violence to the natural meaning of the terms of the publication, if we were to hold it to be published of the plaintiff in the course of his business or occupation or mode of acquiring his livelihood, and not as referring to the disputed title of the shares of the mine.

It has been urged secondly, that, however necessary it may be, according to the antient authorities, to allege some particular damage in cases of unwritten slander of title, the case of written slander stands on different grounds; and that an action may be maintained without an allegation of damage actually sustained, if the plaintiff's right be impeached by a written publication which of itself, it is contended, affords presumption of injury to the plaintiff. No authority whatever has been cited in support of this distinction. And we are of opinion that the necessity for an allegation of actual damage in the case of slander of title, cannot depend upon the medium through which that slander is conveyed; that is, whether it be through words or writing or print; but that it rests on the nature of the action itself, namely, that it is an action for special damage actually sustained, and not an action for slander. The circumstance of the slander of title being conveyed in a letter or other publication, appears to us to make no other difference than that it is more widely and permanently disseminated, and the damages in consequence more likely to be serious, than where the slander of title is by words only: but that it makes no difference whatever in the legal ground of action.

For these reasons, we are of opinion that this action is not maintainable, and that the judgment must be arrested; consequently it becomes unnecessary to inquire whether the innuendo laid in the declaration is more large than it ought to have been. We therefore make the rule for arresting the judgment absolute.

Rule absolute accordingly.

Friday,
Nov. 24th.

STAVERS *v.* CURLING and Another.

By articles of
agreement
entered into
between the
plaintiff, as
captain, and the
defendants, the
owners, of a
South Sea
whaler, th*e*
plaintiff cove-
nanted that he
would preceed
to the fishery,
and procure a
cargo of sperm
oil, ambergris,
&c., or as great
a proportion
thereof as might
be under all
circumstances
within his power
to obtain, and,
having done so,
would return
in and with the
ship to London,
and there at his
own costs dis- ·
charge and de-
liver to the
defendants
whatever cargo
she might have
on board; that
he would obey
such instruc-
tions relative
to the ship and
her voyage as
might from time
to time be re-
ceived by him
from the defen-
dants, their
heirs, &c.; that

THE declaration stated, that, on the 9th February, 1832, by certain articles of agreement, bearing date the day and year aforesaid, between the defendants, therein described as owners of the ship Offley, then lying at Gravesend in the river Thames, of the one part, and the plaintiff of the other part (which said articles of agreement were sealed with the respective seals of the defendants, but, being in the possession of the defendants, the plaintiff could not bring them into court), after reciting that the defendants, as owners of the ship Offley, had fitted out the same with all necessary stores, provisions, casks, and other imple- ments for the prosecuting of a voyage to the Southern whale fishery, and had appointed the plaintiff to be mas- ter of the said vessel, on the terms and conditions therein- after mentioned : it was by the said articles of agreement witnessed, and the said parties did thereby mutually cove- nant and agree to and with each other, in manner follow- ing, that is to say, the plaintiff, for himself, his heirs, exe- cutors, administrators, and assigns, did thereby covenant, promise, and agree to and with the defendants, their heirs, executors, administrators, and assigns, that he, the plain- tiff, would take upon himself the command of the said ship, and proceed in her as soon as she was ready for sea to the Southern whale fishery, and procure a cargo of sperm- oil, head-matter, ambergris, whale-oil, seal-skins, or any other produce, or as great a proportion thereof as might be under all circumstances within his power to obtain, and,

he would be frugal with the ship's stores and provisions, enter in a book the expenditure and appro- priation thereof, and not dispose of any part of them without faithfully accounting with the defen- dants for the produce thereof; that he would not smuggle or trade, or permit it directly or in- directly, whereby the ship or the owners thereof might be prejudicially affected, nor consent or suffer to be committed any illegal act or acts on board the ship whereby the owners might be injured. And the defendants covenanted, *on the performance of the before mentioned terms and conditions on the part of the plaintiff,* that they, their heirs, &c., would pay to the plaintiff, his heirs, &c., a sum equal to one twelfth part of the net proceeds of the cargo:—Held, that the per- formance of the covenants entered into by the plaintiff did not form a condition precedent to his right to recover on the covenants entered into on the part of the defendants.

having done so, would return in and with the said ship to
the port of London, and there, at his own costs, together
with the crew, discharge and deliver to the defendants,
their heirs, executors, administrators, and assigns, whatever cargo the said vessel might have on board; and also
that he, the plaintiff, would obey such instructions relative to the said vessel and her voyage as might from time
to time be received by him from the defendants, their
heirs, executors, administrators, and assigns; and likewise
would be as frugal as possible with the stores and provisions of the said ship, and regularly enter in a book to be
provided for that purpose the expenditure and appropriation thereof, and not dispose of any part of them without
faithfully accounting with the defendants, their heirs, executors, administrators, and assigns for the produce thereof;
and, further, that he would not on any account or pretence
whatsoever smuggle or trade, or permit it directly or indirectly, whereby the said ship or the owners thereof might
be prejudicially affected; or consent or suffer to be committed with his knowledge any illegal act or acts on board
the said ship, whereby the owner or owners might be injured: and he thereby engaged and bound himself, his
heirs, executors, administrators, and assigns, to indemnify,
in case of such an event, the said owners from and against
any claim, loss, or damage which they might sustain
thereby: and the plaintiff thereby engaged on all occasions to act for the interests of the said ship and owners,
according to the utmost of his judgment and abilities: And
the defendants, for themselves, their heirs, executors, administrators, and assigns, did thereby covenant, promise,
and agree, that, *on the performance of the before mentioned
terms and conditions* on the part of the plaintiff, they, the
defendants, their heirs, executors, administrators, and assigns would pay or cause to be paid unto the plaintiff, his
heirs, executors, administrators, and assigns a sum of
money equal to one-twelfth part of the net proceeds which

1836.

STAVERS
v.
CURLING.

Plaintiff's
covenants.

Defendants'
covenants.

might be received from the sale of the cargo, after deducting the cost of the casks sold with the cargo of the ship,
and all custom-house expenses, lighterages, pierages outwards and inwards, convoy, dock, and all other duties
which were or might thereafter be imposed on ship and
cargo or either of them, together with lighterage, landing,
wharfage, quaying, coopering, commissions, and all other
charges and expenses attending the landing and sale of the
said cargo, together with the amount of any disbursements for refreshments or fresh provisions which might
have been made during the voyage by the said master:
and, further, the defendants agreed to allow to the plaintiff
one per cent. upon the aforesaid net proceeds after the
above-recited deductions had been made therefrom: as by
the said articles of agreement, reference being thereunto
had, would more fully and at large appear.   Averment—
that, afterwards, to wit, on the 1st March, in the year aforesaid, the plaintiff took upon himself the command of the
said ship, and, the same being ready for sea, then proceeded in her for the Southern whale fishery; and afterwards, to wit, on &c., and on divers days between that day
and the return of the said ship to the said port of London
as thereinafter mentioned, at and in the said Southern
whale fishery, procured for the said ship a cargo, to wit,
374 tons, of sperm-oil, head-matter, ambergris, whale-oil,
seal-skins, and other produce, of great value, to wit, of the
value of 10,000*l.*, being the best cargo that under all the
circumstances it was in the power of the plaintiff to obtain; that, the said cargo being so obtained and on board
the said ship, afterwards, to wit, on the 1st January, 1835,
the plaintiff, in and with the said ship, the said cargo
being and continuing on board thereof, returned to and
arrived at the said port of London, and then and there at
the said port, at his, the plaintiff's, own cost, together
with the crew of the said ship, discharged and delivered
to the defendants the said cargo, being of the value afore-

said ; that the plaintiff during the voyage aforesaid obeyed all instructions relative to the said vessel and her said voyage from time to time received by him the plaintiff from the defendants, or either of them, and was as frugal as possible with the stores and provisions of the said ship, and regularly entered in a certain book provided for that purpose the expenditure and appropriation thereof, and faithfully accounted to the defendants for the produce of every part of the stores and provisions aforesaid by the plaintiff disposed of during the voyage; that the plaintiff, during the said voyage, did not smuggle or trade, or permit it directly or indirectly, whereby the said ship or owners might be or were prejudicially affected, and did not consent or suffer to be committed with his knowledge any illegal act or acts on board the said ship, whereby the owner or owners might be injured, but on the contrary thereof the plaintiff on all occasions acted for the interest of the said ship and owners to the utmost of his judgment and abilities; of all which several premises the defendants afterwards, and after the return of the said ship to the port of London, to wit, on &c., had notice; that the said cargo, after the return of the said ship as aforesaid to the port of London, to wit, on &c., was by the defendants sold for a large sum, to wit, the sum of 10,000l., and the net proceeds received by the defendants from the said sale, after deducting the cost of the casks sold with the cargo, and all custom-house expenses, lighterages, pierages outwards and inwards, convoy, dock and other duties imposed on the said ship and cargo, or either of them, together with lighterage, landing, wharfage, quaying, coopering, commissions, and all other charges and expenses attending the landing and sale of the cargo, together with the amount of the disbursements for refreshments and fresh provisions made during the said voyage by the plaintiff, amounted to a large sum, to wit, the sum of 6,000l., whereof the defendants then had notice : and

1836.

STAVERS
v.
CURLING.

thereby and by means of the premises an action had accrued to the plaintiff to demand and have of and from the defendants a large sum, to wit, the sum of 500*l.*, being one twelfth part of the said net proceeds, to wit, of the said sum of 6,000*l.*; and thereby also and by means of the premises an action had accrued to the plaintiff to demand and have of and from the defendants a certain other large sum, to wit, the sum of 60*l.*, being one per cent. upon the said net proceeds, to wit, on the said sum of 6,000*l.*; yet the defendants had never at any time paid to the plaintiff the said sums of 500*l.* and 60*l.*, or either of them, or any part thereof.

The declaration also contained counts for work and labour, and money paid, and a count upon an account stated.

The defendants pleaded (amongst others)—secondly— that, after the making of the agreement in the first count mentioned, and before the commencement of the said voyage, to wit, on the 9th February, 1832, the plaintiff received from the defendants certain instructions relative to the said vessel and her said voyage, whereby the defendants instructed the plaintiff, among other things, during the said voyage to pay the strictest attention to the preservation of the stores of all kinds belonging to the ship, and to be careful in bringing the ship and remaining stores home in the best possible order for undertaking a future voyage; that the plaintiff should cautiously abstain himself and strictly prohibit all on board the said vessel from engaging in any sort of trade whatsoever; that the plaintiff should studiously avoid putting in any where except when urgent and unavoidable necessity impelled him to do so; that the plaintiff should use his best exertions to obtain in the least possible time a full cargo for the said ship or vessel, and should endeavour to maintain order and regularity therein, and to promote the health and comfort of all on board the said vessel during the voyage:

that the plaintiff disobeyed the said instructions in this,
to wit, that he did not during the said voyage pay the
strictest attention to the preservation of the stores of all
kinds belonging to the ship, and was not careful in bringing the remaining stores home in the best possible order
for undertaking a future voyage, but, on the contrary
thereof, during the said voyage did carelessly, negligently,
and wilfully damage and suffer to be damaged certain
stores which had been and were provided, and were during the said voyage the stores of the said ship, and which
were not used during the voyage, whereby the same
were rendered unfit for undertaking a future voyage;
and that the plaintiff also disobeyed the said instructions in this, to wit, that he did not cautiously abstain
from engaging in any sort of trade whatsoever, but,
on the contrary thereof, during the time aforesaid, on
divers days between the 9th February, 1832, and the 7th
August, 1835, and during the said voyage, was engaged
in trade, and did trade for his own personal advantage:
that the plaintiff also disobeyed the said instructions in
this, to wit, that he did not avoid putting in any where
except when urgent and unavoidable necessity compelled
him so to do; but, on the contrary thereof, during the
said voyage, put into divers, to wit, ten ports and ten
harbours, and stayed and continued therein for divers
long spaces of time, that is to say, for two months in each
of the said ports and harbours, although not compelled
by any urgent or unavoidable necessity so to do: that the
plaintiff also disobeyed the said instructions in this, to wit,
that the plaintiff did not use his best exertions to obtain
in the least possible time a full cargo for the said ship or
vessel, and did not during the voyage maintain order and
regularity in the said vessel, or promote the comfort of all
who during the said time were on board the said vessel;
but, on the contrary, the plaintiff on divers days and times
during that time and during the said voyage, to wit, on

the 9th February, 1832, and on divers other days and times between that day and the 7th August, 1835, was drunk and intoxicated, and caused and suffered disorder and irregularity in the said vessel, although he might and could then have maintained order and regularity therein: that the plaintiff during the said voyage also disobeyed his said instructions in this, to wit, that, during the whole of the said voyage, he rendered the said vessel and the said voyage uncomfortable to the crew who during that time were on board the said vessel—verification.

Third plea.

Thirdly—that the plaintiff, during the said voyage, to wit, on the said 9th February, 1832, and on divers days between that day and the 7th August, 1835, did trade in such a manner that the owners of the said ship were prejudicially affected thereby—concluding to the country.

Fifth plea.

Fifthly—so far as related to the nonpayment of the said sum of money in which the defendants were alleged to be indebted to the plaintiff, for the price and value of work done by the plaintiff for the defendants at their request— that the said work was done by the plaintiff for the defendants in and about the the taking upon himself the command of the said ship in the first count mentioned, and proceeding in her to the Southern whale fishery as in the said first count mentioned, and in procuring for the the said ship a cargo, and in returning in the said ship and in the command thereof to the port of London, and there discharging and delivering to the defendants the said cargo ; that such work was done and performed by the plaintiff for the defendants under and by virtue of the said articles of agreement in the said first count mention- ed ; and that the plaintiff did, during the said voyage, to wit, on the 9th February, 1832, and on divers days be- tween that day and the 7th August, 1835, trade in such manner that the owners of the said ship were prejudicially affected thereby—verification.

General demurrer, and joinder.

Whateley, in support of the demurrer.—The pleas are
bad. The performance by the plaintiff of the covenants
entered into by him does not constitute a condition precedent to his right to recover for a breach of the defendants'
covenants. The rule is perfectly clear and well ascertained. "Where there are several covenants, promises,
or agreements which are independent of each other, one
party may bring an action against the other for a breach
of his covenants &c., without averring a performance of
the covenants &c. on his the plaintiff's part; and it is no
excuse for the defendant to allege in his plea a breach of
the covenants &c. on the part of the plaintiff; according
to Justinian's rule in the civil law, 'Qui *actiónem* habet
ad rem recuperandam, ipsam rem habere videtur'—Justin.
de Regulis Juris, 361. But, where the covenants &c. are
dependent, it is necessary for the plaintiff to aver and
prove a performance of the covenants &c. on his part, to
entitle himself to an action for the breach of the covenants on the part of the defendant "—1 Wms. Saund. 320 *b*,
n. (4) to *Pordage* v. *Cole*. Where a covenant goes only to
part of the consideration on both sides, and a breach of
such covenant may be paid for in damages, it is an independent covenant, and an action may be maintained for a
breach of the covenant on the part of the defendant,
without averring performance in the declaration. Thus,
in *Boon* v. *Eyre*, 1 H. Blac. 273, n., 2 W. Blac. 1312, where
A. by deed conveyed to B. the equity of redemption of a
plantation in the West Indies, together with the stock of
negroes upon it, in consideration of 500*l.* and an annuity
of 160*l.* for life, and covenanted that he had a good title
to the plantation, was lawfully possessed of the negroes,
and B. should quietly enjoy; and B. covenanted, that, *A.
well and truly performing all and everything therein contained* on his part to be performed, he would pay the annuity: in an action by A. against B. on this covenant, the
breach assigned was, the non-payment of the annuity; the

defendant pleaded that A. was not at the time *legally possessed of the negroes* on the plantation, and so had not a
good title to convey: the court of King's Bench, on demurrer, held the plea to be ill, and added, that, if such
plea were allowed, any one negro not being the property of
A. would bar the action. So, here, if these pleas be good,
should it appear at the trial that a single cask of biscuit
was spoiled through the captain's negligence, or any slight
deviation made from the defendants'. instructions, the
plaintiff would lose all the benefit of the voyage he has
performed. In *Campbell* v. *Jones*, 6 T. R. 579, where it
was agreed between C. and D., that, in consideration of
500*l*., C. should teach B. the art of bleaching materials for
making paper, and permit him during the continuance of
a patent which C. had obtained for that purpose, to bleach
such materials according to the specification; and C., in
consideration of the sum of 250*l*. paid, and of the further
sum of 250*l*. to be paid, by D. to him, covenanted that he
would with all possible expedition teach D. the method of
bleaching such materials, and D. covenanted that he would,
on or before the 24th of February, 1794, or sooner, in case
C. should before that time have taught him the bleaching
of such materials, pay to C. the further sum of 250*l*. In
covenant by C. against D., the breach assigned was, the
non-payment of the 250*l*. The defendant demurred, assigning for cause that it was not averred that C. had taught
D. the method of bleaching such materials: but it was held
by the court, that, the *whole* consideration of the agreement
being, that C. should *permit* D. to bleach materials, as well
as teach him the method of doing it, the covenant by C. to
teach formed but *part* of the consideration, for a breach
of which D. might recover a recompence in damages; and
that C. having in part executed his agreement by transferring to D. a right to exercise the patent, he ought not to
keep that right without paying the remainder of the consideration because he might have sustained some damage

by C.'s not having instructed him: and the demurrer was over-ruled. "Hence," observes Mr. Serjeant Williams (1 Wms. Saund. 320 *d*), "it appears that the reason of the decision in these and other similar cases, besides the inequality of the damages, seems to be, that, where a person has received a *part* of the consideration for which he entered into the agreement, it would be unjust, that, because he has not had the *whole*, he should therefore be permitted to enjoy that part without either paying or doing anything for it. Therefore the law obliges him to perform the agreement on his part, and leaves him to his remedy to recover any damage he may have sustained in not having received the whole consideration." In *Davidson* v. *Gwynne*, 12 East, 381, where the master of a vessel covenanted with the freighter (inter alia) that the vessel should proceed with the first convoy from England for Spain and Portugal, or either, as he should be directed by the freighter or his agents, and there make a right and true delivery of the cargo agreeably to the bills of lading signed for the same; and so take in a home cargo, and return and make a right and true delivery thereof at London, &c.; in consideration whereof, and of every thing above mentioned, the freighter covenanted (inter alia) to load the vessel out and home, and pay certain freight per ton per month, part before and the remainder on the right and true delivery of the homeward cargo at London: it was held, that, the master having proceeded with the outward cargo to Lisbon, under the first order, and brought home a return cargo, and delivered the same to the freighter in London, was entitled to his freight for that voyage, though he had not sailed with the *first* convoy; the sailing with the *first* convoy not being a condition precedent to his right to recover freight for the voyage actually performed under the first order, but a distinct covenant, for the breach of which he was liable in damages; and Lord Ellenborough said: "The principle laid down in *Boon* v. *Eyre* has been recognised in all the subsequent cases, that, unless the non-performance alleged in breach of the contract goes to the whole root and consideration of it; the covenant broken is not to be considered as a condition precedent, but as a distinct covenant, for the breach of which the party injured may be compensated in damages.". So, in *Constable* v. *Cloberie*, Palmer, 397, the covenant being to sail with the *next* wind, upon a certain voyage, in an action for freight (the voyage having been performed), the defendant traversed that the ship did sail with the *next* wind; and the traverse was held bad, on demurrer. In *Ritchie* v. *Atkinson*, 10 East, 295, the rule is thus laid down by Lord Ellenborough—"Where mutual covenants go to the *whole* of the consideration on both sides, they are mutual conditions (and see 1 Wms. Saund. 320 *e*, n.), the one precedent to the other: but, where the covenants go only to *a part*, there a remedy lies on the covenant to recover damages for the breach of it, but it is not a condition precedent." The same principle is laid down and acted upon in the cases of *Hunlocke* v. *Blacklowe*, 2 Wms. Saund. 156, 1 Mod. 64, 2 Keb. 674, *Puller* v. *Stainforth*, 11 East, 232, *Storer* v. *Gordon*, 3 M. & Sel. 308, and *Carpenter* v. *Cresswell*, 1 M. & P. 66, 4 Bing. 409. If the defendants have sustained any injury from the negligence or misconduct of the captain, they have their remedy by a cross action.

R. V. Richards, contrà.—Whether or not the covenants on the part of the plaintiff constitute a condition precedent to his right to enforce performance of the defendants' covenants, depends upon the intention of the parties, to be collected from the agreement. The object in view was a voyage to the Southern whale fishery; a voyage which it is well known is very expensive and lengthy, and requires a greater degree of care and circumspection in the commander than any other description of voyage. It is of the highest importance to the owners that they should have the means of enforcing a proper and faithful performance by the captain of his duty; and therefore it is that he is to receive a proportion of the proceeds upon his doing all that is essential to a successful adventure, or, as the instrument now in question expresses it, "*on the performance of the before-mentioned terms and conditions.*" Unless these words are sufficient to create a condition precedent, no language can create one. The decision in each of the cases cited on the other side has reference entirely to the facts and to the particular form of the instrument the court was called upon to construe. The general rule is well and concisely laid down by Taunton, J., in *Rose v. Poulton*, 2 B. & Ad. 831. "There is a well known distinction," says that learned judge, "between cases where the consideration for doing a thing is the *doing* of some other thing, and where it is merely the *covenanting to do* such thing." In *Carpenter* v. *Cresswell*, the defendant covenanted to do certain things in *consideration of*, and not, as in the present case, *on the performance of*, the plaintiff's covenants. In *Glazebrook* v. *Woodrow*, 8 T. R. 366, where the plaintiff covenanted to sell to the defendant a school-house &c., and to convey the same to him on or before the 1st August, 1797, and to deliver up the possession to him on the 24th June, 1796, and, in consideration thereof, the defendant covenanted to pay the plaintiff 120*l.* on or before the 1st August, 1797—it was held that the covenant to convey and that for the payment of the money were dependent covenants, and that the plaintiff could not maintain an action for the 120*l.*, without averring that he had conveyed or tendered a conveyance to the defendant. And Le Blanc, J., said : "In *Boone* v. *Eyre*, the substantial part of the agreement being the conveyance of the property in respect of which the annuity was to be paid, the court held it to be no answer to an action for the annuity to say that the plaintiff had not a

good title in some of the negroes which were upon the
plantation, because all the material part of the covenant
had been performed, and the plaintiff had a remedy upon
the covenant for any special damage sustained for the non-
performance of the rest : so, in *Campbell* v. *Jones*, the
material part was the conveyance of the patent right, and,
that being performed, the court held that the giving of the
instruction concerning the proper use of it, which might be
given at any time afterwards, need not be averred in order
to sustain the action for the recompence; but that a breach
of that part of the agreement might be compensated in
damages: so, here, the material part of the covenant being
the conveyance, the plaintiff cannot entitle himself to the
money until he has shewn that every thing was done which
he had undertaken to perform on his part as the consideration of that payment." The question in the present case
is, whether there has not been such a substantial infraction
by the plaintiff of the covenants entered into on his part
as to bar his remedy against the defendants, according to
the intention of the parties : and that is a question for a
jury. The facts that stand admitted upon the record must
necessarily have had the effect of entirely ruining the
voyage. It is idle to say that the owners may have a cross
action against the captain.

Whateley, in reply.—No precise form of words is necessary to create a condition precedent—*Hotham* v. *The East
India Company*, 1 T. R. 645, *Porter* v. *Shephard*, 1 T.
R. 665. In *Puller* v. *Stainforth*, which is precisely in point
with the present case, it was urged, that, according to the
terms of the charter-party, the captain was bound to come
direct from Petersburgh to this country, and to bring the
outward cargo with him; that his doing so was a condition
precedent, without performing which he could not claim
the freight or any part of it; and that his going into
Stockholm, and there disposing of part of his outward

cargo, was a breach of that condition: but Lord Ellenborough said : " Many circumstances might occur to make
it prudent and for the interest of all concerned that the
captain should touch at some port in his way home, should
dispose of the outward cargo, and should get a freight
home. Is such a construction, then, to be put upon the
charter-party by implication as to take away from him all
power of availing himself of those circumstances? If he
were to do it improperly, he would be answerable in
damages for whatever injury his misconduct should occasion: so that justice would be done to the freighters,
though this were not held a condition precedent; and the
holding it to be a condition precedent might, in the case I
have just put, be extremely prejudicial to them." Here,
the contract having been executed, and the defendants
having received a considerable benefit from its performance, it is not competent to them now to repudiate it and
to deprive the plaintiff of his stipulated remuneration, for
some slight and immaterial deviation from the prescribed
course of the voyage, or disregard of the instructions delivered to him. The dictum of Taunton, J., in *Rose* v.
Poulton is founded on *Glazebrook* v. *Woodrow;* and in
both those cases, as well as in *Thorpe* v. *Thorpe,* 1 Salk.
171, 1 Ld. Raym. 665, 1 Lutw. 250, 12 Mod. 461, the
covenants were clearly mutual and dependent. In *Davidson* v. *Gwynne,* the terms of the contract were almost exactly those of the present. *Hunlocke* v. *Blacklowe* is a
strong authority in favour of the plaintiff: for, the covenants the breach of which the defendants complain of do
not go to the whole consideration.

Cur. adv. vult.

TINDAL, C. J., delivered the judgment of the court:—
The demurrer to the plea of the defendants raises the
question whether the performance of the covenants entered
into by the plaintiff in the articles of agreement on which

this action is founded, forms a condition precedent to the plaintiff's right to recover on the covenants entered into by the defendants. The rule has been established by a long series of decisions in modern times, that the question whether covenants are to be held dependent or independent of each other, is to be determined by the intention and meaning of the parties as it appears on the instrument, and by the application of common sense to each particular case: to which intention, when once discovered, all technical forms of expression must give way. And one of the means of discovering such intention has been laid down with great accuracy by Lord Ellenborough, in the case of *Ritchie v. Atkinson*, 10 East, 295, to be this—" That, where mutual covenants go to the whole of the consideration on both sides, they are mutual conditions, the one precedent to the other; but, where the covenants go only to *a part*, there a remedy lies on the covenant to recover damages for the breach of it; but it is not a condition precedent." Now, applying that distinction to the consideration of the covenants in question, we think the necessary inference is, that it was not the intention of the contracting parties that any of the covenants entered into by the plaintiff, the captain of the ship, should form a condition precedent to his right to recover on the covenant entered into by the defendants, the ship-owners, for his stipulated remuneration. Thus, for instance, the covenant to procure a cargo of sperm-oil &c., or as great a proportion thereof as might be under all circumstances within the power of the plaintiff to obtain, if held to be a condition precedent, a very small and trifling deficiency from the best possible cargo, if attributable to any the slightest carelessness on the part of the plaintiff, would occasion the total loss of all his profits of the voyage; whereas, if the breach of the covenant were made the subject of an action by the defendants, the compensation to them for such breach would correspond exactly with the extent of their injury. The same observation applies in a still stronger degree to the nonperformance of the several other covenants set out and relied upon in the second and third pleas; which covenants might be broken, to the letter, with very little damage resulting therefrom to the ship-owner; whilst, on the other hand, by treating them as conditions precedent, a trifling injury to the one party would occasion the loss of all the remuneration to the other for long and laborious service. The parties to such a contract may undoubtedly, if they think proper, agree that the captain's right to recover any remuneration for his services shall be conditional only, and shall depend on his strict performance of the covenants he enters into; and if words are used in the contract so precise, express, and strong, that such intention, and such intention only, is compatible with the terms employed, however inconsistent it may be with general principles of reasoning, a court can only give effect to such declared intention of the parties. The sole question in every particular case is, whether such intention is so declared. In this case it is insisted, on the part of the defendants, that such must be considered to be the intention; for that the defendants' covenant is entered into with the plaintiff, not simply in consideration of the plaintiff's covenants and agreements, but "on the performance of the before-mentioned terms and conditions on the part of the plaintiff;" which words, it is argued, must of necessity shew the intention that the performance by the plaintiff must be a condition precedent, and not rest in covenant merely. If this were res integra, the argument would undoubtedly be strong. But, in the case of *Boone v. Eyre*, 1 H. Bl. 273, n., the leading case on this subject, and in which the distinction before adverted to is first clearly established, the defendant covenanted that, "the plaintiff well and truly performing all and every thing therein contained on his part to be performed," he the defendant would pay the annuity. In that case, the per-

formance of the plaintiff's covenant is made the consideration for the defendant's liability, according to the strict
technical frame of the agreement: but in that case it was
held that the obvious intention of the parties was opposed
to it, and such intention was allowed to prevail.   The case
also of *Hunlocke* v. *Blacklowe*, 2 Saund. 155, is strong to
shew that courts of justice are more anxious to discover
and to be governed by the intention of the parties than to
follow the strict and technical form of words used in the
instrument. We think, therefore, the authorities enable us
to give effect in this case to that which appears to us the
intention of the parties, viz. that the ship-owners should
have their remedy in damages on the covenants entered
into by the captain for any loss occasioned by the breach
thereof; but that a failure in the full and literal performance of those covenants on the part of the captain should
not be set up by the ship-owners as an answer to an action
on their own covenants. And we therefore give judgment
for the plaintiff.

                                 Judgment for the plaintiff.

Dow d. WOOD v. ROE.

WILDE, Serjeant, on the 4th November instant, on the
part of the lessor of the plaintiff, obtained a rule under the
1 Geo. 4, c. 87, s. 1, calling upon the tenant to shew cause
why, upon being admitted defendant, besides entering into
the common rule and giving the common undertaking, he
should not undertake, in case a verdict should pass for the
plaintiff, to give the plaintiff a judgment, to be entered up

On a motion by a landlord under the 1 Geo. 4, c. 87, s. 1, the rule should be drawn up on reading the original lease or agreement, or a duplicate or counterpart thereof, and not merely on reading a copy of the lease or agreement.

Where the agreement in such a case appeared to have been stamped after the rule nisi was obtained, the court discharged the rule; holding that, to entitle him to a rule, the landlord must at the time of moving produce a perfect lease or agreement.

against the real defendant of the term next preceding the
time of trial; and also why he should not enter into a recognizance, by himself and two sufficient sureties, in a
reasonable sum, conditioned to pay the costs and damages
which should be recovered by the plaintiff in the action.
The affidavit upon which the rule was obtained contained
the usual allegations as to the execution of an agreement
for a lease between the parties, the enjoyment of the premises by the tenant under that agreement, and the determination of the interest of the latter by efflux of time : but
neither the agreement itself nor a counterpart thereof was
annexed to the affidavit; merely a copy: the rule being
drawn up " on reading a copy," &c.

Stephen, Serjeant, now shewed cause.—In moving this
rule, the lessor of the plaintiff has not followed the course
pointed out by the act. The act says, that, where the
term or interest of any tenant now or hereafter holding,
under a lease or agreement in writing, any lands, tenements,
or hereditaments, for any term or number of years certain,
or from year to year, shall have expired, or been determined either by the landlord or tenant by regular notice
to quit, and such tenant, or any one holding or claiming by
or under him, shall refuse to deliver up possession accordingly, after lawful demand in writing made and signed by
the landlord or his agent, and served personally upon, or
left at the dwelling-house or usual place of abode of such
tenant or person, &c., it shall be lawful for the landlord,
*producing the lease or agreement, or some counterpart or
duplicate thereof*, and proving the execution of the same
by affidavit, and upon affidavit that the premises have been
actually enjoyed under such lease or agreement, and that
the interest of the tenant has expired, or been determined
by regular notice to quit, as the case may be, and that
possession has been lawfully demanded in manner aforesaid, to move the court for a rule, &c. Here, the rule nisi

was not obtained on producing the agreement or any counterpart or duplicate thereof; but merely on the annexation
of a copy of the agreement to the affidavit. There are
good reasons for the act, which is highly beneficial to the
landlord and oppressive to the tenant, requiring the lease
or agreement itself to be produced—that the court may
satisfy themselves before granting the rule that the lease
or agreement is valid. The word "duplicate" in the
statute means a duplicate original, bearing a stamp, and
executed by the parties—a counterpart. The statute has
always been construed strictly—*Doe* d. *Tindal* v. *Roe*, 2 B.
& Ad. 922, 1 Dowl. 146; and, where the title to the premises is disputed, the court will not compel the tenant to
give the undertaking or enter into the recognizance—
Doe d. *Saunders* v. *Roe*, 1 Dowl. 4. Here, the title of the
lessor of the plaintiff is disputed, as appears by the affidavits upon which the rule is opposed.

It was suggested that the agreement was not stamped;
and, on its production, it was found that a stamp had been
impressed upon it on the 11th instant, seven days after the
rule was obtained. This the learned Serjeant contended
was a fatal objection.

Wilde, Serjeant, in support of his rule.—In Tidd's Practice, 9th edit. 1223, it is said, that, "in proceeding on this
statute, the lease or agreement under which the tenant
holds the premises, or a counterpart or duplicate thereof,
must be produced, though it need not, it seems be *left in*
court." Here, the original agreement was in court when
the motion was made, and might have been inspected by
the court had they desired it. The rule is drawn up precisely in the form adopted in *Doe* d. *Sampson* v. *Roe*, 6
Moore, 54. [*Tindal*, C. J.—I cannot get over the difficulty arising from the want of a stamp at the time the rule
was obtained.] The instrument appearing now to be regularly stamped, the court will not inquire when the stamp

was affixed to it. [*Bosanquet*, J.—The agreement is made
evidence on the 4th November, when the rule was moved.
Tindal, C. J.—If we had seen at the time the motion was
made that the agreement was not stamped, we should not
have granted a rule. *Vaughan*, J.—If we ought not to
have granted the rule, how can we make it absolute?]
The object of the act in requiring the production of the
lease or agreement, is, not that the court may see that it is
stamped; but that they may ascertain the fact of the holding, and that the tenancy under it has expired or been determined. In *Clarke* v. *Jones*, 3 Dowl. 277, on a motion
to set aside a cognovit for want of a stamp; Parke, B.,
says: " The objection to the stamp would be of no avail,
as they could get it stamped before cause was shewn."
The like was held in *Rose* v. *Tomblinson*, 3 Dowl. 49. So,
here, the court cannot give effect to the objection unless
taken at a time when there was no stamp on the instrument.

1836.

Doe
d.
Wood
v.
Rot.

TINDAL, C. J.—I am unable to get over the objection
as to the stamp. The statute, which gives new powers to
landlords, enacts, in section 1, that, " where the term or
interest of any tenant holding, under a lease or agreement
in writing, any lands, tenements, or hereditaments, for any
term or number of years certain, or from year to year, shall
have expired, or been determined either by the landlord
or tenant by regular notice to quit, and such tenant, or
any one holding or claiming by or under him, shall refuse
to deliver up possession accordingly, after lawful demand
in writing made and signed by the landland or his agent,
and served personally upon or left at the dwelling-house
or usual place of abode of such tenant or person, and the
landlord shall thereupon proceed by action of ejectment
for the recovery of possession, he may at the foot of the
declaration address a notice to such tenant or person, requiring him to appear on the first day of the term next

1886.

Doe
d.
Wood
v.
Rob.

following, to be made defendant, and to find bail if ordered
by the court; and, upon appearance, or, in case of non-
appearance, on making the usual affidavit of service, it
shall be lawful for the landlord; *producing the lease or
agreement, or some counterpart or duplicate thereof*, and
proving the execution by affidavit, and upon affidavit that
the premises have been actually enjoyed under such lease
or agreement, and that the interest of the tenant has expired, or been determined by regular notice to quit, as the
case may be, and that possession has been lawfully demanded, in manner aforesaid, to move the court for a rule
for such tenant or person to shew cause, within a time to
be fixed by the court on a consideration of the situation
of the premises, why such tenant or person, upon being
admitted defendant, besides entering into the common rule,
and giving the common undertaking, should not undertake,
in case a verdict should pass for the plaintiff, to give the
plaintiff a judgment to be entered up against the real defendant of the term next preceding the time of trial, &c.,
and also why he should not enter into a recognisance, by
himself and two sufficient sureties, in a reasonable sum,
conditioned to pay the costs and damages which shall be
recovered by the plaintiff in the action; and it shall be
lawful for the court, upon cause shewn, or, upon affidavit
of the service of the rule, in case no cause shall be shewn,
to make the same absolute in the whole or in part," &c.
It appears to me, upon reading that clause, that, as a condition precedent to the landlord's right to the rule, he
should produce in court "the lease or agreement, or some
counterpart or duplicate thereof," perfect in all its parts;
and that, such being the condition upon which the landlord is declared entitled to a rule, the rule should be drawn
up on reading the original lease or agreement. Here, at
the time of moving, a copy of the agreement only appears
to have been produced; and it further appears that the
original was not then a perfect agreement, for want of a

stamp. Upon both points, therefore, I think the rule must be discharged.

1836.

Doe
d.
Wood
v.
Rob.

GASELEE, J.—I concur with my Lord Chief Justice in thinking that the rule must be discharged, on the ground that the original agreement was unstamped at the time the rule was obtained. I forbear to express any opinion upon the other point.

VAUGHAN, J.—I am also of opinion that the agreement should have been stamped at the time the rule was moved for; and that, for want of being so stamped, the rule cannot be sustained. With respect to the other point, I will ly add that I would give no encouragement for a second plication similarly circumstanced.

BOSANQUET, J.—I am of opinion that the rule is defective upon both points. It should, I think, have been sworn up on reading the original agreement, or a counterpart or duplicate thereof: a copy will not do.

Rule discharged, without costs.

————◆————

WILLIAMS and Another v. SHARWOOD and Others.

Friday,
Nov. 25th.

ASSUMPSIT for goods sold and delivered, money lent, and money found to be due upon an account stated. The sum claimed by the declaration was 3,000l. By their particular of demand, the plaintiffs claimed a balance of 1,436l. 16s. The defendants delivered twenty-nine pleas. First, as to the several sums in the declaration mentioned, except 1059l. 10s. 7d., non assumpsit—secondly, as to 50l. parcel of the sum of 3,000l. in the first count mentioned,

The defendant is entitled to costs under the 3 & 4 Will. 4, c. 44, s. 33, on a nolle prosequi entered as to *part of the sum claimed* in the declaration, whether consisting of one or more counts.
The plaintiff

cannot object to the allowance of the defendant's pleas after the taxation of costs on the above section.

the delivery by the defendants to the plaintiffs and acceptance by them *before* action brought of a bill of exchange for 50*l.* The third to the nineteenth pleas were similar to the second, alleging the delivery of different bills : and the twentieth to the twenty-sixth averred the delivery to and acceptance by the plaintiffs of bills *after* the commencement of the action. The twenty-seventh was a plea of payment before action brought of 860*l.* 16*s.* 1*d.*: the twenty-eighth, a set-off to the whole declaration except as to 1059*l.* 10*s.* 7*d.*: the twenty-ninth, payment into court of 1059*l.* 10*s.* 7*d.*

Mr. Justice Bosanquet, before whom the summons to plead several matters was attended, allowed all the above pleas : but, at the suggestion of that learned judge, the parties consented that an order should be made for disallowing all the pleas except the first, twenty-seventh, twenty-eighth, and twenty-ninth ; the defendants to be placed in the same situation with respect to their defence as if all the pleas had been pleaded ; and the pleas so struck out being delivered with the rest.

The plaintiffs took the 1059*l.* 10*s.* 7*d.* out of court, and entered a nolle prosequi as to the other three pleas, viz., non-assumpsit, payment, and set-off.

On the taxation of costs, the prothonotary allowed the defendants the costs of the whole of the pleas except that of payment into court, in pursuance of the statute 3 & 4 Will. 4, c. 42, s. 33, which enacts, " that, where any nolle prosequi shall have been entered upon any count, or as to part of any declaration, the defendant shall be entitled to and have judgment for and recover his reasonable costs in that behalf."

Kelly now moved that the prothonotary might be directed to review his taxation. He submitted that the words of the section did not embrace a case like the present, the words " part of any declaration " not being in-

tended to apply to a nolle prosequi entered as to part of a
sum claimed in one of several counts; and that, at all
events, the costs of the whole twenty-nine pleas ought not
to have been allowed, either the plea of non-assumpsit, or
payment, or set-off, if true, being alone a perfectly good
answer to the residue of the plaintiffs' demand. [*Tindal*,
C. J.—Suppose the action had been brought only for the
difference between the balance claimed by the plaintiffs'
particular of demand and the sum paid into court, and
these three pleas had been pleaded, and the plaintiffs had
entered a nolle prosequi; would not the defendants have
been entitled to costs?] If all the pleas were true, one
only was necessary, and the plaintiffs should not be visited
with the costs of all.

Wightman shewed cause in the first instance.—There
is no distinction in principle between a claim which is unfounded as to part, and one that is unfounded as to the
whole. Suppose the plaintiffs had no cause of action at
all, and the defendants had pleaded all these pleas, could
the plaintiffs, by entering a nolle prosequi generally, throw
upon the defendants the costs of all the pleas but one?
All the pleas were necessary, and were properly allowed.

Tindal, C. J.—No doubt the defendants are entitled
to some costs. The act provides, that, where any nolle
prosequi shall have been entered upon any count, or as to
part of any declaration, the defendant shall be entitled to
and have judgment for and recover his *reasonable* costs in
that behalf: and the only question, as it seems to me, is,
whether or not we can hold it to be unreasonable in the
defendants to put in three answers to that part of the
plaintiffs' demand which was uncovered by the payment
into court. I think it would be extremely inconvenient if
such a discussion as this were to be entertained after a
judgment of nolle prosequi. If the plaintiffs conceived

1836.

WILLIAMS
v.
SHARWOOD.

that the pleas had been improperly allowed, their proper course was to apply to have them struck out.

The rest of the court concurring—

Rule refused (*a*).

(*a*) See Goodœ v. Goldsmith, 5 Dowl. 288, 2 Meeson & Welsby, 202, where, to counts in assumpsit for money had and received and on an account stated, the defendant pleaded non-assumpsit except as to 3*l.* 5*s.*, a set-off except as to that sum, and payment of 3*l.* 5*s.* into court; and, the plaintiff having admitted the set-off, taken the money out of court, and declined further to prosecute his action, the court held that the defendant was entitled to the costs of the first two issues.

Friday,
Nov. 25th.

The court has no authority to direct the taxation of an agency bill, either at common law or under the statutes 2 Geo. 2, c. 23, s. 23, and 12 Geo. 2, c. 13.

WEYMOUTH *v.* KNIGHT.

PETERSDORFF, on a former day, obtained a rule on the part of the defendant, a country attorney, calling upon the plaintiff, also an attorney, and the defendant's town agent, to shew cause why the plaintiff's several bills of costs should not be referred to the prothonotary to be taxed, upon the defendant's undertaking to pay into court the sum of 83*l.* 1*s.* 4*d.*, without prejudice to his pleading issuably and taking short notice of trial; proceedings in the meantime to be stayed. It appeared from the affidavits that the plaintiff had transacted the defendant's agency business since the year 1831, and had sent in four several bills; that money had been paid on account from time to time, but no settlement of any of the bills had taken place; that the balance claimed to be due was 108*l.* 17*s.* 8*d.*, for which this action was brought; and that, on the 6th of November instant, the plaintiff attended a summons before Park, J., taken out by the defendant, for the taxation of the bills, when the learned judge refused the order, on the ground that he had no authority under the statute 2 Geo. 2, c. 23, s. 23.

Crowder shewed cause.—The court has no power to order the taxation of these bills. The stat. 2 Geo. 2, c. 23, s. 23, applies only to cases between an attorney and a lay client: and, to exclude all doubt upon the subject, by the 12 Geo. 2, c. 13, s. 6, it is expressly enacted, "that the said act (2 Geo. 2, c. 23), or any matter or thing therein contained, shall not extend to any bill of fees, charges, and disbursements that now are or shall hereafter become due from *any attorney* or solicitor to *any other attorney*, or solicitor, or clerk in court; but that every such attorney, solicitor, or clerk in court may use such remedies for the recovery of his fees, charges, and disbursements, against such other attorney or solicitor, as he might have done before the making of this act." The only power the court has to order the taxation of an attorney's bill, is derived from the 2 Geo. 2, c. 23, s. 23. In Tidd's Practice, 9th edit. 331, it is said : " The statute 2 Geo. 2, c. 23, s. 23, does not extend to any bill of fees &c. due from any attorney or solicitor to any other attorney or solicitor or clerk in court; but every such attorney, solicitor, or clerk in court may use such remedies for the recovery of his fees &c. against such other attorney or solicitor as he might have done before the making of the said act. And there is a case in Wilson's Reports (*Anonymous*, 1 Wils. 266), where a judge of the King's Bench having made an order to refer an *agent's* bill to be taxed, and the master not having obeyed it, the court was applied to, and held that the order was irregular; the master declaring that he had never taxed a bill for agency. It is now the uniform practice, however, in all the courts to refer an agent's bill to be taxed, on the application of his employer, and upon his bringing into court the sum claimed by the plaintiff"— citing an anonymous case in Douglas, 199, where the court considered themselves empowered by their general jurisdiction, independently of the statute, to order the taxation of an agent's bill. The case in Douglas is clearly

1836.

WEYMOUTH
v.
KNIGHT.

D D D 2

not reconcileable with the modern practice. There are, it is true, cases wherein it has been held that the courts have an inherent jurisdiction at common law to tax the bills of attornies practising in them, independently of the powers given by the statutes 2 Geo. 2, c. 23, s. 23, and 30 Geo. 2, c. 19, in cases where no actions have been brought on such bills— *Wilson* v. *Gutteridge*, 4 D. & R. 736, 3 B. & C. 157; *Anonymous*, 2 Chit. Rep. 155; *Watson* v. *Postan*, 2 Tyr. 406, 2 C. & J. 370, 1 Dowl. 556. But this doctrine was disputed in the subsequent case of *Dagley* v. *Kentish*, 2 B. & Adol. 411, 1 Dowl. 331, where, on an application to tax the bill of an attorney against an ordinary client, the bill containing no taxable item, after time taken to consider, Lord Tenterden, in delivering the judgment of the court, said: " We have referred to the other judges on this case, and so much doubt is entertained on the point that we cannot send this bill to be taxed." In *Clutterbuck* v. *Coombs*, 2 N. & M. 209, 5 B. & Ad. 400, the common law jurisdiction of the courts to tax attorneys' bills seems to have been again doubted by the court of King's Bench. And in *Ex parte Bowles*, 1 New Cases, 632, 1 Scott, 583, this court expressly determined that they had no direct power to refer an attorney's bill for taxation, except under the authority of the 2 Geo. 2, c. 23, s. 23. *Doe* d. *Palmer* v. *Roe*, 4 Dowl. 95, is a decision of the court of King's Bench to the same effect.

Wilde, Serjeant, and *Petersdorff*, in support of the rule. The distinction is, that the courts will not refer an agency bill for taxation unless there be an action pending, which gives them authority, in virtue of their general jurisdiction over the parties in the double character of suitors and officers. Unless the power to direct taxation in such case exists, the only mode of discussing the propriety of the charges will be before a jury. The general proposition stated by Mr. Tidd, that " it is the uniform practice of all the courts to refer agents' bills to be taxed, on the application of the employer, and upon his bringing into court the sum claimed by the plaintiff," has never been denied by the courts, and is daily acted upon. *Wildbore* v. *Bryan,* 8 Price, 677, where it was held that the bill of costs of an attorney who is agent to the attorney employed by the party in respect of whose business the agency charges have been incurred, will not be ordered to be referred to the master to be taxed, *on the application of the client,* is in effect a recognition of the general authority of the courts. In *Ex parte Bearcroft,* 1 Doug. 190, it is stated to be the settled practice of the court of Common Pleas to order the taxation of agents' bills. And in *Innes* v. *Hake,* 2 Cox, 173, the Chancellor, on the production of several precedents sanctioning the motion, made an order on an agent to submit his bill to taxation. The court has jurisdiction in all cases where the matter in question is incident to the character of an attorney.

TINDAL, C. J.—The case of attorney and agent is expressly declared by the 12 Geo. 2, c. 13, s. 6, to be excepted out of the 2 Geo. 2, c. 23, s. 23. And the result of the conference of the judges on the case of *Dagley* v. *Kentish,* was, that they almost unanimously concluded that the courts had no authority independently of the statutes to direct the taxation of attorneys' bills; unless under special circumstances, as, where the attorney has been guilty of fraud. I think therefore the rule must be discharged without costs; the defendant having two days' time to plead, on the usual terms.

The rest of the court concurring—

Rule discharged accordingly.

1836.

WEYMOUTH
v.
KNIGHT.

1836.

Friday,
Nov. 25th.

A demand of
oyer must cor-
rectly describe
the parties to
the cause.

POOLE and Another *v.* EDWARD COATES, Executor of
THOMAS COATES, Deceased.

DEBT upon the statute 4 Geo. 2, c. 28, for double the
yearly value of premises held over after the determination
of the term.   The defendant demanded oyer of the lease;
but the demand of oyer omitting to describe the defendant as executor, the plaintiff treated it as a nullity, and
signed judgment.

W. H. Watson, on the part of the defendant, on a
former day obtained a rule nisi to set aside the judgment
for irregularity.

Wilde, Serjeant, now shewed cause.—The description
of the defendant's character is an essential part of the title
of the cause: the demand of oyer, therefore, is not a demand in this cause.

Watson, contrà, submitted that the omission was immaterial, inasmuch as it was not calculated to mislead the
plaintiff; and he produced an affidavit which shewed
something like a waiver of the objection, and a subsequent
promise to give oyer.

THE COURT held the demand to be no demand in the
cause, and therefore a nullity: but the judgment was set
aside, on terms.

Rule absolute, without costs.

Friday,
Nov. 25th.

WYATT *v.* MACDONALD.

A notice to
plead need not
be dated: con-
sequently, it
will not be vitiated by an erroneous date.

THE declaration in this cause was dated the 7th November: the notice to plead was by mistake dated the 7th

August, and required the defendant to plead " within four days from the service hereof." Judgment having on the 12th November been signed for want of a plea—

Humfrey, on the 15th, obtained a rule *nisi* to set it aside for irregularity.

Wilde, Serjeant, shewed cause.—The erroneous date is no objection to the notice: it need not be dated at all; it only becomes operative as a notice from the time of service. Besides, the objection comes too late: the declaration and notice were served on the 7th November; and this motion was not made until the 15th; judgment having been signed on the 12th.

Humfrey, in support of his rule.—There was nothing to warrant a declaration in August: and therefore we had a right to treat the notice to plead as a nullity, until another step taken by the plaintiff in the cause shewed that he intended to abide by it.

TINDAL, C. J.—I am not aware of any necessity for a date to the notice to plead: it only operates from the time of service; and the defendant knows when he is served.

The rest of the court concurring—

Rule discharged.

———◆———

WILES *v.* DODD.

*B*OMPAS, Serjeant, moved to set aside a rule for entering the issue, on the ground that since the rule of Hilary Term, 4 Will. 4, r. 15, no rule to enter the issue was necessary.

*Friday,
Nov. 25th.*

It seems, that, since the new rules (Hilary, 4 Will. 4, s. 15), the plaintiff cannot be ruled to enter the issue.

1836.

WILKS
*.
DODD.

Mansel, who shewed cause in the first instance, submitted that there was nothing in the rule referred to, which applied only to proceedings on the part of the plaintiff, to prohibit the defendant from ruling the plaintiff to enter the issue, as heretofore—" The entry of proceedings on the record for trial, or on the judgment-roll (according to the nature of the case), shall be taken to be, and shall be in fact, the first entry of the proceedings in the cause, or of any part thereof, upon record."

PER CURIAM.—There is nothing upon which the rule can operate.

Rule absolute (a).

(a) The general understanding seems to have been that the plaintiff might, notwithstanding the new rules, be compelled to enter the issue. See Archbold's Practice, 3rd edit. by Chitty, 279—Tidd's New Practice, 446.

Friday,
Nov. 25th.

HELLINGS *v.* YOUNG.

A rule nisi having been granted to reduce the damages, the court allowed the plaintiff to enter up judgment and issue execution for that part of the damages which was unobjected to, on his electing to forego the rest.

THIS was an action of assumpsit on an agreement relative to the sale of shares in the Great Western Railway. At the trial, before Alderson, B., at the last Summer Assizes at Bristol, a verdict was found for the plaintiff, with 1272*l.* damages; leave being reserved to the defendant to reduce the damages by a sum of 115*l.* A rule nisi having been granted accordingly—

Bompas, Serjeant, on a former day, obtained a rule on the part of the plaintiff, calling on the defendant to shew cause why execution should not issue forthwith for the residue of the damages, leaving the 115*l.* to be the subject of future discussion.

Crowder shewed cause.—There is no pretence for the motion. No judgment is yet entered up: and therefore no execution can issue. The plaintiff cannot have two judgments and two executions.

Bompas, Serjeant, in support of his rule.—The court can, at all events, so mould the original rule as to do justice between the parties.

TINDAL, C. J.—That which the plaintiff asks us to do is pregnant with difficulty. Perhaps, if we had been asked at the time the former rule was moved for, we should have refused to grant it unless the defendant had consented to pay to the plaintiff the balance as to which the objection did not apply. The rule must, however, be discharged; or, if the plaintiff will consent to give up the 115*l.*, the subject of the motion to reduce, that rule may be made absolute.

VAUGHAN, J.—It is impossible for the court to entertain this rule: its object is, to have execution, without any judgment to warrant it.

The rest of the court concurring—

Rule accordingly.

———————

STANNARD *v.* ULLITHORNE, HAMILTON, and CROMPTON.

THIS was an action brought against the defendants, solicitors, to recover compensation for damages alleged to have been sustained by the plaintiff, their client, through the negligence of the defendants in allowing the plaintiff (without properly advising him of the extent of his liability) to execute an assignment of a moiety of certain premises for a definite term, and with a general covenant for title, when his interest therein was determinable upon lives.

1836.

HELLINGS
v.
YOUNG.

Friday,
Nov. 25th.

In an action on the case against an attorney for negligence and want of skill in preparing an assignment of a term from the plaintiff to a third person, per quod the latter recovered damages against the plaintiff, the court refused to compel the plaintiff to deliver particulars.

The facts of the case were as follow:—Georgiana Scott
and S. S. Clement, being respectively entitled to undivided moities of a certain messuage and premises as tenants for life, on the 26th of February, 1825, demised the
same to one John Lock, to hold one undivided moiety
thereof from the 25th December, 1824, for the term of
eleven years, if Georgiana Scott should so long live, and
the other undivided moiety for the same term, provided
S. S. Clement should so long live. Mrs. Clement died in
September, 1825.

On the 21st September, 1826, Lock assigned the premises to the plaintiff for all the residue of the said term.
In this assignment, which was prepared by the defendant
Ullithorne, who had before him the original lease, Lock
covenanted, that, " for and notwithstanding any act, deed,
matter, or thing whatsoever *by him the said John Lock*
at any time theretofore made, done, committed, or knowingly occasioned, suffered, or omitted to the contrary, the
said thereinbefore in part recited indenture of lease was,
at the time of the sealing and delivering of the first-mentioned indenture, a good, valid, and effectual lease, in law
and in equity, of and for the premises thereby expressed
to be demised, and thereby assigned or intended so to be,
and that the same and the term of eleven years therein
expressed were respectively in full effect, and in no wise
forfeited, surrendered, assigned, determined, or otherwise
become void or voidable, or prejudicially affected in any
manner howsoever than by effluxion of time, &c." Lock
further covenanted for quiet enjoyment " without any
action, suit, eviction, hindrance, disturbance, or interruption whatsoever of or by the said John Lock, his executors or administrators, *or any person or persons then or
thereafter rightfully claiming or possessing any estate,
right, title, charge, or interest in, to, or out of or upon the
said premises, or any part thereof, by, from, or in trust
for him or them, or by or through his or their acts, deeds,*

defaults, means, consent, or privity, &c." At the time this assignment was executed, neither the plaintiff nor Ullithorne was aware of the death of Mrs. Clement.

In the month of January, 1829, Ullithorne was employed by the plaintiff as his attorney in the negotiation of a partnership about to be entered into between the plaintiff and one Robert James; in furtherance of which the plaintiff had agreed to assign to James a moiety of his interest in the premises for the sum of 350*l.*; and accordingly on the 16th of that month a draft of an assignment, prepared by James's attorney, was delivered to and approved by Ullithorne on behalf of the plaintiff. The assignment was executed by the plaintiff on the 19th of January; the plaintiff therein covenanting "that the thereinbefore-recited indenture of lease was at the time of the sealing and delivering of the same indentures a good and effectual lease, valid in the law, and still subsisting and not surrendered, forfeited, or become void or voidable *in any manner howsoever;*" and also for quiet enjoyment by James " for and during all the residue and remainder to come and unexpired of the said several terms therein of eleven years if the said G. Scott should so long live, and of eleven years if the said S. S. Clement should so long live, without any lawful let, suit, hindrance, interruption, or denial of the plaintiff, his executors or administrators, *or of any other person or persons whomsever;* and that free and clear, and freely and clearly acquitted, exonerated, and discharged of, from, and *against all former and other titles, charges, liens, and incumbrances whatsoever.*"

The partnership between the plaintiff and James was shortly afterwards dissolved ; whereupon, in August, 1829, the plaintiff assigned his share in the premises to James, who thereby became possessed of all that remained of the interest conveyed by the lease of the 26th February, 1825. Ullithorne, though aware of the fact of Mrs. Clement's death at the time the first assignment was executed, omitted to explain to the plaintiff the probable consequences that might result to him from his entering into the general covenants contained in the assignment to James, or the risk he thereby incurred.

In April, 1830, James was ejected from the moiety of the premises, the term in which had determined on the death of Mrs. Clement; and brought an action against the present plaintiff, and recovered damages, who thereupon brought his action against Ullithorne & Co. in which he obtained a verdict.

The life upon which depended the interest in the other moiety conveyed by the assignment of August, 1829, failing before the efflux of the eleven years, James was afterwards ejected therefrom, and brought a second action against the plaintiff, and recovered damages in respect of the second eviction. The present action was brought to recover from the defendants the damages recovered against the plaintiff on the last-mentioned occasion, and also 200*l.* the expenses alleged to have been incurred by the plaintiff in his defence to that action. The declaration was in substance the same as on the former occasion. See 4 Moore & Scott, 359.

Clarke, on a former day in this term, on an affidavit that it was necessary to enable the defendants to plead, obtained a rule for a particular of the plaintiff's demand.

Wilde, Serjeant, now shewed cause, upon an affidavit which stated, that, before the rule nisi was obtained, the plaintiff had offered to furnish particulars of the money items of his demand.—He submitted that particulars were never given in actions of this description; nor, indeed, could they be necessary to enable the defendants to prepare their defence, the whole cause of action being fully set forth on the face of the declaration.

Clarke, in support of his rule, cited *Rex* v. *Curwood*, 1 Harr. 310, where it was held that a prosecutor in an indictment for a nuisance might be compelled to give a particular of the acts of nuisance intended to be relied on.

TINDAL, C. J.—It has never been usual to give particulars in cases of this sort: and I see nothing in the present case to differ it from the ordinary rule. There may, it is true, be cases where it would be difficult, perhaps impossible, for the defendant in an action of this description to make his defence without having a particular of the acts of negligence intended to be charged against him; but here I think the defendants must be fully aware of all the circumstances, and therefore not entitled to the particular sought.

The rest of the court concurring—

Rule discharged.

END OF MICHAELMAS TERM.

REGULA GENERALIS.

—◆—

MICHAELMAS TERM, 7 WILL. IV.

———

1836.

SHERIFFS' RULES.

Rules to return writs, or to bring in the body, except in London and Middlesex, to be eight instead of six day rules.

IT is ordered, that, from and after the last day of this term, all rules upon sheriffs, other than the sheriffs of London and Middlesex, to return writs either of mesne or final process, and rules to bring in the bodies of defendants, be eight day rules, instead of six day rules.

INDEX.

———

ARBITRATION.

Authority of Arbitrator, how revoked—(Continued.)

leave to revoke his authority, under the 3 & 4 Will. 4, c. 42, s. 39. Id. 94.

Award, where final.

5. The cause and all matters in dispute between the parties were referred to arbitration. The arbitrator, reciting that he had heard "the allegations and proofs and answers of the parties touching the matters in difference between them," awarded, "concerning the same," that the defendant should on a given day pay the plaintiff a certain sum "in full of all demands *in the cause :*"—Held, that this award was a sufficiently final adjudication upon the matters in difference. Day v. Bonnin, 597.

Motion to impeach the Award, when made.

6. Where a cause is referred and a verdict entered, a motion to impeach the award must be made within the first four days of the following term. Lyng v. Sutton, 187.

ARREST OF JUDGMENT.

1. In indebitatus assumpsit the day of the promise alleged in the declaration is immaterial; and therefore it is no ground for arresting the judgment, that the promise is stated to have been made at a day subsequent to the issuing of the writ; otherwise, where the day is material. Arnall v. Arnall, 547.

And see PRACTICE, 23, 24.

ATTORNEY.

Examination and Admission.

1. Whereas, by the stat. 4 Hen. 4, c. 18, it was enacted "That all the attorneys shall be examined by the justices, and by their discretion their names put on the roll, and they that be good and vertuous and of good fame shall be received and sworn well and truly to serve in their offices." And whereas by the stat. 3 Jac. 1, c. 7, s. 2, it was enacted, "That none shall from henceforth be admitted attorneys in any of the king's courts of record but such as have been brought up in the same courts, or otherwise well practised in soliciting of causes, and have been found by their dealings to be skilful and of honest disposition, and that none be suffered to solicit any cause or causes in any of the courts aforesaid but only such as are known to be men of sufficient and honest disposition." And whereas by a rule made in Michaelmas Term, 1654, in the courts of King's Bench and Common Pleas, it was ordered that the courts "should, once or more in every year, in Michaelmas Term, nominate twelve or more able and credible practisers, to continue for the ensuing year, to examine such persons as should desire to be admitted attorneys, and appoint convenient times and places for the examination . and the persons desiring to be admitted

ATTORNEY.

were first to attend with their proofs of service, then to repair to the
persons appointed to examine, and, being approved, to be presented
to the court and sworn." And whereas by the stat. 2 Geo. 2, c. 23,
s. 2, it was enacted, "That the judges, or any one or more of them,
should, and they were thereby authorized and required, before they
should admit such person to take the oath, to examine and inquire
by such ways and means as they should think proper, touching his
fitness and capacity to act as an attorney: and if such judge or
judges respectively should be thereby satisfied that such person is
duly qualified to be admitted to act as an attorney, then, and not
otherwise, the said judge or judges of the said courts respectively
should, and they were thereby authorized to administer to such person the oath thereinafter directed to be taken by attorneys, and,
after such oath taken, to cause him to be admitted an attorney of
such court respectively." And whereas, in order to carry the last-
mentioned statute more fully into effect, it is expedient annually to
appoint examiners, subject to the control of the judges in manner
hereinafter mentioned: It is ordered that the several masters and
prothonotaries for the time being of the courts of King's Bench,
Common Pleas, or Exchequer respectively, together with twelve
attorneys or solicitors, be appointed, by a rule of court, in Easter Term in every year, to be examiners for one year; any five of
whom (one whereof to be one of the said masters or prothonotaries) shall be competent to conduct the examination; and that,
from and after the last day of next Easter Term, subject to such
appeal as hereinafter mentioned, no person shall be admitted to be
sworn an attorney of any of the courts, except on production of a
certificate signed by the major part of such examiners actually
present at and conducting his examination, testifying his fitness and capacity to act as an attorney; such certificate to
be in force only to the end of the term next following the date
thereof, unless such time shall be specially extended by the order of
a judge. Reg. Gen., Hilary Term, 6 Will. 4.

2. It is further ordered, that the examiners so to be appointed
shall conduct the said examinations under regulations to be first submitted to and approved by the judges. Id.

3. And it is further ordered, that, in case any person shall be dissatisfied with the refusal of the examiners to grant such certificate,
he shall be at liberty to apply for admission by petition in writing
to the judges, to be delivered to the clerk of the Lord Chief Justice
of the court of King's Bench, upon which no fee or gratuity shall
be received, which application shall be heard in Serjeant's Inn Hall,
by no less than three of the judges. Id.

4. And whereas the hall or building of the Incorporated Law So-

ATTORNEY.

Examination and Admission—(Continued.)

ciety of the United Kingdom, in Chancery Lane, will be a fit and convenient place for holding the said examination, and the said society have consented to allow the same to be used for that purpose: it is further ordered, that, until further order, such examinations be there held on such days, being within the last ten days of every term, as the said examiners or any five of them shall appoint; and that any person not previously admitted an attorney of any of the three courts, and desirous of being admitted, shall, in addition to the notices already required, give a term's notice to the said examiners of his intention to apply for examination, by leaving the same with the secretary of the said society at their said Hall; which notice shall also state his place or places of residence or service for the last preceding twelve months; and, in case of application to be admitted on a refusal of the certificate, shall give ten days' notice, to be served in like manner, of the day appointed for hearing the same. Id.

5. And it is further ordered, that, three days at the least before the commencement of the term next preceding that in which any person not before admitted shall propose to be admitted an attorney of either of the courts, he shall cause to be delivered at the masters' or prothonotaries' office, as the case may be, instead of affixing the same on the walls of the courts, as now required, the usual written notices, which shall state, in addition to the particulars now required, his place or places of abode or service for the last preceding twelve months; and the master or prothonotary, as the case may be, shall reduce all such notices as in this rule first mentioned into an alphabetical table or tables, under convenient heads, and affix the same, on the first day of term, in some conspicuous place within or near to and on the outside of each court. Id.

6. And whereas it is expedient, that, upon the re-admission of attornies, the judges should have further means of inquiring as to the circumstances under which persons applying to be re-admitted discontinued to practise, and as to their conduct and employment during the time of such discontinuance; it is further ordered, that, at the time of giving the usual notice of the intention to apply for such re-admission, the party shall cause to be filed the affidavit on which he seeks to be re-admitted, with the master or prothonotary, as the case may be; which affidavit shall contain, in addition to the particulars now required, a statement of his place or places of abode during the last preceding year; and such person shall also at the same time cause to be left a copy of such affidavit with the clerk of the Lord Chief Justice of the court of King's Bench; and the rule for the re-admission of such person shall be drawn up on reading such affidavit, and also an affidavit of such copy having been left in compliance with this rule. Id.

ATTORNEY.

Examination and Admission—(Continued.)

Regulations approved by the Judges in Easter Term, 1836, for the Ex-
amination of Persons applying to be admitted as Attorneys of the Courts
of King's Bench, Common Pleas, or Exchequer, pursuant to the Rule
of Court made in Hilary Term, 1836.

7. Whereas, by a rule of the courts of King's Bench, Common Pleas,
and Exchequer, made in Hilary Term, 1836, it was ordered, that the
several masters and prothonotaries for the time being of the said
courts respectively, together with twelve attorneys or solicitors, should
be appointed by a rule of court in Easter Term in every year, to be
examiners, for one year, of persons applying to be admitted attorneys
of the said courts, any five of whom (one whereof to be one of the
said masters or prothonotaries) should be competent to conduct the
examination; and that, from and after the last day of the present
Easter Term, subject to such appeal as thereinafter mentioned, no
person should be admitted to be sworn an attorney of any of the said
courts, except on production of a certificate, signed by the major
part of such examiners actually present at and conducting his examination, testifying his fitness and capacity to act as an attorney;
such certificate to be in force only to the end of the term next following the date thereof, unless such time should be specially extended by
the order of a judge: And it was further ordered, that the examiners
so to be appointed should conduct the said examinations under regulations to be first submitted to and approved by the judges; and that,
until further order, such examinations should be held in the hall or
building of the Incorporated Law Society of the United Kingdom, in
Chancery Lane, on such days (being within the last ten days of every
term) as the said examiners, or any five of them, should appoint;
and that any person not previously admitted of any of the three
courts, and desirous of being admitted, should give a term's notice of
his intention to apply for examination, by leaving the same with the
secretary of the said society, at their said hall. Id.

8. And whereas, by a rule of all the said courts, made in this present
Easter Term, it was ordered, that the several masters and prothonotaries for the time being of the said courts respectively, together with
Thomas Adlington, Jonathan Brundrett, George Frere, James William
Freshfield, James Hall, Bryan Holme, William Lowe, Edward Rowland Pickering, Samuel White Sweet, William Tooke, Richard White,
and Edward Archer Wilde, gentlemen, attorneys, should be, and the
same were thereby appointed examiners for one year then next ensuing, to examine all such persons as should desire to be admitted
attorneys of all or either of the said courts from and after the last
day of that term; and that any five of the said examiners, one of
them being one of the said masters or prothonotaries, should be competent to conduct the said examination, in pursuance of and subject
to the provisions of the said rule of Hilary Term last. Id.

ATTORNEY.

Examination and Admission—(Continued.)

9. In pursuance of the said rules, the following regulations for conducting the said examinations have been submitted to and approved by the judges of the said courts. Id.

(1). That every person applying to be admitted an attorney of any of the said courts pursuant to the said rules, shall, within the first seven days of the term in which he is desirous of being admitted, leave or cause to be left with the secretary of the said Incorporated Law Society, his articles of clerkship, duly stamped, and also any assignment which may have been made thereof, together with answers to the several questions hereunto annexed, signed by the applicant, and also by the attorney or attorneys with whom he shall have served his clerkship. Id.

(2). That, in case the applicant shall shew sufficient cause, to the satisfaction of the examiners, why the first regulation cannot be fully complied with, it shall be in the power of the said examiners, upon sufficient proof being given of the same, to dispense with any part of the first regulation that they may think fit and reasonable. Id.

(3). That every person applying for admission shall also, if required, sign and leave, or cause to be left, with the secretary of the said society, answers in writing to such other written or printed questions as shall be proposed by the said examiners touching his said service and conduct; and shall also, if required, attend the said examiners personally, for the purpose of giving further explanation touching the same; and shall also, if required, procure the attorney or attorneys with whom he shall have served his clerkship as aforesaid, to answer, either personally or in writing, any question touching such service or conduct, or shall make proof to the satisfaction of the said examiners of his inability to procure the same. Id.

(4). That every person so applying shall also attend the said examiners at the hall of the said society, at such time or times as shall be appointed for that purpose, pursuant to the said rule, as the said examiners shall appoint, and shall answer such questions as the said examiners shall then and there put to him by written or printed papers, touching his fitness and capacity to act as an attorney. Id.

(5). That, upon compliance with the aforesaid regulations, and if the major part of the said examiners actually present at and conducting the said examination (one of them being one of the said masters or prothonotaries) shall be satisfied as to the fitness and capacity of the person so applying to act as an attorney, the said examiners present, or the major part of them, shall certify the same under their hands in the following form, viz.:—

"In pursuance of the rules made in Hilary and Easter Terms, 1836, of the courts of King's Bench, Common Pleas, and Exchequer, We, being the major part of the examiners actually present at and

ATTORNEY.

Examination and Admission—(Continued.)

conducting the examination of A. B., of &c., do hereby certify that we have examined the said A. B., as required by the said rules; and we do testify that the said A. B. is fit and capable to act as an attorney of the said courts." Id.

10. *Questions as to due Service, to be answered by the Clerk.*

(1). What was your age on the day of the date of your articles?

(2). Have you served the whole term of your articles at the office where the attorney or attorneys to whom you were articled or assigned carried on his or their business? and, if not, state the reason.

(3). Have you, at any time during the term of your articles, been absent without the permission of the attorney or attorneys to whom you were articled or assigned? and, if so, state the length and occasions of such absence.

(4). Have you, during the period of your articles, been engaged or concerned in any profession, business, or employment, other than your professional employment as clerk to the attorney or attorneys to whom you were articled or assigned?

(5). Have you, since the expiration of your articles, been engaged or concerned, and for how long time, in any and what profession, trade, business, or employment, other than the profession of an attorney or solicitor? Id.

11. *Questions as to due Service, to be answered by the Attorney.*

(1). Has A. B. served the whole term of his articles at the office where you carry on your business? and, if not, state the reason.

(2). Has the said A. B., at any time during the term of his articles, been absent without your permission? and, if so, state the length and occasions of such absence.

(3). Has the said A. B., during the period of his articles, been engaged or concerned in any profession, business, or employment, other than his professional employment as your articled clerk?

(4). Has the said A. B., during the whole term of his clerkship, with the exceptions above mentioned, been faithfully and diligently employed in your professional business of an attorney or solicitor?

(5). Has the said A. B., since the expiration of his articles, been engaged or concerned, and for how long time, in any and what profession, trade, business, or employment, other than the profession of an attorney and solicitor?

And I do hereby certify that the said A. B. hath duly and faithfully served under his articles of clerkship, (or assignment, *as the case may be*), bearing date &c., for the term therein expressed; and that he is a fit and proper person to be admitted an attorney. Id.

Authority of.

12. A motion to reverse an outlawry cannot be entertained, unless

ATTORNEY.

Authority of—(Continued.)

it expressly appear by the affidavits that the attorney making the application is duly authorized by the outlaw. Houlditch v. Swinfen, 169.

Summary Jurisdiction of the Court over.

13. This court cannot exercise a summary jurisdiction over a party who is not one of its own officers, although the matter be pending here. Sharp v. Hawker, 396.

14. The writ issued on the 5th September, and was sent to the under-sheriff of Hants on the 16th October. An order for a stay of proceedings was made on the 20th, on which day the plaintiff's attorney wrote to the under-sheriff at Winchester, desiring to be informed what was the amount of his and the officer's charges, and informing the under-sheriff that a judge's order had been obtained for staying the proceedings. The debt and costs were paid on the 31st October. On the 4th November, the defendant was arrested on the same writ in Hampshire, and gave a bail-bond. A judge's order having been obtained for cancelling the bail-bond, with costs, and those costs having been paid by the plaintiff, he obtained a rule calling upon his attorney to shew cause why he should not repay to him the sum so paid for costs :—Held, that the attorney had not under the circumstances been guilty of such a degree of negligence as to render him liable—at least on motion. Meggs v. Binns, 52.

Action against, for Negligence or Breach of Duty.

15. In an action against an attorney for negligence in procuring insufficient security upon an advance of money, per quod the plaintiff lost the money—the court allowed the defendant to plead, in addition to non assumpsit and several other pleas, that the loss was not the result of the alleged negligence. Wright v. Newton, 595.

16. The defendant was retained as an attorney to raise money for the plaintiff by way of mortgage. In the course of his employment on this retainer, the defendant discovered that the legal estate in certain of the property intended to be comprised in the mortgage was in the plaintiff's brother, J. H. T., whose attorney the defendant was. The defendant communicated the discovery to J. H. T., who thereupon instituted proceedings for the recovery of the premises, whereby the plaintiff was put to expense, delayed in procuring the advance he required, and ultimately compelled to pay a higher rate of interest :— Held, that this was such a breach of duty on the part of the defendant as to render him liable to an action. Taylor v. Blacklow, 614.

Taxation of Bill.

17. The court has no authority to direct the taxation of an agency

ATTORNEY.

Taxation of Bill—(Continued.)

bill, either at common law or under the statutes 2 Geo. 2, c. 23, s. 23, and 12 Geo. 2, c. 13, s. 6.   Weymouth v. Knight, 764.

And see Costs, 4, 5.

ATTORNEY'S LIEN—See Set-off.

AWARD—See Arbitration.

BAIL.

Time for inquiring as to.

Where the regular notice of bail has been given, the court will, under special circumstances, allow time for inquiry into their sufficiency, on payment of costs.   Dicas v. Smith, 600.

BANKRUPT.

Protected Payments.

1. L. & C., silk merchants, deposited silk warrants with the defendants, who advanced money to them thereon; on the 27th November, one W. handed to the defendants an order (which the jury found to be a fraudulent preference) from L. & C., directing the defendants to make to the bearer a further advance of 500*l.* on the silks; no money was advanced on this order until the 6th December, when the defendants gave W. 150*l.* and it was agreed that they should retain the remaining 350*l.* to meet certain acceptances of W.'s which they held, and which were due on the 14th December.   On the 3rd December, L. & C. committed an act of bankruptcy, and on the 5th a fiat issued against them:—Held, that the payments made by the defendants on the 6th and 14th December were not protected by the 6 Geo. 4, c. 16, s. 82.   Green v. White, 387.

Mutual Credits.

2. The plaintiffs, as assignees, declared in trover for a policy of insurance.   The defendant pleaded an antient custom in the city of London for insurance brokers to retain in their possession all policies effected by them, under a lien for their general balance, and then set up a balance due to him *at the time of the demand and refusal.*   The plaintiffs replied that the sum for which the lien was claimed was the price of certain canvass which the defendant had sold to the bankrupt at a credit of twelve months, and which credit had not expired at the time of the conversion; and further, that the defendant had drawn a bill of exchange at twelve months upon the bankrupt, which bill was accepted by him, and was received by the defendant on account of the price of the canvass, *before the time of the conversion.*   To this replication the defendant demurred:—Held, that it was not competent to the defendant under this plea to set up a right to retain the property in question for a balance due to him on mutual credits between himself and the bankrupt; and that, even if it were, it did not sufficiently appear upon the record that the mutual credits, upon the

BANKRUPT.

Mutual Credits—(Continued.)

result of which the balance was claimed, were given *before the bankruptcy*, so as to make the balance claimed *a balance due at the time of the bankruptcy*. Hewison v. Guthrie, 298.

3. If a security is taken for a debt for which the party has a lien upon property of the debtor, such security being payable at a distant day, the lien is gone. Ibid.

Fraudulent Preference.

4. Whether or not a voluntary payment made by a trader in insolvent circumstances and on the verge of bankruptcy to a particular creditor, is void as being a fraud upon the bankrupt laws, is a question of fact for the jury, depending upon the mind and intention of the party at the time of making the payment, to be collected from the surrounding circumstances. If his condition and conduct be such as to evince clearly a contemplation on the part of the trader that his embarrassments must of necessity end in *bankruptcy*, the jury will not be warranted in coming to any other conclusion than that the transaction is fraudulent. But, inasmuch as every man has down to the time of committing an act of bankruptcy the sole right of dominion over his property, such a payment cannot be held to be a fraudulent preference where the bankrupt at the time of making it appears to entertain a bona fide hope or expectation that he may be extricated from his difficulties without being made a bankrupt. Gibson v. Boutts, 229.

Committal for not answering Questions.

5. A bankrupt detained in the Fleet prison in several actions, not answering to the satisfaction of the commissioners certain questions which they had put to him, they issued their warrant, addressed "to the keeper of Newgate, or whom else it might concern," authorizing the detention of the bankrupt until he should make answer to their satisfaction. This warrant was delivered to the Warden of the Fleet. To a writ of habeas corpus issued at the instance of the prisoner, the Warden returned that he held him by virtue of the detainers in the civil suits; and added, that, on a certain day, the above warrant was left with him:—Held, that, the warrant not being a cause of the prisoner's detainer in the Fleet, it was not necessary to set it forth in the return ; and that, under the circumstances, the court could not inquire into the validity of the warrant. In re Garcia, 662.

BARON AND FEME—See HUSBAND AND WIFE.

BEYOND SEAS—See IRELAND.

BILLS OF EXCHANGE AND PROMISSORY NOTES.

The defendants made and delivered to the plaintiffs a promissory note in payment for goods. Before the note became due, and before the plaintiffs

BILLS OF EXCHANGE AND PROMISSORY NOTES—(*Continued.*)

had indorsed it, it was stolen by a clerk of the plaintiffs', who forged their indorsement thereon, and presented the note with such forged indorsement at the defendants' bankers', who paid the amount, and in the usual course handed the note over to the defendants. The plaintiffs did not discover the felony till six weeks after the note had arrived at maturity and been paid. Upon a special case stating these facts, and containing no allegation of negligence on the part of the plaintiffs:—Held, that the plaintiffs were entitled to recover the value of the note from the defendants, in an action of trover. Johnson v. Windle, 608.

BLOCKADE—See SHIP AND SHIPPING, 1.

BOND—See APOTHECARY.

BOTTOMRY BOND.

1. In assumpsit for money lent, &c., the defendant pleaded—first, non assumpsit—secondly, that the causes of action arose out of disbursements made for and on account of a vessel belonging to the defendant, and that the master made and sealed a bottomry bond, which was accepted and received by the plaintiff in satisfaction of the promises in the declaration mentioned, &c. The plaintiff replied that he did not accept or receive the bond in satisfaction of the promises, modo et formâ. At the trial it appeared that the bond was given by the master the day after the transaction as to the advances on the ship's account was closed, and by way of collateral security only: the issue thereon having been found for the plaintiff:—Held, that the plaintiff's right to sue the owner in respect of the implied contract was not destroyed by his taking such *additional* security. Weston v. Foster, 155.

2. Held, also, that it was not competent to the defendant under non assumpsit to give in evidence the making and delivery of the bond. Ibid.

BREACH OF DUTY—See ATTORNEY, 16.

BREACH OF PROMISE OF MARRIAGE.

1. To an action for a breach of promise of marriage, the defendant pleaded—first, that, after the making of the promise, the defendant discovered that the plaintiff was an immodest, lewd, unchaste, and immoral person, and, being sole and unmarried, had had carnal intercourse with one H. P.—and secondly, that, after the making of the promise, the defendant had notice that the plaintiff, being so sole and unmarried, had committed fornication with some person or persons to defendant unknown, and was pregnant with a child likely to be born a bastard (averring the fact to be so), of which he had no notice or knowledge at the time of making the promise:—Held, sufficient. Young v. Murphy, 379.

2. The court refused to order satisfaction to be entered upon the roll in an action for breach of promise of marriage, without a warrant of attorney from the plaintiff, notwithstanding a judge's order had been obtained for the purpose by consent. Wood v. Hurd, 368.

BRISTOL DOCK.

In relation to the rates and duties payable on goods imported into the port of Bristol, by the Bristol Dock act, 48 Geo. 3, c. xi, Ireland is in parts beyond the seas. Battersby v. Kirk, 11.

CASE.

For Negligence in removing Buildings.

1. The first count of the declaration stated that the plaintiffs were possessed of a certain vault adjoining certain other vaults and walls of the defendant, and which in part rested upon and was of right in part supported by parts of those adjoining vaults and walls; that the plaintiffs were of right entitled that their vault should be so supported in part by the said parts of the said adjoining vaults and walls without the hindrance or disturbance of any person; and that there were certain foundations belonging to and supporting the said vault which the plaintiffs ought to enjoy: yet that the defendant wrongfully took down and removed the said vaults and walls so adjoining the plaintiffs' vault, without shoring up or otherwise securing, or taking other reasonable or proper precautions to support or secure the plaintiffs' said vault, so as to prevent the same from giving way or being weakened or destroyed; and wrongfully dug the earth and disturbed the foundations, without taking due and proper precautions to prevent the said foundations from being weakened and giving way; and by reason thereof the said foundations became and were injured, loosened, and weakened, and also by reason of certain timber &c. falling upon the plaintiffs' vault (which by reason of the acts complained of was unable to bear the weight of the timber &c.), the vault fell in, and its contents were injured:—Held, that the count contained a clear and substantial ground of action, viz. that of negligence and carelessness in the exercise of the defendant's rights, by reason whereof the plaintiffs' rights were injured. Trower v. Chadwick, 699.

2. The second count stated, that the plaintiffs were possessed of a vault; that the defendant was about to pull down and remove and did pull down and remove certain other vaults and walls next adjoining the plaintiffs' vault; and thereupon it became and was the duty of the defendant, in the event of his not shoring up or protecting the plaintiffs' vault, to give due and reasonable notice to the plaintiffs of his intention to pull down and remove the said vaults and walls so adjoining the plaintiffs' vault, before he pulled down the same, so as to enable the plaintiffs to protect themselves; and also to use due care and skill, and take due, reasonable, and proper precautions in and about the pulling down and removing his vaults and walls, so that for want of such care, skill, and precaution, the plaintiffs' vault and its contents might not be damaged or destroyed:—Held, that the using due care, skill, and precaution in removing his own vaults and walls, so as to prevent injury resulting to the plaintiffs from the absence of such care, skill, and precaution, was a duty clearly imposed upon the

CASE.

For Negligence in removing Buildings—(Continued.)

defendant by law; that a breach alleging that he conducted himself so carelessly, negligently, and unskilfully in pulling down his vaults and walls as by reason thereof to injure the plaintiffs' vault, was well assigned; and that this allegation of duty being severable from the former (as to the defendant's duty to give notice), the count disclosed a good ground of action. Ibid.

3. Quære, whether any obligation on the part of the defendant to give the plaintiffs notice of his intention to pull down his own vaults, if he did not himself shore up their vault, resulted as an inference of law from the mere juxta-position of the respective premises. Ibid.

4. To the first count the defendant pleaded—as to the not shoring or propping up the walls, or taking other reasonable or proper precautions to support or secure the plaintiffs' vault, so as to prevent the same from being weakened—that he was not bound by law or otherwise, nor was there any duty, obligation, or liability imposed upon him by law or otherwise to shore up or secure, or take means to secure the plaintiffs' vault: and—as to so much of the count as related to the defendant's not having taken due and proper precaution to prevent the foundations of the plaintiffs' vault from being injured and giving way—that the defendant was not bound by law or otherwise, nor was there any duty, obligation, or liability imposed upon him by law or otherwise to take any precautions to prevent the foundations of the plaintiffs' vault from being weakened and injured:—Held, that both these pleas were bad, the traverses therein respectively not being the traverse of any allegation to be found in the count; and that they raised an issue in law for the consideration of the jury, viz. as to whether or not a duty was cast upon the defendant by law or otherwise. Ibid.

5. The defendant further pleaded that the falling of the timber &c. upon the plaintiffs' vault was not occasioned by any act, default, &c. of the defendant, or the breach or neglect of any duty, obligation, or liability imposed upon him by law or otherwise. The count stating the inability of the plaintiffs' vault to bear the weight of the timber &c. to have arisen solely from the wrongful act of the defendant:—Held, that he was the proximate cause of the damage thereby occasioned, and responsible for it; and therefore that the plea was bad, inasmuch as it confessed without avoiding that part of the charge in the count to which it professed to be an answer:—Held, also, that the plea was bad, as being pleaded to part of the special damage alleged in the count; and also on the ground that it traversed an obligation in law (and one not even alleged in the count), thereby tendering an issue improper to be tried by a jury. Ibid.

6. Another plea, professing to be an answer to the whole of the first count, omitted to give any answer as to the digging the earth and disturbing the foundations of the plaintiffs' vault:—Held, bad. Ibid.

CASE.

For Negligence in removing Buildings—(Continued.)

7. Pleas to the second count—that the defendant was not bound by law to shore up the plaintiffs' vault, or, in the event of his not doing so, to give the plaintiffs notice of his intention to pull down his own vaults—and that it was not the defendant's duty to use due and proper or any precautions in and about the pulling down his vaults and walls, so that the plaintiffs' vault might not be damaged:—Held bad, as raising issues of law, instead of issues of fact for the jury. Ibid.

For Negligence in constructing a Sewer—See COMMISSIONERS OF SEWERS.

Against Attornies—See ATTORNEY, 15, 16.

CERTIFICATE.

To deprive Plaintiff of Costs, under 43 Eliz. c. 6, s. 2.

In trespass for an assault, battery, and imprisonment of the plaintiff's wife, the defendants pleaded—first, not guilty—secondly, that the individual was not the plaintiff's wife—thirdly, a justification under process issued against her. A verdict was found for the plaintiffs on the first and second pleas, with a farthing damages, and for the defendants on the third:—Held, that it was competent to the judge to certify under the 43 Eliz. c. 6, s. 2, to deprive the plaintiffs of costs, notwithstanding that, on the issue joined on the plea of not guilty, the postea had been entered up generally for the plaintiffs; there being no necessary admission of a battery on the face of the record. Wilson v. Lainson, 676.

CHARTERPARTY—See SHIP AND SHIPPING, 2.

COMMISSIONERS.

For taking Acknowledgments under 3 & 4 Will. 4, c. 74—See ACKNOWLEDGMENT.

COMMISSIONERS OF SEWERS.

1. In order to render commissioners acting in the bona fide performance of a public duty liable to an action for an injury to an individual resulting from an act so done by them, it must appear that they have been guilty of negligence or want of skill in the conduct of it. Grocers' Co. v. Donne, 356.

2. In case against commissioners of sewers for an injury done to the plaintiffs' premises by the construction of an adjoining sewer, the cause was referred to an arbitrator, who found, that there were two modes of making a sewer practised in London, the one by what is called tunnelling, the other by what is called open cutting; that, in this case, a deep sewer could not be made either by the one method or the other without risk of damage to the adjoining buildings; that the amount of risk varied according to the nature of the soil, which here was of a nature to make the risk considerable; that the probability of damage accruing was *in some degree less* where the sewer was made by open cutting than by tunnelling; that

COMMISSIONERS OF SEWERS—(*Continued.*)

the sewer was made by the mode of tunnelling; that the commissioners, in directing it to be made, and in the making of it, were acting bona fide in the honest discharge of their duty as commissioners; that the sewer was fit and proper to be made for the convenient drainage of the city of London, and was made in a workmanlike, skilful, and proper manner in all respects, provided that the commissioners were justified in making it by the mode of tunnelling; and that, in consequence of the making of the sewer, the plaintiffs' house was damaged to a certain amount. It did not appear that the plaintiffs had had any notice of the progress of the work or of the mode of doing it:—Held, that the commissioners were not responsible for the injury so occasioned. Ibid.

COMMON.

Right of, how pleaded.

In trespass quare clausum fregit, the defendant pleaded an uninterrupted enjoyment, under a claim of right, of common over the locus in quo "for the full period of thirty years before the commencement of the suit:"—Held, sufficient, without alleging the enjoyment to have been for thirty years *next* before the commencement of the suit. Jones v. Price, 376.

CONDITION PRECEDENT.

By articles of agreement entered into between the plaintiff, as captain, and the defendants, the owners, of a South Sea whaler, the plaintiff covenanted that he would proceed to the fishery, and procure a cargo of sperm-oil, ambergris, &c., or as great a proportion thereof as might be under all circumstances within his power to obtain, and, having done so, would return in and with the ship to London, and there at his own cost discharge and deliver to the defendants whatever cargo she might have on board; that he would obey such instructions relative to the ship and her voyage as might from time to time be received by him from the defendants, their heirs &c.; that he would be frugal with the ship's stores and provisions, enter in a book the expenditure and appropriation thereof, and not dispose of any part of them without faithfully accounting with the defendants for the produce thereof; that he would not smuggle or trade, or permit it directly or indirectly, whereby the ship or the owners thereof might be prejudicially affected, nor consent or suffer to be committed any illegal act or acts on board the ship whereby the owners might be injured. And the defendants covenanted, *on the performance of the before mentioned terms and conditions on the part of the plaintiff,* that they, their heirs, &c., would pay to the plaintiff, his heirs, &c., a sum equal to one-twelfth part of the net proceeds of the cargo:—Held, that the performance of the covenants entered into by the plaintiff did not form a condition precedent to his right to recover on the covenants entered into on the part of the defendants. Stavers v. Curling, 740.

COPYHOLD.

A devisee in fee of a copyhold tenement, on his admittance, paid the lord the full fine due by the custom of the manor. He afterwards made a surrender of the premises to the use of himself and his assigns for life, with divers remainders over; and, on being admitted tenant for life of the surrendered premises, he paid a fine of 1s. to the lord:—Held, that, in the absence of a custom within the manor to sanction it, no fine was payable on the admission of the remainder-man—the admission of the tenant for life being the admission of the remainder-man. Phypers v. Eburn, 634.

COSTS.

Taxation of.

1. Upon writs of inquiry before the sheriff, where the damages are under 20l., the costs are taxed on the same scale as upon trials before the sheriff. Hooppell v. Leigh, 188.

2. In assumpsit on a bill of exchange drawn in London, the venue was laid in Surrey, for the purpose of obtaining speedier execution: the parties and witnesses all residing in London, the prothonotary, on a verdict for the plaintiff, refused to allow him larger costs than he would have been entitled to had the cause been tried in London: The court directed a review of the taxation. Vere v. Wood, 646.

3. The court has no authority to direct the taxation of an agency bill, either at common law or under the statutes 2 Geo. 2, c. 23, s. 23, and 12 Geo. 2, c. 13, s. 6. Weymouth v. Knight, 764.

4. A bailable writ having been sued out of this court against an attorney of the King's Bench, he, after some attempts to compromise, obtained a judge's order to stay the proceedings on payment of the debt and such costs as the prothonotary should under the circumstances think reasonable. The prothonotary having allowed the costs of bailable process:—Held, that the parties were concluded by his determination. Meggs v. Binns, 52.

5. The writ issued on the 5th September, and was sent to the under-sheriff of Hants on the 16th October. The order for a stay of proceedings was made on the 20th, on which day the plaintiff's attorney wrote to the under-sheriff at Winchester, desiring to be informed what was the amount of his and the officer's charges, and informing the under-sheriff that a judge's order had been obtained for staying the proceedings. The debt and costs were paid on the 31st October. On the 4th November, the defendant was arrested on the same writ in Hampshire, and gave a bail-bond. A judge's order having been obtained for cancelling the bail-bond, with costs, and those costs having been paid by the plaintiff, he obtained a rule calling upon his attorney to shew cause why he should not repay to him the sum so paid for costs:—Held, that the attorney had not under the circumstances been guilty of such a degree of negligence as to render him liable—at least on motion. Ibid.

COSTS—(*Continued.*)

How affected by Defendant's Discharge under 7 Geo. 4, c. 57.

    6. In trover for goods, the plaintiff recovered a verdict. Before the taxation of costs or the entry of final judgment, the defendant obtained his discharge under the insolvent debtors act, 7 Geo. 4, c. 57, having inserted the amount of the verdict and the supposed amount of costs in his schedule:—Held, that, under the 50th section of the statute, the defendant was discharged from the damages and costs. Goldsmid v. Lewis, 369.

Under 43 Geo. 3, c. 46, s. 3.

    7. On a motion for costs under 43 Geo. 3, c. 46, s. 3, the amount of the verdict is not the criterion by which the discretion of the court is to be guided. Graham v. Beaumont, 287.

Under 9 Geo. 4, c. 22.

    8. The judgment entered up on the speaker's certificate for costs under the 9 Geo. 4, c. 22, s. 63, can only be for the sum mentioned in such certificate, and not for the costs of the motion for leave to enter up the judgment thereon. Ranson v. Dundas, 501.

Under 3 & 4 Will. 4, c. 42, s. 31.

    See Executors and Administrators.

On Nolle Prosequi.

    9. The defendant is entitled to costs under the 3 & 4 Will. 4, c. 42, s. 33, on a nolle prosequi entered as to *part of the sum* claimed in the declaration, whether consisting of one or more counts. Williams v. Sharwood, 761.

Certificate under 43 Eliz. c. 6, s. 2.

    10. In trespass for an assault, battery, and imprisonment of the plaintiff's wife, the defendants pleaded—first, not guilty—secondly, that the individual was not the plaintiff's wife—thirdly, a justification under process issued against her. A verdict was found for the plaintiffs on the first and second pleas, with a farthing damages, and for the defendants on the third:—Held, that it was competent to the judge to certify under the 43 Eliz. c. 6, s. 2, to deprive the plaintiffs of costs, notwithstanding that, on the issue joined on the plea of not guilty, the postea had been entered up generally for the plaintiffs; there being no necessary admission of a battery on the face of the record. Wilson v. Lainson, 676.

COVENANT.

    1. On a mortgage of premises held under a corporation on a renewable lease, the sum originally advanced was 130*l.*; in the mortgage deed there was an absolute covenant on the part of the *mortgagor* to renew, and a power to the mortgagee to renew in case of default by the mortgagor, with a proviso that the money paid by the mortgagor for such renewal should

COVENANT—*(Continued.)*

not be a charge upon the premises to an amount exceeding 70*l.*: the deed was stamped with a 2*l.* stamp, as a deed for securing a sum not exceeding 200*l.*:—Held, sufficient. Doe d. Jarman v. Larder, 407.

In Indenture of Lease, Construction of.

2. A lessee covenanted to preserve and keep, and at the end of the term leave the demised premises in good and tenantable repair:— Held, that this covenant would be satisfied by leaving the premises in such a state as, regard being had to the age of the building at the time of the demise, might be considered tenantable. Stanley v. Towgood, 313.

3. The lessee during the term erected a lean-to, with a roof so ill constructed that it did not exclude the weather, and so left it at the end of the term:—Held, that this was a breach of his covenant to repair. Ibid.

Limitation in Action of.

4. Quære whether the limitation of six years imposed by the 3 & 4 Will. 4, c. 27, s. 42, in actions for " arrears of rent or of interest in respect of any sum of money charged upon or payable out of land," applied to an action of covenant for arrears of rent accruing under an indenture—Tindal, C. J., and Bosanquet, J., accord.—Park, J., and Vaughan, J., dis. Paget v. Foley, 120.

5. The limitation in actions of covenant for arrears of rent under indenture, is governed by the 3 & 4 Will. 4, c. 42, s. 3, this provision being virtually a repeal pro tanto of the former. Ibid.

CRIMINAL CONVERSATION.

1. The court granted a commission for the examination of a witness in an action for criminal conversation with the plaintiff's wife. Norton v. Lord Melbourne, 398.

2. In an action for crim. con., evidence was offered on the part of the *defendant* to shew the affectionate terms upon which he lived with his own wife and family, which, being unobjected to, was admitted, and was observed upon by the judge in his summing up as affording an inference in the defendant's favour:—Held, that this was no mis-direction. Mellin v. Taylor, 513.

3. The jury having found for the defendant, and it appearing from the report of the learned judge who tried the cause that there was a manifest preponderance of evidence the other way, and that he himself was not satisfied with the verdict—The court granted a new trial, on payment of costs. Ibid.

4. The 48 Geo. 3, c. 123, applies to the case of a prisoner in execution for damages not exceeding 20*l.* recovered against him in an action for criminal conversation with the plaintiff's wife. Goodfellow v. Rollings, 319.

ECCLESIASTICAL LEASES—(*Continued.*)

used for the habitation of the vicar, nor having ground to the same belonging above the quantity of ten acres, is a valid lease, notwithstanding the restraining statutes of Elizabeth. Vivian v. Blomberg, 681.

ERECTIONS—See LANDLORD AND TENANT, 3.

EJECTMENT—See LANDLORD AND TENANT, 1, 5, 6.

ESTOPPEL.

W. purchased from the assignees of G. lands which had been devised to G. as freehold, and which were described as freehold in the conveyance to W.:—Held, that W. was not estopped by the deed, as against the widow of G., from shewing that the lands were not freehold, and consequently not chargeable with dower. Gaunt v. Wainmain, 413.

And see EVIDENCE, 8.

EVIDENCE.

Family Papers.

1. In quare impedit to recover the presentation to the church of K., the advowson whereof was claimed to be part of the temporalities of the Bishop of Meath, a case dated the 28th February, 1695, purporting to be a case stated for the opinion of counsel on the part of Anthony Dopping, then Bishop of Meath, wherein it was, among other things, stated, " that, in the year 1637, Ulick, Earle of Clanricarde, granted to Dr. Donnellan, incumbent of Rathweir, his executors and administrators, the next presentation to the rectory and vicarage of Rathweir, dated the 28th March, 1637; that, in 1642, both rectory and vicarage being void by the death of Dr. Donnellan, his widow and executrix presented pro hac vice tantum William Barry to both, who was instituted by the Bishop June 13th, 1642, but not inducted till the 27th of February, 1660; and that by a mandate from the bishop's successor, the bishop that instituted being dead before William Barry's induction." This case was produced by a descendant of Anthony Dopping, into whose possession it had come from the family mansion of the Doppings, where it was found among other papers, the house being occupied by a member of the Dopping family :—Held, that the case, being found in a place in which and under the care of persons with whom papers of Bishop Dopping might naturally and reasonably be expected to be found, was properly receivable in evidence against the bishop's successors:—Held, also, that the grant referred to in the case, being found in the same place and under precisely the same circumstances, was also admissible. The Bishop of Meath v. The Marquis of Winchester, 561.

Declarations.

2. In trover for a watch, the defendant pleaded that it was not the property of the plaintiff. At the trial, the defendant proved that the watch (which had belonged to his father, whose personal representative he was) had been in his, the defendant's, possession for four years

EVIDENCE.

Declarations—(Continued.)

previously to the father's death; and then put in evidence letters of administration :—Held, that declarations of the intestate as to the ownership of the watch, were evidence against the defendant. Smith v. Smith, 352.

As to what may be given in Evidence under the General Issue.

3. Quære whether, in an action of tort against the sheriff, by the assignees of a bankrupt, for seizing goods of the bankrupt, the defendant may, without specially pleading them, give in evidence payments necessarily made by him out of the proceeds, *in reduction of the damages.* Goldsmith v. Raphael, 385.

Parol Explanation of a written Contract.

4. The defendant contracted to sell to the plaintiff " Scott & Co., 75 barrels mess pork, at 53*s*. per barrel." At the trial it was proved that mess pork cured by Scott & Co. obtained in the market a higher price by 2*s*. 6*d*. per barrel than pork cured by any other house; and witnesses (connected with the trade) were allowed to state their construction of the contract :—Held, that, by the terms of the contract, the pork was expressly warranted to be pork *cured* by Scott & Co., and not merely *consigned* by that firm :—Held, also, that the witnesses were properly admitted to explain the meaning of the contract. Powell v. Horton, 110.

Of Enjoyment of a Right of Way.

5. Under a replication (pursuant to the 2 & 3 Will. 4, c. 71, s. 5) denying that the defendant had used the way for forty years as of right and without interruption, the plaintiff is at liberty to shew the character and description of the user and enjoyment of the way during any part of the time; as that it was used by stealth, or in the absence of the occupier of the close and without his knowledge, or that it was merely a precarious enjoyment by leave and license, or any other circumstances which negative that it was an user or enjoyment under a claim of right: the words of the 5th section, " not inconsistent with the simple fact of enjoyment," being referable to the fact of enjoyment as before stated in the act, viz. an enjoyment claimed and exercised " as of right." Beasley v. Clarke, 258.

Generally.

6. In quare impedit, the plaintiff, in his fifth count, alleged that Richard, fourth Earl of Clanricarde, was in 1626 seised in fee of the manor of Rathweir, to which the advowson of the church of Killuean, otherwise Rathweir, was then appendant; and, after deducing title through the successive earls, averred that one H. P. W. and himself became possessed of the advowson in gross for a term of five hundred years; and that, in 1810, H. P. W. died, leaving the plaintiff him surviving, who thereupon " became and was possessed of the advowson for the residue of the term ;" that the church became vacant;

EVIDENCE.

Generally—(Continued.)

and that it then belonged to him to present. The bishop in his fifth plea (averring that he, as Bishop of Meath, was seised of the advowson in gross in right of his see), and the clerk in his eighth plea, traversed this allegation in these terms—" without this that the plaintiff is possessed of the said advowson of the said church of Killucan, otherwise Rathweir, in manner and form as the said plaintiff hath in his said fifth count alleged. The clerk concluded his fifth plea with a special traverse that Michael, the fifth earl, was seised; and his seventh plea with a special traverse that it now belonged to the plaintiff to present:—Held, that a fine stated to have been levied in Trinity Term, 1 Jac. 2, by William, seventh Earl of Clanricarde, and Hester, his wife, to John Brown, Gerard Dillon, and Anthony Mulledy, and the heirs of the said John Brown, of the manors of Rathweir and Killucan, with the appurtenances, and also of the advowson and right of patronage of the parish of Killucan, was not admissible in evidence under the above issues—the traverse being, by the fair and natural import of the plaintiff's allegation, confined to the possession of the plaintiff by reason of the term for years, and of his surviving his co-joint-tenant in the term : and that, admitting that the averment in the declaration would amount to an allegation, that, by reason of all the various steps in the title of the plaintiff which were set out in the fifth count, the plaintiff was possessed of the right to the advowson, and admitting the traverse to be equally extensive, and to put all those steps of the title in issue, still, by analogy to the rules of pleading, the utmost effect that could be given to such a traverse is, that it is a simple denial of the different allegations of the descent and of the other steps of the title, so as thereby to put the plaintiff to the proof of his whole declaration; but that the traverse would not admit of new affirmative evidence on the part of the defendant, taking the title out of the plaintiff, and vesting it in another person. The Bishop of Meath v. The Marquis of Winchester, 561.

7. Held, also, that the legal effect of such fine as a bar to the action of quare impedit, was a matter of law merely, and not of fact; and therefore, if the fine were received in evidence, it ought not to be left to the jury to say whether or not it operated as a bar to the action. Ibid.

8. Held, also, that the fine did not, if properly received in evidence, absolutely of itself bar the action; not on the ground of estoppel, because the parties to the suit did not both claim respectively under the parties to the fine; nor as a conveyance, there being ground for presuming that it was a conveyance by way of mortgage and that the mortgage had been paid off, and there being no evidence of any dealing with the advowson or presentation by the conusees of the fine, or any one claiming under them. Ibid.

HOLIDAYS.

To be kept in the Law Offices.

Whereas by the act of the 3 & 4 Will. 4, c. 42, s. 43, it is enacted, that none of the several days mentioned in the statute passed in the sessions of parliament holden in the 5th and 6th year of the reign of King Edward the 6th, intituled, " An Act for keeping Holidays and Fasting Days," shall be kept or observed in the courts of common law, or in the several offices belonging thereto, except Sundays, the day of the Nativity of our Lord, and the three following days, and Monday and Tuesday in Easter week : it is hereby ordered, that, henceforth, in addition to the said days, the following and none other shall be observed or kept as holidays in the several offices belonging to the said courts, viz. Good Friday and Easter Eve, and such of the five days following as may not fall in the time of term, but not otherwise; the Birthday of our Lord the King, the Birthday of our Lady the Queen, the day of the Accession of our Lord the King, Whit Monday, and Whit Tuesday. Reg. Gen., Hilary Term, 6 Will. 4.

HUSBAND AND WIFE.

After plaint in the county court, the plaintiff (a female) married ; the defendant removed the plaint into this court by a re. fa. lo., and then pleaded in abatement the plaintiff's marriage :—Held, that the plea was good. Hollis v. Freer, 284.

INDEMNITY.

The plaintiff published a libel at the request of the defendant, and on his undertaking to indemnify him against the consequences of such publication, and defended an action brought against him for the libel at the defendant's request and on his promise to indemnify him against the costs of such action :—Held that the consideration was illegal, and the promise void. Shackell v. Rosier, 59.

INSOLVENT DEBTOR.

From what Liabilities discharged under 7 Geo. 4, c. 57.

In trover for goods, the plaintiff recovered a verdict. Before the taxation of costs or the entry of final judgment, the defendant obtained his discharge under the insolvent debtors act, 7 Geo. 4, c. 57, having inserted the amount of the verdict and the supposed amount of costs in his schedule :—Held, that, under the 50th section of the statute, the defendant was discharged from the damages and costs. Goldsmid v. Lewis, 369.

And see PRISONER.

INSURANCE.

Insurable Interest.

One B. contracted to sell to the plaintiff 500 to 700 barrels of oats, to be shipped by J. & Son at Youghall, and to be delivered at Portsmouth. Shortly afterwards, B. wrote to the plaintiff to inform him

INSURANCE.

Insurable Interest—(Continued.)

that room had been engaged in the G. Packet for about 600 barrels on his (the defendant's) account; and on the following day the plaintiff sent instructions to his agent in London to insure 400*l.* on oats per the G. Packet from Youghall to Southampton and Portsmouth. J. & Son shipped 486 barrels of oats on account of the above contract on board the G. Packet bound for Southampton, and transmitted a bill of lading (indorsed generally) to their agent there. The plaintiff insisting upon the vessel going round to Portsmouth, B. sold the oats to a third party. The G. Packet was afterwards lost :—Held, that the plaintiff having at the time of effecting the insurance an insurable interest in the oats shipped on board the G. Packet, no subsequent change in the property in the oats would relieve the underwriters from their liability on the policy. Sparkes v. Marshall, 172.

INSURANCE BROKERS.

Lien of—See LIEN, 1.

INTEREST—See INSURANCE—LIMITATION OF ACTIONS, 1.

INTERPLEADER—See PRACTICE, 29.

IRELAND.

In relation to the rates and duties payable on goods imported into the port of Bristol, by the Bristol Dock act, 48 Geo. 3, c. xi, Ireland is in parts beyond the seas. Battersby v. Kirk, 11.

ISSUE.

Entering—See PRACTICE, 18.

IRREGULARITY—See PRACTICE, 17.

JUDGE'S ORDER.

Setting aside.

The court refused to set aside an order made by a judge at chambers for the issuing of a distringas, though the affidavit on which the order was obtained did not shew that three calls and two appointments had been previously made for the purpose of serving the writ of summons. Gale v. Winkes, 667.

LANDLORD AND TENANT.

Tenancy from Year to Year, how created.

1. The defendant held premises under lease from one F., and assigned the same by way of mortgage to one R. The lease being forfeited, it was agreed between F., R., and the defendant, that a new lease should be granted to R., and that R. should grant an underlease to the defendant. The lease from F. to R. was accordingly executed. The underlease from R. to the defendant was not prepared : but possession was given to the latter, to whom R. said on delivering him the key—" Go on as before ; pay me the money as fast as you can ;

LANDLORD AND TENANT.

Tenancy from Year to Year, how created—(Continued.)

and when you have paid it you shall have your underlease." No rent was ever paid under the tenancy thus created, though a quarter was demanded:—Held, that the defendant did not thereby become tenant from year to year; but a mere tenant by sufferance. Doe d. Rogers v. Pullen, 271.

Covenant to repair.

2. A lessee covenanted to preserve and keep, and at the end of the term leave the demised premises in good and tenantable repair:—Held, that this covenant would be satisfied by leaving the premises in such a state as, regard being had to the age of the building at the time of the demise, might be considered tenantable. Stanley v. Towgood, 313.

Erections.

3. The lessee during the term erected a lean-to, with a roof so ill constructed that it did not exclude the weather, and so left it at the end of the term:—Held, that this was a breach of his covenant to repair. Ibid.

Costs of preparing Lease, by whom defrayed.

4. Pending a negotiation between the defendant and one P. for a lease of certain premises belonging to the latter, P. died. A suit in Chancery was instituted for the purpose of carrying his will into effect. The agreement between the defendant and P. not being in writing, and therefore not capable of being enforced in equity, the plaintiffs, the executors of P., consented to grant the defendant the lease upon the terms originally agreed on by their testator. The lease was accordingly prepared by their solicitor, and executed, but was retained by him, a part of the purchase money remaining unpaid. The defendant afterwards paid the balance of the purchase money, and demanded the lease, but refused to pay the expenses of preparing the same. The plaintiffs having paid such expenses out of a fund in Chancery belonging to them as executors:—Held, that, on proof of the usual course of business in such cases being for the lessor's solicitor to prepare the lease, and for the lessee to pay the expenses, the plaintiffs were entitled to recover the amount as money paid to the defendant's use; and that they need not sue in their representative character. Grissell v. Robinson, 329.

Motion under the 1 Geo. 4, c. 87, s. 1.

5. On a motion by a landlord under the 1 Geo. 4, c. 87, s. 1, the rule should be drawn up on reading the original lease or agreement, or a duplicate or counterpart thereof, and not merely on reading a copy of the lease or agreement. Doe d. Wood v. Roe, 756.

6. Where the agreement in such a case appeared to have been

LANDLORD AND TENANT.

Motion under the 1 *Geo.* 4, *c.* 87, *s.* 1—(*Continued.*)

stamped after the rule nisi was obtained, the court discharged the rule ; holding that, to entitle him to a rule, the landlord must at the time of moving produce a *perfect* lease or agreement. Ibid.

LEASE.

Costs of preparing—See LANDLORD AND TENANT, 4.

LIBEL.

1. The plaintiff published a libel at the request of the defendant, and on his undertaking to indemnify him against the consequences of such publication, and defended an action brought against him for the libel at the defendant's request and on his promise to indemnify him against the costs of such action :—Held, that the consideration was illegal, and the promise void.   Shackell v. Rosier, 59.

2. Where a libel contains several distinct charges, the defendant may justify a part only : but, if the part not justified contain libellous matter, he is liable in damages for that which is so left uncovered by the justification.   Clarke v. Taylor, 95.

3. The defendants published in the Manchester Guardian a statement reflecting upon the plaintiff, and charging him with having been connected with a " grand swindling concern."   The whole of the alleged libel related to transactions said to have taken place at Manchester, with the exception of the following passages: " As we have already stated, Clarke (the plaintiff) had been at Leeds for one or two days before his arrival in this town, and is supposed to have made considerable purchases there.   It is hoped, however, that the detection of his plans in Manchester will be learnt in time to prevent any very serious losses from taking place"— " We have already stated that Clarke referred Mr. N. to a stockbroker in London, a Mr. P., we believe, to whom Mr. N. wrote for information respecting Clarke's circumstances.   He received a reply from Mr. P., stating that Clarke had been introduced to him by a very respectable party ; that he had sold stock for Clarke amounting to 1700*l.*, and had introduced him to Messrs. Jones, Lloyd, & Co., with whom he had opened an account by depositing 2000*l.*   We believe there is not the slightest reason to doubt the truth of Mr. P.'s statement; and the probability is that Clarke had been furnished with the stock and an introduction to the stockbroker, for the purpose of giving colour to his proceedings here and in Yorkshire."   The defendants, in their plea, justified the whole libel with the exception of the paragraphs above set out.   The declaration containing no allegation that the defendants intended to impute to the plaintiff the commission of any fraud at Leeds:—Held, that the passages not justified were not so clearly libellous as to entitle the plaintiff to a verdict thereon. Ibid.

4. A plea of justification in an action for a libel contained three material allegations, as to one of which the jury in the course of the summing up expressed themselves satisfied that the proof failed.   The judge, told

LIEN—(*Continued.*)

for his own individual fees; and also for those of his co-commissioner, provided he be authorised by him to do so. Ex parte Grove, 671.

And see SHIP AND SHIPPING,2.

LIMITATION OF ACTION.

Covenant for Arrears of Rent by Indenture.

1. Quære whether the limitation of six years imposed by the 3 & 4 Will. 4, c. 27, s. 42, in actions for "arrears of rent or of interest in respect of any sum of money charged upon or payable out of land," applied to an action of covenant for arrears of rent accruing under an indenture—Tindal, C. J., and Bosanquet, J., accord.—Park, J., and Vaughan, J., dis. Paget v. Foley, 120.

2. The limitation in actions of covenant for arrears of rent under indenture, is governed by the 3 & 4 Will. 4, c. 42, s. 3, this provision being virtually a repeal pro tanto of the former. Ibid.

21 *Jac.* 1, *c.* 16.

3. To a declaration on a promissory note made in 1819 (about sixteen years before the commencement of the suit), payable on demand, with interest for the same from the day of the date of the note—averring that defendant " did not pay the amount of the note and interest, or any part thereof, &c., except interest on the said note from the day of the date of the said note up to a certain day within six years next before the commencement of the suit"—the defendant pleaded that the cause of action did not nor did any part thereof accrue at any time within six years next before the commencement of the suit:—Held, on special demurrer, that the plea was a sufficient answer to the action; the allegation as to the payment of interest being prematurely introduced into the declaration, and at most amounting to matter of evidence. Hollis v. Palmer, 265.

9 *Geo.* 4, *c.* 14, *s.* 1.

4. The written acknowledgment required by the 9 Geo. 4, c. 14, s. 1, to take a case out of the statute of limitations, must bear the actual signature of *the party to be charged thereby :* the signature of an agent will not suffice. Hyde v. Johnson, 289.

LORDS' ACT.

In Trinity Term the defendant was brought up at the instance of the plaintiff under the compulsory clauses of the lords' act, and, claiming his sixty days, was remanded. The sixty days expired in June; and in August the defendant had been twelve months in execution in the action. On the first day of the following term, the defendant applied for his discharge under the 48 Geo. 3, c. 123, the debt being less than 20*l.* The notice required by the 90th rule of Hilary Term, 2 Will. 4, not having been given, the court granted only a rule nisi. On the next day, the prisoner was brought up at the suit of the creditor under the lords' act.

LORDS' ACT—(*Continued.*)

The prisoner was called upon by the court to deliver in a schedule of his effects in pursuance of the act; which he declined to do:—Held, that, notwithstanding such refusal, he was entitled to his discharge under the 48 Geo. 3, c. 123.   Davis v. Curtis, 321.

MASTER AND SERVANT.

Authority.

1. The only ground upon which the authority of a servant is traverseable in an action of trespass, is, the protection of the person or property of a party from the officious and wanton interference of a stranger, where the principal might have been willing to waive his right.   Dobree v. Napier, 201.

2. Where the act of the principal is lawful in the country where it is done, and the authority under which such act is done is complete, binding, and unquestionable there, the servant who does the act cannot be made responsible in the courts of this country (of which he is a subject) for the consequences of such act, merely by reason of a personal disability imposed by the law of this country upon him for contracting such engagement.   Ibid.

Dissolution of Contract of Hiring.

3. The plaintiff, a domestic servant, entered into the defendant's service on the 19th November.   On the 15th January, her mistress caused her to be taken before a magistrate on a charge of stealing some small articles of plate : the magistrate remanded her till the 20th, when she was again brought up, and discharged.   On the 22nd, the plaintiff went to demand her clothes and wages, including 1*l.* 1*s.* in lieu of a month's warning.   The defendant tendered 2*l.* 2*s.* for the two months' actual service, but refused to pay the additional guinea:—Held, that, inasmuch as the placing the plaintiff in custody on a charge that was afterwards abandoned was no dissolution of the contract of hiring, the plaintiff was under the circumstances entitled to wages for the third month, which had been entered upon ; and that the whole might be recovered under the common count for work and labour.   Smith v. Kingsford, 279.

MEMBER OF PARLIAMENT—See PARLIAMENT.

MESSUAGE.

An allegation that the plaintiff was possessed of a messuage and premises, is supported by proof of his occupation of *a part* of a house; the word "messuage" importing no more than "dwelling-house."   Fenn v. Grafton, 56.

MISDIRECTION.

In an action for crim. con., evidence was offered on the part of the *defendant* to shew the affectionate terms upon which he lived with his own

MISDIRECTION—(*Continued.*)

wife and family, which, being unobjected to, was admitted, and was observed upon by the judge in his summing up as affording an inference in the defendant's favour:—Held, that this was no misdirection. Mellin v. Taylor, 513.

MONITION—See Ecclesiastical Law.

NEGLIGENCE—See Attorney, 15, 16—Bills of Exchange and Promissory Notes—Commissioners of Sewers.

NEW TRIAL.

1. After verdict for the plaintiff in debt on bond (the defendant not appearing at the trial), the court granted a new trial on the ground that in the issue delivered the pleas were not dated, pursuant to the rule of Hilary Term, 4 Will. 4. Worthington v. Wigley, 555.

2. In an action for crim. con., the jury having found for the defendant, and it appearing from the report of the learned judge who tried the cause that there was a manifest preponderance of evidence the other way, and that he himself was not satisfied with the verdict—The court granted a new trial, on payment of costs. Mellin v. Taylor, 513.

NOLLE PROSEQUI—See Costs, 9.

NOTICE OF DECLARATION—See Practice, 10.

NOTICE TO PLEAD—See Practice, 9.

OUTLAWRY.

Mode of proceeding to.

1. The summons and distringas given by the statute 2 Will. 4, c. 39, are not the only mode of proceeding to outlawry. Houlditch v. Swinfen, 170.

Reversal of.

2. A motion to reverse an outlawry cannot be entertained, unless it expressly appear by the affidavits that the attorney making the application is duly authorized by the outlaw. Id. 169.

3. A bailable capias, upon which the defendant was outlawed, having issued upon a defective affidavit—The court, on motion, reversed the outlawry, on payment of costs, the defendant entering a common appearance. Id. 170.

OXFORD.

The municipal corporation act, 5 & 6 Will. 4, c. 76, s. 61, has effected no change in the mode of executing process from the superior courts in the city of Oxford; they are still to be executed by the sheriff *of the county.* Grainger v. Taunton, 393.

OYER.

A demand of oyer must correctly describe the parties to the cause. Poole v. Coates, 768.

PARLIAMENT.

1. A petition presented to the house of commons, complaining of an undue return, and charging the sitting members with having been guilty of bribery by themselves and their agents, incidentally complained also of misconduct and partiality in the returning officers; but, in its prayer, the petition merely called upon the house to determine the validity of the election, and was altogether silent as to any claim for redress against the returning officers on the ground of their alleged misconduct:—Held, that the returning officers, notwithstanding they appeared before the committee in opposition to the petition, were not to be considered as *parties* entitled to assist in striking the committee, under the 9 Geo. 4, c. 22, s. 36—the necessary construction of that clause being, that it does not comprehend the case where the sitting members are called upon to appear, do actually appear at the bar of the house, and are the parties opposing the petition; and, consequently, that the want of a notice to the returning officers, and an order upon them to attend the house at the striking of the committee, did not invalidate the appointment of such committee. Ranson v. Dundas, 429.

2. The petition was subscribed by three individuals *in the same interest*, and the recognizance taken in pursuance of the 5th section of the statute, and in the form given in the schedule, was entered into by *one* of them only, and was conditioned for payment of the costs of witnesses summoned on his behalf (being altogether silent as to the other two petitioners), and also for the costs and expenses of the party who should appear *before the house* in opposition to the petition, in the event of its being unsuccessful: Held, sufficient. Ibid.

3. The report of the committee failing to decide anything with respect to the charge, or the opposition to the charge, made against the returning officers, being frivolous or vexatious:—Held, that it was not therefore void as against the sitting members. Ibid.

4. The committee having reported the opposition of the sitting members to the petition to be frivolous and vexatious, a request was made to the speaker to refer the bill of costs of the petitioners to taxation. The speaker thereupon directed two examiners appointed by him to tax the costs, and the examiners reported that the costs and expenses allowed by them on such taxation amounted to a certain sum, and that the sitting members, whose opposition to the petition appeared to the committee to be frivolous and vexatious, were liable to pay the same:—Held, that the speaker's certificate being, by the 60th section of the statute, declared to be conclusive evidence of the amount of the demand, in all cases and for all purposes whatsoever, the court had no power to try the propriety of the examiners' allowance of costs, or the principle upon which it was conducted. Ibid.

5. Judgment having been given for the plaintiffs in an action of debt upon the speaker's certificate, under the 9 Geo. 4, c. 22, s. 63, for the costs therein mentioned, the court refused to allow a suggestion to be entered

PARLIAMENT—(*Continued.*)

on the record of the circumstances upon which the judgment was founded. Id. 497.

6. The judgment entered up on the speaker's certificate for costs under the 9 Geo. 4, c. 22, s. 63, can only be for the sum mentioned in such certificate, and not for the costs of the motion for leave to enter up the judgment thereon. Id. 501.

PARTICULARS OF DEMAND—See Practice, 6, 7.

PAYMENT.

Plea of.

1. A plea of part payment, or the delivery of bills, in satisfaction of a bond, after the day on which the money was by the condition made payable, is bad on general demurrer. Worthington v. Wigley, 558.

Evidence of.

2. Quære whether, in an action of tort against the sheriff, by the assignees of a bankrupt, for seizing goods of the bankrupt, the defendant may, without specially pleading them, give in evidence payments necessarily made by him out of the proceeds, *in reduction of the damages.* Goldsmid v. Raphael, 385.

Protected Payments—See Bankrupt, 1.

PLEADING.

Declarations.

Allegation of Promise.

1. In indebitatus assumpsit the day of the promise alleged in the declaration is immaterial; and therefore it is no ground for arresting the judgment, that the promise is stated to have been made at a day subsequent to the issuing of the writ; otherwise, where the day is material. Arnall v. Arnall, 547.

Pleas in Abatement.

Marriage of Plaintiff.

2. After plaint in the county court, the plaintiff (a female) married; the defendant removed the plaint into this court by re. fa. lo., and then pleaded in abatement the plaintiff's marriage :—Held, that the plea was good. Hollis v. Freer, 284.

Pleas in Bar.

3. In trespass for seizing and converting the plaintiff's ship, the defendant pleaded—first, that he was retained in the service of the Queen of Portugal, being at peace with our sovereign; that enemies were waging war against her by sea and land; that the defendant by her command established and proclaimed an effective blockade along the coast of Portugal; that the plaintiff's ship broke the blockade; and that thereupon the defendant, as the servant and by the command

PLEADING.

Pleas in Bar—(Continued.)

of the Queen of Portugal, seized the ship—secondly, that the plaintiff's ship, laden with warlike stores, was on the high seas aiding and assisting the queen's enemies, wherefore the defendant, as the servant and by the command of the queen, seized her—thirdly, that the vessel was in a port in Portugal, and had just discharged a cargo there destined for the use of the queen's enemies, whereupon the defendant, as the servant and by the command of the queen, seized her as lawful prize, and that she was in due course and form of law condemned as lawful prize by a court of competent jurisdiction in that behalf. To these pleas the plaintiffs replied that they and the defendant were natural-born subjects of the kingdom of England; that the vessel in question was a British registered vessel; and that the defendant, in breach of the foreign enlistment act, 59 Geo. 3, c. 69, s. 2, entered the service of the Queen of Portugal, and whilst in such service committed the trespass complained of:—Held, that, notwithstanding the statute, the authority of the Queen of Portugal was a justification of the seizure—whether " as prize," for breaking the blockade, or for supplying warlike stores to her enemies ; and therefore that the pleas were a sufficient bar to the plaintiff's right of action. Dobree v. Napier, 201.

4. In trespass for seizing and converting the plaintiffs' ship the defendant pleaded that the plaintiffs, contrary to 59 Geo. 3, c. 69, s. 7, were, without the license or consent of his majesty, knowingly concerned in equipping the vessel, with intent that the same should be employed in the service of a foreign prince as a transport and store-ship ; and that, by force of the statute, the vessel became forfeited to his majesty. On special demurrer, for that the plea did not allege that the vessel was ever seized or condemned as forfeited, or that the defendant had any authority from his majesty to seize her :—Held, that the plea was insufficient, for want of the allegation of authority. Ibid.

5. To an action for a breach of promise of marriage, the defendant pleaded—first, that, after the making of the promise, the defendant discovered that the plaintiff was an immodest, lewd, unchaste, and immoral person, and, being sole and unmarried, had had carnal intercourse with one H. P.—and secondly, that, after the making of the promise, the defendant had notice that the plaintiff, being so sole and unmarried, had committed fornication with some person or persons to defendant unknown, and was pregnant with a child likely to be born a bastard (averring the fact to be so), of which he had no notice or knowledge at the time of making the promise:—Held, sufficient. Young v. Murphy, 379.

PLEADING.

Pleas in Bar—(Continued.)

6. In case for negligently navigating a vessel, whereby the plaintiffs' bridge was damaged, the defendants pleaded that the plaintiffs had, wrongfully, and without the knowledge of the defendants, contracted and narrowed the channel, and that, in consequence of such contraction of the waterway, and the increased rapidity of the current thereby occasioned, and without the default of the defendants, the vessel was driven against the bridge; *without this that the vessel of the defendants ran foul of and struck against the bridge by and through the carelessness and negligence of the defendants as in the declaration alleged*—concluding to the country:—Held, that, under this plea, it was competent to the defendants to offer evidence to disprove the carelessness charged in the declaration, notwithstanding they had failed in establishing the preceding matter, or inducement in the plea, as to the alleged obstruction by the plaintiffs. Cross Keys Bridge Co. v. Rawlings, 400.

7. To debt on bond the defendant pleaded, that the bond was given in pursuance of a corrupt and illegal agreement between the obligee and obligor that the obligee should take the obligor's son as his apprentice to learn the art, mystery, and profession of a surgeon, *apothecary*, and man-midwife, *for the term of two years only*, but that in the articles it should be made to appear that the son had been articled for the full term of five years—in order that by such corrupt contrivance the parties might fraudulently and illegally procure the obligor's son to be admitted to examination for the purpose of practising as an *apothecary* upon serving an apprenticeship for two years, instead of an apprenticeship for five years, as required by the 55 Geo. 3, c. 194, s. 15:—Held, that the bond was void, and the plea a sufficient answer to the action. Prole v. Wiggins, 601.

Non assumpsit infra sex Annos.

8. To a declaration on a promissory note made in 1819 (about sixteen years before the commencement of the suit), payable on demand, with interest for the same from the day of the date of the note—averring that defendant "did not pay the amount of the note and interest, or any part thereof, &c., except interest on the said note from the day of the date of the said note up to a certain day within six years next before the commencement of the suit"—the defendant pleaded that the cause of action did not nor did any part thereof accrue at any time within six years next before the commencement of the suit:—Held, on special demurrer, that the plea was a sufficient answer to the action; the allegation as to the payment of interest being prematurely introduced into the declaration, and at most amounting to matter of evidence. Hollis v. Palmer, 265.

PLEADING.

Pleas in Bar—(Continued.)

Argumentative and amounting to the General Issue.

9. In assumpsit for money paid to the use of the defendants, they pleaded specially circumstances shewing that the policy of insurance in respect of which the payments were made had been so framed as to be utterly unavailing. Upon special demurrer, on the ground, amongst others, that the plea was argumentative and amounted to the general issue—The court inclined to think the plea good, but allowed the plaintiff to withdraw his demurrer and reply de novo, without costs. Cole v. Le Souef, 188.

Solvit post Diem.

10. A plea of part payment, or the delivery of bills, in satisfaction of a bond, after the day on which the money was by the condition made payable, is bad on general demurrer. Worthington v. Wigley, 558.

Right of Common.

11. In trespass quare clausum fregit, the defendant pleaded an uninterrupted enjoyment, under a claim of right, of common over the locus in quo "for the full period of thirty years before the commencement of the suit:—Held, sufficient, without alleging the enjoyment to have been for thirty years *next* before the commencement of the suit. Jones v. Price, 376.

Date of Pleadings, Effect of Absence of.

12. After verdict for the plaintiff in debt on bond (the defendant not appearing at the trial), the court granted a new trial on the ground that in the issue delivered the pleas were not dated, pursuant to the rule of Hilary Term, 4 Will. 4. Worthington v. Wigley, 555.

What may be given in Evidence under Non assumpsit.

13. In assumpsit for money lent, &c., the defendant pleaded—first, non assumpsit—secondly, that the causes of action arose out of disbursements made for and on account of a vessel belonging to the defendant, and that the master made and sealed a bottomry bond, which was accepted and received by the plaintiff in satisfaction of the promises in the declaration mentioned, &c. The plaintiff replied that he did not accept or receive the bond in satisfaction of the promises modo et forma:—Held, that it was not competent to the defendant under non assumpsit to give in evidence the making and delivery of the bond. Weston v. Foster, 155.

*Time for Pleading—*See PRACTICE, 11, 12.

*Rule to Plead—*See PRACTICE, 10.

And see CASE, 1, 2, 4, 5, 6, 7—SLANDER OF TITLE, 2, 3.

PRACTICE.

Process.

Indorsement on Writ of Distringas.

1. A distringas to compel appearance, under the 2 Will. 4, c. 39, s. 3, must be indorsed with the amount of the debt and costs. Gale v. Winkes, 667.

2. The court refused to set aside an order made by a judge at chambers for the issuing of a distringas, though the affidavit on which the order was obtained did not shew that three calls and two appointments had been previously made for the purpose of serving the writ of summons. Ibid.

Execution of.

3. The municipal corporation act, 5 & 6 Will. 4, c. 76, s. 61, has effected no change in the mode of executing process from the superior courts in the city of Oxford : they are still to be executed by the sheriff *of the county.* Grainger v. Taunton, 393.

Alias or Pluries Writ.

4. It is not essential to the validity of an alias or pluries that the writ of summons or capias should be previously returned, except where the object is to save the statute of limitations, or where the capias is made the foundation of proceedings to outlawry. Gregory v. Des Anges, 584.

Bail, Sufficiency of.

5. Where the regular notice of bail has been given, the court will, under special circumstances, allow time for inquiry into their sufficiency, on payment of costs. Dicas v. Smith, 600.

Particulars of Demand.

6. Where the plaintiff declares only on a bill of exchange, the defendant is not, except under very special circumstances, entitled to particulars of demand. Brooks v. Farlar, 654.

7. In an action on the case against an attorney for negligence and want of skill in preparing an assignment of a term from the plaintiff to a third person, per quod the latter recovered damages against the plaintiff, the court refused to compel the plaintiff to deliver particulars. Stannard v. Ullithorne, 771.

Demand of Oyer.

8. A demand of oyer must correctly describe the parties to the cause. Poole v. Coates, 768.

Notice to plead.

9. A notice to plead need not be dated: consequently it will not be vitiated by an erroneous date. Wyatt v. Macdonald, 768.

Rule to plead.

10. Where a declaration is filed, the rule to plead must not be left at the office until notice of the filing of the declaration has been duly

PRACTICE.

Rule to plead—(Continued.)

served; the time for pleading only beginning to reckon from the time of service of the notice of declaration. Bennett v. Smith, 673.

Time for pleading.

11. The declaration was delivered on the 28th October, with notice to plead in four days. On the 29th the defendant took out a summons for four days' *further* time to plead. An order was thereupon drawn up by consent on the 29th for "four days' time to plead:"— Held, that the time was to be reckoned from the date of the order, and not from the expiration of the original four days; and consequently that a judgment signed on the 3rd November was regular. Lane v. Parsons, 652.

12. Where a declaration is filed, the rule to plead must not be left at the office until notice of the filing of the declaration has been duly served; the time for pleading only beginning to reckon from the time of service of the notice of declaration. Bennett v. Smith, 673.

Pleading several Matters.

13. Semble, that no rule to plead several matters is necessary in the case of pleas added under a judge's order. Monck v. Shenstone, 661.

14. The plaintiff cannot object to the allowance of the defendant's pleas after the taxation of costs under the 3 & 4 Will. 4, c. 42, s. 33. Williams v. Sharwood, 761.

15. In an action against an attorney for negligence in procuring insufficient security upon an advance of money, per quod the plaintiff lost the money—the court allowed the defendant to plead in addition to non assumpsit and several other pleas, that the loss was not the result of the alleged negligence. Wright v. Newton, 595.

Marking Points for Argument on Special Cases or Demurrers.

16. On demurrer to a replication, the court will not permit the plaintiff to attack the defendant's plea, unless the point has been marked for argument pursuant to the rule of Hilary Term, 4 Will. 4, s. 2. Bayley v. Homan, 384.

Setting aside and staying Proceedings.

17. A defect in the copy delivered to a defendant at the time of execution of process under the 2 Will. 4, c. 39, s. 4, is not an irregularity that can be taken advantage of on a summons or motion to set aside the bail-bond for irregularity. Yeates v. Chapman, 648.

And see JUDGE'S ORDER.

Entering Issue.

18. It seems, that, since the new rules (Hilary Term, 4 Will. 4, s. 15), the plaintiff cannot be ruled to enter the issue. Wilks v. Dodd, 769.

PRACTICE—(*Continued.*)

Entering Suggestion.

19. Judgment having been given for the plaintiffs in an action of debt upon the speaker's certificate under the 9 Geo. 4, c. 22, s. 63, for the costs therein mentioned, the court refused to allow a suggestion to be entered on the record of the circumstances upon which the judgment was founded. Ranson v. Dundas, 497.

20. The court refused to enter the judgment as of a past term, on a suggestion that one of the plaintiffs had died pending the rule. Id. 500.

Entering Verdict under the Rule of Hilary Term, 4 Will. 4, Trespass, V., ss. 4—6.

21. In trespass, the defendant in his third plea justified under an alleged right of way with horses, carts, and carriages, for the purpose of fetching goods and water from a navigable river. The jury affirmed the right set up so far as it related to the fetching of water, but negatived it as to the rest. The court directed the verdict to be entered distributively (for the plaintiff as to the goods, for the defendant as to the water,) under the rules of Hilary Term, 4 Will. 4, *Trespass*, V., ss. 4—6. Knight v. Moore, 326.

Setting aside Verdict.

22. A plea of justification in an action for a libel contained three material allegations, as to one of which the jury in the course of the summing up expressed themselves satisfied that the proof failed. The judge told them, that, to warrant a finding in favour of the defendant, they must be satisfied that all three of the allegations were substantially made out. The jury, after two hours' deliberation, returned a verdict for the defendant upon that plea:—The court refused to set it aside. Napier v. Daniell, 417.

Motion in Arrest of Judgment, when to be made.

23. Where a cause is tried in vacation, a motion in arrest of judgment, in this court, must, pursuant to the old practice, be made within the first four days of the ensuing term. Weston v. Foster, 164.

24. Semble, that the Reg. Gen., Hilary, 2 Will. 4, s. 65, as to motions in arrest of judgment, does not apply to the case of a trial out of term. Ibid.

Signing Judgment.

25. The court will permit judgment to be signed on a sqi. fa. after eight days from the return (r. 81, H. T., 4 Will. 4), where the defendant resides abroad, he having had *reasonable notice of the proceeding.* Weatherhead v. Landles, 406.

PRACTICE—*Continued.*)

Execution.

26. A rule nisi having been granted to reduce the damages, the court allowed the plaintiff to enter up judgment and issue execution for that part of the damages which was unobjected to, on his electing to forego the rest. Hellings v. Young; 770.

Charging Plaintiff in Execution.

27. In order to render a party liable to be brought up by writ of habeas corpus ad satisfaciendum to be charged in execution, it is not necessary that he should be in custody *in the particular suit :* and such writ may issue at the suit of a defendant to charge the plaintiff in execution for the costs of a nonsuit. Furnival v. Stringer, 551.

Entering Satisfaction on the Roll.

28. The court refused to order satisfaction to be entered upon the roll in an action for breach of promise of marriage, without a warrant of attorney from the plaintiff, notwithstanding a judge's order had been obtained for the purpose by consent. Wood v. Hurd, 368.

Motions under the Interpleader Act, 1 & 2 *Will.* 4, c. 58.

29. Practice under the interpleader act, where the parties called upon by a rule obtained on behalf of the sheriff decline to appear. Eveleigh v. Salsbury, 674.

Motions under the 1 *Geo,* 4, c. 87, s. 1.

30. On a motion by a landlord under the 1 Geo. 4, c. 87, s. 1, the rule should be drawn up on reading the original lease or agreement, or a duplicate or counterpart thereof, and not merely on reading a copy of the lease or agreement. Doe d. Wood v. Roe, 756.

31. Where the agreement in such a case appeared to have been stamped after the rule nisi was obtained, the court discharged the rule; holding that, to entitle him to a rule, the landlord must at the time of moving produce a *perfect* lease or agreement. Ibid.

Summary Proceedings.

32. This court cannot exercise a summary jurisdiction over a party who is not one of its own officers, although the matter be pending here. Sharp v. Hawker, 396.

And see SET-OFF.

PREDECESSORS.

"Progenitors" and "predecessors," in some cases synonymous. The Bishop of Meath v. The Marquis of Winchester, 583.

PRISONER.

Discharge of under 48 *Geo.* 3, c. 123.

1. In Trinity Term, the defendant was brought up at the instance of the plaintiff under the compulsory clauses of the lords' act, and,

PRISONER.

Discharge of under 48 *Geo.* 3, *c.* 123—(*Continued.*)

claiming his sixty days, was remanded. The sixty days expired in June; and in August. the defendant had been twelve months in execution in the action. On the first day of the following term, the defendant applied for his discharge under the 48 Geo. 3, c. 123, the debt being less than 20*l.* The notice required by the 90th rule of Hilary Term, 2 Will. 4, not having been given, the court granted only a rule nisi. On the next day the prisoner was brought up at the suit of the creditor under the lords' act. The prisoner was called upon by the court to deliver in a schedule of his effects in pursuance of the act; which he declined to do :—Held, that, notwithstanding such refusal, he was entitled to his discharge under the 48 Geo. 3, c. 123. Davis v. Curtis, 321.

2. The 48 Geo. 3, c. 123, applies to the case of a prisoner in execution for damages not exceeding 20*l.*, recovered against him in an action for criminal conversation with the plaintiff's wife. Goodfellow v. Rollings, 319.

PRIZE.

In trespass for seizing and converting the plaintiffs' ship, the defendant pleaded that the plaintiffs, contrary to the 59 Geo. 3, c. 69, s. 7, were, without the license or consent of his majesty, knowingly concerned in equipping the vessel, with intent that the same should be employed in the service of a foreign prince as a transport and store-ship ; and that, by force of the statute, the vessel became forfeited to his majesty. On special demurrer, for that the plea did not allege that the vessel was ever seized or condemned as forfeited, or that the defendant had any authority from his majesty to seize her :—Held, that the plea was insufficient, for want of the allegation of authority. Dobree v. Napier, 204.

And see SHIP AND SHIPPING, 1.

PROGENITORS.

" Progenitors" and " predecessors," in some cases synonymous. The Bishop of Meath v. the Marquis of Winchester, 583.

PROMISSORY NOTES—See BILLS OF EXCHANGE AND PROMISSORY NOTES.

PROTECTED PAYMENTS—See BANKRUPT, 1.

PUBLIC OFFICERS—See COMMISSIONERS OF SEWERS.

QUARE IMPEDIT—See EVIDENCE, 1, 6, 7, 8.

RECOVERY—See FINES AND RECOVERIES.

REFERENCE—See AWARD.

REGULÆ GENERALES.

Rules to return Writs.

From and after the last day of this term, all rules upon sheriffs, other than the sheriffs of London and Middlesex, to return writs

REGULÆ GENERALES.

Rules to return Writs—(Continued.)

either of mesne or final process, and rules to bring in the bodies of defendants, be eight day rules, instead of six day rules. Michaelmas Term, 7 Will. 4, 776.

And see ATTORNEY, 1—11—HOLLIDAYS.

REPAIRS—See LANDLORD AND TENANT, 2, 3.

RESTRAINT OF TRADE.

1. By an award the defendants were directed to pay a certain sum to the plaintiffs and to sign a memorandum containing an engagement on the part of the defendants to abstain for a certain time from pirating the plaintiffs' patterns.—Quære whether such an engagement amounts to a contract in restraint of trade? Stuart v. Nicholson, 536.

RETURN OF WRIT.

It is not essential to the validity of an alias or pluries that the writ of summons or capias should be previously returned, except where the object is to save the statute of limitations, or where the capias is made the foundation of proceedings to outlawry. Gregory v. Des Anges, 534.

RETURNING OFFICER—See PARLIAMENT, 1, 3.

RIGHT OF COMMON—See COMMON.

RIGHT OF WAY.

1. In trespass, the defendant in his third plea justified under an alleged right of way with horses, carts, and carriages, for the purpose of fetching goods and water from a navigable river. The jury affirmed the right set up so far as it related to the fetching of water, but negatived it as to the rest:—The court directed the verdict to be entered distributively (for the plaintiff as to the goods, for the defendant as to the water), under the rules of Hilary Term, 4 Will. 4, *Trespass,* V., ss. 4—6. Knight v. Woore, 326.

2. Under a replication (pursuant to the 2 & 3 Will. 4, c. 71, s. 5) denying that the defendant had used the way for forty years as of right and without interruption, the plaintiff is at liberty to shew the character and description of the user and enjoyment of the way during any part of the time; as that it was used by stealth, or in the absence of the occupier of the close and without his knowledge, or that it was merely a precarious enjoyment by leave and license, or any other circumstances which negative that it was an user or enjoyment under a claim of right: the words of the 5th section, "not inconsistent with the simple fact of enjoyment," being referable to the fact of enjoyment as before stated in the act, viz. an enjoyment claimed and exercised " as of right." Beasley v. Clarke, 258.

RULE OF COURT.

How drawn up.

On a motion by a landlord under the 1 Geo. 4, c. 87, s. 1, the rule should be drawn up on reading the original lease or agree-

RULE OF COURT.

How drawn up—Continued.

ment, or a duplicate or counterpart thereof, and not merely on reading a copy of the lease or agreement. Doe d. Wood v. Roe, 756.

And See ATTORNEY, 1—11—HOLIDAYS—REGULÆ GENERALES.

RULE TO PLEAD—See PRACTICE, 10.

SALE.

Construction of Contract.

1. The defendant contracted to sell to the plaintiff "Scott & Co., 75 barrels mess pork, at 53s. per barrel." At the trial it was proved that mess pork cured by Scott & Co. obtained in the market a higher price by 2s. 6d. per barrel than pork cured by any other house; and witnesses (connected with the trade) were allowed to state their construction of the contract:—Held, that, by the terms of the contract, the pork was expressly warranted to be pork *cured* by Scott & Co., and not merely *consigned* by that firm:—Held, also, that the witnesses were properly admitted to explain the meaning of the contract. Powell v. Horton, 110.

2. One B. contracted to sell to the plaintiff 500 to 700 barrels of oats, to be shipped by J. & Son at Youghall, and to be delivered at Portsmouth. Shortly afterwards, B. wrote to the plaintiff to inform him that room had been engaged in the G. Packet for about 600 barrels on his (the defendant's) account; and on the following day the plaintiff sent instructions to his agent in London to insure 400l. on oats per the G. Packet from Youghall to Southampton and Portsmouth. J. & Son shipped 486 barrels of oats on account of the above contract on board the G. Packet bound for Southampton, and transmitted a bill of lading (indorsed generally) to their agent there. The plaintiff insisting upon the vessel going round to Portsmouth, B. sold the oats to a third party. The G. Packet was afterwards lost:—Held, that the plaintiff having at the time of effecting the insurance an insurable interest in the oats shipped on board the G. Packet, no subsequent change in the property in the oats would relieve the underwriters from their liability on the policy. Sparkes v. Marshall, 172.

By Auction.

3. A contract of purchase (of leasehold property sold by auction) written on the back of the particulars of sale (which contains the name of the owner of the property), and signed by the *purchaser* only, is a sufficient note or memorandum of the *agreement* between the parties to satisfy the 4th section of the statute of frauds: the *vendor's* signature is not essential. Laythoarp v. Bryant, 238.

SATISFACTION.

Entering Satisfaction on the Roll—See PRACTICE, 28.

SCIRE FACIAS.

Signing Judgment on.

The court will permit judgment to be signed on a sci. fa. after eight days from the return (r. 81, H. T., 2 Will. 4), where the defendant resides abroad, he having had *reasonable notice of the proceeding.* Weatherhead v. Landles, 406.

SEQUESTRATION—See Ecclesiastical Law.

SET-OFF.

On a reference to arbitration of an action of ejectment and all matters in difference between the parties, the arbitrator directed that a sum of 50l. should be paid by the lessor of the plaintiff to the defendants by way of compensation for certain buildings erected by them, and that a verdict should be entered for the former. On motion, the court directed the sum awarded to the defendants to be set off against the costs of the lessor of the plaintiff, saving the lien of their attorney. Doe d. Swinton v. Sinclair, 42.

SHERIFF.

Liability for Acts of Bailiff's Assistant.

A ca. sa. against one G. was delivered to the sheriff, who thereupon made his warrant commanding one W. a bailiff to arrest G. The bailiff W. and his assistant R. proceeded to execute the warrant. The latter, in the absence of the former, arrested G., and, in order to secure him till he could procure the attendance of W. who had the warrant in his possession, placed him in the custody of a policeman on a false charge of felony, and caused him to be conveyed to a police-station. R. then fetched W., who, with full knowledge of the illegal manner in which the caption had been effected, took G. on the warrant, and carried him to prison :—Held, that these facts were sufficient to establish the affirmative of an issue as to whether or not W. illegally seized and imprisoned G. Humphrey v. Mitchell, 44.

And see Practice, 29.

SHIP AND SHIPPING.

1. In trespass for seizing and converting the plaintiffs' ship, the defendant pleaded—first, that he was retained in the service of the Queen of Portugal, being at peace with our sovereign ; that enemies were waging war against her by sea and land; that the defendant by her command established and proclaimed an effective blockade along the coast of Portugal ; that the plaintiffs' ship broke the blockade; and that thereupon the defendant, as the servant and by the command of the Queen of Portugal, seized the ship—secondly, that the plaintiffs' ship, laden with warlike stores, was on the high seas aiding and assisting the queen's enemies, wherefore the defendant, as the servant and by the command of the queen, seized her—thirdly, that the vessel was in a port in Portugal, and had just discharged a cargo there destined for the use of the queen's enemies, whereupon the defendant, as the servant and by the command of

SHIP AND SHIPPING—(*Continued.*)

the queen, seized her as lawful prize, and that she was in due course and forth of law condemned as lawful prize by a court of competent jurisdiction in that behalf. To these pleas the plaintiffs replied that they and the defendant were natural-born subjects of the kingdom of England; that the vessel in question was a British registered vessel; and that the defendant, in breach of the foreign enlistment act, 59 Geo. 3, c. 69, s. 2, entered the service of the Queen of Portugal, and whilst in such service committed the trespass complained of:—Held, that, notwithstanding the statute, the authority of the Queen of Portugal was a justification of the seizure— whether " as prize," for breaking the blockade, or for supplying warlike stores to her enemies; and therefore that the pleas were a sufficient bar to the plaintiffs' right of action. Dobree v. Napier, 201.

Construction of Charterparty.

2. The plaintiff, owner of the ship Hero, entered into a charter- party with one J. B. G., a merchant in London, for a voyage from London to Calcutta and back, covenanting, amongst other things, to take in a cargo in London, and proceed therewith to Calcutta, receive on board a homeward cargo, and deliver the same agreeably to bills of lading; the ship *to take her regular turn in the East India Docks for the purpose of delivering her cargo;* the freighter to pay a certain sum for every passenger; and all the cabins except one for the use of the captain to be at the disposal and for the benefit of the freighter, who was to appoint a supercargo, not only to act as super- cargo, but to take upon him the authority of the captain in the stow- age of the cargo, which was to be done under his entire direction, but he was not in any other particular to interfere with the duties of the captain. And the freighter, J. B. G., covenanted to load the ship, and to pay for the freight or hire of the ship for the voyage, at the rate of 14*l.* per ton register tonnage, with primage, to be paid as fol- lows—500*l.* in cash at the expiration of six months from the date of the charterparty, a moiety of the remainder by bills at two months after date from *the day of the ship's arrival in the Thames* on her return voyage, and *and the residue by bills at four months' date from the same period.* The defendants and C. & Co. of Calcutta, to whom the out- ward cargo was consigned, were cognizant of this charterparty. The ship sailed with a captain and crew appointed and paid by the owner. Arrived at Calcutta, C. & Co., as agents of J. B. G., received the cargo, and put up the ship as a general ship, but, not being able to fill her, they purchased and shipped on account of J. B. G. (but in their own name) 511 bales of cotton wool, which by the bill of lad- ing were made deliverable to the defendants, and the freight for which was in the bill of lading expressed to have been paid by bills on London. It was found as a fact that the cotton wools in question were the property of J. B. G.:—Held, that the owner had a lien upon these goods for the general freight due under the charterparty,

SHIP AND SHIPPING.

Construction of Charterparty—(Continued.)

the payment of the entire freight being by the charterparty to precede the delivery of the cargo. Campion v. Colvin, 838.

And see BOTTOMRY BOND.

SLANDER OF TITLE.

1. An action for slander of title is not properly an action for words spoken or for a libel written and published, but an action on the case for special damage sustained by reason of the speaking or publication of the slander of the plaintiff's title. Malachy v. Soper, 723.

2. Therefore, an action to recover damages by reason of the publication of a paragraph in a newspaper, stating that "the petition in a bill filed in the court of Chancery against the plaintiff and certain other persons as shareholders in a certain mine, for an account and an injunction, had been granted by the Vice-Chancellor, and that persons duly authorised had arrived on the workings," cannot be maintained without an allegation of special damage. Ibid.

3. And, held, that an allegation "that the plaintiff was injured in his rights, and the shares so possessed by him and in which he was interested had been and were much depreciated and lessened in value, and divers persons had believed and still believe that he had little or no right to the shares, and that the mine could not be lawfully worked or used for his benefit, and that he had been hindered and prevented from selling or disposing of his said shares in the said mine, and from working and using the same in so ample and beneficial a manner as he otherwise would have done, and was prevented from gaining divers profits which otherwise would have accrued to him"—was not a sufficient allegation of special damage. Ibid.

4. Held, also, that the publication was not a libel on the plaintiff in his business, but a mere slander of his title to the shares. Ibid.

SOLVIT POST DIEM—See PLEADING, 10.

SPECIAL ARGUMENT.

Marking Points.

On demurrer to a replication, the court will not permit the plaintiff to attack the defendant's plea, unless the point has been marked for argument pursuant to the rule of Hilary Term, 4 Will. 4, s. 2. Bayley v. Homan, 384.

SPECIAL DAMAGE—See CASE, 5—SLANDER OF TITLE, 2, 3.

STAMP.

On Mortgage Deed.

1. On a mortgage of premises held under a corporation on a renewable lease, the sum originally advanced was 130*l.*; in the mortgage deed there was an absolute covenant on the part of the mortgagor to

STAMP.

On Mortgage Deed—(Continued.)

renew, and a power to the mortgagee to renew in case of default by the mortgagor, with a proviso that the money paid by the mortgagor for such renewal should not be a charge upon the premises to an amount exceeding 70*l.:* the deed was stamped with a 2*l.* stamp, as a deed for securing a sum not exceeding 200*l.*:—Held, sufficient. Doe d. Jarman v. Larder, 407.

On Lease or Agreement.

2. Where the agreement (on a motion by the landlord under the 1 Geo. 4, c. 87, s. 1), appeared to have been stamped after the rule nisi was obtained, the court discharged the rule; holding that, to entitle him to a rule, the landlord must at the time of moving produce a *perfect* lease or agreement. Doe d. Wood v. Roe, 756.

STATUTE OF FRAUDS.

What a sufficient Memorandum.

A contract of purchase (of leasehold property sold by auction) written on the back of the particulars of sale (which contains the name of the owner of the property), and signed by the *purchaser* only, is a sufficient note or memorandum of the *agreement* between the parties to satisfy the 4th section of the statute of frauds : the *vendor's* signature is not essential. Leythoarp v. Bryant, 238.

STATUTE OF LIMITATIONS—See LIMITATION OF ACTION.

STATUTES:

Decisions on.

STAYING PROCEEDINGS—See PRACTICE, 17.

STOCK-BROKER.

1. Time bargains in foreign funds are not illegal or void at the common law. Wells v. Porter, 141.

STOCK-JOBBING—(*Continued.*)

    2. If they were so, semble that the broker employed in effecting them would still be entitled to sue for his commission in respect thereof. Ibid.

STOCK-JOBBING.

    1. The stock-jobbing act, 7 Geo. 2, c. 8, operates only upon time bargains in the funds of this country. Oakley v. Rigby, 194.

    2. The stock-jobbing act, 7 Geo. 2, c. 8, is confined to the stocks of this country. Wells v. Porter, 141.

    3. Time bargains in foreign funds are not illegal or void at the common law. Ibid.

STOLEN NOTE—See BILLS OF EXCHANGE AND PROMISSORY NOTES.

SUGGESTION—See PRACTICE, 19, 20.

SURGEON—See APOTHECARY.

SURRENDER—See COPYHOLD.

TAXATION—See COSTS, 1—5.

TENANT BY SUFFERANCE—See LANDLORD AND TENANT, 1.

TENANT FROM YEAR TO YEAR—See LANDLORD AND TENANT, 1.

TIME BARGAINS—See STOCK-JOBBING.

TITLE—See ATTORNEY, 16.

TRADE, RESTRAINT OF—See RESTRAINT OF TRADE.

TRESPASS—See PLEADING, 3, 4, 11.

TROVER—See BILLS OF EXCHANGE AND PROMISSORY NOTES—COSTS, 6— LIEN, 1, 2, 3—EVIDENCE; 2—SHIP AND SHIPPING, 2.

VENDOR AND PURCHASER—See SALE, 3.

VICAR.

    Lease by.—See ECCLESIASTICAL LEASES.

WAY, RIGHT OF—See RIGHT OF WAY.

WITNESS.

    Commission for Examination of.

        The court granted a commission for the examination of a witness in an action for criminal conversation with the plaintiff's wife. Norton v. Lord Melbourne, 398.

WRIT OF INQUIRY.

    Upon writs of inquiry before the sheriff, where the damages are under 20*l.*, the costs are taxed on the same scale as upon trials before the sheriff. Hooppell v. Leigh, 188.

END OF VOL. III.

Lightning Source UK Ltd.
Milton Keynes UK
UKHW052335301118
333023UK00008BA/267/P